Mass Transfer Concepts

K Asokan

Deputy Director and Head, Chlor-Alkali Division,
Central Electro Chemical Research Institute (CECRI), Karaikudi

Universities Press

UNIVERSITIES PRESS (INDIA) PRIVATE LIMITED

Registered Office
3-6-747/1/A & 3-6-754/1, Himayatnagar, Hyderabad 500 029 (A.P.), India
E-mail: info@universitiespress.com; Web: www.universitiespress.com

Distributed by
Orient Blackswan Private Limited

Registered Office
3-6-752 Himayatnagar, Hyderabad 500 029 (A.P.), India

Other Offices
Bangalore / Bhopal / Bhubaneshwar / Chandigarh / Chennai / Ernakulam / Guwahati
Hyderabad / Jaipur / Kolkata / Lucknow / Mumbai / New Delhi / Noida / Patna

First published 2011

ISBN 978 81 7371 727 7

Typeset in Times New Roman BT 11/13 *by*
OSDATA, Hyderabad 500 049

Printed at
Aegean Offset, Greater Noida

Published by
Universities Press (India) Private Limited
3-6-747/1/A & 3-6-754/1, Himayatnagar
Hyderabad 500 029 (A.P.), India

Dedication

This book is dedicated to
my grandchild, Oneeka, the great.
Her comforting presence and willingness to sacrifice her time with me
enabled me to concentrate fully on my work.

Preface

In chemical process industries, a frequent requirement is to separate a mixture into its individual components. Mass transfer refers to the group of operations available for this purpose. These operations are based on the transfer of material from one homogenous phase to another. They make use of the differences in the physical properties of the components to be separated, such as vapour pressure, solubility or diffusivity. The driving force for mass transfer is the existence of a concentration difference or a concentration gradient within the system. Mass transfer operations include techniques such as gas absorption, distillation, leaching, extraction, crystallisation, humidification, drying, adsorption and membrane based separation processes. A process engineer has to be well versed with all these operations. A course on mass transfer equips the process engineer with the tricks of the trade.

In this book, the subject matter is divided into ten chapters based on the concept involved. In each chapter, the fundamental principles are explained in a simple manner followed by illustrations for clarity of concepts. At the end of each chapter, problems have been given for the learner to solve. Answers for these problems have been provided at the end of the book. In all, there are 154 worked examples and 169 exercise problems.

The book is intented as a textbook for students pursuing a diploma in chemical technology, undergraduate chemical engineering, biotechnology, petroleum and petrochemical technology, and pharmaceutical engineering courses. The book will also be useful for practicing process engineers as well for refreshing the basic concepts quickly.

K Asokan

Karaikudi
2010

Acknowledgements

I take this opportunity to express my deep sense of gratitude to the following people: Professor A K Shukla, Director, Central Electrochemical Research Institute, Karaikudi, for the encouragement; my colleague, Dr K Subramanian, for the moral support; Ms Sornam Pandivelan, for the neat and patient typing of the material; my student, Mr P Venkatesh Kumar, for the wonderful sketches and drawings and my daughter, Ms A Ishwarya for the computational help and effective formatting of the material.

K Asokan

Contents

1 Diffusion

The group of operations available for the separation of the component of interest from its mixture with another component, are termed as mass transfer operations. The mechanism in most of these operations is molecular diffusion. This chapter provides all the necessary information regarding molecular diffusion as well as mass transfer analogies and correlations that are required for a thorough understanding of the mass transfer operations to be discussed in the later chapters.

Mass transfer operations are characterised by the transfer of one substance through another. The transfer is on a molecular scale. The driving force for mass transfer operations may be one or more of the following:

1. Deviation from equilibrium behaviour; $x \sim x^{\star}$ or $y \sim y^{\star} > 0$
2. Concentration gradient; $\dfrac{\Delta C}{\Delta Z} > 0$

The diffusing component moves from a region of high concentration to one of low concentration.

Most of the mass transfer operations involve a two phase system with several components. When the two phases are initially brought into contact, the composition of each of the components will not be the equilibrium composition. The system attempts to reach equilibrium by a relatively slow diffusive movement of components between the phases.

MOLECULAR DIFFUSION IN FLUIDS

Molecular diffusion refers to the random movement of individual molecules within a system, from a region of higher concentration to one of lower concentration at a given temperature and pressure. The net distance the molecule moves in one direction in a given time is known as the *rate of diffusion* and the process is known as *molecular diffusion*. At ordinary conditions, the rate of diffusion is very slow. The rate of diffusion can be increased by increasing the temperature which increases the molecular velocity, or by decreasing the pressure which decreases the number of collisions between molecules.

Molecular diffusion is a slow process. It is different from rapid mixing, which can be brought about by mechanical stirring or convective movement of fluid. Mechanical agitation produces rapid movement of relatively large chunks or eddies of fluid characteristic of turbulent motion, which carries the substance with it. This mode of transfer is known as *eddy* or *turbulent diffusion*.

Molecular diffusion is the mechanism of mass transfer in stagnant fluids and in fluids which are moving in laminar flow. In the case of fluids in turbulent flow, molecular diffusion is supplemented by eddy diffusion. However, within each eddy, uniformity is achieved only by molecular diffusion, which is the ultimate process.

DIFFUSION IN LIQUID PHASE

When a concentration gradient exists within a fluid consisting of two or more components, there is a tendency for each component to flow in such a direction as to nullify the concentration gradient.

The rate of transfer of A in a mixture of two components A and B, will be determined by the rate of diffusion of A and the behaviour of the other component.

Fick's first law [1], states that the rate of diffusion of a component in a mixture of components is directly proportional to the concentration gradient of that component. If component A is diffusing, then

$$N_A \propto -\frac{dC_A}{dZ} \tag{1.1}$$

$$N_A = -D_{AB}\frac{dC_A}{dZ} \tag{1.2}$$

The proportionality constant, D_{AB}, is known as the diffusivity of A in the mixture.

N_A	=	Rate of diffusion per unit area or diffusion flux, kmol m^{-2} s^{-1}.
D_{AB}	=	Diffusivity of A in B, m^2 s^{-1}.
C_A	=	Molar concentration of A, kmol m^{-3}.
Z	=	distance in the direction of diffusion, m.

The negative sign indicates that the concentration drops in the direction of diffusion. The corresponding rate of diffusion of B is given by

$$N_B = -D_{BA}\frac{dC_B}{dZ} \tag{1.3}$$

where D_{BA} is the diffusivity of B in A and C_B is the concentration of B.

When the fluid is turbulent, eddy diffusion takes place in addition to molecular diffusion and the rate of diffusion increases.

$$N_A = -(D_{AB} + \varepsilon_D)\frac{dC_A}{dZ} \tag{1.4}$$

where ε_D is known as eddy diffusivity. Eddy diffusivity will increase as the turbulence is increased.

DIFFUSIVITY

The diffusivity of a component is defined as the ratio of its diffusion flux to its concentration gradient. The SI unit of diffusivity is $m^2\ s^{-1}$.

DIFFUSION IN THE GAS PHASE

Consider a system consisting of two gases (or vapours) A and B. Let their partial pressures be P_A and P_B, and the total pressure be P. If A and B are ideal gases,

$$P_A V = n_A RT$$

where n_A is the number of moles of A, R is the universal gas constant and T is the temperature.

$$P_A = \frac{n_A}{V}RT \tag{1.5}$$

The number of moles of the substance in unit volume is the molar concentration.

$$P_A = C_A RT \quad \text{or} \quad \frac{P_A}{RT} = C_A \tag{1.6}$$

$$\text{Hence } N_A = -\frac{D_{AB}}{RT} \times \frac{dP_A}{dZ} \tag{1.7}$$

$$N_B = -\frac{D_{BA}}{RT} \times \frac{dP_B}{dZ} \tag{1.8}$$

TYPES OF MOLECULAR DIFFUSION

Molecular diffusion is of three types. They are

1. Equimolecular counter diffusion; $N_A, N_B > 0; N_A = N_B$
2. Diffusion of one component through another stationary or stagnant component; $N_A > 0;\ N_B = 0$
3. Differential diffusion; $N_A, N_B > 0; N_A \neq N_B$

When the first type of diffusion occurs, the rates of diffusion of the two components are equal but they diffuse in opposite directions. So, the total pressure and hence the total molar concentration is constant throughout. Such a situation occurs in distillation operations. If the two components have equal molar latent heats, the condensation of one mole of the less volatile component releases just sufficient heat for the vaporisation of one mole of the more volatile component. Hence, equimolecular counter diffusion takes place with the two components diffusing at equal but opposite rates.

In the absorption process, there is a net transfer of one of the components, that is, diffusion of one of the components through the other component, which is stationary. Pressure variation exists from point to point.

In many processes, one of the components neither remains stationary nor diffuses at an equal but opposite molar rate. When the two components have unequal molar latent heats, both diffuse at different rates in different directions. Exact calculations for these types of problems is difficult.

Equimolar Counter Diffusion

In equimolecular counter diffusion, the two components diffuse at equal rates but in opposite directions; the total pressure at any point in the system will remain constant as a result of diffusion. This is because equal numbers of molecules diffuse in each direction. In other words, $N_A = N_B$. In this case, $D_{AB} = D_{BA} = D$, where D is the diffusivity of component A or B, in the presence of the other component. In short, D is the diffusivity of the mixture, when there is equimolar counter diffusion of the components.

$$N_A = -D_{AB}\frac{dC_A}{dZ} \quad \text{or} \quad -\frac{D_{AB}}{RT} \times \frac{dP_A}{dZ} \tag{1.9}$$

$$N_B = +D_{BA}\frac{dC_B}{dZ} \quad \text{or} \quad +\frac{D_{BA}}{RT} \times \frac{dP_B}{dZ} \tag{1.10}$$

The above equations give the transfer rate in terms of a point value of a concentration gradient or a partial pressure gradient. It can be integrated directly.

The two different points in the system are denoted by the suffixes 1 and 2 and integrated.

$$N_A \int_{Z_1}^{Z_2} dZ = -D \int_{C_{A1}}^{C_{A2}} dC_A \tag{1.11}$$

$$N_A(Z_2 - Z_1) = -D(C_{A2} - C_{A1}) \tag{1.12}$$

$$N_A = \frac{D(C_{A1} - C_{A2})}{(Z_2 - Z_1)} \tag{1.13}$$

The diffusion flux may also be reported in terms of the partial pressures as given below.

$$N_A = \frac{D(P_{A1} - P_{A2})}{RT(Z_2 - Z_1)} \tag{1.14}$$

Note: Z_1 is the distance between a point in the system denoted by the suffix 1 and the reference point, the wall of the confining vessel. Similarly, Z_2 is the distance between the point in the system denoted by the suffix 2 and the reference point. Thus, the distance between points 1 and 2 is $(Z_2 - Z_1)$, assuming that point 2 is the farthest location.

ILLUSTRATIONS

1A Calculate the flux of O_2 in an O_2–N_2 gas mixture at a total pressure of 1 000 kN m^{-2} and 298 K assuming equimolar counter diffusion of the two gases. The concentrations of O_2 at two planes 2 mm apart are 10 and 20 volume%. Diffusivity of the mixture may be taken as 1.81×10^{-5} m^2 s^{-1}.

Solution

Diffusivity of the mixture (D)	=	1.81×10^{-5} m^2 s^{-1}
Total pressure	=	1 000 000 N m^{-2}
Partial pressure of O_2 at plane 1(P_{A1})	=	Total pressure × mole fraction
	=	1 000 000 × 0.2 = 200 000 kN m^{-2}
Partial pressure of O_2 at plane 2(P_{A2})	=	1 000 000 × 0.1 = 100 000 kN m^{-2}
Universal gas constant (R)	=	8 314 J kmol^{-1} K^{-1}
Temperature (T)	=	298 K
Distance between the planes ($Z_2 - Z_1$)	=	0.002 m

For equimolar counter diffusion, the diffusion flux can be calculated using the equation,

$$N_A = \frac{D(P_{A1} - P_{A2})}{RT(Z_2 - Z_1)}$$

$$= \frac{1.81 \times 10^{-5} \times (200\,000 - 100\,000)}{8314 \times 298 \times 0.002}$$

$$= 3.65 \times 10^{-4} \text{ kmol m}^{-2} \text{ s}^{-1}$$

Note: Problems can be easily solved by merely substituting the values of the parameters involved in the equation, appropriate for the given conditions.

1B A simple rectifying column consists of a tube arranged vertically and supplied at the bottom with a mixture of benzene and toluene as vapour. At the top, a condenser returns some of the product of a reflux which flows in a thin film down the inner wall of the tube. The tube is insulated and heat losses can be neglected. At one point in the column, the vapour contains 70 mol% benzene and the adjacent liquid reflux contains 59 mol% benzene. The temperature at this point is 365 K. Assuming that the resistance to diffusion is due to a vapour layer of 0.2 mm thickness, calculate the rate of interchange of benzene and toluene between the vapour and the liquid. The molar latent heats of vaporisation can be taken to be almost equal. The vapour pressure of toluene at 365 K is 54 kN m^{-2} and the diffusivity of the vapours is 0.05 cm^2 s^{-1}. The pressure remains constant at 1 atm throughout the operation.

Solution

As the latent heat of vaporisation of benzene and toluene are equal, equimolar counter diffusion takes place.

Diffusivity of the mixture (D) = 0.051×10^{-4} m^2 s^{-1}
Total pressure = 101.3 kN m^{-2}

At plane 1, the mole fraction of toluene is 0.41 and at plane 2, the mole fraction of toluene is 0.30. The partial pressure of toluene at the two planes is found using Raoult's law.

Partial pressure of toluene at plane 1 (P_{T1}) = Vapour pressure $\times$ mole fraction
= $54 \times 0.41 = 22.14$ kN m^{-2}
Partial pressure of toluene at plane 2 (P_{T2}) = $54 \times 0.30 = 16.2$ kN m^{-2}
Universal gas constant (R) = 8.314 kJ kmol^{-1} K^{-1}
Temperature (T) = 365 K
Distance between the planes ($Z_2 - Z_1$) = 0.000 2 m

For equimolar counter diffusion, diffusion flux for toulene can be calculated using the equation,

$$N_A = \frac{-D(P_{T2} - P_{T1})}{RT(Z_2 - Z_1)}$$

$$= \frac{-0.051 \times 10^{-4} \times (16.2 - 22.14)}{8.314 \times 365 \times 0.0002}$$

$$= 4.99 \times 10^{-5} \text{ kmol m}^{-2} \text{ s}^{-1}$$

Partial pressure of benzene at plane 1 (P_{B1})=Total pressure – Partial pressure of toluene
$=101.3 - 22.14 = 79.16$ kN m^{-2}

Partial pressure of benzene at plane 2 (P_{B2})=Total pressure – Partial pressure of toluene
$=101.3 - 16.20 = 85.10$ kN m^{-2}

For equimolar counter diffusion, the diffusion flux for benzene can be calculated using the equation,

$$N_A = \frac{-D(P_{B2} - P_{B1})}{RT(Z_2 - Z_1)}$$

$$= \frac{-0.051 \times 10^{-4} \times (85.10 - 79.16)}{8.314 \times 365 \times 0.0002}$$

$$= -4.99 \times 10^{-5} \text{ kmol m}^{-2} \text{ s}^{-1}$$

The rates of diffusion of toluene and benzene are equal but in opposite directions.

Table 1.1 will be helpful in the correct usage of units for the various physical quantities involved in the diffusion flux calculations.

Table 1.1 Correct usage of units in diffusion flux calculations

Diffusivity	Pressure	Gas constant	Distance	Diffusion flux
cm^2 s^{-1}	atm	82.06 cm^3 atm mol^{-1} K^{-1}	cm	mol cm^{-2} s^{-1}
m^2 s^{-1}	kN m^{-2}	8.314 kJ kmol^{-1} K^{-1}	m	kmol m^{-2} s^{-1}
m^2 s^{-1}	N m^{-2}	8 314 J kmol^{-1} K^{-1}	m	kmol m^{-2} s^{-1}
m^2 s^{-1}	N m^{-2}	8.314 J mol^{-1} K^{-1}	m	mol m^{-2} s^{-1}

Diffusion of One Component through a Stagnant Component

Consider a two component system, consisting of A and B separated by a liquid surface which absorbs only A. As A is absorbed, a partial pressure gradient is set up, which causes A to diffuse towards the liquid.

$$N_A = -D_{AB} \frac{dC_A}{dZ} \tag{1.2}$$

If this process is allowed to proceed for some time, diffused A will be absorbed by the liquid. A total pressure gradient will be set up, causing the bulk motion of A and B towards the liquid. Since there is no transfer of B across the interface, the molecules of B transferred to the interface by bulk flow must diffuse back into the bulk in order to maintain uniform concentration throughout. The driving force for the bulk flow is the concentration gradient of A and hence the concentration gradient of A determines the bulk flow rate of B. Bulk flow of B is accompanied by bulk flow of A as well. Figure 1.1 shows the direction of diffusion of the various components.

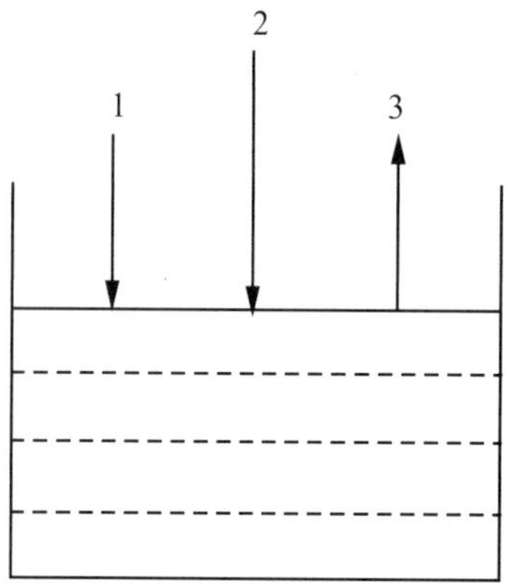

1. Diffusion of A
2. Bulk flow of A and B
3. Bulk diffusion of B.

Fig. 1.1 Diffusion through a stagnant component

Bulk rate of flow of B, $$N_B = -D_{AB}\frac{dC_A}{dZ} \tag{1.15}$$

Bulk flow rate of $A = N_B \times \frac{C_A}{C_B}$ $\left(\frac{C_A}{C_B}\text{ is the ratio of molecules of A to B at any point}\right)$

$$= -D_{AB} \times \frac{dC_A}{dZ} \times \frac{C_A}{C_B}$$

$$= -D_{AB} \times \frac{dC_A}{dZ} \times \frac{C_A}{(C_T - C_A)} \tag{1.16}$$

Total rate of transfer A is obtained by summing up the transfer by diffusion and by bulk flow.

$$N'_A = -D_{AB} \times \frac{dC_A}{dZ} - D_{AB} \times \frac{dC_A}{dZ} \times \frac{C_A}{(C_T - C_A)}$$

$$= -D_{AB} \times \frac{dC_A}{dZ}\left[1 + \frac{C_A}{(C_T - C_A)}\right]$$

$$= -D_{AB} \times \frac{dC_A}{dZ} \times \frac{C_T}{(C_T - C_A)}$$

$$= -D_{AB} \times \frac{dC_A}{dZ} \times \frac{C_T}{C_B} \quad (\text{since } C_T - C_A = C_B) \tag{1.17}$$

This relation is known as *Stefan's law* [2].

$$N'_A = -D_{AB} \times \frac{dC_A}{dZ} \times \frac{C_T}{(C_T - C_A)} \tag{1.17}$$

Integration of this, between two positions denoted by suffixes 1 and 2 give

$$N_A^1 \int_{Z_1}^{Z_2} dZ = -D_{AB}C_T \int_{C_{A1}}^{C_{A2}} \frac{dC_A}{(C_T - C_A)} \tag{1.18}$$

$$N_A^1(Z_2 - Z_1) = +D_{AB}C_T \ln \frac{(C_T - C_{A2})}{(C_T - C_{A1})} \tag{1.19}$$

$$N_A^1 = \frac{D_{AB}}{(Z_2 - Z_1)} \times \frac{C_T}{(C_T - C_A)_{lm}} \times [(C_T - C_{A2}) - (C_T - C_{A1})] \tag{1.20}$$

$$N_A^1 = \frac{D_{AB}}{(Z_2 - Z_1)} \times \frac{C_T}{C_{Blm}} \times (C_{A2} - C_{A1}) \quad \text{since } (C_T - C_A) = C_B \tag{1.21}$$

C_{Blm} is the log mean value of concentration of the non-diffusing component B at locations 1 and 2 and it is given by,

$$C_{Blm} = \frac{C_{B2} - C_{B1}}{\ln \frac{C_{B2}}{C_{B1}}} \tag{1.22}$$

For gases, $$N_A^1 = \frac{D_{AB}}{RT(Z_2 - Z_1)} \times \frac{P}{P_{Blm}} \times (P_{A2} - P_{A1}) \tag{1.23}$$

where P is the total pressure, P_{A2} and P_{A1} are the partial pressures of the diffusing component A at locations 2 and 1 respectively, P_{Blm} is the log mean value of the partial pressure of the non-diffusing component B at locations 1 and 2 and is given by,

$$P_{Blm} = \frac{P_{B2} - P_{B1}}{\ln \dfrac{P_{B2}}{P_{B1}}} \tag{1.24}$$

The equation, $N'_A = \dfrac{D_{AB} \times C_T}{(Z_2 - Z_1)} \ln \dfrac{(C_T - C_{A2})}{(C_T - C_{A1})}$ can be simplified when the concentration of the diffusing component A, C_A, is very small when compared to C_T.

$$N_A^1 = \frac{D_{AB} \times C_T}{(Z_2 - Z_1)} \ln \left[1 - \frac{(C_{A2} - C_{A1})}{(C_T - C_{A1})}\right] \tag{1.25}$$

$$N_A^1 = \frac{D_{AB} \times C_T}{(Z_2 - Z_1)} \ln \left[-\frac{(C_{A2} - C_{A1})}{(C_T - C_{A1})} - \frac{1}{2} \left\{ \frac{C_{A2} - C_{A1})}{(C_T - C_{A1})} \right\}^2 \right] \tag{1.26}$$

For small values of $C_A, C_T - C_A \approx C_T$.

$$N_A^1 = \frac{D_{AB}}{(Z_2 - Z_1)} \times (C_{A2} - C_{A1}) \tag{1.27}$$

This is equal to the equation for equimolecular counter diffusion. Thus, the effect of bulk flow can be neglected for low concentrations of the diffusing component.

ILLUSTRATIONS

1C O_2 is diffusing through CO under steady state conditions with the CO being non-diffusing. The total pressure is 1×10^5 N m^{-2} and the temperature is 273 K. The partial pressure of O_2 at two planes 2 mm apart is 13 000 N m^{-2} and 6 500 N m^{-2}. The diffusivity of the mixture may be taken as 1.87×10^{-5} m^2 s^{-1}. Calculate the diffusion of O_2 in kmol s^{-1} through each m^2 of two planes.

Solution

For gaseous systems, the diffusion flux when one component is diffusing while the other remains stagnant is given by the equation,

$$N_A^1 = \frac{D_{AB}}{RT(Z_2 - Z_1)} \times \frac{P}{P_{Blm}} \times (P_{A2} - P_{A1})$$

where P is the total pressure, P_{A2} and P_{A1} are the partial pressures of the diffusing component A at locations 2 and 1 respectively, P_{Blm} is the log mean value of the partial pressure of the non-diffusing component B at locations 1 and 2 and it is given by,

$$P_{Blm} = \frac{P_{B2} - P_{B1}}{\ln \dfrac{P_{B2}}{P_{B1}}}$$

Total pressure (P)	=	100 000 N m^{-2}
Partial pressure of O_2 at plane 1 (P_{A1})	=	13 000 N m^{-2}
Partial pressure of O^2 at plane 2 (P_{A2})	=	6 500 N m^{-2}
Partial pressure of CO at plane 1 (P_{B1})	=	$P - P_{A1} = 1\,00\,000 - 13\,000$ N m^{-2}
	=	87 000 N m^{-2}

Partial pressure of CO at plane 1 (P_{B2}) $= P - P_{A2} = 1\ 00\ 000 - 6\ 500$ N m^{-2}

$= 93\ 500$ N m^{-2}

$$P_{Blm} = \frac{P_{B2} - P_{B1}}{\ln \dfrac{P_{B2}}{P_{B1}}} = \frac{93\ 500 - 87\ 000}{\ln \dfrac{93\ 500}{87\ 000}} = 90\ 200 \text{ N m}^{-2}$$

Universal gas constant (R) $= 8\ 314$ J kmol^{-1}K^{-1}

Temperature (T) $= 273$ K

Distance between the planes ($Z_2 - Z_1$) $= 0.002$ m

Substituting the values of the parameters in the equation,

$$N_A^1 = \frac{D_{AB}}{RT(Z_2 - Z_1)} \times \frac{P}{P_{Blm}} \times (P_{A2} - P_{A1})$$

$$= \frac{1.87 \times 10^{-5}}{8\ 314 \times 273 \times 0.002} \times \frac{100\ 000}{90\ 200} \times (13\ 000 - 6\ 500)$$

$$= 2.97 \times 10^{-5} \text{ kmol m}^{-2} \text{ s}^{-1}$$

1D A vertical glass tube with a 3 mm diameter is filled with liquid toluene to a depth of 20 mm from the top. The diffusivity of toluene in air is 0.031 m^2 h^{-1}. Vapour pressure at 312 K is 7.64 kN m^{-2}. The density of toluene is 850 kg m^{-3}. Estimate the rate of diffusion at 1 atm pressure and 312 K. Assume that diffusion takes place under steady state conditions and air is stagnant.

Solution

For gaseous systems, the diffusion flux when one component is diffusing while the other remains stagnant is given by the equation,

$$N_A^1 = \frac{D_{AB}}{RT(Z_2 - Z_1)} \times \frac{P}{P_{Blm}} \times (P_{A2} - P_{A1})$$

where P is the total pressure, P_{A2} and P_{A1} are the partial pressures of the diffusing component A at locations 2 and 1 respectively, P_{Blm} is the log mean value of the partial pressure of the non-diffusing component B at locations 1 and 2 and is given by,

$$P_{Blm} = \frac{P_{B2} - P_{B1}}{\ln \dfrac{P_{B2}}{P_{B1}}}$$

Diffusivity of the mixture (D) $= 0.031$ m^2 h^{-1}

Total pressure (P) $= 101\ 325$ N m^{-2}

Partial pressure of C_7H_8 at plane 1 (P_{A1}) = 7 640 N m^{-2}
Partial pressure of C_7H_8 at plane 2 (PA_2) = 0 N m^{-2}
Partial pressure of air at plane 1 (P_{B1}) = $P - P_{A1} = 101\ 325 - 7\ 640$ N m^{-2}
= 93 685 N m^{-2}

Partial pressure of air at plane 1 (P_{B2}) = $P - P_{A2} = 101\ 325 - 0$ N m^{-2}
= 101 325 N m^{-2}

$$P_{Blm} = \frac{P_{B2} - P_{B1}}{\ln \dfrac{P_{B2}}{P_{B1}}} = \frac{101\ 325 - 93\ 685}{\ln \dfrac{101\ 325}{93\ 685}} = 97\ 455 \text{ N m}^{-2}$$

Universal gas constant (R) = 8.314 J mol^{-1} K^{-1}
Temperature (T) = 312 K
Distance between the planes ($Z_2 - Z_1$) = 0.02 m

Substituting the values of the parameters in the equation below,

$$N_A^1 = \frac{D_{AB}}{RT(Z_2 - Z_1)} \times \frac{P}{P_{Blm}} \times (P_{A2} - P_{A1})$$

$$= \frac{0.031}{8.314 \times 312 \times 0.02} \times \frac{101\ 325}{97\ 455} \times (7\ 640 - 0) = 4.75 \text{ mol m}^{-2} \text{ h}^{-1}$$

Rate of evaporation = Diffusion flux × Area of cross section
= 4.75 mol m^{-2} h^{-1} × 3.14 × $(0.001\ 5)^2$ m^2
= 3.36×10^{-5} mol h^{-1}

1E A service attendant accidentally spills 50 litres of gasoline which quickly spreads over a level surface of area 8 m^2. Estimate the time required for the gasoline to evaporate into the stagnant air above the surface of the liquid. The diffusivity of gasoline in air is 0.65 m^2 h^{-1}. The air temperature is 298 K. Evaporation may be assumed to take place through a film of air of 2 m thickness. Vapour pressure of gasoline at 298 K is 76 mm Hg. The density of gasoline is 720 kg m^{-3} and the molecular weight of gasoline is 200. The operation takes place at 1 atm pressure.

Solution

For gaseous systems, the diffusion flux when one component is diffusing while the other remains stagnant, is given by the equation,

$$N_A^1 = \frac{D_{AB}}{RT(Z_2 - Z_1)} \times \frac{P}{P_{Blm}} \times (P_{A2} - P_{A1})$$

where P is the total pressure, P_{A2} and P_{A1} are the partial pressures of the diffusing component A at locations 2 and 1 respectively, P_{Blm} is the log mean value of the partial pressure of the non-diffusing component, B at locations 1 and 2 and is given by,

$$P_{Blm} = \frac{P_{B2} - P_{B1}}{\ln \frac{P_{B2}}{P_{B1}}}$$

Diffusivity of the mixture (D) = $0.65 \text{ m}^2 \text{ h}^{-1}$

Total pressure (P) = 101.3 kN m^{-2}

Partial pressure of gasoline at plane 1 (P_{A1}) = $\frac{101.3 \times 76}{760} = 10.13 \text{ kN m}^{-2}$

Partial pressure of gasoline at plane 2 (P_{A2}) = 0 N m^{-2}

Partial pressure of air at plane 1 (P_{B1}) = $P - P_{A1} = 101.3 - 10.13 \text{ kN m}^{-2}$

= 91.17 N m^{-2}

Partial pressure of air at plane 1 (P_{B2}) = $P - PA_2 = 101.3 - 0 \text{ kN m}^{-2}$

= 101.3 kN m^{-2}

$$P_{Blm} = \frac{P_{B2} - P_{B1}}{\ln \frac{P_{B2}}{P_{B1}}} = \frac{101.3 - 91.17}{\ln \frac{101.3}{91.17}} = 96.14 \text{ kN m}^{-2}$$

Universal gas constant (R) = $8.314 \text{ kJ kmol}^{-1} \text{ K}^{-1}$

Temperature (T) = 298 K

Distance between the planes ($Z_2 - Z_1$) = 2 m

Substituting the values of the parameters in the equation,

$$N_A^1 = \frac{D_{AB}}{RT(Z_2 - Z_1)} \times \frac{P}{P_{Blm}} \times (P_{A2} - P_{A1})$$

$$= \frac{0.65}{8.314 \times 298 \times 2} \times \frac{101.3}{96.14} \times (10.13 - 0)$$

$$= 1.4 \times 10^{-3} \text{ kmol m}^{-2} \text{ h}^{-1}$$

$$= 1.4 \text{ mol m}^{-2} \text{ h}^{-1}$$

Rate of evaporation = Diffusion flux × Area

= $1.4 \text{ mol m}^{-2} \text{ h}^{-1} \times 8 \text{ m}^2 = 11.2 \text{ mol h}^{-1}$

Moles of gasoline to be evaporated = (volume × density) ÷ molecular weight

= $50 \times \frac{720}{1\,000} \div 200 = 180 \text{ mol } (0.18 \text{ kmol})$

Time required = (amount to be evaporated ÷ rate of evaporation)
= $180 \div 11.2 = 16.07$ h

1F Water has spilled out through the accidental opening of the valve of a pipe line on the floor of an industrial plant. The water layer is 1 mm thick and is at 298 K. The air is at 298 K and 1 atm pressure. The water vapour content of air is 2 g per kg of dry air. Determine the time required for the complete evaporation of the water. Evaporation takes place by molecular diffusion through an air film of 5 mm thickness. The diffusivity of water vapour in air is 0.256 $cm^2\ s^{-1}$. The vapour pressure of water at 298 K is 24.56 mm Hg.

Solution

For gaseous systems, the diffusion flux when one component is diffusing while the other remains stagnant, is given by the equation,

$$N_A^1 = \frac{D_{AB}}{RT(Z_2 - Z_1)} \times \frac{P}{P_{Blm}} \times (P_{A2} - P_{A1})$$

where P is the total pressure, P_{A2} and P_{A1} are the partial pressures of the diffusing component A at locations 2 and 1 respectively, P_{Blm} is the log mean value of the partial pressure of the non-diffusing component B at locations 1 and 2 and is given by,

$$P_{Blm} = \frac{P_{B2} - P_{B1}}{\ln \dfrac{P_{B2}}{P_{B1}}}$$

Diffusivity of the mixture (D) = $0.256 \times 10^{-4}\ m^2\ s^{-1}$

Total pressure (P) = 1 atm

Partial pressure of water vapour at plane 1 (P_{A1}) = $\dfrac{24.56}{760} = 0.032\ 3$ atm

The partial pressure of water vapour at plane 2 (P_{A2}) has to be found from the water vapour content of air. The weight ratio of water vapour to dry air is converted to molar ratio of water vapour to dry air, which is equal to the partial pressure ratio of water vapour to dry air.

$$\frac{\dfrac{2}{18}}{\dfrac{1\ 000}{29}} = 0.003\ 2 = \frac{P_{A2}}{1 - P_{A2}}$$

Partial pressure of water vapour at plane 2 (P_{A2}) = 0.003 2 atm

Partial pressure of air at plane 1 (P_{B1}) = $P - P_{A1} = 1 - 0.032\ 3$ atm

= 0.967 7 atm

Partial pressure of air at plane 1 (P_{B2}) = $P - P_{A2} = 1 - 0.003\ 2$ atm

= 0.996 8 atm

$$P_{Blm} = \frac{P_{B2} - P_{B1}}{\ln \dfrac{P_{B2}}{P_{B1}}} = \frac{0.996\ 8 - 0.967\ 7}{\ln \dfrac{0.996\ 8}{0.967\ 7}} = 0.983\ 1 \text{ atm}$$

Universal gas constant (R) = 0.082 05 m^3 atm kmol^{-1} K^{-1}

Temperature (T) = 298 K

Distance between the planes ($Z_2 - Z_1$) = 5×10^{-3} m

Substituting the values of the parameters in the equation below,

$$N_A^1 = \frac{D_{AB}}{RT(Z_2 - Z_1)} \times \frac{P}{P_{Blm}} \times (P_{A2} - P_{A1})$$

$$= \frac{0.256 \times 10^{-4}}{0.082\ 05 \times 298 \times 5 \times 10^{-3}} \times \frac{1}{0.9831} \times (0.032\ 3 - 0.003\ 2)$$

$$= 6.19 \times 10^{-6} \text{ kmol m}^{-2} \text{ s}^{-1}$$

$$= 1.115 \times 10^{-4} \text{ kg m}^{-2} \text{ s}^{-1}$$

Water to be evaporated = Water film thickness × area × density

= $1 \times 10^{-3} \times 1 \times 1000 = 1$ kg m^{-2}

Time required = (amount to be evaporated ÷ rate of evaporation)

= $1.0 \div (1.115 \times 10^{-4}) = 8\ 968.6$ s

1G An open bowl, 0.5 m in diameter, contains water at 360 K which is evaporating into the atompherc. If the air currents are sufficiently strong to remove the water vapour as it is formed and if the resistance to its mass transfer in air is equivalent to that of a 2 mm layer for conditions of molecular diffusion, what will be the rate of cooling due to evaporation? Water can be considered as well mixed (that is, all the water in the bowl is at the same temperature) and the water equivalent of the sytem can be taken as 20 kg. Diffusivity of water vapour in air can be taken as 0.20 cm^2 s^{-1}. Vapour pressure of water at 360 K is 62.5 kN m^{-2}.

Solution

For gaseous systems, the diffusion flux when one component is diffusing while the other remains stagnant, is given by the equation below,

$$N_A^1 = \frac{D_{AB}}{RT(Z_2 - Z_1)} \times \frac{P}{P_{Blm}} \times (P_{A2} - P_{A1})$$

where P is the total pressure, P_{A2} and P_{A1} are the partial pressures of the diffusing component A at locations 2 and 1 respectively, P_{Blm} is the log mean value of the partial pressure of the non-diffusing component B at locations 1 and 2 and is given by,

$$P_{Blm} = \frac{P_{B2} - P_{B1}}{\ln \dfrac{P_{B2}}{P_{B1}}}$$

Diffusivity of the mixture (D) = 0.2×10^{-4} m^2 h^{-1}

Total pressure (P) = 101. 3 kN m^{-2}

Partial pressure of water vapour at plane 1 (P_{A1}) = 62.5 kN m^{-2}

Partial pressure of water vapour at plane 2 (P_{A2}) = 0 N m^{-2}

Partial pressure of air at plane 1 (P_{B1}) = $P - P_{A1} = 101.3 - 62.5$ kN m^{-2}

= 38.8 N m^{-2}

Partial pressure of air at plane 1 (P_{B2}) = $P - P_{A2} = 101.3 - 0$ kN m^{-2}

= 101.3 kN m^{-2}

$$P_{Blm} = \frac{P_{B2} - P_{B1}}{\ln \dfrac{P_{B2}}{P_{B1}}} = \frac{101.3 - 38.8}{\ln \dfrac{101.3}{38.8}} = 65.13 \text{ kN m}^{-2}$$

Universal gas constant (R) = 8.314 kJ kmol^{-1} K^{-1}

Temperature (T) = 360 K

Distance between the planes ($Z_2 - Z_1$) = 0.002 m

Substituting the values of the parameters in the equation,

$$N_A^1 = \frac{D_{AB}}{RT(Z_2 - Z_1)} \times \frac{P}{P_{Blm}} \times (P_{A2} - P_{A1})$$

$$= \frac{0.2 \times 10^{-4}}{8.314 \times 360 \times 0.002} \times \frac{101.3}{65.13} \times (62.5 - 0)$$

$$= 3.25 \times 10^{-4} \text{ kmol m}^{-2} \text{ s}^{-1} = 5.85 \times 10^{-3} \text{ kg m}^{-2} \text{ s}^{-1}$$

Rate of evaporation	=	Diffusion flux × Area of cross section
	=	5.85×10^{-3} kg m^{-2} s^{-1} $\times 3.14 \times (0.25)^2$ m^2
	=	1.15×10^{-3} kg s^{-1}

Latent heat of vaporisation of water at 360 K	=	2 288 kJ kg^{-1}
Rate of heat removal	=	$1.15 \times 10^{-3} \times 2\,288 = 2.63$ kJ s^{-1}

This is equal to the water equivalent of the system × Specific heat of water × Rate of fall in temperature

$20 \times 4.187 \times$ Rate of fall in temperature	=	2.63 kJ s^{-1}
Rate of fall in temperature	=	0.031 K s^{-1}

1H Estimate the rate of diffusion of chloropicrin in air, which is stagnant at 298 K and 1 atm pressure. The diffusivity is 0.088 cm^2 s^{-1}; vapour pressure of chloropicrin at 298 K is 23.81 mm Hg; density of chloropicrin is 1.65 g cm^{-3}; surface area of liquid exposed to evaporation is 2.29 cm^2; distance from the liquid level to the top of the tube is 11.14 cm.

Solution

For gaseous systems, the diffusion flux when one component is diffusing while the other remains stagnant is given by the equation,

$$N_A^1 = \frac{D_{AB}}{RT(Z_2 - Z_1)} \times \frac{P}{P_{Blm}} \times (P_{A2} - P_{A1})$$

where P is the total pressure, P_{A2} and P_{A1} are the partial pressures of the diffusing component A at locations 2 and 1 respectively, P_{Blm} is the log mean value of partial pressure of the non-diffusing component B at locations 1 and 2 and is given by,

$$P_{Blm} = \frac{P_{B2} - P_{B1}}{\ln \dfrac{P_{B2}}{P_{B1}}}$$

Diffusivity of the mixture (D)	=	0.088 cm^2 s^{-1}
Total pressure (P)	=	1 atm
Partial pressure of chloropicrin at plane 1 (P_{A1})	=	$23.81 \div 760 = 0.031\,3$ atm
Partial pressure of chloropicrin at plane 2 (P_{A2})	=	0 atm
Partial pressure of air at plane 1 (P_{B1})	=	$P - P_{A1} = 1.0 - 0.0313$
	=	0.968 7 atm
Partial pressure of air at plane 2 (P_{B2})	=	$P - P_{A2} = 1.0 - 0 = 1.0$ atm

$$P_{Blm} = \frac{P_{B2} - P_{B1}}{\ln \dfrac{P_{B2}}{P_{B1}}} = \frac{1.0 - 0.968\,7}{\ln \dfrac{1.0}{0.968\,7}} = 0.984\,3 \text{ atm}$$

Universal gas constant (R) = 82.05 cm^3 atm mol^{-1} K^{-1}

Temperature (T) = 298 K

Distance between the planes ($Z_2 - Z_1$) = 11.14 cm

Substituting the values of the parameters in the equation,

$$N_A^1 = \frac{D_{AB}}{RT(Z_2 - Z_1)} \times \frac{P}{P_{Blm}} \times (P_{A2} - P_{A1})$$

$$= \frac{0.088}{82.05 \times 298 \times 11.14} \times \frac{1.0}{0.984\,3} \times (0.031\,3 - 0)$$

$$= 1.027 \times 10^{-8} \text{ mol cm}^{-2} \text{ s}^{-1}$$

Rate of evaporation = Diffusion flux × Surface area

$$= 1.027 \times 10^{-8} \times 2.29 = 2.352 \times 10^{-8} \text{ mol s}^{-1}$$

1I In a packed column operating at atmospheric pressure and 295 K, 10% ammonia–air mixture is scrubbed with water and the concentration of ammonia in the air is reduced to 0.1%. The entire resistance to mass transfer may be regarded as lying within a thin laminar film on the gas side of the gas–liquid interface. At some intermediate point, where the ammonia concentration in the gas phase has been reduced to 5%, the partial pressure of ammonia in equilibrium with the average solution is 66 kN m^{-2} and the transfer rate has been determined to be 10^{-3} kmol m^{-2} s^{-1}. Compute the thickness of the hypothetical gas film. Diffusivity of ammonia in air may be taken as 0.24 cm^2 s^{-1}.

Solution

For gaseous systems, the diffusion flux when one component is diffusing while the other remains stagnant is given by the equation,

$$N_A^1 = \frac{D_{AB}}{RT(Z_2 - Z_1)} \times \frac{P}{P_{Blm}} \times (P_{A2} - P_{A1})$$

where P is the total pressure, P_{A2} and P_{A1} are the partial pressures of the diffusing component A at locations 2 and 1 respectively, P_{Blm} is the log mean value of partial pressure of the non-diffusing component B at locations 1 and 2 and is given by,

$$P_{Blm} = \frac{P_{B2} - P_{B1}}{\ln \dfrac{P_{B2}}{P_{B1}}}$$

Diffusivity of the mixture (D) $= 0.24 \times 10^{-4}$ m^2 s^{-1}

Total pressure (P) $= 101.3$ kN m^{-2}

Partial pressure of ammonia at plane 1 (P_{A1}) = Total pressure $\times$ Mole fraction

$= 101.3 \times 0.05 = 5.065$ kN m^{-2}

Partial pressure of ammonia at plane 2 (P_{A2}) = 66 kN m^{-2}

Partial pressure of air at plane 1 (P_{B1}) $= P - P_{A1} = 101.3 - 5.065$

$= 96.235$ kN m^{-2}

Partial pressure of air at plane 1 (P_{B2}) $= P - P_{A2} = 101.3 - 66.0 = 35.3$ kN m^{-2}

$$P_{Blm} = \frac{P_{B2} - P_{B1}}{\ln \dfrac{P_{B2}}{P_{B1}}} = \frac{93.235 - 35.3}{\ln \dfrac{93.235}{35.3}} = 59.65 \text{ kN m}^{-2}$$

Universal gas constant (R) $= 8.314$ kJ kmol^{-1} K^{-1}

Temperature (T) $= 295$ K

Distance between the planes ($Z_2 - Z_1$) = Z m

Diffusion flux(N_A^1) $= 1.0 \times 10^{-3}$ kmol m^{-2} s^{-1}

Substituting the values of the parameters in the equation,

$$Z = \frac{D_{AB}}{RTN_A^1} \times \frac{P}{P_{Blm}} \times (P_{A2} - P_{A1})$$

$$= \frac{0.24 \times 10^{-4}}{8.314 \times 295 \times 1.0 \times 10^{-3}} \times \frac{101.3}{59.65} \times (66 - 5.065)$$

$$= 0.001\,01 \text{ m} = 1.01 \text{ mm}$$

1J Calculate the rate of diffusion of NaCl at 291 K through a stagnant film of water of thickness 1 mm, when the concentrations are 25% and 5% by weight respectively on either side of the film. The diffusivity of NaCl in water is 1.22×10^{-9} m^2 s^{-1} under the given conditions. The densities of the 25% and 5% NaCl solutions are 1.19 g cm^{-3} and 1.027 g cm^{-3} respectively.

Solution

For liquid systems, the diffusion flux when one component is diffusing while the other remains stagnant is given by the equation,

$$N_A^1 = \frac{D_{AB}}{(Z_2 - Z_1)} \times \frac{C_T}{C_{Blm}} \times (C_{A2} - C_{A1})$$

where C_T is the total concentration which is the mean of the total concentrations C_{T1} and C_{T2} at the planes 1 and 2 respectively, C_{A1} and C_{A2} are the concentrations of the diffusing component A at planes 1 and 2 respectively, C_{Blm} is the log mean value of concentration of the non-diffusing component B at planes 1 and 2 and is given by,

$$C_{Blm} = \frac{C_{B2} - C_{B1}}{\ln \dfrac{C_{B2}}{C_{B1}}}$$

The concentration of the diffusing component A in kmol m^{-3} at the two planes is found using the relation, concentration of A = weight of one cubic meter of solution in kg × weight fraction of A ÷ molecular weight of A.

Concentration of NaCl at plane 1 (C_{A1}) $= \dfrac{1\,190 \times 0.25}{58.46} = 5.09$ kmol m^{-3}

Concentration of water at plane 1 (C_{B1}) $= \dfrac{1\,190 \times 0.75}{18} = 49.58$ kmol m^{-3}

Total concentration at plane 1 (C_{T1}) $= C_{A1} + C_{B1} = 54.67$ kmol m^{-3}

Concentration of NaCl at plane 2 (C_{A2}) $= \dfrac{1\,027 \times 0.05}{58.46} = 0.88$ kmol m^{-3}

Concentration of water at plane 2 (C_{B2}) $= \dfrac{1\,027 \times 0.95}{18} = 54.20$ kmol m^{-3}

Total concentration at plane 2 (C_{T2}) $= C_{A2} + C_{B2} = 55.08$ kmol m^{-3}

Mean total concentration (C_T) $= \dfrac{C_{T1} + C_{T2}}{2} = 54.88$ kmol m^{-3}

$$C_{Blm} = \frac{C_{B2} - C_{B1}}{\ln \dfrac{C_{B2}}{C_{B1}}} = \frac{54.20 - 49.58}{\ln \dfrac{54.20}{49.58}} = 51.91 \text{ kmol m}^{-3}$$

Diffusivity of NaCl in water (D_{AB}) $= 1.22 \times 10^{-9}$ m^2 s^{-1}

Distance between the planes ($Z_2 - Z_1$) $= 0.001$ m

Substituting the values of the parameters in the equation,

$$N_A^1 = \frac{D_{AB}}{(Z_2 - Z_1)} \times \frac{C_T}{C_{Blm}} \times (C_{A2} - C_{A1}) = \frac{1.22 \times 10^{-9}}{0.001} \times \frac{54.88}{51.91} \times (5.09 - 0.88)$$

$$= 5.43 \times 10^{-6} \text{ k mol m}^{-2} \text{ s}^{-1}$$

1K Calculate the rate of diffusion of acetic acid across a film of non-diffusing water solution of 2 mm thickness at 290 K. The concentration on opposite sides of the film are respecitvely 8% and 4% by weight of acid respectively. The diffusivity of acetic acid in the solution is 0.95×10^{-9} m^2 s^{-1}. The densities of 8% and 4% by weight acetic acid solutions are 1.01 g cm^{-3} and 1.004 g cm^{-3} respectively.

Solution

For liquid systems, the diffusion flux when one component is diffusing while the other remains stagnant is given by the equation,

$$N_A^1 = \frac{D_{AB}}{(Z_2 - Z_1)} \times \frac{C_T}{C_{Blm}} \times (C_{A2} - C_{A1})$$

where C_T is the total concentration which is the mean of the total concentrations C_{T1} and C_{T2} at the planes 1 and 2 respectively, C_{A1} and C_{A2} are the concentrations of the diffusing component A at planes 1 and 2 respectively, C_{Blm} is the log mean value of the concentration of the non-diffusing component B at planes 1 and 2 and is given by,

$$C_{Blm} = \frac{C_{B2} - C_{B1}}{\ln \dfrac{C_{B2}}{C_{B1}}}$$

The concentration of the diffusing component A in kmol m^{-3} at the two planes is found using the relation, concentration of A = weight of one cubic meter of solution in kg × weight fraction of A ÷ molecular weight of A.

Concentration of acetic acid at plane 1 (C_{A1}) = $\dfrac{1\,004 \times 0.04}{60} = 0.67$ kmol m^{-3}

Concentration of water at plane 1 (C_{B1}) = $\dfrac{1\,004 \times 0.96}{18} = 53.55$ kmol m^{-3}

Total concentration at plane 1 (C_{T1}) = $C_{A1} + C_{B1} = 54.22$ kmol m^{-3}

Concentration of acetic acid at plane 2 (C_{A2}) = $\dfrac{1\,010 \times 0.08}{60} = 1.35$ kmol m^{-3}

Concentration of water at plane 2 (C_{B2}) = $\dfrac{1\,010 \times 0.92}{18} = 51.62$ kmol m^{-3}

Total concentration at plane 2 (C_{T2}) = $C_{A2} + C_{B2} = 52.97$ kmol m^{-3}

Mean total concentration (C_T) = $\dfrac{C_{T1} + C_{T2}}{2} = 53.60$ kmol m^{-3}

$$C_{Blm} = \frac{C_{B2} - C_{B1}}{\ln \dfrac{C_{B2}}{C_{B1}}} = \frac{53.55 - 51.62}{\ln \dfrac{53.55}{51.62}} = 52.58 \text{ kmol m}^{-3}$$

Diffusivity of acetic acid in water (D_{AB}) = 0.95×10^{-9} m^2 s^{-1}

Distance between the planes $(Z_2 - Z_1)$ = 0.002 m

Substituting the values of the parameters in the equation,

$$N_A^1 = \frac{D_{AB}}{(Z_2 - Z_1)} \times \frac{C}{C_{Blm}} \times (C_{A2} - C_{A1})$$

$$= \frac{0.95 \times 10^{-9}}{0.002} \times \frac{53.60}{52.58} \times (1.35 - 0.67)$$

$$= 3.29 \times 10^{-7} \text{ kmol m}^{-2} \text{ s}^{-1}$$

MAXWELL'S LAW OF DIFFUSION

Maxwell [3] postulated that the partial pressure gradient in the direction of diffusion for a component of a two component gaseous mixture is proportional to

1. the relative velocity of the molecules in the direction of diffusion, and
2. the product of the molar concentrations of the components.

$$-\frac{dP_A}{dZ} \propto C_A C_B (u_A - u_B)$$

$$= F C_A C_B (u_A - u_B) \tag{1.28}$$

Here, C_A and C_B are molar concentrations of A and B, u_A and u_B are the mean molecular velocities of A and B in the direction of mass transfer and F is the coefficient.

But $u_A = \frac{N_A}{C_A}$; $u_B = \frac{N_B}{C_B}$

$$P_A V = n_A RT \text{ and } \frac{n_A}{V} = C_A$$

So $P_A = C_A RT$ (for ideal gas)

Substituting these in equation (1.28), we get

$$-\frac{dC_A RT}{dZ} = F \times C_A C_B \left(\frac{N_A}{C_A} - \frac{N_B}{C_B} \right) \tag{1.29}$$

$$-\frac{dC_A}{dZ} = \frac{F}{RT}(N_A C_B - N_B C_A) \tag{1.30}$$

For equimolecular counter diffusion, put $N_A = -N_B$ in equation (1.30)

So $$-\frac{dC_A}{dZ} = \frac{F N_A}{RT}(C_B + C_A) = \frac{F N_A}{RT} C_T \tag{1.31}$$

$$N_A = -\frac{RT}{FC_T}\frac{dC_A}{dZ} \tag{1.32}$$

By comparison with Fick's law.

$$D = +\frac{RT}{FC_T}$$

or $$F = +\frac{RT}{DC_T} \tag{1.33}$$

For diffusion of A through stagnant B, $N_B = 0$ and $N_A = N_A^1$ in equation (1.30)

$$-\frac{dC_A}{dZ} = \frac{F}{RT}N_A^1 C_B \tag{1.34}$$

$$N_A^1 = -\frac{RT}{FC_B} \times \frac{dC_A}{dZ}$$

$$= -\frac{RT}{DC_T} \times \frac{C_T}{C_B} \times \frac{dC_A}{dZ}$$

$$= -D \times \frac{C_T}{C_B} \times \frac{dC_A}{dZ} \tag{1.35}$$

This is Stefan's law (equation 1.17). It has been derived from Maxwell's law of diffusion.

MULTI-COMPONENT MASS TRANSFER

Consider the transfer of component A through a stationary gas consisting of components B, C and so on. The total partial pressure gradient can be regarded as being made up of a series of terms, each representing the contribution of the individual component gases.

$$-\frac{dC_A}{dZ} = \frac{F}{RT}(N_A C_B - N_B C_A) \tag{1.36}$$

$$-\frac{dC_A}{dZ} = \frac{F}{RT}N_A^1 C_B \tag{1.37}$$

When $N_B = 0, N_A = N_A^1$

For the multi-component system,

$$-\frac{dC_A}{dZ} = \frac{F_{AB}}{RT} C_B \ N_A^1 + \frac{F_{AC}}{RT} C_C \ N_A^1 + \ldots$$

$$= \frac{N_A^1}{RT}(F_{AB}C_B + F_{AC}C_c + \ldots) \tag{1.38}$$

But $F_{AB} = \dfrac{RT}{D_{AB}C_T}$ and hence $\dfrac{F_{AB}}{RT} = \dfrac{1}{D_{AB}C_T}$

$$-\frac{dC_A}{dZ} = +\frac{N^1 A}{C_T}\left(\frac{C_B}{D_{AB}} + \frac{C_C}{D_{AC}} + \ldots\ldots\right) \tag{1.39}$$

$$\frac{-C_T \dfrac{dC_A}{dZ}}{\left(\dfrac{C_B}{D_{AB}} + \dfrac{C_C}{D_{AC}} + \ldots\right)} = N_A^1 \tag{1.40}$$

$$N_A^1 = \frac{\dfrac{-C_T}{C_T - C_A}\dfrac{dC_A}{dZ}}{\dfrac{C_B}{C_T - C_A}\dfrac{1}{D_{AB}} + \dfrac{C_C}{C_T - C_A}\dfrac{1}{D_{AC}} + \ldots\ldots}$$

$$= \frac{-1}{\left(\dfrac{y_B^1}{D_{AB}} + \dfrac{y_C^1}{D_{AC}} + \ldots\right)} \frac{C_r}{C_T - C_A}\frac{dC_A}{dZ}$$

$$= -D^1 \frac{C_T}{C_T - C_A}\frac{dC_A}{dZ} \tag{1.41}$$

Comparing this with Stefan's law, which states that,

$$N_A^1 = -D\frac{C_T}{C_B}\frac{dC_A}{dZ} \tag{1.17}$$

we can get, $D^1 = \dfrac{1}{\left(\dfrac{y_B^1}{D_{AB}} + \dfrac{y_C^1}{D_{AC}} + \ldots\ldots\right)}$ (1.42)

D^1 is the effective diffusivity of A in the mixture and $y_B^1, y_C^1, \ldots$ are the mole fractions of the stationary components.

ILLUSTRATION

1L Calculate the diffusion of O_2 (A) in a non-diffusing gaseous mixture of CH_4 (B) and H_2 (C) in the volume ratio of 2:1, at a total pressure of 1×10^5 N m^{-2} and a temperature of 273 K. The partial pressures of O_2 at two planes 2.0 mm apart are 13 000 and 6 500 N m^{-2} respectively. The diffusivity has been estimated to be 6.99×10^{-5} m^2 s^{-1} for the O_2–H_2 mixture and 1.86×10^{-5} m^2 s^{-1} for the O_2–CH_4 mixture.

Solution

For gaseous systems, the diffusion flux when one component is diffusing while the other remains stagnant is given by the equation,

$$N_A^1 = \frac{D^1}{RT(Z_2 - Z_1)} \times \frac{P}{P_{Blm}} \times (P_{A2} - P_{A1})$$

where P is the total pressure, P_{A2} and P_{A1} are the partial pressures of the diffusing component A at locations 2 and 1 respectively, P_{Blm} is the log mean value of the partial pressure of the non-diffusing component B at locations 1 and 2 and is given by,

$$P_{Blm} = \frac{P_{B2} - P_{B1}}{\ln \dfrac{P_{B2}}{P_{B1}}}$$

Effective diffusivity of the mixture (D^1)

$$= \frac{1}{\left(\dfrac{Y_B^1}{D_{AB}} + \dfrac{Y_C^1}{D_{AC}} + \ldots\right)} = \frac{1}{\dfrac{0.667}{1.86 \times 10^{-5}} + \dfrac{0.333}{6.99 \times 10^{-5}}}$$

$$= 2.46 \times 10^{-5} \text{ m}^2 \text{ s}^{-1}$$

Total pressure (P) = 1×10^5 N m^{-2}

Partial pressure of O_2 at plane 1 (P_{A1}) = 13 000 N m^{-2}

Partial pressure of O_2 at plane 2 (P_{A2}) = 6 500 N m^{-2}

Partial pressure of non diffusing components at plane 1 (P_{B1}) = $P - P_{A1} = 87\,000$ N m^{-2}

Partial pressure of non diffusing components at plane 2 (P_{B2}) = $P - P_{A2} = 93\,500$ N m^{-2}

$$P_{Blm} = \frac{P_{B2} - P_{B1}}{\ln \dfrac{P_{B2}}{P_{B1}}} = \frac{87\ 000 - 93\ 500}{\ln \dfrac{87\ 000}{93\ 500}} = 90\ 211 \text{ N m}^{-2}$$

Universal gas constant (R)	=	8. 314 J mol^{-1} K^{-1}
Temperature (T)	=	273 K
Distance between the planes ($Z_2 - Z_1$)	=	0.002 m

Substituting the values of the parameters, in the equation,

$$N_A^1 = \frac{D^1}{RT(Z_2 - Z_1)} \times \frac{P}{P_{Blm}} \times (P_{A2} - P_{A1})$$

$$= \frac{2.46 \times 10^{-5}}{8.314 \times 273 \times 0.002} \times \frac{100\ 000}{90\ 211} \times (13\ 000 - 6\ 500)$$

$$= 3.90 \times 10^{-2} \text{ mol m}^{-2} \text{ s}^{-1}$$

DIFFUSIVITIES OF VAPOURS

Diffusivities of vapours can be determined by the Winkelmann [4] method. The liquid of the vapours of which diffusivity has to be determined, is allowed to evaporate in a vertical glass tube (Fig. 1.2). Over the top of the glass tube, a stream of vapour-free gas is passed sufficiently rapidly so that the vapour pressure at the top is zero. The apparatus is maintained at a constant temperature to avoid eddy currents in the vertical tube and to ensure that mass transfer takes place only by molecular diffusion. The rate of evaporation is followed by the rate of fall in the liquid level using a travelling microscope. Using this information, the concentration gradient and the diffusivity can be calculated. Care must be taken to avoid any distrubance of the gas at the mouth of the tube which will reduce the effective distance through which diffusion occurs. It is a case of diffusion of vapours of the liquid through the non diffusing or stagnant air.

The rate of mass transfer is equal to the diffusion flux. The diffusion flux under these conditions is given by

$$N_A^1 = \frac{D_{AB}}{RT(Z_2 - Z_1)} \times \frac{P}{P_{Blm}} \times (P_{A2} - P_{A1}) \tag{1.23}$$

where P is the total pressure, P_{A2} and P_{A1} are the partial pressures of the diffusing component – vapour of the liquid A – at the liquid surface and at the top of the tube respectively. Clearly, P_{A2} is the vapour pressure of the liquid at the experimental temperature and P_{A1} is zero, as mentioned earlier. P_{Blm} is the mean value of the partial pressure of the non-diffusing component air (B), at locations 1 and 2 and is given by,

$$P_{Blm} = \frac{P_{B2} - P_{B1}}{\ln \dfrac{P_{B2}}{P_{B1}}}$$

D_{AB} is the diffusivity of the mixture and $Z_2 - Z_1$ is the distance between the liquid level and the top open end of the tube.

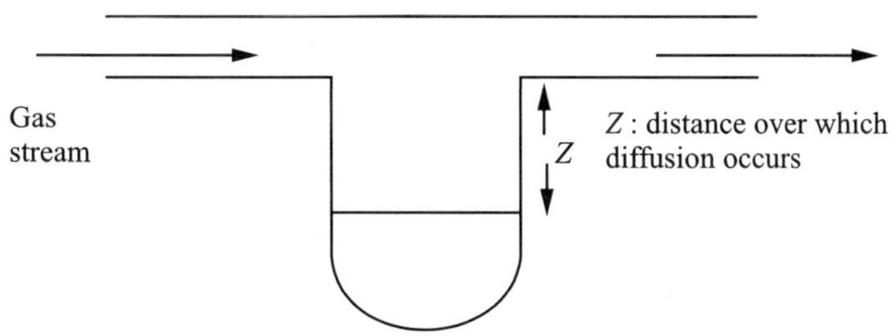

Fig. 1.2 Determination of diffusivity

The rate of mass transfer is also equal to the rate of evaporation, which can be found by following the ratc of fall in liquid level.

$$N_A^1 = \left(\frac{\rho}{M}\right)_L \times \left(\frac{dZ}{dt}\right) \tag{1.43}$$

where ρ is the density of the liquid, M is the molecular weight of the liquid and $\frac{dZ}{dt}$ is the rate of fall in liquid level.

$$N_A^1 = \frac{D_{AB}}{RT(Z_2 - Z_1)} \times \frac{P}{P_{Blm}} \times (P_{A2} - P_{A1}) = \left(\frac{\rho}{M}\right)_L \times \left(\frac{dZ}{dt}\right) \tag{1.44}$$

Separating the variables, $\dfrac{D_{AB}}{RT} \times \dfrac{P}{P_{Blm}} \times (P_{A2} - P_{A1})dt = \left(\dfrac{\rho}{M}\right)_L \times (Z_2 - Z_1)dZ$ (1.45)

At zero time, the liquid level is Z_1 and when the time is t, the level drops to Z_2. Integrating the above equation between two limits,

$$\frac{D_{AB}}{RT} \times \frac{P}{P_{Blm}} \times (P_{A2} - P_{A1}) \int_0^t dt = \left(\frac{\rho}{M}\right)_L \times \int_{Z1}^{Z2} dZ \tag{1.46}$$

$$\frac{D_{AB}}{RT} \times \frac{P}{P_{Blm}} \times (P_{A2} - P_{A1})t = \left(\frac{\rho}{M}\right)_L \times \frac{(Z_2^2 - Z_1^2)}{2} \tag{1.47}$$

From the above, D_{AB} can be found.

$$D_{AB} = \left(\frac{\rho}{M}\right)_L \times \frac{(Z_2^2 - Z_1^2)}{2} \times \frac{RTP_{Blm}}{P(P_{A2} - P_{A1})t} \tag{1.48}$$

ILLUSTRATIONS

1M A tube of small diameter was filled with acetone to a depth of 1.10 cm from the top and maintained at a temperature of 293 K in a gentle current of air. After 5 hours, the level of liquid had fallen to 2.05 cm. The barometric pressure is 750 mm Hg, the vapour pressure of acetone at 293 K is 180 mm Hg and the density of acetone is 0.79 g cm^{-3}. Calculate the diffusivity of acetone vapour in air.

Solution

The problem can be solved using the equation,

$$D_{AB} = \left(\frac{\rho}{M}\right)_L \times \frac{(Z_2^2 - Z_1^2)}{2} \times \frac{RTP_{Blm}}{P(P_{A2} - P_{A1})t}$$

where P is the total pressure, P_{A2} is the vapour pressure of the liquid at the experimental temperature and P_{A1} is zero, as only atmospheric air is present at the top of the tube. P_{Blm} is the log mean value of the partial pressure of the non-diffusing component air (B), at the liquid surface (P_{B2}) and at the top of the tube (P_{B1}) and is given by,

$$P_{Blm} = \frac{P_{B2} - P_{B1}}{\ln \dfrac{P_{B2}}{P_{B1}}}$$

Total pressure (P) $= \dfrac{750}{760} = 0.986$ atm

Vapour pressure of liquid at the liquid surface (P_{A1}) $= \dfrac{180}{760} = 0.236$ atm

Partial pressure of vapour at the top of the tube (P_{A1})$=$ 0.986 atm

Partial pressure of air at the liquid surface (P_{B1}) $= P - P_{A1}$

$= 0.986 - 0.236 = 0.75$ atm

Partial pressure of air at the top of the tube (P_{B2}) $= P - P_{A2}$

$= 0.986 - 0 = 0.986$ atm

$$P_{Blm} = \frac{P_{B2} - P_{B1}}{\ln \dfrac{P_{B2}}{P_{B1}}} = \frac{0.986 - 0.75}{\ln \dfrac{0.986}{0.75}} = 0.861 \text{ atm}$$

Universal gas constant (R)	=	$0.082\ 05\ m^3\ atm\ kmol^{-1}\ K^{-1}$
Temperature (T)	=	293 K
Initial level (Z_1)	=	1.1×10^{-2} m
Final level (Z_2)	=	2.05×10^{-2} m
Duration of experiment (t)	=	$5 \times 3\ 600$ s
Density of the liquid (ρ)	=	$0.79\ g\ cm^{-3} = 790\ kg\ m^{-3}$
Molecular weight of acetone (M)	=	58

Substituting the values of the parameters in the equation,

$$D_{AB} = \left(\frac{\rho}{M}\right)_L \times \frac{(Z_2^2 - Z_1^2)}{2} \times \frac{RTP_{Blm}}{P(P_{A2} - P_{A1})t}$$

$$= \frac{790}{58} \times \frac{(2.05 \times 10^{-2})^2 - (1.1 \times 10^{-2})^2}{2} \times \frac{0.082\ 05 \times 293 \times 0.861}{0.986 \times 0.236 \times 5 \times 3\ 600}$$

$$= 1.01 \times 10^{-5}\ m^2\ s^{-1}$$

1N A vertical galss tube of 3 mm inner diameter was filled with liquid toluene (density = 0.82 g cm^{-3}) to a depth of 2 cm from the top open end. After 200 hours at 303 K and at a total pressure of 1 atm, the level dropped to 8 cm from the top. The vapour pressure of toluene at 303 K is 57 mm Hg. Neglecting the counter current diffusion of air to replace the evaporating liquid, calculate the diffusivity of toluene in air. Make suitable assumptions, if required.

Solution

The problem can be solved using the equation,

$$D_{AB} = \left(\frac{\rho}{M}\right)_L \times \frac{(Z_2^2 - Z_1^2)}{2} \times \frac{RTP_{Blm}}{P(P_{A2} - P_{A1})t}$$

where P is the total pressure, P_{A2} is the vapour pressure of the liquid at the experimental temperature and P_{A1} is zero, as only atmospheric air is present at the top of the tube. P_{Blm} is the log mean value of the partial pressure of the non-diffusing component air (B), at the liquid surface (P_{B2}) and at the top of the tube (P_{B1}) and is given by,

$$P_{Blm} = \frac{P_{B2} - P_{B1}}{\ln \dfrac{P_{B2}}{P_{B1}}}$$

Total pressure (P)	=	1.0 atm
Vapour pressure of liquid at the liquid surface (P_{A1})	=	$\frac{57}{760} = 0.075$ atm

Partial pressure of vapour at the top of the tube (P_{A2}) = 0 atm

Partial pressure of air at the liquid surface (P_{B1}) = $P - P_{A1}$

= $1.0 - 0.075 = 0.925$ atm

Partial pressure of air at the top of the tube (P_{B2}) = $P - P_{A2}$

= 1.0 atm

$$P_{Blm} = \frac{P_{B2} - P_{B1}}{\ln \dfrac{P_{B2}}{P_{B1}}} = \frac{1.0 - 0.925}{\ln \dfrac{1.0}{0.925}} = 0.962 \text{ atm}$$

Universal gas constant (R)	=	0.082 05 m^3 atm $kmol^{-1}$ K^{-1}
Temperature (T)	=	303 K
Initial level (Z_1)	=	8×10^{-2} m
Final level (Z_2)	=	2×10^{-2} m
Duration of experiment (t)	=	$200 \times 3\,600$ s
Density of the liquid (ρ)	=	0.82 g cm^{-3} = 820 kg m^{-3}
Molecular weight of toluene (M)	=	92

Substituting the values of the parameters in the equation,

$$D_{AB} = \left(\frac{\rho}{M}\right)_L \times \frac{(Z_2^2 - Z_1^2)}{2} \times \frac{RTP_{Blm}}{P(P_{A2} - P_{A1})t}$$

$$= \frac{820}{92} \times \frac{(8 \times 10^{-2})^2 - (2 \times 10^{-2})^2}{2} \times \frac{0.082\,05 \times 303 \times 0.962}{1 \times 0.075 \times 200 \times 3\,600}$$

$$= 1.18 \times 10^{-5} \text{ m}^2 \text{ s}^{-1}$$

10 In an experiment to determine the diffusivity of chloropicrin (CCl_3NO_2) in a steady state diffusion of the former in air, liquid chloropicrin is allowed to evaporate from a free surface and diffuse into a column of air. When the steady state was attained, the following data were collected.

Total pressure	=	1 atm
Vapour pressure of CCl_3NO_2	=	23.8 mm Hg
Length of air column	=	11.14 cm
Temperature	=	298 K
Area of cross reaction of air column	=	2.3 cm^2
Density of CCl_3NO_2	=	1.65 gpL
Evaporation	=	0.014 g h^{-1}

Calculate the diffusivity of the system.

Solution

For gaseous systems, the diffusion flux when one component is diffusing while the other remains stagnant is given by the equation,

$$N_A^1 = \frac{D_{AB}}{RT(Z_2 - Z_1)} \times \frac{P}{P_{Blm}} \times (P_{A2} - P_{A1})$$

where P is the total pressure, P_{A2} and P_{A1} are the partial pressures of the diffusing component A at locations 2 and 1 respectively, P_{Blm} is the log mean value of the partial pressure of the non-diffusing component B at locations 1 and 2 and is given by,

$$P_{Blm} = \frac{P_{B2} - P_{B1}}{\ln \dfrac{P_{B2}}{P_{B1}}}$$

Diffusivity of the mixture = To be calculated, D_{AB}

Total pressure (P) = 1 atm

Partial pressure of chloropicrin at plane 1 (P_{A1}) = $23.81 \div 760 = 0.031\ 3$ atm

Partial pressure of chloropicrin at plane 2 (P_{A2}) = 0 atm

Partial pressure of air at plane 1 (P_{B1}) = $P - P_{A1} = 1.0 - 0.031\ 3 = 0.968\ 7$ atm

Partial pressure of air at plane 1 (P_{B2}) = $P - P_{A2} = 1.0 - 0 = 1.0$ atm

$$P_{Blm} = \frac{P_{B2} - P_{B1}}{\ln \dfrac{P_{B2}}{P_{B1}}} = \frac{1.0 - 0.968\ 7}{\ln \dfrac{1.0}{0.968\ 7}} = 0.984\ 3 \text{ atm}$$

Universal gas constant (R) = 82.05 cm^3 atm $mol^{-1}K^{-1}$

Temperature (T) = 298 K

Distance between the planes ($Z_2 - Z_1$) = 11.14 cm

Molecular weight of chloropicrin = 164.38

Rate of evaporation = 0.014 g h^{-1}

$$= \frac{0.014}{3\ 600} \text{ g s}^{-1}$$

$$= \frac{0.014}{3\ 600 \times 164.38} \text{ mol s}^{-1}$$

Diffusion flux = Rate of evaporation ÷ surface area

$$= \frac{0.014}{3\ 600 \times 164.38 \times 2.3}$$

$$= 1.026 \times 10^{-8} \text{ mol cm}^{-2} \text{ s}^{-1}$$

Substituting the values of the parameters in the equation,

$$N_A^1 = \frac{D_{AB}}{RT(Z_2 - Z_1)} \times \frac{P}{P_{Blm}} \times (P_{A2} - P_{A1})$$

$$1.026 \times 10^{-8} = \frac{D_{AB}}{82.05 \times 298 \times 11.14} \times \frac{1.0}{0.984\ 3} \times (0.0313 - 0)$$

$$D_{AB} = 0.0879\ \text{cm}^2\ \text{s}^{-1}$$

EMPIRICAL EQUATIONS FOR DIFFUSIVITY

Diffusivity of gases and vapours can also be found from their physical properties using the empirical equation proposed by Gilliland [5].

$$D_{AB} = \frac{4.3 \times 10^{-3} T^{3/2} \sqrt{\left(\frac{1}{M_A} + \frac{1}{M_B}\right)}}{P(V_A^{1/3} + V_B^{1/3})} \tag{1.49}$$

where D_{AB} is the diffusivity in m^2 s^{-1}, T is the temperature (in the absolute scale) at which the measurement is made, M_A and M_B are the molecular weights of A and B, V_A and V_B are molecular volumes of A and B in their liquid state at their boiling point in m^3 kmol^{-1} and P is the pressure at which the measurement is carried out.

This equation indicates the dependence of diffusivity on temperature and pressure. Diffusivity is directly proportional to the 1.5th power of temperature and inversely proportional to pressure.

$$D_{AB} \propto \frac{T^{3/2}}{P} \tag{1.50}$$

The diffusivity of dilute solutions of non-electrolytes can be calculated using the equation proposed by Wilke and Chang [6]. This equation is not dimentionally consistent and hence the values of the coefficient depends on the units employed. For SI units, the following equation has to be employed.

$$D_{AB} = \frac{1.173 \times 10^{-16} \times T\sqrt{\phi_B \times M_B}}{\mu \times V_A^{0.6}} \tag{1.51}$$

where D_{AB} is the diffusivity of solute A in solvent B in m^2 s^{-1}, T is the temperature (in the absolute scale) at which the measurement is made, M_B is the molecular weight of solvent, V_A is the molecular volume of the solute of A in m^3 kmol^{-1}, μ is the viscosity of the solution in kg m^{-1} s^{-1} and ϕ_B is the association factor for the solvent (2.26 for water, 1.9 for methanol, 1.5 for ethanol and 1.0 unassociated solvents like hydrocarbons and ethers).

ILLUSTRATIONS

1P The diffusivity of gases is often estimated by the Gilliland equation,

$$D_{AB} = \frac{0.0043\, T^{3/2}\sqrt{\left(\frac{1}{M_A} + \frac{1}{M_B}\right)}}{P(V_A^{1/3} + V_B^{1/3})}$$

Estimate the diffusity of ethanol in air at 298 K and at atmospheric pressure, if the atomic volumes of C, H and O are 14.8, 3.7 and 7.4 respectively. The molar volume of air is 29.9 cm^3 mol^{-1}.

Solution

The molecular formula of ethanol is CH_3CH_2OH. By Kopp's rule, the molar volume is obtained by the summation of atomic volumes of the constitutent atoms.

Molar volume of ethanol (V_A) = $(2 \times 14.8) + (6 \times 3.7) + 7.4 = 59.2$ cm^3 mol^{-1}

Molecular weight of ethanaol (M_A) $= 46$

Molecular weight of air (M_B) $= 29$

Substituting all the other parameters, in the equation,

$$D_{AB} = \frac{0.0043\, T^{3/2}\sqrt{\left(\frac{1}{M_A} + \frac{1}{M_B}\right)}}{P(V_A^{1/3} + V_{M_B}^{1/3})} = \frac{0.004\,3(298)^{3/2}\sqrt{\left(\frac{1}{46} + \frac{1}{29}\right)}}{1(59.2^{1/3} + 29.9^{1/3})}$$

$$= 0.749 \text{ cm}^2 \text{ s}^{-1}$$

1Q Ammonia is diffusing through an inert air film of 2 mm thickness at a temperature of 273 K and 1 atm pressure. The concentration of ammonia is 10% by volume on one side and zero on the other side. The diffusivity of ammonia in air at 273 K and 1 atm pressure is 0.198 cm^2 s^{-1}. Estimate the rate of diffusion of ammonia. Also estimate the rate of diffusion if the temperature is 293 K and pressure is 2 atm.

Solution

For gaseous systems, the diffusion flux when one component is diffusing while the other remains stagnant is given by the equation,

$$N_A^1 = \frac{D_{AB}}{RT(Z_2 - Z_1)} \times \frac{P}{P_{Blm}} \times (P_{A2} - P_{A1})$$

where P is the total pressure, P_{A2} and P_{A1} are the partial pressures of the diffusing component A at locations 2 and 1 respectively, P_{Blm} is the log mean value of the partial pressure of the non-diffusing component B at locations 1 and 2 and is given by,

$$P_{Blm} = \frac{P_{B2} - P_{B1}}{\ln \dfrac{P_{B2}}{P_{B1}}}$$

At 273 K and 1 atm pressure

Total pressure (P) = 1 atm

Partial pressure of NH_3 at plane 1(PA_1) = Total pressure × Mole fraction

= $1 \times 0.1 = 0.1$ atm

Partial pressure of NH_3 at plane 2(PA_2) = 0 atm

Partial pressure of air at plane 1(P_{B1}) = $P - P_{A1} = 1.0 - 0.1 = 0.9$ atm

Partial pressure of air at plane 1(P_{B2}) = $P - P_{A2} = 1.0 - 0 = 1.0$ atm

$$P_{Blm} = \frac{P_{B2} - P_{B1}}{\ln \dfrac{P_{B2}}{P_{B1}}} = \frac{1 - 0.9}{\ln \dfrac{1}{0.9}} = 0.948\,8 \text{ atm}$$

Universal gas constant (R) = $0.082\,05$ m^3 atm kmol^{-1} K^{-1}

Temperature (T) = 273 K

Distance between the planes ($Z_2 - Z_1$) = 0.002 m

Diffusivity of NH_3 in air (D_{AB}) = 0.198 cm^2 s^{-1}

= 1.98×10^{-5} m^2 s^{-1}

Substituting the values of the parameters, in the equation,

$$N_A^1 = \frac{D_{AB}}{RT(Z_2 - Z_1)} \times \frac{P}{P_{Blm}} \times (P_{A2} - P_{A1})$$

$$= \frac{1.98 \times 10^{-5}}{0.082\,05 \times 273 \times 0.002} \times \frac{1}{0.948\,8} \times (0.1 - 0)$$

$$= 4.658 \times 10^{-5} \text{ k mol m}^{-2} \text{ s}^{-1}$$

At 293 K and 2 atm pressure

Diffusivity is directly proportional to the 1.5th power of temperature and inversely proportional to pressure.

$$D \propto \frac{T^{3/2}}{P}$$

$$\frac{D_{AB,\,273\text{ K},1\text{ atm}}}{D_{AB,\,293\text{ K},2\text{ atm}}} = \left(\frac{273}{293}\right)^{3/2} \times \frac{2}{1}$$

$$\frac{1.98\times10^{-5}}{D^1} = 0.899\,4\times2$$

Diffusivity at the new conditions (D^1) = 1.10×10^{-5} m^2 s^{-1}

Total pressure (P) = 2 atm

Partial pressure of NH_3 at plane 1 (P_{A1})= Total pressure $\times$ Mole fraction

= $2\times0.1 = 0.2$ atm

Partial pressure of NH_3 at plane 2 (P_{A2})= 0 atm

Partial pressure of air at plane 1 (P_{B1}) = $P - P_{A1} = 2.0 - 0.2 = 1.8$ atm

Partial pressure of air at plane 1 (P_{B2}) = $P - P_{A2} = 2.0 - 0 \quad = 2.0$ atm

$$P_{Blm} = \frac{P_{B2}-P_{B1}}{\ln\dfrac{P_{B2}}{P_{B1}}} = \frac{2-1.8}{\ln\dfrac{2}{1.8}} = 1.898\text{ atm}$$

The rest of the parameters are the same. Substituting the values of the parameters in the equation below,

$$N_A^1 = \frac{D_{AB}}{RT(Z_2-Z_1)} \times \frac{P}{P_{Blm}} \times (P_{A2}-P_{A1})$$

$$= \frac{1.1\times10^{-5}}{0.082\,05\times293\times0.002} \times \frac{2}{1.898} \times (0.2-0)$$

$$= 4.821\times10^{-5}\text{ kmol m}^{-2}\text{ s}^{-1}$$

If there is no change in temperature, then $D^1 = 1/2D$ and $(P_{A2} - P_{A1}) = 0.2$. There will be no change in N_A^1 due to increase of presssure alone, as the diffusivity becomes half, although the partial pressure difference becomes double.

1R By what percentage would the rate of absorption be increased or decreased by increasing the total pressure from 100 to 200 kN m^{-2} in the following:

(a) the absorption of NH_3 from a mixture of NH_3 and air containing 10% NH_3 by volume using pure water as solvent. Assume all the resistance lies in the gas phase.

(b) The same continues as in (a) but the absorbing liquid exerts a partial pressure of NH_3 equal to 5 kN m^{-2}. The diffusivity may be assumed to be inversely related to absorption pressure.

Solution

For gaseous systems, the diffusion flux when one component is diffusing while the other remains stagnant is given by the equation,

$$N_A^1 = \frac{D_{AB}}{RT(Z_2 - Z_1)} \times \frac{P}{P_{Blm}} \times (P_{A2} - P_{A1})$$

where P is the total pressure, P_{A2} and P_{A1} are the partial pressures of the diffusing component A at locations 2 and 1 respectively, P_{Blm} is the log mean value of the partial pressure of the non-diffusing component B at locations 1 and 2 and is given by,

$$P_{Blm} = \frac{P_{B2} - P_{B1}}{\ln \dfrac{P_{B2}}{P_{B1}}}$$

At 100 kN m^{-2} pressure

Total pressure (P) = 100 kN m^{-2}

Partial pressure of NH_3 at plane 1 (P_{A1}) = Total pressure $\times$ Mole fraction

= $100 \times 0.1 = 10$ kN m^{-2}

Partial pressure of NH_3 at plane 2 (P_{A2}) = 0 kN m^{-2}

Partial pressure of air at plane 1 (P_{B1}) = $P - P_{A1} = 100 - 10 = 90$ kN m^{-2}

Partial pressure of air at plane 1 (P_{B2}) = $P - P_{A2} = 100 - 0 = 100$ kN m^{-2}

$$P_{Blm} = \frac{P_{B2} - P_{B1}}{\ln \dfrac{P_{B2}}{P_{B1}}} = \frac{100 - 90}{\ln \dfrac{100}{90}} = 94.91 \text{ kN m}^{-2}$$

Let the universal gas constant be R, temperature be T, distance between the planes be Z and diffusivity of NH_3 in air be D_{AB}. Substituting the values of the parameters in the equation,

$$N_A^1 = \frac{D_{AB}}{RT(Z_2 - Z_1)} \times \frac{P}{P_{Blm}} \times (P_{A2} - P_{A1}) = \frac{D_{AB}}{RTZ} \times \frac{100}{94.91} \times (10 - 0)$$

$$= 10.54 \frac{D_{AB}}{RTZ} = \text{k mol m}^{-2} \text{ s}^{-1}$$

At 200 kN m^{-2} pressure

The diffusivity is inversely proportional to pressure.

Diffusivity at the new conditions (D_1) = $\dfrac{D_{AB}}{2}$

Total pressure (P) = 200 kN m^{-2}

Partial pressure of NH_3 at plane 1 (P_{A1})= Total pressure × Mole fraction

= $200 \times 0.1 = 20$ kN m^{-2}

Partial pressure of NH_3 at plane 2 (P_{A2})= 0 kN m^{-2}

Partial pressure of air at plane 1 (P_{B1}) = $P - P_{A1} = 200 - 20 = 180$ kN m^{-2}

Partial pressure of air at plane 1 (P_{B2}) = $P - P_{A2} = 200 - 0 = 200$ kN m^{-2}

$$P_{Blm} = \frac{P_{B2} - P_{B1}}{\ln \dfrac{P_{B2}}{P_{B1}}} = \frac{200 - 180}{\ln \dfrac{200}{180}} = 189.82 \text{ kN m}^{-2}$$

The rest of the parameters are the same. Substituting the values of the parameters in the equation,

$$N_A^1 = \frac{D_{AB}}{RT(Z_2 - Z_1)} \times \frac{P}{P_{Blm}} \times (P_{A2} - P_{A1}) = \frac{D_{AB}}{2RTZ} \times \frac{200}{189.82} \times (20 - 0)$$

$$N_A^1 = \frac{D_{AB}}{RT(Z_2 - Z_1)} \times \frac{P}{P_{Blm}} \times (P_{A2} - P_{A1}) == 10.54\frac{D_{AB}}{RTZ} \text{ kmol m}^{-2} \text{ s}^{-1}$$

Therefore, there will be no change in N_A^1 as a result of presssure change.

(b) If the absorbing solution has a partial pressure of $NH_3 = 5$ kN m^{-2}.

At 100 kN m^{-2} pressure

Total pressure (P) = 100 kN m^{-2}

Partial pressure of NH_3 at plane 1 (P_{A1})= Total pressure × Mole fraction

= $100 \times 0.1 = 10$ kN m^{-2}

Partial pressure of NH_3 at plane 2 (P_{A2})= 5 kN m^{-2}

Partial pressure of air at plane 1 (P_{B1}) = $P - P_{A1} = 100 - 10 = 90$ kN m^{-2}

Partial pressure of air at plane 1 (P_{B2}) = $P - P_{A2} = 100 - 5 \quad = 95$ kN m^{-2}

$$P_{Blm} = \frac{P_{B2} - P_{B1}}{\ln \dfrac{P_{B2}}{P_{B1}}} = \frac{95 - 90}{\ln \dfrac{95}{90}} = 92.48 \text{ kN m}^{-2}$$

Let the universal gas constant be R, the temperature be T, the distance between the planes be Z and the diffusivity of NH_3 in air be D_{AB}. Substituting the values of the parameters in the equation,

$$N_A^1 = \frac{D_{AB}}{RT(Z_2 - Z_1)} \times \frac{P}{P_{Blm}} \times (P_{A2} - P_{A1})$$

$$= \frac{D_{AB}}{RTZ} \times \frac{100}{92.48} \times (10 - 5)$$

$$= 5.406\frac{D_{AB}}{RTZ} \text{ kmol m}^{-2} \text{ s}^{-1}$$

At 200 kN m^{-2} pressure

The diffusivity is inversely proportional to pressure.

Diffusivity at the new conditions (D_1) $= \dfrac{D_{AB}}{2}$

Total pressure (P) $= 200$ kN m^{-2}

Partial pressure of NH^3 at plane 1 (P_{A1})= Total pressure × Mole fraction

$= 200 \times 0.1 = 20$ kN m^{-2}

Partial pressure of NH_3 at plane 2 (P_{A2})= 5 kN m^{-2}

Partial pressure of air at plane 1 (P_{B1}) $= P - P_{A1} = 200 - 20 = 180$ kN m^{-2}

Partial pressure of air at plane 1 (P_{B2}) $= P - P_{A2} = 200 - 5 = 195$ kN m^{-2}

$$P_{Blm} = \frac{P_{B2} - P_{B1}}{\ln \frac{P_{B2}}{P_{B1}}} = \frac{195 - 180}{\ln \frac{195}{180}} = 187.40 \text{ kN m}^{-2}$$

The rest of the parameters are the same. Substituting the values of the parameters in the equation,

$$N_A^1 = \frac{D_{AB}}{RT(Z_2 - Z_1)} \times \frac{P}{P_{Blm}} \times (P_{A2} - P_{A1})$$

$$= \frac{D_{AB}}{2RTZ} \times \frac{200}{187.47} \times (20 - 5)$$

$$= 8.00\frac{D_{AB}}{RTZ} = \text{kmol m}^{-2} \text{ s}^{-1}$$

Then diffusion flux increases by 48%.

DIFFUSION IN SOLIDS

Diffusion of fluids through solids occurs in leaching, drying, adsorption and membrane separations like dialysis, electrodialysis and reverse osmosis. The mechanism of diffusion in solids is different from the mechanism of diffusion in fluids. Fick's law is applicable to diffusion in solids with certain limitations. When the rate of diffusion is constant, the diffusivity is independent of concentration and there is no bulk flow, Fick's law can be applied to diffusion in solids. Diffusion flux, N_A is given by

$$N_A = -D_A \times \frac{dC_A}{dZ} \tag{1.2}$$

where D_A is the diffusivity of A through the solid. For diffusion through a flat slab of thickness Z,

$$N_A = -D_A \times \frac{(C_{A2} - C_{A1})}{Z} \tag{1.52}$$

where C_{A2} and C_{A1} are the concentrations at the opposite sides of the slab. The rate of diffusion J_A for any solid shape is given by

$$J_A = N_A S_{av} = -D_A S_{av} \frac{(C_{A2} - C_{A1})}{Z} \tag{1.53}$$

where S_{av} is the average cross section for diffusion. For radial diffusion through a solid cylinder of inner radius r_i, outer radius r_o and length l, the average cross section is given by

$$S_{av} = \frac{2\pi\lambda(r_0 - r_i)}{\ln\frac{r_o}{r_i}} \text{ and } Z = (r_o - r_i) \tag{1.54}$$

For radial diffusion through a spherical shell of inner radius r_i and outer radius r_o,

$$S_{av} = 4\pi\lambda r_i r_0 \text{ and } Z = r_0 - r_i \tag{1.55}$$

ILLUSTRATION

1S Hydrogen gas at 2.5 atm pressure and 298 K flows through a pipe made of unvulcanised rubber with ID = 40 mm and OD = 50 mm. The solubility of H_2 is 5.3×10^{-2} cm^3 (STP) cm^{-3} atm and the diffusivity of H_2 through rubber is 1.8×10^{-6} cm^2 s^{-1}. Estimate the rate of loss of H_2 by diffusion per metre of pipe length.

Solution

Solubility of H_2 at 1atm = 5.3×10^{-2} cm^3 (STP) cm^{-3} atm

$$
\begin{aligned}
\text{Solubility of } H_2 \text{ at 2.5 atm} &= 5.3 \times 10^{-2} \times 2.5 \\
&= 0.132\ 5\ \text{cm}^3\ \text{(STP) cm}^{-3} \\
&= 0.132\ 5\ \text{m}^3\ \text{(STP) m}^3 \\
&= \frac{0.132\ 5 \times 273}{22.4 \times 298} = 5.418 \times 10^{-3}\ \text{kmol m}^{-3}
\end{aligned}
$$

This is equal to concentration of H_2 at the plane 2 (C_{A2}).

Concentration of H_2 at plane 1 (C_{A1}) = 0 kmol m^{-3} (since H_2 diffuses away immediately)

Diffusivity of H_2 through rubber (D_A) = 1.8×10^{-10} m^2 s^{-1}

Length (l) = 1 m

$$
S_{av} = \frac{2\pi\lambda(r_o - r_i)}{\ln \dfrac{r_o}{r_i}} = \frac{2\pi \times 1(25 - 20)}{100\ 0 \times \ln \dfrac{25}{20}} = 0.140\ 7\ \text{m}^2
$$

$$
Z = (r_o - r_i) = 25 - 20 = 5 \times 10^{-3}\ \text{m}
$$

The rate of diffusion of H_2 per metre length of the rubber tube is given by the formula,

$$
W = N_A S_{av} = -D_A S_{av} \frac{(C_{A2} - C_{A1})}{Z}
$$

Substituting the parameters in the above equation,

$$
W = 1.8 \times 10^{-10} \times 0.140\ 7 \times \frac{5.418 \times 10^{-3} - 0)}{5 \times 10^{-3}} = 2.74 \times 10^{-11}\ \text{kmol s}^{-1}
$$

$$
= 2.74 \times 10^{-11} \times 2.018 \times 360\ 0 = 2.00 \times 10^{-4}\ \text{g h}^{-1}
$$

TYPES OF SOLID DIFFUSION

The mechanism of diffusion and the rate of diffusion depend to a large extent on the structure of the solid and its interaction with the diffusing material.

Diffusion Through Polymers

If a polymeric membrane separates two bodies of a gas at different pressures, the gas dissolves in the solid at the high pressure side. The extent of dissolution is governed by Henry's law; that is, the concentration of the dissolved gas is directly proportional to the pressure. The gas then diffuses from the high pressure side to the low pressure side. Polymeric chains are in a state of constant thermal motion. Diffusing molecules jump from one position to another over a potential barrier. A successful jump requires a hole or passage of sufficient size. The size of the hole is fixed by the size and shape of the diffusing molecules. Hence diffusivity is temperature dependent and it follows an Arrhenius type expression.

$$D_A = D_o e^{-H_D/RT}$$

where H_D is the activation energy for diffusion and D_o is a constant. The diffusivity for simple gases is independent of concentration but is a strong function of the pressure of molding of the polymer. This type of diffusion is generally observed in the case of gases like hydrogen, helium and the like for which the molecular diameter is extremely small. It may be noted that the diffusivity of such gases is very low and is of the order of 10^{-10} m^2 s^{-1}.

Liquids which can act as solvents alone diffuse through polymers, by plasticising them. Solvents like benzene or methyl ethyl ketone (MEK) diffuse at rates very much higher than for permanent gases. Their diffusivities are strongly dependent on the solute concentration in the solid. In the case of oxygenated polymers like cellulose acetate, solvents like water, ammonia and ethanol form hydrogen bonds with the polymer and move from one bond site to the other at a faster rate.

The diffusion characteristics of the solid are usually described in terms of permeability. Permeability is defined as

$$\rho_A = D_A S_A \tag{1.56}$$

where ρ_A is the permeability for component A in cm^3 gas (STP) cm^{-2} s^{-1} (cm Hg cm^{-1})$^{-1}$, D_A is the diffusivity of A in cm^2 s^{-1} and S_A is the solubility coefficient or Henry's law constant in cm^3 for a gas (STP) and cm^{-3} for a solid (cm Hg)$^{-1}$. At the two faces of the membrane, the equilibrium solubility of the gas in the polymer is directly proportional to pressure.

Hence, $$V_A = \frac{-\rho_A(P_{A2} - P_{A1})}{Z} \tag{1.57}$$

where V_A = diffusion flux in terms of volume in m^3 gas (STP) cm^{-2}s^{-1}, P_A is the partial pressure of the diffusing gas in cm Hg and Z is thickness of the polymeric membrane, in cm. An important commercial application of diffusion of gases through solids is the separation of hydrogen from waste refinery gases using shell and tube devices made of polymer fibre tubes cased inside a metallic shell.

ILLUSTRATION

1T Calculate the rate of diffusion of CO_2 through a membrane of vulcanised rubber, 5 mm thick at 298 K, if the partial pressure of CO_2 is 5 cm Hg on one side and 0 on the other. Also, calculate the permeability of the membrane for CO_2. At

298 K, the solubility coefficient is 0.9 m^3 gas (STP) m^{-3} atm^{-1}. The diffusivity is 1.1×10^{-10} m^2 s^{-1}.

Solution

Permeability is given by $\rho_A = D_A S_A$

ρ_A is permeability for component A, in cm^3 gas (STP) cm^{-2} s^{-1} (cm Hg)$^{-1}$, D_A is diffusivity of A in cm^2 s^{-1} and S_A is solubility coefficient in cm^3 gas (STP) cm^{-3} solid (cm Hg)$^{-1}$.

$$D_A = 1.1 \times 10^{-10} \text{ m}^2 \text{ s}^{-1} = 1.1 \times 10^{-6} \text{ cm}^2 \text{ s}^{-1}$$

S_A is given in terms of m^3 gas (STP) m^{-3} atm^{-1}. It has to be converted to cm^3 gas (STP) cm^{-3} solid (cm Hg)$^{-1}$.

$$S_A = \frac{0.9}{76} = 0.01184 \text{ cm}^3 \text{ gas (STP) cm}^{-3} \text{ solid (cm Hg)}^{-1}$$

We know that,

$$\rho_A = D_A S_A$$

$$= 1.1 \times 10^{-6} \times 0.0118\,4 \text{ cm}^3 \text{ (STP) cm}^{-1} \text{ s}^{-1} \text{ solid (cm Hg)}^{-1}$$

$$= 1.3 \times 10^{-8} \text{ cm}^3 \text{ (STP) cm}^{-1} \text{ s}^{-1} \text{ (cm Hg)}^{-1}$$

We also know that, $V_A = \dfrac{-\rho_A(P_{A2} - P_{A1})}{Z}$

where V_A = diffusion flux in terms of volume in m^3 gas (STP) cm^{-2} s^{-1}, P_A is the partial pressure of the diffusing gas in cm Hg and Z is the thickness of the polymeric membrane, in cm.

Partial pressure of CO_2 on one side of the membrane (P_{A1})	=	5 cm Hg
Partial pressure of CO_2 on other side of the membrane (P_{A2})	=	0 cm Hg
Thickness of the membrane (Z)	=	0.5 cm

$$V_A = \frac{-1.3 \times 10^{8} \times (0.5)}{0.5} = 1.3 \times 10^{-7} \text{ cm}^3 \text{ (STP) cm}^{-2} \text{ s}^{-1}$$

Diffusion Through Crystalline Solids

The mechanism of diffusion through crystalline solids varies greatly depending upon the crystalline structure and the nature of solute. The principal mechanisms are:

1. **Interstitial mechanism** Places between the atoms of a crystal lattice are known as interstitial sites. Tiny atoms of the diffusing solute may pass from an interstitial site to

the adjacent one, if the matrix atoms of the crystal lattice move apart temporarily to provide the necessary space.

2. **Vacancy mechanism** If vacancies exist in the crystal lattice, an atom in an adjacent site may jump into such a vacancy.

3. **Crowd-ion mechanism** In a chain of closely packed atoms, an extra atom, if present can displace several atoms from their equilibrium position, leading to a diffusion flux.

4. **Diffusion along grain boundaries** In the case of multi-crystalline samples, diffusion occurs along the grain boundaries or crystal interfaces.

Diffusion in Porous Solids

In porous solids, the solute movement may occur by diffusion from one fluid body to the other by virtue of a concentration gradient or it may be hydrodynamic as a result of pressure difference. The pores of a solid may be interconnected, dead end or isolated. The pores in most solids are neither straight nor of constant diameter. It is more practical to base the flux upon the gross external surface area. Fluxes will be smaller than the true values based on true fluid cross section and length. Hence an effective diffusivity $D_{A,\text{eff}}$ smaller than the true D_A must be used. $D_{A,\text{eff}}$ is usually determined by experiments. It varies inversely with pressure and is approximately directly proportional to $T^{3/2}$.

The type of diffusive movement of gases through pores depends on the ratio of pore diameter d, to the mean free path of the gas molecules, λ. The mean free path is given by the relation

$$\lambda = \frac{3.2\mu}{P}\left(\frac{RT}{2\pi M}\right)^{1/2} \tag{1.58}$$

If the d/λ ratio is greater than 20, ordinary molecular diffusion predominates. If the d/λ ratio is less than 0.2, the rate of diffusion is controlled by collisions of gas molecules with the pore walls and Knudsen's law is followed. For a standard circular pore of diameter d and length l, the diffusion flux is given by,

$$N_A = -\frac{du_A}{3RTl}(P_{A2} - P_{A1}) \tag{1.59}$$

where u_A is mean molecular velocity of A. According to the kinetic theory of gases, mean molecular velocity is given by

$$u_A = \left(\frac{8RT}{\pi M_A}\right)^{1/2} \tag{1.60}$$

Substituting this in the expression for N_A, we get

$$N_A = \left(\frac{8RT}{\pi M_A}\right)^{1/2} \frac{d}{3RTl}(P_{A2} - P_{A1})$$

$$= \frac{-D_{K,A}(P_{A2} - P_{A1})}{RTl} \tag{1.61}$$

where $D_{K,A}$ is the Knudsen diffusion coefficient. Hence,

$$D_{K,A} = \frac{d}{3} \times \left(\frac{8RT}{\pi M_A}\right)^{1/2} \tag{1.62}$$

Usually, the pore diameter is not constant and pore length is not known precisely. So for all practical purposes, $D_{K,A}$ is replaced by $D_{K,A,\text{eff}}$ which is determined by experiments. $D_{K,A,\text{eff}}$ is independent of pressure and varies as $\left(\frac{T}{M}\right)^{1/2}$. Knudsen diffusion is not known for liquids.

Hydrodynamic Flow of Gases

Hydrodynamic flow of gas through the solid will occur, if there is a difference in absolute pressure across a porous solid. If the solid consists of uniform straight capillary tubes of diameter d and length l at ordinary temperatures, the flow of gas in the capillaries will be laminar. Diffusion flux for a single gas can be described by Poiseuille's law for a compressible fluid.

$$N_A = -\frac{d^2}{32\mu l RT}\overline{P}(P_2 - P_1) \tag{1.63}$$

where $\overline{P} = \dfrac{(P_2 - P_1)}{2}$ (1.64)

Here, it is assumed that the entire pressure difference is only due to fluid friction in the pores. As the pores are neither straight nor of constant diameter, diffusion flux should be based on the gross external cross section of the solid.

ILLUSTRATION

1U An unglazed porcelain plate of 8 mm thickness has an average pore diameter of 0.3 μm. Pure O_2 at 25 mm Hg and 323 K is on one side of the plate and it passes through the pores in the plate. The pressure on the downstream side is negligible.

Estimate the rate of passage of O_2 under these conditions. Take the viscosity of O_2 as 20×10^{-6} kg m^{-1} s^{-1}.

Solution

First we have to fix the type of diffusion based on the d/λ ratio. λ is determined using the expression, $\lambda = \frac{3.2\mu}{P}\left(\frac{RT}{2\pi M}\right)^{1/2}$

$\mu = 20 \times 10^{-6}$ kg m^{-1}s^{-1}; $R = 8\ 314$ J kmol^{-1} K^{-1}; $T = 373$ K

$P = \frac{25 \times 101\ 325}{760} = 3\ 338$ N m^{-2}; $M = 32$ kg kmol^{-1}; $l = 8 \times 10^{-3}$ m

Substituting the values of the parameters in the above expression,

$$\lambda = \frac{3.2 \times 20 \times 10^{-6}}{3\ 338} \times \left(\frac{8\ 314 \times 323}{2 \times 3.14 \times 32}\right)^{1/2} = 2.22 \times 10^{-6} \text{ m}$$

$\frac{d}{\lambda} = \frac{0.3 \times 10^{-6}}{2.22 \times 10^{-6}} = 0.135$, which is < 0.2, hence mass transfer is by Knudsen diffusion.

Knudsen diffusivity is calculated using

$$D_{K,A} = \frac{d}{3} \times \left(\frac{8RT}{\pi M_A}\right)^{1/2}$$

$$= \frac{0.3 \times 10^{-6}}{3} \times \left(\frac{8 \times 8\ 314 \times 323}{3.14 \times 32}\right)^{1/2}$$

$$= 4.62 \times 10^{-5} \text{ m}^2\text{s}^{-1}$$

Rate of passage of O_2 (N_A)= $\frac{D_{k,A}(P_{A2} - P_{A1})}{RTl}$

$$= \frac{4.62 \times 10^{-5} \times (3\ 338 - 0)}{8\ 314 \times 323 \times 8 \times 10^{-3}}$$

$$= 7.18 \times 10^{-6} \text{ kmol m}^{-2}\text{s}^{-1}$$

MASS TRANSFER COEFFICIENTS

Mass transfer coefficient (k_c) is defined as the molecular diffusion flux for unit concentration difference.

$$k_c = \frac{N_A}{(C_{A2} - C_{A1})} \tag{1.65}$$

where N_A is the diffusion flux for component A in kmol m^{-2} s^{-1}, C_{A2} and C_{A1} are the concentrations of A in kmol m^{-3} at plane 2 and 1 respectively, separated by a distance of Z in metre. The SI unit of the mass transfer coefficient is m s^{-1}. The diffusion flux can also be found by multiplying the mass transfer coefficient by the concentration difference.

$$N_A = k_c \times \Delta C_A \tag{1.66}$$

The composition of a system can also be expressed in terms of partial pressure or mole fraction.

$N_A = k_P \times \Delta P_A$, if the composition of A is represented in partial pressure.

$N_A = k_y \times \Delta y_A$, if the composition of A is represented in mole fraction and A is present in the light phase.

$N_A = k_x \times \Delta x_A$, if the composition of A is represented in mole fraction and A is present in the heavy phase.

COLBURN ANALOGY

Theories of heat transfer tell us that the variables affecting the coefficient of heat transfer to fluids flowing inside tubes h_i, include terms descriptive of the system geometry, fluid flow and fluid thermal properties. The system geometry depends on diameter if the cross section is circular, or equivalent diameter if the cross section is other than circular (d). The variables that control the character of the fluid flow are fluid velocity (u), fluid density (ρ) and fluid viscosity (μ). Thermal conductivity (k) and specific heat capacity (C_P) are the thermal properties concerned.

$$h_i = f(d_i, u, \rho, \mu, C_P, k)$$

Dimensional analysis leads to the following functional relation.

$$\frac{h_i d}{k} = \psi\left(\frac{dG}{\mu}, \frac{C_p}{\mu k}\right) \tag{1.67}$$

The dimensionless grouping $\frac{h_i d}{k}$ is known as the Nusselt number (Nu); the dimensionless grouping $\frac{dG}{\mu}$ is known as Reynolds number (Re); the dimensionless grouping $\frac{C_P}{\mu k}$ is known as Prandtl number (Pr).

$$Nu = \psi(Re, Pr) \tag{1.68}$$

For flow inside pipes, experimental studies indicate the following empirical relation.

$$\frac{Nu}{Re\ \ Pr} = 0.023Re^{0.8}Pr^{0.33} \tag{1.69}$$

This can be expressed in the j form. Dividing both sides of the above equation by $Re.\ Sc$,

$$\frac{Nu}{Re\ Pr} = 0.023Re^{-0.2}Pr^{-2/3} \tag{1.70}$$

The expression on the right hand side of the equation is known as Stanton's number for heat transfer.

$$St_H = 0.023Re^{-0.2}Pr^{-2/3} \tag{1.71}$$

$$St_H Pr^{2/3} = 0.023Re^{-0.2} \tag{1.72}$$

The expression on the right hand side of the above equation is known as j_H, which is the j factor for heat transfer.

$$j_H = 0.023Re^{-0.2} \tag{1.73}$$

$$j_H = \frac{1}{2}(0.046Re^{-0.2}) \tag{1.74}$$

$$j_H = \frac{f}{2} \text{ where } f \text{ is Fanning's friction factor.} \tag{1.75}$$

The above equation is known as Colburn equation or Colburn analogy [7].

CHILTON–COLBURN ANALOGY

Mechanisms of mass transfer predict that the mass transfer coefficient k_c can be expected to depend on diffusivity (D) and the variables that control the character of the fluid flow, namely, diameter if the cross section is circular, or equivalent diameter if the cross section is other than circular (d), fluid velocity (u), fluid density (ρ) and fluid viscosity (μ). Since the shape of the interphase also influences the process, different relations should appear for each shape.

For any given shape,

$$k_c = f(D, d, u, \rho, \mu) \tag{1.76}$$

Dimensional analysis leads to the following functional relation.

$$\frac{k_c d}{D} = \psi\left(\frac{dG}{\mu}, \frac{\mu}{\rho D}\right) \tag{1.77}$$

The dimensionless grouping $\frac{k_c d}{D}$ is known as Sherwood number (Sh); the dimensionless grouping $\frac{dG}{\mu}$ is known as Reynolds number (Re); the dimension less grouping $\frac{\mu}{\rho D}$ is known as Schmidt number (Sc).

$$Sh = \psi(Re, Sc) \tag{1.78}$$

For flow inside pipes, experimental studies indicate the following empirical relation.

$$Sh = 0.023 \quad Re^{0.8} \quad Sc^{0.33} \tag{1.79}$$

This can be expressed in the j form. Dividing both sides of the above equation by $Re.Sc$,

$$\frac{Sh}{ReSc} = 0.023Re^{-0.2}Sc^{-2/3} \tag{1.80}$$

The expression on the right hand side of the equation is known as Stanton's number for mass transfer.

$$St_M = 0.023Re^{-0.2}Sc^{-2/3} \tag{1.81}$$

$$St_M Sc^{2/3} = 0.023Re^{-0.2} \tag{1.82}$$

The expression on the right hand side of the above equation is known as j_M, which is the j factor for mass transfer.

$$j_M = 0.023Re^{-0.2} \tag{1.83}$$

$$j_M = 1/2(0.046Re^{-0.2}) \tag{1.84}$$

$$j_M = \frac{f}{2} \tag{1.85}$$

where f is Fanning's friction factor.

So we have $j_H = \frac{f}{2} = j_M$ (1.86)

This is known as Chilton–Colburn equation or Chilton–Colburn analogy [8]. This analogy is the result of Fick's law for mass transfer and Fourier law for heat conduction being analogous.

OTHER ANALOGIES

Taylor–Prandtl Analogy

This analogy is represented by the following equation:

$$St_H = St_M = \frac{\frac{f}{2}}{\left[1 + 5\sqrt{\frac{f}{2}}(Sc - 1)\right]} = \frac{\frac{f}{2}}{\left[1 + 5\sqrt{\frac{f}{2}}(Pr - 1)\right]} \tag{1.87}$$

The Chilton–Colburn analogy assumes that only a turbulent core is present in the fluid while the Taylor–Prandtl analogy [9] assumes the presence of a turbulent core and a laminar sub-layer in the fluid.

Von–Karman analogy

This analogy is represented by the following equation:

$$St_M = \frac{\frac{f}{2}}{\left[1 + 5\sqrt{\frac{f}{2}}(Sc - 1) + \ln\left(\frac{5Sc + 1}{6}\right)\right]}$$

$$= \frac{\frac{f}{2}}{\left[1 + 5\sqrt{\frac{f}{2}}(Pr - 1) + \ln\left(\frac{5Pr + 1}{6}\right)\right]} \tag{1.88}$$

The Von–Karman analogy [9] assumes the presence of a turbulent core, a laminar sub-layer and buffer layers in the fluid. When $Sc = Pr = 1$, equations (1.85), (1.86) and (1.87) lead to the Colburn analogy.

SOME USEFUL MASS TRANSFER CORRELATIONS

Table 1.2 gives some of the most widely used mass transfer correlations.

Table 1.2 Mass transfer correlations

Fluid flow pattern	Range of conditions	Equation	Ref
Inside circular tubes	$Re : 4\,000 - 60\,000$	$j_M = 0.023R_e^{-0.17}$	10
Unconfined flow parallel to flat plates	$Re_x < 50\,000$	$j_M = 0.664$	11
Confined flow parallel to flat plates in a duct	$Re' = 2\,000 - 26\,000$	$j_M = 0.023(Re')^{-0.17}$	12
Perpendicular to single cylinders	$Re = 10 - 10\,000$	$Sh = 0.61Re^{0.5}\ Sc^{0.33}$	13
Past single spheres	$Re < 1\,000$	$Sh = 2 + 0.6Re^{0.5}\ Sc^{0.33}$	14

NOTATIONS

C_A	Molar concentration of diffusing component, kmol m^{-3}.
C_B	Molar concentration of non-diffusing component, kmol m^{-3}.
C_T	Molar concentration of A and B, kmol m^{-3}.
C_{A1}	Molar concentration of diffusing component at plane 1, kmol m^{-3}.
C_{A2}	Molar concentration of diffusing component at plane 2, kmol m^{-3}.
C_{B1}	Molar concentration of non-diffusing component at plane 1, kmol m^{-3}.
C_{B2}	Molar concentration of non-diffusing component at plane 2, kmol m^{-3}.
C_{Blm}	Log mean value of molar concentration of the non-diffusing component, at locations 1 and 2, kmol m^{-3}.
C_P	Heat capacity at constant pressure, J kg^{-1} K^{-1}.
d	Pore diameter, m.
d_e	Equivalent diameter, ratio of cross sectional area to perimeter, m.
D	Diffusivity of diffusing component in the mixture, m^2 s^{-1}.
D_{AB}	Diffusivity of A in B, m^2 s^{-1}.
D_{BA}	Diffusivity of B in A, m^2 s^{-1}.
D'	Effective diffusivity of the diffusing component in the mixture, m^2 s^{-1}.
$D_{K,A}$	Knudsen diffusivity of component A, m^2 s^{-1}.
$D_{K,A,eff}$	Effective Knudsen diffusivity of component A, m^2 s^{-1}.
f	Fanning's friction factor, dimensionless.
F	Constant.
h_i	Heat transfer coefficient for the inside fluid, W m^{-2} K^{-1}.
H_D	Activation energy for diffusion, J mol^{-1}.
j_M	Colburn factor for mass transfer, dimensionless.
j_H	Colburn factor for heat transfer, dimensionless.
J_A	Rate of diffusion of component A, kmol s^{-1}.
k	Thermal conductivity, W m^{-1} K^{-1}.
k_c	Mass transfer coefficient based on concentration, m s^{-1}

k_P	Mass transfer coefficient based on partial pressure, m s^{-1}
k_y	Mass transfer coefficient based on mole fraction of the component in the light phase, m s^{-1}.
k_x	Mass transfer coefficient based on mole fraction of the component in the heavy phase, m s^{-1}.
M	Molecular weight of diffusing component.
M_A	Molecular weight of component A.
M_B	Molecular weight of component B.
n_A	Number of moles of A.
n_B	Number of moles of B.
N_A	Rate of diffusion per unit area or diffusion flux of A, kmol $m^{-2}s^{-1}$.
N_B	Rate of diffusion per unit area or diffusion flux of B, kmol $m^{-2}s^{-1}$.
Nu	Nusselt number, the dimensionless grouping $\frac{h_i d}{k}$.
P	Total pressure, N m^{-2}.
P_A	Partial pressure of A, N m^{-2}.
P_B	Partial pressure of B, N m^{-2}.
P_{A1}	Partial pressure of diffusing component at plane 1, N m^{-2}.
P_{A2}	Partial pressure of diffusing component at plane 2, N m^{-2}.
P_{B1}	Partial pressure of non-diffusing component at plane 1, N m^{-2}.
P_{B2}	Partial pressure of non-diffusing component at plane 2, N m^{-2}.
P_{Blm}	Log mean value of partial pressure of the non-diffusing component, B at locations 1 and 2, N m^{-2}.
P_A	Permeability for component A, in cm^3 gas (STP) $cm^{-2}s^{-1}$ (cm Hg $cm^{-1})^{-1}$.
Pr	Prandtl number, the dimension less grouping $\frac{C_P \mu}{k}$.
r_i	Inner radius, m.
r_o	Outer radius, m.
R	Universal gas constant, 8 314 J $kmol^{-1}K^{-1}$.
Re	Reynolds number, dimensionless grouping $\frac{dG}{\mu}$.
Re'	Reynolds number based on equivalent diameter, dimensionless grouping $\frac{d_e G}{\mu}$.
S_{av}	Average cross section for diffusion, m^2.
S_A	Solubility coefficient or Henry's law constant, cm^3 gas (STP) cm^{-3} solid (cm $Hg)^{-1}$.
Sc	Schmidt number, dimensionless grouping $\frac{\mu}{\rho D}$.
Sh	Sherwood number, dimensionless grouping $\frac{k_c d}{D}$.
St_H	Stanton's number for heat transfer, dimensionless grouping $\frac{Nu}{Re.Pr}$.
St_M	Stanton's number for mass transfer, dimensionless grouping $\frac{Sh}{Re.Sc}$.
t	Time, s.
T	Temperature, K.
u_A	Mean molecular velocity of A in the direction of mass transfer, m s^{-1}.

u_B	Mean molecular velocity of B in the direction of mass transfer, m s^{-1}.
V	Volume of the system, m^3.
V_A	Diffusion flux in terms of volume, m^3 gas (STP) $cm^{-2}s^{-1}$.
V_A	Molar volume of component A, m^3 $kmol^{-1}$.
V_B	Molar volume of component B, m^3 $kmol^{-1}$.
x	Mole fraction of component A in the heavy phase.
x^*	Mole fraction of component A in the heavy phase at equilibrium.
y	Mole fraction of component A in the light phase.
y^*	Mole fraction of component A in the light phase at equilibrium.
y_B^1	Mole fraction of the stationary component.
z	Thickness of the polymeric membrane, m.
Z	Distance in the direction of diffusion, m.
$Z_2 - Z_1$	Distance between the planes 1 and 2, m.
$\frac{\Delta C}{\Delta Z}$	Concentration gradient, kmol m^{-2}.
Δ	Difference.
ϵ_D	Eddy diffusivity, m^2 s^{-1}.
l	Length, m.
ρ	Density of the diffusing component in its liquid state, kg m^{-3}.
λ	Mean free path of the gas molecules, m.
μ	Viscosity, kg $m^{-1}s^{-1}$.

REFERENCES

1. Fick A, *Ann. Phys.*, **94**: 59 (1855).
2. Stefan J, *Ann. Physik.*, **41**: 723 (1890).
3. Maxwell JC, *Phil. Trans. Roy. Soc.*, **157**: 49 (1867).
4. Winkelmann A, *Ann. Physik.*, **22**: 1152 (1884).
5. Gilliland ER, *Ind. Eng. Chem.*, **26**: 681 (1934).
6. Wilke CR and Chang P, *A.I.Ch. E. J.*, **1**: 264 (1955).
7. Colburn AP, *Trans. Am. Inst. Chem. Eng.*, **29**: 174 (1933).
8. Chilton TH and Colburn AP, *Ind. Eng. Chem.*, **26**: 1183 (1934).
9. Danckwerts PV, *Gas Liquid Reactions*, McGraw–Hill Book Company, New York, 1970.
10. Linton WH and Sherwood TK, *Chem. Eng. Prog.*, **46**: 258 (1950).
11. Kays WM, *Convective Heat and Mass Transfer*, McGraw–Hill Book Company, New York, 1966.
12. O'Brien LJ and Stutzman LF, *Ind. Eng. Chem.*, **42**: 1181 (1950).
13. Sherwood TK, Pigford RL and Wilke CR, *Mass Transfer*, McGraw–Hill Book Company, New York, 1975.
14. Schlichting H, *Boundary Layer Theory*, McGraw–Hill Book Company, New York, 1979.

Problems for Practice

1.1 Ammonia gas diffuses through nitrogen gas under steady state conditions with nitrogen being non-diffusing. The total pressure is 1.013×10^5 Pa and the temperature is 298 K, the diffusion path is 0.15 m. The partial pressure of ammonia at one point is 1.5×10^4 Pa and at the other point is 5×10^3 Pa. The diffusion coefficient for the mixture at 1.013×10^5 Pa and 298 K is 2.3×10^{-5} m^2 s^{-1}. Calculate (a) the flux of ammonia and (b) equimolal counter diffusion flux assuming that nitrogen also diffuses.

1.2 Calculate the rate of diffusion of acetic acid across a film of non-diffusing water solution 2 mm thick at 290 K, when the concentrations on opposite sides of the film are 10 wt% and 5 wt% acid respectively. The diffusivity of acetic acid in the solution is 0.95×10^{-9} m^2 s^{-1}. The density of the 10 wt% and 5 wt% solution are 1 013 kg m^{-3} and 1 006 kg m^{-3} respectively.

1.3 A vertical glass tube of 3 mm diameter is filled with toluene to a depth of 1.9 cm from the top. After 300 hours at 309 K and a total pressure of 1 atm, the level fell to 7.9 cm from the top. Neglecting the counter diffusion of air to replace the liquid, calculate the diffusivity if the density and vapour pressure of toluene at 309 K are 0.85 g cm^{-3} and 57.5 mm Hg respectively.

1.4 Hydrogen and air are in equimolar diffusion with each other. The total pressure is 1 atm and the temperature is 298 K. The mass diffusivity for the mixture is 0.410 cm^2 s^{-1}. The partial pressures at the two planes 0.5 cm apart, perpendicular to the direction of diffusion, are 120 and 40 mm Hg respectively. Calculate the rate of diffusion of the mixture in mol cm^{-2} s^{-1}.

1.5 In an oxygen–nitrogen gas mixture at 1 atm and 298 K, the concentrations of oxygen at two planes 0.2 cm apart are 10 and 20 volume% respectively. Calculate the rate of diffusion of oxygen expressed as mol cm^{-2} s^{-1} for the case where (a) nitrogen is non-diffusing and (b) there is equimolar counter diffusion of the two gases. The diffusivity for the mixture is 0.2 cm^2 s^{-1}.

1.6 Oxygen is diffusing through carbon monoxide under steady state conditions. The total pressure is 1 atm and the temperature is 301 K. The partial pressures of oxygen at two places 0.2 cm apart are 13 330 and 6 665 N m^{-2} respectively. Calculate the rate of diffusion of oxygen in mol cm^{-2} s^{-1}. The diffusivity of gas in the mixture is 1.85×10^{-5} m^2 s^{-1}.

1.7 Oxygen is diffusing through a stagnant layer of methane 5 mm thick. The temperature is 273 K and the pressure is 1 atm. Calculate the rate of diffusion of oxygen through 1 m^2 of the methane film when the concentration changes across the film from 15% to 5% oxygen by volume. The diffusivity may be taken as 0.184 cm^2 s^{-1}.

1.8 There are two bulbs connected by a straight tube 0.001 m in diameter and 0.15 m in length. Initially the bulb at end '1' contains nitrogen and the bulb at end '2' contains hydrogen. The pressure and temperature are maintained at 298 K and 1 atm respectively. At a certain time after allowing the diffusion to occur between the two bulbs, the nitrogen content of the gas at the end '1' of the tube is 80 mol% and the other end is 25 mol%. If the diffusion coefficient is 0.784 $cm^2\ s^{-1}$, determine the rates and direction of transfer of hydrogen and nitrogen.

1.9 Calculate the rate of diffusion of oxygen through the non-diffusing gas mixture of methane and hydrogen in the volume ratio 2:1. The total pressure is 1 atm and the temperature is 273 K. The partial pressures of oxygen at two planes 0.2 cm apart are respectively 100 and 50 mm Hg. The diffusivities are 0.690 and 0.184 $cm^2\ s^{-1}$ for the oxygen–hydrogen mixture and oxygen–methane mixture respectively.

1.10 In an oxygen–nitrogen gas mixture at 1 atm and 298 K, the concentration of oxygen at two places 0.2 cm apart are 10 and 20 volume% respectively. Calculate the rate of diffusion of oxygen expressed as mole $cm^{-2}\ s^{-1}$ for the following cases: (a) nitrogen is non-diffusing and (b) equimolar counter diffusion of the two gases. The diffusivity for the mixture is 0.181 $cm^2\ s^{-1}$.

1.11 A crystal of $CuSO_4.5H_2O$ falls through a large tank of pure water at 293 K. Estimate the rate at which the crystal dissolves. Molecular diffusion occurs through a 0.03 mm thick uniform film of water surrounding the crystal. At the inner side of the film adjacent to the crystal surface, the concentration of $CuSO_4$ is 0.023 mole fraction. The outer surface of the film is pure water. The density of the solution is 1 200 kg m^{-3} and the diffusivity of $CuSO_4$ is $7.3 \times 10^{-10}\ m^2\ s^{-1}$.

1.12 Calculate the rate of diffusion of sodium chloride at 293 K through a stationary film of water 1 mm thick where the concentrations are 20% and 10% by weight respectively on either side of the film. $D_{AB} = 1.35 \times 10^{-5}\ mm^2\ s^{-1}$.

1.13 Hydrogen gas at 1 atm and 298 K flows through a pipe made of unvulcanised neoprene rubber tube with ID and OD of 25 and 50 mm respectively. If the concentration of hydrogen at the inner surface of the pipe is 2.37×10^{-3} kmol m^{-3} and the diffusivity of hydrogen through the rubber is $1.8 \times 10^{-6}\ cm^2\ s^{-1}$, estimate the rate of loss of hydrogen by diffusion through a pipe of 2 m length. The outside air may be assumed to be free from hydrogen.

1.14 Calculate the amount of diffusion of acetic acid in two hours across a film of non-diffusing water solution 1 mm thick at 290 K, when the concentrations on opposite sides of the film are 9% and 3% by weight respectively. The diffusivity of the acid in solution is $0.95 \times 10^{-9}\ m^2\ s^{-1}$. The density of the 9% solution = 1 012 kg m^{-3}, density of the 3% solution = 1 003.2 kg m^{-3}.

1.15 A mixture of benzene and toluene is distilled in a laboratory distillation unit. At one plane in the vertical tube where benzene and toluene are condensing, the vapour contains 85.3 mol% benzene and the adjacent liquid film contains 70 mol% benzene. The temperature is at 360 K. The gas layer which is assumed to be stagnant is 0.254 cm thick. The molal latent heat of vaporisation of benzene and toluene are the same implying equimolal counter diffusion. The vapour pressure of toluene at this temperature is 368 mm Hg. Calculate the rate of interchange of benzene and toluene between vapour and liquid at atmospheric pressure. The diffusion coefficient is 0.050 6 $cm^2\ s^{-1}$.

1.16 Ammonia gas diffuses at a constant rate through a layer of stagnant air 0.25 cm thick. Conditions are fixed so that the gas contains 50% NH_3 by volume at one boundary of the stagnant layer. The ammonia diffusing at the other boundary is quickly absorbed and the concentration is negligible at that plane. The temperature is 303 K and the pressure is 1 atm under which conditions the diffusivity value of the ammonia–air system may be assumed to be 0.25 $cm^2\ s^{-1}$. Calculate the rate of diffusion of ammonia through the air layer.

1.17 Alcohol is diffusing through water at 308 K and 1 atm pressure. Concentrations of alcohol on the two sides of the water film 3 mm thick are 80% and 10% by weight respectively. Calculate the rate of diffusion of alcohol through water. The diffusivity of alcohol is found to be $0.6 \times 10^{-9}\ m^2\ s^{-1}$. The densities of 80% and 10% alcohol by weight are 0.830 $g\ cm^{-3}$ and 0.977 $g\ cm^{-3}$ respectively.

1.18 A vertical glass tube of 3 mm ID is filled with liquid toluene (density 0.82 $g\ cm^{-3}$) to a depth of 2 cm from the top open end. After 200 hours at 303 K and a total pressure of 1 atm, the level dropped to 8 cm from the top of the tube. The vapour pressure of toluene at 303 K is 57 mm Hg. Neglecting counter current diffusion of air to replace liquid, calculate the diffusivity of toluene into air. Make suitable assumptions if required.

1.19 Calculate the rate of diffusion of water vapour from the bottom of a well 6 m deep to dry air flowing over the top of the well. Assume the entire system is at 298 K and atmospheric pressure. If the well diameter is 3 m, find out the total weight of water diffusing per second from the surface of the water in the well. The diffusion coefficient for the system is $0.256 \times 10^{-4}\ m^2\ s^{-1}$. The partial pressure of water vapour at 298 K is 0.032 3 atm.

1.20 Calculate the amount of oxygen diffusing in one hour under steady state conditions through a non-diffusing gas mixture of methane and hydrogen in the volume ratio of 2:1. The diffusivities are estimated to be $6.99 \times 10^{-5}\ m^2\ s^{-1}$ and $1.86 \times 10^{-5}\ m^2\ s^{-1}$ for the oxygen–hydrogen mixture and oxygen–methane mixture respectively. The total pressure is $1 \times 10^5\ N\ m^{-2}$ and temperature is 273 K. The partial pressures of oxygen at two planes 2 mm apart are 13 000 and 6 500 $N\ m^{-2}$ respectively. R may be taken as 8 314 $Nm\ kmol^{-1}\ K^{-1}$.

1.21 A polyethylene film, 0.15 mm thick, is being considered for use in packaging a pharmaceutical product at 303 K. If the partial pressure of O_2 outside is 0.21 atm and inside the package is 0.01 atm, calculate the diffusion flux of O_2 at the steady state. Use permeability coefficient as $4.17 \times 10^{-12}\ m^3$ solute STP $(s\ m^2\ atm\ m^{-1})^{-1}$. Assume that the resistances to diffusion outside and inside are negligible compared to the resistance of the film.

1.22 An open circular tank 6.0 m in diameter contains benzene at 298 K which is exposed to the atmosphere in such a manner that the liquid is covered with a stagnant air film having an estimated thickness of 5.0 mm. The concentration of benzene beyond the stagnant film is negligible. The vapour pressure of benzene at 298 K is 100 mm Hg. If benzene is worth one rupee a litre, what is the value of the loss of benzene from this tank in rupees per day? The molar diffusivity of benzene in air at 298 K and 1.0 atm pressure is 277.7 $cm^2\ h^{-1}$. The density of benzene at 298 K is 0.88 g cm^{-3}.

1.23 Methane diffuses at a steady state through a tube containing He. At point A, the partial pressure of methane is 15.55 kPa and at point B, which is 20 mm apart, the partial pressure of methane is 10 kPa. The total pressure is 101.32 kPa and the temperature is 293 K. At this pressure and temperature, the diffusivity of methane in He is $6.75 \times 10^{-5}\ m^2\ s^{-1}$. (a) Calculate the flux of methane at steady state equimolar counter diffusion. (b) Calculate the partial pressure of methane at the midpoint between A and B layers.

2 Interphase Mass Transfer

Many important applications of mass transfer pertain to the transfer of material across a phase boundary. The rate of mass transfer between the two fluid phases depends on the physical properties of the two phases, the concentration difference, the interfacial area and the degree of turbulence. This chapter deals with the methods available for the determination of the rate of mass transfer, various theories of mass transfer and general concepts of mass transfer equipment design.

Interphase mass transfer involves simultaneous diffusion of material in each phase of the combined system. The rate of diffusion in each phase depends on the concentration gradient existing within that phase. The existence of a concentration gradient in each of the phases indicates that the two phases are not in equilibrium. Once equilibrium is established, the concentration gradients will vanish and the net rate of diffusion will become zero. So mass transfer between phases depends on

1. diffusion phenomena, and
2. equilibrium between phases.

EQUILIBRIUM

Let us consider the equilibrium characteristics of the gas absorption operation. Let a fixed amount of water be placed in a closed container along with a gaseous mixture of ammonia and air. Let the temperature and pressure be maintained constant. As ammonia is very soluble in water, ammonia molecules will transfer from the gas phase into the liquid phase, crossing the interphase between the gas and liquid. A portion of the ammonia molecules will escape back into the gas phase at a rate proportional to its concentration in the liquid. As more ammonia enters the liquid phase, its concentration in this phase will increase and the rate at which ammonia returns back to the gas phase also will increase. This will go on till the rate at which ammonia goes into the liquid phase equals the rate at which ammonia escapes from the liquid. At the same time, the concentration throughout each phase will become uniform by diffusion. A dynamic equilibrium now exists. The ammonia molecules continue to transfer back and forth from one phase to the other. The net transfer rate falls to zero.

If additional ammonia is injected into the container, a new set of equilibrium concentrations will be established with higher concentrations in each phase. In this manner, we can obtain a complete relationship between equilibrium concentrations in both phases which gives rise to an equilibrium distribution curve. Figure 2.1 shows a typical equilibrium curve. The curve is independent of the amount of ammonia and air and is influenced only by the temperature and pressure of the system. At equilibrium, the concentrations of the solute in the two phases need not be equal; but the chemical potential of the solute is the same in both phases. This equality of chemical potential causes the net transfer of the solute to stop. Though the above results have been obtained for a particular system, similar results are expected for any system involving the distribution of substances between two insoluble phases. In general,

1. At a fixed temperature and pressure, there exists an equilibrium relation between the concentrations of the substance distributed between the two phases.
2. For a system in equilibrium, there is no net diffusion of components between phases.
3. For a system not in equilibrium, diffusion of components between phases will occur in order to establish equilibrium.

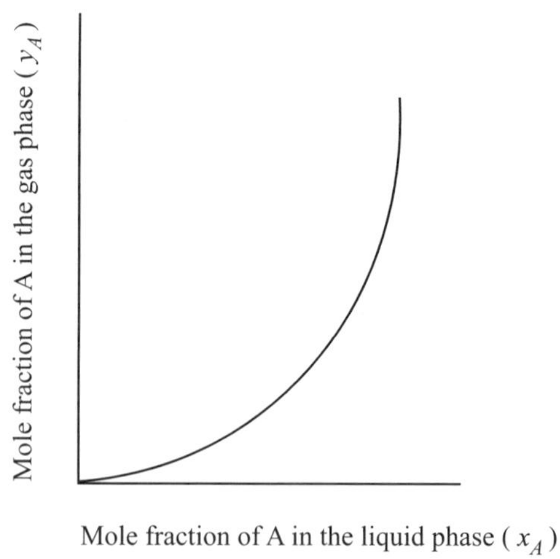

Fig. 2.1 Equilibrium curve

MASS TRANSFER COEFFICIENT FOR INDIVIDUAL PHASES

Let us investigate the situation at a point mid way between the top and bottom of a gas absorber. Ammonia–air mixture enters at the bottom and flows upwards while water flows downwards. The composition of the gas mixture changes from a high to low solute concentration as it flows up while water dissolves ammonia and leaves at the bottom as an aqueous ammonia solution. When a steady state is attained, the concentrations at any point do not change with time. Since the solute diffuses from the gas phase to the liquid phase, there must be a concentration gradient in the direction of transfer in each phase.

The concentration of A in the bulk of the gas is y_{AG} mole fraction and it falls to y_{Ai} at the interphase. In the liquid, the concentration of A falls from x_{Ai} at the interphase to x_{AL} in the bulk of the liquid phase. The bulk concentrations y_{AG} and x_{AL} are clearly not the equilibrium concentrations, since otherwise diffusion of A would not occur. Figure 2.2 shows the variation of concentration with distance.

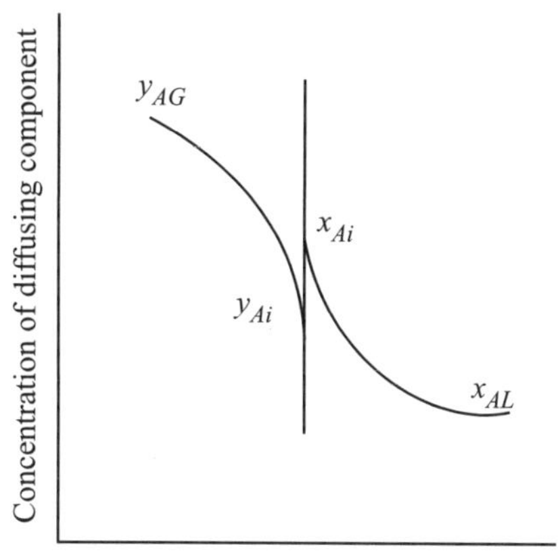

Fig. 2.2 Concentration variation with distance

Lewis and Whitman [1] proposed that there is no resistance to solute transfer across the interface separating the phases and the entire resistance lies only in the fluids. Therefore, the concentration rise at the interphase from y_{Ai} to x_{Ai} is not a barrier to diffusion in the direction of gas to liquid. They are merely equilibrium concentrations and hence correspond to equal chemical potentials of substance A in both phases at the interphase.

Various concentrations are shown graphically in Fig. 2.3. The point P represents the two bulk phase concentrations and point M represents those at the interphase.

For steady state mass transfer, the rate at which A reaches the interphase from the bulk must be equal to the rate at which A diffuses from the interphase into the bulk so that there is no accumulation or depletion of A at the interphase.

$$N_A = k_y(y_{AG} - y_{Ai}) = k_x(x_{Ai} - x_{AL}) \tag{2.1}$$

k_y and k_x are the gas phase and liquid phase mass transfer coefficients.

$$\frac{y_{AG} - y_{Ai}}{x_{AL} - x_{Ai}} = -\frac{k_x}{k_y} \tag{2.2}$$

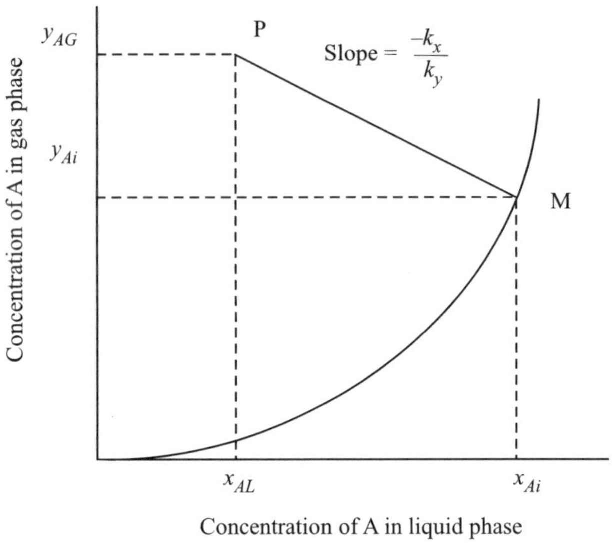

Fig. 2.3 Equilibrium distribution curve

This is the slope of the line PM, which is the operating line, as it denotes the operating conditions.

OVERALL MASS TRANSFER COEFFICIENT

Experimental determination of the rate of mass transfer can be carried out by the determination of solute concentrations in the bulk and at the interphase by sampling and analysing. Sampling in the bulk is possible but sampling at the interphase is not possible using ordinary sampling devices. Thus, only an overall effect can be determined in terms of bulk concentrations. The entire two phase mass transfer effect can be measured in terms of an overall mass transfer coefficient. The various concentrations are shown graphically in Fig. 2.4.

$$N_A = K_y(y_{AG} - x_{AL}) \tag{2.3}$$

$$N_A = K_y(y_{AG} - y_A^*) \text{ where } y_A^* \text{ is a measure of } x_{AL}. \tag{2.4}$$

$$\frac{N_A}{K_y} = (y_{AG} - y_A^*) \tag{2.5}$$

From equation (2.1), $$\frac{N_A}{k_y} = (y_{AG} - y_{Ai}) \tag{2.6}$$

and $$\frac{N_A}{kx} = (x_{Ai} - x_{AL}) \tag{2.7}$$

We also know that,

$$(y_{AG} - y_A^*) = (y_{AG} - y_{Ai}) + (y_{Ai} - y_A^*)$$
$$= (y_{AG} - y_{Ai}) + m^I(x_{Ai} - x_{AL}) \tag{2.8}$$

From equations (2.5), (2.6), (2.7) and (2.8),

$$\frac{N_A}{K_y} = \frac{N_A}{k_y} + \frac{m^I N_A}{k_x} \tag{2.9}$$

$$\frac{1}{K_y} = \frac{1}{k_y} + \frac{m^I}{k_x} \tag{2.10}$$

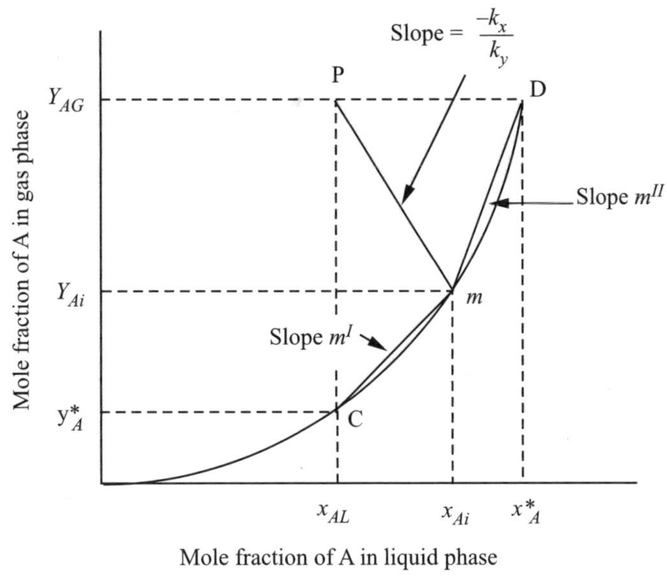

Fig. 2.4 Equilibrium curve

This gives the relationship between individual phase transfer coefficients and the overall mass transfer coefficient in the form of addition of resistances [1]. x_A^* is a measure of y_{AG} and can be used to define the other overall coefficient, K_x.

$$N_A = K_x(x_A^* - x_{AL}) \tag{2.11}$$

$$\frac{1}{Kx} = \frac{1}{m^{II} k_y} + \frac{1}{k_x} \tag{2.12}$$

$$\frac{\text{Resistance in gas phase}}{\text{Total resistance in both phases}} = \frac{1/k_y}{1/K_y} \tag{2.13}$$

$$\frac{\text{Resistance in liquid phase}}{\text{Total resistance in both phases}} = \frac{1/k_x}{1/K_x} \tag{2.14}$$

Assuming the numerical values of k_x and k_y to be roughly equal, the importance of the slope of the equilibrium curve chord can readily be demonstrated. If m^I is small, the equilibrium concentration of A in the gas phase will be small and the concentration of A in the liquid will be very large. Then, m^I/k_x will be very insignificant. The major resistance is represented by $1/K_y$. It is said that the rate of mass transfer is gas phase controlled.

$$\frac{1}{K_y} \approx \frac{1}{k_y} \tag{2.15}$$

$$y_{AG} - y_A^* \approx y_{AG} - y_{Ai} \tag{2.16}$$

Under these circumstances, even large percentage changes in K_x will not affect K_y significantly and efforts to increase the rate of mass transfer would be directed towards decreasing the gas phase resistance.

Conversely when m^{II} is very large, solute A is relatively insoluble in the liquid phase. With nearly equal K_x and K_y, $1/m^{II}k_y$ becomes insignificant and the major resistance is represented by $1/K_x$. The rate of mass transfer is said to be liquid phase controlled.

$$\frac{1}{K_x} \approx \frac{1}{k_x} \tag{2.17}$$

$$x_A^* - x_{AL} \approx x_{Ai} - x_{AL} \tag{2.18}$$

Efforts to increase the rate of mass transfer in such cases must be directed towards decreasing the liquid phase resistance. A typical equilibrium distribution curve for a gas phase controlled reaction and a liquid phase controlled reaction are shown in Fig. 2.5.

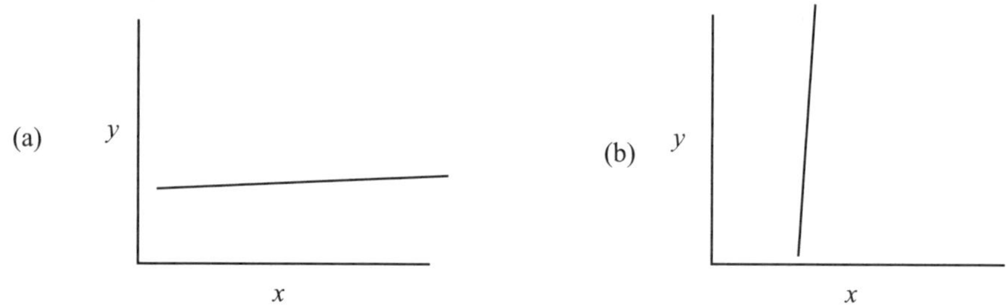

Fig. 2.5 Equilibrium distribution curve for (a) Gas phase controlled reaction (b) Liquid phase controlled reaction

For cases where k_x and k_y are not nearly equal, the relative size of the ratio k_x/k_y and the value of m^I or m^{II} will determine the location of the controlling mass transfer resistance.

The composition of the gas phase can be represented in partial pressure (atmosphere) and the composition of the liquid phase can be represented in terms of concentration (kmol m^{-3}). Then, the gas phase mass transfer coefficient is denoted by k_g and the liquid phase mass transfer coefficient is denoted by k_l. The overall mass transfer coefficient based on the gas phase is denoted by K_g and the overall mass transfer coefficient based on the liquid phase is denoted by K_l. The mass flux in this case is given by

$$N_A = k_g(P_{AG} - P_{Ai}) = k_\ell(C_{Ai} - C_{AL}) \tag{2.19}$$

$$N_A = K_g(P_{AG} - P_A^*) = K_\ell(C_A^* - C_{AL}) \tag{2.20}$$

(C_{AL}, P_{AG}) represents a bulk point and (C_{Ai}, P_{Ai}) represents the interphase. C_A^* is a measure of P_{AG} and P_A^* is a measure of C_{AL}. The relationship between individual phase transfer coefficients and the overall mass transfer coefficient is given by

$$\frac{1}{K_g} = \frac{1}{k_g} + \frac{m}{k_\ell} \text{ and } \frac{1}{K_\ell} = \frac{1}{mk_g} + \frac{1}{k_\ell} \tag{2.21}$$

where m is the slope of the equilibrium curve or the Henry's law constant. It is also the coefficient of C_A, if the equilibrium relation is expressed in the form of $P_A = mC_A$.

ILLUSTRATIONS

2A A wetted wall tower is fed with water as the wall liquid, and air–ammonia mixture as the central core gas. The operation is carried out at 299 K and 1 atm. Compute the interphase composition and mass transfer flux using the overall coefficient or film coefficient. The values of k_x and k_y are 0.53 and 0.49 kmol m^{-2} h^{-1} (Δ mole fraction)$^{-1}$ in the respective phases.

Equilibrium data

x	0	0.05	0.10	0.25	0.30
y	0	0.07	0.14	0.59	0.92

x and y denote mole fraction of ammonia in the liquid and gas phases respectively.

Solution

The equilibrium curve is drawn using the equilibrium data given. It is given that, at a particular level in the tower, the ammonia concentration in the bulk gas is 0.8 mole fraction and in the bulk liquid is 0.05 mole fraction. It means that y_{AG} = 0.8 and x_{AL} = 0.05. Then the bulk point P is located at (0.05, 0.8). The slope of the operating line is $-k_x/k_y$ and it is calculated using the values given in the problem. The operating line PM is drawn as a point on the line and its slope is known. The operating line intersects the equilibrium curve at (x_{Ai}, y_{Ai}). x_{Ai} and y_{Ai} are the interfacial compositions, x_{Ai} is the mole fraction of ammonia in the liquid side of the interface and y_{Ai} is the mole fraction of ammonia in the gas side of the interface. From the graph, one can get $x_{Ai} = 0.25$ and $y_{Ai} = 0.59$. Then y_A^* is a measure of x_{AL} and is found from the graph to be 0.07. The graphical solution for this illustration is given in Fig. 2.6.

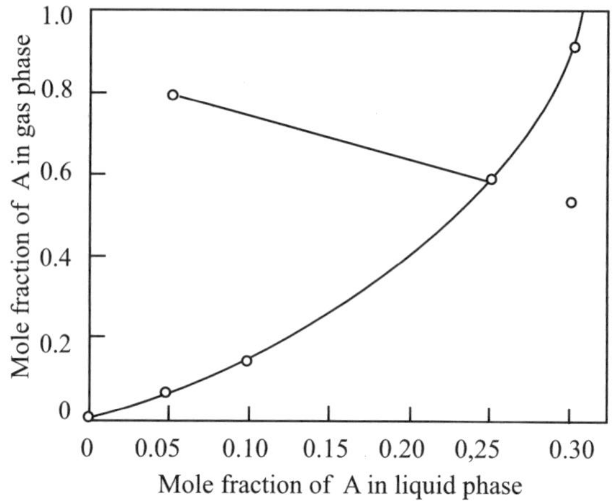

Fig. 2.6 Graphical solution for 2A

The slope of the equilibrium curve chord, $m^I = \dfrac{y_{Ai} - y_A^*}{x_{Ai} - x_{AL}} = \dfrac{0.59 - 0.07}{0.25 - 0.05} = 2.6$

$$\frac{1}{K_y} = \frac{1}{k_y} + \frac{m^I}{k_x}$$

$$= \frac{1}{0.49} + \frac{2.6}{0.53} = 6.947 \text{ and } K_y = 0.144 \text{ kmol m}^{-2} \text{ h}^{-1} (\Delta \text{ mole fraction})^{-1}$$

Mass transfer flux, N_A is given by $N_A = K_y(y_{AG} - y_A^*)$

$$= 0.144(0.80 - 0.07) = 0.105 \text{ kmol m}^{-2} \text{ h}^{-1}$$

$$N_A = k_y(y_{AG} - y_{Ai})$$

$$= 0.49(0.80 - 0.59) = 0.103 \text{ kmol m}^{-2} \text{ h}^{-1}$$

$$N_A = k_x(x_{Ai} - x_{AL})$$

$$= 0.53(0.2 - 0.05) = 0.106 \text{ kmol m}^{-2} \text{ h}^{-1}$$

2B In a certain apparatus used for the absorption of sulphur dioxide from air by means of water, at one point in the equipment, the gas contained 10% sulphur dioxide by volume and was in contact with liquid containing 0.4% sulphur dioxide (density

990 kg m^{-3}). The temperature was 323 K and the total pressure was 1 atm. The overall mass transfer coefficient based on gas concentration was $K_g = 7.36 \times 10^{-5}$ kmol m^{-2} s^{-1} atm^{-1}. Of the total resistance, 50% lies in the gas phase and 50% in the liquid phase.

Equilibrium data:

kg of SO_2 per 100 kg of H_2O	0.2	0.3	0.5	0.7
Partial pressure of SO_2 in mm Hg	2.9	46	83	119

Calculate (a) the overall coefficient based on liquid concentration, (b) the interphase composition in both phases and (c) the mass flux.

Solution

The equilibrium relation provided has to be converted to the usual mole fraction form. The composition of the liquid is given in kg of solute per 100 kg of solvent. Weight divided by molecular weight gives the number of moles of any substance. The number of moles of solute and solvent are found and from these; the mole fraction of the solute is then calculated.

Let us take the first data, kg of SO_2 per 100 kg of H_2O = 0.2

$$\text{Number of kilomoles of } SO_2 \text{ in the solution} = \frac{0.2}{64}$$

$$\text{Number of kilomoles of } H_2O \text{ in the solution} = \frac{100}{18}$$

$$\text{Mole fraction of } SO_2 \text{ in the solution } (x) = \frac{\text{Moles Of } SO_2}{\text{Moles of } SO_2 + \text{Moles of } H_2O}$$

$$= \frac{\dfrac{0.2}{64}}{\dfrac{0.2}{64} + \dfrac{100}{18}} = 0.000\,5$$

Partial pressure of SO_2 in the gas phase in equilibrium with the above liquid = 29 mm Hg

$$\text{Mole fraction of } SO_2 \text{ in the gas } (y) = \frac{\text{Partial presuure of } SO_2}{\text{Total pressure}} = \frac{29}{760} = 0.038$$

Similarly the entire equilibrium data has to be converted.

The equilibrium data now becomes

x	0.000 5	0.000 9	0.001 4	0.002
y	0.038	0.060	0.109	0.157

x and y denote the mole fraction of ammonia in the liquid and gas phases respectively.

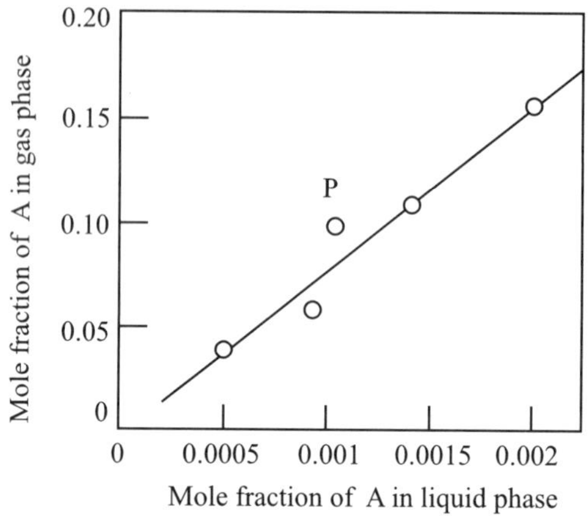

Fig. 2.7 Graphical solution for 2B

It is given that at one point in the equipment, the gas contained 10% sulphur dioxide by volume and was in contact with liquid containing 0.4% sulphur dioxide. It means that $y_{AG} = 0.1$. x_{AL} is found as given below.

Weight of 1 m^3 of solution $= 990$ kg

Wt% of SO_2 in the solution $= 0.4\%$

Weight of SO_2 in the solution $= \dfrac{990 \times 0.4}{100} = 3.96$ kg

Weight of H_2O in the solution $= 990 - 3.96 = 986.04$ kg

Number of kmole of SO_2 in the solution $= \dfrac{3.96}{64}$

Number of kmole of H_2O in the solution $= \dfrac{986.04}{18}$

Mole fraction of SO_2 in the solution (x_{AL}) $= \dfrac{\text{Moles of } SO_2}{\text{Moles of } SO_2 + \text{Moles of } H_2O}$

$$= \frac{\dfrac{3.96}{64}}{\dfrac{3.96}{64} + \dfrac{986.04}{18}} = 0.00113$$

The overall mass transfer coefficient based on gas concentration is given on partial pressure basis, as $K_g = 7.36 \times 10^{-5}$ kmol m^{-2} s^{-1} atm^{-1}. This has to be converted to the mole fraction form.

$$N_A = K_g(P_{AG} - P_A^*) = K_g(Py_{AG} - Py_A^*) = K_gP(y_{AG} - y_A^*) \tag{2.1}$$

$$N_A = K_y(y_{AG} - y_A^*) \tag{2.2}$$

From equations (2.1) and (2.2), $K_g P = K_y$

In the present case, the total pressure is 1 atm. Hence, K_g and K_y are numerically equal.

$$K_y = 7.36 \times 10^{-5} \text{ kmol m}^{-2} \text{ s}^{-1} \ (\Delta \text{ mole fraction})^{-1}$$

The equilibrium curve is drawn using the equilibrium data. The bulk point P is located at (0.00113, 0.1). Then, y_A^*, which is a measure of x_{AL} and x_A^* which is a measure of y_{AG} are found from the graph.

$$y_A^* = 0.08 \text{ and } x_A^* = 0.001\ 35$$

$$\begin{aligned}
\text{Mass flux, } N_A &= K_y(y_{AG} - y_A^*) \\
&= 7.36 \times 10^{-5}(0.10 - 0.08) \\
&= 1.472 \times 10^{-6} \text{ kmol m}^{-2} \text{ s}^{-1} \\
\text{Mass flux is also given by } N_A &= K_x(x_A^* - x_{AL}) \\
1.472 \times 10^{-6} \text{ kmol m}^{-2} \text{ s}^{-1} &= K_x(0.001\ \ 35 - 0.001\ \ 13) \\
K_x &= 6.682 \times 10^{-3} \text{ kmol m}^{-2} \text{ s}^{-1} \ (\Delta \text{ mole fraction})^{-1}
\end{aligned}$$

We know that, $\dfrac{\text{Resistance in gas phase}}{\text{Total resistance in both phases}} = \dfrac{1/k_y}{1/K_y}$

$$0.5 = \frac{1/k_y}{1/K_y} \quad \text{or} \quad k_y = \frac{K_y}{0.5} = \frac{7.36 \times 10^{-5}}{0.5}$$

$$= 1.472 \times 10^{-4} \text{ kmol m}^{-2} \text{ s}^{-1} (\Delta \text{ mole fraction})^{-1}$$

$$N_A = k_y(y_{AG} - y_{Ai})$$

$$1.472 \times 10^{-6} \text{ kmol m}^{-2} \text{ s}^{-1} = 1.472 \times 10^{-4}(0.10 - y_{Ai})$$

and hence $\quad y_{Ai} = 0.09$

We also know that, $\dfrac{\text{Resistance in liquid phase}}{\text{Total resistance in both phases}} = \dfrac{1/k_x}{1/K_x}$

$$0.5 = \frac{1/k_x}{1/K_x} \text{ or } k_x = \frac{K_x}{0.5} = \frac{6.682 \times 10^{-3}}{0.5}$$

$$= 1.34 \times 10^{-2} \text{ kmol m}^{-2} \text{ s}^{-1} \ (\Delta \text{ mole fraction})^{-1}$$

$$N_A = k_x(x_{Ai} - x_{AL})$$

$$1.472 \times 10^{-6} \text{ kmol m}^{-2} \text{ s}^{-1} = 1.34 \times 10^{-2}(x_{Ai} - 0.001\ 13)$$

and hence $x_{Ai} = 0.001\,24$

The graphical solution for this illustration is given in Fig. 2.7.

2C In a mass transfer apparatus operating at 1 atm pressure, the individual mass transfer coefficients are $k_x = 22$ kmol m^{-2} h^{-1} and $k_y = 1.07$ kmol m^{-2} h^{-1}. The equilibrium composition of the gas and liquid phases are characterised by Henry's law. $P_A = 0.08 \times 10^6 x_A$ mm Hg, where P_A is the partial pressure of the solute in the gas phase and x_A is the mole fraction of the solute in the liquid phase.

(a) Determine the overall mass transfer coefficients.

(b) By how many times does the diffusion resistance of the liquid phase differ from that of the gas phase?

Solution

The equilibrium relation is given by $P_A = 0.08 \times 10^6 x_A$ mm Hg, where P_A is the partial pressure of the solute in the gas phase and x_A is the mole fraction of the solute in the liquid phase. This has to be transformed to the usual mole fraction form.

$$\text{Partial pressure} = \text{Total pressure} \times \text{Mole fraction}$$

$$P_A = P y_A$$

$$P y_A = 0.08 \times 10^6 x_A \text{ mm Hg}$$

$$760 y_A = 0.08 \times 10^6 x_A \text{ mm Hg}$$

$$y_A = \frac{0.08 \times 10^6}{760} x_A$$

This reduces to $y_A = 105.263 x_A$ or simply $y = 105.263x$

The slope of the equilibrium curve $m = m^I = m^{II} = 105.263$

The relationship between individual phase transfer coefficients and the overall mass transfer coefficients is given by

$$\frac{1}{K_y} = \frac{1}{k_y} + \frac{m^I}{k_x}$$

$$\frac{1}{K_y} = \frac{1}{1.07} + \frac{105.263}{22}$$

Overall mass transfer coefficient based on gas phase $(K_y) = 0.175$ kmol m^{-2} h^{-1}

$$\frac{1}{Kx} = \frac{1}{m^{II}k_y} + \frac{1}{k_x}$$

$$\frac{1}{Kx} = \frac{1}{105.263 \times 1.07} + \frac{1}{22}$$

Overall mass transfer coefficient based on liquid phase (K_x) = 18.423 kmol m^{-2} h^{-1}

$$\frac{\text{Resistance in liquid phase}}{\text{Resistance in gas phase}} = \frac{1/k_x}{1/k_y} = \frac{k_y}{k_x} = \frac{1.07}{22} = 0.048\,6$$

Hence, the resistance in the liquid phase is 0.048 6 times that of the gas phase.

2D At 293 K, the solubility of ammonia in water is given by $P = 0.021\,6C$, where P is the partial pressure of ammonia in the gas phase in atm and C is the concentration of ammonia in the liquid phase in kg m^{-3}. A mixture of 10% ammonia and 90% air by volume at 1 atm pressure is in contact with an aqueous solution containing 2.5 g L^{-1} ammonia. The air velocity is such that $k_g/k_l = 1$. Find the concentration and partial pressure of ammonia at the interphase.

Solution

It is given that, a mixture of 10% ammonia and 90% air by volume at 1 atm pressure is in contact with an aqueous solution containing 2.5 g L^{-1} ammonia. It means that P_{AG} = 0.1 and C_{AL} = 2.5 g L^{-1} = 2.5 kg m^{-3}.

Diffusion flux is given by

$$N_A^{\mathrm{I}} = k_g(P_{AG} - P_{Ai}) = k_\ell(C_{Ai} - C_{AL})$$

$$\frac{k_g}{k_\ell} = \frac{(C_{Ai} - C_{AL})}{(P_{AG} - P_{Ai})}$$ The value of this is given as 1 in the problem.

$$\frac{(C_{Ai} - C_{AL})}{(P_{AG} - P_{Ai})} = 1$$

$$\frac{(C_{Ai} - 2.5)}{(0.1 - P_{Ai})} = 1$$

$$C_{Ai} = 2.545 \text{ kg m}^{-3}$$

$$P_{Ai} = 0.021\,6C_{Ai} = 0.021\,6 \times 2.545 = 0.055 \text{ atm}$$

Interfacial composition: Gas phase contains 5.5% NH_3 by volume. Liquid phase contains 2.545 g L^{-1} NH_3.

2E In an experimental study of the absorption of ammonia from an air–ammonia mixture by water, in a wetted wall tower, the value of the overall gas mass transfer coefficient K_g was found to be 0.932 5 kmol m^{-2} h^{-1} atm^{-1} from an air–ammonia mixture in a wetted wall tower. The operating pressure and temperature are 2 atm and 288 K respectively. For dilute solutions of ammonia at 288 K, the equilibrium relation is given by $P_A = 4C_A$, where P_A is the partial pressure of ammonia in atm and C_A is the concentration of ammonia in water in kmol m^{-3} of solution. At the top of the tower, the outlet gas contained 1% ammonia by volume and the input liquid in contact is pure water. 85% of the total resistance to mass transfer was contributed by the gas phase. Calculate (a) the overall coefficient based on liquid concentration, (b) the individual phase transfer coefficients, (c) interphase compositions and (d) the mass transfer flux.

Solution

It is given that at the top of the tower, the outlet gas contained 1% ammonia by volume and the input liquid in contact is pure water. It means that $P_{AG} = 0.02$ atm and $C_{AL} = 0$ kmol m^{-3}.

$$K_g = 0.932\ 5 \text{ kmol m}^{-2}\text{ h}^{-1}\text{ atm}^{-1}$$

The equilibrium relation is given by $P_A = 4C_A$, where P_A is the partial pressure of ammonia in the atmosphere and C_A is the concentration of ammonia in water in kmol m^{-3} of solution.

So the slope of the equilibrium curve, $m = 4$.

$$\frac{\text{Resistance in gas phase}}{\text{Total resistance in both phases}} = \frac{1/k_g}{1/K_g} = \frac{K_g}{k_g} = \frac{0.9365}{k_g} = 0.85$$

Gas phase mass transfer coefficient $(k_g) = 1.097$ kmol m^{-2} h^{-1} atm^{-1}

$$\frac{1}{K_g} = \frac{1}{k_g} + \frac{m}{k_l}$$

$$\frac{1}{0.932\ 5} = \frac{1}{1.097} + \frac{4}{k_l}$$

Liquid phase mass transfer coefficient $(k_l) = 24.87$ kmol m^{-2} h^{-1} (kmol m^{-3})$^{-1}$

$$\frac{\text{Resistance in liquid phase}}{\text{Total resistance in both phases}} = \frac{1/k_\ell}{1/K_\ell} = \frac{K_\ell}{k_\ell} = \frac{K_\ell}{24.87} = 0.15$$

Overall mass transfer coefficient based on liquid phase (K_l)

$$= 3.73 \text{ kmol m}^{-2}\text{ h}^{-1}\text{ (kmol m}^{-3})^{-1}$$

Mass transfer flux $(N_A) = K_\ell(C_A^* - C_{AL})$

C_A^* is a measure of P_{AG}. $P_{AG} = 4\ C_A^*$ and $0.02 = 4C_A^*$. Hence $C_A^* = 0.005$ kmol m^{-3}.

Substituting the parameters in the above equation,

$$N_A = K_\ell(C_A^* - C_{AL})$$

$$= 3.73(0.005 - 0) = 1.867 \times 10^{-3} \text{ kmol m}^2 \text{ h}^{-1}$$

Mass transfer flux, N_A is also $= k_\ell(C_{Ai} - C_{AL})$

$$24.87(C_{Ai} - C_{AL}) = 1.867 \times 10^{-3} \text{ kmol m}^2 \text{ h}^{-1}$$

$$24.87(C_{Ai} - 0) = 1.867 \times 10^{-3} \text{ kmol m}^2 \text{ h}^{-1}$$

$$C_{Ai} = 7.5 \times 10^{-4} \text{ kmol m}^{-3}$$

$$P_{Ai} = 4C_{Ai} = 4 \times 7.5 \times 10^{-4} = 3 \times 10^{-3} \text{ atm}$$

At the interphase, the liquid has a concentration of 7.5×10^{-4} kmol m^{-3} ammonia and the gas phase has an ammonia partial pressure of 3×10^{-3} atm.

2F Component A is being transferred from the liquid phase to the gas phase in a mass transfer apparatus. The equilibrium relation is given by $y = 0.75x$. At one point in the apparatus, the liquid contains 90 mol% A and the gas in contact with the liquid contains 40 mol% A. The gas film coefficient at the above point is 2 kmol m^{-2} h^{-1} $(\Delta y_A)^{-1}$ and 72% of the total resistance to mass transfer lies in the gas phase. Determine the molar flux of A, the interphase concentration of A in both phases and the overall mass transfer coefficient based on the gas phase.

Solution

It is given that at one point in the apparatus, the liquid contains 90 mol% A and the gas in contact with the liquid contains 40 mol% A. It means that $y_{AG} = 0.4$ and $x_{AL} = 0.9$. The gas film coefficient, k_y at the above point is 2 kmol m^{-2} h^{-1} $(\Delta y_A)^{-1}$ and 72% of the total resistance to mass transfer lies in the gas phase.

$$\frac{\text{Resistance in gas phase}}{\text{Total resistance in both phases}} = \frac{1/k_y}{1/K_y} = \frac{K_y}{k_y} = \frac{K_y}{2} = 0.72$$

Overall mass transfer coefficient based on gas phase $(K_y) = 1.44$ kmol m^{-2} h^{-1} $(\Delta y_A)^{-1}$

Mass transfer flux $(N_A) = K_y(y_{AG} - x_{AL}) = K_y(y_{AG} - y_A^*)$

y_A^* is a measure of x_{AL}.

Equilibrium relation is given by $y = 0.75x$. So $y_A^* = 0.75x_{AL}$

$$= 0.75 \times 0.9 = 0.675$$

Substituting the parameters in the above equation,

$$N_A = K_y(y_{AG} - y_A^*)$$
$$= 1.44(0.4 - 0.675)$$
$$= -0.396 \text{ kmol m}^2 \text{ h}^{-1}$$

The $-$ve sign indicates that mass transfer is from the liquid to the gas phase.

$$\text{Mass transfer flux, } N_A \text{ is also} = k_y(y_{AG} - y_{Ai})$$
$$2(0.4 - y_{Ai}) = -0.396 \text{ kmol m}^2 \text{ h}^{-1}$$
$$y_{Ai} = 0.598$$

Equilibrium relation is given by $y_{Ai} = 0.75x_{Ai}$

So $\quad 0.598 = 0.75x_{Ai}$

$$x_{Ai} = 0.797$$

At the interphase, the liquid contains 79.7 mol% A and the gas phase contains 59.8 mol% A.

2G Ammonia is absorbed at 1 bar from an ammonia–air stream by passing it up a vertical tube. Dilute sulphuric acid is flowing down the same tube. The following data are available. The length and diameter of the tube are 825 mm and 5 mm respectively. The partial pressures of ammonia at the inlet and the outlet are 7.5 kN m^{-2} and 2.0 kN m^{-2} respectively. If the air rate is 2×10^{-5} kmol s^{-1}, compute the gas phase mass transfer coefficient, k_g.

Solution

Driving force at the inlet $= 7.5 \text{ kN m}^{-2}$

Driving force at the outlet $= 2.0 \text{ kN m}^{-2}$

Mean driving force $= \dfrac{7.5 - 2.0}{\ln \dfrac{7.5}{2.0}} = 4.2 \text{ kN m}^{-2}$

Moles of ammonia per mole of air at the inlet $= \dfrac{7.5}{92.5} = 0.081\ 1$

Moles of ammonia per mole of air at the outlet $= \dfrac{2}{98} = 0.020\ 4$

Ammonia absorbed $= 2\times10^{-5}(0.081\ 1 - 0.020\ 4) = 1.214 \times 10^{-6}$ kmol s^{-1}

Wetted area $= \pi \times 0.015 \times 0.825 = 0.038\ 8$ m^2

Mass transfer coefficient is the diffusion flux for unit average driving force.

$$k_g = \frac{1.214 \times 10^{-6}}{0.0388 \times 4.2} = 7.45 \times 10^{-6} \text{ kmol m}^{-2} \text{ (kN m}^{-2})^{-1}$$

THEORIES OF MASS TRANSFER

In all mass transfer operations, material is transferred across an interphase. As no material accumulates at the interphase, the rate of transfer on each side of the interphase must be the same. Therefore, concentration gradients automatically adjust themselves so that they are proportional to the resistance to transfer in that particular phase. If there is no resistance to transfer at the interphase, the concentrations on each side will be related to each other by the phase equilibrium relationship. There are conflicting opinions regarding the existence or otherwise of a resistance to transfer at the phase boundary.

Two Film Theory

Whitman [2] proposed the first theory known as the *two film theory* to represent the conditions occurring when the material is transferred from one fluid to another. In this theory, it is assumed that the turbulence dies at the interphase and that a laminar layer exists in each of the two fluids. In the laminar layer, mass transfer is entirely by molecular diffusion and outside the laminar layer, eddies supplement diffusion so that the resistance to mass transfer becomes progressively smaller.

A schematic representation of the variation in concentration with distance is shown in Fig. 2.8. The concentration gradient is linear close to the interphase and gradually becomes less at greater distances. The basis of the theory is the assumption that the zones in which the resistance to transfer lies can be represented by two hypothetical layers, one on each side of the interphase. Within these layers, mass transfer is entirely by molecular diffusion. The concentration gradient is therefore linear in each of these layers and zero outside. The broken lines AGC and DHF indicate the hypothetical concentration distribution. Z_1 and Z_2 represent the thickness of the two layers or films. An equilibrium exists at the interphase and therefore the relative position of points C and D is determined by the equilibrium relation between the phases. Mass transfer is assumed to be a steady state process. Therefore, this theory can be applied only if the time taken for the establishment of concentration gradient is very small.

According to the two film theory, for equimolecular counter diffusion, the rate of transfer per unit area for I phase is as follows.

$$N_A = \frac{D_1}{Z_1}(C_{A01} - C_{Ai1}) = k_{C1}(C_{A01} - C_{Ai1}) \tag{2.22}$$

where Z_1 is the thickness of the film, C_{A01} is the molar concentration of A outside the film and C_{Ai1} is the concentration at the interphase. For the second phase,

$$N_A = \frac{D_2}{Z_2}(C_{Ai2} - C_{A02}) = k_{C2}(C_{Ai2} - C_{A02}) \tag{2.23}$$

where Z_2 is the thickness of the film, C_{A02} is the molar concentration of A outside the film and C_{Ai2} is the concentration at the interphase.

$$k_c = \frac{D}{Z} \tag{2.24}$$

$$k_c \ \alpha \ D_n, \text{ where } n = 1 \tag{2.25}$$

k_c varies with the first power of D. This theory cannot explain values of n less than 1.

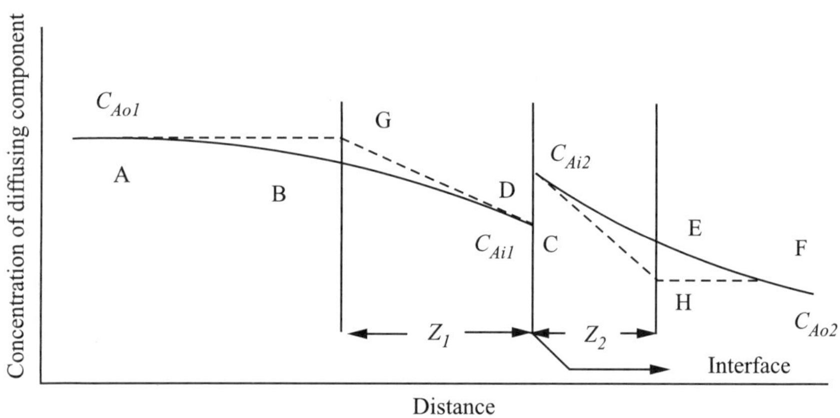

Fig. 2.8 Concentration–distance diagram

Penetration Theory

Higbie [3] proposed the penetration theory to explain the dependence of mass transfer rate on fractional powers of diffusivity. He said that material transfer across the interphase cannot occur if the contact time is short. According to him, eddy diffusion supplements molecular diffusion in the case of interfacial mass transfer. Eddies in one phase bring an element of fluid to the interphase from the bulk. At the interphase, the element is exposed to the second phase for a definite interval of time. After the exposure, the element is driven back to the bulk from the interphase by the eddy movement. Thus, the fluid whose initial composition corresponds to that of the bulk fluid away from the interphase, is suddenly exposed to the second phase. The surface layers attain equilibrium at a definite time and then a process of unsteady state molecular diffusion occurs. Thus, the expression for the transient rate of diffusion into a relatively thick mass of fluid with a constant concentration is given by

$$\frac{\partial C_A}{\partial t} = D \times \frac{\partial^2 C_A}{\partial Z^2} \tag{2.26}$$

The following boundary conditions apply.

$$\text{At } t = 0 \qquad Z = 0 - \infty \quad C_A = C_{Ao} \tag{2.27}$$

$$\text{At } t > 0 \qquad Z = 0 \qquad C_A = C_{Ai} \tag{2.28}$$

$$\text{At } t > 0 \qquad Z = 8 \qquad C_A = C_{Ao} \tag{2.29}$$

The rate of mass transfer can be obtained by solving the above equation for the boundary conditions.

$$N_A = (C_{Ai} - C_{Ao})\sqrt{D/\pi\, t} \tag{2.30}$$

$$k_c \ \alpha \ D^{0.5} \tag{2.31}$$

The rate is a linear function of the driving force and the concentration gradient as in the two film theory, but it is proportional to the square root of diffusivity instead of diffusivity.

Surface Renewal Theory

Danckwerts [4] pointed out that the Higbie's theory with its constant time of exposure of eddies of fluid at the surface is only a special case. In reality, eddies are exposed for varying lengths of time.

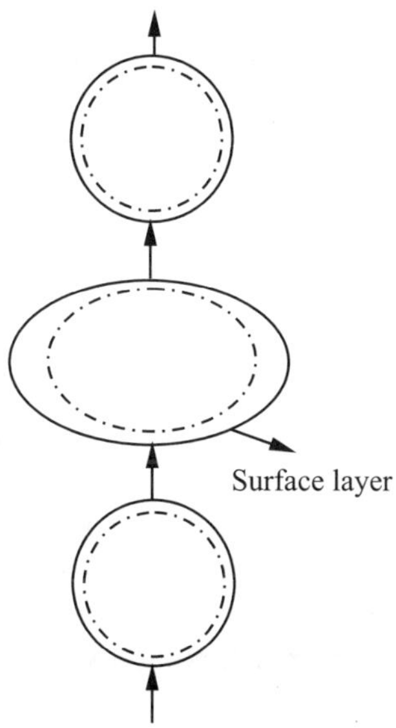

Fig. 2.9 Surface stretch theory

He proved that the probability of any element of the surface becoming destroyed and mixed with the bulk of the fluid was independent of the age of the element. The interphase is a mosaic of surface elements of different exposure times. Since the rate of solute penetration depends upon the exposure time, the average rate for a unit surface area must be determined by summing up the individual values.

He calculated the diffusion flux as $N_A = (C_{Ai} - C_{Ao})\sqrt{D\,s}$ (2.32)

and estimated the average transfer coefficient as $\overline{k_c} = \sqrt{D\,s}$ (2.33)

where s is the fractional rate of surface renewal. The rate of mass transfer is time dependent and proportional to the concentration difference and to the square root of diffusivity. In practice, the numerical value of s is difficult to estimate, but s will increase as the fluid becomes more turbulent.

The Film-Penetration Theory

This theory, proposed by Toor and Marchello [5], combines most of the principles of the two film theory and the penetration theory. The entire resistance to mass transfer is assumed to lie within a laminar film at the interphase as in the two film theory. However, mass transfer is regarded as an unsteady state process, which is the main postulate of the penetration theory. It is assumed that a fresh surface is formed at intervals from the fluid which is brought from the bulk to the interphase by the action of eddies. Mass transfer then takes place as in the penetration theory with the exception that the resistance is confined to the finite film and the material which crosses the film is immediately completely mixed with the bulk of the fluid. For short times of exposure, when none of the diffusing material has reached the far side of the interphase, the process is identical to that proposed in the penetration theory. For prolonged periods of exposure when a steady concentration gradient has developed, conditions are similar to those described in the two film theory.

Surface Stretch Theory

Lightfoot et al [6] have extended the penetration–surface renewal principles to situations where the interphase through which mass transfer occurs, changes periodically with time. Situations like this occur when drops and bubbles are formed at nozzles and when liquid surfaces are wavy or rippled. A classical example is a liquid drop rising through a denser solution with mass transfer of the solute from the solution to the drop (Fig. 2.9). If the drop is large, it will wobble, oscillate and change its shape. If the central portion of the drop is thoroughly turbulent, the mass transfer resistance of the drop resides in a surface layer of varying thickness. For such cases, as per this theory,

$$k_c = \frac{A/A_r\sqrt{D/\pi\,t}}{\sqrt{\int_0^{t/t_r}\left(\frac{A}{A_r}\right)^2 dt}} \tag{2.34}$$

where A is the time dependent surface area of the interphase, A_r is the reference value of A defined for each situation and t_r is the drop formation time, which is a constant with the dimensions of time.

CONCEPT OF STAGE WISE CONTACTORS

The stage wise contactor is a type of mass transfer device consisting of assemblies of individual units or stages that are interconnected so that the materials being processed pass through each stage in turn (Fig. 2.10). The two streams move in a counter current mode through the assembly.

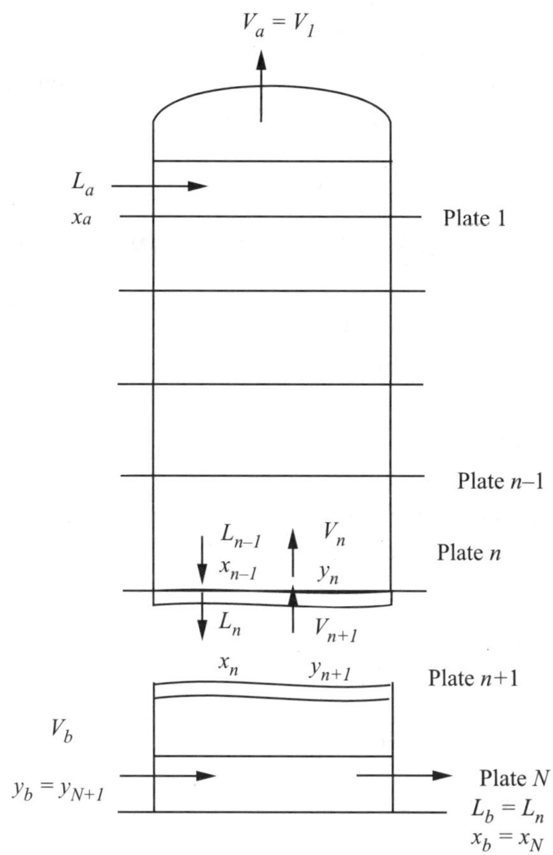

Fig. 2.10 Stage wise contactors

In each stage, they are brought into contact and then separated. Such multistage systems are called cascades. For mass transfer to take place, the streams entering each stage must not be in equilibrium with each other, because it is the departure from equilibrium which provides the driving force for mass transfer. The leaving streams are closer to equilibrium than the entering streams. The closeness to equilibrium depends on the effectiveness of mass transfer between the phases. To simplify the design of a cascade, the streams leaving each stage are assumed to be in equilibrium; that is, each stage is assumed to be ideal. If stage n is ideal, then the effluent concentrations (x_n, y_n) are coordinates of a point on the equilibrium curve. Then a correction or efficiency factor is applied to account for any departure from equilibrium.

The individual contact units in a cascade are numbered serially starting from one end. The stages are numbered in general in the direction of flow of the heavy phase and the last stage is that discharging the heavy phase. A general stage in the system is the nth stage which is the number *n* counting from the entrance of the heavy phase. The stage immediately above or ahead of stage n in the sequence is stage $n-1$ and that immediately following it is stage $n+1$. If the total number of stages is N, then the last stage in the plant is the Nth stage. Streams and concentrations originating from a stage carry the number of the stage as a subscript. For a two component system, y_{n+1} is the mole fraction of A in the vapour phase leaving the stage $n+1$ and L_n is the molal flow rate of the liquid phase leaving the nth stage.

GRAPHICAL METHOD FOR A TWO COMPONENT SYSTEM

For binary systems, mass transfer problems can be solved graphically. The method is based on material balance and equilibrium relationship.

Operating Line Diagram

For a binary system, the components of the two phases in a cascade can be shown on an arithmetic graph where x is abscissa and y the ordinate (Fig. 2.10).

Overall material balance: $L_a + V_b = L_b + V_a$ (2.35)

Component A balance : $L_a x_a + V_b y_b = L_b x_b + V_a y_a$ (2.36)

$$y_b = \frac{L_b}{V_b} x_b + \frac{V_a y_a - L_a x_a}{V_b} \tag{2.37}$$

If the changes in L and V are neglected

$$y_b = \frac{L}{V} x_b + y_a - \frac{L}{V} x_a \tag{2.38}$$

So the operating line is a straight line with $\frac{L}{V}$ as slope and $y_a - \frac{L}{V} x_a$ as the intercept. The operating line can also be constructed by drawing a straight line connecting the two points corresponding to the terminal compositions (x_a, y_a) and (x_b, y_b).

When the flow rates are not constant in the column, the operating line is not a straight line but is slightly curved. This usually happens when the mole fraction of the solute in the entering gases is more than 0.1. Terminal compositions may still be used to locate the ends of the line. Material balance calculations over sections of the column can be made to find one or two intermediate points. For the construction of the operating line, a maximum of two intermediate points other than the terminal compositions will do.

Determination of Number of Ideal Stages

To find the number of ideal stages, the operating line and equilibrium curve are to be plotted on the same graph sheet. Consider a gas absorber. Let the terminal concentrations be (x_a, y_a) and (x_b, y_b). We have to find the ideal stages needed to accomplish the gas phase concentration change y_b to y_a and liquid phase concentration change x_a to x_b. The concentration of the gas leaving the top stage which is stage 1 is y_a or y_1. If this stage is ideal, the liquid leaving it will be in equilibrium with the vapour leaving. So, the point (x_1, y_1) must lie on the equilibrium line. This fact fixes point m which is the point of intersection of the equilibrium line and a line drawn through a parallel to the x axis.

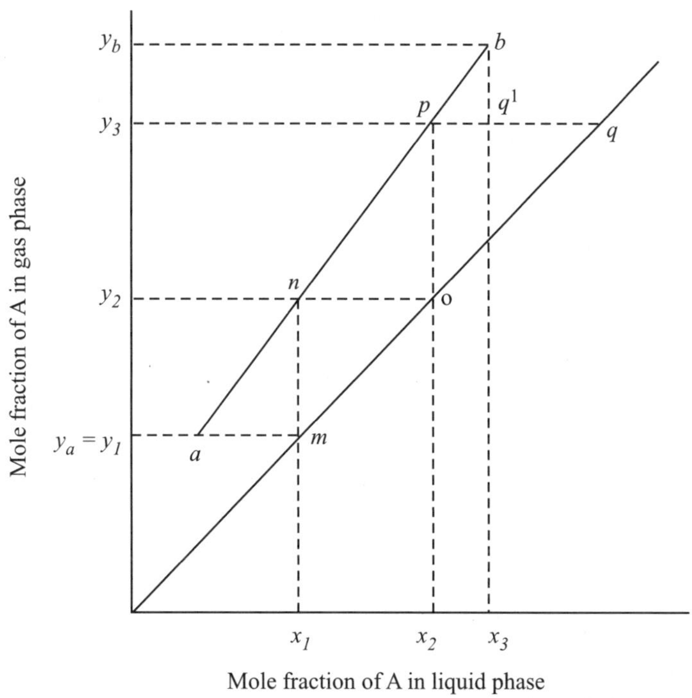

Fig. 2.11 Graphical construction for finding ideal stages

The abscissa of point m is x_1. Now, the operating line has to be used. The operating line passes through all points having coordinates of the type (x_n, y_{n+1}). If x_1 is known we can find y_2. y_2 is found by moving vertically upwards from point m till the point n on the operating line is reached. The coordinates of the point n are (x_1, y_2). The triangle amn represents one ideal stage (Fig. 2.11).

By repeating the same construction, that is, passing horizontally to the equilibrium curve and passing vertically to the operating line till point b is reached, the number of ideal stages can be found out. This graphical step-by-step construction utilising the equilibrium curve and operating line alternately to find the number of ideal stages is known as the *McCabe–Thiele method* [7]. It can be used for other mass transfer operations like rectification, leaching, extraction and others. The construction can be started at either end of the column. In general, the last step will not exactly meet the terminal concentration. A fractional stage may be assigned or the number of ideal stages may be rounded up to the next whole number.

ILLUSTRATION

2H It is desired to absorb 95% acetone from a feed mixture of acetone and air containing 2 mol% acetone using 20% more than the minimum water rate. Pure water is introduced at the top of the tower and the gas flow rate at the bottom of the tower is 450 kg h^{-1}. The gas mixture enters at 298 K and atmospheric pressure, which is the operating condition inside the tower. The equilibrium relationship is given by $y = 2.5x$ where x and y are the mole fractions of acetone in the liquid and gas phases respectively. Calculate the flow rate of water and the number of theoretical stages required.

Solution

Basis: 1 hour operation.

Mole fraction of acetone in the entering gases (y_b)	=	0.02
Mole fraction of air in the entering gases	=	0.98
Average molecular weight of the entering gases	=	$(58 \times 0.02) + (29 \times 0.98) = 29.58$
Mass flow rate of entering gases	=	450 kg
Molal flow rate of the entering gases	=	$450 \div 29.58 = 15.213$ kmol
Amount of acetone in the entering gases	=	$15.213 \times 0.02 = 0.304$ kmol
Amount of air in the entering gases	=	$15.213 - 0.304 = 14.909$ kmol

95% of acetone in the entering gases is absorbed by water.

Amount of acetone absorbed	=	$0.304 \times 0.95 = 0.289$ kmol
Amount of acetone in the leaving gases	=	$0.304 \times 0.05 = 0.015$ kmol
Amount of gases leaving	=	Inert air + Unabsorbed acetone
	=	$14.909 + 0.015 = 14.924$ kmol
Mole fraction of acetone in the leaving gases (y_a)	=	$0.015 \div 14.924 = 0.001$

The entering water is acetone free.

Mole fraction of acetone in the entering water (x_a) = 0

Amount of acetone in the liquid effluent = 0.289 kmol

Let the minimum water rate be L kmol h^{-1}. At the minimum water rate, the mole fraction of ammonia in the liquid effluent is x_b^*.

$$y_b = mx_b^*$$

That is, 0.02 = 2.5x_b^* and x_b^* = 0.008

$$\frac{0.289}{0.289 + L} = 0.008$$

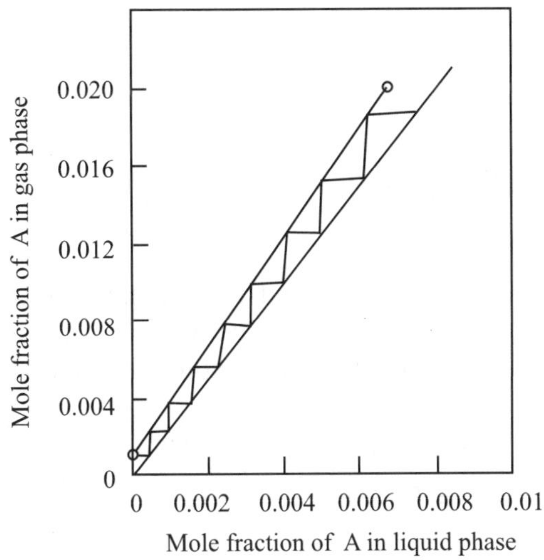

Fig. 2.12 Graphical solution for 2H

Hence L = 35.84 k mol

Actual water rate is 1.20 times the minimum.

Actual water rate = 35.84 ×1.20 = 43.005 k mol = 774.09 kg h^{-1}

Mole fraction of ammonia in the liquid effluent $(x_b) = \dfrac{0.289}{0.289 + 43.005} = 0.00668$

In this case, $y_b < 0.1$. So the operating line is drawn using the extreme ends (x_a, y_a) and (x_b, y_b). On the same graph sheet, the equilibrium curve is also drawn. The number of theoretical stages required is found by the McCabe–Thiele method, as shown in Fig. 2.12. The number of theoretical units required for this operation = 8.33, that is, 9.0.

STAGE EFFICIENCY

An ideal stage is defined as one where the effluent phases are in equilibrium so that a longer time of contact will bring about no additional change in composition. But in practice, no stage is ideal. To get the actual number of stages, the number of ideal stages found by graphical means has to be divided by a factor, the stage efficiency.

$$\text{Number of actual stages} = \frac{\text{Number of ideal stages}}{\text{Stage efficiency}}$$

The stage efficiency (η) is defined as the fractional approach to equilibrium which a real stage produces. It is also the ratio of actual solute transfer to that if equilibrium were attained.

$$\eta = \frac{y_b - y_a}{y_b^* - y_a^*} \text{ or } \frac{x_b - x_a}{x_b^* - x_a^*}$$

DIFFERENTIAL CONTACTORS

In a differential contact plant such as a packed absorption tower, there are no sudden discrete changes in composition. A schematic representation of a differential contactor is shown in Fig. 2.13. The variations in concentration are continuous from one end of the equipment to the other.

Overall material balance based on terminal streams:

$$\text{Total material: } L_a + V_b = L_b + V_a \tag{2.39}$$

$$\text{Component A: } L_a x_a + V_b y_b = L_b x_b + V_a y_a \tag{2.40}$$

Material balance for the portion of the column above the section:

$$\text{Total material: } L_a + V = L + V_a \tag{2.41}$$

$$\text{Component A: } L_a x_a + V_y = L_x + V_a y_a \tag{2.42}$$

$$V_y = L_x + (V_a y_a - L_a x_a) \tag{2.43}$$

$$y = \frac{L}{V}x + \frac{(V_a y_a - L_a x_a)}{V} \tag{2.44}$$

This is the equation of the operating line for a differential contactor. x and y are the bulk concentrations of the liquid and gas respectively in contact with each other at any given section through the column. Absorption of the soluble component from the gas mixture makes the total gas rate V decrease and the flow of liquid L increase as the gas passes through the column. These changes make the operating line slightly curved. For dilute gas mixtures containing less than 10% of soluble gas, the effect of changes in the total flow can be neglected and the design can be based on the above flow rates.

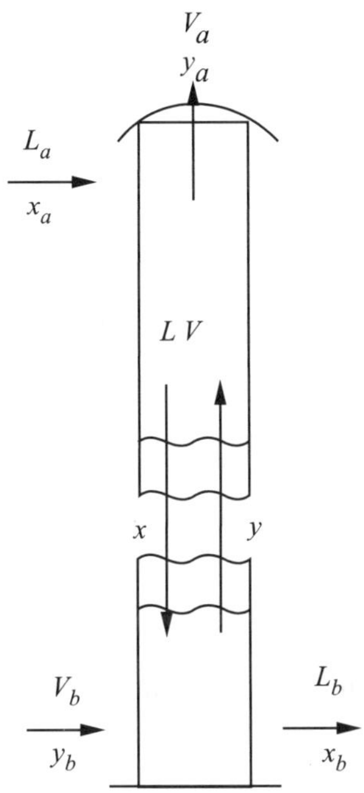

Fig. 2.13 Differential contactor

Limiting Gas–Liquid Ratio

From equation (2.44), it is clear that the slope of the operating line is $\frac{L}{V}$, the ratio of the molar flow rates of liquid to gas. For a given gas flow, a reduction in liquid flow decreases the slope of the operating line. If the gas flow rate and the terminal concentrations x_a, y_a and y_b are held constant and the liquid flow rate is decreased, the upper end of the operating line then shifts in the direction of the equilibrium line and x_b, the concentration of the strong liquid, increases. The maximum possible liquid concentration and the minimum possible liquid rate are obtained when the operating line just touches the equilibrium line as in the case of 'ab', in Fig. 2.14.

At this condition, the height of the packed column becomes infinity, as the concentration difference for mass transfer becomes zero at the bottom of the tower. For an actual absorber, the liquid rate must be greater than this minimum to achieve the specified change in gas composition. In general, the liquid rate to the absorber should be in the range 1.1 to 1.5 times the minimum.

In a counter current operation, the $\frac{L}{V}$ ratio is important in the economics of absorption. The driving force for mass transfer is $y - y^*$, which is proportional to the vertical distance between the operating line and equilibrium line. Increasing $\frac{L}{V}$ increases the driving force everywhere in the column except at the very top and also, the absorption column need not be tall.

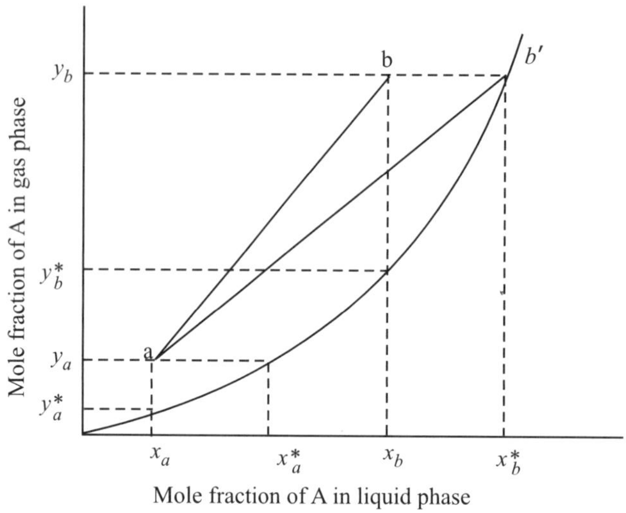

Fig. 2.14 Graphical representation for minimum liquid rate

HTU AND NTU

Consider a packed column functioning as an absorber. A schematic representation of a differential contactor is given in Fig. 2.15. Let the cross section be S. The differential volume in height dZ is SdZ. If the change in the molar flow rate is neglected, the amount of solute absorbed in section dZ can be obtained by multiplying the molar flow rate of the vapour (V) by the change in vapour composition (dy), which is also equal to the mass transfer coefficient multiplied by the difference in mole fraction multiplied by the differential volume.

$$-V \times dy = K_y\, a\, (y - y^*) S\, dZ \tag{2.45}$$

Here, the negative sign indicates that the concentration drops in the direction of mass transfer.

To get the overall effect, the above equation has to be integrated.

$$-\frac{dy}{y - y^*} = \frac{K_y a S}{V} \int dZ \tag{2.46}$$

$$-\int_b^a \frac{dy}{y - y^*} = \frac{K_y a S}{V} \int_0^{Z_T} dZ \tag{2.47}$$

$$\int_a^b \frac{dy}{y - y^*} = \frac{K_y a S}{V} \int_0^{Z_T} dZ \tag{2.48}$$

$$\int_a^b \frac{dy}{y-y^*} = \frac{K_y a S}{V} Z_T \tag{2.49}$$

$$Z_T = \frac{(V/S)}{K_y a} \int_a^b \frac{dy}{y-y^*} \tag{2.50}$$

where Z_T is the total height of the packing. The integral in the equation represents the change in vapour concentration for unit average driving force. It is called number of transfer units (N_{Oy}), as it is based on the overall driving force for the gas phase [8]. The other part, $\frac{(V/S)}{K_y a}$, which has the unit of the length, is known as height of a transfer unit (H_{Oy}).

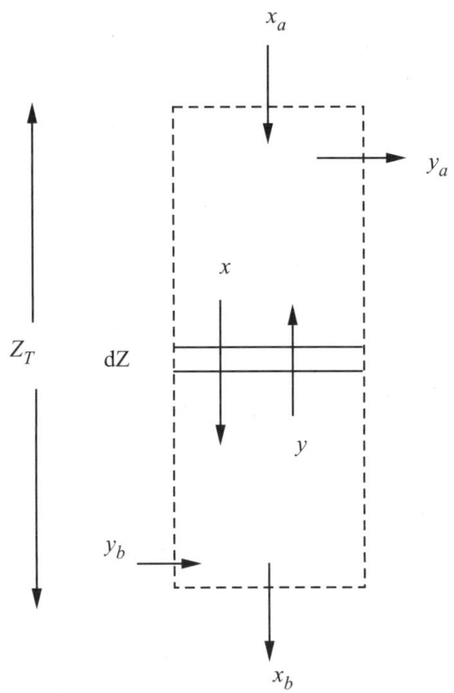

Fig. 2.15 Differential contactor

$$Z_T = N_{Oy} \times H_{Oy} \tag{2.51}$$

N_{OY} is also equal to $\frac{y_b - y_a}{\Delta y_{lm}}$, where y_b is the mole fraction of the solute in the gas phase at the bottom of the column, y_a is the mole fraction of the solute in the gas phase at the top of the column and Δy_{lm} is the log mean of the driving forces in the gas phase at the extreme ends of the column. In other words, Δy_{lm} is the log mean of $y_b - y_b^*$ and $y_a - y_a^*$. The above derivation for NTU and HTU are for overall resistance based on the gas phase. Similar derivations are possible for overall resistance based on the liquid phase, gas phase resistance and liquid phase resistance. The results are given below:

$$N_{Oy} = \int_a^b \frac{dy}{y - y^*} \text{ and } H_{Oy} = \frac{(V/S)}{K_y a}, \text{ for overall resistance based on gas phase.} \tag{2.52}$$

$$N_{Ox} = \int_a^b \frac{dx}{x^* - x} \text{ and } H_{Ox} = \frac{(L/S)}{K_x a}, \text{ for overall resistance based on liquid phase.} \tag{2.53}$$

$$N_y = \int_a^b \frac{dy}{y - y_i} \text{ and } H_y = \frac{(V/S)}{k_y a}, \text{ for resistance based on gas phase.} \tag{2.54}$$

$$N_x = \int_a^b \frac{dx}{x_i - x} \text{ and } H_x = \frac{(L/S)}{k_x a}, \text{ for resistance based on liquid phase.} \tag{2.55}$$

Figure 2.16 shows the graphical procedure for finding the equilibrium concentrations.

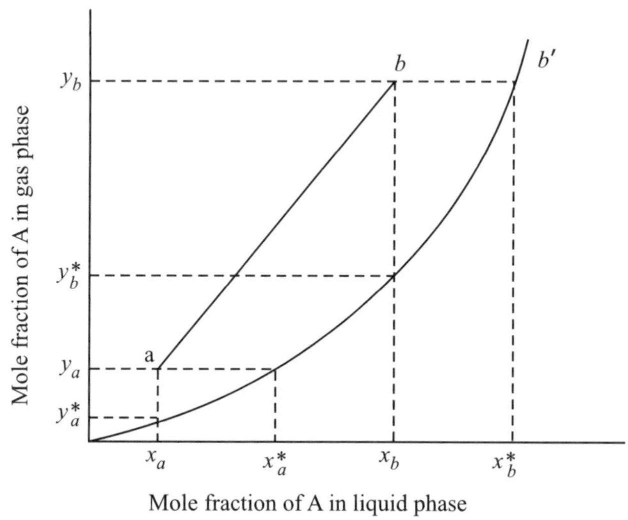

Fig. 2.16 Graphical representation of equilibrium values

ILLUSTRATION

2I In an air–ammonia mixture containing 5 vol% ammonia, ammonia is absorbed in water using a packed tower to recover 98% of ammonia at an inlet flow rate of 1200 kg h^{-1} m^{-2}. The tower operates at 293 K and atmospheric pressure. Determine (a) minimum mass flow rate of liquid (b) number of transfer units using 1.25 times the minimum liquid flow rate. The equilibrium relationship for the system is given by $y = 1.154x$, where x and y are mole fractions and (c) height of the tower assuming Kga to be 128 kmol m^{-3} h^{-1} atm^{-1}.

Solution

Basis: 1 hour operation.

Average molecular weight of gas at the inlet = (29 × 0.95) + (17 × 0.05) = 28.40

Mass flow rate of the gas	=	1200 kg
Molal flow rate of the gas at the inlet (V_b) = 1200 ÷ 28.40	=	42.25 kmol
Mole fraction of ammonia at the gas inlet (y_b)	=	0.05
Ammonia at the gas inlet = 42.25 × 0.05	=	2.113 kmol
Air at the gas inlet = 42.25 – 2.113	=	40.137 kmol
98% of ammonia is absorbed in water.		
Ammonia absorbed in water = 2.113 × 0.98	=	2.07 k mol
Ammonia in the gas output = 2.113 – 2.07	=	0.043 kmol
Mole fraction of ammonia in the gas outlet (y_a) = $\dfrac{0.043}{40.137 + 0.043}$	=	0.001
Molal flow rate of the gas at the outlet (V_a) = 40.137 + 0.043	=	40.18 kmol

Water used for absorption is pure.

Mole fraction of ammonia in water entering the absorption tower (x_a) = 0

Let the minimum water rate be L kmol h^{-1}. At a minimum water rate, the mole fraction of ammonia in the liquid effluent is, x_b^*.

$$y_b = mx_b^*$$

That is, 0.05 = 1.154x_b^* and x_b^*= 0.0433

$$\frac{2.07}{2.07 + L} = 0.0433$$

Hence L = 45.74 k mol = 823.32 kg h^{-1}m^{-2}

The actual water rate is 1.25 times the minimum.

Actual water rate = 45.74 × 1.25 = 57.175 k mol

Mole fraction of ammonia in the liquid effluent (x_b) = $\dfrac{2.07}{57.175 + 2.07} = 0.0349$

y_b^*= 1.154 x_b = 1.154 × 0.0349 = 0.0403 and y_a^*= 1.154 *xa* = 1.154 × 0 = 0

$$N_{oy} = \frac{y_b - y_a}{\Delta y_{lm}}, \text{ where } \Delta y_{lm} = \frac{(y_b - y_b^*) - (y_a - y_a^*)}{\ln \dfrac{(y_b - y_b^*)}{(y_a - y_a^*)}}$$

Substituting the value of the parameters,

$$N_{oy} = 12.79$$

$$H_{oy} = \frac{\overline{(V/S)}}{K_y a}$$

$$\overline{V} = \frac{(V_a + V_b)}{2} = \frac{42.25 + 40.18}{2} = 41.22 \; K_{ga} = 128 \text{ kmol m}^{-3} \text{ h}^{-1} \text{ atm}^{-1}$$

$$= P \times K_{ya}$$

where P is the total pressure, here it is 1 atm.

Hence K_{ya} = 128 kmol m^{-3} h^{-1}

$$H_{oy} = \frac{41.22}{128} = 0.322 \text{ m}$$

$$Z_T = N_{oy} \times H_{oy} = 12.79 \times 0.322 = 4.12 \text{ m}$$

NOTATIONS

a	Interfacial area per unit volume of packing, m^{2}m^{-3}.
a	Top of the column, when used as subscript.
A	Time dependent interfacial surface, m^2.
A_r	Reference value of A, m^2.
b	Bottom of the column, when used as subscript.
C_A	Molar concentration of A, mol m^{-3}.
C_{A0}	Initial molar concentration of A, mol m^{-3}.
C_{Ai}	Molar concentration of A at the interphase, mol m^{-3}.
C_{AO1}	Molar concentration of A outside the film in the first phase, mol m^{-3}.
C_{Ai1}	Molar concentration of A at the first phase side of the interphase, mol m^{-3}.
C_{AO2}	Molar concentration of A outside the film in the second phase, mol m^{-3}.
C_{Ai2}	Molar concentration of A at the second phase side of the inter phase, mol m^{-3}.
C_{AL}	Concentration of the solute in the bulk of the heavy phase (liquid phase), mol m^{-3}.
C_{Ai}	Concentration of the solute at the liquid side of the interphase, mol m^{-3}.
C_A^*	Equilibrium value of solute in the heavy phase, corresponding to P_{AG}, mol m^{-3}.
D	Diffusivity of the solute, m^2 s^{-1}.
D_1	Diffusivity of the solute in the first phase, m^2 s^{-1}.
D_2	Diffusivity of the solute in the second phase, m^2 s^{-1}.
H_x	Height of a transfer unit based on resistance in liquid phase, m.
H_y	Height of a transfer unit based on resistance in vapour phase, m.
H_{ox}	Height of a transfer unit based on overall resistance in terms of liquid phase, m.
H_{oy}	Height of a transfer unit based on overall resistance in terms of vapour phase, m.
k_c	Mass transfer coefficient based on concentration, m s^{-1}.
k_g	Mass transfer coefficient for the light phase (gas phase), kmol m^{-2} s^{-1} (mol m^{-3})$^{-}$

k_l	Mass transfer coefficient for the heavy phase (liquid phase), kmol m^{-2} s^{-1} (mol m^{-3})$^{-1}$.
k_y	Mass transfer coefficient for the light phase (gas phase), kmol m^{-2} s^{-1} (Δ mole fraction)$^{-1}$.
k_x	Mass transfer coefficient for the heavy phase (liquid phase), kmol m^{-2} s^{-1} (Δ mole fraction)$^{-1}$.
K_y	Overall mass transfer coefficient based on light phase (gas phase), kmol m^{-2} s^{-1} (Δ mole fraction)$^{-1}$.
K_x	Overall mass transfer coefficient based on heavy phase (liquid phase), kmol m^{-2} s^{-1} (Δ mole fraction)$^{-1}$.
K_g	Overall mass transfer coefficient based on light phase (gas phase), kmol m^{-2} s^{-1} (N m^{-2})$^{-1}$.
K_l	Overall mass transfer coefficient based on heavy phase (liquid phase), kmol m^{-2} s^{-1} (N m^{-2})$^{-1}$.
L	Molal flow rate of the liquid, kmol h^{-1}.
L_a	Molal flow rate of the liquid entering the tower, kmol h^{-1}.
L_b	Molal flow rate of the liquid leaving the tower, kmol h^{-1}.
L_n	Molal flow rate of liquid leaving the nth plate or stage, kmol h^{-1}.
m	Slope of the equilibrium curve.
m_1	Slope of the equilibrium curve chord.
m_{11}	Slope of the equilibrium curve chord at an another location.
N_x	Number of transfer units based on resistance in the liquid phase.
N_y	Number of transfer units based on resistance in the vapour phase.
N_{ox}	Number of transfer units based on overall resistance in terms of the liquid phase.
N_{oy}	Number of transfer units based on overall resistance in terms of the vapour phase.
N_A	Rate of diffusion per unit area or diffusion flux of A, kmol m^{-2} s^{-1}.
P_{AG}	Partial pressure of the solute in the bulk of the light phase (gas phase), N m^{-2}.
P_{Ai}	Partial pressure of the solute at the gas side of the interphase, N m^{-2}.
P_A^*	Equilibrium value of solute in the light phase, corresponding to C_{AL}, N m^{-2}.
s	Fractional rate of surface renewal, s.
S	Cross sectional area of the tower, m^2.
t	Time, s.
t_r	Drop formation time, s.
V	Molal flow rate of the vapour, kmol h^{-1}.
V_a	Molal flow rate of the vapour leaving the tower, kmol h^{-1}.
V_b	Molal flow rate of the vapour entering the tower, kmol h^{-1}.
V_n	Molal flow rate of vapour leaving the nth plate or stage, kmol h^{-1}.

x	Mole fraction of the solute in the liquid.
x^*	Equilibrium value of mole fraction of solute in the liquid.
x_a	Mole fraction of solute in the heavy phase entering the tower.
x_b	Mole fraction of solute in the heavy phase leaving the tower.
x_A	Mole fraction of the solute in the liquid.
x_{AL}	Mole fraction of the solute in the bulk of the liquid.
x_{Ai}	Mole fraction of the solute at the liquid side of the interphase.
x_n	Mole fraction of the solute at the liquid leaving the nth plate.
x_A^*	Equilibrium value of solute in the heavy phase, corresponding to y_{AG}.
dx	Change in liquid composition in terms of mole fraction.
y	Mole fraction of the solute in the vapour.
y_a	Mole fraction of solute in the light phase leaving the tower.
y_b	Mole fraction of solute in the light phase entering the tower.
y^*	Equilibrium value of mole fraction of solute in the vapour.
y_A	Mole fraction of the solute in the light phase.
y_{AG}	Mole fraction of the solute in the bulk of the light phase.
y_{Ai}	Mole fraction of the solute at the gas side of the interphase.
y_n	Mole fraction of the solute at the vapour leaving the nth plate.
y_b^*	Equilibrium value in terms of mole fraction, corresponding to x_a.
y_a^*	Equilibrium value in terms of mole fraction, corresponding to x_b.
y_A^*	Equilibrium value of solute in the light phase, corresponding to x_{AL}.
dy	Change in vapour composition in terms of mole fraction.
Δy_{lm}	Log mean of the driving forces in the light phase at the extreme ends of the column.
Z_1	Thickness of the film on the first phase, m.
Z_2	Thickness of the film on the second phase, m.
dz	Differential height, m.
Z_T	Total height of the tower, m.

REFERENCES

1. King CJ, *A.I.Ch.E. J.*, **10**: 671 (1964).
2. Whitman WG, *Chem. and Met. Eng.*, **29**: 147 (1923).
3. Higbie R, *Trans. Am. Inst. Chem. Eng.*, **31**: 365 (1935).
4. Danckwerts PV, *Ind. Eng. Chem.*, **43**: 1460 (1951).
5. Toor HL and Marchello JM, *A.I.Ch.E. J.*, **4**: 97 (1958).
6. Lightfoot EN, Angelo JB and Stewart WE, *A.I.Ch.E. J.*, **16**: 771 (1970).
7. McCabe WL and Thiele EW, *Ind. Eng. Chem.*, **17**: 605 (1925).
8. Chilton TH and Colburn AP, *Ind. Eng. Chem.*, **27**: 255 (1935).

Problems for Practice

2.1 In an experimental study of absorption of ammonia by water in a wetted wall column, the overall gas phase mass transfer coefficient was estimated to be 2.718×10^{-5} mol cm^{-2} s^{-1} atm^{-1}. At one point in the column, the gas contained 8 mol% ammonia and the liquid phase concentration was 6.415×10^{-5} mol NH_3 per cm^3 of solution. The temperature was 293 K and the total pressure 1.0 atm. 85% of the total resistance to mass transfer was found to be in the gas phase. If Henry's law constant at 293 K is 9.354 atm mol^{-1} cm^{-3}, calculate the film coefficients and the interphase composition.

2.2 In an experimental study of the absorption of NH_3 by water in a wetted wall column, the value of K_G was found to be 1 kmol NH_3 h^{-1} m^{-2} atm^{-1}. At one point in the column, the gas contained 8 mol% NH_3 and the liquid phase concentration was 0.07 kmol NH_3 m^{-3} of solution. The temperature was 303 K and the total pressure was 1 atm. 80% of the total resistance to mass transfer was found to be in the gas phase. If Henry's constant is 0.008 atm (kmol NH_3)$^{-1}$ m^{-3} of solution, calculate the individual film coefficients and the interphase compositions.

2.3 In a wetted wall tower, an air–H_2S mixture is flowing up, while a thin film of water is flowing down. H_2S is being absorbed from air to the water at a total pressure of 1.5 atm and 303 K. A value of 9.567×10^{-4} m s^{-1} has been predicted for the gas phase mass transfer coefficient k_c. At a given point, the mole fraction of H_2S in the liquid at the liquid–gas interface is 2.0×10^{-5} and partial pressure of H_2S in the gas is 0.05 atm. Using the Henry's law equilibrium relation $p_A = 609x_A$, calculate the rate of absorption of H_2S.

2.4 In the absorption of ammonia from an ammonia–air mixture by water in a certain apparatus at 2 atm and 303 K, the average value of k_y was found to be 2 kmol h^{-1}m^{-2} atm^{-1} and that of k_x as 0.33 kmol h^{-1} m^{-2} (kmol m^{-3})$^{-1}$. For dilute solutions of ammonia in water at 303 K, the equilibrium partial pressure of ammonia is given by $p = 645x$, where p is the partial pressure of ammonia in mm Hg and x is the mole fraction of ammonia in the liquid. Compute the overall mass transfer coefficient expressed in kmol h^{-1} m^{-2} atm^{-1} and the relative size of the resistances of gas and liquid phases.

2.5 In an experimental study of absorption of ammonia by water in a wetted wall column, the overall gas phase mass transfer coefficient was estimated to be 2.72×10^{-4} kmol m^{-2} s^{-1} atm^{-1}. At one point in the column, the gas contained 10 mol% ammonia and the liquid phase concentration was 6.42×10^{-2} kmol NH_3 m^{-3} of the solution. The temperature was 293 K and the total pressure was 1 atm. 80% of the total resistance to mass transfer was found to be in the gas phase. If Henry's law constant at 293 K is 9.35×10^{-3} atm m^3 kmol^{-1}, calculate the individual film coefficient, interphase composition and molar flux.

3

Gas Absorption

The removal of a soluble vapour from its mixture with an inert gas using a liquid is termed as gas absorption. Later, the solute is recovered from the liquid by distillation and the residual absorbing liquid is reused. This chapter deals with the basics of gas absorption and the methods available for designing gas absorbers.

The selective removal of one of the components of a mixture of gases by contact with a suitable liquid solvent is known as *absorption*. The operation is also known as *scrubbing*. A major application of absorption technology involves the removal of carbon dioxide [1] and hydrogen sulphide from natural gas or synthesis gas by absorption in aqueous solutions of monoethanolamine, diethanolamine, triethanolamine or alkaline salts [2]. Another example is the washing of ammonia from a mixture of ammonia and air by means of liquid water.

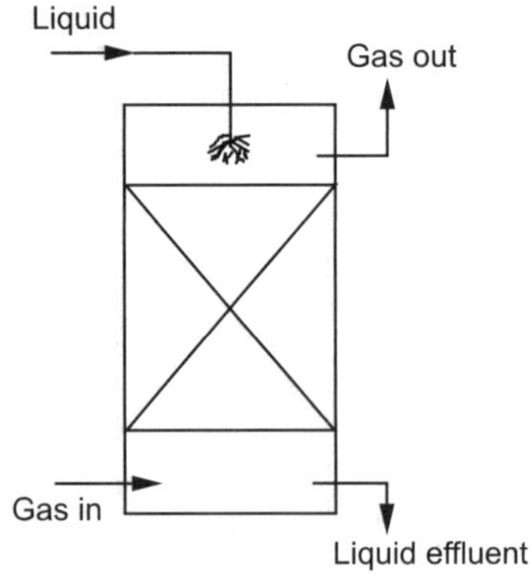

Fig. 3.1 Schematic representation of a gas absorption operation

Absorption processes can be divided into two groups. They are

1. Processes which are solely physical, and

2. Processes which are accompanied by a chemical reaction.

$$CO_2 + Na_2CO_3 + H_2O \rightarrow 2NaHCO_3 \tag{3.1}$$

$$SO_3 + H_2O \rightarrow H_2SO_4 \tag{3.2}$$

In absorption, the feed is a gaseous mixture and is introduced at the bottom of a packed tower which often acts as an absorption column. The liquid solvent is fed from the top. As it trickles down the column, the solvent selectively absorbs one of the components of the gaseous mixture and leaves with it through the bottom of the column. The unabsorbed components of the gaseous mixture leave the column from the top (Fig. 3.1).

In absorption, only the component absorbed by the liquid diffuses through the gas phase and into the liquid phase while all the other components remain stationary. For the diffusion in the gas phase, the following equations are applicable.

$$N_A^I = \frac{D_g \times P \times (P_{A2} - P_{A1})}{z_g \times RT \times P_{Blm}} \tag{3.3}$$

$$= k_g(P_{A2} - P_{A1}) \tag{3.4}$$

$$k_g = \frac{D_g \times P}{z_g \times RT \times P_{Blm}} \tag{3.5}$$

$$k_g \times P = k_y \tag{3.6}$$

Similarly, for diffusion in the liquid phase, the following equations can be used.

$$N_A^I = \frac{D_\ell \times \overline{C_T} \times (C_{A2} - C_{A1})}{z_l \times C_{Blm}} \tag{3.7}$$

$$= k_l(C_{A2} - C_{A1}) \tag{3.7}$$

$$k_l = \frac{D_\ell \times \overline{C_T}}{z_l \times C_{Blm}} \tag{3.8}$$

The solubility of gases in liquids is governed by Henry's law. It states that the partial pressure of a component in the gas phase over a solution is directly proportional to its mole fraction in the liquid phase.

$$P_A \propto x_A \tag{3.9}$$

$$P_A = mx_A \tag{3.10}$$

where m is the Henry's law constant.

All dilute solutions obey Henry's law and when the solution obeys Henry's law, m is the average slope of the equilibrium curve.

FACTORS INFLUENCING THE TRANSFER COEFFICIENT

The shape of the equilibrium curve and the film as well as the overall coefficients depend to a large extent on the solubility of the gas. For a very soluble gas, the equilibrium curve lies very close to the concentration in the liquid phase axis and its slope is very low. $K_y \sim k_y$ and the mass transfer is controlled by the gas phase.

For an almost insoluble gas, the equilibrium curve rises very steeply and the slope of the equilibrium curve is very large. $K_x \sim k_x$ and the mass transfer is controlled by the liquid phase.

For a moderately soluble gas, both films offer appreciable resistance. Mass transfer is controlled by the resistances in both phases.

PACKED TOWERS

A packed tower is an essential equipment used in gas absorption (Fig. 3.2). It consists of a cylindrical column. The column has a gas inlet and gas distribution space at the bottom, a liquid inlet and a liquid distributor at the top, liquid and gas outlets at the bottom and top respectively and a supported mass of solid shapes. The solid shapes are called tower packing. The liquid fed to the tower may be a pure solvent or a dilute solution of the solute in the solvent known as weak liquor. It is distributed over the top of the packing by the liquid distributor. Under ideal conditions, the liquid should flow down, wetting the packing with a thin film of liquid of uniform thickness. The gaseous mixture containing the soluble vapour and the inert gas (known as rich gas) enters the gas distribution space below the packing and flows upwards through the interstices in the packing, counter current to the flow of the liquid. The packing increases the retention time of the gas mixture inside the tower due to reduced cross section for gas flow, provides a large area of contact between the gas and the liquid and thereby encourages intimate contact between the phases. The solute in the rich gas is absorbed by the liquid entering the tower and dilute or lean gas leaves the top of the tower. The liquid gets enriched in solute as it flows down the tower and the concentrated liquid (also called strong liquor) leaves the bottom of the tower. Packed columns have been studied extensively [3, 4].

Principal requirements to be met by the tower packing

1. Should be chemically inert to the fluids in the tower.
2. Should provide large interfacial surface between the liquid and the gas.
3. Should be mechanically strong but light weight.
4. Must have adequate passages for both the streams, so that the pressure drop for the gas is low.
5. Should not lead to excessive liquid hold up or pressure drop.
6. Must induce good contact between the liquid and the gas.
7. The cost must be reasonable.

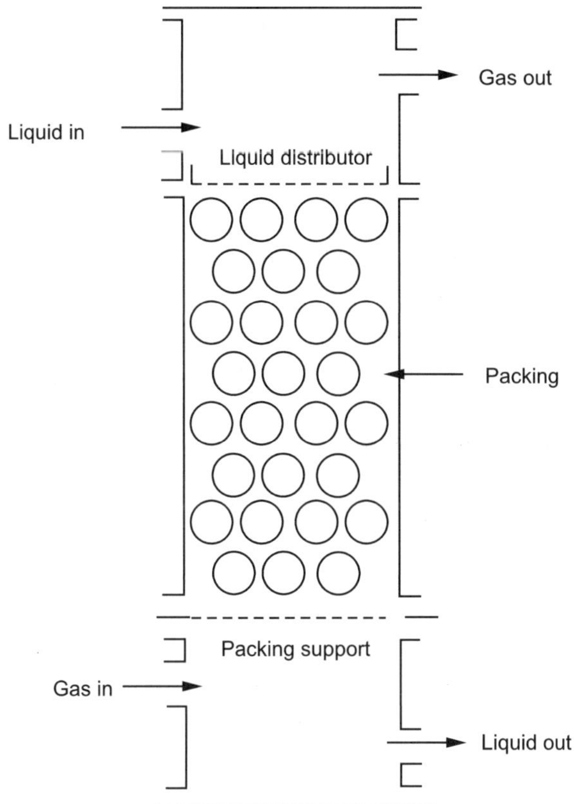

Fig. 3.2 Gas absorber

Most of the tower packing is made of clay, porcelain, plastics or thin walled metal rings. Large passages for the fluids is obtained by making the units irregular or hollow so that they interlock into open structures with 60%–90% porosity.

The packing can be of two different types.

1. Dumped or random packing: They are dumped at random. Their dimensions are in the range of 6–75 mm.
2. Stacked regular packing: They are stacked by hand. Their dimensions are in the range of 50–200 mm.

CHARACTERISTICS OF SOLVENT USED FOR ABSORPTION

1. **Gas solubility**: The solubility of the gas should be high so that the rate of absorption will be high and the solvent requirement will be low. If the solvent and the solute

to be absorbed are of the same chemical nature, the solubility will be good. For example, hydrocarbon oils are excellent solvents for removing benzene vapours from coke oven gas. Chemical reaction of the solvent with the solute results in very high gas solubility. Absorption of carbon dioxide in aqueous sodium carbonate solution can be cited as an example. If the solvent has to be recovered for reuse, the reaction must be reversible. H_2S can be removed from gas mixtures using ethanolamine solutions since it is readily absorbed by ethanolamines at low temperatures and easily stripped at high temperatures. NaOH absorbs H_2S well but will not release it in the subsequent stripping operation.

2. **Volatility**: The solvent should have a low vapour pressure, since the gas leaving the absorption operation is saturated with vapours of the solvent, leading to substantial loss of solvent.
3. Chemically inert to the equipment.
4. Inexpensive.
5. Readily available.
6. Non-toxic.
7. Non-flammable.
8. Chemically stable.
9. Low freezing point.
10. Low viscosity to have good absorption rates, improved flooding characteristics, low pressure drop in absorption towers and good heat transfer characteristics.

DESIGN OF INDUSTRIAL ABSORBERS

If the composition of the gaseous feed, the feed rate and the percentage of absorption in the absorber are known, the rate and composition of the gaseous output from the absorption column can be calculated. If the liquid feed rate is also known, the rate and composition of the liquid effluent can also be computed. The number of theoretical stages or the height of the packed column required to accomplish the desired percentage of absorption can be determined as discussed in detail in Chapter 2.

ILLUSTRATIONS

3A It is required to absorb 95% acetone from a feed mixture containing 2 mol% of acetone and the rest air, using pure water. 800 kg h^{-1} of water is introduced at the top of the tower. The gas flow at the bottom of the tower is 450 kg h^{-1}. Find the composition of acetone in the liquid effluent flowing out of the tower.

Solution

Basis: 1 hour operation.

The composition of the gas is given in mol%. The gas flow rate is given in terms of mass. The gas flow rate has to be converted to number of moles to find its acetone content.

The gas fed to the tower contains 2 mol% acetone and 98 mol% air.

Average molecular weight of air is 29 and molecular weight of acetone is 58.

Average molecular weight of the gas fed to the tower $= 58 \times 0.02 + 29 \times 0.98 = 29.58$

Number of kmol of the gas is found by dividing the mass by average molecular weight.

Number of kmol of entering gas $= 450 \div 29.58 = 15.213$

Acetone in the entering gas $= \dfrac{15.213 \times 2}{100} = 0.304$ kmol

$= 0.304 \times 58 = 17.632$ kg

95% of acetone is removed by absorption in water.

Acetone in water $= 17.632 \times \dfrac{95}{100} = 16.75$ kg

Water in the effluent from the absorber $=$ 800 kg

Weight of liquid effluent leaving the absorber $=$ 816.75 kg

Wt% of acetone in the liquid effluent flowing out $= \dfrac{16.75 \times 100}{816.75} = 2.051\%$

3B An air–ammonia mixture containing 5 mol% ammonia enters a packed tower at the rate of 500 kmol h^{-1}. It is necessary to recover 90% of ammonia using 700 kmol h^{-1} pure water. Compute the composition of ammonia in the liquid effluent and the gas effluent from the absorption tower.

Solution

Basis: 1 hour operation.

Gas entering the absorber = 500 kmol

The entering gas is an air–ammonia mixture. It contains 5 mol% ammonia.

Ammonia in the gas entering the absorber $= \dfrac{500 \times 5}{100} = 25$ kmol

Air in the gas entering the absorber $=$ 475 kmol

90% ammonia is absorbed by water.

Ammonia absorbed by water $= \dfrac{25 \times 90}{100} = 22.5$ kmol

Ammonia in the outgoing air = ammonia entering – ammonia absorbed

= $25 - 22.5 = 2.5$ kmol

Water absorbs only ammonia. The amount of air in the outgoing gas is the same as the entering gas.

Number of kmols of outgoing gas = air in entering gas + unabsorbed ammonia

= $475 + 2.5 = 477.5$

Mol% of ammonia in the gaseous effluent from the tower = $\dfrac{2.5 \times 100}{477.5} = 0.524\%$

The valid assumption for expressing the composition of the gaseous effluent is mol%.

Water fed to the tower = 700 kmol = $700 \times 18 = 12\,600$ kg

Ammonia absorbed by water = 22.5 kmol = $22.5 \times 17 = 382.5$ kg

Molecular weights of water and ammonia are 18 and 17 respectively.

Weight of the liquid effluent = 12 982.5 kg

Wt% of ammonia in the liquid effluent from the tower = $\dfrac{382.5 \times 100}{12\,982.5} = 2.946\%$

The valid assumption for expressing the composition of the liquid effluent is wt%.

3C Benzene–air mixture is to be scrubbed in a counter current absorption tower using non-volatile hydrocarbon oil as a solvent. The inlet gas contains 10% benzene and the flow rate of the entering gas is 1 500 $m^3\ h^{-1}$. 80% of benzene in the entering gas is proposed to be recovered. The average molecular weight of the oil is 200. Find the required oil flow rate in kg h^{-1} and the composition of the outgoing gases. The mole fraction of benzene in the liquid outlet from the tower has to be 0.3.

Solution

Basis: 1 hour operation.

The gas input to the tower is on a volume basis. It is assumed that the composition of the gaseous mixture is expressed in mol%. The gas composition is in mol%. The gas feed rate has to be converted to molar basis using the relation,

$$\text{Number of kmols of entering gas } (n) = \frac{PV}{RT} = \frac{1\,500 \times 1}{0.082\,05 \times 303} = 60.34$$

The entering gas contains 10 mol% benzene.

$$\text{Benzene in entering gas} = \frac{60.34 \times 10}{100} = 6.034 \text{ kmol}$$

80% of benzene in the entering gas is recovered by absorption in hydrocarbon oil.

$$\text{Benzene absorbed in hydrocarbon oil} = \frac{6.034 \times 80}{100} = 4.827 \text{ kmol}$$

Mole fraction of benzene in the liquid outlet from the tower has to be 0.3.

Therefore, the mole fraction of hydrocarbon oil in the liquid outlet from the tower is 0.7.

$$\text{Hydrocarbon oil in the liquid output} = \frac{4.827 \times 0.7}{0.3} = 11.263 \text{ kmol}$$

Average molecular weight of oil is 200.

Oil rate to the tower = $11.263 \times 200 = 2\,252.6$ kg h^{-1}

Benzene free gas entering the tower = number of kmol of entering gas – number of kmol of benzene in the entering gases

= $60.340 - 6.034 = 54.306$ kmol

Benzene in the outgoing gas = benzene in the input – benzene absorbed

= $6.034 - 4.827 = 1.207$ kmol

Number of kmols of outgoing gases = benzene free gas in the gas input + unabsorbed benzene

= $54.306 + 1.207 = 55.513$ kmol

Composition of benzene in the outgoing gases = $\dfrac{1.207 \times 100}{55.513} = 2.174\%$ by mol

3D H_2S is to be removed from a gas by scrubbing with water at 298 K. The gas contains 2% H_2S and is to be scrubbed to a concentration of 0.1% H_2S. The water is H_2S free. Henry's law describes the solubility and $\frac{P_A}{x_A} = 0.545$ atm/mol fraction. For a counter current absorber, calculate the liquid to gas ratio for 1.2 times the minimum liquid rate and composition of exit liquid if the pressure is 1 atm.

Solution

Basis: 100 kmol of entering gases.

Molal flow rate of the entering gases (V_b)	=	100 kmol
Mole fraction of H_2S in the entering gases (y_b)	=	0.02
Amount of H_2S in the entering gases	=	2.0 kmol
Amount of inerts in the entering gases	=	98.0 kmol

H_2S in the entering gases is scrubbed by water.

Mole fraction of H_2S in the leaving gases (y_a) = 0.001

$$0.001 = \frac{H_2S}{H_2S + 98}$$

So H_2S in the leaving gases	=	0.0979 kmol
Molal flow rate of leaving gases (V_b)	=	Inert gases + unscrubbed H_2S
	=	$98 + 0.0979 = 98.0979$ kmol
Mole fraction of H_2S in the entering water (x_a)	=	0
Amount of H_2S in the liquid effluent	=	H_2S in entering gases – H_2S in leaving gases
	=	$2.0 - 0.0979 = 1.9021$ kmol

Equilibrium relation is given by $\dfrac{p_A}{x_A} = 0.545$ atm/mol fraction. It has to be converted to the usual mole fraction form.

$$\frac{p_A}{x_A} = \frac{y_A P}{x_A} = 0.545$$

As total pressure, $P = 1$ atm, $y_A = 0.545x_A$ and equilibrium relation is $y = 0.545x$.

Let the minimum water rate be L kmol h^{-1}.

At minimum water rate, the mole fraction of ammonia in the liquid effluent is x_b^*.

$$y_b = mx_b^*$$

That is, $0.02 = 0.545x_b^*$ and $x_b^* = 0.0367$

$$\frac{1.9021}{1.9021 + L} = 0.0367$$

Hence $L = 49.93$ kmol

Actual water rate is 1.20 times the minimum.

Water input rate (L_a)	=	$49.93 \times 1.20 = 59.92$ kmol
Liquid effluent rate (L_b)	=	$L_a +$ H_2S scrubbed
	=	$59.92 + 1.9021 = 61.82$ kmol
Mean gas rate $\overline{V}$	=	$\dfrac{V_a + V_b}{2} = 99.05$ kmol
Mean Liquid rate $\overline{L}$	=	$\dfrac{L_a + L_b}{2} = 60.87$ kmol
Molar ratio of $\dfrac{L}{V}$	=	$\dfrac{60.87}{99.05} = \dfrac{\overline{L}}{\overline{V}} = 0.6145$
Mole fraction of H_2S in the exit liquor (x_b)	=	$\dfrac{1.9021}{1.9021 + 59.92} = 0.030\,76$

3E 500 m^3 h^{-1} of a gas at 760 mm Hg and 308 K and containing 3% by volume of toluene is absorbed using wash oil as an absorbent to remove 95% of toluene. The wash oil enters the tower at 308 K, contains 0.5 mol% toluene and has an average molecular weight of 250. The oil rate used is 1.5 times the minimum. Wash oil is assumed to behave ideally. At 308 K, the vapour pressure of toluene is 110 mm Hg. Calculate the weight of wash oil used and the number of theoretical stages.

Solution

Basis: 1 hour operation.

The equilibrium relation is given in vapour pressure form. It has to be converted to the usual mole fraction form.

By Rauolt's law, we have $P_A = P_A^* x_A$ and by Dalton's law we have $P_A = P y_A$

Combining these, we get, $P y_A = P_A^* x_A$

$$y_A = \frac{P_A^*}{P} x_A \text{ or } y = \frac{P^*}{P} x$$

$$y = \frac{110}{760} x = 0.1447x$$

This is the equilibrium relation.

Volumetric flow rate of entering gases = 500 m^3

This has to be converted to molal flow rate using the relation,

$$n = \frac{PV}{RT} = \frac{500 \times 1}{0.082\,06 \times 308} = 19.783 \text{ kmol}$$

Molal flow rate of the entering gases	=	19.783 kmol
Mole fraction of toluene in the entering gases (y_b)	=	0.03
Amount of toluene in the entering gases	=	$19.783 \times 0.03 = 0.593$ kmol
Amount of inerts in the entering gases	=	$19.783 - 0.593 = 19.19$ kmol

95% of toluene in the entering gases is absorbed by wash oil.

Amount of toluene absorbed	=	$0.593 \times 0.95 = 0.564$ kmol
Amount of toluene in the leaving gases	=	$0.593 - 0.564 = 0.029$ kmol
Amount of gases leaving	=	inerts + unabsorbed acetone
	=	$19.19 + 0.029 = 19.219$ kmol

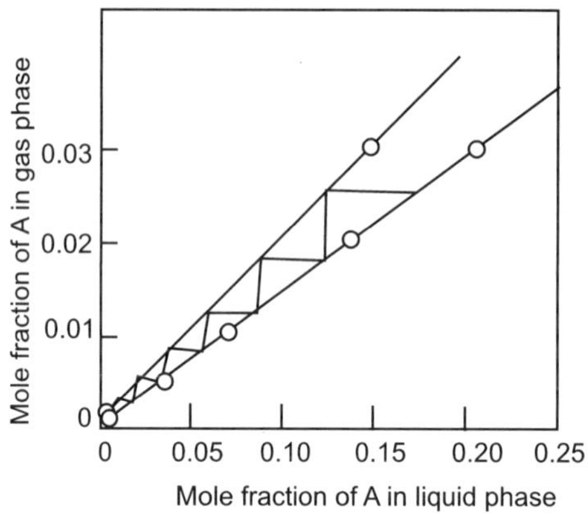

Fig. 3.3 Graphical solution for 3E

Mole fraction of toluene in the leaving gases (y_a)	=	$0.029 \div 19.219 = 0.0015$
Mole fraction of toluene in the entering wash oil (x_a)	=	0.005
Amount of toluene in the liquid effluent	=	0.564 kmol

Let the minimum wash oil rate be L kmol h^{-1}.

At minimum wash oil rate, mole fraction of ammonia in the liquid effluent is x_b^*.

$$y_b = mx_b^*$$

That is, $0.03 = 0.1447x_b^*$ and $x_b^* = 0.207\,3$

$$\frac{0.005L + 0.564}{0.564 + L} = 0.207\,3$$

Hence $L = 2.21$ k mol

Actual wash oil rate is 1.5 times the minimum.

Actual wash oil rate $= 2.21 \times 1.50 = 3.315$ kmol $= 3.315 \times 250 = 828.75$ kg

Mole fraction of toluene in the liquid effluent (x_b)

$$= \frac{(0.005 \times 3.315) + 0.564}{3.315 + 0.564} = 0.149\,8$$

In this case, $y_b < 0.1$. So the operating line is drawn using the extreme ends (x_a, y_a) and (x_b, y_b). On the same graph sheet, the equilibrium curve is also drawn. The number of theoretical stages required is found by the McCabe–Thiele method as shown in Fig. 3.3. The number of theoretical units required for this operation = 6.5. That is, 7.0.

3F A mixture of air and acetone vapour containing 85% air by volume is stripped of 95% of its acetone content by counter current contact with a stream of water in a bubble plate column operating at 298 K and 1 atm. An overall plate efficiency of 30% can be assumed. If 1.25 times the minimum liquid rate is used, find the actual number of plates required.

Equilibrium data:

Mole % of acetone in liquid	3.33	7.20	11.70	17.10
Partial pressure of acetone in gas (mm Hg)	3.0	29.6	61.8	103

Solution

Basis: 100 kmol of entering gases.

The equilibrium relation given has to be converted to the usual mole fraction form. The composition of the liquid is given in mol%. Mol% divided by 100 gives the mole fraction of the solute in the liquid phase.

Let us take the first data, mol% of solute in the liquid	=	3.33
Mole fraction of solute in the liquid = 3.33 ÷ 100	=	0.033
Partial pressure of solute in the gas phase in equilibrium with the liquid	=	29 mm Hg

$$\text{Mole fraction of solute in the gas } (y) = \frac{\text{Partial pressure of acetone}}{\text{Total pressure}} = \frac{3}{760} = 0.004$$

Similarly the entire equilibrium data has to be converted.

The equilibrium data now becomes

x	0.033	0.072	0.117	0.171
y	0.004	0.039	0.081	0.136

Mole fraction of air in the entering gases (y_b)	=	0.85
Amount of air in the entering gases	=	$100 \times 0.85 = 85$ kmol
Amount of acetone in the entering gases	=	$100 - 85 = 15$ kmol

95% of acetone in the entering gases is absorbed in water.

Amount of acetone absorbed	=	$15 \times 0.95 = 14.25$ kmol
Amount of acetone in the liquid effluent	=	14.25 kmol
Amount of acetone in the leaving gases	=	$15 - 14.25 = 0.75$ kmol
Amount of gases leaving = inert air – unabsorbed acetone	=	$85 + 0.75 = 85.75$ kmol
Mole fraction of acetone in the leaving gases (y_a)	=	$0.75 \div 85.75 = 0.008\,7$

The entering water is acetone free. The mole fraction of acetone in the entering water (x_a) is 0.

Let the minimum water rate be L kmol h^{-1}.

At minimum water rate, mole fraction of ammonia in the liquid effluent is x_b^*.

$$y_b = mx_b^*$$

The value of x_b^* is found from the equilibrium curve corresponding to $y_b = 0.15$ and it is $x_b^* = 0.19$

$$\frac{14.25}{14.25 + L} = 0.19$$

Hence $L = 60.75$ k mol

The actual water rate is 1.25 times the minimum.

Actual water rate $= 60.75 \times 1.25 = 75.94$ kmol

Mole fraction of ammonia in the liquid effluent (x_b) $= \dfrac{14.25}{14.25 + 75.94} = 0.158$

As $y_b > 0.1$, the operating line has to be constructed using two intervening points, in addition to the terminal ones.

Let us consider a location in the column where 10 kmol of acetone is remaining in the gas. As the gas leaving the tower has 0.75 kmol acetone, acetone in the liquid phase at that location will be 10 – 0.75 = 9.25 kmol. Details of gas–liquid phase compositions at various locations are given in Fig. 3.4.

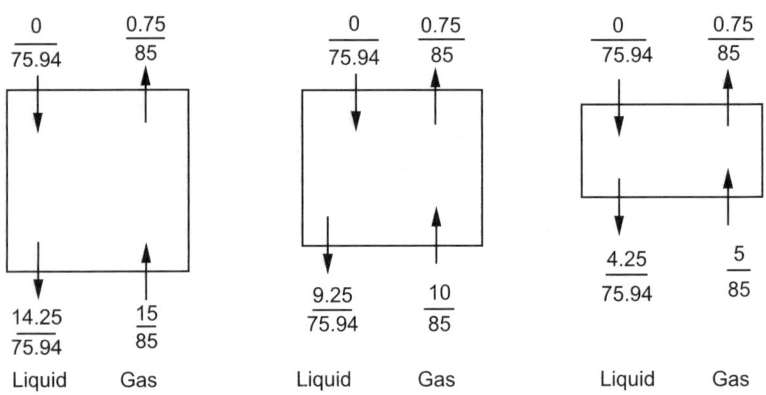

Fig. 3.4 Gas–liquid phase compositions at various locations

$$\text{Mole fraction of acetone in the gas phase } (y_1) = \frac{10}{10 + 85} = 0.105$$

$$\text{Mole fraction of acetone in the liquid phase } (x_1) = \frac{9.25}{9.25 + 75.94} = 0.109$$

Let us consider one more location in the column where 5 kmol of acetone is remaining in the gas. As the gas leaving the tower has 0.75 kmol acetone, acetone in the liquid phase at that location will be 5 – 0.75 = 4.25 kmol.

$$\text{Mole fraction of acetone in the gas phase} \quad (y_2) = \frac{5}{5+85} = 0.055$$

$$\text{Mole fraction of acetone in the liquid phase } (x_2) = \frac{4.25}{4.25 + 75.94} = 0.059$$

The operating line is drawn using the four points (x_a, y_a), (x_1, y_1), (x_2, y_2) and (x_b, y_b). On the same graph sheet, the equilibrium curve also is drawn. The number of theoretical stages required is found by the McCabe–Thiele method, as shown in Fig. 3.5.

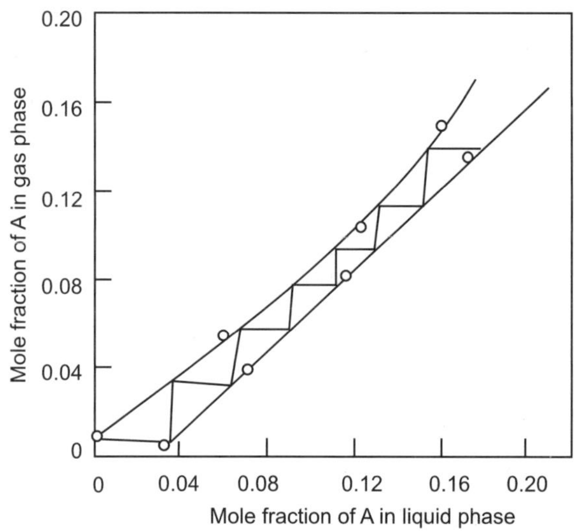

Fig. 3.5 Graphical solution for 3F

Number of theoretical units required for this operation $= 6.23$

The plate efficiency is only 30%.

So the actual number of plates required $= 6.23 \div 0.3 = 20.77$. That is, 21.0.

3G Compute the number of ideal stages for a plate column where acetone is absorbed from its mixture with air in a non-volatile oil. The entering gas contains 30 mol% acetone and the entering oil is acetone free. 97% of acetone has to be recovered. The strong liquor should not contain more than 10 mol% of acetone. The equilibrium relationship is given by $y = 2x$, where x and y refer to the mole fraction of acetone in the liquid and vapour phases respectively.

Solution

Basis: 100 kmol of entering gases.

Mole fraction of acetone in the entering gases (y_b)	=	0.3
Amount of acetone in the entering gases	=	$100 \times 0.3 = 30$ kmol
Amount of air in the entering gases	=	$100 - 30 = 70$ kmol

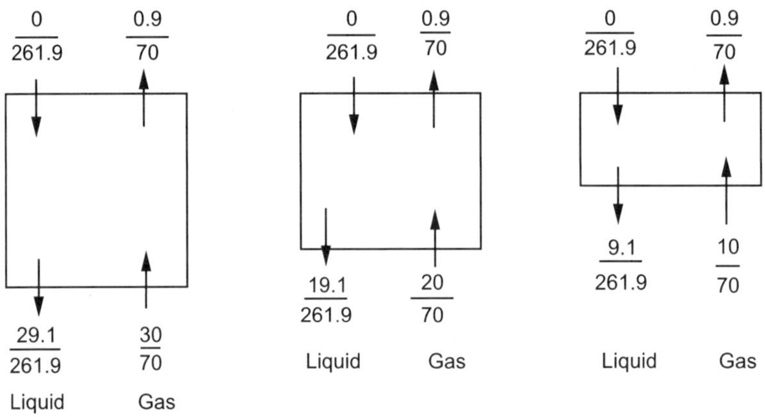

Fig. 3.6 Gas–liquid phase compositions at various locations

97% of acetone in the entering gases is absorbed.

Amount of acetone absorbed	=	$30 \times 0.97 = 29.1$ kmol
Amount of acetone in the leaving gases	=	$30 \times 0.03 = 0.9$ kmol
Amount of gases leaving = inert air – unabsorbed acetone	=	$70 + 0.9 = 70.9$ kmol
Mole fraction of acetone in the leaving gases	=	$0.9 \div 70.9 = 0.012\,7$
Amount of acetone in the liquid effluent	=	29.1 kmol
Mole fraction of acetone in the liquid effluent (x_b)	=	0.1
Oil in the liquid effluent	=	$\dfrac{29.1 \times 0.9}{0.1} = 261.9$ kmol

The entering oil is acetone free. The mole fraction of acetone in the entering oil (x_a) = 0. As $y_b > 0.1$, the operating line has to be constructed using two intervening points, in addition to the terminal ones. Details of gas–liquid phase compositions at various locations are given in Fig. 3.6. Let us consider a location in the column where 20 kmol of acetone is remaining in the gas. As the gas leaving the tower has 0.9 kmol acetone, acetone in the liquid phase at that location will be $20 - 0.9 = 19.1$ kmol.

$$\text{Mole fraction of acetone in the gas phase } (y_1) = \frac{20}{20 + 70} = 0.222$$

Mole fraction of acetone in the liquid phase (x_1) $= \dfrac{19.1}{261.9 + 19.1} = 0.068$

Let us consider one more location in the column where 10 kmol of acetone is remaining in the gas. As the gas leaving the tower has 0.9 kmol acetone, acetone in the liquid phase at that location will be $10 - 0.9 = 9.1$ kmol.

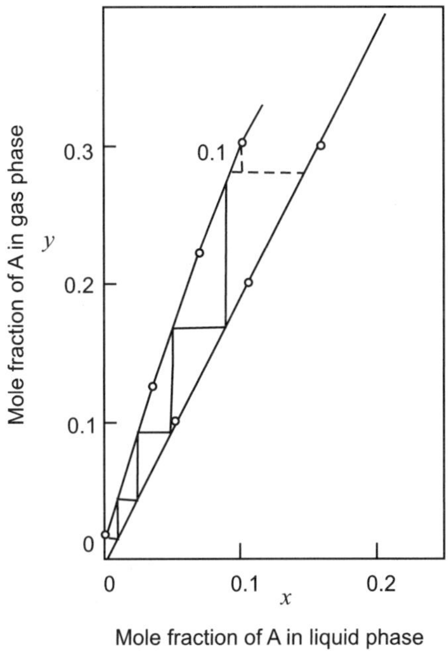

Fig. 3.7 Graphical construction for 3G

Mole fraction of acetone in the gas phase (y_2) $= \dfrac{10}{10 + 70} = 0.125$

Mole fraction of acetone in the liquid phase (x_2) $= \dfrac{9.1}{261.9 + 9.1} = 0.033\,6$

The operating line is drawn using the four points (x_a, y_a), (x_1, y_1), (x_2, y_2) and (x_b, y_b). On the same graph sheet, the equilibrium curve is also drawn as shown in Fig. 3.7. The number of theoretical stages required is found by the McCabe–Thiele method.

The number of theoretical units required for this operation = 4.18. That is, 5.0.

3H An acetone–air mixture containing 0.015 mole fraction of acetone has the mole fraction reduced to 1% of this value by counter current absorption with water in a packed tower. The gas flow rate is 1 kg m^{-2} s^{-1} of air and the water entering is 1.6 kg m^{-2} s^{-1}. For this system the equilibrium relationship is $y = 1.75x$. Determine N_{oy} and N_{ox}.

Solution

Basis: 1 second operation.

The concentration of acetone in the gas and liquid mixture is extremely low and the flow rate of the mixture can be taken as that of air in the case of the gaseous mixture and that of water in the case of the liquid mixture and the composition in terms of mole fraction can be taken to be that of the mole ratio.

Mole fraction of acetone in the entering gases (y_b) $= 0.015$

This is reduced to 1% of this value by absorption of acetone in water.

Mole fraction of acetone in the leaving gases (y_a)	=	$0.015 \div 100 = 0.000\ 15$
Mole fraction of acetone in the entering water (x_a)	=	0
Mass flow rate of gaseous mixture	=	1.0 kg m^{-2} s^{-1}
Molal flow rate of gaseous mixture	=	$\frac{1.0}{29} = 0.034\ 5$ kmol m^{-2} s^{-1}
Mass flow rate of liquid mixture	=	1.6 kg m^{-2} s^{-1}
Molal flow rate of liquid mixture	=	$\frac{1.6}{18} = 0.088\ 9$ kmol m^{-2} s^{-1}

Mole fraction of acetone in the liquid effluent (x_b), can be found by an acetone balance for the absorber. Acetone lost by the gaseous stream is gained by the liquid stream.

$$0.0345(0.015 - 0.000\ 15) = 0.088\ 9(x_b - 0) \text{ and hence } x_b = 0.005\ 76$$

$$y_b^* = 1.75x_b = 1.75 \times 0.005\ 76 = 0.010\ 1 \text{ and } y_a^* = 1.75x_a = 1.75 \times 0 = 0$$

$$N_{oy} = \frac{y_b - y_a}{\Delta y_{lm}}, \text{ where } \Delta y_{lm} = \frac{(y_b - y_b^*) - (y_a - y_a^*)}{\ln \dfrac{(y_b - y_b^*)}{(y_a - y_a^*)}}$$

Substituting the value of the parameters,

	N_{oy}	=	10.92
	$1.75x_a^*$	=	$y_a = 0.000\ 15$
Hence	x_a^*	=	$0.000\ 086$
	$1.75x_b^*$	=	$y_b = 0.015$
Hence	x_a^*	=	$0.008\ 6$

$$N_{ox} = \frac{x_b - x_a}{\Delta x_{lm}}, \quad \text{where} \quad \Delta x_{lm} = \frac{(x_b - x_b^*) - (x_a - x_a^*)}{\ln \dfrac{(x_b - x_b^*)}{(x_a - x_a^*)}}$$

Substituting the value of the parameters, $N_{ox} = 7.31$.

3I An air–ammonia mixture containing 5 mol% ammonia enters a packed tower at the rate of 500 kmol h^{-1} m^{-2}. It is necessary to recover 95% of ammonia using a liquid flow rate of 1.5 times the minimum. Estimate the height of the packing needed for this operation. Height of a transfer unit is 0.25 m. Equilibrium relation is given by $y = 1.08x$ where x and y refer to the mole fractions of ammonia in the liquor and vapour phases respectively. Fresh solvent enters the tower.

Solution

Basis: 1 hour operation.

Molal flow rate of the gas at the inlet	=	500 kmol
Mole fraction of ammonia at the gas inlet (y_b)	=	0.05
Ammonia at the gas inlet	=	$500 \times 0.05 = 25$ kmol
Air at the gas inlet	=	$500 - 25 = 475$ kmol
95% of ammonia is absorbed in water.		
Ammonia absorbed in water	=	$25 \times 0.95 = 23.75$ kmol
Ammonia in the gas output	=	$25 - 23.75 = 1.25$ kmol
Mole fraction of ammonia in the gas outlet (y_a)	=	$\dfrac{1.25}{475 + 1.25} = 0.002\,6$

Water used for absorption is pure.

Mole fraction of ammonia in water entering the absorption tower $(x_a) = 0$

Let the minimum water rate be L kmol h^{-1}.

At minimum water rate, mole fraction of ammonia in the liquid effluent is x_b^*.

$$y_b = mx_b^*$$

That is, $0.05 = 1.08x_b^*$ and $x_b^* = 0.046\,3$

$$\frac{23.75}{23.75 + L} = 0.0463$$

Hence $L = 466.33$ kmol

Actual water rate is 1.5 times the minimum.

Actual water rate $= 466.33 \times 1.5 = 699.5$ kmol

Mole fraction of ammonia in the liquid effluent $(x_b) = \dfrac{23.75}{23.75 + 699.5} = 0.033$

$y_b^* = 1.08x_b = 1.08 \times 0.033 = 0.0356$ and $y_a^* = 1.08x_a = 1.08 \times 0 = 0$

$$N_{oy} = \frac{y_b - y_a}{\Delta y_{lm}} \quad \text{where } \Delta y_{lm} = \frac{(y_b - y_b^*) - (y_a - y_a^*)}{\ln \dfrac{(y_b - y_b^*)}{(y_a - y_a^*)}}$$

Substituting the value of the parameters,

$$N_{oy} = 6.89$$

$$H_{oy} = 0.25 \text{ m}$$

$$Z_T = N_{oy} \times H_{oy} = 6.89 \times 0.25 = 1.72 \text{ m}$$

3J Gas from a petroleum distillation column has its concentration of H_2S reduced from 0.03 kmol H_2S per kmol of inert hydrocarbon gas to 1% of this value by scrubbing with triethanolamine–water mixture in a counter current tower of height 7.79 m operating at 300 K and 1 atm pressure. The equilibrium relation is given by $y = 2x$, where y = kmol H_2S per kmol inert gas and x = kmol H_2S per kmol solvent. Pure solvent enters the tower and leaves it containing 0.013 kmol H_2S per kmol of solvent. If the flow rate of the gas is 0.015 kmol m^{-2} s^{-1} and gas phase resistance controls the process, calculate the overall gas absorption coefficient $K_g a$.

Solution

Basis: 1 second operation.

The concentration of H_2S in the gas and liquid mixture is extremely low and the flow rate of the mixture can be taken as that of air in the case of the gaseous mixture and that of water in the case of the liquid mixture. The composition in terms of mole fraction can be taken to be that of the mole ratio.

Mole ratio of H_2S to inert gas in the entering gases (y_b) = 0.03

This is reduced to 1% of the value by absorption of H_2S in liquid.

Mole ratio of H_2S to inert gas in the leaving gases (y_a)	=	$0.03 \div 100 = 0.000\ 3$
Mole ratio of H_2S to the absorbent in the entering liquid (x_a)	=	0
Mole ratio of H_2S to the absorbent in the leaving liquid (x_b)	=	0.013

$$y_b^* = 2x_b = 2 \times 0.013 = 0.026 \text{ and } y_a^* = 2x_a = 2 \times 0 = 0$$

$$N_{oy} = \frac{y_b - y_a}{\Delta y_{lm}} \quad \text{where } \Delta y_{lm} = \frac{(y_b - y_b^*) - (y_a - y_a^*)}{\ln \dfrac{(y_b - y_b^*)}{(y_a - y_a^*)}}$$

Substituting the value of the parameters,

$$N_{oy} = 20.79$$

$$Z_T = N_{oy} \times H_{oy} = 20.79 \times H_{oy} = 7.79 \text{ m and so } H_{oy} = 0.375$$

$$H_{oy} = 0.375$$

Molal flow rate of the gas (V/S) $= 0.015 \text{ kmol m}^{-2} \text{ s}^{-1}$

$$0.375 = \frac{V/S}{K_y a} = \frac{0.015}{K_y a}$$

$$K_{ya} = 0.04 \text{ kmol m}^{-3} \text{ s}^{-1} \text{ (mole fraction)}^{-1}$$

$$K_g a = K_y a \times P = 0.04 \text{ kmol m}^{-3} \text{ s}^{-1} \text{ atm}^{-1} = 144 \text{ kmol m}^{-3} \text{ h}^{-1} \text{ atm}^{-1}$$

3K A mixture containing 10% solute by volume and the rest inerts is fed to a packed tower in which 90% of the solute is absorbed. Solute-free water is used for absorption and it contains 5 mol% solute when it leaves the tower. The equilibrium relation is given by $y = 0.05x$ where x and y denote the mole fractions of the solute in the liquid phase and the gas phase respectively. If $H_x = 0.5$ m and $H_y = 0.4$ m, what is the height of the packed section?

Solution

Basis: 100 kmol entering gases (V_b).

Mole fraction of solute at the gas inlet (y_b)	=	0.1
Solute at the gas inlet	=	$100 \times 0.1 = 10$ kmol
Air at the gas inlet	=	$100 - 10 = 90$ kmol

90% of the solute is absorbed in water.

Solute absorbed in water	=	$10 \times 0.90 = 9$ kmol
Solute in the gas output	=	$10 - 9 = 1$ kmol
Volume of the leaving gases (V_a)	=	inerts + unabsorbed solute
	=	$90 + 1 = 91$ kmol
Mole fraction of solute in the gas outlet (y_a)	=	$1 \div 91 = 0.011$

Water used for absorption is pure.

Mole fraction of solute in water entering the absorption tower $(x_a) = 0$

Solute in the liquid effluent	=	9 kmol
Mole fraction of solute in the liquid effluent (x_b)	=	0.05
Flow rate of liquid effluent (L_b)	=	$9 \div 0.05 = 180$ kmol
Flow rate of absorbent (L_a) = Effluent – solute in it	=	$180 - 9 = 171$ kmol

$$y_b^* = 0.05x_b = 0.05 \times 0.05 = 0.0025 \text{ and } y_a^* = 0.05x_a = 0.05 \times 0 = 0$$

$$N_{oy} = \frac{y_b - y_a}{\Delta y_{lm}} \quad \text{where} \quad \Delta y_{lm} = \frac{(y_b - y_b^*) - (y_a - y_a^*)}{\ln \dfrac{(y_b - y_b^*)}{(y_a - y_a^*)}}$$

Substituting the value of the parameters,

$$N_{oy} = 1.99$$

The relationship between the overall mass transfer coefficient and the film transfer coefficients is given by

$$\frac{1}{K_y} = \frac{1}{k_y} + \frac{m}{k_x}$$

Dividing the denominator throughout by a,

$$\frac{1}{K_y a} = \frac{1}{k_y a} + \frac{m}{k_x a}$$

Multiplying the numerator through out by (V/S)

$$\frac{V/S}{K_y a} = \frac{V/S}{k_y a} + \frac{m(V/S)}{k_x a}$$

$$\frac{V/S}{K_y a} = \frac{V/S}{k_y a} + \frac{m(V/S)(L/S)}{k_x a(L/S)}$$

$$H_{oy} = H_y + \frac{mV}{L} H_x$$

This is the relationship between H_{oy}, H_y and H_x.

$$V = \frac{V_a + V_b}{2} = \frac{100 + 91}{2} = 95.5 \text{ and } L = \frac{L_a + L_b}{2} = \frac{171 + 180}{2} = 175.5$$

Substituting the value of the parameters,

$$H_{oy} = 0.4 + \frac{0.5 \times 0.05}{175.5} \times 95.5 = 0.4 + 0.0136 = 0.4136 \text{ m}$$

$$Z = N_{oy} \times H_{oy} = 1.99 \times 0.4136 = 0.823 \text{ m}$$

3L 500 0 kg h^{-1} of SO_2–air mixture containing 5% by volume of SO_2 is to be scrubbed with 200 000 kg h^{-1} of H_2O in a packed tower. The SO_2 concentration in the exit air is 0.15%. The tower operates at 1 atm. The equilibrium relation is given by $y = 30x$, where y is the mole ratio of SO_2 to air in the gas phase and x is the mole ratio of SO_2 to water in the liquid phase. If the packed height of the tower is 420 cm, estimate the height of the transfer unit.

Solution

Basis: 1 hour operation.

The composition of the gas is given in mol%. The gas flow rate is given in terms of mass. The gas flow rate has to be converted to the molar basis to find its SO_2 content. The gas fed to the tower contains 5 mol% SO_2 and 95 mol% air. The average the molecular weight of air is 29 and the molecular weight of SO_2 is 64.

Average molecular weight of the gas fed to the tower $= 64 \times 0.05 + 29 \times 0.95 = 30.75$

Number of kmol of the gas is found by dividing the mass by average molecular weight.

Number of kmol of entering gas $= 500\,0 \div 30.75 = 162.6$

SO_2 in the entering gas $= \dfrac{162.6 \times 5}{100} = 8.13$ kmol

Air at the gas inlet $= 162.6 - 8.13 = 154.47$ kmol

As equilibrium data is based on the mole ratios, the problem should be solved based on the mole ratios.

Mole ratio of SO_2 to air at the gas inlet $(y_b) = \dfrac{8.13}{154.47} = 0.052\,6$

The exit concentration of SO_2 is reduced to 0.15%. That is, in the exit gas, air makes up 99.85% and SO_2 makes up 0.15%.

SO_2 in the exit air $= \dfrac{162.6 \times 0.15}{99.85} = 0.244\,2$ kmol

Mole ratio of SO_2 to air at the gas outlet $(y_a) = \dfrac{0.244\,2}{154.47} = 0.001\,58$

Water used for absorption is pure.

Mole ratio of SO_2 to water at the liquid inlet $(x_a) = 0$

Water input to the absorber $= \dfrac{200\,000}{18} = 11\,111.11$ kmol

Mole ratio of SO_2 to water at the liquid outlet $(x_b) = \dfrac{7.9}{11\,111.11} = 0.000\,71$

$$y_b^* = 30x_b = 30 \times 0.000\,71 = 0.021\,3 \text{ and } y_a^* = 30x_a = 30 \times 0 = 0$$

$$N_{oy} = \frac{y_b - y_a}{\Delta y_{lm}} \quad \text{where} \quad \Delta y_{lm} = \frac{(y_b - y_b^*) - (y_a - y_a^*)}{\ln \dfrac{(y_b - y_b^*)}{(y_a - y_a^*)}}$$

Substituting the value of the parameters,

$$N_{oy} = 5.13 \approx 6$$

$$Z_T = N_{oy} \times H_{oy}$$

That is, 4.2 = 6 × H_{oy} and $H_{oy} = 0.7$ m.

3M A gas stream containing a valuable hydrocarbon (molecular weight = 44) and air is to be scrubbed with a non-volatile oil (molecular weight = 300) in a tower packed with 2.54 cm Raschig rings. The entering gas contains 10 mol% hydrocarbon and 95% of this has to be removed. The gas stream enters the bottom of the column at the rate of 227 0 kg h^{-1} and the hydrocarbon-free oil used is 1.5 times the minimum. Determine the number of gas phase mass transfer units.

Equilibrium data:

Mole fraction of hydrocarbon in liquid phase	0	0.10	0.20	0.30	0.400	0.458
Mole fraction of hydrocarbon in gas phase	0	0.01	0.02	0.06	0.118	0.200

Solution

The composition of the gas is given in mol%. The gas flow rate is given in terms of mass. The gas flow rate has to be converted to the molar basis to calculate its hydrocarbon content. The gas fed to the tower contains 10 mol% hydrocarbon and 90 mol% air. The average molecular weight of air is 29 and molecular weight of the hydrocarbon is 44.

Average molecular weight of the gas fed to the tower $= 44 \times 0.1 + 29 \times 0.9 = 30.5$

Number of kmol of the gas is found by dividing the mass by average molecular weight.

Number of kmol of entering gas $= 227\,0 \div 30.5 = 74.43$

Hydrocarbon in the entering gas $= 74.43 \times 0.1 = 7.443$ kmol

Air at the gas inlet $= 74.43 - 7.443 = 66.987$ kmol

Mole fraction of hydrocarbon at the gas inlet (y_b) $= 0.10$

95% of the hydrocarbon is absorbed in non-volatile oil.

Solute absorbed in oil $= 7.443 \times 0.95 = 7.071$ kmol

Solute in the gas output $= 7.443 - 7.071 = 0.372$ kmol

Volume of the leaving gases (V_a) = inerts + unabsorbed solute

$= 66.987 + 0.372 = 67.359$ kmol

Mole fraction of hydrocarbon at the gas outlet (y_a) $= \dfrac{0.372}{67.359} = 0.005\,5$

Volatile oil used for absorption is pure.

Mole fraction of hydrocarbon at the liquid inlet $(x_a) = 0$

Let the minimum water rate be L kmol h^{-1}.

At minimum oil rate, mole fraction of hydrocarbon in the liquid effluent is x_b^*.

From the equilibrium curve, as shown in Fig. 3.7, $x_b^* = 0.37$, corresponding to $y_b = 0.1$.

$$\frac{7.071}{7.071 + L} = 0.37$$

Hence $L = 12.04$ kmol

Actual oil rate is 1.5 times the minimum.

Actual oil rate $= 12.04 \times 1.5 = 18.06$ kmol

Mole fraction of hydrocarbon in the liquid effluent $(x_b) = \dfrac{7.071}{7.071 + 18.06} = 0.281$

From the equilibrium curve, $y_b^* = 0.05$, corresponding to $x_b = 0.281$ and $y_a^* = 0$, corresponding to $x_a = 0$.

$$N_{oy} = \frac{y_b - y_a}{\Delta y_{lm}} \quad \text{where} \quad \Delta y_{lm} = \frac{(y_b - y_b^*) - (y_a - y_a^*)}{\ln \dfrac{(y_b - y_b^*)}{(y_a - y_a^*)}}$$

Substituting the value of the parameters, $N_{oy} = 4.687 \approx 5$

3N Benzene is to be absorbed from a benzene vapour–air mixture containing 5 mol of benzene vapour per 100 moles of air. For every 105 mol of gas mixture, 10 mol of absorption oil is available. The operation takes place at 300 K and 100 kPa pressure. Calculate the percentage of benzene vapour absorbed if the gas mixture and oil are brought into contact with each other and allowed to stand for a long time. Assume that oil–benzene solutions obey Raoult's law and the vapour pressure of benzene at 300 K is 13.33 kPa.

Solution

The equilibrium relation is given in vapour pressure form. It has to be converted to the usual mole fraction form.

By Rauolt's law, we have $P_A = P_A^* x_A$ and by Dalton's law we have $P_A = P y_A$.

Combining these, we get, $P y_A = P_A^* x_A$

$$y_A = \frac{P_A^*}{P} x_A \quad \text{or} \quad y = \frac{P^*}{P} x$$

$$y = \frac{13.33}{100} x = 0.133\,3x$$

This is the equilibrium relation.

Mole fraction of benzene vapour in the entering gases $(y_b) = \dfrac{5}{105} = 0.047\,62$

It is given that the gas mixture and oil are brought into contact with each other and allowed to stand for a long time. This means that the process attains equilibrium. When equilibrium is attained, the final concentration of benzene in the oil $x_b = x_b^*$.

$$y_b = mx_b^*$$

That is, $0.047\ 62 = 0.133\ 3x_b^*$ and $x_b^* = 0.357$

$$x_b^* = \frac{\text{Benzene}}{\text{Benzene} + \text{Oil}} = \frac{\text{Benzene}}{\text{Benzene} + 10} = 0.357$$

Solving, benzene = 5.555 mol, while benzene at the inlet itself is only 5 mol. So all the benzene vapour in the incoming gas will be absorbed.

TWO PHASE FLOW THROUGH PACKED TOWER

Achieving good contact between the liquid and gas is difficult in large towers. Ideally, once the liquid is distributed over the top of the packing, it flows in thin films over the packing surface all the way down the tower. In practice, the film tends to grow thicker in some places and thinner in others. The liquid collects into small rivulets and flows along localised paths through the packing. With most of the packing, this is the usual phenomenon at low liquid rates. This effect is known as *channeling*. This is the chief reason for the poor performance of a packed tower. Channeling is

1. More severe in towers packed with stacked packing.
2. Less severe in towers packed with dumped packing of crushed solid.
3. Least severe in dumped packing of regular units.

Channeling can be minimised by having the diameter of the tower at least equal to 8 times the packing diameter. In tall towers filled with large packing, the effect of channeling may be reduced by providing redistributors for the liquid at 3–5 metre intervals of the packed section.

Pressure Drop Through the Packing

Power required to force the gas through the packing frequently represents the principal operating cost of the packed tower. The power cost is proportional to the product of the gas rate and the pressure drop through the tower, ΔP. So, data on ΔP at various gas rates are important for design purposes. The principal factors affecting the pressure drop in packed towers are:

1. Size and shape of the packing.
2. Ratio of tower diameter to packing diameter.
3. ΔP in the packing supports.

4. Gas and liquid flow rates.
5. Physical properties of the gas and liquid.

Most of the ΔP in the turbulent range is due to contraction and expansion losses and changes in direction, as the gas flows through the irregular orifices formed by the packing. It has been estimated that only 10% of the drop is due to skin friction. Contraction losses, expansion losses and skin friction are all approximately proportional to the square of the gas rate.

The effect of the gas flow rate on the behaviour of the packed column can be best described by a plot of pressure drop per unit depth of packing ($\frac{\Delta P}{Z}$) versus the mass velocity of gas (G_y) as given in Fig. 3.8. For dry packing, ΔP increases as the 1.8th power of the mass velocity of gas (G_y). The plot is a straight line, indicating that the flow through the packing is turbulent. With counter current flow of liquid, approximately the same variation of ΔP with G_y is observed till a critical G_y is reached, at which ΔP begins to increase rapidly and the plot of $\frac{\Delta P}{Z}$ versus G_y passes into a curve.

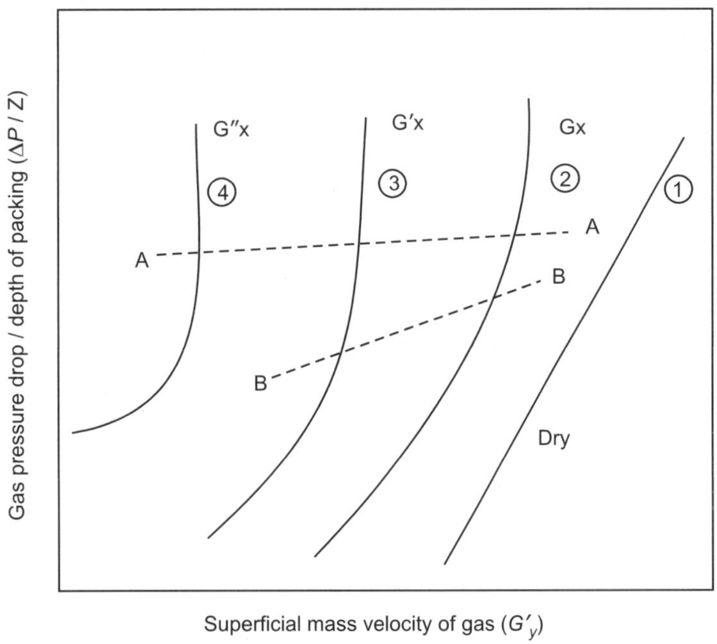

Fig. 3.8 Loading and flooding points in packed towers

The corresponding gas velocity is known as the *loading point*. At gas velocities below the loading point, the liquid hold up depends only on the liquid flow rate and is virtually independent of the gas velocity. In this region, the ΔP is increased by liquid flow owing to the reduction in the free space available for gas flow, but the gas has no influence on the liquid flow. Above the loading point, the gas friction hinders the downward flow of the liquid and causes an increase in the liquid holdup which further reduces the free space and increases the ΔP more rapidly. This goes on till a second critical G_y is reached at which the plot of $\frac{\Delta P}{Z}$ versus G_y turns abruptly upward and the liquid becomes a continuous phase in the packing. The second critical G_y is known as the *flooding point*.

This is the point where the friction between the gas and the liquid is great enough to back up the liquid into a continuous layer across the tower. The gas can then pass through the tower in occasional slugs. During flooding, the liquid phase becomes continuous and the gas phase becomes discontinuous in the voids of the bed. The flooding point represents the maximum loading the packing can accommodate. It is a fairly definite point and is needed in all tower calculations. Operation above the flooding point is impractical. Operation between the loading point and flooding point is unstable. Most towers operate just below or in the lower part of the loading region. The usual gas velocities are 50%–60% of the flooding velocity which corresponds to a $\frac{\Delta P}{Z}$ value of 200–400 N m^{-2} per meter of packed depth. Using Sherwood's flooding correlation (Fig. 3.9), the flooding velocity for the system is determined [5].

In the equation, L is the mass flow rate of the liquid (kg s^{-1}), V is the mass flow rate of the gas (kg s^{-1}), ρ_y is the density of the gas (kg m^{-3}), ρ_x is the density of the liquid (kg m^{-3}), G_y is the mass velocity of the gas (kg m^{-2} s^{-1}), C_f is the empirical packing factor based on interfacial surface area and voidage or porosity and μ_x is the viscosity of the liquid (kg m^{-1} s^{-1}).

An operational value of 50%–60% of the flooding velocity is used to calculate the column cross section from the flow rate of the gas. The tower diameter can be computed from this.

$$S = \frac{V_b}{0.5\,\text{to}\,0.6\,G_y}\,\frac{\text{kg}\,\text{s}^{-1}}{\text{kg}\,\text{m}^{-2}\,\text{s}^{-1}} = \frac{\Pi}{4}d^2 \tag{3.11}$$

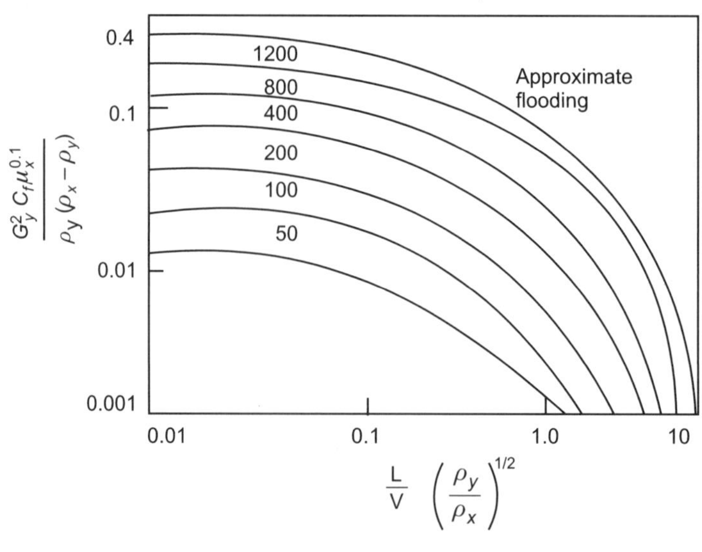

Fig. 3.9 Sherwood's flooding correlation

Another approach is to fix a particular $\frac{\Delta P}{Z}$ value and get the G_y corresponding to that. S can be found by dividing V_b by G_y. Larger flow quantities are at the bottom of the absorber. Hence, the diameter has to be chosen to accommodate the bottom conditions.

$$S = \frac{V_b}{G_y} = \frac{\Pi}{4} d^2 \tag{3.12}$$

ILLUSTRATION

30 It is required to absorb 96% of acetone in a 2 mol% mixture of acetone in air in a continuous counter current absorption tower using 20% more than the minimum liquid rate. Pure water is used as the solvent and it is introduced at the top of the tower and the gas mixture is blown into the bottom of the tower at 450 kg h^{-1}. Find the height and the diameter of the tower packed with 2.54 cm wet stone ware, Raschig rings and operating at 50% of the flooding velocity. The tower may be assumed to be operating at atmospheric pressure and 300 K. The equilibrium relation is $y = 2.5x$ where y and x are mole fractions of acetone in air and water respectively. The following relationship and data are available. $H_{oy} = H_y + \frac{mG}{L} H_x$ where $H_y = 0.54$ m and $H_x = 0.32$ m. The density of the acetone–air mixture = 1.181 kg m^{-3} and that of the solution and also of water = 998.4 kg m^{-3}. Viscosity of solution = 0.86 cP. Characteristic factor of packing = 160.

Solution

Basis: 1 hour operation.

Mole fraction of acetone in the entering gases (y_b) = 0.02

Mole fraction of air in the entering gases = 0.98

Average molecular weight of the entering gases = $(58 \times 0.02) + (29 \times 0.98) = 29.58$

Mass flow rate of entering gases = 450 kg

Molal flow rate of the entering gases = $450 \div 29.58 = 15.213$ kmol

Amount of acetone in the entering gases = $15.213 \times 0.02 = 0.304$ kmol

Amount of air in the entering gases = $15.213 - 0.304 = 14.909$ kmol

96% of acetone in the entering gases is absorbed by water.

Amount of acetone absorbed = $0.304 \times 0.96 = 0.292$ kmol

Amount of acetone in the leaving gases = $0.304 \times 0.04 = 0.012$ kmol

Amount of gases leaving = inert air + unabsorbed acetone

= $14.909 + 0.012 = 14.921$ kmol

Mole fraction of acetone in the leaving gases (y_a) = $0.012 \div 14.921 = 0.000\,8$

The entering water is acetone free.

Mole fraction of acetone in the entering water (x_a)	=	0
Amount of acetone in the liquid effluent	=	0.292 kmol

Let the minimum water rate be L kmol h^{-1}.

At the minimum water rate, the mole fraction of ammonia in the liquid effluent is x_b^*.

$$y_b = mx_b^*$$

That is, $0.02 = 2.5x_b^*$ and $x_b^* = 0.008$

$$\frac{0.292}{0.292 + L} = 0.008$$

Hence $L = 36.21$ kmol

The actual water rate is 1.20 times the minimum.

Actual water rate = $36.21 \times 1.20 = 43.45$ kmol $= 782.09$ kg h^{-1}

Mole fraction of ammonia in the liquid effluent $(x_b) = \dfrac{0.292}{0.292 + 43.45} = 0.006\,68$

$y_b^* = 2.5x_b = 2.5 \times 0.00668 = 0.0167$ and $y_a^* = 2.5x_a = 2.5 \times 0 = 0$

$$N_{oy} = \frac{y_{b'} - y_a}{\Delta y_{lm}} \quad \text{where} \quad \Delta y_{lm} = \frac{(y_b - y_b^*) - (y_a - y_a^*)}{\ln \dfrac{(y_b - y_b^*)}{(y_a - y_a^*)}}$$

Substituting the value of the parameters,

$$N_{oy} = 10.91$$

It is given that $H_{oy} = H_y + \dfrac{mG}{L} H_x$, where m is the slope of the equilibrium line, G is the gas rate, L is the liquid rate, $H_y = 0.54$ m and $H_x = 0.32$ m.

Substituting the value of the parameters,

$$H_{oy} = 0.54 + 2.5 \times \frac{15.21}{43.45} \times 0.32 = 0.82 \text{ m}$$

Packed height of the tower $Z_T = N_{oy} \times H_{oy} = 0.82 \times 10.91 = 8.95$ m

Diameter of the Tower

Using Sherwood's flooding correlation, flooding velocity for the system is determined. Here, L is the mass flow rate of the liquid (kg s^{-1}), V is the mass flow rate of the gas (kg s^{-1}), ρ_y is the density of the gas (kg m^{-1}), ρ_x is the density of the liquid (kg m^{-3}), G_y is the mass velocity of the gas (kg m^{-2} s^{-1}), C_f is the empirical packing factor based on interfacial surface area and voidage or porosity and μ_x is the viscosity of the liquid (kg m^{-1} s^{-1}).

$$\frac{L}{G}\left(\frac{\rho_y}{\rho_x}\right)^{0.5} = \frac{782.1}{450}\left(\frac{1.181}{998.4}\right)^{1/2} = 0.06$$

From the flooding correlation graph, the ordinate for this abscissa is 0.26.

$$0.26 = \frac{G_y^2 C_f \ \mu_x^{0.1}}{\rho_y(\rho_x - \rho_y)} = \frac{G_y^2 \times 160 \times (0.86 \times 10^{-3})^{0.1}}{1.181 \times (998.4 - 1.181)}$$

So G_y flooding = 1.969 kg m^{-2} s

50% of the flooding velocity has to be used to calculate column cross section from the flow rate of gas. The tower diameter can be computed from this.

$$S = \frac{V_b}{0.5\,G_y}\ \frac{\text{kg s}^{-1}}{\text{kg m}^{-2}\text{s}^{-1}} = \frac{\Pi}{4}d^2$$

$$G_y \text{ actual} \quad = 0.5 \times 1.969 = 0.984\,5 \text{ kg m}^{-2}\text{ s}^{-1}$$

$$\frac{\pi}{4}d^2 \quad = \frac{450}{3\,600} \times 0.984\,5$$

Diameter, $d = 0.402$ m

ABSORPTION FACTOR METHOD FOR CALCULATING THE NUMBER OF IDEAL STAGES

The absorption factor (A) is defined as the ratio of actual absorption to ideal or maximum possible absorption.

$$A = \frac{(y_b - y_a)}{(y_b^* - y_a^*)} \tag{3.13}$$

Here $(y_b - y_a)$ refers to the actual absorption while $(y_b^* - y_a^*)$ represents the ideal or maximum possible absorption.

$$A = \frac{\dfrac{(y_b - y_a)}{(x_b - x_a)}}{\dfrac{(y_b^* - y_a^*)}{(x_b - x_a)}} = \frac{\text{Slope of the operating line}}{\text{Slope of the eqilibrium curve}} = \frac{L}{mV} \tag{3.14}$$

as $\frac{L}{V}$ is the slope of the operating line and m is the slope of the equilibrium curve.

The operating line is a straight line if the solute content of the gaseous input is less than 10 mol% ($y_b < 0.1$). If the equilibrium relation is of the form $y = mx$, then the equilibrium curve is a straight line. When the operating line and the equilibrium curve are both straight lines, the number of ideal stages can be found by a formula which is derived as follows.

Equation of equilibrium curve is $y = mx + B$, where m and B are constants.

If stage n is ideal, $y_n = mx_n + B$. So, $x_n = \frac{y_n - B}{m}$. When the molal flow rates are constant throughout the tower, then the equation of the operating line is

$$\begin{aligned}
y_{n+1} &= \frac{L}{V}x_n + y_a - \frac{L}{V}x_a \\
&= \frac{L}{V}\frac{(y_n - B)}{m} + y_a - \frac{L}{V}\frac{m}{m}x_a \\
&= A(y_n - B) + y_a - Amx_a \\
&= Ay_n + y_a - Amx_a - AB \\
&= Ay_n + y_a - A(mx_a - B) \\
&= Ay_n + y_a - Ay_a^* \qquad (\text{since } mx_a - B = y_a^*) \\
&= Ay_n - Ay_a^* + y_a
\end{aligned} \tag{3.15}$$

For stage 1, put $n = 1$ and $y_1 = y_a$

$$\begin{aligned}
y_2 &= Ay_1 - Ay_a^* + y_a \\
&= Ay_a - Ay_a^* + y_a \\
&= Ay_a + y_a - Ay_a^* \\
&= y_a(1 + A) - Ay_a^*
\end{aligned} \tag{3.16}$$

For stage 2, put $n = 2$

$$\begin{aligned}
y_3 &= A[y_a(1 + A) - Ay_a^*] + y_a - Ay_a^* \\
&= y_a(1 + A + A_2) - y_a^*(A + A_2)
\end{aligned} \tag{3.17}$$

For the nth stage,

$$y_{n+1} = y_a(1 + A + A^2 + \ldots + A^n) - y_a^*(A + A^2 + \ldots + A^n) \tag{3.18}$$

For the entire cascade, $n = N$, the total number of stages and $y_{n+1} = y_{N+1} = y_b$ (3.19)

$$y_b = y_a(1 + A + A^2 + \ldots + A^N) - y_a^*(A + A^2 + \ldots + A^N) \tag{3.20}$$

$$y_b = y_a\left[\frac{(1 - A^{N+1})}{1 - A}\right] - y_a^* A\left[\frac{(1 - A^N)}{1 - A}\right] \tag{3.21}$$

This is known as the *Kremser equation* [6].

$$y_b(1 - A) = y_a(1 - A^{N+1}) - y_a^* A(1 - A^N) \tag{3.22}$$

$$y_b - A_{yb} = y_a - A^{N+1}y_a - Ay_a^* + A^{N+1}y_a^* \tag{3.23}$$

$$y_b - y_a = A_{yb} - Ay_a^* - A^{N+1}(y_a - y_a^*) \tag{3.24}$$

We know that $A - \dfrac{(y_b - y_a)}{(y_b^* - y_a^*)}$ (from equation 3.13)

$$A(y_b^* - y_a^*) = Ay_b - Ay_a^* - A^{N+1}(y_a - y_a^*) \tag{3.25}$$

$$Ay_b^* - Ay_a^* = Ay_b - Ay_a^* - A^{N+1}(y_a - y_a^*) \tag{3.26}$$

$$Ay_b^* - Ay_b = -A^{N+1}(y_a - y_a^*) \tag{3.27}$$

$$Ay_b - Ay_b^* = A^{N+1}(y_a - y_a^*) \tag{3.28}$$

$$A(y_b - y_b^*) = A^{N+1}(y_a - y_a^*) \tag{3.29}$$

$$(y_b - y_b^*) = A^N(y_a - y_a^*) \tag{3.30}$$

$$\frac{(y_b - y_b^*)}{(y_a - y_a^*)} = A^N \tag{3.31}$$

Taking log on both sides,

$$\log\frac{(y_b - y_b^*)}{(y_a - y_a^*)} = N\log A \tag{3.32}$$

$$N = \frac{\log\dfrac{(y_b - y_b^*)}{(y_a - y_a^*)}}{\log\dfrac{(y_b - y_a)}{(y_b^* - y_a^*)}} = \frac{\log\left[\dfrac{\text{driving force at the bottom}}{\text{driving force at the top}}\right]}{\log\left[\dfrac{\text{actual absorption}}{\text{max imum possible absorption}}\right]} \tag{3.33}$$

ILLUSTRATIONS

3P Benzene–air mixture is to be scrubbed in a simple counter current absorption tower using non-volatile hydrocarbon oil as a solvent. The inlet gas contains 5% benzene and the entering gas flow rate is 600 k mol h^{-1}. The solubility of benzene in oil follows Rauolt's law. The tower operates isothermally at 299 K and 1 atm. The average molecular weight of oil is 200. Compute (a) the minimum oil rate in kg h^{-1} needed to recover 90% of the entering benzene and (b) how many theoretical stages are required if the oil rate is 1.5 times the minimum. The vapour pressure of benzene at 299 K is 103 mm Hg.

Solution

Basis: 1 hour operation.

The equilibrium relation is given in the vapour pressure form. It has to be converted to the usual mole fraction form. By Rauolt's law, we have $P_A = P_A^* x_A$ and by Dalton's law we have $P_A = Py_A$.

Combining these, we get, $Py_A = P_A^* x_A$

$$y_A = \frac{P_A^*}{P} x_A \quad \text{or} \quad y = \frac{P^*}{P} x$$

$$y = \frac{103}{760} x = 0.135\,5x$$

This is the equilibrium relation and the equilibrium curve is a straight line.

Molal flow rate of the gas at the inlet (V_b) = 600 kmol
Mole fraction of benzene at the gas inlet (y_b) = 0.05

Hence, the operating line is a straight line.

Benzene at the gas inlet = $600 \times 0.05 = 30$ kmol
Air at the gas inlet = $600 - 30 = 570$ kmol

90% of benzene is absorbed in a non-volatile oil.

Benzene absorbed in oil = $30 \times 0.90 = 27$ kmol
Benzene in the gas output = $30 - 27 = 3$ kmol
Mole fraction of benzene in the gas outlet (y_a) = $\dfrac{3}{570 + 3} = 0.005\,2$

The oil used for absorption is pure.

Mole fraction of benzene in water entering the absorption tower (x_a)= 0

Let the minimum oil rate be L kmol h^{-1}.

At the minimum oil rate, the mole fraction of benzene in the liquid effluent is x_b^*.

$$y_b = mx_b^*$$

That is, $0.05 = 0.1355x_b^*$ and $x_b^* = 0.369$

$$\frac{27}{27 + L} = 0.369$$

Hence $L = 47.17$ kmol $= 9\,234$ kg h^{-1}

The actual oil rate is 1.5 times the minimum.

Actual oil rate $= 47.17 \times 1.5 = 69.255$ kmol

Mole fraction of benzene in the liquid effluent $(x_b) = \dfrac{27}{27 + 69.255} = 0.280\,5$

As the operating line and equilibrium curve are both straight lines, the number of ideal stages can be found by the formula,

$$N = \frac{\log \dfrac{(y_b - y_b^*)}{(y_a - y_a^*)}}{\log \dfrac{(y_b - y_a)}{(y_b^* - y_a^*)}}$$

$$y_b^* = 0.1355 x_b = 0.135\,5 \times 0.280\,5 = 0.038 \text{ and } y_a^* = 0.135\,5 x_a = 0.135\,5 \times 0 = 0$$

Substituting the values of the parameters in the above equation, $N = 5.08$.

3Q Carbondisulphide–nitrogen mixture containing 7% carbondisulphide is to be absorbed by using absorption oil. The gas mixture enters at 297 K and atmospheric pressure at a rate of 0.4 m^3 s^{-1}. The vapour content is to be brought down to 0.5%. Oil free from carbondisulphide enters. Determine (a) the minimum liquid to gas ratio, (b) determine the kg of oil entering the tower for a liquid to gas ratio of 1.5 times the minimum, and (c) the theoretical number of stages needed. Vapour pressure of carbon disulphide at 297 K is 346 mm Hg and the average molecular weight of oil is 180.

Solution

Basis: 1 hour operation.

The equilibrium relation is given in the vapour pressure form. It has to be converted to the usual mole fraction form.

By Rauolt's law, we have $P_A = P_A^* x_A$ and by Dalton's law we have $P_A = P y_A$.

Combining these, we get, $P y_A = P_A^* x_A$

$$y_A = \frac{P_A^*}{P} x_A \quad \text{or} \quad y = \frac{P^*}{P} x$$

$$y = \frac{346}{760} x = 0.455 x$$

This is the equilibrium relation.

Volumetric flow rate of entering gases $= 0.4 \times 3\,600 = 1\,440$ m^3

This has to be converted to molal flow rate using the relation,

$$n = \frac{PV}{RT} = \frac{1\,440 \times 1}{0.082\,06 \times 297} = 59.092 \text{ kmol}$$

Molal flow rate of the entering gases	=	59.092 kmol
Mole fraction of CS_2 in the entering gases (y_b)	=	0.07
Amount of CS_2 in the entering gases	=	$59.092 \times 0.07 = 4.136$ kmol
Amount of nitrogen in the entering gases	=	$59.092 - 4.136 = 54.956$ kmol
Mole fraction of CS_2 in the outgoing gases (y_a)	=	0.005
CS_2 in the outgoing gases	=	$\frac{54.956 \times 0.005}{0.995} = 0.276$ kmol
CS_2 absorbed by the non-volatile oil	=	$4.136 - 0.276 = 3.86$ kmol

Mole fraction of CS_2 in water entering the absorption tower $(x_a) = 0$

Let the minimum oil rate be L kmol h^{-1}.

At minimum oil rate, mole fraction of CS_2 in the liquid effluent is x_b^*.

$$y_b = mx_b^*$$

That is, $0.07 = 0.455x_b^*$ and $x_b^* = 0.154$

$$\frac{3.86}{3.86 + L} = 0.154$$

Hence $L = 21.21$ kmol

The actual oil rate is 1.5 times the minimum.

Actual oil rate $= 21.21 \times 1.5 = 31.815$ kmol	=	$31.815 \times 180 = 5\ 726.7$ kg h^{-1}
Mole fraction of CS_2 in the liquid effluent (x_b)	=	$\frac{3.86}{3.86 + 31.815} = 0.108\ 2$

As the operating line and equilibrium curve are both straight lines, the number of ideal stages can be found by the formula,

$$N = \frac{\log \dfrac{(y_b - y_b^*)}{(y_a - y_a^*)}}{\log \dfrac{(y_b - y_a)}{(y_b^* - y_a^*)}}$$

$y_b^* = 0.455x_b = 0.455 \times 0.1082 = 0.0492$ and $y_a^* = 0.455x_a = 0.455 \times 0 = 0$

Substituting the values of the parameters in the above equation, $N = 5.12$.

3R Coal gas is to be freed of its light oil by scrubbing with wash oil as an absorbent. The gas flow rate to the absorber is at the rate of 0.8 million litres per hour at 800 mm Hg, 299 K containing 2% by volume of light oil. The light oil containing exclusively benzene has a vapour pressure of 100 mm Hg at the operating temperature. 95% of benzene has to be removed. The wash oil enters the absorber at 299 K containing 0.005 mole fraction benzene. The average molecular weight of the wash oil is 260. An oil circulation rate of 1.5 times the minimum is used. The wash oil–benzene solution behaves ideally. Compute the minimum oil rate and the number of ideal stages required.

Solution

Basis: 1 hour operation.

The equilibrium relation is given in the vapour pressure form. It has to be converted to the usual mole fraction form.

By Rauolt's law, we have $P_A = P_A^* x_A$ and by Dalton's law we have $P_A = P y_A$.

Combining these, we get, $P y_A = P_A^* x_A$

$$y_A = \frac{P_A^*}{P} x_A \quad \text{or} \quad y = \frac{P^*}{P} x$$

$$y = \frac{100}{800} x = 0.125x$$

This is the equilibrium relation.

Volumetric flow rate of entering gases = $0.8 \times 1\,000\,000\ L = 800\ \text{m}^3$

This has to be converted to the molal flow rate using the relation,

$$n = \frac{PV}{RT} = \frac{800 \times 800}{0.082\,06 \times 299 \times 760} = 34.32\,\text{kmol}$$

Molal flow rate of the entering gases	=	34.32 kmol
Mole fraction of benzene at the gas inlet (y_b)	=	0.02

Hence, the operating line is a straight line.

Benzene at the gas inlet	=	$34.32 \times 0.02 = 0.686\,4$ kmol
Inert gases at the gas inlet	=	$34.32 - 0.686\,4 = 33.634$ kmol

95% of benzene is absorbed in wash oil.

Benzene absorbed in oil	=	$0.686\,4 \times 0.95 = 0.652$ kmol
Benzene in the gas output	=	$0.6864 - 0.652 = 0.034$ kmol
Mole fraction of benzene in the gas outlet (y_a)	=	$\dfrac{0.034}{0.034 + 33.634} = 0.001$

Let the minimum oil rate be L kmol h^{-1}.

At minimum oil rate, the mole fraction of benzene in the liquid effluent is x_b^*.

$$y_b = mx_b^*$$

That is, $0.02 = 0.125x_b^*$ and $x_b^* = 0.16$

Mole fraction of benzene in the entering wash oil (x_a)= 0.005

$$\frac{0.005L + 0.652}{0.652 + L} = 0.16$$

Hence, $L = 3.534$ kmol

The actual wash oil rate is 1.5 times the minimum.

Actual wash oil rate $= 3.534 \times 1.50 = 5.301$ kmol

Mole fraction of toluene in the liquid effluent (x_b) $= \dfrac{(0.005 \times 5.301) + 0.652}{5.301 + 0.652} = 0.114$

As the operating line and equilibrium curve are both straight lines, the number of ideal stages can be found by the formula,

$$N = \frac{\log \dfrac{(y_b - y_b^*)}{(y_a - y_a^*)}}{\log \dfrac{(y_b - y_a)}{(y_b^* - y_a^*)}}$$

$$y_b^* = 0.125x_b = 0.125 \times 0.114 = 0.014\ 5$$

and $\quad y_a^* = 0.125x_a = 0.125 \times 0.005 = 0.000\ 625$

Substituting the values of the parameters in the above equation, $N = 7.21$.

ABSORPTION ASSOCIATED WITH CHEMICAL REACTION

In a number of cases, the gas on absorption reacts chemically with a component of the liquid phase. Absorption of CO_2 by NaOH or diethanolamine and absorption of NH_3 by HCl or H_2SO_4 are typical examples for absorption accompanied by chemical reaction. In such processes, the conditions in the gas phase are similar to those for physical absorption, but in the liquid phase there is a liquid film followed by a reaction zone. The process of diffusion and chemical reaction can be represented by an extension of the film theory.

Assume that the chemical reaction is irreversible. Let the solute gas A be absorbed from a mixture by a substance B in the liquid phase which combines with A, according to the equation: A + B $\rightarrow$ AB. As the gas approaches the liquid phase, it dissolves and reacts at once with B. The new product AB thus formed diffuses towards the main body of the liquid. The concentration of B at the interphase falls. This results in the diffusion of B from the bulk of the liquid phase to the interphase. Since the chemical reaction is rapid B is removed very quickly so that it is necessary for the gas A to diffuse through part of the liquid film before meeting B. There is a zone of reaction between A and B which moves away from the gas–liquid interphase taking up some position towards the bulk of the liquid. The final position of this reaction zone will be such that the rate of diffusion of A from the interphase is equal to the rate of diffusion of B from the bulk of the liquid. The situation can be summarised in the form of a diagram (Fig. 3.10).

A diffuses through the gas phase as a result of the driving force $P_{AG} - P_{Ai}$ and diffuses to the reaction zone as a result of the driving force $C_{Ai} - 0 = C_{Ai}$ in the liquid phase. Component B diffuses from the bulk of the liquid to the reaction zone under the driving force, $C_{BL} - 0 = C_{BL}$. The non-volatile product, AB diffuses back to the bulk of the liquid under the driving force, $C_{AB,i} - C_{AB,L}$.

For the transfer in the gas phase, $N_A^I = k_g\ (P_{AG} - P_{Ai})$ from equation (3.4), and for transfer in the liquid phase, $N_A^I = k_l(C_{Ai} - C_{AL})$ from equation (3.7). The effect of the chemical reaction is to accelerate the removal of A from the interphase. If the rate is r times greater, then

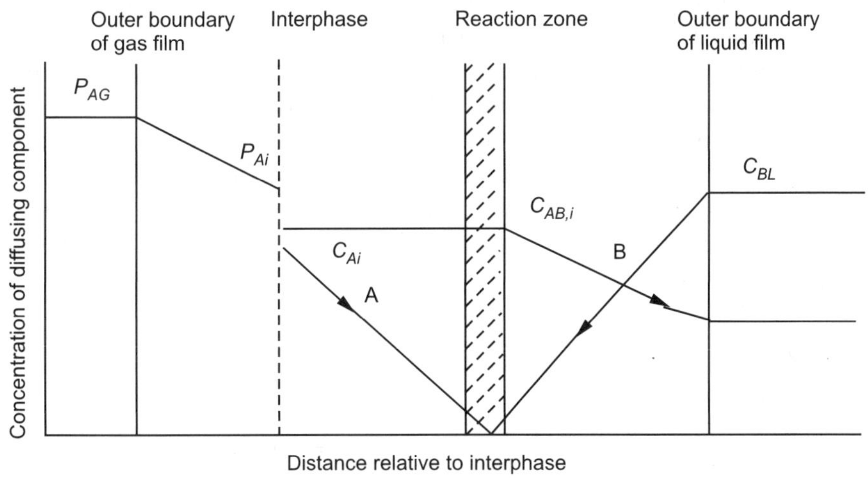

Fig. 3.10 Concentration–distance diagram

$$N_A^{II} = rk_l(C_{Ai} - C_{AL}) \tag{3.34}$$

The factor r has been found [7] to be related to C_{Ai}, D_l, k_l, C_{BL} and the chemical reaction rate constant j.

1. If j is very small, $r \approx 1$ and the conditions are those of physical absorption.
2. If j is very large, $r \approx \frac{C_{BL}}{C_{Ai}}$ and the rate of the process is determined by the transport of B towards the phase boundary.
3. At moderate values of $j, r \approx \left(j\frac{D_l}{C_{BL}}\right)^{1/2}/k_l$ and the rate of the process is determined by the rate of the chemical reaction. Hence, in all cases the controlling factor is j.

HEIGHT EQUIVALENT TO A THEORETICAL PLATE (HETP)

This constitutes the height of packing that will give the same separation as one theoretical plate, that is, a section of packing in which the vapour leaving the top of the section will be in equilibrium with the liquid leaving the bottom of the section. HETP is characteristic for each packing. It depends on the type and size of packing, flow rate of each fluid and the components. If the packed height of the tower is Z_T and the number of theoretical plates is N, then HETP = $\frac{Z_T}{N}$. If the operating line and equilibrium curve are straight lines and parallel, then HETP = H_{oy}. The usual value of HETP ranges from 0.3–0.6 m.

ILLUSTRATION

3S A tower packed with 0.5 cm Raschig rings of 12 m height is to be used for absorption of H_2S from CH_4 using monoethanolamine (MEA) as solvent. The operation is carried out at 303 K and 1 atm in a counter current manner. The entering gas contains 18% H_2S by volume and 90% of this has to be absorbed. The gas flow rate is 2 000 $m^3\ m^{-2}\ h^{-1}$. The equilibrium line is straight and in the operating limit, it is given by $y = 1.1x$, where x and y have the usual significance. The operating line is straight and is parallel to the equilibrium line. Find (a) the liquid flow rate and (b) the number of stages and height equivalent to a theoretical plate (HETP).

Solution

Basis: 1 hour operation.

Volumetric flow rate of entering gases = 2 000 m^3

This has to be converted to molal flow rate using the relation,

$$n = \frac{PV}{RT} = \frac{2\,000 \times 1}{0.082\,06 \times 303} = 80.45\ \text{kmol}$$

Molal flow rate of the entering gases = 80.45 kmol

Mole fraction of H_2S in the entering gases (y_b) = 0.18

Amount of H_2S in the entering gases = $80.45 \times 0.18 = 14.48$ kmol

Amount of inerts in the entering gases = $80.45 - 14.48 = 65.97$ kmol

90% of H_2S in the entering gases is absorbed by MEA.

Amount of H_2S absorbed	=	$14.48 \times 0.90 = 13.03$ kmol
Amount of H_2S in the leaving gases	=	$14.48 - 13.03 = 1.45$ kmol
Amount of gases leaving	=	inerts + unabsorbed acetone
	=	$65.97 + 1.45 = 67.42$ kmol
Mole fraction of H_2S in the leaving gases (y_a)	=	$1.45 \div 67.42 = 0.021\ 5$
Mole fraction of H_2S in the entering wash oil (x_a)	=	0
Amount of H_2S in the liquid effluent	=	13.03 kmol

The operating line and the equilibrium line are parallel. Therefore, the equation of the operating line is also $y = 1.1x$.

$$y_b = 1.1x_b \text{ and } 0.18 = 1.1x_b$$

Thus, $\quad x_b = 0.1636$

$$0.1636 = \frac{13.03}{L_a + 13.03}$$

So the liquid rate, $L_a = 66.63$ kmol m^{-2} h^{-1} = 4 064 kg m^{-2} h^{-1}

The operating line is drawn using the extreme ends (x_a, y_a) and (x_b, y_b). On the same graph sheet, the equilibrium curve is also drawn. The number of theoretical stages required is found by the McCabe–Thiele method.

The number of theoretical units required for this operation = 9.71.

$$\text{HETP} = \frac{12}{9.71} = 1.236\,\text{m}$$

NOTATIONS

A	Absorption factor, dimensionless.
C_{Ai}	Concentration of reactant A at the liquid side of the interphase, mol m^{-3}.
C_{A1}	Molar concentration of solute A at plane 1, kmol m^{-3}.
C_{A2}	Molar concentration of solute A at plane 2, kmol m^{-3}.
$C_{AB,i}$	Concentration of the product AB at the liquid side of the interphase, mol m^{-3}.
C_{AL}	Concentration of the reactant A in the bulk of the heavy phase (liquid phase), mol m^{-3}.
C_{BL}	Concentration of reactant B in the bulk of liquid, mol m^{-3}.
C_f	Empirical packing factor based on interfacial surface area and voidage or porosity.
$\overline{C_T}$	Average of total molar concentration of A and B at locations 1 and 2, kmol m^{-3}.
d	Diameter of the tower, m.
D_g	Diffusivity of the solute in the gas phase, m^2 s^{-1}.
D_ℓ	Diffusivity of the solute in the liquid phase, m^2 s^{-1}.
G_y	Mass velocity of gas, kg m^{-2} s^{-1}.

H_{ox}	Height of a transfer unit based on overall resistance in terms of liquid phase, m.
H_{oy}	Height of a transfer unit based on overall resistance in terms of vapour phase, m.
H_x	Height of a transfer unit based on resistance in the liquid phase, m.
H_y	Height of a transfer unit based on resistance in the vapour phase, m.
HETP	Height equivalent to a theoretical plate.
j	Rate constant for the chemical reaction.
k_g	Mass transfer coefficient based on partial pressure of solute in the gas phase, m s^{-1}.
k_l	Mass transfer coefficient based on solute concentration in the liquid, m s^{-1}.
k_x	Mass transfer coefficient for the heavy phase (liquid phase), kmol m^{-2} s^{-1} (Δ mole fraction)$^{-1}$.
k_y	Mass transfer coefficient for the light phase (gas phase), kmol m^{-2} s^{-1} (Δ mole fraction)$^{-1}$.
K_x	Overall mass transfer coefficient based on the heavy phase (liquid phase), kmol m^{-2} s^{-1} (Δ mole fraction)$^{-1}$.
K_y	Over all mass transfer coefficient based on light phase (gas phase), kmol m^{-2} s^{-1} (Δ mole fraction)$^{-1}$.
L	Mass flow rate of liquid, kg s^{-1}.
m	Henry's law constant.
N	Number of theoretical stages.
N_{ox}	Number of a transfer unit based on the overall resistance in terms of the liquid phase.
N_{oy}	Number of a transfer unit based on the overall resistance in terms of the vapour phase.
N_x	Number of a transfer unit based on resistance in the liquid phase.
N_y	Number of a transfer unit based on resistance in the vapour phase.
N_A^1	Diffusion flux of A, while the other component B remains stagnant, kmol m^{-2} s^{-1}.
P	Total pressure, N m^{-2}.
P_A	Partial pressure of solute A in the gaseous mixture, N m^{-2}.
P_{Ai}	Partial pressure of the reactant at the gas side of the interphase, N m^{-2}.
P_{A1}	Partial pressure of solute A at plane 1, N m^{-2}.
P_{A2}	Partial pressure of solute A at plane 2, N m^{-2}.
P_{Blm}	Log mean value of partial pressure of the non-diffusing component B at locations 1 and 2, N m^{-2}.
P_{AG}	Partial pressure of the reactant A in the bulk of the light phase (gas phase), N m^{-2}.
r	Factor for absorption accompanied by chemical reaction.
R	Universal gas constant, 8 314 J kmol^{-1} K^{-1}.
S	Cross sectional area of the tower, m^2.
T	Temperature, K.
V	Mass flow rate of gas, kg s^{-1}.
x_a	Mole fraction of solute in the liquid entering the tower.
x_A	Mole fraction of solute A in the gas phase.
x_b	Mole fraction of solute in the liquid leaving the tower.
y_a	Mole fraction of solute in the gas phase leaving the tower.
y_b	Mole fraction of solute in the gas phase entering the tower.

y_a^* Equilibrium value in terms of the mole fraction, corresponding to x_b.
y_b^* Equilibrium value in terms of the mole fraction, corresponding to x_a.
Δy Change in vapour composition in terms of the mole fraction.
Δy_{lm} Log mean of the driving forces in the light phase at the extreme ends of the column.
Z_g Thickness of the film in the gas phase, m.
Z_l Thickness of the film in the liquid phase, m.
Z_T Total height of the tower, m.
$\frac{\Delta P}{Z}$ Pressure drop per unit depth of packing, N m^{-3}.
ρ_x Density of the liquid, kg m^{-3}.
ρ_y Density of the gas, kg m^{-3}.
μ_x Viscosity of the liquid, kg m^{-1} s^{-1}.
Δ Difference.

REFERENCES

1. Danckwerts PV and McNeil KM, *Trans. Inst. Chem. Eng.*, **45**: 32 (1967).
2. Danckwerts PV and Sharma MM, *Chem. Engr. London*, **CE 244**: 202 (1967).
3. Sahay BN and Sharma MM, *Chem. Eng. Sci.*, **28**: 41 (1973).
4. Eckert JS, *Chem. Engg.*, **82**: 70 (1975).
5. Eckert JS, *Chem. Engg. Prog.*, **66**: 39 (1970).
6. Kremser A, *Nat. Petroleum News*, **22**: 43 (1930).
7. Van Krevelen DW and Hoftuzer PJ, *Rec. Trav. Chim.*, **67**: 563 (1948).

Problems for Practice

3.1 A gas is absorbed in water using a packed tower. The equilibrium relationship is $y = 0.05x$. The terminal conditions are

x	0	0.08
y	0.001	0.009

where x and y are mole fractions of the solute in the liquid and gas phase respectively.

(i) Calculate the number of transfer units needed.
(ii) The height of packing needed if the height of a transfer unit is 40 cm.

3.2 A mixture of air and acetone vapour containing 90% air (by volume) is stripped off 95% acetone by counter current contact with a stream of water in a bubble plate column operated at 298 K and 1 atm. An overall plate efficiency of 35% can be assumed. If the water rate used is 1.3 times the minimum value, calculate the actual number of plates required.

Equilibrium data:

Mole % acetone in liquid	3.33	7.2	11.7	17.1
Partial pressure of acetone, mm Hg	3.0	62.8	85.4	103.0

3.3 A soluble gas is absorbed in water using a packed tower. The equilibrium relationship may be taken as $y = 0.06x$, where y and x represent the ratio of moles of solute to moles of inert component.

The terminal conditions are

	Top	Bottom
x	0	0.08
y	0.001	0.009

If the individual heights of the transfer units based on the liquid and gas phases respectively are $H_x = 0.24$ m and $H_y = 0.36$ m, what is the height of the packed section?

3.4 An SO_2–air mixture containing 5% SO_2 is scrubbed with water to remove SO_2. 500 kg h^{-1} of gas mixture is to be processed with 20 000 kg h^{-1} of water to reduce the SO_2 in the exit gas to 0.15%. Calculate the height of packing required, assuming dilute solutions are involved. The equilibrium relationship is given by $y = 30x$, where x and y are the mole fractions of SO_2 in the liquid and vapour phases respectively. Take the height of the transfer unit as 30 cm.

3.5 Sulphur dioxide is removed from air by scrubbing the gas with water in a packed tower. The entering gas contains 20% SO_2 by volume. 95% of SO_2 entering is to be removed. The entering water is SO_2 free. Find the minimum water rate. If the water rate is twice the minimum, estimate the concentration of SO_2 in the solution leaving the tower. The slope of the equilibrium line is 19.5.

3.6 Ammonia is absorbed from a gas by water in a scrubber. The initial ammonia content in the gas is 0.03 kmol per kmol of inert gas. The absorption factor is 0.9. The water leaving the absorber contains 0.02 kmol ammonia per kmol water. The absorber operates isothermally. Determine the number of transfer units.

Equilibrium data:

kmol NH_3 per kmol of water	0.005	0.01	0.012 5	0.015	0.02	0.023
kmol of NH_3 per kmol of inert gas	0.005	0.010 2	0.013	0.018	0.027	0.033

3.7 An air–ammonia mixture containing 8 mole% NH_3 is being scrubbed with water in a counter current packed tower to recover 95% ammonia. The mass velocity of gas and water at their respective inlets are 3 000 kg h^{-1} m^{-2} and 2 500 kg h^{-1} m^{-2} respectively. The tower is maintained at 298 K and 1 atm. Estimate the number of transfer units needed and hence the packed height of the tower. The equilibrium relationship is given by $y = 0.98x$ where x and y are the liquid and gas phase concentrations of ammonia in mole fraction. $K_{ga} = 65$ kmol $h^{-1}m^{-3}$ atm^{-1}.

3.8 95% of acetone in an air–acetone mixture with an initial composition of 5 mol% is to be absorbed by scrubbing it with water in a packed counter current absorber at 298 K and 1 atm pressure. Calculate the height of the tower.

Equilibrium data:

Mole fraction of acetone in liquid phase	0	0.01	0.02	0.03	0.04
Mole fraction of acetone in gas phase	0	0.02	0.038	0.055	0.07

Total gas flow rate: 3 000 kg h^{-1}, inlet water flow rate: 5 000 kg h^{-1}, diameter of the tower: 1.5 m, $K_{ga} = 100$ mol h^{-1} L^{-1} atm^{-1}.

3.9 It is desired to absorb 95% of acetone from a feed mixture of acetone and air containing 2 mol% of acetone using 20% more than the minimum water rate. Pure water is introduced at the top of the tower and the gas flow rate at the bottom of the tower is 450 kg h^{-1}. The gas mixture enters at 298 K and 1 atm pressure which is the operating condition inside the tower. The operation is carried out in a plate tower. The equilibrium relationship is $y = 2.5x$, where x and y are the mole fractions of acetone in the liquid and gas phases respectively. Calculate (i) the flow rate of water and (ii) the number of theoretical plates. The operation is carried out using counter current.

3.10 An air–SO_2 mixture containing 5% SO_2 is scrubbed with water to remove SO_2 in a packed tower. 20 kmol h^{-1} of gas mixture is to be processed to reduce the SO_2 concentration at the exit to 0.15%. If the water used is twice the minimum required, estimate the number of transfer units needed. The equilibrium relationship is $y = 30x$. If the height of a transfer unit is 30 cm, estimate the height of packing to be used.

3.11 NH_3 is to be absorbed from air at 303 K and 1 atm pressure in a counter current packed tower, using water at 303 K as the absorbent. An inlet gas rate of 50 m^3 h^{-1} and an NH^3-free water rate of 35 kg h^{-1} will be used. If the NH_3 concentration is reduced from 3.52% to 1.29% by volume, Calculate the ratio of (L_s/G_s) actual to (L_s/G_s) minimum.

Equilibrium data for the system at 303 K and 1 atm:

kmol NH_3 per kmol H_2O	0.016	0.025	0.035	0.045	0.072
kmol NH_3 per kmol air	0.021	0.032	0.042	0.053	0.080

3.12 Ammonia is to be removed from 20% NH_3 and 80% air mixture by counter current scrubbing with water at 1 atm and 293 K. The scrubber is to be designed to remove 99% NH_3 in the entry gas. Calculate the minimum amount of water and the number of theoretical stages necessary for absorption at 1.2 times the minimum water rate if the gas rate is 1 kg s^{-1}.

Equilibrium data:

Partial pressure of NH_3 in gas (mm Hg)	12	18	32	50	70	166
Concentration of NH_3 in water (g per100 g water)	2	3	5	7.5	10	20

3.13 An absorption tower is to be designed to absorb SO_2 from air by scrubbing the gas with water. The entering gas contains 20% SO_2 by volume and the leaving gas is to contain 0.5% SO_2 by volume. The entering water is free from SO. The water flow is to be twice the minimum. The air flow on SO_2-free basis is 975 kg h^{-1} m^{-2}. The temperature is 303 K and 1 atm. The equilibrium relationship is $y = 21x$, where x and y are the mole fractions of SO_2 in the liquid and vapour phases respectively. Compute the number of overall gas phase transfer units.

3.14 A mixture containing 10% mole solute and rest inert is fed to a packed tower in which 95% of the solute is absorbed. Solute-free water is used as the solvent. The water leaves with 5 mol% solute at the bottom of the tower. If the equilibrium relation is $y = 0.05x$, $H_y = 0.5$ m and $H_x = 0.4$ m, what is the height of the packed section?

3.15 Ammonia is to be absorbed from air at 298 K and atmospheric pressure in a co-current tower using water as absorbent. An inlet gas rate of 500 m^3 h^{-1} will be used. The ammonia concentration is to be reduced from 3.52% to 1.29% by volume using a water stream 1.37 times the minimum liquid rate. Determine (i) the minimum (L/G) ratio (ii) the actual water rate and (iii) the concentration in the exiting aqueous stream.

Equilibrium data:

x	0.016 4	0.025 2	0.034 9	0.045 5	0.072 2
y	0.021	0.032	0.042	0.053	0.08

where x and y are the mole ratios of the solute to solvent in the liquid and vapour phases respectively.

4 Distillation

Distillation is concerned with the separation of solutions, where all the components are appreciably volatile. The difference in volatility of the components is exploited to make the separation. The solution is partially vaporised by the application of heat. The composition of the newly formed vapour phase will be different from that of the residual liquid. Near complete separation of the phases is achieved by repeated vaporisations and condensations. This chapter deals with the theories governing different distillation methods and the procedure for designing an appropriate distillation column for the problem on hand.

Distillation is the separation of a liquid–liquid mixture based on the difference in boiling points of the constituents. Figure 4.1 shows a typical distillation column.

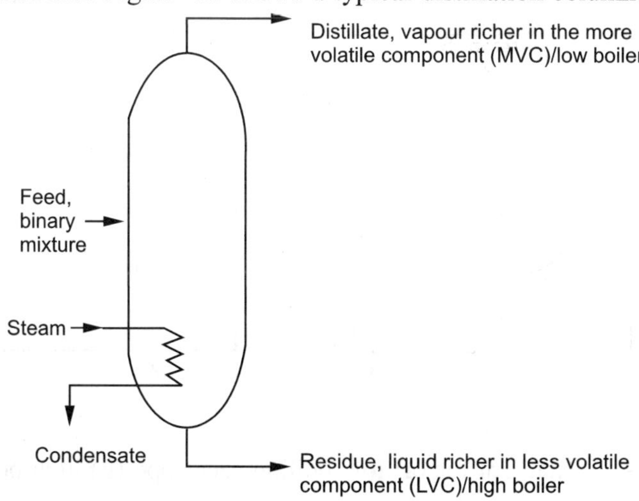

Fig. 4.1 Distillation column

VAPOUR–LIQUID EQUILIBRIUM [1]

The composition of the vapour in equilibrium with a liquid of known composition is determined experimentally using an equilibrium still. The results are conveniently shown on a temperature–composition diagram. In the normal case, ABC shows the composition of the liquid that boils at a given temperature and ADC, the corresponding composition of the vapour at that temperature. A liquid of composition x_1 will boil at a temperature T_1 and the vapour in equilibrium has a composition y_1. The vapour formed will be richer in the more volatile component (Fig. 4.2). Mixtures such as C_6H_6–C_7H_8, C_7H_{16}–C_7H_8 and CS_2–CCl_4 exhibit this type of behaviour.

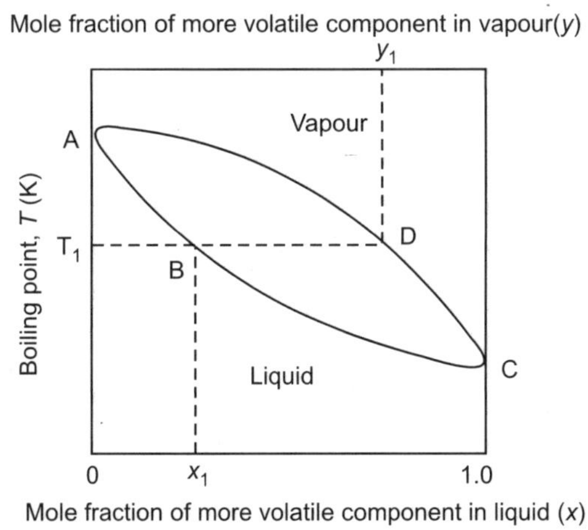

Fig. 4.2 T–x–y diagram for a normal binary mixture

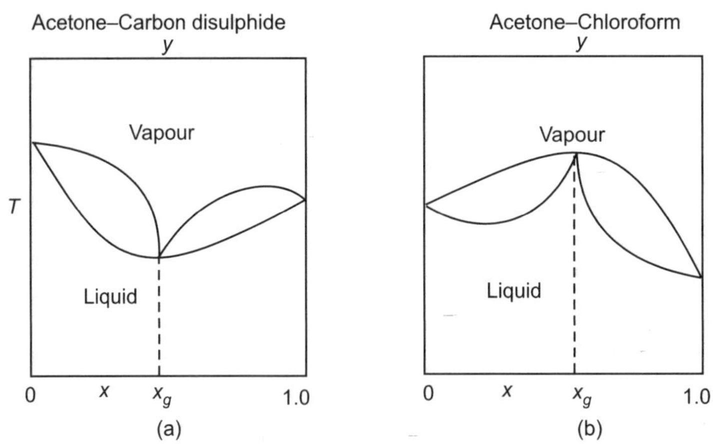

Fig. 4.3 T–x–y diagram for (a) low boiling azeotrope (b) high boiling azeotrope

In the other types, there is a critical composition x_g where the vapour has the same composition as the liquid so that no change occurs on boiling (Fig. 4.3). Such critical mixtures are called *azeotropes*. Special methods are required for their separation.

LAWS OF PARTIAL PRESSURES

Dalton's Law

The total pressure is equal to the summation of the partial pressures.

$$P = \Sigma P_i \tag{4.1}$$

For an ideal gas or vapour, the partial pressure is the mole fraction multiplied by the total pressure.

$$P_A = y_A P \tag{4.2}$$

Raoult's Law

The partial pressure of a component in a mixture is equal to the mole fraction of that component multiplied by its vapour pressure in the pure state at that temperature.

$$P_A = P_A^* x_A \tag{4.3}$$

This relation is true for high values of x_A or when A is a solvent.

Henry's Law

The partial pressure of a component over a solution is proportional its mole fraction in the solution.

$$P_A \alpha x_A = m x_A \tag{4.4}$$

where m is Henry's law constant. This is true for low values of x_A or where A is a solute.

If a mixture follows Raoult's law, the composition of the liquid and vapour phases in equilibrium at different temperatures can be found from the knowledge of vapour pressures of the two pure components. For a binary mixture, by Rauolt's law,

$$P_A = P_A^* x_A \tag{4.3}$$

$$P_B = P_B^* x_B$$

and $$P = P_A + P_B \tag{4.5}$$

$$P = P_A^* x_A + P_B^* x_B = P_A^* x_A + P_B^*(1 - x_A)$$

$$= P_A^* x_A + P_B^* - P_B^* x_A \tag{4.6}$$

$$P - P_B^* = P_A^* x_A - P_B^* x_A = x_A(P_A^* - P_B^*) \tag{4.7}$$

$$x_A = \frac{P - P_B^*}{P_A^* - P_B^*} \tag{4.8}$$

When x_A is known, y_A can be found as given below.

By Raoult's law, $P_A = P_A^* x_A$ and by Dalton's law $P_A = P_{yA}$

$$P y_A = P_A^* x_A \tag{4.9}$$

$$y_A = \frac{P_A^*}{P} x_A \tag{4.10}$$

Relative Volatility

The ratio of the partial pressure of a component in the vapour phase to its mole fraction in the liquid phase is defined as volatility.

$$\text{Volatility of A, } \alpha_A = \frac{P_A}{x_A} \tag{4.11}$$

$$\text{Volatility of B, } \alpha_B = \frac{P_B}{x_B} \tag{4.12}$$

The ratio of the two volatilities is known as relative volatility.

$$\alpha_{AB} = \frac{\alpha_A}{\alpha_B}$$

$$= \frac{P_A}{x_A}\frac{x_B}{P_B} \text{ but } P_A = y_A P \text{ and } P_B = y_B P$$

$$= \frac{y_A x_B}{x_A y_B} \tag{4.13}$$

$$\frac{y_A}{y_B} = \alpha_{AB} \frac{x_A}{x_B} \tag{4.14}$$

For binary mixtures, $y_B = 1 - y_A$ and $x_B = 1 - x_A$

$$\frac{y_A}{1 - y_A} = \alpha_{AB} \frac{x_A}{1 - x_A} \tag{4.15}$$

$$y_A(1 - x_A) = \alpha_{AB} x_A (1 - y_A) \tag{4.16}$$

If we assume that A is always the component of our interest and relative volatility α_{AB} always denotes the volatility of component A to that of B, the subscripts can be omitted.

$$y(1 - x) = \alpha x(1 - y) \tag{4.17}$$

$$y - xy = \alpha x - \alpha xy \tag{4.18}$$

$$y - xy + \alpha xy = \alpha x \tag{4.19}$$

$$y\{1 - x + \alpha x\} = \alpha x \tag{4.20}$$

$$y\{1 + x(\alpha - 1)\} = \alpha x \tag{4.21}$$

$$y = \frac{\alpha\, x}{1 + x\,(\alpha - 1)} \tag{4.22}$$

Similarly we can prove that,

$$x = \frac{y}{y + \alpha\,(1 - y)} \tag{4.23}$$

From these relations, the compositions of vapour and liquid can be found if one of them and α are known. Also if α is known, the equilibrium relation can be derived.

For an ideal solution,

$$P_A = P_A^* x_A \text{ and } P_B = P_B^* x_B$$

$$\alpha_{AB} = \frac{\alpha_A}{\alpha_B}$$

$$= \frac{P_A}{x_A}\frac{x_B}{P_B} = \frac{P_A^* x_A x_B}{P_B^* x_B x_A} = \frac{P_A^*}{P_B^*} \tag{4.24}$$

α is temperature dependent. If the change in the value of α with the temperature is moderate, then a geometric mean of the extreme values is recommended for average α.

$$\alpha_{av} = \sqrt{\alpha_{\min} \times \alpha_{\max}} \tag{4.25}$$

ILLUSTRATION

4A The vapour pressure data for the benzene–toluene system is given below:

Temperature (ºC)	80.1	85	90	95	100	105	110.6
Vapour pressure of benzene (mm Hg)	760	877	1010	1168	1344	1 532	1 800
Vapour pressure of toluene (mm Hg)	—	345	405	475	557	645	760

(i) Compute the equilibrium (x–y) data and plot the T–x–y diagram
(ii) Determine the average relative volatility.

Solution

From the data given, we can infer that the boiling point of benzene is 80.1°C and that of toluene is 110.6°C, as at these temperatures the vapour pressure is equal to the atmospheric pressure. Hence, benzene is the more volatile component (MVC) or low boiler or component A and toluene is the less volatile component (LVC) or high boiler or component B. We can compute the mole fraction of MVC in the heavy phase—liquid phase (x), the mole fraction of MVC in the light phase—vapour phase (y) and relative volatility (α) of the benzene–toluene system using the formulae derived earlier.

They are $x = \dfrac{P - P_B^*}{P_A^* - P_B^*}$, $y = \dfrac{P_A^*}{P} x_A$ and $\alpha = \dfrac{P_A^*}{P_B^*}$. The results are given in Table 4.1

Table 4.1 T–x–y data

Temperature (T)	Mole fraction of MVC in the liquid phase $x = \dfrac{P - P_B^*}{P_A^* - P_B^*}$	Mole fraction of MVC in the vapour phase $y = \dfrac{P_A^*}{P} x_A$	Relative volatility $\alpha = \dfrac{P_A^*}{P_B^*}$
80.1	1	1	—
85.0	$\dfrac{760 - 345}{877 - 345} = 0.783$	$\dfrac{877}{760} \times 0.783 = 0.90$	$\dfrac{877}{345} = 2.54$
90.0	$\dfrac{760 - 405}{1010 - 405} = 0.586$	$\dfrac{1010}{760} \times 0.586 = 0.78$	$\dfrac{1010}{405} = 2.49$
95.0	$\dfrac{760 - 475}{1168 - 475} = 0.411$	$\dfrac{1168}{760} \times 0.411 = 0.63$	$\dfrac{1168}{475} = 2.46$
100.0	$\dfrac{760 - 557}{1344 - 557} = 0.258$	$\dfrac{1344}{760} \times 0.258 = 0.456$	$\dfrac{1344}{557} = 2.413$
105.0	$\dfrac{760 - 645}{1532 - 645} = 0.13$	$\dfrac{1532}{760} \times 0.13 = 0.261$	$\dfrac{1532}{645} = 2.375$
110.6	0	0	$\dfrac{1800}{760} = 2.368$

$$\alpha_{av} = \sqrt{\alpha_{\min} \times \alpha_{\max}}$$

$$\alpha_{av} = \sqrt{2.368 \times 2.54} = 2.452$$

Using the above results, the T–x–y diagram is drawn (Fig. 4.4).

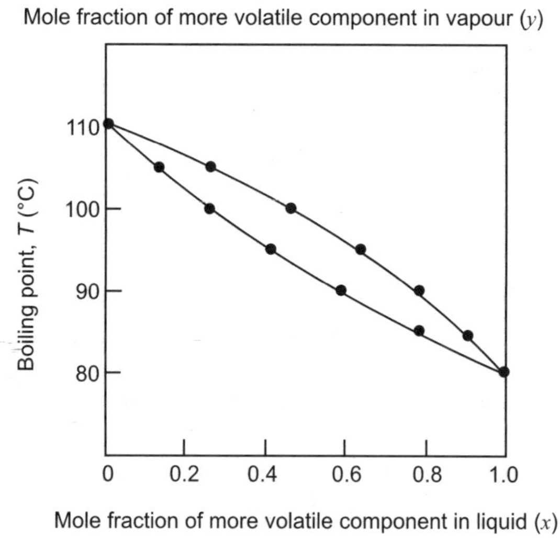

Fig. 4.4 Graphical solution for 4A

PARTIAL CONDENSATION AND PARTIAL VAPORISATION

Consider a mixture of C_6H_6 and C_7H_8 to be heated in closed vessel at constant pressure. Let no material be allowed to escape. If the mole fraction of the more volatile component (MVC) in the liquid is plotted as abscissa and the temperature at which the mixture boils as ordinate, it results in a diagram similar to Fig. 4.5.

ABCJ is the boiling point or bubble point curve. It gives the variation of boiling point with composition. ADEJ is the dew point curve. This gives the variation of the dew point with the composition of the vapour. Consider a mixture of composition x_2 at a temperature T_3 below its boiling point T_2 as shown by G. On heating at constant pressure, the following changes will occur.

1. When the temperature reaches T_2 the liquid will boil at B. The composition of the vapour will be y_2 corresponding to E.
2. On further heating, the composition of the liquid will change, because of the loss of MVC to the vapour. The boiling point will therefore rise to some temperature T_1. At this temperature, the liquid will have a composition represented by point K and the vapour will have the composition represented by D. Since no material is lost from the system, there will be a change in the proportion of liquid to vapour, the ratio being $\frac{\text{Liquid}}{\text{Vapour}} = \frac{\text{MN}}{\text{ML}}$.

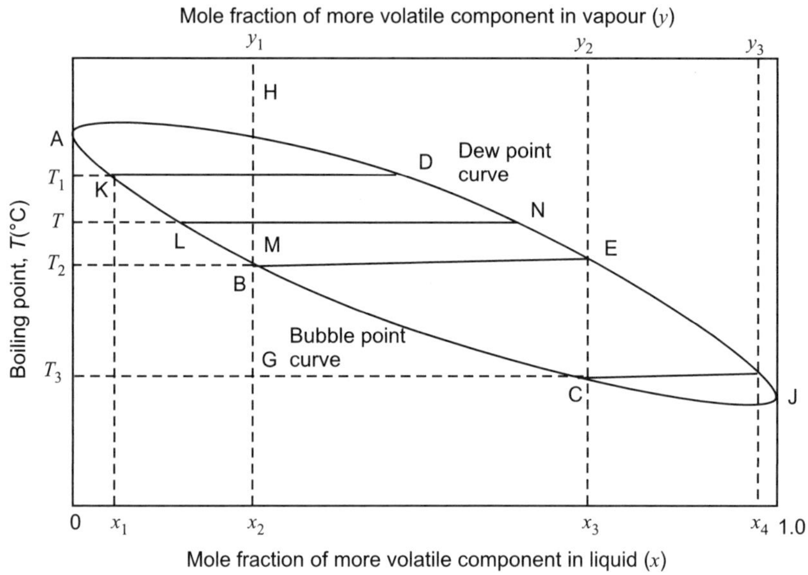

Fig. 4.5 Effect of partial vaporisation / partial condensation on temperature and composition

Partial vaporisation of a liquid results in a vapour richer in the MVC than the liquid. If the vapour initially formed – for instance at point E – is at once removed by condensation, then a liquid of composition x_3 is obtained represented by point C. The step BEC represents an ideal stage since the liquid passes from composition x_2 to liquid of composition x_3 which is the greatest possible enrichment in the MVC.

Starting with super heated vapour represented by point H, on cooling to D, condensation will commence and the first drop of liquid will have the composition K. Further cooling to T will give liquid L and vapour N. Thus partial condensation brings about enrichment of the vapour in the MVC in the same manner as partial vaporisation. The individual distillation column is in essence, a series of units in which the two processes of partial condensation and partial vaporisation are effected simultaneously.

DISTILLATION OF TWO COMPONENT MIXTURES

For a binary mixture with a normal T–x–y curve, the vapour is always richer in the more volatile component than the liquid from which it is formed. For distillation, mainly three methods are practiced. All of them rely on this fact. They are

1. Batch or differential distillation,
2. Equilibrium or flash distillation and
3. Rectification.

In the first two methods, all the vapours are removed as such and condensed as product (Fig. 4.6a). In the third method, part of the vapour is condensed and returned to the still. In this way, rectification is different from the rest (Fig. 4.6b). Rectification is important from the point of view of industrial applications.

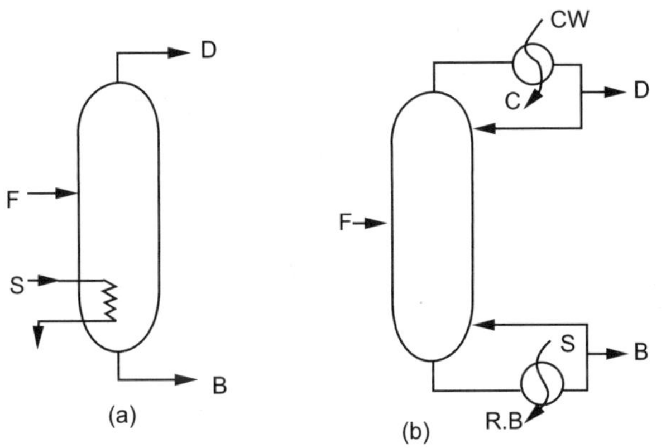

Fig. 4.6 Schematic representation of (a) differential / flash distillation and (b) rectification C: Condenser, R.B: Reboiler, CW: Cooling water, S: Steam

DIFFERENTIAL DISTILLATION

Let a batch of liquid be charged to a still fitted with a heating device. The charge is boiled slowly and the vapours are withdrawn as rapidly as they form to a condenser where they are liquefied and the condensate, that is the distillate, is collected in a receiver. A typical differential distillation setup is shown in Fig. 4.7. The equipment is merely a large scale laboratory distillation flask and condenser. The distillate is richer in MVC than the liquid. The liquid remaining in the still becomes steadily lean in that component and the composition of the distillate progressively changes. While the vapour formed over a short period is in equilibrium with the liquid, the total vapour formed is not in equilibrium with the residual liquid. At the end of the process, the liquid which has not been vaporised is removed as the bottom product. This process was first analysed by Rayleigh.

Rayleigh Equation

Let F moles of liquid consisting of a MVC (A) and a LVC (B) be charged to a still. Let n be the number of moles of liquid left in the still at any time, y and x be the vapour and liquid compositions in mole fractions respectively of MVC and the number of moles of A left in the still be n_A. n_A is also equal to nx. If a small amount of liquid dn is vaporised, the change in the number of moles of component A is dn_A which is also equal to $y\ dn$.

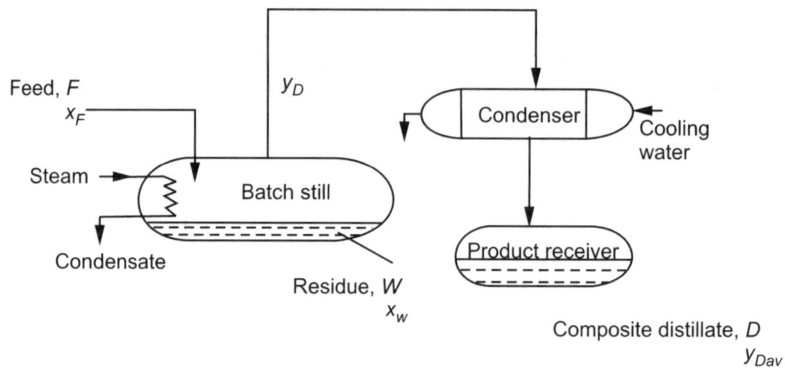

Fig. 4.7 Differential distillation setup

$$dn_A = d(nx)$$

$$= ndx + xdn \tag{4.26}$$

$$ydn = ndx + xdn \tag{4.27}$$

$$(y - x)dn = ndx \tag{4.28}$$

$$\frac{dn}{n} = \frac{dx}{y - x} \tag{4.29}$$

The above equation can be integrated between the initial and final concentrations, x_F and x_W.

$$\int_W^F \frac{dn}{n} = \int_{x_W}^{x_F} \frac{dx}{y - x} \tag{4.30}$$

$$\ln \frac{F}{W} = \int_{x_W}^{x_F} \frac{dx}{y - x} \tag{4.31}$$

This equation is known as the *Rayleigh equation.*

The function $\frac{dx}{y-x}$ can be integrated numerically if an algebraic equilibrium relationship between y and x is available such as $y = \frac{\alpha x}{1+x(\alpha-1)}$ or graphically by plotting $\frac{1}{y-x}$ as ordinate against x as abscissa and determining the area under the curve between the indicated limits. The data for this may be taken from the vapour–liquid equilibrium relationship. The composition y_{Dav} of the composite distillate can be determined by the simple material balance.

$$Fx_F = Dy_{D\ av} + Wx_w \tag{4.32}$$

ILLUSTRATIONS

4B 100 moles of a liquid mixture containing 50 mol% n-heptane and 50 mol% n-octane is subjected to differential distillation at atmospheric pressure with 60 moles of the liquid distilled. Compute the composition of composite distillate and residue.

Equilibrium data:

x	0.5	0.46	0.42	0.38	0.34	0.32
y	0.689	0.648	0.608	0.567	0.523	0.497

where x and y refer to the mole fraction of the more volatile component in the liquid and vapour respectively.

Solution

Feed is 100 moles. It is given that 60 moles of the liquid feed is differentially distilled. Feed $F = 100$ mol, distillate $D = 60$ mol, so the residue $W = 40$ mol.

Of the hydrocarbons in the liquid mixture, the lower hydrocarbon is the MVC.

Mole fraction of MVC in the feed $x_F = 0.5$.

Data required for the graphical integration are given in Table 4.2.

By the Rayleigh equation, we have $\ln \frac{F}{W} = \int_{x_W}^{x_F} \frac{dx}{y - x}$

$$\ln \frac{100}{40} = \int_{x_W}^{0.5} \frac{dx}{y - x}$$

$$0.916 = \int_{x_W}^{0.5} \frac{dx}{y - x}$$

The function $\frac{dx}{y-x}$ is integrated graphically by plotting $\frac{1}{y-x}$ as ordinate against x as abscissa and the area under the curve from $x = 0.5$, is integrated. The integration is stopped when the area is equal to 0.916. The value of x_W is 0.33 at that point. The composition y_{Dav} of the composite distillate is determined by the simple material balance, $Fx_F = Dy_{Dav} + Wx_w$.

$$100 \times 0.5 = 60 \times y_{Dav} + 40 \times 0.33$$

So $\quad y_{Dav} = 0.614$

Table 4.2 Data required for graphical integration

x	y	$\frac{1}{y-x}$
0.5	0.689	5.29
0.46	0.648	5.32
0.42	0.608	5.32
0.38	0.567	5.35
0.34	0.523	5.50
0.32	0.497	5.65

The composite distillate contains 61.4mol% n-heptane and the residue contains 33mol% n-heptane. The graphical solution is shown in Fig. 4.8.

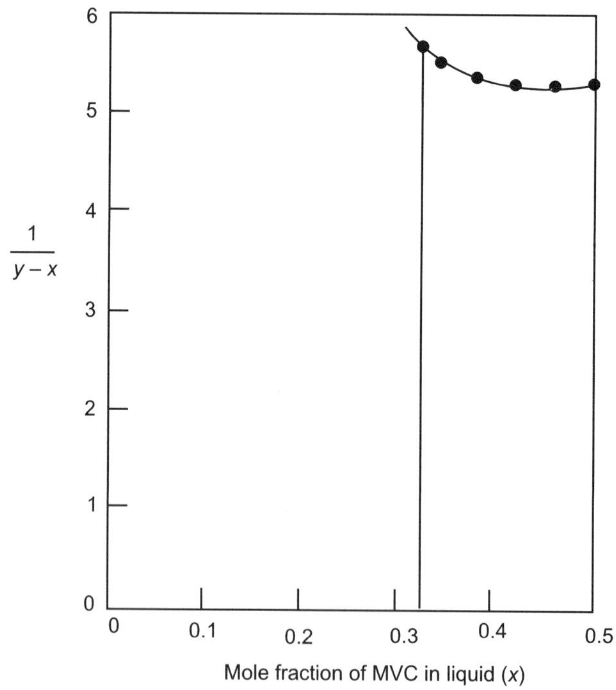

Fig. 4.8 Graphical solution for 4B

4C A liquid mixture containing 60 mol% acetone and 40 mol% water is to be distilled differentially at 1 atm pressure to vaporise 30 mol% of feed. Compute the composition of the composite distillate and residue. The equilibrium data is as follows:

x	0.1	0.2	0.3	0.5	0.6	0.8	0.9
y	0.755	0.815	0.83	0.85	0.86	0.9	0.935

where x and y refer to the mole fraction of the more volatile component in the liquid and in the vapour respectively.

Solution

Let the feed be 100 moles. It is given that 30 mol% of the liquid feed is differentially distilled.

$F = 100$ mol, distillate $D = 30$ mol, so the residue = 70 mol.

In the liquid mixture, acetone is the MVC.

Mole fraction of the MVC in the feed, $x_F = 0.6$

Data required for the graphical integration are given in Table 4.3.

By Rayleigh equation, we have $\ln \frac{F}{W} = \int_{x_W}^{x_F} \frac{dx}{y - x}$

$$\ln \frac{100}{70} = \int_{x_W}^{0.6} \frac{dx}{y - x}$$

$$0.3567 = \int_{x_W}^{0.6} \frac{dx}{y - x}$$

Table 4.3 Data required for graphical integration

x	y	$\frac{1}{y - x}$
0.6	0.86	3.85
0.3	0.83	1.89
0.2	0.815	1.63
0.1	0.755	1.53

The function $\frac{dx}{y-x}$ is integrated graphically by plotting $\frac{1}{y-x}$ as ordinate against x as abscissa and the area under the curve from $x = 0.6$ is integrated. The integration is stopped when the area is equal to 0.3567. The value of x_W is 0.49 at that point.

The composition y_{Dav} of the composite distillate is determined by the simple material balance, $Fx_F = Dy_{Dav} + Wx_w$

$$100 \times 0.6 = 30 \times y_{Dav} + 70 \times 0.49$$

So, $y_{Dav} = 0.86$

The composite distillate contains 86 mol% acetone and the residue contains 49 mol% acetone.

The graphical solution is shown in Fig. 4.9.

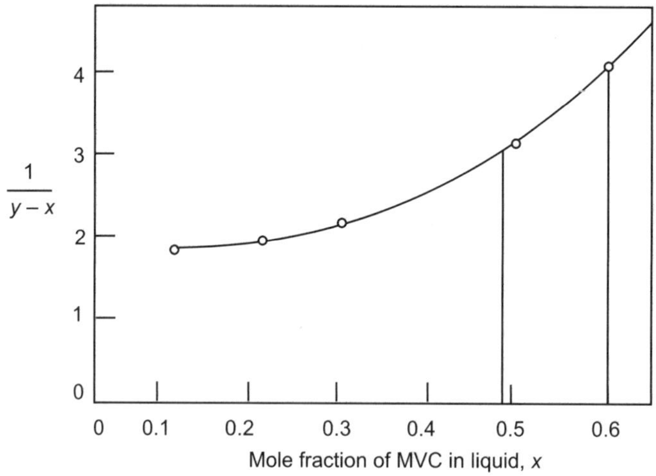

Fig. 4.9 Graphical solution for 4C

4D 100 moles of benzene (A) and toluene (B) mixture containing 50 mol% of benzene is subjected to a differential distillation at atmospheric pressure till the composition of the benzene in the residue is 33%. Calculate the total moles of the mixture distilled. The average relative volatility may be assumed to be 2.16. The equilibrium data may be obtained using the following relation.

$$y = \frac{\alpha\, x}{1 + (\alpha - 1)x}.$$

Solution

First, the equilibrium data is obtained using the information given.

x	0	0.157	0.312	0.487	0.655
y	0	0.279	0.492	0.674	0.810

where x and y are mole fractions of benzene in liquid and vapour phases respectively.

Feed is 100 moles. Feed $F = 100$ mol

Of the hydrocarbons in the liquid mixture, the lower hydrocarbon is the MVC.

Mole fraction of MVC in the feed, x_F = 0.50

Mole fraction of MVC in the residue, x_W = 0.33

Data required for the graphical integration are given in Table 4.4.

By Rayleigh equation, we have

$$\ln\frac{F}{W} = \int_{x_W}^{x_F} \frac{dx}{y-x}$$

$$\ln\frac{F}{W} = \int_{0.33}^{0.5} \frac{dx}{y-x}$$

Table 4.4 Data required for graphical integration

x	y	$y-x$	$\dfrac{1}{y-x}$
0.33	0.52	0.19	5.26
0.35	0.54	0.19	5.26
0.40	0.59	0.19	5.26
0.45	0.64	0.19	5.26
0.50	0.68	0.18	5.50

The function $\dfrac{dx}{y-x}$ is integrated graphically by plotting $\dfrac{1}{y-x}$ as ordinate against x as abscissa and the area under the curve from $x = 0.5$ to $x = 0.33$ is determined. The area is 0.9 square units.

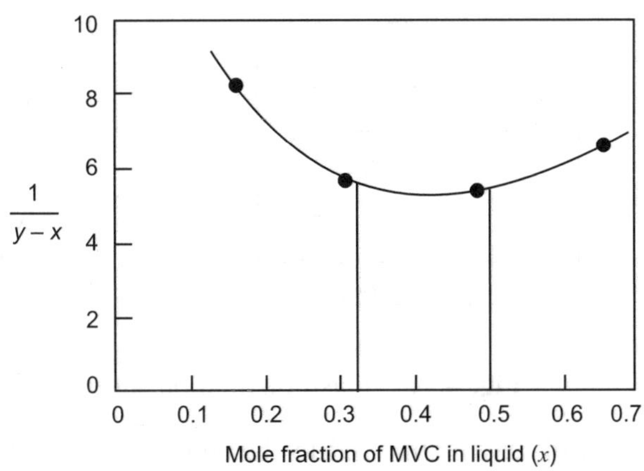

Fig. 4.10 Graphical solution for 4D

$$\ln\frac{F}{W} = 0.9$$

$$\frac{F}{W} = 2.46$$

$$\frac{100}{W} = 2.46$$

Hence, $W = 40.65$ mol

The overall balance is $F = D + W$

D moles distilled $= 100 - 40.65 = 59.35$ mol

The graphical solution is shown in Fig. 4.10.

FLASH DISTILLATION

It consists of vaporising a definite fraction of the liquid in such a way that the evolved vapour is in equilibrium with the residual liquid separating the vapour from the liquid and condensing it. The feed is pumped through a heater and the pressure is reduced by a valve (Fig. 4.11). An intimate mixture of vapour and liquid enters the vapour–liquid separator. Sufficient time is allowed for the vapour and liquid portions to separate. Because of the intimate contact between the liquid and vapour before separation, the streams are in equilibrium. The vapour and liquid leave through separate lines. This is largely done in petroleum refining. Petroleum fractions are heated in pipe stills and the heated fluid is flashed into overhead vapour and residual liquid streams each containing a number of components.

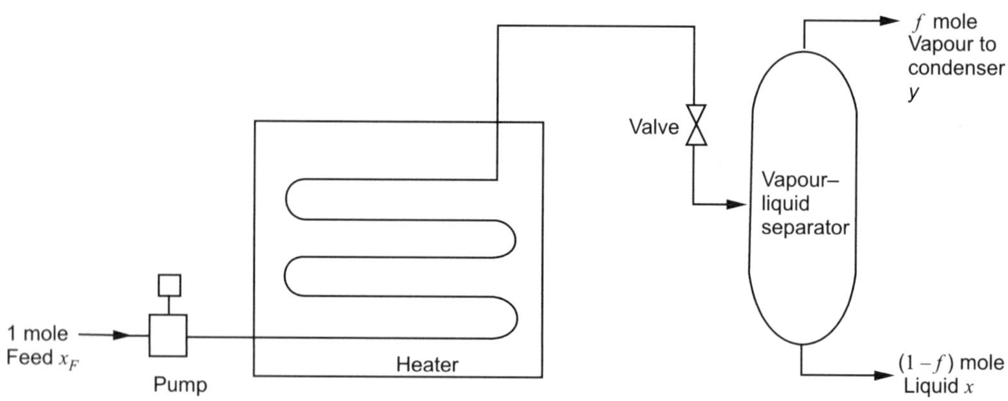

Fig. 4.11 Flash distillation setup

Consider one mole of a binary mixture fed to the equipment. Let the concentration of the feed be x_F in terms of mole faction of the MVC. Let f be the moles of feed vaporised and withdrawn continuously as vapour, $(1 - f)$ be the mole fraction of feed that leaves continuously as a liquid and y and x be the concentrations in mole fraction of the MVC in the vapour and liquid respectively.

Overall balance: $1 = f + (1 - f)$ (4.33)

Material balance for the MVC based on one mole of feed gives,

$$x_F = fy + (1 - f)x \tag{4.34}$$

$$x_F - (1-f)x = fy \tag{4.35}$$

$$\frac{x_F}{y} - \frac{1-f}{f}x = y \tag{4.36}$$

This is the equation of a straight line with slope $-\left(\frac{1-f}{f}\right)$ and is known as the operating line as it denotes the operating conditions. The point of intersection between the operating line and the diagonal can be found by letting $x = x_F$ in the above equation.

$$y = -\left(\frac{1-f}{f}\right)x_F + \frac{x_F}{f} = x_F \tag{4.37}$$

So the operating line passes through (x_F, x_F) and has a slope of $-\left(\frac{1-f}{f}\right)$. As (x, y) represents a point on the equilibrium curve, the operating line intersects the equilibrium curve on (x, y). Thus if x_F and f are known, the composition of the vapour and liquid can be obtained by plotting the operating line, diagonal and equilibrium curve on the same equilibrium diagram.

ILLUSTRATIONS

4E A liquid mixture containing 60 mol% heptane and 40% octane is flash distilled such that 60 mol% of the feed is distilled. Estimate the composition of the residue and distillate.

x	0	0.157	0.312	0.489	0.655	1.0
y	0	0.279	0.492	0.674	0.810	1.0

where x and y are mole fractions of heptane in the liquid and vapour phase respectively.

Solution

Let the feed be 100 mol. Feed $F = 100$ mol. Of the hydrocarbons in the liquid mixture, the lower hydrocarbon is the MVC. $x_F = 0.60$

It is given that 60 mol% of the feed is flash distilled. That is, $f = 0.6$

$$\text{Slope of operating line} = -\left(\frac{1-f}{f}\right) = \frac{-0.4}{0.6} = \frac{-2}{3}$$

The equilibrium curve is plotted making use of the equilibrium data. The diagonal is drawn by connecting the opposite corners of the graph sheet. Then the operating line is drawn using the facts, it passes through (x_F, x_F) and has a slope of $-\frac{2}{3}$. The operating line intersects the equilibrium curve on (x, y). Here it is (0.67, 0.49). The graphical solution is given in Fig. 4.12.

So, the distillate contains 67 mol% heptane and 33 mol% octane and the residue contains 49 mol% heptane and 51 mol% octane.

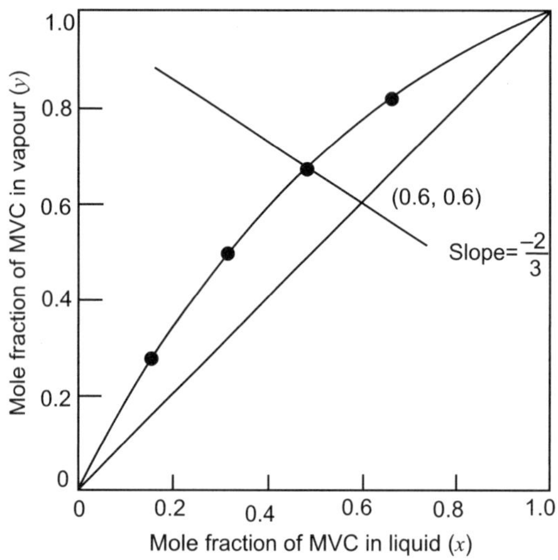

Fig. 4.12 Graphical solution for 4E

4F Using Raoult's law, calculate T–x–y of the system hexane (P_1) – heptane (P_2) at 760 mm Hg pressure and prepare the boiling point and vapour–liquid equilibrium diagram and calculate the average relative volatility of this system. 60% of the hexane–heptane mixture containing 50 mol% hexane is vaporised at the atmospheric pressure. If the vapour–liquid portions are in equilibrium, compute their composition.

Data:

Temperature (°C)	69	70	75	85	95	99.2
P_1 (mm Hg)	760	780	915	1 225	1 571	1 765
P_2 (mm Hg)	295	302	348	498	675	760

Solution

(i) From the data given, we can infer that the boiling point of hexane is 69°C and that of heptane is 99.2°C, as at these temperatures, the vapour pressure is equal to the atmospheric pressure. Hence hexane is the more volatile component (MVC) or low boiler or component A and heptane is the less volatile component (LVC) or high boiler or component B. We can compute the mole fraction of MVC in the heavy phase—liquid phase (x), the mole fraction of MVC in the light phase—vapour phase (y) and the relative volatility (α) of the benzene–toluene system using the formulae derived earlier.

They are, $x = \dfrac{P - P_2}{P_1 - P_2}$, $y = \dfrac{P_1}{P} x_A$ and $\alpha = \dfrac{P_1}{P_2}$

The results are given in Table 4.5.

Table 4.5 T–x–y data

T(°C)	$x = \dfrac{P - P_2}{P_1 - P_2}$	$y = \dfrac{P_1}{P} x_A$	$\alpha = \dfrac{P_1}{P_2}$
69	1	1	2.576
70	0.958	0.983	2.583
75	0.727	0.875	2.629
85	0.360	0.58	2.460
95	0.095	0.196	2.327
99.2	0	0	2.322

$$\alpha_{av} = \sqrt{2.322 \times 2.629} = 2.471$$

Figure 4.13 gives the T–x–y diagram.

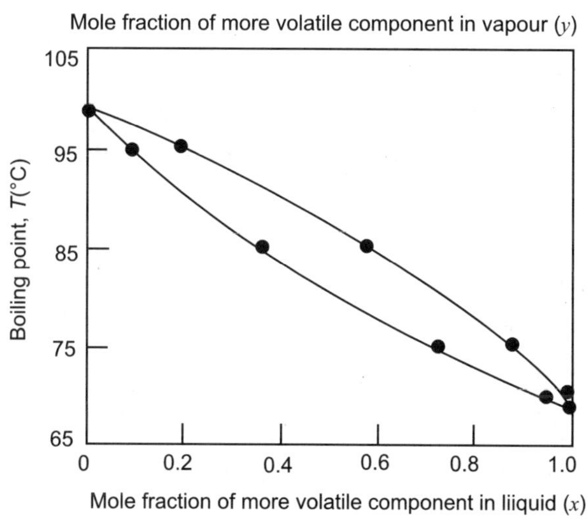

Fig. 4.13 Graphical solution for 4F

(ii) Let the feed be 100 mol. Feed $F = 100$ mol. Of the hydrocarbons in the liquid mixture, the lower hydrocarbon is the MVC. $x_F = 0.50$

It is given that 60 mol% of the feed is distilled, such that the vapour and liquid portions are in equilibrium. So, it is flash distillation and is $f = 0.6$

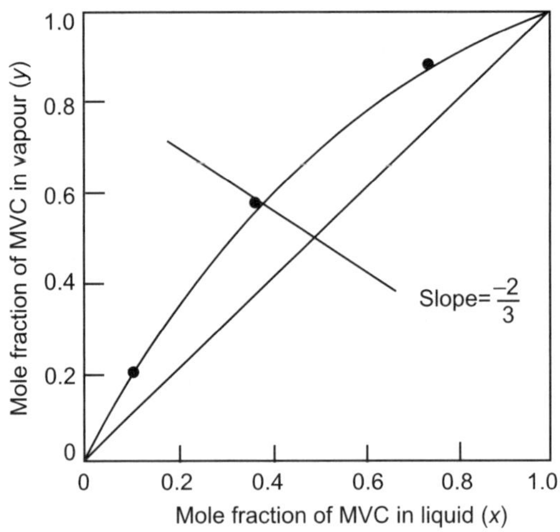

Fig. 4.14 Graphical solution for 4F

$$\text{Slope of operating line} = -\left(\frac{1-f}{f}\right) = \frac{-0.4}{0.6} = \frac{-2}{3}$$

The equilibrium curve is plotted making use of the equilibrium data. The diagonal is drawn by connecting the opposite corners of the graph sheet. Then the operating line is drawn using the facts, it passes through (x_F, x_F) and has a slope of $-\frac{2}{3}$. The operating line intersects the equilibrium curve on (x, y). Here it is (0.58, 0.37).

So ,the distillate contains 58 mol% hexane and 42 mol% heptane and the residue contains 37 mol% hexane and 63 mol% heptane. Fig. 4.14 shows the graphical solution for this illustration.

4G An equimolar liquid mixture of A and B is flash distilled such that 70 mol% of the feed is distilled. Estimate the composition of residue and distillate.

x	0	0.08	0.185	0.251	0.335	0.489	0.651	0.788	0.914	1.0
y	0	0.233	0.428	0.514	0.608	0.729	0.814	0.904	0.963	1.0

where x and y are mole fractions of heptane in the liquid and vapour phase respectively.

Solution

Let the feed be 100 mol. Feed $F = 100$ mol

Of the components in the liquid mixture, A is the MVC. $x_F = 0.50$

It is given that 70 mol% of the feed is flash distilled. That is $f = 0.7$

$$\text{Slope of operating line} = -\left(\frac{1-f}{f}\right) = \frac{-0.3}{0.7}$$

The equilibrium curve is plotted making use of the equilibrium data. The diagonal is drawn by connecting the opposite corners of the graph sheet. Then the operating line is drawn using the facts, it passes through (x_F, x_F) and has a slope of $-\frac{3}{7}$. The operating line intersects the equilibrium curve on (x,y). Here it is (0.59, 0.32). The graphical solution is given in Fig. 4.15.

So the distillate contains 59 mol% A and 41 mol% B and the residue contains 32 mol% A and 68 mol% B.

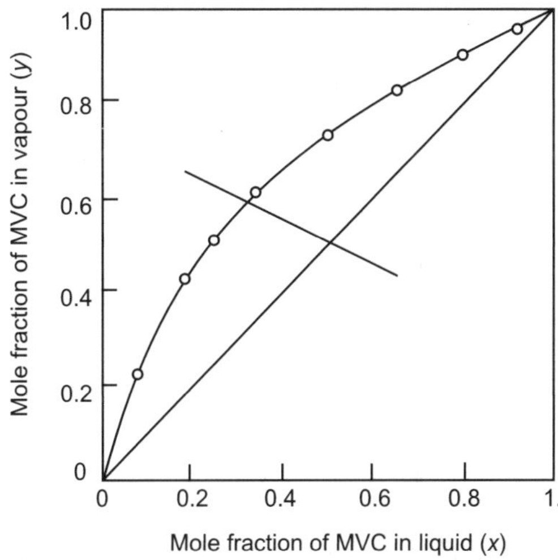

Fig. 4.15 Graphical solution for 4G

Flash distillation versus differential distillation

Flash distillation	Differential distillation
Involves vaporising a definite fraction of a batch of liquid keeping the liquid and the vapour in intimate contact so that at the end of the operation V is in equilibrium with L.	Involves operation in such a way that the vapour generated by boiling the liquid is withdrawn from contact with the liquid and condensed as fast as it is formed.
The relationship between L and V at the end of the operation is established by the equilibrium curve.	There is continuous change in composition of L and V during the process.

RECTIFICATION

Flash distillation and differential distillation lead only to partial enrichment. They are not effective if the components to be separated are of comparable volatility. The condensed vapour and residual liquid will be far from pure. Even after successive re-distillations, only small amounts of nearly pure components can be recovered. In such cases, rectification has to be resorted to. It is a multistage, counter current distillation operation which enables the separation of a solution into its components, recovering each at any desired purity level.

The rectification column consists of a cascade of ideal plates. The plates are numbered serially from the top. In the nth plate (Fig. 4.16), a stream of liquid, L_{n-1} mol h^{-1} of composition x_{n-1}, is brought into intimate contact with a stream of vapour, V_{n+1} mol h^{-1} of composition y_{n+1}.

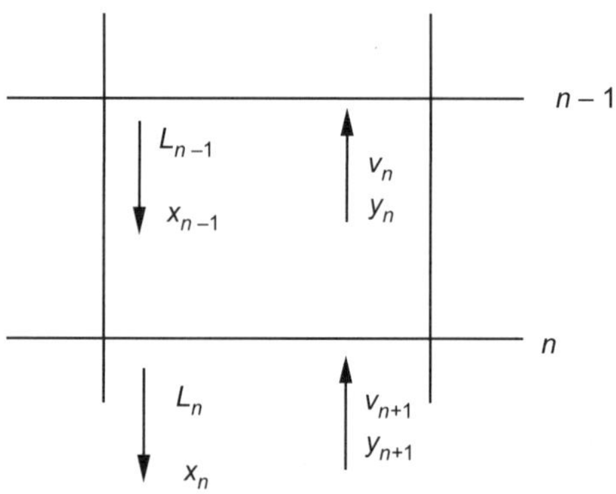

Fig. 4.16 Fluid streams of the nth plate

If plate n is ideal, the vapour and liquid streams leaving the plate will be in equilibrium. So x_n, y_n are in equilibrium or a point on the equilibrium curve. The streams leaving the plate are in equilibrium while those entering are not. When the vapour from plate $n + 1$ and the liquid from plate $n - 1$ are brought into intimate contact, their concentrations move towards an equilibrium state. Some of the MVC is vaporised from the liquid decreasing the liquid concentration from x_{n-1} to x_n and some of the LVC is condensed from the vapour increasing the vapour concentration from y_{n+1} to y_n. Since the liquid and the vapour are at their respective bubble and dew points, the heat necessary to vaporise the MVC must be supplied by the heat released by the condensation of the LVC. Each plate then acts as an interchange apparatus in which the MVC is transferred to the vapour phase and the LVC is transferred to the liquid phase.

CONTINUOUS RECTIFICATION

A continuous fractionating column (Fig. 4.17) consists of rectifying and stripping sections. The column is fed near the centre with a definite flow of feed of definite concentration. The feed is mostly a liquid at its boiling point. The plate on which the feed enters is known as the feed plate. All plates above the feed plate form the rectifying section and all plates below the feed plate including the feed plate itself, form the stripping section. The feed flows down the stripping section to the bottom of the column in which a definite level of liquid is maintained. The liquid flows by gravity to the reboiler which is a steam-heated vaporiser that generates vapour and returns it to the bottom of the column. The vapour passes up the entire column. At one end of the reboiler is a weir. The bottom product is withdrawn from the pool of the liquid on the downstream side of the weir and flows through the cooler. The cooler can preheat the feed by heat exchange with the hot products at the bottom.

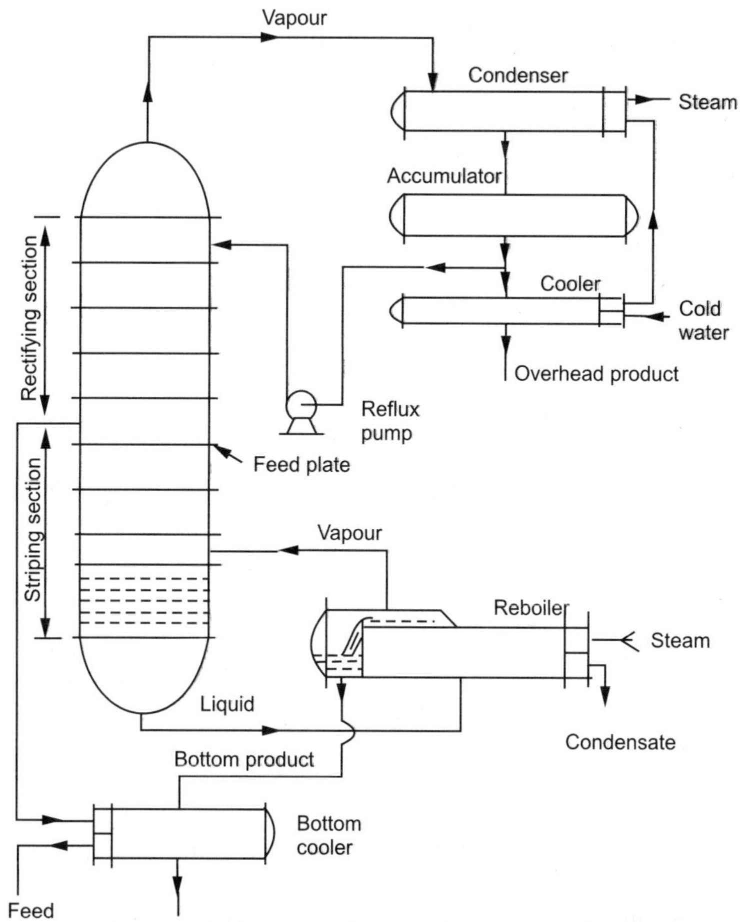

Fig. 4.17 Fractionating column

The vapours rising through the rectifying section are completely condensed in the condenser and the condensate is collected in an accumulator, in which a definite level is maintained. The reflux pump takes the excess liquid from the accumulator and delivers it to the top plate of the tower. This liquid stream is called reflux. It provides the down-flowing stream in the rectifying section that is needed to act on the ascending vapours. Without reflux, no rectification would occur in the rectifying section and the concentration of the overhead product would be no greater than that of the vapour rising from the feed plate. The condensate that is not picked by the reflux pump is cooled in the product cooler, which is a heat exchanger, and is withdrawn as the overhead product. *If no azeotropes are involved, both the overhead and bottom products may be obtained in any desired purity, if enough plates and adequate reflux are provided.*

Overall Material Balance for a Two Component System

The column is fed with a feed F mol h^{-1} of concentration x_F and delivers D mol h^{-1} of overhead product of concentration x_D and B mol h^{-1} of bottom product of concentration x_B.

Then overall balance: $F = D + B$ (4.38)

MVC balance: $Fx_F = Dx_D + Bx_B$ (4.39)

Rectifying Section

The quantity D is the difference between the flow rates of the streams entering and leaving the top of the column.

$$D = V_a - L_a \tag{4.40}$$

As equimolar overflow is assumed along with the assumption of equal molar latent heats for the components of the mixture, the difference between the flow rates of vapour and liquid anywhere in the upper section of the column is also equal to D.

$$D = V_{n+1} - L_n \tag{4.41}$$

In other words, D is the net upward flow rate of material in the upper section of the column.

Component balance gives $Dx_D = V_a y_a - L_a x_a = V_{n+1} y_{n+1} - L_n x_n$ (4.42)

Dx_D is the net upward flow rate of component A in the rectifying section of the column. This too is constant throughout the section. These details are shown in Fig. 4.18.

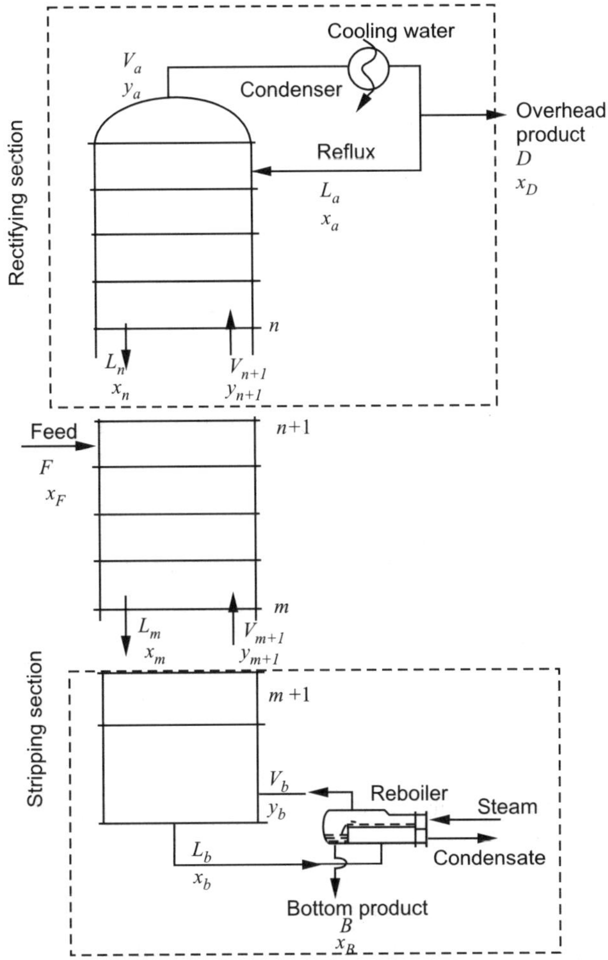

Fig. 4.18 Material balance

Stripping Section

In the lower part of the column too, the net flow rates are assumed to be constant but in a downward direction. The net flow rate of total material equals B.

$$B = L_b - V_b = L_m - V_{m+1} \tag{4.43}$$

The net flow rate of component A is Bx_B.

$$Bx_B = L_b x_b - V_b y_b = L_m x_m - V_{m+1} y_{m+1} \tag{4.44}$$

Operating Lines

As there are two sections in the column, there are two operating lines—one for the rectifying section and the other for the stripping section.

$$y_{n+1} = \frac{L_n}{V_{n+1}}x_n + \frac{V_a y_a - L_a x_a}{V_{n+1}} \tag{4.45}$$

On substitution of the values of $V_a y_a - L_a x_a$

$$y_{n+1} = \frac{L_n}{V_{n+1}}x_n + \frac{D x_D}{V_{n+1}} \tag{4.46}$$

The slope of the line is as usual the ratio of flow of the liquid stream to that of the vapour stream.

$$y_{n+1} = \frac{L_n}{L_n + D}x_n + \frac{D x_D}{L_n + D} \tag{4.47}$$

For the stripping section, the composition material balance gives

$$V_{m+1} y_{m+1} = L_m x_m - B x_B \tag{4.48}$$

$$y_{m+1} = \frac{L_m}{V_{m+1}}x_m - \frac{B x_B}{V_{m+1}} \tag{4.49}$$

Here also, the slope is the ratio of liquid rate to vapour rate. V_{m+1} can also be eliminated.

$$y_{m+1} = \frac{L_m}{L_m - B}x_m - \frac{B x_B}{L_m - B} \tag{4.50}$$

Analysis of the performance of the plate columns are based on

1. Material balance
2. Energy balance
3. Phase equilibria

McCABE–THIELE'S METHOD FOR FRACTIONATING COLUMNS

When the operating lines are plotted on the x–y diagram along with the equilibrium curve, McCabe–Thiele's step by step construction [2] can be used for computing the number of ideal plates needed to effect a definite concentration difference in either the rectifying section or the stripping section. For most cases of distillation, the molal flow rates of vapour and liquid are nearly constant in each section. For these cases, the operating line is almost straight. This results from equal molal latent heat of vaporisation, as a result of which each mole of condensing LVC vaporises one mole of MVC.

Hence in the rectifying section,

$$V_n = V_{n+1} = V_{n-1} = V \tag{4.51}$$

$$L_n = L_{n+1} = L_{n-1} = L \tag{4.52}$$

and in the stripping section,

$$V_m = V_{m+1} = V_{m-1} = \overline{V} \tag{4.53}$$

$$L_m = L_{m+1} = L_{m-1} = \overline{L} \tag{4.54}$$

Under these conditions, the operating line becomes a straight line and it can be plotted if the coordinates of any two points are known. If L_n, V_n, L_m and V_m are not constant, the operating lines will be curved. Then, plotting them requires energy balance.

REFLUX RATIO AND REFLUX LINE

Reflux ratio is defined as the ratio of reflux to the overhead product

$$R_D = \frac{L}{D} = \frac{V - D}{D} \tag{4.55}$$

This is very useful in the analysis of the fractionating column.

For constant molal overflow, the operating line for the rectifying section is given by,

$$y_{n+1} = \frac{L}{L+D}x_n + \frac{D\,x_D}{L+D}$$

$$= \frac{\frac{L}{D}}{\frac{L}{D}+1}x_n + \frac{\frac{D\,x_D}{D}}{\frac{L}{D}+1}$$

$$= \frac{R_D}{R_D+1}x_n + \frac{x_D}{R_D+1} \tag{4.56}$$

The y-intercept of the operating line for the rectifying section, rectifying line is $\dfrac{x_D}{R_D+1}$. The concentration x_D is set by the conditions of the design. R_D is an operating variable, that can be controlled at will by adjusting the split between reflux and overhead product. A point on the upper end of the rectifying line can be obtained by setting x_n equal to x_D.

$$y_{n+1} = \frac{R_D}{R_D+1}x_D + \frac{x_D}{R_D+1} = \frac{x_D(R_D+1)}{(R_D+1)} = x_D \tag{4.57}$$

So, the rectifying line intersects the diagonal at (x_D, x_D).

CONDENSER AND TOP PLATE

The concentration of the vapour from the top plate is y_1 and that of the reflux is x_C, (Fig. 4.19). So, the upper end of the rectifying line is (x_C, y_1). But the concentrations of the vapour from the top plate, of the reflux to the top plate and of the overhead product all are equal and can be denoted by x_D. So, the starting point of the operating line is (x_D, x_D) which is the point of intersection of the rectifying line and the diagonal.

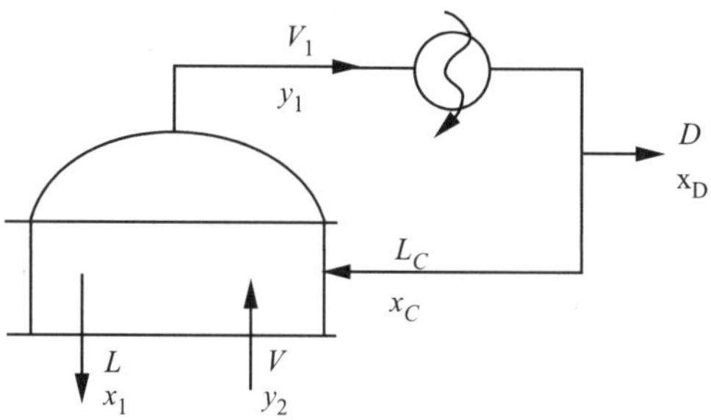

Fig. 4.19 Top plate and condenser

BOTTOM PLATE AND REBOILER

The lowest point of the operating line for the stripping section, stripping line is (x_b, y_r), the concentrations of the liquid leaving the bottom plate and the vapour coming from the reboiler are as shown in Fig. 4.20.

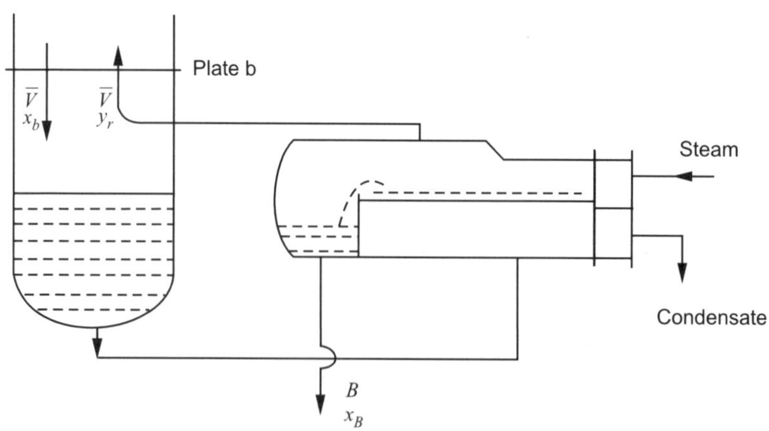

Fig. 4.20 Bottom plate and reboiler

The vapour leaving the reboiler is in equilibrium with the liquid leaving the reboiler as product. That is, (x_B, y_r) is a point on the equilibrium curve. In other words, the reboiler acts as an ideal plate. It is a necessary requirement to attain the composition of the bottom product, x_B. So, the stripping line terminates at (x_B, x_B) on the diagonal.

FEED PLATE

At the plate where feed is admitted, the liquid rate, the vapour rate or both change, depending on the thermal condition of the feed. The feed may be a cold liquid, saturated liquid, partially vaporised, saturated vapour or super-heated vapour. All five feed types can be characterised by the use of a single factor q, where q is the number of moles of liquid flow in the stripping section of the column resulting from the introduction of one mole of feed on the feed plate.

As shown in Fig. 4.21, when the feed is a cold liquid, some amount of vapour in the rectifying section condenses to supply the heat required to raise the temperature of the feed from the feed temperature to its boiling point. Hence, the number of moles of liquid flow in the stripping section of the column resulting from the introduction of one mole of feed on the feed plate will be more than one. When the feed is a liquid at its boiling point, there is no sensible heat load and the number of moles of liquid flow in the stripping section of the column resulting from the introduction of one mole of feed on the feed plate will be one. When the feed is a mixture of liquid and vapour, the number of moles of liquid flow in the stripping section of the column resulting from the introduction of one mole of feed on the feed plate will be more than zero but less than one. When the feed is a vapour at its dew point, the number of moles of liquid flow in the stripping section of the column resulting from the introduction of one mole of feed on the feed plate will be zero. When the feed is a super-heated vapour, the sensible heat brought in by the feed vaporises some amount of liquid present in the rectifying section and the number of moles of liquid flow in the stripping section of the column resulting from the introduction of one mole of feed on the feed plate will be less than zero.

The numerical value of a q will be

> 1	if the feed is a cold liquid
$= 1$	if it is a saturated liquid
> 0 but < 1	if it is partially vaporised
$= 0$	if it is a saturated vapour
< 0	if it is a super-heated vapour

The value of q for liquid feed can be found from the equation given below.

$$q = 1 + \frac{C_{P,L}(T_b - T_F)}{\lambda} \tag{4.58}$$

For vapour,
$$q = \frac{C_{P,V}(T_F - T_d)}{\lambda} \tag{4.59}$$

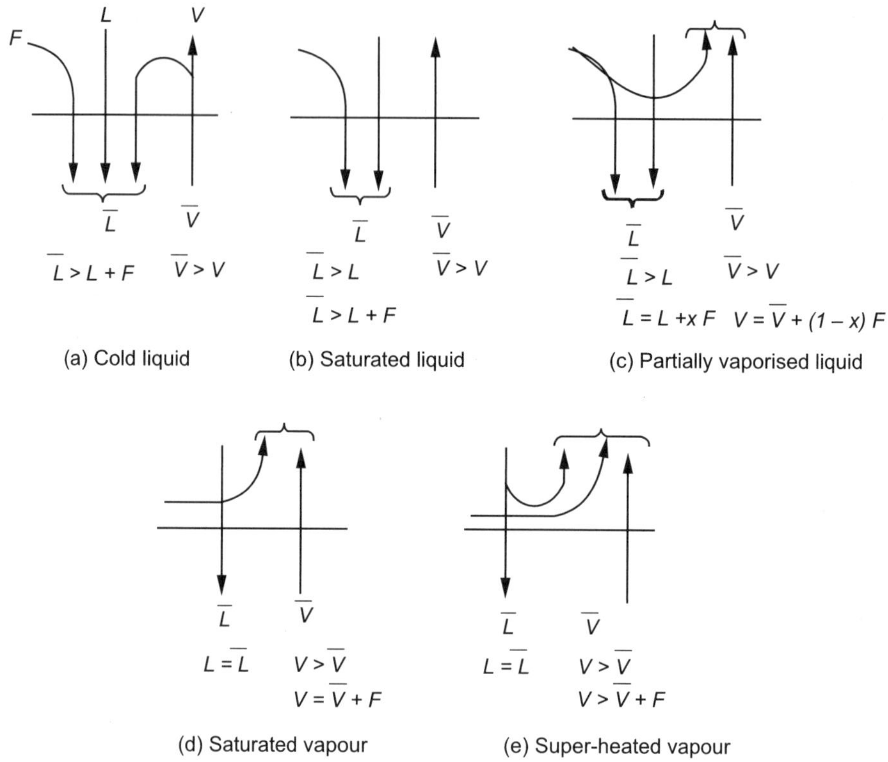

Fig. 4.21 Liquid and vapour rates after the feed plate for various feed conditions
F: feed, L: liquid in Rs. $\bar{L}$: liquid in SS, V: vapour in Rs, V: vapour in SS
x: mole fraction of liquid in feed, RS: rectifying section, SS: striping section

Here, T_b is the boiling point of the liquid, T_d is the dew point of the vapour, T_F is the temperature of the feed and λ is latent heat of vaporisation. The value of q can also be found using the expression $q = \frac{[H_V - H_F]}{[H_V - H_L]}$, where H_V, H_F and H_L represent specific enthalpies of the vapour, feed and liquid respectively.

FEED LINE

The feed line is the locus of the point of intersection of the operating lines for the rectifying and stripping sections. Equation of the feed line can be found as follows.

Total flow rate of liquid in the stripping section is

$$\overline{L} = L + qF \quad \text{or} \quad \overline{L} - L = qF \tag{4.60}$$

The total flow rate of vapour in the rectifying section is

$$V = \overline{V} + (1 - q)F \quad \text{or} \quad V - \overline{V} = (1 - q)F \tag{4.61}$$

For constant molal overflow, the material balance equations are

$$V y_{n+1} = L x_n + D x_D \tag{4.62}$$

$$\overline{V}\, y_{m+1} = \overline{L}\, x_m - B\, x_B \tag{4.63}$$

Let their point of intersection be (x, y). Then $y_{n+1} = y_{m+1} = y$ and $x_n = x_m = x$

Equation (4.62) becomes $\quad V y = L x + D x_D$ and (4.64)

Equation (4.63) becomes $\quad \overline{V}\, y = \overline{L}\, x - B\, x_B$ (4.65)

(4.64) – (4.65) becomes $\quad y\,(V - \overline{V}) = (L - \overline{L})\, x + D\, x_D + B\, x_B$

$$= (L - \overline{L})x + F\, x_F \tag{4.66}$$

Because, from equation (4.39), $D x_D + B x_B = F x_F$

Substituting the values of $(V - \overline{V})$ and $(L - \overline{L})$

$$(1 - q)F y = -qF x + F x_F \tag{4.67}$$

$$y = -\left(\frac{q}{1 - q}\right) x + \frac{x_F}{(1 - q)} \tag{4.68}$$

This is the equation of the feed line; the point of intersection of the rectifying line and stripping line lies on this. Its position depends only on x_F and q. This line crosses the diagonal at $x = x_F$. Hence, the feed line passes through (x_F, x_F) and has a slope of $\frac{-q}{1-q}$. The feed line can be drawn making use of a point on the line and the slope.

McCABE–THIELE METHOD FOR FINDING THEORETICAL NUMBER OF PLATES

1. Draw the diagonal and mark (x_F, x_F), (x_D, x_D), (x_B, x_B) on the diagonal.
2. Draw the equilibrium curve on the same graph using given equilibrium data or relative volatility value.
3. Locate the feed line. It passes through (x_F, x_F). Its slope is $\frac{-q}{(1-q)}$ where q is the number of moles of liquid in the stripping section for every mole of feed fed on the feed plate. The feed line depends on the thermal conditions of the feed.

   (a) If it is cold liquid, the feed line slopes upward to the right.
   (b) If it is a saturated liquid, the feed line is vertical.
   (c) If it is a mixture of liquid and vapour, the feed line slopes upward and to the left.
   (d) If it is a saturated vapour, the feed line is horizontal.

(e) If it is super-heated vapour, the feed line slopes downward and to the left.

Figure 4.22 shows the feed lines for the five different thermal conditions.

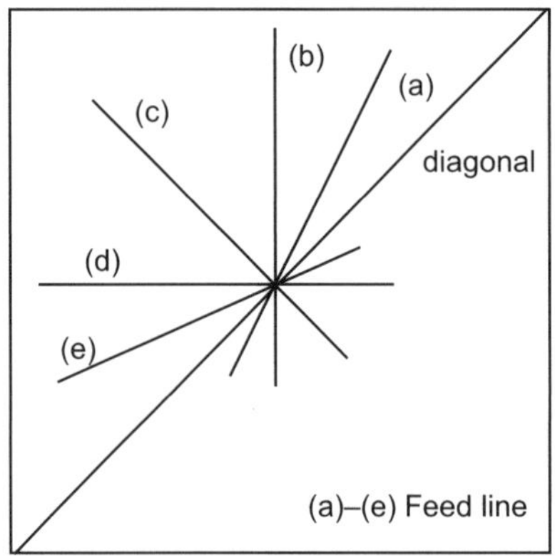

Fig. 4.22 Dependence of feed line on thermal condition of feed

4. Calculate the y intercept of the rectifying line using $\frac{x_D}{R_D+1}$. Join the intercept with (x_D, x_D) to get the rectifying line. The rectifying line is drawn making use of a point on the line and the y intercept.
5. Join the point of intersection of the rectifying line and the feed line with (x_B, x_B) to get the stripping line. The stripping line is drawn making use of two points on the line.
6. After the operating lines have been plotted, the number of ideal plates is found by the usual step by step construction which may be started either at the bottom of the stripping line or at the top of rectifying line.

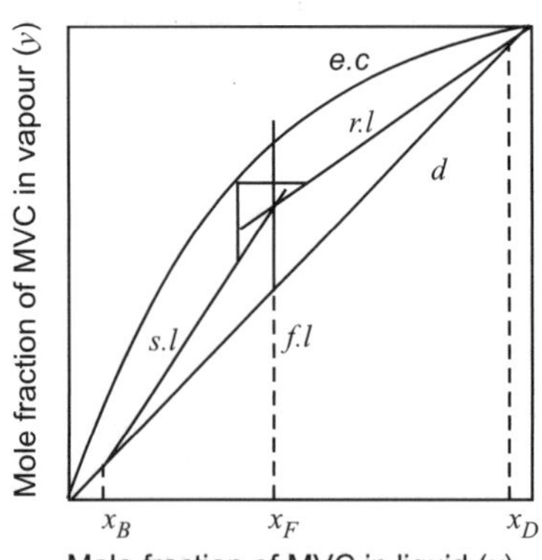

Fig. 4.23 Feed plate location
d: diagonal, $e.c$: equilibrium curve, $f.l$: feed line
$r.l$: rectification line, $s.l$: striping line

7. As the point of intersection of the operating lines is approached, the steps should be transferred from the rectifying line to the stripping line as soon as a value of x less than the x-coordinate of the point of intersection of the two operating lines is reached. The feed plate is represented by a triangle that has one corner on the rectifying line and the other on the stripping line. Figure 4.23 shows the location of a typical feed plate.

ILLUSTRATIONS

4H A continuous fractionating column is to be designed to separate 10 000 kg h^{-1} of a mixture of 50 mol% benzene and 50 mol% toluene to give an overhead product containing 98 mol% benzene and a bottom product of 97 mol% toluene. A molar reflux ratio of 3 is to be used. Calculate (a) moles of overhead and bottom products obtained per hour and (b) number of ideal plates and location of the feed plate: feed is at its boiling point.

Equilibrium data:

Mole fraction of benzene in liquid	1.0	0.77	0.66	0.46	0.29	0.14	0.01	0
Mole fraction of benzene in vapour	1.0	0.90	0.83	0.68	0.50	0.28	0.03	0

Solution

The distillation column splits the feed (F) into a distillate (D) richer in the MVC and a bottom product (B), richer in the LVC.

Average molecular weight of feed $= 0.5 \times 78 + 0.5 \times 92 = 85$

Feed = 10 000 kg $= \dfrac{10\,000}{85} = 117.65$ kmol

Mole fraction of benzene in the feed (x_F) $= 0.5$

Mole fraction of benzene in the overhead product (x_D) $= 0.98$

Mole fraction of benzene in the bottom product (x_B) $= 0.03$

Overall material balance: $F = B + D$

$$117.65 = B + D \tag{1}$$

Benzene balance: $Fx_F = Bx_B + Dx_D$

$$0.5 \times 117.65 = 0.03B + 0.98D \tag{2}$$

From (1) and (2) $B = 59.45$ kmol h^{-1}

$$D = 58.20 \text{ kmol h}^{-1}$$

Draw the diagonal and mark (x_F, x_F), (x_D, x_D) and (x_B, x_B) on the diagonal. Draw the equilibrium curve on the same graph using the given equilibrium data. Locate the feed line. The feed line passes through (x_F, x_F). The feed is a saturated liquid, so the feed line is vertical. Calculate the y intercept of the rectifying line using $\frac{x_D}{R_D+1} = \frac{0.98}{3+1} = 0.245$. Join the intercept with (x_D, x_D) to get the rectifying line. Join the point of intersection of the rectifying line and the feed line with (x_B, x_B) to get the stripping line.

After the operating lines have been plotted, the number of ideal plates is found by the usual step by step construction which may be started either at the bottom of the stripping line or at the top of the rectifying line. As the point of intersection of the operating lines is approached, the steps should be transferred from the rectifying line to the stripping line as soon as a value of x less than the x-coordinate of the point of intersection of the two operating lines is reached. The feed plate is represented by a triangle that has one corner on the rectifying line and the other on the stripping line. The number of theoretical stages is 9.7 inclusive of the reboiler. The feed plate is the sixth plate from the bottom. Figure 4.24 gives the graphical solution for this illustration.

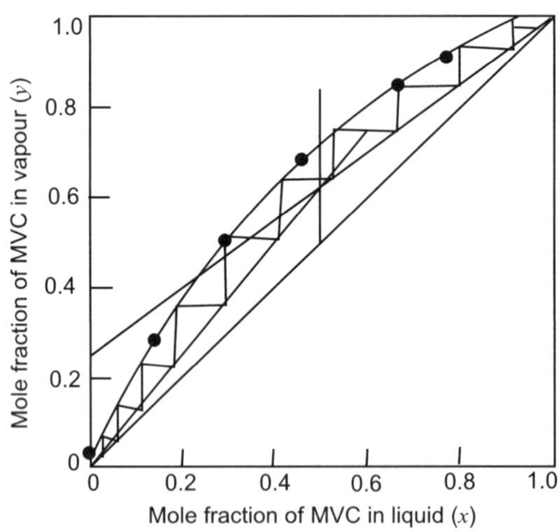

Fig. 4.24 Graphical solution for 4H

MINIMUM REFLUX

The slope of the rectifying line is $\frac{R_D}{R_D+1}$. If R_D increases, the slope of the rectifying line also increases. When R_D is infinity, that is, $V = L$ or $D = 0$ (as $R_D = \frac{L}{D}$), the slope is one and the operating lines merge with the diagonal. This condition is called total reflux. At total reflux $F = D = B = 0$. It represents one limiting case in the operation of fractionating columns. At total reflux, the number of plates is minimum. As the reflux is reduced from total reflux, the number of plates becomes higher. At a definite minimum reflux, the number of plates becomes infinity.

The minimum reflux ratio can be found by following the movement of the operating lines as the reflux is reduced. At total reflux, the operating lines follow bfa. As the reflux is reduced, the operating lines become bea, bda and so on. As the reflux is reduced, the point of intersection of the rectifying line and the stripping line moves along the feed line towards the equilibrium curve. When the operating lines touch the equilibrium curve, the reflux ratio is minimum or the reflux ratio corresponding to the point of intersection of the feed line and equilibrium curve is the minimum reflux ratio (R_{Dm}). If (x^1, y^1) is the point of intersection of the feed line and equilibrium curve, then the slope of the rectifying line is

$$\frac{R_{Dm}}{R_{Dm}+1} = \frac{x_D - y^1}{x_D - x^1} \quad (4.69)$$

$$R_{Dm} = \frac{x_D - y^1}{y^1 - x^1} \quad (4.70)$$

Graphical construction for finding R_{Dmin} is shown in Fig. 4.25.

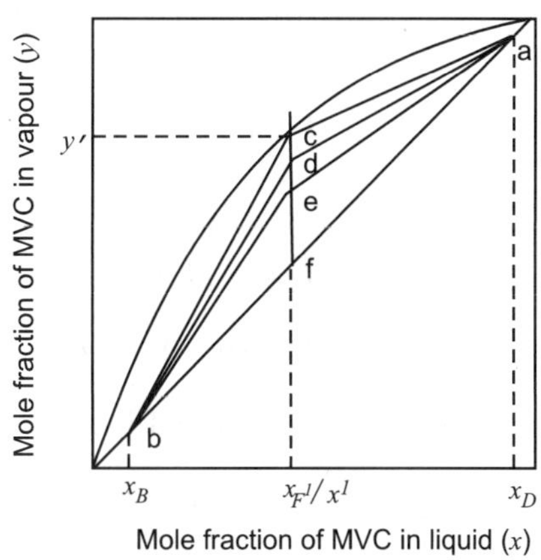

Fig. 4.25 Graphical construction for finding R_{Dmin}

ILLUSTRATIONS

4I A solution CCl_4 and CS_2 containing 50 mol% each is to be continuously fractionated at 1 atm to get a top product of 95 mol% CS_2 and a bottom product of 6 mol% CS_2. The feed is a saturated liquid at its boiling point and fed to the column at 5 000 kg h^{-1}. A total condenser is used and the reflux is returned to the top plate as a saturated liquid. The equilibrium data at one atmosphere is given below.

x	0	0.06	0.11	0.26	0.39	0.53	0.66	0.76	0.86	1.0
y	0	0.16	0.27	0.50	0.63	0.75	0.83	0.88	0.93	1.0

where x and y are mole fractions of the CS_2 in liquid and vapour respectively. Determine (i) the product rate in kg h^{-1}, (ii) minimum reflux ratio and (iii) the number of theoretical plates required and feed plate if the tower is operated at a reflux ratio of twice the minimum ratio.

Solution

The distillation column splits the feed (F) into a distillate (D) richer in the MVC and a bottom product (B) richer in the LVC.

Average molecular weight of feed (F) $= (153.8 \times 0.5) + (76 \times 0.5) = 114.9$

Average molecular weight of distillate (D) $= (76 \times 0.95) + (153.8 \times 0.05) = 79.89$

Average molecular weight of bottom product (B) $= (76 \times 0.06) + (153.8 \times 0.94) = 149.13$

Mole fraction of benzene in the feed (x_F) $= 0.50$

Mole fraction of benzene in the overhead product (x_D) $= 0.95$

Mole fraction of benzene in the bottom product (x_B) $= 0.06$

Kilomoles of feed $= \dfrac{5\,000}{114.9} = 43.52$

Overall material balance: $F = B + D$

$$43.52 = B + D \qquad (1)$$

Benzene balance: $F_{xF} = B_{xB} + D_{xD}$

$$0.5 \times 43.52 = 0.06B + 0.95D \qquad (2)$$

From (1) and (2)

$$B = 22.00 \text{ kmol h}^{-1} = 3\,280.86 \text{ kg}$$

$$D = 21.52 \text{ kmol h}^{-1} = 1\,719.23 \text{ kg}$$

Draw the diagonal and mark (x_F, x_F), (x_D, x_D) and (x_B, x_B) on the diagonal. Draw the equilibrium curve on the same graph using the given equilibrium data. Locate the feed line. It passes through (x_F, x_F). The feed is a saturated liquid, so the feed line is vertical. Let (x^1, y^1) be the point of intersection of the feed line and the equilibrium curve. Here, $y^1 = 0.76$ and $x^1 = 0.50$.

Then minimum reflux ratio (R_{Dm}) $= \dfrac{x_D - y^1}{y^1 - x^1} = \dfrac{0.95 - 0.76}{0.76 - 0.50} = 0.73$

$$R_D = \text{twice } R_{Dm} = 2 \times 0.73 = 1.46$$

Calculate the y intercept of the rectifying line using $\dfrac{x_D}{R_D + 1} = \dfrac{0.95}{1.46 + 1} = 0.386$

Join the intercept with (x_D, x_D) to get the rectifying line. Join the point of intersection of the rectifying line and feed line with (x_B, x_B) to get the stripping line. After the operating lines have been plotted, the number of ideal plates is found by the usual step by step construction which may be started either at the bottom of the stripping line or at the top of the rectifying line. As the point of intersection of the operating lines is approached, the steps should be transferred from the rectifying line to the stripping line as soon as a value of x less than the x-coordinate of the point of intersection of the two operating lines is reached. The feed plate is represented by a triangle that has one corner on the rectifying line and the other on the stripping line.

The number of theoretical stages is 10.6 and is inclusive of the reboiler. The feed plate is the sixth plate from the top. Figure 4.26 gives the graphical solution for this illustration.

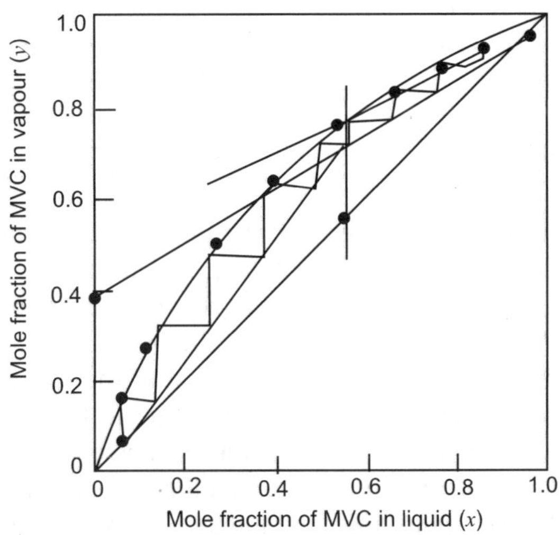

Fig. 4.26 Graphical solution for 4I

4J A continuous distillation column is used to separate methanol from water from a mixture containing 40 mol% methanol. The feed is a saturated vapour. The distillate is to contain 98 mol% methanol and bottom product to contain 98 mol% water. A reflux ratio of 1.5 times the minimum is to be maintained. If the overall plate efficiency is 80%, determine the actual number of plates needed for the separation and also the location of the feed plate.

Equilibrium data:

x	0	0.1	0.2	0.3	0.4	0.5	0.6	0.7	0.8	0.9	1.0
y	0	0.42	0.58	0.67	0.73	0.78	0.83	0.87	0.92	0.96	1.0

where x and y are the mole fractions of the methanol in the 'iquid and vapour respectively.

Solution

Mole fraction of methanol in the feed (x_F)	=	0.40
Mole fraction of methanol in the overhead product (x_D)	=	0.98
Mole fraction of methanol in the bottom product (x_B)	=	0.02

Draw the diagonal and mark (x_F, x_F), (x_D, x_D) and (x_B, x_B) on the diagonal. Draw the equilibrium curve on the same graph using the given equilibrium data. Locate the feed line. It passes through (x_F, x_F). The feed is a saturated vapour, so the feed line is horizontal. Let (x^1, y^1) be the point of intersection of the feed line and the equilibrium curve. Here $y^1 = 0.40$ and $x^1 = 0.095$.

$$\text{Then minimum reflux ratio } (R_{Dm}) = \frac{x_D - y^1}{y^1 - x^1} = \frac{0.98 - 0.40}{0.40 - 0.095} = 1.90$$

$$R_D = 1.5 \text{ times } R_{Dm} = 1.5 \times 1.90 = 2.85$$

$$\text{Calculate the } y \text{ intercept of the rectifying line using } \frac{x_D}{R_D + 1} = \frac{0.98}{2.85 + 1} = 0.2545$$

Join the intercept with (x_D, x_D) to get the rectifying line. Join the point of intersection of the rectifying line and the feed line with (x_B, x_B) to get the stripping line. After the operating lines have been plotted, the number of ideal plates is found by the usual step by step construction which may be started either at the bottom of the stripping line or at the top of the rectifying line. As the point of intersection of the operating lines is approached, the steps should be transferred from the rectifying line to the stripping line as soon as a value of x less than the x-coordinate of the point of intersection of the two operating lines is reached. The feed plate is represented by a triangle that has one corner on the rectifying line and the other on the stripping line. The number of theoretical stages is 8 inclusive of the reboiler. The number of actual plates is $\frac{8}{0.8} = 10$. The feed plate is the sixth theoretical plate from the top. Figure 4.27 gives the graphical solution for this illustration.

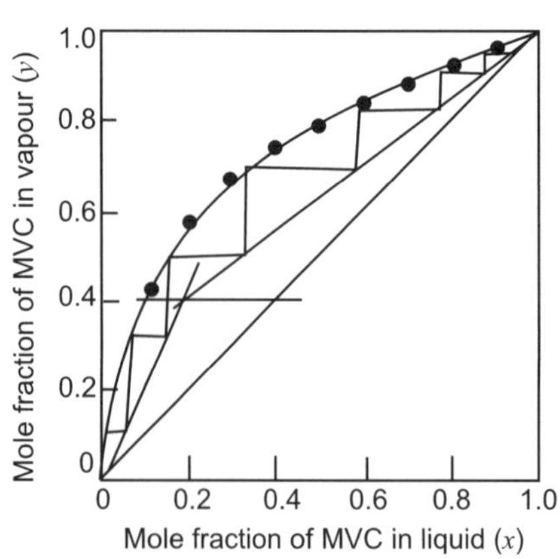

Fig. 4.27 Graphical solution for 4J

4K A continuous fractionating column is to be designed to separate a binary mixture containing 40 mol% A and the rest B to give an overhead product containing 95 mol% A and residue 98 mol% B. If the column operates at 1.5 times the minimum reflux ratio, calculate the number of theoretical plates and the location of the feed plate. Assume that the feed is 40% liquid and 60% vapour. The relative volatility of the mixture is 1.8.

Solution

The equilibrium data is obtained using the relative volatility, using the relation

$$y = \frac{\alpha\, x}{1 + (\alpha - 1)x} = \frac{1.8\, x}{1 + 0.8\, x}$$

x	0	0.1	0.2	0.4	0.6	0.8	0.9	1
y	0	0.17	0.31	0.55	0.73	0.88	0.94	1

Mole fraction of A in the feed (x_F) = 0.40
Mole fraction of A in the overhead product (x_D) = 0.95
Mole fraction of A in the bottom product (x_B) = 0.02

Draw the diagonal and mark (x_F, x_F), (x_D, x_D) and (x_B, x_B) on the diagonal. Draw the equilibrium curve on the same graph using the given equilibrium data. Locate the feed line. It passes through (x_F, x_F). The slope of the feed line is $\frac{-q}{(1-q)}$ where q is the number of moles of liquid in the stripping section for every mole of feed fed on the feed plate. q has been given in the problem as 0.4. The slope of the feed line is $\frac{-0.4}{(1-0.4)} = \frac{-2}{3}$. Using the above information, draw the feed line. Let (x^1, y^1) be the point of intersection of the feed line and the equilibrium curve. Here $y^1 = 0.45$ and $x^1 = 0.32$.

$$\text{Then, minimum reflux ratio } (R_{Dm}) = \frac{x_D - y^1}{y^1 - x^1} = \frac{0.95 - 0.45}{0.45 - 0.32} = 3.85$$

$$R_D = 1.5 \text{ times } R_{Dm} = 1.5 \times 3.85 = 5.77$$

$$\text{Calculate the } y \text{ intercept of the rectifying line using } \frac{x_D}{R_D + 1} = \frac{0.95}{5.77 + 1} = 0.14$$

Join the intercept with (x_D, x_D) to get the rectifying line. Join the point of intersection of the rectifying line and the feed line with (x_B, x_B) to get the stripping line. After the operating lines have been plotted, the number of ideal plates is found by the usual step by step construction which may be started either at the bottom of the stripping line or at the top of the rectifying line. As the point of intersection of the operating lines is approached, the steps should be transferred from the rectifying line to the stripping line as soon as a value of x less than the x-coordinate of the point of intersection of the two operating lines is reached. The feed plate is represented by a triangle that has one corner on the rectifying line and the other on the stripping line. Figure 4.28 gives the graphical solution for this illustration. The number of theoretical stages is 14.8 inclusive of the reboiler. The feed plate is eighth plate from the bottom.

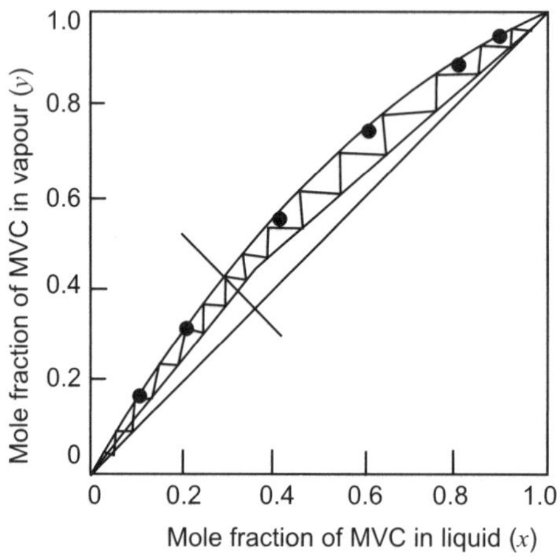

Fig. 4.28 Graphical solution for 4K

4L

It is desired to design a plate type distillation column for the separation of a mixture of A and B. The feed is an equimolar mixture of liquid and vapour. The feed contains 45 mol% A. The top and bottom products contain 96 mol% A and 5 mol% A respectively. Find the minimum reflux. For a reflux ratio of twice the minimum, estimate the theoretical number of plates needed. Equilibrium data:

x	0	5	10	15	20	30	40	50	60	70	80	90	100
y	0.	11	21	30	38	51	63	72	78	85	91	96	100

where x and y are the mole percentages of A in the liquid and vapour respectively.

Solution

Mole fraction of A in the feed (x_F)	=	0.45
Mole fraction of A in the overhead product (x_D)	=	0.96
Mole fraction of A in the bottom product (x_B)	=	0.05

Draw the diagonal and mark (x_F, x_F), (x_D, x_D) and (x_B, x_B) on the diagonal. Draw the equilibrium curve on the same graph using the given equilibrium data. Locate the feed line. The feed line passes through (x_F, x_F). The slope of the feed line is $\frac{-q}{(1-q)}$ where q is the number of moles of liquid in the stripping section for every mole of feed fed on the feed plate. q has been given in the problem as 0.5. The slope of the feed line is $\frac{-0.5}{(1-0.5)} = -1$. Using the above information, draw the feed line. Let (x^1, y^1) be the point of intersection of the feed line and the equilibrium curve. Here $y^1 = 0.55$ and $x^1 = 0.34$.

$$\text{Then minimum reflux ratio } (R_{Dm}) = \frac{x_D - y^1}{y^1 - x^1} = \frac{0.96 - 0.55}{0.55 - 0.34} = 1.95$$

$$R_D = 2.0 \text{ times } R_{Dm} = 2.0 \times 1.95 = 3.90$$

$$\text{Calculate the } y \text{ intercept of the rectifying line using } \frac{x_D}{R_D + 1} = \frac{0.96}{3.90 + 1} = 0.196$$

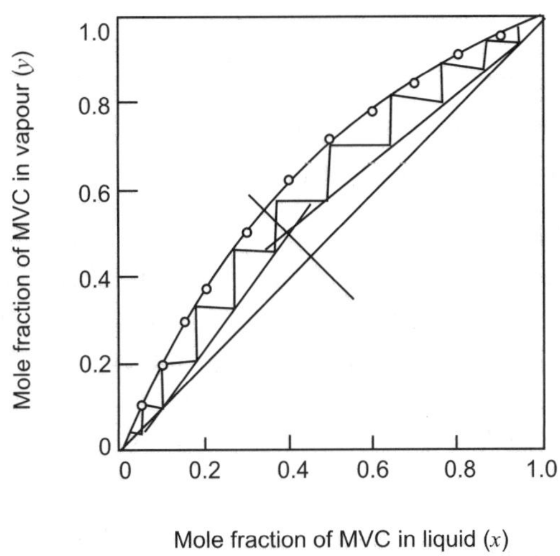

Fig. 4.29 Graphical solution for 4L

Join the intercept with (x_D, x_D) to get the rectifying line. Join the point of intersection of the rectifying line and feed line with (x_B, x_B) to get the stripping line. After the operating lines have been plotted, the number of ideal plates is found by the usual step by step construction which may be started either at the bottom of the stripping line or at the top of the rectifying line. As the point of intersection of the operating lines is approached, the steps should be transferred from the rectifying line to the stripping line as soon as a value of x less than the x-coordinate of the point of intersection of the two operating lines is reached. The feed plate is represented by a triangle that has one corner on the rectifying line and the other on the stripping line. Figure 4.29 gives the graphical solution for this illustration. The number of theoretical stages is 9.5 inclusive of the reboiler.

4M It is desired to separate by distillation at 760 mm Hg, a mixture of 40 mol% n-heptane and 60 mol% ethyl benzene to produce a distillate containing 95 mol% n-heptane and a residue containing 96 mol% ethyl benzene. The feed enters as a liquid at its boiling point. Determine the minimum reflux. Using a reflux ratio of 2.5 times the minimum, determine the number of theoretical stages.

Equilibrium data:

x	0	0.08	0.185	0.251	0.335	0.487	0.651	0.914	1.00
y	0.	0.233	0.428	0.514	0.608	0.729	0.840	0.963	1.00

where x and y are mole fractions of the n-heptane in liquid and vapour respectively.

Solution

Mole fraction of A in the feed (x_F) = 0.40

Mole fraction of A in the overhead product (x_D) = 0.95

Mole fraction of A in the bottom product (x_B) = 0.04

Draw the diagonal and mark (x_F, x_F), (x_D, x_D) and (x_B, x_B) on the diagonal. Draw the equilibrium curve on the same graph using the given equilibrium data. Locate the feed line. The feed line passes through (x_F, x_F). The slope of the feed line is $\frac{-q}{(1-q)}$ where q is the number of moles of liquid in the stripping section for every mole of feed fed on the feed plate. q has been given in the problem as 1. So, the feed line is vertical. Let (x^1, y^1) be the point of intersection of the feed line and the equilibrium curve. Here, $y^1 = 0.65$ and $x^1 = 0.40$.

$$\text{Then minimum reflux ratio } (R_{Dm}) = \frac{x_D - y^1}{y^1 - x^1} = \frac{0.95 - 0.65}{0.65 - 0.40} = 1.20$$

$$R_D = 2.5 \text{ times } R_{Dm} = 2.5 \times 1.2 = 3.0$$

Calculate the y intercept of the rectifying line using $\frac{x_D}{R_D + 1} = \frac{0.95}{3.0 + 1} = 0.237\,5$

Join the intercept with (x_D, x_D) to get the rectifying line. Join the point of intersection of the rectifying line and the feed line with (x_B, x_B) to get the stripping line. After the operating lines have been plotted, the number of ideal plates is found by the usual step by step construction which may be started either at the bottom of the stripping line or at the top of the rectifying line. As the point of intersection of the operating lines is approached, the steps should be transferred from the rectifying line to the stripping line as soon as a value of x less than the x-coordinate of the point of intersection of the two operating lines is reached. The feed plate is represented by a triangle that has one corner on the rectifying line and the other on the stripping line. Figure 4.30 gives the graphical solution for this illustration. The number of theoretical stages is 8 inclusive of the reboiler.

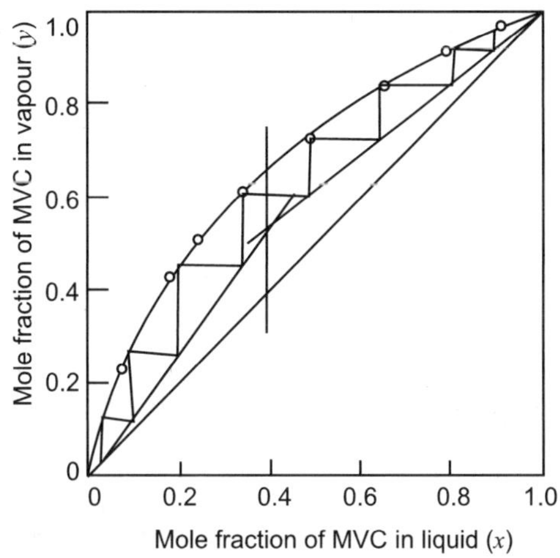

Fig. 4.30 Graphical solution for 4M

4N A continuous fractionating column operating at atmospheric pressure is to separate a feed mixture containing 30 mol% CS_2 and 70 mol% CCl_4 into an overhead product of 95 mol% CS_2 and a bottom product of 95 mol% CCl_4. The feed is a liquid at its boiling point. Assuming an overall plate efficiency of 70% and a reflux ratio of 3:1, estimate the number of theoretical plates required. The equilibrium data at 1 atm is given below.

x	0	0.0296	0.0615	0.258	0.39	0.532	0.663	0.758	0.86	1.0
y	0	0.0823	0.1555	0.494	0.634	0.747	0.80	0.88	0.932	1.0

Solution

Mole fraction of A in the feed (x_F) = 0.30

Mole fraction of A in the overhead product (x_D) = 0.95

Mole fraction of A in the bottom product (x_B) = 0.05

Draw the diagonal and mark (x_F, x_F), (x_D, x_D) and (x_B, x_B) on the diagonal. Draw the equilibrium curve on the same graph using the given equilibrium data. Locate the feed line. It passes through (x_F, x_F). The slope of the feed line is $\frac{-q}{(1-q)}$ where q is the number of moles of liquid in the stripping section for every mole of feed fed on the feed plate. q has been given in the problem as 1. So, the feed line is vertical. Let (x^1, y^1) be the point of intersection of the feed line and the equilibrium curve.

Calculate the y intercept of the rectifying line using $\dfrac{x_D}{R_D+1} = \dfrac{0.95}{3.0+1} = 0.237\,5$

Join the intercept with (x_D, x_D) to get the rectifying line. Join the point of intersection of the rectifying line and the feed line with (x_B, x_B) to get the stripping line. After the operating lines have been plotted, the number of ideal plates is found by the usual step by step construction which may be started either at the bottom of the stripping line or at the top of the rectifying line. As the point of intersection of the operating lines is approached, the steps should be transferred from the rectifying line to the stripping line as soon as a value of x less than the x-coordinate of the point of intersection of the two operating lines is reached. The feed plate is represented by a triangle that has one corner on the rectifying line and the other on the the stripping line. Figure 4.31 gives the graphical solution for this illustration. The number of theoretical stages is 9.3 inclusive of the reboiler and the actual number of theoretical stages is 14 inclusive of the reboiler.

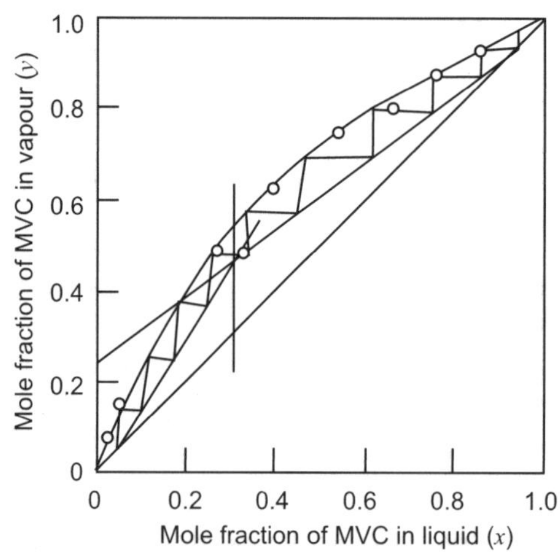

Fig. 4.31 Graphical solution for 4N

UNDERWOOD EQUATION [3]

The minimum reflux ratio (R_{Dm}) can be found from the point of intersection of the feed line and the equilibrium curve. If (x^1, y^1) is the point of intersection of the feed line and the equilibrium curve, then the slope of the rectifying line is

$$\frac{R_{Dm}}{R_{Dm}+1} = \frac{x_D - y^1}{x_D - x^1} \tag{4.71}$$

$$R_{Dm} = \frac{x_D - y^1}{y^1 - x^1} \tag{4.72}$$

If α is known, y^1 can be replaced by x^1.

$$y^1 = \frac{\alpha x^1}{1 + (\alpha - 1)\, x^1}$$

Substituting this in the above equation, we get

$$R_{Dm} = \frac{x_D - \dfrac{\alpha x^1}{1 + (\alpha - 1)x^1}}{\dfrac{\alpha x^1}{1 + (\alpha - 1)x^1} - x^1}$$

$$= \frac{1}{(\alpha - 1)} \left[\frac{x_D}{x^1} - \frac{\alpha (1 - x_D)}{(1 - x^1)} \right] \tag{4.73}$$

The above equation is known as the *Underwood equation.* R_{Dm} can be found from the physical properties of the system. If the feed is a liquid at its boiling point then $x^1 = x_F$ and the equation becomes,

$$R_{Dm} = \frac{1}{(\alpha - 1)} \left[\frac{x_D}{x_F} - \frac{\alpha (1 - x_D)}{(1 - x_F)} \right] \tag{4.74}$$

MINIMUM NUMBER OF PLATES—FENSKE EQUATION [4]

The minimum number of plates ($N_{\min}$) for a given separation can be found graphically by constructing steps on an $x - y$ diagram between compositions x_D and x_B using the diagonal as the operating line for both sections. $N_{\min}$ can also be found using the *Fenske equation*, which is derived as discussed below.

The ratio of the partial pressure of a component in the vapour phase to its mole fraction in the liquid phase is defined as volatility.

Volatility of A, $\alpha_A = \dfrac{P_A}{x_A}$ (4.11)

Volatility of B, $\alpha_B = \dfrac{P_B}{x_B}$ (4.12)

The ratio of the two volatilities is known as relative volatility.

$$\alpha_{AB} = \frac{\alpha_A}{\alpha_B}$$

$$= \frac{P_A}{x_A}\frac{x_B}{P_B} \quad \text{but } P_A = y_A P \text{ and } P_B = y_B P$$

$$= \frac{y_A x_B}{x_A y_B} \tag{4.13}$$

$$\frac{y_A}{y_B} = \alpha_{AB}\frac{x_A}{x_B} \tag{4.14}$$

For binary mixtures, $y_B = 1 - y_A$ and $x_B = 1 - x_A$

$$\frac{y_A}{1-y_A} = \alpha_{AB}\frac{x_A}{1-x_A} \tag{4.15}$$

If we assume that A is always the component of our interest and the relative volatility α_{AB} always denotes the volatility of component A to that of B, the subscripts can be omitted.

$$\frac{y}{1-y} = \alpha\frac{x}{1-x} \tag{4.75}$$

For the $n+1^{\text{th}}$ plate of the fractionating column,

$$\frac{y_{n+1}}{1-y_{n+1}} = \alpha\frac{x_{n+1}}{1-x_{n+1}} \tag{4.76}$$

Operating line for the rectifying section is

$$y_{n+1} = \frac{L_n}{L_n+D}x_n + \frac{D\,x_D}{L_n+D} \tag{4.47}$$

Operating line for the stripping section is

$$y_{m+1} = \frac{L_m}{L_m-B}x_n + \frac{B\,x_B}{L_m-B} \tag{4.48}$$

At total reflux, $D = B = 0$. So the equations for the above operating lines will be $y_{n+1} = x_n$ and $y_{m+1} = x_m$. Substituting this in equation (4.76),

$$\frac{x_n}{1-x_n} = \alpha\frac{x_{n+1}}{1-x_{n+1}} \tag{4.77}$$

At the top of the column, $y_1 = x_D$

$$\frac{x_D}{1-x_D} = \alpha\frac{x_1}{1-x_1} \tag{4.78}$$

Writing for the next n plates,

$$\frac{x_1}{1-x_1} = \alpha\frac{x_2}{1-x_2}$$

$$\frac{x_2}{1-x_2} = \alpha\frac{x_3}{1-x_3} \tag{4.79}$$

– – – – – – – – – – –

– – – – – – – – – – –

– – – – – – – – – – –

$$\frac{x_{n-1}}{1-x_{n-1}} = \alpha\frac{x_n}{1-x_n}$$

If all the equations are multiplied together, the intermediate terms will get cancelled.

$$\frac{x_D}{1-x_D} = \alpha^n\frac{x_n}{1-x_n} \tag{4.80}$$

A reboiler is required to reach the bottom discharge.

$$\frac{x_D}{1-x_D} = \alpha^{n+1}\frac{x_B}{1-x_B} \tag{4.81}$$

$$n+1 = \frac{\log\dfrac{x_D(1-x_B)}{x_B(1-x_D)}}{\log\alpha} \tag{4.82}$$

This equation is known as the Fenske equation. If α varies with temperature, the geometric mean of the extreme values has to be used.

ILLUSTRATIONS

40 A mixture of benzene and toluene containing 40 mol% benzene is to be separated to give a product of 90 mol% benzene at the top and a bottom product containing 10 mol% benzene. The feed is a liquid at its boiling point. If the average relative volatility of benzene relative to toluene is 2.4, find the minimum number of plates and the minimum reflux ratio.

Solution

Mole fraction of benzene in the feed (x_F)	=	0.40
Mole fraction of benzene in the overhead product (x_D)	=	0.90
Mole fraction of benzene in the bottom product (x_B)	=	0.10
Relative volatility of the mixture (α)	=	2.4

The minimum number of plates can be found using Fenske equation and the minimum reflux ratio can be found using the Underwood equation.

$$n+1 = \frac{\log\dfrac{x_D(1-x_B)}{x_B(1-x_D)}}{\log\alpha}$$

$$= \frac{\log\dfrac{0.9\times0.9}{0.1\times0.1}}{\log 2.4} = 5.0$$

5 plates inclusive of a reboiler is required. If the feed is a liquid at its boiling point then $x^1 = x_F$ and the equation becomes,

$$R_{Dm} = \frac{1}{(\alpha - 1)}\left[\frac{x_D}{x_F} - \frac{\alpha(1 - x_D)}{(1 - x_F)}\right]$$

$$\frac{1}{2.4 - 1}\left[\frac{0.9}{0.4} - \frac{2.4(1 - 0.9)}{(1 - 04)}\right] = 1.32$$

4P A plant distils a mixture containing 80 mol% methanol and 20 mol% water. The overhead product is to contain 99.99 mol% methanol and the bottom product 0.005 mol% methanol. The feed is cold and for each mole of feed, 0.4 moles of vapour is condensed on the feed plate. Calculate the (i) minimum number of plates (ii) minimum reflux ratio.

Equilibrium data:

x	0.1	0.2	0.3	0.4	0.5	0.6	0.7	0.8	0.9	1.0
y	0.417	0.579	0.669	0.729	0.78	0.825	0.871	0.915	0.959	1.0

where x and y are mole fractions of methanol in the liquid and vapour respectively.

Solution

Mole fraction of methanol in the feed (x_F) = 0.80

Mole fraction of methanol in the overhead product (x_D) = 0.999 9

Mole fraction of methanol in the bottom product (x_B) = 0.005

Draw the diagonal and mark (x_F, x_F), (x_D, x_D) and (x_B, x_B) on the diagonal. Draw the equilibrium curve on the same graph using the given equilibrium data. Locate the feed line. It passes through (x_F, x_F). The slope of the feed line is $\frac{-q}{(1-q)}$ where q is the number of moles of liquid in the stripping section for every mole of feed fed on the feed plate. It is given that the feed is cold and for each mole of feed, 0.4 moles of vapour is condensed on the feed plate. So q is 1.4. The slope of the feed line is $\frac{-1.4}{(1-1.4)} = 3.5$. Using the above information, draw the feed line. Let (x^1, y^1) be the point of intersection of the feed line and the equilibrium curve.

Here $y^1 = 0.93$ and $x^1 = 0.84$.

Then, the minimum reflux ratio $(R_{Dm}) = \dfrac{x_D - y^1}{y^1 - x^1} = \dfrac{0.999\,9 - 0.93}{0.93 - 0.84} = 0.777$

The minimum number of plates is found graphically by constructing steps on an x–y diagram between the compositions x_D and x_B using the diagonal as the operating line for both sections.

For this operation, the minimum number of theoretical plates required is 9 inclusive of reboiler. Figure 4.32 gives the graphical solution for this illustration.

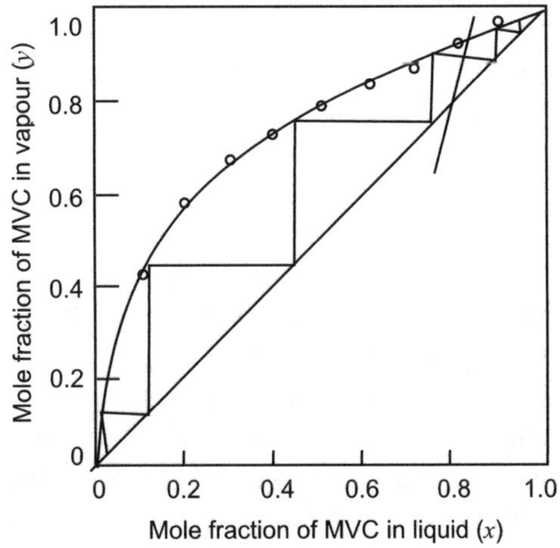

Fig. 4.32 Graphical solution for 4P

OPTIMUM REFLUX RATIO

The most economical R_D or the R_D for which cost is the least is known as the *optimum* R_D. At R_D minimum, the column requires an infinite number of plates and the fixed cost is infinity but the operating costs (heat for the reboiler, cooling water requirement for the condenser and power for the reflux pump) are the least. As R_D increases from R_D minimum, the numbers of plates decrease, but the column diameter increases, owing to the large quantities of recycled liquor and vapour per unit quantity of feed. The condenser, reflux pump and reboiler must also be large. So, the fixed cost therefore falls to a minimum and rises again to infinity at total reflux. The heating and cooling requirements increase almost directly with R_D. The total cost which is the sum of the fixed and operating costs must also fall through a minimum (Fig. 4.33). The R_D corresponding to this minimum is the optimum R_D and this will be in the range of 1.2–1.5 times the R_D minimum.

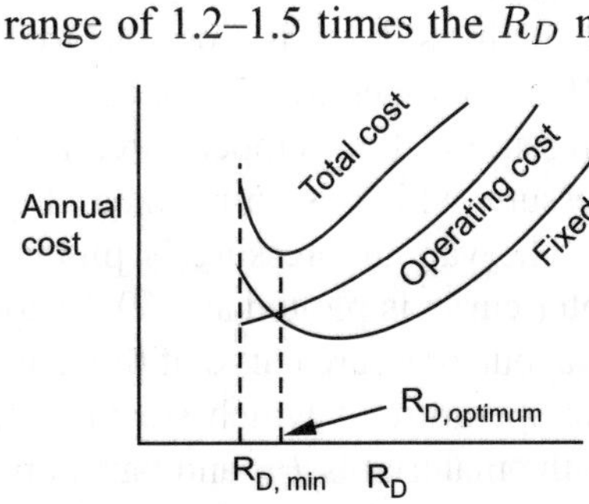

Fig. 4.33 Optimum reflux ratio

STEAM DISTILLATION

Steam distillation is often used to distill a material (i) that has a relatively high boiling point under atmospheric pressure and (ii) that is liable to decompose at boiling point. This method is often used to separate high boiling organic materials from non-volatile impurities. It can be applied only when the product is almost or completely immiscible with water. Steam distillation is practiced in industry for the purification of nitrobenzene, aniline and turpentine.

The material to be distilled is placed in a batch still and the steam is blown directly into the material. This process can be done in either of the following two ways. In the first method, the only heat input is that due to the latent heat of the steam and a certain proportion of steam must condense to provide the latent heat of vaporisation for the product that is taken overhead. As a result, a layer of liquid water is formed in the still. In the second case, either the steam is superheated or another external source of heat is supplied so that steam does not condense but passes out with the product. In either case, when the sum of partial pressures of the steam and the material distilled reaches the total pressure in the apparatus, both materials will pass over in the molecular ratio of their partial pressures. If the mixed vapours are condensed, two layers are formed in the condensate receiver; they can be separated by gravity and any non-volatile impurity will be left behind in the still.

In either case

$$\frac{n_A}{n_B} = \frac{P_A}{P_B} \tag{4.83}$$

$$\frac{W_A}{M_A}\frac{M_B}{W_B} = \frac{P_A}{P_B} \tag{4.84}$$

$$\frac{W_A}{W_B} = \frac{P_A}{P_B}\frac{M_A}{M_B} = \frac{P - P_B}{P_B}\frac{M_A}{M_B} \tag{4.85}$$

Here, P_A and P_B are partial pressures of components of A and B respectively, P is the total pressure, M_A and M_B are molecular weights of A and B respectively and component A is the more volatile component—steam.

If two liquid layers collect in the still, it is possible to fix either the temperature or total pressure, but not both. If the temperature is fixed, each liquid will exert a partial pressure equal to its vapour pressure at that temperature. The sum of the partial pressures will be equal to the total pressure which is thus fixed. Figure 4.34 is very useful for steam distillation calculations. The vapour pressure is plotted against temperature for the material to be distilled. The water curve is plotted as 760 – vapour pressure of water against temperature. It cuts across the vapour pressure curve of the material to be distilled. The point of intersection represents the temperature at which steam distillation takes places. At this temperature, partial pressure of the material is P_B and partial pressure of water is 760 – P_B. The weight ratio of material to water can be found using the equation derived earlier.

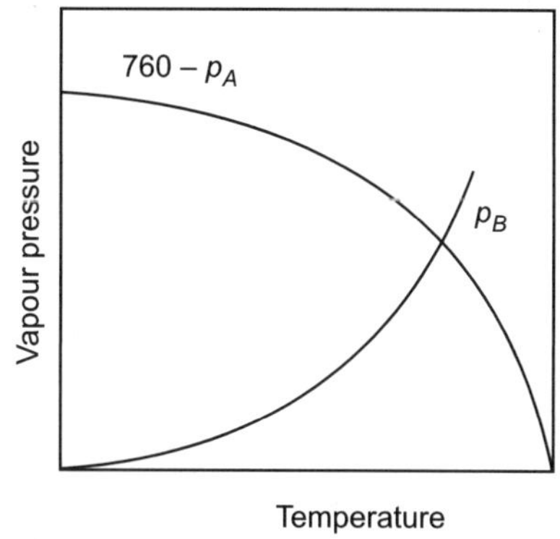

Fig. 4.34 Temperature–vapour pressure data

ILLUSTRATIONS

4Q For steam distillation of benzaldehyde at atmospheric pressure with condensed steam as the only source of heat, calculate the amount of steam (kg) required per kg of benzaldehyde.

Data:

Benzaldehyde charged to the still:	100 kg
Initial temperature of benzaldehyde:	305 K
Steam pressure:	0.7 atm g
Vaporisation efficiency:	90%
Latent heat of vaporisation of benzaldehyde:	356 kJ kg^{-1}
Specific heat of benzaldehyde:	1.792 kJ kg^{-1} K^{-1}
Molecular weight of benzaldehyde:	106

Temperature–vapour pressure data is given in Table 4.6.

Table 4.6 Temperature–vapour pressure data

Temperature (K)	Vapour pressure (mm Hg)	
	Benzaldehyde	Water
335	10	163.8
348	20	289.1
363	40	527.8
372.6	60	749.2

Solution

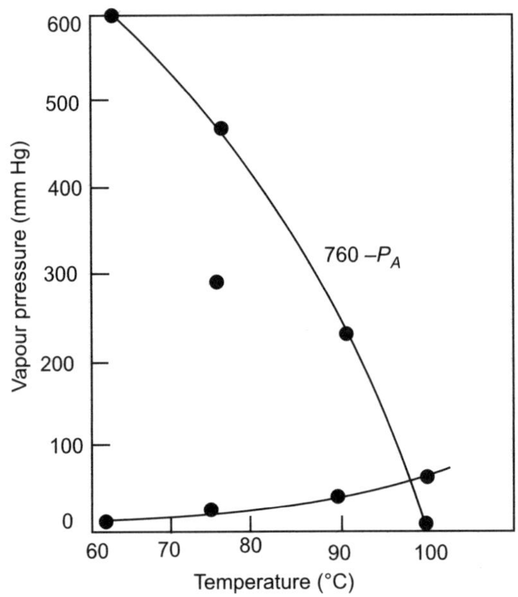

Fig. 4.35 Graphical solution for 4Q

Data required for drawing the graph are given in Table 4.7.

Table 4.7 Temperature–vapour pressure data

Temperature (K)	P_A (mm Hg)	760 – P_A(mm Hg)	P_B (mm Hg)
335	163.8	596.2	10
348	289.1	470.9	20
363	527.8	232.2	40
372.6	749.2	10.8	60

Steam distillation temperature = 371 K (Fig. 4.35)

Vapour pressure of benzaldehyde (P_B) = 55 mm Hg (Fig. 4.35)

$$\frac{W_A}{W_B} = \frac{P - P_B}{P_B}\frac{M_A}{M_B} = \frac{760 - 55}{55} \times \frac{18}{106} = 217.68 \text{ kg}$$

This is carrier steam. But vaporisation efficiency of steam is only 90%.

Actual carrier steam required is $\dfrac{217.68}{0.9} = 241.87$ kg

Total heat required for the vaporisation of benzaldehyde = $100\{1.792(371 - 305) + 356\}$

$= 47\ 427.2$ kJ

The carrier steam is at 1.7 atm pressure and its pressure drops to 1 atm when it goes out of the still carrying benzaldehyde with it and there by loses heat.

Heat lost by carrier steam due to pressure drop = 23.2 kJ kg^{-1}

Total heat supplied by carrier steam = $241.87 \times 23.2 = 5\ 611.4$ kJ

Heat to be supplied by the heating steam = $47\ 427.2 - 5\ 611.4 = 41\ 815.8$ kJ

Latent heat of vapourisation of steam at 1.7 atm = 2 288.8 kJ kg^{-1}

Steam required as heating medium = $\dfrac{41\,815.8}{2\,288.8} = 18.27$ kg

Total steam required = weight of carrier steam + weight of heating steam

$= 241.87 + 18.27 = 260.14$ kg

Steam requirement $= \dfrac{260.14}{100} = 2.2014$ kg per kg of benzaldehyde

4R 100 L h^{-1} of turpentine is to be steam distilled at atmospheric pressure. For turpentine, the latent heat of vaporisation is 309.84 kJ kg^{-1}; molecular weight is 136 and specific gravity is 0.865. No external heat is supplied. How much of steam at 35 kPa g will be used per hour? Neglect the heat required to heat up the charge and the heat lost by radiation. From the vapour pressure data curve for steam distillation of turpentine, the temperature of distillation was found to be 368.5 K and the vapour pressure of turpentine at that temperature was 114 mm.

Solution

Weight of turpentine to be steam distilled (W_B) $= 100 \times 0.865 = 86.5$ kg

Making use of the relationship between weight, partial pressure and molecular weight of the components in the case of steam distillation, we have

$$\frac{W_A}{W_B} = \frac{P_A M_A}{P_B M_B} = \frac{646 \times 18}{114 \times 136} = 0.75$$

Weight of steam, $W_A = 0.75 W_B = 0.75 \times 86.5$ = 64.875 kg

Steam passing over along with turpentine = 64.875 kg h^{-1}

Heat required to vapourise turpentine = $86.5 \times 309.84 = 26\ 801$ kJ h^{-1}

Saturation temperature of 35 kPa g steam is 381.3 K. The steam that goes along with turpentine cools from 381.3 K to 368.5 K.

Sensible heat furnished by the steam leaving along with turpentine

$$= 64.875 \times 2.01 \times (381.3 - 368.5) = 131 \text{ kJ}$$

Rest of the heat, that is 26 801 – 131 = 26 670 kJ must be supplied by steam condensing and then cooling to 368.5 K.

Condensing steam supplies 2233.7 kJ kg^{-1} as latent heat and 53.6 kJ kg^{-1} as sensible heat. In all it supplies 2 287.3 kJ kg^{-1} of heat energy.

$$\text{Weight of steam condensing required} = \frac{26\,670}{2\,287.3} = 11.66 \text{ kg h}^{-1}$$

Total steam required = weight of carrier steam and condensing steam

$$= 64.875 + 11.66 = 76.535 \text{ kg h}^{-1}$$

AZEOTROPIC DISTILLATION [5]

In the separation of binary mixtures by distillation, the formation of a binary azeotrope makes it impossible to produce nearly pure parts by ordinary fractionation. Under these circumstances a third component sometimes called the entrainer, may be added to the binary mixture to form a new low boiling azeotrope with one of the original components whose volatility is such that it can be easily separated from the other original component.

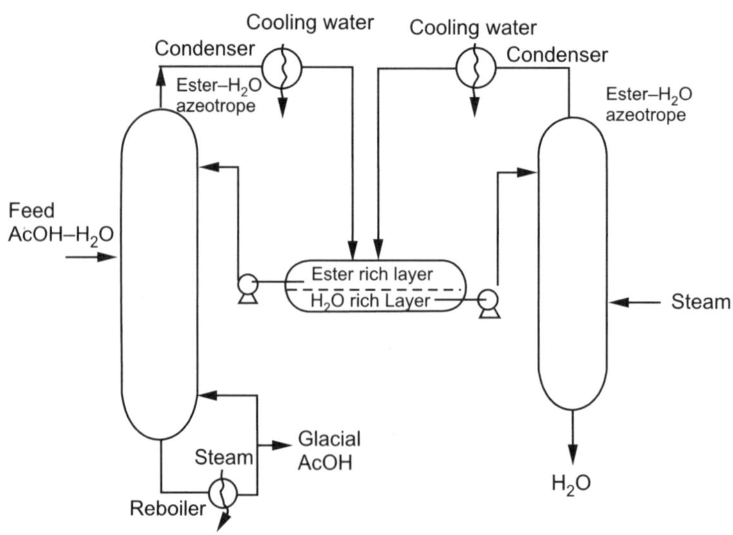

Fig. 4.36 Azeotropic distillation

Consider the azeotropic distillation of acetic acid (boiling point: 391 K)–water (boiling point: 383 K) solutions using butyl acetate as entrainer. The acetic acid–water mixture is relatively hard to separate due to the formation of the azeotrope. Butyl acetate is only slightly soluble in water and hence forms a hetero-azeotrope with it (boiling point 363 K). If sufficient butyl alcohol is added to the top of the column to form an azeotrope with all the water in the binary feed, the azeotrope can be distilled from the high boiling acetic acid, which leaves as residue. The hetero-azeotrope on condensation forms two insoluble liquid layers—one nearly pure water saturated with ester and the other nearly pure ester saturated with water. The latter is returned to the top of the column as reflux and is the source of entrainer in the column. The former can be stripped off its small amount of entrainer in a second small column. A schematic representation of an azeotropic distillation process is given in Fig. 4.36.

Characteristics of a Good Entrainer

1. The entrainer should preferably form a low boiling azeotrope with only one of the components of the binary mixture, preferably the constituent present in the lowest amount in order to reduce the heat requirement.
2. The new azeotrope must have sufficient volatility to make it separable from the remaining component so that the residue will be nearly pure, that is, almost free from the entrainer.
3. The new azeotrope formed should be heterogeneous so that the recovery of the entrainer from the azeotrope will be simple.
4. It should be cheap and readily available.
5. It should be chemically stable.
6. It should be inactive towards the components of the mixture being separated.
7. It should be non-corrosive to common construction materials.
8. It should be non-toxic.
9. It should have a low latent heat of vaporisation.
10. It should have a low freezing point (easily storable and outdoor handling possible).
11. It should have low viscosity and hence high tray efficiency.

EXTRACTIVE DISTILLATION [5]

Extractive distillation is a method of rectification used for binary mixtures having relative volatility close to one which are difficult or impossible to separate by fractional distillation. In this case also, a third component known as solvent is added which alters the relative volatility of the original components thus permitting separation. The solvent has low volatility and is itself not appreciably vaporised in the fractionator.

For a non-ideal mixture,

$$P_A = \gamma_A P_A^* x_A; \; P_B = \gamma_B P_B^* x_B \tag{4.86}$$

where γ_A and γ_B are activity coefficients. They take care of the deviation from ideality. The solvent added to the mixture in extractive distillation differentially alters the activities of the components and hence the relative volatility. In the case of toluene (boiling point: 383 K)–isooctane (boiling point: 372 K), phenol (boiling point: 454 K) is used as a solvent. Both form a non-ideal mixture with phenol. But, the extent of non-ideality with isooctane is greater than that with toluene. As a result, the relative volatility of isooctane with respect to toluene increases. We get isooctane as an overhead product with negligible amount of phenol. The residue is a mixture of toluene and phenol. Phenol can be separated from the residue without much difficulty due to the appreciable difference in boiling points. A schematic representation of a typical extractive distillation operation is given in Fig. 4.37.

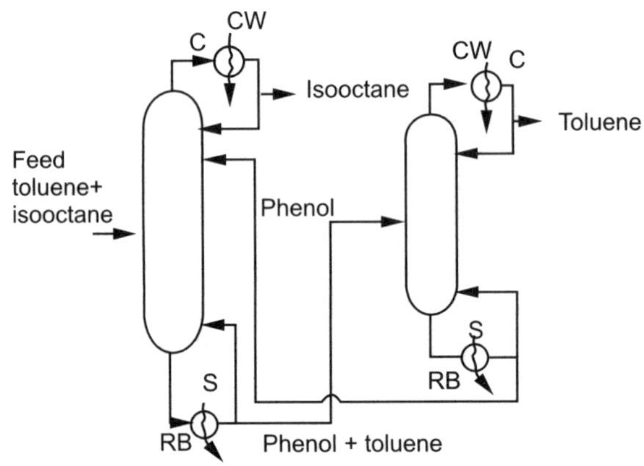

Fig. 4.37 Extractive distillation
C: Condenser, CW: Cooling water, RB: Reboiler, S: Steam

Essential Requirements of a Good Solvent

1. High selectivity, ability to alter the vapour–liquid equilibria of the original mixture.
2. High capacity, ability to dissolve the components of the original mixture.
3. Low volatility so that the overhead product will not contain the solvent.
4. Separability, that is, the solvent should be easily separated from the mixture to which it is added.
5. Cheap and readily available.
6. Chemically stable.
7. Inactive towards the components of the mixture being separated.
8. Non-corrosive to common construction materials.
9. Non-toxic.
10. Low latent heat of vaporisation.
11. Low freezing point (easily storable and outdoor handling possible).
12. Low viscosity and hence high tray efficiency.

ANALYSIS OF FRACTIONATING COLUMNS BY ENTHALPY–CONCENTRATION METHOD OR PONCHON–SAVARIT METHOD [6,7]

The assumptions made in McCabe–Thiele method of analysis of fractionating column are

1. negligible heat of mixing,
2. equal molal latent heating, and
3. hence, constant molal overflow.

The limitations imposed by the above may be removed if the analysis of fractionating columns is based on enthalpy balances as well as material balances. Then, reflux and vapour at any point in the column are found by a rigorous enthalpy balance which replaces the approximate heat balance based on

$$\lambda_n = \lambda_{n+1}; \lambda_m = \lambda_{m-1} \tag{4.87}$$

$$V_n\lambda_n = V_{n+1}\lambda_{n+1}; L_m\lambda_m = L_{m-1}\lambda_{m-1} \tag{4.88}$$

This method is known as the Ponchon–Savarit method and is based on graphical construction of the H–x diagram.

H–x Diagram

In most of the distillation problems, it is necessary to take into account the latent heat, heat of mixing and sensible heat of the components of the mixture. For binary systems, all these quantities and equilibrium data may be shown on a H–x diagram.

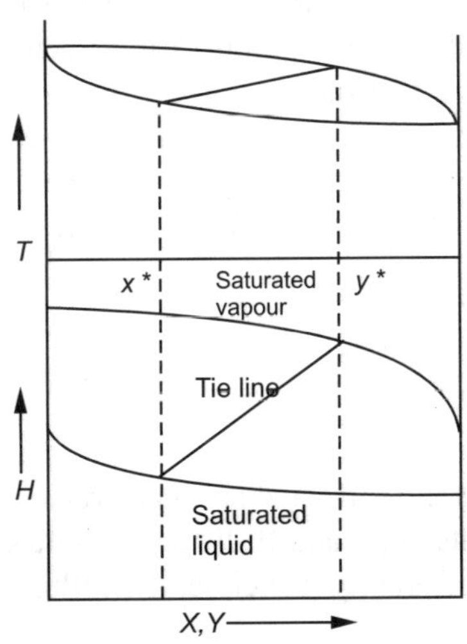

Fig. 4.38 H, T–x–y diagram

This diagram (Fig. 4.38), may be constructed on either mass or mole basis. Enthalpies referred to are at standard state conditions of 298 K and a specified constant pressure. At constant pressure, the specific enthalpy of saturated liquid or saturated vapour depends only on the boiling point; the boiling point depends only on concentration. Enthalpies (ordinate) are plotted as functions of concentration (abscissa). The lower curve shows specific enthalpies of saturated liquids H^L versus x and the upper curve shows specific enthalpies of saturated vapour H^V versus y. All points above the saturated line represent saturated vapour. All points below the saturated liquid line pertain to liquids below their boiling point. All points between these lines represent mixtures of saturated liquid and saturated vapour.

Equilibrium between the liquid and vapour phases is shown by straight lines connecting the saturated liquid line and the saturated vapour line. These straight lines are called tie lines. The abscissas of the terminals of any one tie line represent the corresponding values of x^* and y^*—the coordinates of a point on the equilibrium curve. These tie lines correspond to the horizontal lines between the boiling point and dew point curves of the boiling point diagram. Tie lines can be constructed using equilibrium data.

Overall Enthalpy Balance for a Fractionating Column

Let H_F, H_D and H_B be the specific enthalpies of feed, overhead product and bottom product represented in kJ kg^{-1}respectively. Points F, D and B representing feed, overhead and bottom are plotted on the H–x diagram. The details required for energy balance are given in Fig. 4.39.

Both products are at their respective bubble points. So points B and D are on the saturated liquid line. The feed may have any thermal condition from cold liquid to super-heated vapour. In the present case, the feed is shown as a mixture of vapour and liquid. Based on the centre of gravity principle, the ratio of vapour to liquid in the feed is given by the ratio of the distance aF to bF where a and b are the points of intersection of the tie line passing through F with the saturated liquid line and the saturated vapour line respectively (Fig. 4.40).

The overall process is a non-adiabatic splitting of the feed into overhead and bottom products. To use adiabatic construction, the stream D has to be corrected for $-q_c$, the heat removed from the condenser and stream B for q_r, the heat added to the reboiler.

$$H'_D = H_D - \frac{-q_C}{D} = H_D + \frac{q_C}{D} \tag{4.89}$$

$$H'_B = H_B - \frac{q_r}{B} \tag{4.90}$$

The points D′ and B′ represent the corrected product streams. Now the process with corrected streams is adiabatic. The points D′, F and B′ lie on a single straight line, which is the overall enthalpy line. By the centre of gravity principle, the reflux ratio is

$$R_D = \frac{H'_D - H_1^V}{H_1^V - H_D} \tag{4.91}$$

where H_1^V is the specific enthalpy of the vapour leaving the top plate (plate 1) and entering the condenser.

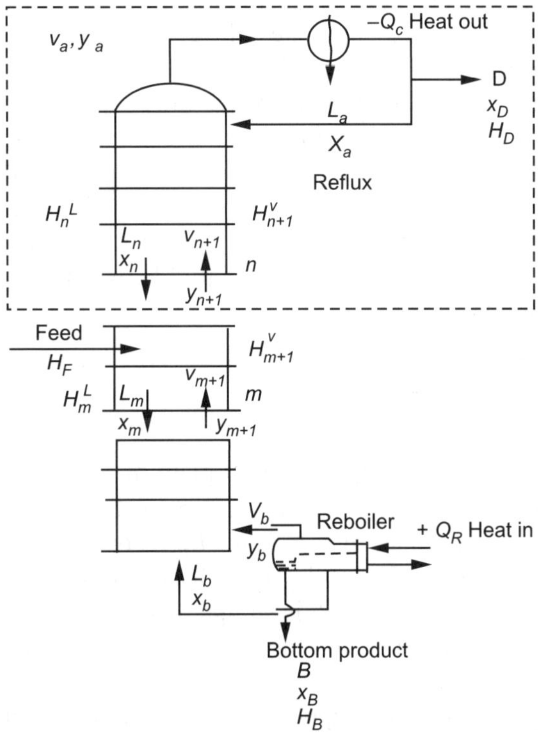

Fig. 4.39 Overall enthalpy balance

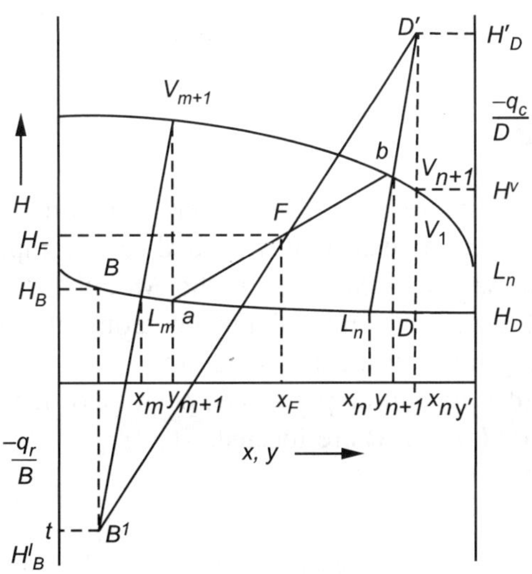

Fig. 4.40 H–x–y diagram for a theoretical plate

Enthalpy Balance in the Rectifying and Stripping Sections

Let the specific enthalpy of the vapour stream entering plate n in the rectifying section be H^V_{n+1} and let the liquid stream leaving plate n be H^L_n. Let point V_{n+1} represent the vapour from plate n+1 and point L_m represent the liquid from plate n. Point V_{n+1} lies on the boiling point curve and L_n on the dew point curve. Since the column is adiabatic, points D', V_{n+1} and L_n are collinear. The straight line through these points is the enthalpy operating line. Such lines exist for each plate and all the lines for all plates above the feed pass through D'. Like the operating lines in the McCabe–Thilele method, the enthalpy operating lines relate the concentration of the vapour rising to a plate with that of the liquid leaving it. They also show the ratio of flow rates of the vapour and liquid between the plates.

By the centre of gravity principle,

$$\frac{V_{n+1}}{L_n} = \frac{D'L_n}{D'V_{n+1}} = \frac{x_D - x_n}{x_D - y_{n+1}} \tag{4.92}$$

Let the specific enthalpy of the vapour rising to plate m in the stripping section be H^V_{m+1} and let that of the liquid from plate m be H^L_m. Let point L_m represent the liquid from plate m and V_{m+1} the vapour from plate $m+1$. Point L_m is on the boiling point line and V_{m+1} is on the dew point line. Points V_{m+1}, L_m and B$'$ are the terminal points of an adiabatic mixing process. So, the line V_{m+1}, L_mB' is straight and is an enthalpy operating line. There is a separate enthalpy operating line for each plate below the feed and all such lines pass through B'.

The ratio of the flow rates of the vapour and liquid at any point in the stripping section can be found from the equation

$$\frac{V_{m+1}}{L_m} = \frac{x_m - x_B}{y_{m+1} - x_B} \tag{4.93}$$

Number of Ideal Plates

The enthalpy operating lines are used alternatively with tie lines to give a step by step determination of the number of ideal plates needed to accomplish a given separation. In comparing the Ponchon–Savarit method with the McCabe–Thiele method, the tie lines correspond to the equilibrium curve and enthalpy operating lines on the H–x diagram to the material balance operating lines on the x–y diagram.

Let the feed be a liquid at its boiling point. The position of feed F (H_F, x_F) on the boiling point line and top product (H_D, x_D) are located.

$$H_D' = H_D + \frac{q_C}{D} \tag{4.94}$$

Then B$'$ is located on the extension of D$'$F with coordinates (x_B, H_B) where

$$H_B' = H_B - \frac{q_r}{B} \tag{4.95}$$

The condition of the vapour leaving the top plate is shown at V_1 on the dew point curve with abscissa x_D. The condition of liquid leaving the top plate is then found by drawing the tie line T_1, (x_1, y_1) connecting V_1 on the dew point curve and L_1 on the boiling point curve using equilibrium data. The condition V_2 of the vapour on the second plate is found by drawing L_1D' to intersect the dew point curve on V_2. L_2 is then found by the tie line T_2. The conditions of the other vapour and liquid upto F are found in the same way. When the feed composition F is crossed, the operating lines are drawn based on B′.

After passing over point F, the first point on the dew point curve gives the vapour composition of the top plate in the stripping section. Other liquid and vapour compositions are found by similar construction but using B′ till x_B is reached. The construction can also be started from B′ and can go upwards. The procedure is shown in Fig. 4.41.

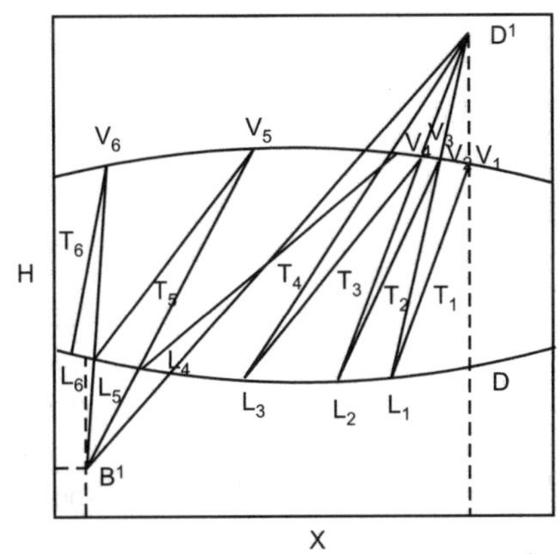

Fig. 4.41 Ponchon–Savarit construction for finding theoretical plates

ILLUSTRATION

4S The enthalpy–concentration data for a binary system is given in Table 4.8.

Table 4.8 Enthalpy–concentration data

Mole fraction of A in liquid	0.25	0.407	0.62	0.839
Mole fraction of A in vapour	0.396	0.566	0.756	0.906
Specific enthalpy of liquid, kcal kmol^{-1}	180	145	195	260
Specific enthalpy of vapour, kcal kmol^{-1}	1030	955	895	885

The rest of the data can be obtained by extrapolation. A feed mixture containing

30 mol% A is to be separated into an overhead product containing 90 mol% A and a bottom product containing 6 mol% A. Determine the ideal number of plates needed if the reflux ratio is 3. The feed enters as a liquid at its boiling point.

Solution

Figure 4.42 shows the x–y diagram for this illustration. The feed is a liquid at its boiling point. It is given that $x_F = 0.3$. Locate F on the bubble point curve using $x_F.x_D = 0.9$ and locate D on the dew point curve using $x_D.\ x_B = 0.06$. Locate B on the bubble point curve using x_B.

R_D is given and from the enthalpy data, corrected heat content of the distillate, $H_D^{'}$ is found.

$$R_D = \frac{H_D^{'} - H_1^V}{H_1^V - H_D}$$

$$3 = \frac{H_D^{'} - 890}{890 - 280}$$

$$H_D^{'} = 2\ 720 \text{ kcal kmol}^{-1}$$

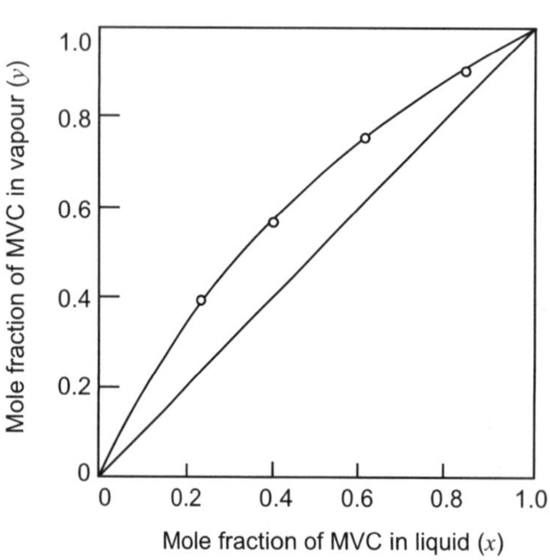

Fig. 4.42 x–y diagram for 4S

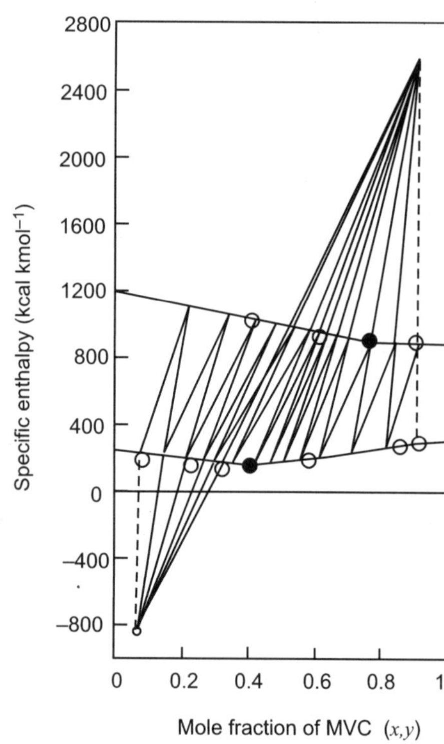

Fig. 4.43 Graphical construction for 4S

Using x_D and $H_D^{'}$ locate D'. Join D′F and extend to B′. Locatc B′ using x_B. The condition of the vapour leaving the top plate is shown at V_1 on the dew point curve with abscissa x_D. The condition of the liquid leaving the top plate is then found by drawing the tie line $T_1, (x_1, y_1)$ connecting V_1 on the dew point curve and L_1 on the boiling point curve using equilibrium data. The condition V_2 of the vapour on the second plate is found by drawing $L_1 D'$ to intersect the dew point curve on V_2. L_2 is then found by the tie line T_2. The conditions of the other vapour and liquid up to F are found in the same way. When the feed composition F is crossed, the operating lines are drawn based on B′. After passing over point F, the first point on the dew point curve gives the vapour composition of the top plate in the stripping section. The other liquid and vapour compositions are found by similar construction but using B′ till x_B is reached. Construction can also be started from B′ and can go upwards. The procedure is shown in Fig. 4.41. The number of ideal plates required for this operation is 13. The graphical solution is shown in Fig. 4.43.

PLATE EFFICIENCY

To translate ideal plates into actual plates, the plate efficiency must be known. In fact three types of plate efficiencies are possible.

1. overall efficiency, denoting the efficiency of the entire column,
2. Murphree efficiency, denoting the efficiency of a single plate and
3. local efficiency, denoting the efficiency at a specific location on a single plate.

The overall efficiency (η_o) is defined as the ratio of the number of ideal plates needed in an entire column to the actual number of plates. If 5 ideal plates are required for a desired separation whereas 10 actual plates are used then efficiency is 0.5 or 50%.

Murphree efficiency (η_M) is the change in vapour composition from one plate to the next divided by the change that would have occurred if the vapour leaving were in equilibrium with the liquid leaving.

$$\eta_M = \frac{y_n - y_{n+1}}{y_n^* - y_{n+1}^*} \tag{4.96}$$

The local efficiency (η^1) is defined by $\eta^1 = \frac{y_n^I - y_{n+1}^I}{y_n^{*I} - y_{n+1}^I}$, where y_n^I is the concentration of vapour leaving a specific location on plate n, y_{n+1}^I is concentration of vapour entering the same location on plate $n+1$ and y_n^{*I} is the concentration of vapour in equilibrium with liquid at the same location on plate n.

NOTATIONS

D	Moles of distillate.
f	Fraction of feed that has been flashed.
F	Moles of feed.
H	Enthalpy, kJ kmol^{-1}.
H_F	Enthalpy of feed, kJ kmol^{-1}.
H_B	Enthalpy of bottom product, kJ kmol^{-1}.
H_D	Enthalpy of distillate, kJ kmol^{-1}.
L	Molar flow rate of liquid, kmol s^{-1}.
L_n	Molar flow rate of liquid leaving the nth plate, kmol s^{-1}.
L_{n-1}	Molar flow rate of liquid leaving the $n-1^{\text{th}}$ plate, kmol s^{-1}.
LVC	Less volatile component, component B.
m	Henry's law constant; a general plate in the stripping section.
M_A	Molecular weight of the MVC.
M_B	Molecular weight of the LVC.
MVC	More volatile component, component A.
n	Total moles of feed; a general plate in the rectifying section.
n_A	Number of moles of MVC in the feed.
n_B	Number of moles of LVC in the feed.
P	Total pressure, N m^{-2}.
P_A	Partial pressure of component A in the gaseous mixture, N m^{-2}.
P_B	Partial pressure of component B in the gaseous mixture, N m^{-2}.
P_i	Partial pressure of the ith component in the gaseous mixture, N m^{-2}.
P_A^*	Vapour pressure of pure A in the liquid state, N m^{-2}.
P_B^*	Vapour pressure of pure B in the liquid state, N m^{-2}.
q	q factor.
q_c	Heat removed from the condenser.
q_r	Heat added to the reboiler.
R_D	Molar reflux ratio.
$R_{D,\min}$	Minimum reflux ratio.
R_S	Rectifying section.
S_S	Stripping section.
T	Boiling point, K.
T_F	Boiling point of the feed, K.
T_b	Boiling point of the liquid, K.
T_d	Dew point of the vapour, K.
V	Molar flow rate of vapour, kmol s^{-1}.
V_n	Molar flow rate of vapour leaving the nth plate, kmol s^{-1}.
V_{n+1}	Molar flow rate of vapour leaving the $n+1^{\text{th}}$ plate, kmol s^{-1}.
W	Moles of residue.

W_A	Weight of MVC in the feed.
W_B	Weight of LVC in the feed.
x	Mole fraction of more volatile component in the heavy phase, liquid.
x	Mole fraction of MVC in the residue.
x_b	Mole fraction of MVC in the liquid phase leaving the distillation column.
x_n	Mole fraction of MVC in the liquid phase leaving the nth plate.
x_{n-1}	Mole fraction of MVC in the liquid phase leaving the $n - 1^{\text{th}}$ plate.
x_A	Mole fraction of component A in the liquid phase; also denoted by x.
x_B	Mole fraction of component B in the liquid phase; also denoted by $(1 - x)$.
x_B	Mole fraction of MVC in the bottom product.
x_F	Mole fraction of MVC in the feed; mole fraction of MVC in the distillate.
x_W	Mole fraction of MVC in the residue.
y	Mole fraction of more volatile component in the light phase, gas.
y	Mole fraction of MVC in the distillate.
y_a	Mole fraction of MVC in the vapour phase leaving the distillation column.
y_n	Mole fraction of MVC in the vapour phase leaving the nth plate.
y_{n+1}	Mole fraction of MVC in the vapour phase leaving the $n + 1^{\text{th}}$ plate.
y_r	Mole fraction of MVC in the vapour phase leaving the reboiler.
y_A	Mole fraction of component A in the vapour phase; also denoted by y.
y_B	Mole fraction of component B in the vapour phase; also denoted by $(1-y)$.
y_D	Mole fraction of MVC in the distillate.
α_A	Volatility of component A.
α_B	Volatility of component B.
α_{AB}	Volatility of component A relative to component B; also known as relative volatility and denoted by α
α_{av}	Average value of relative volatility.
α_{min}	Minimum value of relative volatility.
α_{max}	Maximum value of relative volatility.
γ_A	Activity coefficient of component, A.
γ_B	Activity coefficient of component, B.
λ	Molar latent heat of vaporisation, kJ kmol^{-1}.
η_o	Overall efficiency.
η_M	Murphree efficiency.
η^1	Local efficiency.

REFERENCES

1. Hala EJ, Pick VF and Velim O, *Vapour–liquid Equilibria*, Newyork, Elsevier, 1973.
2. McCabe WL and Thiele EW, *Ind. Eng. Chem.*, **17**: 605 (1925).
3. Underwood AJV, *Chem. Eng. Prog.*, **44**: 603 (1948).
4. Fenske MR, *Ind. Eng .Chem.*, **24**: 482 (1931).

5. Furter WF, *Adv. Chem. Ser.*, **115**: 45 (1972).
6. Poncon M, *Tech. Mod.*, **13**: 55 (1921).
7. Savarit R, *Arts Metiers*, **1922**: 65, 142, 178, 241, 266, 307.

Problems for Practice

4.1 A liquid mixture containing 60 mol% benzene and rest toluene is differentially distilled at 1 atm pressure to yield a residue containing 30 mol% benzene. Calculate the composition of the distillate and the percentage vapourisation.

The vapour–liquid equilibrium data is as follows:

Mole fraction of benzene in liquid	0.06	0.16	0.30	0.40	0.50	0.70	0.82	1.00
Mole fraction of benzene in vapour	0.13	0.30	0.45	0.60	0.72	0.83	0.92	1.00

4.2 A continuous rectifying column treats a mixture consisting of 40% of benzene by weight and 60% of toluene by weight at the rate of 4 kg s^{-1} and separates it into a product containing 95% benzene and a liquid containing 97% toluene. The feed is a liquid at its boiling point. Determine (i) the weights of distillate and waste liquor per unit time, (ii) if a reflux of 3.5 to 1 is employed, how many plates are required in the rectifying part of the column, (iii) what is the actual number of plates if the plate efficiency is 60%? Use the equilibrium data given for 4.1.

4.3 A continuous fractionator is to be designed for separating a feed mixture containing equimolar amounts of CCl_4 and CS_2 into a top product containing 95% CS_2 and bottom product containing 6% CS_2. The feed is saturated vapour and is fed at a rate of 5000 kg h^{-1}. A total condenser is used and the reflux is returned to the top plate as a saturated liquid. The equilibrium data is given below:

Mole fraction of CS_2 in liquid	0.06	0.11	0.26	0.39	0.53	0.66	0.76	0.86	1.00
Mole fraction of CS_2 in vapour	0.13	0.30	0.45	0.60	0.72	0.83	0.88	0.93	1.00

(a) Determine the flow rate of the top and bottom product.
(b) Calculate the theoretical number of trays required if a reflux ratio of 2 times R_D min is used.
(c) Locate the feed tray.

4.4 A benzene–toluene solution containing 50% benzene is to be fractionated continuously in a distillation column to get a top product of 80% benzene. The bottom product should not contain more than 12% benzene. The feed is at its bubble point. The relative volatility is 2.5. Find the following. (i) Minimum reflux ratio, (ii) minimum number of plated required, (iii) if twice the minimum reflux ratio is used, theoretical number of plates required.

4.5 A continuous distillation column is used to separate a feed mixture containing 25 mol% acetone and the remaining methanol. The top product should contain 80% acetone. The residue should not contain more than 5% acetone. The feed is 40% liquid and 60% vapour. A reflux of twice the minimum is used. Determine the number of theoretical plates required.

Data:

Mole fraction of acetone in liquid	0.05	0.1	0.2	0.3	0.4	0.5	0.6	0.7	0.8	1.0
Mole fraction of acetone in vapour	0.102	0.186	0.322	0.428	0.513	0.586	0.656	0.725	0.8	1.0

4.6 Compute the vapour–liquid equilibria at a constant pressure of 1 atm for mixtures of n-heptane and n-octane which forms an ideal solution.

Temperature (K)	371.4	378	383	388	393	398.6
Vapour pressure of n-heptane (kPa)	101.3	125.3	140.0	159.9	179.9	205.3
Vapour pressure of n-octane (kPa)	44.4	55.6	64.5	74.8	86.6	101.3

Draw the x–y diagram. Estimate the relative volatility.

4.7 It is desired to separate a mixture containing of 40 mol% n-heptane and 60 mol% ethylbenzene by distillation at 1 atm pressure to produce a distillate containing 95 mol% n-heptane and a residue containing 96 mol% ethylbenzene. The feed enters as a liquid at its boiling point. (i) Determine the minimum reflux ratio, (ii) using a reflux ratio of 2.5 times the minimum, determine the theoretical number of stages.

Mole fraction of n-heptane in liquid	0	0.08	0.185	0.251	0.335	0.487	0.651	0.788	0.914	1.0
Mole fraction of n-heptane in vapour	0	0.233	0.428	0.514	0.608	0.729	0.814	0.904	0.963	1.0

4.8 A liquid mixture containing 50 mol% heptane and 50 mol% octane is distilled in a continuous fractionating column to a top product containing 95% heptane and a bottom product containing 94% octane. The feed enters at its boiling point. The reflux ratio used is 1.5 times the minimum. Estimate the theoretical number of plates needed.

Data:

Mole fraction of n-heptane in liquid	0	0.157	0.312	0.487	0.655	1.0
Mole fraction of n-heptane in vapour	0	0.279	0.492	0.674	0.810	1.0

4.9 An equimolar mixture of A and B is flash distilled such that 70 mol% of the feed is distilled out at 1 atm. Estimate the composition of the residue and distillate.

Equilibrium data:

Mole fraction of n-heptane in liquid	0	0.08	0.185	0.251	0.335	0.487	0.651	0.788	0.914	1.0
Mole fraction of n-heptane in vapour	0	0.233	0.428	0.514	0.608	0.729	0.814	0.904	0.963	1.0

4.10 An equimolal feed of ethylacetate and acetic acid at its bubble point is to be distilled to yield an overhead product of 98 mol% of ethylacetate and a residue having 2 mol% of ethylacetate. If the reflux ratio is 1.5 times the minimum, estimate the number of ideal stages required and the location of the feed point.

Equilibrium data:

Mole fraction of ethylacetate in liquid	0	0.1	0.2	0.4	0.6	0.8	1.0
Mole fraction of ethylacetate in vapour	0	0.31	0.5	0.7	0.93	0.93	1.0

4.11 A fractionating column separates a liquid mixture of 50 wt% chloroform and 50 wt% CS_2 at 1 atm at the rate of 5 000 kg h^{-1} into a distillate containing 94 wt% CS_2 and a residue of 4 wt% CS_2. The feed is 28 mol% vapour before entering the tower. A total condenser and reflux at its bubble point are used. The equilibrium data are as follows:

x	0.03	0.06	0.11	0.14	0.26	0.39	0.53	0.66	0.76	0.86	1.00
y	0.08	0.16	0.27	0.33	0.50	0.63	0.71	0.83	0.88	0.93	1.00

x and y refer to the mole fraction of CS_2 in the liquid and vapour respectively. Determine the number of theoretical trays required at a reflux ratio of 2.2 times the minimum and the composition of liquid and vapour leaving the second plate from top.

4.12 A continuous rectifying column treats a mixture containing 40 mol% benzene and 60 mol% toluene and separates into distillate product containing 98 mol% benzene and a bottom product containing 98 mol% toluene. The feed enters as a liquid at its boiling point. If a reflux ratio of 3.5 is used, estimate the height of the tower. The average height of a transfer unit is 0.7 m. The overall resistance to mass transfer lies in the vapour phase. Equilibrium data:

x	0	0.1	0.2	0.3	0.4	0.5	0.6	0.7	0.8	0.9	1.00
y	0	0.22	0.38	0.51	0.63	0.7	0.78	0.85	0.91	0.96	1.00

x and y refer to the mole fraction of benzene in the liquid and vapour respectively.

4.13 A mixture of 35 mol% A and 65 mol% B is to be separated in a distillation column. The concentration of A in the distillate is 93% and concentration of B in the residue is 96%. The feed enters at its bubble point. If the reflux ratio is 2.1 times the minimum, estimate the theoretical number of stages needed and the feed plate location. The relative volatility is 2.0.

4.14 A binary mixture containing 60 mol% n-heptane and 40 mol% n-octane at 300 K is subjected to differential distillation at atmospheric pressure with 75 mol% of the feed liquid distilled. Assuming the relative volatility as 2.17, determine the composition of the charge in the still and that of distillate.

4.15 A mixture of 50 mol of liquid benzene and 50 mol of H_2O is boiling at 101.32 kPa pressure. Liquid benzene is immiscible in water. Determine the boiling point of the mixture and the composition of the vapour. Which component will first be removed completely from the still? The vapour pressure data of the pure components follows:

Temperature (K)	308.3	325.7	345.6	353.1
Vapour pressure of water (kPa)	5.33	16.7	18.7	21.3
Vapour pressure of benzene (kPa)	20.0	40.0	80.0	101.3

4.16 The enthalpy–concentration data for a binary system of volatile liquids is given below:

Mole fraction of A in liquid	0.25	0.407	0.62	0.839
Mole fraction of A in vapour	0.396	0.566	0.756	0.906
Specific enthalpy of liquid, kJ kmol^{-1}	754	607	816	1089
Specific enthalpy of vapour, kJ kmol^{-1}	4313	4000	3747	3706

The rest of the data can be obtained by extrapolation. A feed mixture with an initial composition of 30 mol% A is to be separated into an overhead product of 95 mol% A and 4 mol% of A at the bottom. Determine the ideal number of stages if the reflux ratio is 2.4. The feed enters as a saturated liquid.

4.17 A feed mixture containing equimolar quantities of A and B is distilled differentially such that 60 mol% of the feed is distilled out. Estimate the composition of residue and distillate. Equilibrium data is given below.

x	0	0.1	0.2	0.3	0.4	0.5	0.6	0.7	0.8	0.9	1.00
y	0	0.21	0.38	0.51	0.63	0.72	0.78	0.85	0.91	0.96	1.00

x and y refer to the mole fraction of A in the liquid and vapour respectively.

4.18 A continuous fractionating column is to be designed for separating 4 000 kg h^{-1} of liquid mixture containing an equimolar mixture of methanol and water into an overhead product containing 95% methanol and a residue containing 3% methanol. The feed is 30% vaporised. Calculate (i) molar flow rate of overhead and bottom product, (ii) the number of actual plates assuming overall tray efficiency of 0.7, (iii) use reflux of 1.75 times minimum and locate the feed tray. Equilibrium data:

x	0	0.1	0.2	0.3	0.4	0.5	0.6	0.7	0.8	0.9	1.00
y	0	0.417	0.579	0.669	0.729	0.78	0.825	0.879	0.915	0.959	1.00

x and y refer to the mole fraction of methanol in the liquid and vapour respectively.

4.19 100 kmol h^{-1} of benzene–toluene mixture containing 50 mol% benzene is to be separated in a continuous plate column operating at 1 atm pressure. The distillate is to contain 90 mol% benzene and the bottom products to contain 10 mol% benzene. The feed is a liquid at its boiling point. The reflux ratio is 4.5. Find the number of theoretical plates. Use the equilibrium data given for problem 4.12.

4.20 It is desired to design a plate column for separating a equimolar feed mixture of A and B to get a product of 95% A and 5% A in the distillate and residue respectively. The reflux enters the column at its bubble point and the reflux ratio of 1.5 times the minimum is to be used. Estimate the number of plates needed if the plate efficiency is 80%.

Mole fraction of A in liquid	0	0.16	0.31	0.49	0.66	1.0
Mole fraction of A in vapour	0	0.28	0.49	0.67	0.81	1.0

4.21 Methanol and ethanol form an ideal solution. Compute VLE data and prepare plots of x Vs y and T–x–y at 1 atm pressure. The following pure component vapour pressure data may be used.

Vapour pressure (kPa)	26.7	53.3	101.3	202.6
Temperature for ethanol (K)	321.4	335.5	361.4	370.5
Temperature for methanol (K)	301.8	322.9	337.7	357

4.22 It is required to distill 100 mol h^{-1} of an ethyl alcohol and n-butyl alcohol mixture containing 40 mol% of ethyl alcohol. The top product contains 95 mol% ethyl alcohol and the bottom product contains 95 mol% n-butyl alcohol. Assume a reflux ratio of 1.5 times the minimum; the feed enters at its boiling point. Calculate the actual number of plates required if the overall plate efficiency is 45%. The equilibrium data is as follows:

Mole fraction of ethanol in liquid	0	0.11	0.25	0.43	0.6	0.74	0.94	1.0
Mole fraction of ethanol in vapour	0	0.32	0.60	0.78	0.9	0.95	0.99	1.0

4.23 1 000 kg of a binary mixture containing 30% benzene by weight and the rest toluene is differentially distilled at 1 atm pressure to yield a residue containing 18% by weight of benzene. Determine the composition and weight of the distillate and residue using the equilibrium data.

Mole fraction of benzene in liquid	0	0.06	0.16	0.26	0.38	0.51	0.66	0.82	1.00
Mole fraction of benzene in vapour	0	0.13	0.30	0.45	0.60	0.72	0.83	0.92	1.00

4.24 A continuous fractionating column is to be designed to separate a mixture containing of 50 mol% each of n-heptane and ethylbenzene into a top product containing 95 mol% heptane and a bottom product containing 95 mol% ethylbenzene. The column will be equipped with a reboiler and a total condenser. The feed is at its bubble point. How many plates are necessary if the reflux ratio is thrice the minimum value? The overall efficiency is 70%.

Mole fraction of heptane in liquid	0	0.08	0.185	0.335	0.487	0.651	0.788	0.914	1.0
Mole fraction of heptane in vapour	0	0.23	0.43	0.61	0.73	0.85	0.90	0.96	1.0

4.25 100 kmol h^{-1} of a benzene–toluene mixture containing 50 mol% benzene is to be separated in a continuous plate column operating at 1 atm pressure. The distillate is to contain 90 mol% benzene and the bottom products to contain 10 mol% benzene. Calculate the minimum number of plates using the Fenske equation. Use the equilibrium data given in problem 4.24.

4.26 A mixture of 100 mol containing 50 mol% n-pentane and the rest n-heptane is distilled at differential conditions at 101.3 kPa until 40 mol is distilled. What is the average composition of total vapour distilled and of the liquid left?

Equilibrium data:

Mole fraction of pentane in liquid	1	0.867	0.594	0.398	0.254	0.145	0.059	0
Mole fraction of pentane in vapour	0	0.984	0.925	0.836	0.701	0.521	0.271	0

4.27 Compute the vapour–liquid equilibrium data at constant pressure of 1 bar for mixtures of n-heptane with n-octane. The vapour pressure is given below:

Temperature (K)	371.3	378	383	388	393	398.6
Vapour pressure of n-heptane (bar)	1.00	1.237	1.381	1.579	1.776	2.036
Vapour pressure of n–octane (bar)	0.438	0.549	0.637	0.738	0.855	1.0

Also compute the average relative volatility.

5

Leaching and Extraction

Selective dissolution of one of the components of a solid mixture by a liquid solvent is known as leaching. If the mixture to be separated is in the liquid state, the operation is extraction. Basic concepts and design considerations of leaching and extraction operations are described in this chapter.

Leaching and extraction are concerned with preferential removal of one component from a mixture using a liquid solvent. When the mixture and the component to be removed are in the form of solids, the operation is termed *leaching* and when the mixture and the component to be removed are liquids, the operation is termed *extraction*. To a large extent, the fundamentals of both the processes are similar. The difference mainly lies in the equipment used for carrying out the operation.

The three different methods of leaching are

1. Leaching by percolation (Shank's process).
2. Moving bed leaching (the equipment for this is Hildebrandt extractor or Bollman extractor).
3. Dispersed solid leaching.

CONTINUOUS COUNTER CURRENT LEACHING [1]

A continuous counter current leaching battery consists of a series of units. The feed solid is fed to the last unit and fresh solvent to the first unit. In each unit, the solid from the previous unit is mixed with the liquid from the succeeding unit and the mixture is allowed to settle. The solid is then transferred to the succeeding unit and the liquid to the previous unit. A schematic representation for a continuous counter current leaching set up consisting of three units is given in Fig. 5.1. As the liquid flows from unit to unit, it becomes enriched in the solute and as the solid flows from unit to unit it becomes lean in solute. The solid discharged at one end is well extracted and the solution leaving at the other end is strong in solute. The thoroughness of the extraction depends on the

1. Amount of solvent.
2. Number of units.

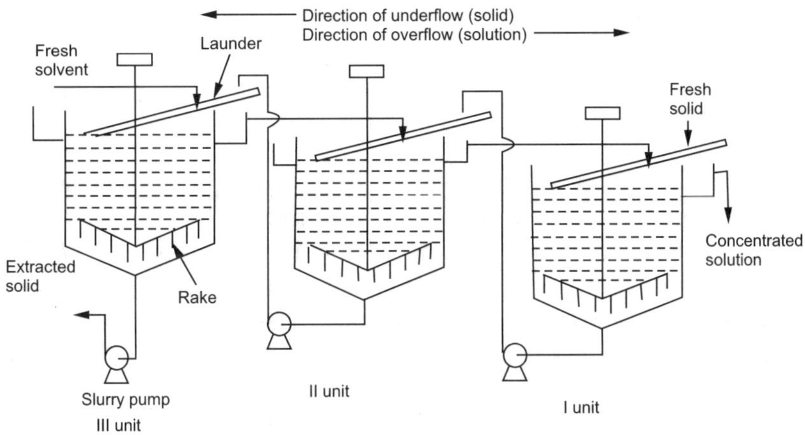

Fig. 5.1 Continuous counter current leaching

IDEAL STAGES IN COUNTER CURRENT LEACHING

A multi-stage counter current leaching unit is shown in Fig. 5.2. The stages are numbered in the direction of flow of the solid. The liquid phase is the liquid that overflows from stage to stage in a direction counter to that of the flow of the solid-dissolving solute as it moves from stage N to 1. The solid phase is the solid flowing from stage 1 to stage N. Exhausted solids leave stage N and the concentrated solution overflows from stage one. It is assumed that the solute-free solid is insoluble in the solvent and that the flow rate of this solid is constant throughout the cascade.

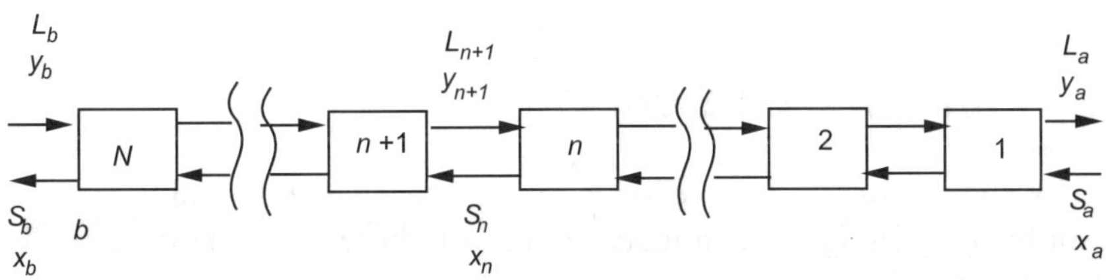

Fig. 5.2 Multistage counter current leaching
S: flow rate of solid, L: flow rate of liquid, x: solute fraction in solid, y: solute fraction in liquid

The solid is porous and carries with it an amount of solution which may or may not be constant. Let L refer to the flow rate of overflow solution and S refer to that of the retained solution. S and L may be expressed as mass per unit time or mass per unit mass of solute-free solid. Let y_a refer to the solute concentration in the leaving solution, y_b the solute concentration in the feed solvent, x_a the solute concentration in the solution contained by the feed solid and x_b the solute concentration in the leaving solid. The performance of the equipment can be analysed by studying the equilibrium curve and operating line as in the case of absorption and distillation.

Equilibrium Curve

If sufficient solvent is provided to dissolve all the solute in the entering solid and if there is no adsorption of solute by the solid, equilibrium is attained when the solute is completely dissolved and the concentration of solution is uniform. When equilibrium is attained, the concentration of the solution retained by the solid leaving any stage is equal to the concentration of liquid overflow from that stage. That is, $x = y$. Hence, the diagonal is the equilibrium curve in the case of leaching.

Operating Line

As usual, the equation of the operating line is the material balance equation for the first n stages.

Overall balance: $$S_a + L_{n+1} = S_n + L_a \tag{5.1}$$

Solute balance: $$S_a x_a + L_{n+1} y_{n+1} = S_n x_n + L_a y_a \tag{5.2}$$

$$y_{n+1} = \frac{S_n}{L_{n+1}} x_n + \frac{L_a y_a - S_a x_a}{L_{n+1}} \tag{5.3}$$

So, the operating line passes through (x_a, y_a) and (x_b, y_b) and if the flow rates are constant the slope is $\frac{S}{L}$.

CONSTANT AND VARIABLE UNDERFLOW

If the density and viscosity of the solution change considerably with solute concentration, the solids of the initial stages retain more liquid than those of the later stages. This mode is known as variable underflow. Then the slope of the operating line varies from unit to unit.

If the mass of the solution retained by the solid is independent of concentration then S_n, the amount of solution retained by the solid from any stage, is constant and the operating line is a straight line. This condition is called constant solution underflow. If the underflow is constant, the overflow also will be constant.

NUMBER OF IDEAL STAGES FOR CONSTANT UNDERFLOW

For this case, the operating line is straight and it can be drawn if the extreme ends are known. The equilibrium curve, which is the diagonal, is also drawn on the same graph sheet. The number of theoretical stages can be determined by the usual McCabe–Thiele method [2].

ILLUSTRATIONS

5A In a leaching unit, feed solid containing 25% solute and 75% inert is treated with fresh solvent. After allowing sufficient time, the contents of the unit are filtered. The filtrate contains 10% solute and 90% solvent. The filter cake contains 2% solid solute and carries with it 0.2 kg of solution per kg of solid. Compute (i) the percentage recovery of solute and (ii) the weight of solvent used for this operation.

Solution

Basis: 100 kg of feed solid.

Weight of solute in the feed solid = 25 kg

Weight of inert in the feed solid = 75 kg

Inerts, which weigh 75 kg, form 98% of the filter cake and the balance 2% is solute.

Solute lost in the filter cake $= 75 \times \dfrac{2}{98} = 1.53$ kg

Filter cake = weight of inert + weight of solute

$= 75 + 1.53$ kg $= 76.53$ kg

Each kg of filter cake carries with it 0.2 kg of solution.

Solution carried by the filler cake $= 76.53 \times 0.2 = 15.31$ kg

This solution has the same composition as the filtrate. The filtrate contains 10% solute and 90% solvent.

Weight of solute in the solution carried by the filter cake $= 15.31 \times \dfrac{10}{100} = 1.53$ kg

Weight of solvent in the solution carried by the filler cake

= weight of solution – weight of solute $= 15.31 - 1.53 = 13.78$ kg

Weight of total solute lost in cake

= weight of solute in the cake + weight of solute in the solution

$= 1.53 + 1.53 = 3.06$ kg

Weight of solute recovered

= weight of solute in feed – weight of solute lost in filter cake

= 25 – 3.06 = 21.94 kg

Percentage recovery of solute $= \dfrac{21.94}{25} \times 100 = 87.76\%$

The filtrate contains 10% solute and 90% solvent.

Weight of solvent in filtrate $= 21.94 \times \dfrac{90}{10} = 197.46$ kg

Weight of solvent lost in filter cake = 13.78 kg

Weight of solvent used in the operation

= weight of solvent in the filtrate + weight of solvent lost in the filter cake

= 197.46 + 13.78 = 211.24 kg per 100 kg of feed solid

5B A counter current extraction battery is used to extract the sludge of the reaction

$$Na_2CO_3 + Ca(OH)_2 \rightarrow CaCO_3 + 2\ NaOH$$

$CaCO_3$ carries with it 1.5 times its weight of solution in flowing from one unit to another. It is desired to recover 95% of the NaOH to produce an aqueous solution of 10 wt% concentration. The products from the reactor enter the first unit with no excess reactants but with 0.5 kg H_2O per kg of $CaCO_3$. Calculate the number of kg of neutral wash water that must be used per kg of $CaCO_3$. How many ideal stages are required?

Solution

Basis: Products from the reactor with 0.5 kg H_2O per kg of $CaCO_3$.

In the reactor, 80 kg of NaOH is produced and it is accompanied by 100 kg $CaCO_3$. The slurry is mixed with 0.5 kg water per kg of $CaCO_3$ and fed to the leaching unit.

NaOH in the input to the leaching unit = 80 kg

$CaCO_3$ in the input to the leaching unit = 100 kg

Water in the input to the leaching unit = $100 \times 0.5 = 50$ kg

Weight fraction of NaOH in the feed solution (x_a) $= \dfrac{80}{80+50} = 0.615\,4$

Recovery of 95% of NaOH is desired.

NaOH recovered = $80 \times 0.95 = 76$ kg

Recovered NaOH leaves the leaching unit as 10 wt% aqueous solution and it forms the final overflow.

Weight fraction of NaOH in the final overflow $(y_b) = 0.1$

Water in the final overflow $= 76 \times \dfrac{90}{10} = 684$ kg

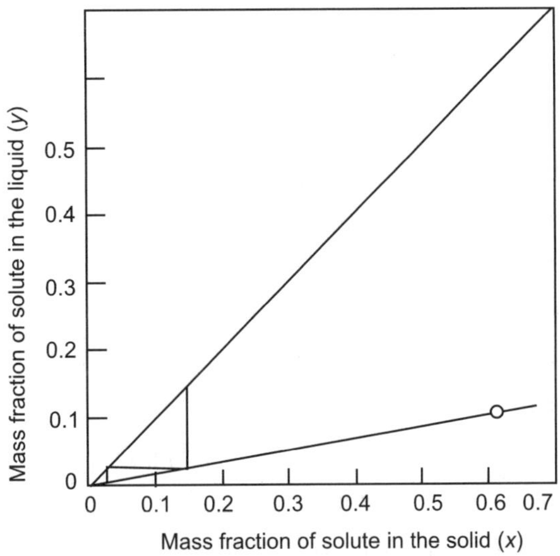

Fig. 5.3 Graphical solution for 5B

NaOH that is not recovered leaves the leaching unit as final underflow. The inert $CaCO_3$, as it flows from stage to stage, carries with it 1.5 times its weight of solution.

Solution in the final underflow $= 100 \times 1.5 = 150$ kg

Water in the final underflow $= 150 - 4 = 146$ kg

Weight fraction of NaOH in the final underflow (x_b) $= \dfrac{4}{150} = 0.027$

The leaching unit is fed with neutral water.

Weight fraction of NaOH in the water fed (y_a) $= 0$

Amount of neutral water fed to the leaching unit can be calculated by a water balance.

Neutral water fed = Water in the final overflow + water in the final underflow – water in the input $= 684 + 146 - 50 = 780$ kg

Neutral wash water required $= 780 \div 100 = 7.8$ kg per kg of $CaCO_3$

It is a case of constant underflow. So, the operating line is a straight line and can be plotted using the extreme ends, (x_a, y_a) and (x_b, y_b). The equilibrium curve which is the diagonal, is also drawn on the same graph sheet. The number of theoretical stages is then determined by the usual McCabe–Thiele method (Fig. 5.3).

Number of theoretical stages required $= 1.6 \approx 2.0$

5C A groundnut oil cake containing 10% oil by weight is to be extracted at the rate of 2 000 kg h^{-1} using 1 500 kg h^{-1} of pure hexane in a counter current multistage extraction unit. The cake retains 0.35 kg of solution per kg of oil free cake. Determine the number of ideal stages required to reduce the oil content of the cake to 1%.

Solution

In this problem, the entering solid does not have a solution. So, we have to separate the first unit from the rest. Determine the number of stages required to do the job based on a material balance for the $n - 1$ units and add one to get the actual number of theoretical stages. Figures 5.4a to 5.4c give the material balance details.

Basis: 1 hour operation.

The leaching unit is fed with 2 000 kg of oil cake and 1 500 kg of pure hexane.

Cake contains 10% oil by weight.

Oil in cake $= 2\ 000 \times 0.1 = 200$ kg

Oil free cake $= 1\ 800$ kg

It is desired that oil content of the cake should be reduced to 1%.

Oil in the cake leaving the leaching unit $= \dfrac{1 \times 1800}{99} = 18.18$ kg

Weight fraction of oil in the final overflow $(y_a) = \dfrac{181.82}{181.82 + 888.18} = 0.169\ 9$

Weight fraction of oil in the final underflow $(x_b) = \dfrac{18.18}{611.82 + 18.18} = 0.028\ 9$

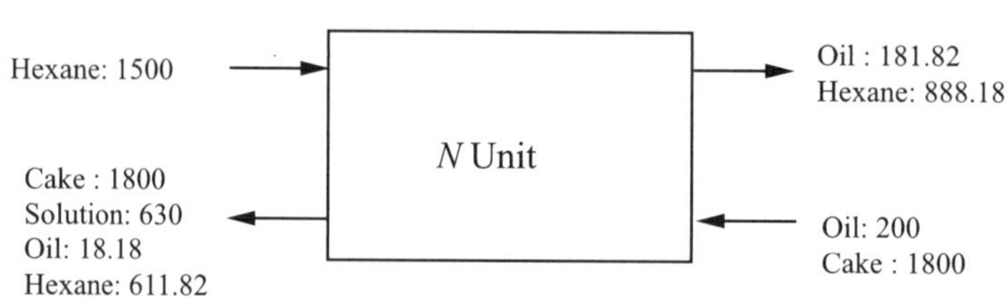

Fig. 5.4a Material balance for *N* units

The first stage has to be separated from the rest of the cascade. The composition of the liquid output and solid input to the first unit are known. The composition of the liquid input to the first unit and solid output from it has to be calculated. If the first stage is an ideal one, the leaving streams are in equilibrium. That is $y_a = x_1 = 0.169\ 9$. This fixes the weight fraction of oil in the solution retained by the solid output from the first unit. The cake retains 0.35 kg of solution per kg of oil free cake, as it flows from stage to stage.

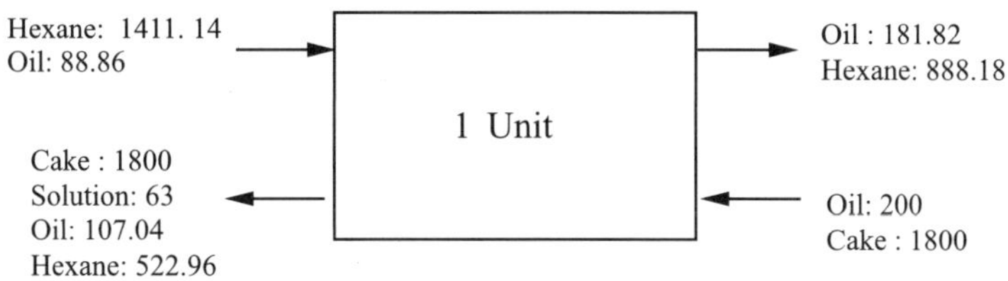

Fig. 5.4b Material balance for the I unit

Solution retained by the solid output from the first unit	=	$1\ 800 \times 0.35 = 630$ kg
Oil in this solution	=	$630 \times 0.169\ 9 = 107.04$ kg
Hexane is the balance, which is	=	$630 - 107.04 = 522.96$ kg
Weight fraction of oil in the underflow from the I Unit (x_1)	=	$\dfrac{107.04}{107.04 + 522.96} = 0.169\ 9$

By an oil and hexane balance over the first unit, the composition of the liquid input to the first unit can be found out.

Oil in liquid input to the first unit	=	$181.18 + 107.04 - 200 = 88.22$ kg
Hexane in liquid input to the first unit	=	$522.96 + 888.18 = 1\ 411.14$ kg
Weight fraction of oil in the liquid input to the I unit (y_2)	=	$\dfrac{88.22}{1411.14 + 88.22} = 0.058\ 8$

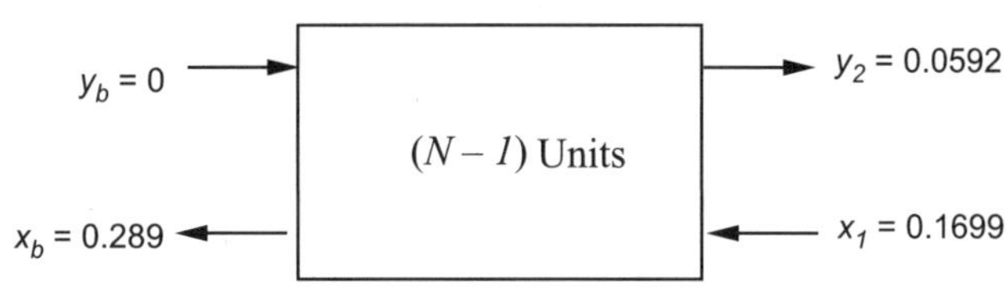

Fig. 5.4c Material balance for the *(N – 1)*units

Now for the $N - 1$ units, the input and output compositions are known. It is a case of constant underflow. So, the operating line is a straight line and can be plotted using the extreme ends, (x_1, y_2) and (x_b, y_b). The equilibrium curve, which is the diagonal is also drawn on the same graph sheet. The number of theoretical stages is then determined by the usual McCabe–Thiele method (Fig. 5.5). The number of theoretical stages required (N – 1) is 1.55. The actual number of theoretical stages is obtained by adding one. $N = 2.55 \approx 3$.

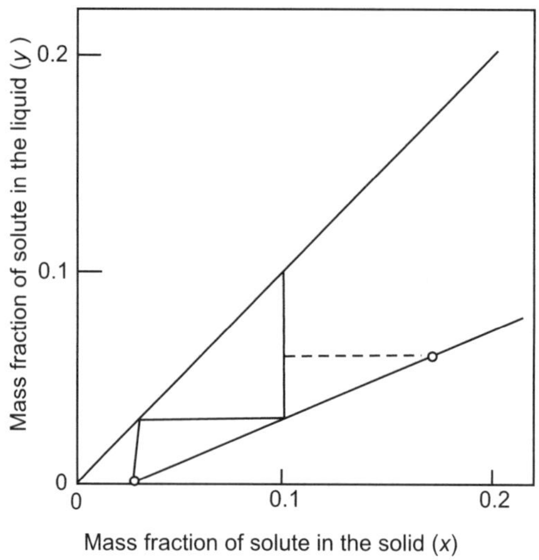

Fig. 5.5 Graphical solution for 5C

5D Seeds containing 20% oil by weight are to be extracted in a counter current multistage extraction unit. 90% of the oil is recovered as a solution containing 50% by weight of oil. If the seeds are extracted with fresh solvent and 1 kg of solution is removed in the underflow in association with every 2 kg of insoluble matter, how many ideal stages are required?

Solution

In this problem, the entering solid does not have a solution. So, we have to separate the first unit from the rest. Determine the number of stages required to do the job based on a material balance for the $n - 1$ units and add one to get the actual number of theoretical stages. Figures 5.6a to 5.6c give the material balance details.

Basis: 100 kg of seeds fed to the extractor.

Seeds contain 20% oil by weight.

Oil in seeds $= 100 \times 0.2 = 20$ kg

Oil free insoluble matter or meal $= 80$ kg

90% of the oil is recovered as a solution containing 50% by weight of oil.

Oil in the final overflow leaving the leaching unit $= 20 \times 0.9 = 18$ kg

Solvent in the final overflow leaving the leaching unit $=$ 18 kg

Weight fraction of oil in the final overflow (y_a) $=$ 0.50

Seeds are extracted with fresh solvent.

Weight fraction of oil in the entering solvent (y_a) $= 0$

Oil that is not recovered leaves the leaching unit as final underflow. The meal, as it flows from stage to stage carries with it 1 kg of solution for every 2 kg of meal.

Solution in the final underflow	=	$80 \times \frac{1}{2} - 40$ kg
Oil in the final underflow = oil fed – oil recovered	=	$20 - 18 = 2$ kg
Solvent in the final underflow = Weight of solution – weight of oil	=	$40 - 2 = 38$ kg
Weight fraction of oil in the final underflow (x_b)	=	$\frac{2}{40} = 0.05$

Amount of solvent fed to the leaching unit can be calculated by a solvent balance.

Solvent fed = Solvent in the final overflow + solvent in the final underflow $= 18 + 38 = 56$ kg

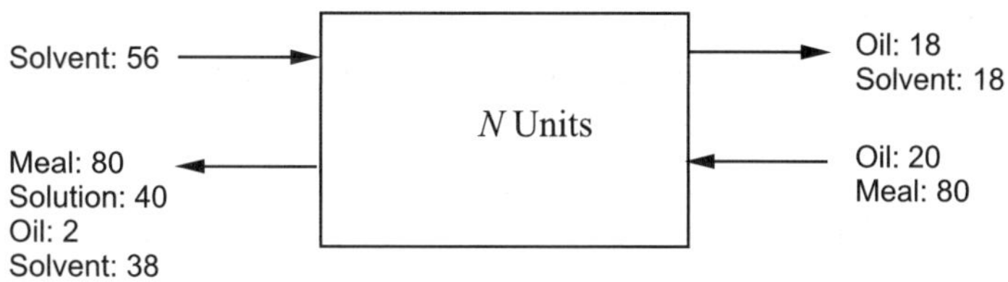

Fig. 5.6a Material balance for the N unit

The first stage has to be separated from the rest of the cascade. The composition of the liquid output and the solid input to the first unit are known. The composition of the liquid input to the first unit and solid output from it has to be calculated. If the first stage is an ideal one, the leaving streams are in equilibrium. That is, $y_a = x_1 = 0.50$. This fixes the weight fraction of oil in the solution retained by the solid output from the first unit. Every kg of meal retains 0.5 kg of solution as it flows from stage to stage.

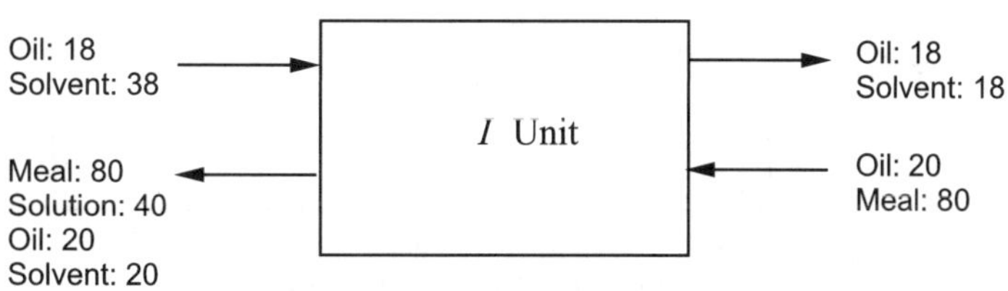

Fig. 5.6b Material balance for the I unit

Solution retained by the solid output from the first unit	=	$80 \times 0.5 = 40$ kg
Oil in this solution	=	$40 \times 0.5 = 20$ kg
Solvent is the balance, which is	=	$40 - 20 = 20$ kg

By an oil and solvent balance over the first unit, the composition of the liquid input to the first unit can be found out.

Oil in liquid input to the first unit	$=$	$20 + 18 - 20 = 18$ kg
Solvent in liquid input to the first unit	$=$	$20 + 18 = 38$ kg
Weight fraction of oil in the liquid input to the I unit (y_2)	$=$	$\dfrac{18}{18 + 38} = 0.321$

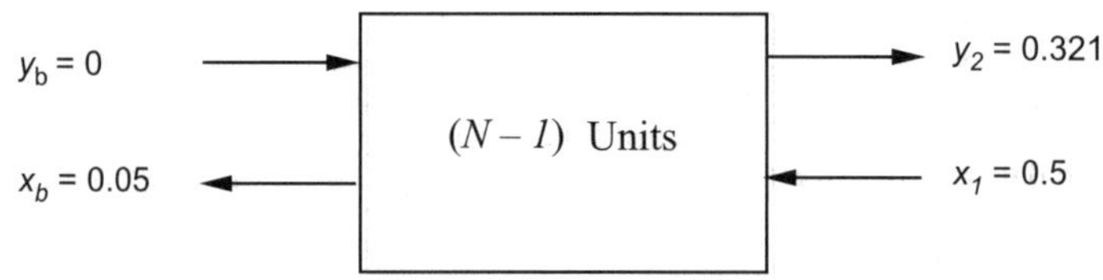

Fig. 5.6c Material balance for the $(N - 1)$ units

Now for the $N - 1$ units, the input and output compositions are known. It is a case of constant underflow. So, the operating line is a straight line and can be plotted using the extreme ends, (x_1, y_2) and (x_b, y_b).

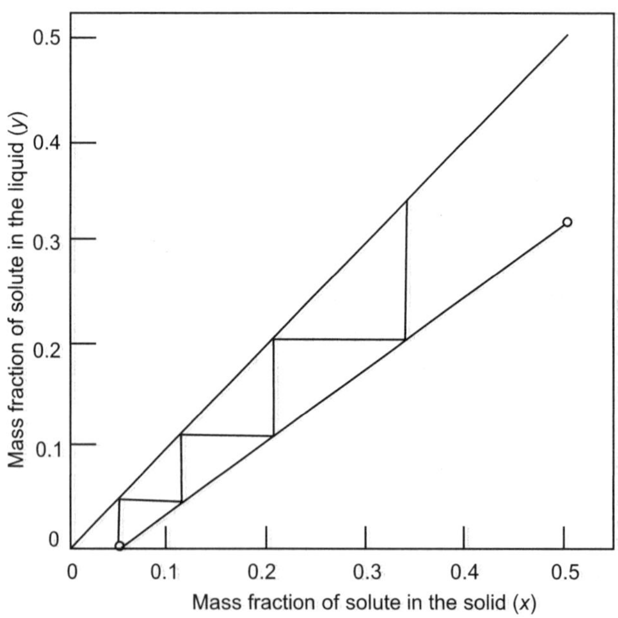

Fig. 5.7 Graphical solution for 5D

The equilibrium curve which is the diagonal, is also drawn on the same graph sheet. The number of theoretical stages is then determined by the usual McCabe–Thiele method (Fig. 5.7). The number of theoretical stages required $(N - 1)$ is 3.85. The actual number of theoretical stages is obtained by adding one. $N = 4.85 \approx 5$.

5E 2 000 kg h^{-1} tung meal containing 60% oil by weight is to be extracted in a counter current multiple extractor process using 3 000 kg h^{-1} of hexane containing 0.5 wt% of oil. After extraction, the meal contains 1 kg of solution per kg of oil free meal. The overflow contains 0.05 kg of fine meal particles per kg of solution. How many ideal stages are required to recover 95% of oil?

Solution

In this problem, the entering solid does not have a solution. So, we have to separate the first unit from the rest. Determine the number of stages required to do the job based on a material balance for $N - 1$ units and add one to get the actual number of theoretical stages. The entering solvent contains solute. The final overflow contains fine meal particles. Both have to be taken into account properly. Figures 5.8a to 5.8c give the material balance details.

Basis: 1 hour operation.

The leaching unit is fed with 2 000 kg of meal and 3 000 kg of hexane containing solute.

Cake contains 60% oil by weight.

Oil in meal = $2\ 000 \times 0.6 = 1\ 200$ kg

Oil free meal = 800 kg

It is desired to recover 95% of oil.

Oil in the final underflow leaving the leaching unit = $1\ 200 \times 0.05 = 60$ kg

After extraction, the meal contains 1 kg of solution per kg of oil free meal.

Solution in the final underflow leaving the leaching unit = 800 kg

Solvent entering the unit = 3 000 kg

Oil in it = $3\ 000 \times 0.005 = 15$ kg

Pure hexane fed = 2985 kg

Let the final overflow be L_a. The final overflow contains 0.05 kg of fine meal particles per kg of solution.

Meal in the final overflow = $0.05L_a$

Meal in final underflow = $800 - 0.05L_a$

Solution in final underflow = $800 - 0.05L_a$

Solvent in final underflow = solution – oil = $800 - 0.05L_a - 60 = 740 - 0.05L_a$

Oil in final overflow is found by an oil balance.

Oil in final overflow = $1\ 200 + 15 - 60 = 1155$

Hexane in final overflow = $2\ 985 - (740 - 0.05L_a)$

= $2\ 245 + 0.05L_a$

Final overflow, L_a is the sum of the two above.

$$L_a = 1\ 155 + 2\ 245 + 0.05 L_a \text{ and } L_a = 3\ 578.95 \text{ kg}$$

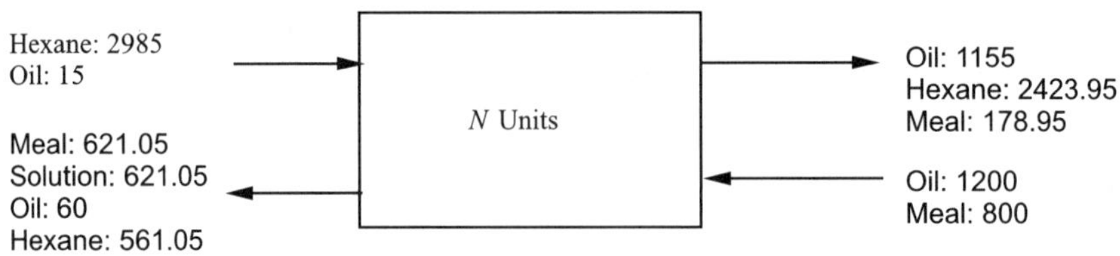

Fig. 5.8a Material balance for the N units

Weight fraction of oil in the final overflow (y_a) $= \dfrac{1155}{3578.95} = 0.322\ 7$

Weight fraction of oil in the final underflow (x_b) $= \dfrac{60}{621.05} = 0.097$

The first stage has to be separated from the rest of the cascade. The composition of the liquid output and solid input to the first unit are known. The composition of the liquid input to the first unit and solid output from it has to be found out. If the first stage is an ideal one, the leaving streams are in equilibrium. That is, $y_a = x_1 = 0.3227$. This fixes the weight fraction of oil in the solution retained by the solid output from the first unit. The meal contains 1 kg of solution per kg of oil free meal as it flows from stage to stage.

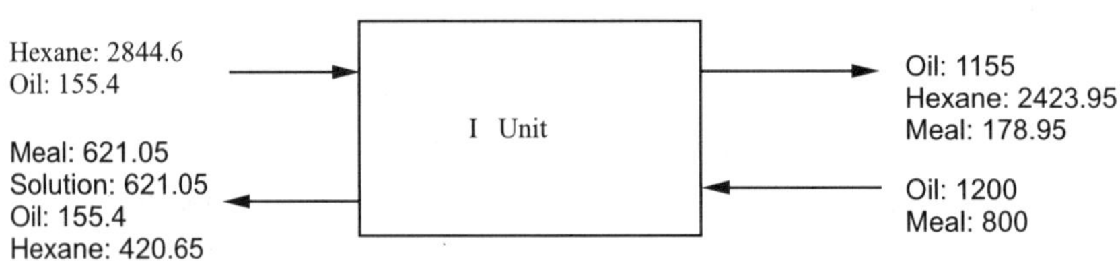

Fig. 5.8b Material balance for the I unit

Solution retained by the solid output from the first unit $= 621.05 \times 1 = 621.05$ kg

Oil in this solution $= 621.05 \times 0.322\ 7 = 200.4$ kg

Hexane is the balance, which is $= 621.05 - 200.4 = 420.65$ kg

Weight fraction of oil in the underflow from the I Unit (x_1) $= \dfrac{200.4}{621.05} = 0.322\ 7$

By an oil and hexane balance over the first unit, the composition of the liquid input to the first unit can be found out.

Oil in liquid input to the first unit $= 1\ 155 + 200.4 - 1\ 200 = 155.4$ kg

Hexane in liquid input to the first unit $= 2\ 423.95 + 420.65 = 2\ 844.6$ kg

Weight fraction of oil in the liquid input to the I unit (y_2) $= \dfrac{155.4}{155.4 + 2\,844.6} = 0.051\,8$

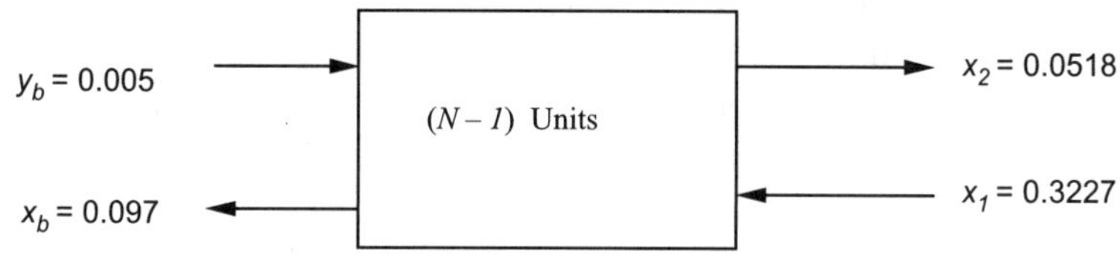

Fig. 5.8c Material balance for the $(N - 1)$ units

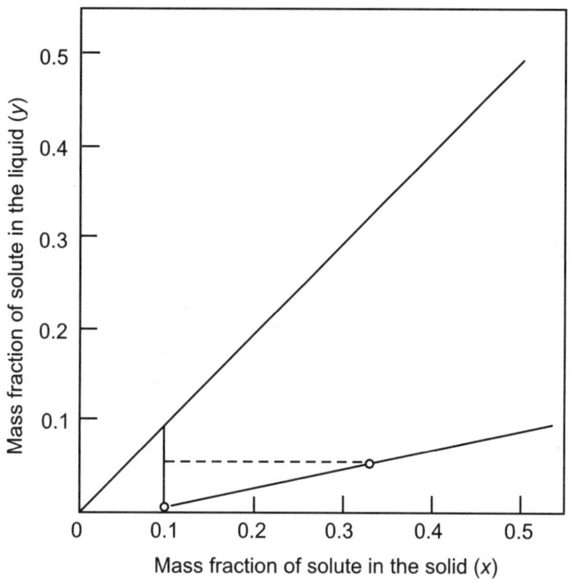

Fig. 5.9 Graphical solution for 5E

Now for the $N - 1$ units, the input and output compositions are known. It is a case of constant underflow. So, the operating line is straight line and can be plotted using the extreme ends, (x_1, y_2) and (x_b, y_b). The equilibrium curve which is the diagonal, is also drawn on the same graph sheet. The number of theoretical stages is then determined by the usual McCabe–Thielle method (Fig. 5.9). The number of theoretical stages required $(N - 1)$ is 1.55. The actual number of theoretical stages is obtained by adding one. $N = 2.55 \approx 3$.

NUMBER OF IDEAL STAGES FOR VARIABLE UNDERFLOW

When the density and viscosity of the solution vary with solute concentration, the underflow and hence the overflow will vary from stage to stage. In this case, the operating line will be curved. So, it cannot be plotted with (x_a, y_a) and (x_b, y_b) alone and at least one additional point is required. The data regarding the amount of underflow as a function of underflow composition is also required. The intermediate point is found by the following procedure.

An intermediate value of x_n is chosen. The corresponding S_n is found from the x_n versus S_n data. Once S_n is found, L_{n+1} is found from the material balance equation and hence y_{n+1}. The operating line is plotted using the terminal points and (x_n, y_{n+1}). The number of stages is determined using the usual McCabe–Thiele method.

ILLUSTRATION

5F A counter current extraction battery is used to extract the sludge using the equation

$$Na_2CO_3 + CaO + H_2O \rightarrow CaCO_3 + 2\ NaOH$$

The sludge retains solution varying with concentration as given below:

Wt% of NaOH in the solution	0	5	10	15	20
kg of solution per kg of $CaCO_3$	1.50	1.75	2.20	2.70	3.60

The products from the reaction enter the first unit with no excess reactants but with 0.5 kg of H_2O per kg of $CaCO_3$. If a 10% NaOH solution is to be produced, how many stages must be used to recover 95% NaOH. What is the wash water requirement per kg of $CaCO_3$?

Solution

Basis: Products from the reactor with 0.5 kg H_2O per kg of $CaCO_3$.

In the reactor, 80 kg of NaOH is produced and is accompanied by 100 kg of $CaCO_3$. The slurry is mixed with 0.5 kg water per kg of $CaCO_3$ and fed to the leaching unit.

NaOH in the input to the leaching unit = 80 kg

$CaCO_3$ in the input to the leaching unit = 100 kg

Water in the input to the leaching unit = $100 \times 0.5 = 50$ kg

Weight fraction of NaOH in the feed solution (x_a) = $\dfrac{80}{80+50} = 0.615\ 4$

It is desired that 95% of NaOH should be recovered.

NaOH recovered $= 80 \times 0.95 = 76$ kg

Recovered NaOH leaves the leaching unit as 10 wt% aqueous solution and it forms the final overflow.

Weight fraction of NaOH in the final overflow (y_b) = 0.1

Water in the final overflow = $76 \times \dfrac{90}{10} = 684$ kg

The NaOH which is not recovered leaves the leaching unit as final underflow. The inert $CaCO_3$, as it flows from stage to stage, carries with it the NaOH solution whose weight varies with solute concentration in the solution.

NaOH in the final underflow = 4 kg

NaOH concentration	Weight of solution retained	NaOH in solution
5 wt%	$100 \times 1.75 = 175$ kg	8.75 kg
0 wt%	$100 \times 1.5 = 150$ kg	0 kg

Solution in the underflow when NaOH in the solution is 4 kg =

$$150 + \frac{175 - 150}{8.75 - 0} \times 4 = 100 \times 1.5 = 161.43 \text{ kg}$$

Water in the final underflow = $161.43 - 4 = 157.43$ kg

Weight fraction of NaOH in the final underflow (x_b) = $\dfrac{4}{161.43} = 0.024\,8$

The leaching unit is fed with neutral water.

Weight fraction of NaOH in the water fed (y_a) = 0

Amount of neutral water fed to the leaching unit can be calculated by a water balance.

Neutral water fed = Water in the final overflow + water in the final underflow – water in the input

= $684 + 157.43 - 50 = 791.43$ kg

Neutral wash water required = $791.43 \div 100 = 7.914\,3$ kg per kg of $CaCO_3$

It is a case of varying underflow. In this case, the operating line will be curved. So, it cannot be plotted with (x_a, y_a) and (x_b, y_b) alone and at least one additional point is required. The intermediate point is found by the following procedure. An intermediate value of x_n is chosen. The corresponding S_n is found from the x_n versus S_n data. Once S_n is found, L_{n+1} is found from the material balance equation and hence y_{n+1}.

Solution retained when the solute fraction in the retained solution (x^I) is 0.1.

Weight of solution retained (S_n) = $100 \times 2.2 = 220$ kg

Weight of NaOH in the solution = $220 \times 0.1 = 22$ kg

Weight of water in the solution = $220 \times 0.9 = 198$ kg

Weight of NaOH in the liquid overflow at this point

= NaOH in the final overflow + NaOH in the final underflow – NaOH in the solid input to the cascade

= $76 + 22 - 80 = 18$ kg

Weight of H_2O in the liquid overflow at this point

= H_2O in the final overflow + H_2O in the final underflow – H_2O in the solid input to the cascade

= $684 + 198 - 50 = 832$ kg

Liquid overflow at this point (L_{n+1}) = weight of NaOH + weight of H_2O

= $18 + 832 = 850$ kg

Solute fraction in the liquid overflow at this point $(y^I) = \dfrac{18}{850} = 0.021$

Solution retained, when the solute fraction in the retained solution (x^{II}) is 0.2.

Weight of solution retained (S_n), from the data given = $100 \times 3.6 = 360$ kg
Weight of NaOH in the solution = $360 \times 0.2 = 72$ kg
Weight of water in the solution = $360 \times 0.8 = 288$ kg

Weight of NaOH in the liquid overflow at this point

= NaOH in the final overflow + NaOH in the final underflow – NaOH in the solid input to the cascade

= $76 + 72 - 80 = 68$ kg

Weight of H_2O in the liquid overflow at this point

= H_2O in the final overflow + H_2O in the final underflow – H_2O in the solid input to the cascade

= $684 + 288 - 50 = 922$ kg

Liquid overflow at this point (L_{n+1}) = weight of NaOH + weight of H_2O

$= 68 + 922 = 990$ kg

Solute fraction in the liquid overflow at this point $(y^{II}) = \dfrac{68}{990} = 0.069$

The operating line is plotted using the terminal points and the two intervening points. The number of stages is determined using the usual McCabe–Thiele method as 1.875 (Fig. 5.10).

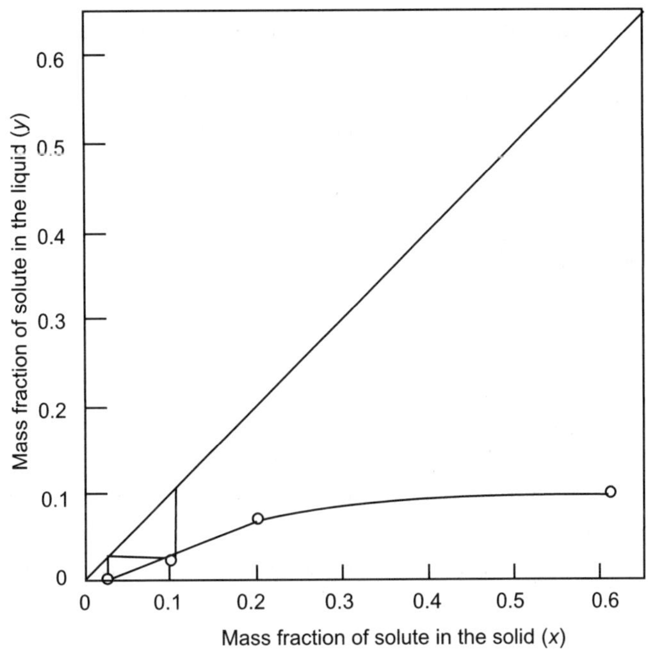

Fig. 5.10 Graphical solution for 5F

EXTRACTION

Extraction is resorted to

1. When separation by distillation is ineffective or very difficult.
2. If the boiling points of the components to be separated are very close.
3. Components do not withstand the temperature of distillation.
4. Azeotropes are formed, limiting the degree of separation by distillation.

Extraction utilises the chemical difference rather than vapour pressure difference.

In extraction, the phases must be brought into good contact to permit transfer of material and then they are separated. If the two phases have comparable density, then the energy available for mixing and separation by gravity flow is small. If the viscosities of the two phases are high, then they are hard to mix and harder to separate. In such cases, the energy for mixing and separation are supplied mechanically.

In extraction, the liquid mixture containing the two components to be separated is mixed thoroughly with the extraction solvent and allowed to stand till it separates into two layers—extract and raffinate. The extract is the layer of extraction solvent plus the extracted solute. The raffinate is the layer from which the solute has been removed. If the extract is light, it will be removed from the top of the equipment. If it is heavy, it is removed from the bottom of the equipment. For the desired separation, if more than one contact is required, the operation has to be repeated.

The simple mixer–settler is the most used extraction equipment. Spray towers, packed towers, perforated plate towers, baffle towers, agitated towers and pulse columns can also be used for extraction.

TERNARY SYSTEMS [3]

The addition of a new solvent to a binary mixture of a solute in a solvent may lead to the formation of several types of mixtures.

1. A homogenous solution may be formed; then the new solvent is unsuitable.
2. The new solvent may be completely immiscible with the initial solvent.
3. The new solvent may be partially miscible with the original solvent resulting in the formation of one pair of partially miscible liquids.
4. The new solvent may lead to the formation of two or three pairs of partially miscible liquids.

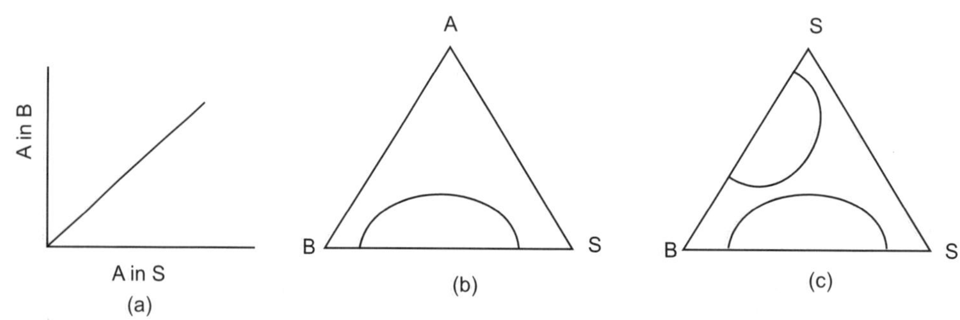

Fig. 5.11 Equilibrium diagram for ternary systems
(a) B and S are immiscible, (b) B and S form one pair of miscible liquids (c) B and S form two pairs of miscible liquids

For (2), equilibrium curves can be drawn on rectangular coordinates; for (3) and (4), equilibrium curves have to be drawn on triangular diagrams. Figure 5.11 gives the possible equilibrium diagrams. Of all these possibilities (2), (3) and (4) are workable systems.

USE OF TRIANGULAR DIAGRAMS

The acetone (A)–water (B)–methyl isobutyl ketone (S) system forms only one two-phase region. Solute A is completely miscible with the solvents B and S. But, the two solvents are partially miscible with each other. As shown in Fig. 5.12, a mixture indicated by H consists of three components, A, B and S in the ratio of the perpendiculars, HL, HJ and HK. BN represents the solubility of S in B and MS that of B in S. The area A under the curve NPFQM represents a two phase region which will split into two layers in equilibrium with each other.

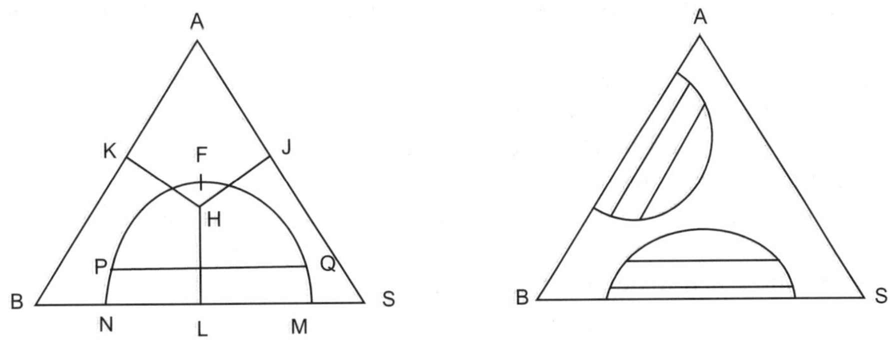

Fig. 5.12 Equilibrium diagram for a partially miscible system

These layers have compositions represented by the points P and Q; and PQ is known as a tie line. Tie lines connect together two phases in equilibrium with each other. They may be found by experiments. There will be only one point F on the curve which represents a single phase that does not split into two phases. F is known as the plait point, again found by experiments. In the case of the aniline (A)–water (B)–phenol (S) system, there are two two-phase regions. A and S are miscible in all proportions. But A and B as well as B and S are only partially miscible.

REQUIREMENTS TO BE MET BY THE EXTRACTION SOLVENT

1. An important factor in assessing the value of a solvent is the ratio of the concentrations of the desired component in the two-phase region rather than their actual concentrations. The selectivity ratio can be defined as

$$\beta = \frac{\left(\frac{x_A}{x_B}\right)_E}{\left(\frac{x_A}{x_B}\right)_R} \tag{5.4}$$

   where x_A and x_B are the mass or mole fractions of A and B in the two phases—extract (E) and raffinate (R). The selectivity has the same significance in extraction as relative volatility α has, in distillation. So separation is directly related to the numerical value of β. When $\beta = 1$ separation is impossible. When β approaches unity, a large number of stages are required to get a given degree of separation and the fixed and operating costs are large.
2. The distribution coefficient, $K = \frac{C_E}{C_R} = \frac{\text{Solute concentration in E}}{\text{Solute concentration in R}}$ should be larger than 1, since less solvent will be required for extraction.
3. The extraction solvent and the original solvent should be immiscible.

4. The extraction solvent should be recoverable for reuse. If distillation has to be carried out for its recovery, then it should not form an azeotrope. It should have high volatility for low cost of recovery. Its latent heat of vaporisation must be low.
5. The density of the extraction solvent should be different from that of the original solvent. Only then, the saturated liquid phases will also have a density difference.
6. If the interfacial tension is larger, then the dispersion of one liquid in another will be difficult and the equilibrium phases will separate out on their own.
7. The solvent should be chemically stable and inert towards the solute and common materials of construction.
8. Viscosity, vapour pressure and freezing point must all be low for ease of handling and storage.
9. It should be non-toxic, non-flammable and low cost.

PLAIT POINT

The point where the B-rich and S-rich solubility curves merge is called the plait point. It is ordinarily not at the maximum value of A on the solubility curve.

SOLUTROPIC SYSTEMS

In triangular charts, the tie lines in the two-phase region are rarely parallel and they usually change their slope slowly in one direction. In relatively few systems, the direction of the tie line changes and one tie line will be horizontal. Such systems are said to be solutropic. Examples of solutropic systems are given in Table 5.1.

Table 5.1 Solutropic systems

A	B	S
Acetaldehyde	Toluene	Water
Acetone	Water	Monochlorobenzene
Dioxane	Water	Benzene
Nicotine	Water	Kerosene

Lixiviation refers to leaching of alkali from wood ashes.

Decoction refers to the leaching operation wherein the solvent is at its boiling point.

Elutriation or elution refers to the operation of the solute being washed off by the solvent when the solute is largely on the surface of an insoluble solid.

SINGLE STAGE EXTRACTION

Let a feed of mass F containing a solution of a solute A in solvent B be in contact with an extraction solvent S of mass S to give an extract E of mass E and a raffinate R of mass R. Let the solute content of the feed be x_F, that of the raffinate be x and that of the extract be y, all in mass fractions. Let y_s be the mass fraction of the solute in the extraction solvent.

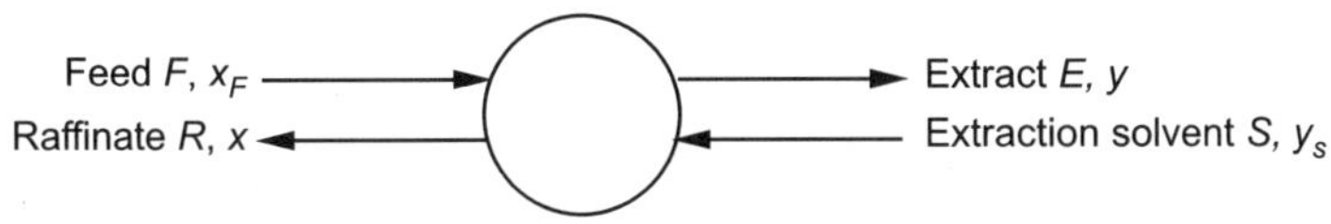

Fig. 5.13 Schematic representation of single stage extraction

The schematic representation of a single stage extraction is shown in Fig. 5.13. The equipment used for this operation is a mixer–settler. The flow can be cocurrent or counter current. When S and B are miscible, the operation has to be followed on a phase diagram in triangular coordinates. If S and B are immiscible, the operation can be followed on rectangular coordinates. When S and B are immiscible, the entire S would be present in E and entire B would be present in R. Solute A would be distributed between B and S.

$$\text{Overall balance: } F + S = E + R \tag{5.5}$$

Let x' and y' be the mass fractions of the solute on solute-free basis, that is, mass ratio of solute to solvent.

$$x' = \frac{x}{1-x} \text{ or } \left(\frac{A}{S}\right) \text{ and } y' = \frac{y}{1-y} \text{ or } \left(\frac{A}{B}\right) \tag{5.6}$$

Solute balance:

$$Sy'_S + Fx'_F = Ey' + Rx' \tag{5.7}$$

$$= Sy' + Bx' \tag{5.8}$$

$$Sy'_S + Fx'_F - Bx' = Sy' \tag{5.9}$$

$$\frac{(Fx'_F + Sy'_S)}{S} - \frac{B}{S}x' = y' \tag{5.10}$$

So, the operatingline passes through (x_F^1, y_S^1) and has a slope of $\frac{-B}{S}$. The point of intersection between the operating line and the equilibrium curve gives the values of x^1 and y^1. The graphical solution is shown in Fig. 5.14.

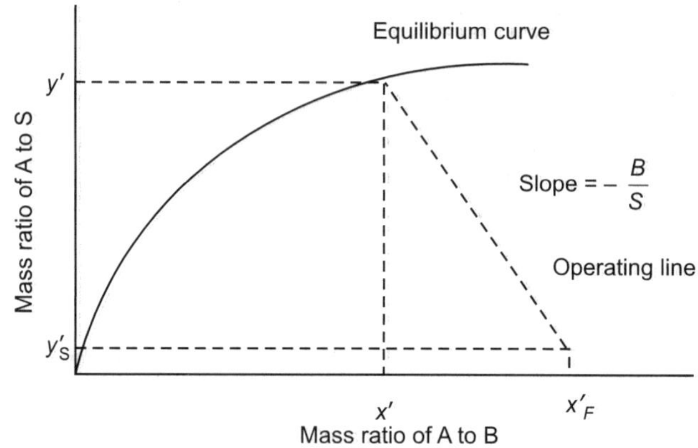

Fig. 5.14 Graphical solution for single stage extraction

MULTI-STAGE CROSS CURRENT EXTRACTION

This is an extension of the single stage operation, wherein the raffinate is successively contacted with fresh extraction solvent. A single final raffinate results and the extracts can be combined to provide a composite extract. The raffinate from a stage is fed to the next stage and it acts as feed for that stage. Since B and S are immiscible, there will be B kg of this in all raffinates and S kg of this in all extracts. The schematic representation of a two stage cross current extraction is given in Fig. 5.15.

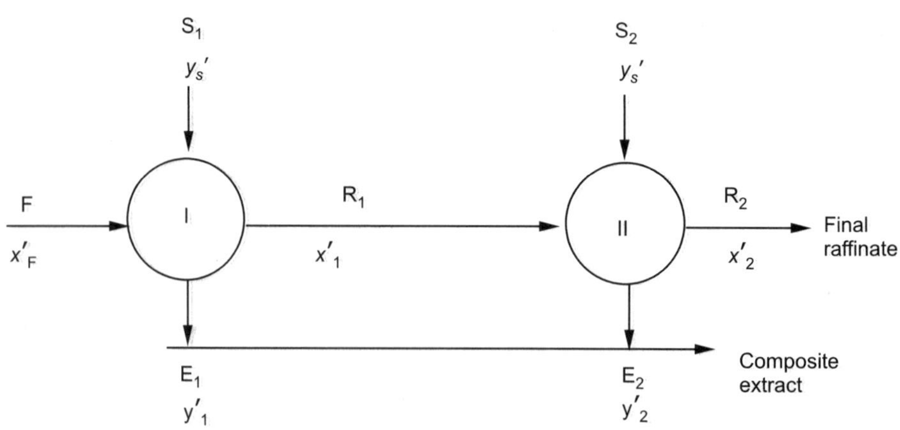

Fig. 5.15 Schematic representation of multi-stage cross current extraction

A solute balance about any stage n is then

$$Bx'_{n-1} + S_n y'_S = S_n y'_n + Bx'_n \tag{5.11}$$

$$-\frac{B}{S_n} = \frac{y_S^1 - y_n^1}{x_{n-1}^1 - x_n^1} \tag{5.12}$$

This is the operating line for the nth stage. It has a slope of $-\frac{B}{S_n}$ and passes through points (x_{n-1}^1, y_S^1) and (x_n^1, y_n^1). The construction of a two stage unit is shown in Fig. 5.16. Each stage has an operating line of appropriate slope. Each operating line intersects the equilibrium curve at the raffinate and extract concentrations.

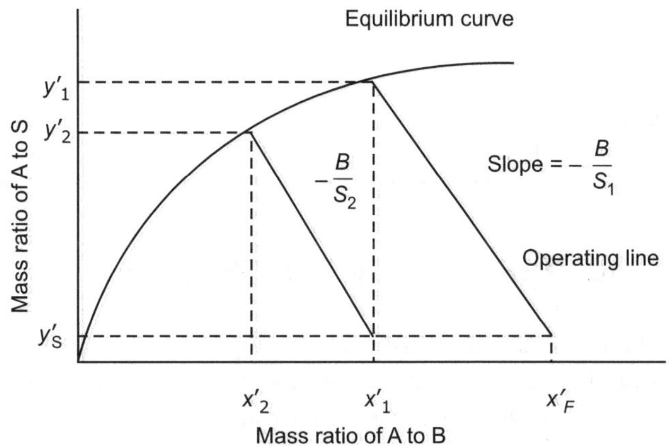

Fig. 5.16 Graphical solution for multi-stage cross current extraction

If the equilibrium relation is given by an equation of the type, $y = mx$, then the material balance of the solute for the I stage in terms of solute free coordinates will be

$$Bx_F^1 = Bx_1^1 + Sy_1^1$$

$$= Bx_1^1 + Smx_1^1$$

$$= x_1^1(B + mS) \tag{5.13}$$

$$\left(\frac{B}{B + mS}\right) x_F^1 = x_1^1 \tag{5.14}$$

For the second stage

$$Bx_1^1 = Bx_2^1 + Sy_2^1$$

$$= Bx_2^1 + Smx_2^1$$

$$= x_2^1(B + mS) \tag{5.15}$$

$$\left(\frac{B}{B + mS}\right) x_1^1 = x_2^1 \tag{5.16}$$

But $$x_1^1 = \left(\frac{B}{B+mS}\right) x_F^1 \tag{5.14}$$

Hence $$\left(\frac{B}{B+mS}\right)^2 x_F^1 = x_2^1 \tag{5.17}$$

Similarly for n stages, $$\left(\frac{B}{B+mS}\right)^n x_F^1 = x_n^1 \tag{5.18}$$

The number of stages, $$n = \frac{\log \dfrac{x_n^1}{x_F^1}}{\log \dfrac{B}{B+mS}} \tag{5.19}$$

MULTI-STAGE COUNTER CURRENT OPERATION

If a series of mixing and separating vessels are arranged so that the flow is counter current, then the conditions of flow can be represented as shown in Fig. 5.17. F is the solution of solute A in solvent B and is fed to the first unit and leaves as raffinate R_1. This stream passes through all the units and leaves the nth unit as stream R_n.

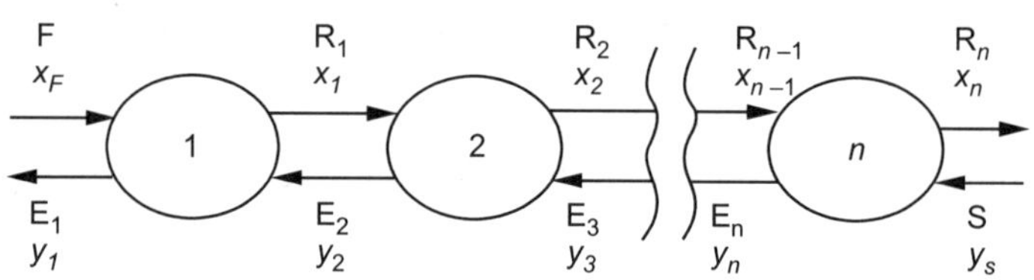

Fig. 5.17 Schematic representation of multi-stage counter current extraction

The extraction solvent S enters the last (n^{th}) unit and passes through the other units in the reverse direction and leaves the first unit as extract E_1. Let x be the mass fraction of solute in the raffinate and y be the mass fraction of solute in the extract stream. Since B and S are immiscible, S remains in E and B in R. The following material balance for the solute can be written.

For the first stage,

$$Bx_F^1 + Sy_2^1 = Bx_1^1 + Sy_1^1 \tag{5.20}$$

For the nth stage,

$$Bx_{n-1}^1 + Sy_{n+1}^1 = Bx_n^1 + Sy_n^1 \tag{5.21}$$

Overall

$$Bx_F^1 + Sy_{n+1}^1 = Bx_n^1 + Sy_1^1 \tag{5.22}$$

$$y_{n+1} = \frac{B}{S}(x_n^1 - x_F^1) + y_1^1 \tag{5.23}$$

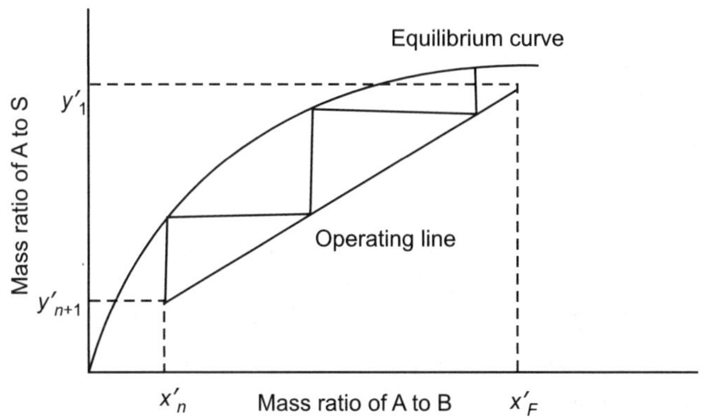

Fig. 5.18 Graphical solution for multi-stage counter current extraction

This is the equation of the operating line with slope $\frac{B}{S}$. This line passes through points (x_F^1, y_1^1) and (x_n^1, y_{n+1}^1). The equilibrium curve can be drawn using the relation $y = f(x)$. The number of theoretical stages can be found by the usual McCabe–Thiele method. The graphical solution is shown in Fig. 5.18.

ILLUSTRATIONS

5G Methylethylketone (MEK) and water are partially miscible and hence form a mutually soluble two phase system. At 298 K, the MEK rich layer contains 12% water and the water rich layer contains 25% MEK. If 100 kg each of water and MEK are mixed at 298 K and allowed to reach equilibrium, estimate the weights of the two layers.

Solution

Basis: 100 kg of water mixed with 100 kg of MEK at 298 K.

On mixing, two layers, one rich in MEK and the other rich in water are formed.

Total weight of the two layers = 200 kg

Let the weight of the MEK rich layer be x kg then the weight of H_2O rich layer will be $(200 - x)$ kg. We have one unknown, x and to find its value, only one equation is required. The required equation is framed from a water balance.

Water balance:

Weight of water in the MEK rich layer + weight of water in the water rich layer = weight of total water.

MEK rich layer contains 12% water and the water rich layer contains 25% MEK.

$$0.12x + 0.75(200 - x) = 100$$

$$x = 79.37 \text{ kg}$$

Weight of MEK rich layer = 79.37 kg

Weight of water rich layer = 200 − 79.37 = 120.63 kg

5H Under certain conditions of temperature and composition, a mixture of phenol and water forms two separate liquid phases, one rich is phenol and the other rich in water. At 303 K, the composition of the upper and lower layers is 70% and 9% phenol respectively. If 40 kg of phenol and 60 kg of water are mixed and the layers are allowed to separate at 303 K, what will be weights of the two layers?

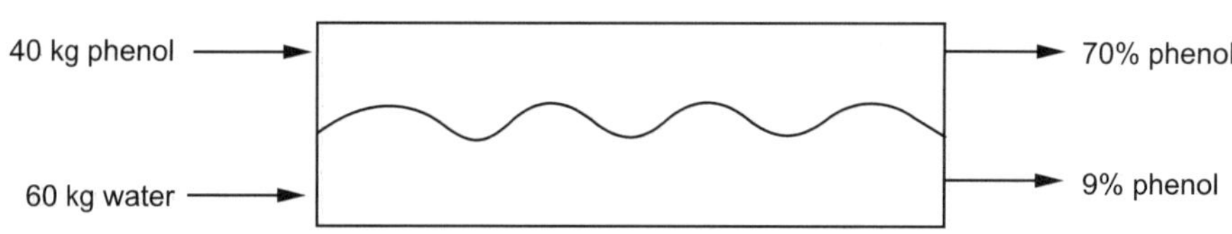

Fig. 5.19 Mixing of phenol and water

Solution

Basis: Mixture of 40 kg phenol and 60 kg water.

The process is represented in Fig. 5.19. The total weight is 100 kg. Let the weight of the upper layer be x kg. Then the weight of the lower layer is $(100 - x)$. We have one unknown x, and to find its value, one equation is required. The required equation is framed from a phenol balance. Phenol forms 70% of upper layer and 9% of lower layer.

Phenol balance:

Phenol in upper layer + phenol in lower layer = total phenol

$$0.7x + 0.09(100 - x) = 40$$

$$x = 50.82 \text{ kg}$$

Weight of upper layer = 50.82 kg

Weight of lower layer = 100 − 50.82 = 49.18 kg

5I A 4% CH_3CHO solution in toluene is to be extracted with water in a four stage cross current unit. If 30 kg of water is used per stage for 100 kg of feed, find the amount of CH_3CHO in the final raffinate. The equilibrium relation is given by $y = 2.2x$, where y = kg of CH_3CHO per kg of water and x = kg of CH_3CHO per kg of toluene. Also, find the amount of CH_3CHO extracted if 120 kg of water is added in one lot.

Solution

Equilibrium data is given on a weight ratio basis. So the problem should be solved using the weight ratio basis.

Feed, F	=	100 kg
Solute content of feed (x_F)	=	0.04
Solute, acetaldehyde (A)	=	4 kg
Solvent, toluene (B)	=	96 kg

1. Extraction solvent, water (S) for each stage = 30 kg

   So the slope of the operating line $= -\dfrac{A}{S} = -\dfrac{96}{30} = -3.2$

   The equilibrium curve is drawn using the relation $y = 2.2x$.

   As 30 kg of water is added in each of the four stages, the operating lines will be parallel. The raffinate from the first stage is the feed to the second stage, the raffinate from the second stage is the feed to the third stage and so on. The extraction solvent, toluene, is solute free. The weight ratio of solute in toluene (y'_s) is zero. On the x axis, locate the feed point, which is (x'_F, y'_s). The operating line for the first stage passes through this point and has a slope of -3.2. Draw this line. It intersects the equilibrium line at (x'_1, y'_1). Locate (x'_1, y'_1) on the x axis.

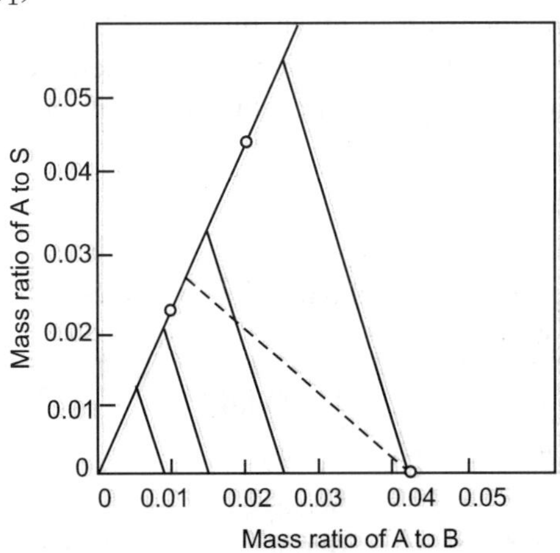

Fig. 5.20 Graphical solution for 5I

The operating line for the second stage passes through this point and has a slope of −3.2. Draw this line. It intersects the equilibrium line at (x_2^1, y_2^1). Repeat the above two more times to find x_4', which is the weight ratio of CH_3CHO in toluene after 4 stages as 0.005 5.

Number of kg of acetaldehyde per kg of toluene in the final raffinate = 0.005 5

Weight of acetaldehyde in the final raffinate = 96 × 0.005 5 = 0.528 kg

Amount of CH_3CHO extracted = amount in feed – amount in final raffinate

$$= 4 - 0.528 = 3.472 \text{ kg}$$

2. Extraction solvent, water (S) in the single stage operation = 120 kg

So the slope of the operating line $= -\dfrac{A}{S} = -\dfrac{96}{120} = -0.8$

As water is added in a single lot, there is only one operating line. On the x axis, locate the feed point, which is (x'_F, y'_s). The operating line passes through this point and has a slope of −0.8. Draw this line. It intersects the equilibrium line at (x'_1, y'_1) which is the weight ratio of CH_3CHO in toluene after the single stage as 0.012.

Number of kg of acetaldehyde per kg of toluene in the final raffinate = 0.012.

Weight of acetaldehyde in the final raffinate = 96 × 0.012 = 1.152 kg

Amount of CH_3CHO extracted = amount in feed – amount in final raffinate

$$= 4 - 1.152 = 2.848 \text{ kg}$$

The graphical solution is given in Fig. 5.20.

5J A solution of acetaldehyde in toluene with 5% by weight acetaldehyde is extracted in 5 stages with water in a cross current extraction unit. The feed rate is 1 000 kg h^{-1}. Water used is 250 kg h^{-1} in each stage. Toluene and water are completely immiscible. The equilibrium relationship is given by $y = 2.2x$. Calculate the % extraction of acetaldehyde, if x is the weight fraction of acetaldehyde in the toluene–acetaldehyde mixture and y is weight fraction of acetaldehyde in the water–acetaldehyde mixture.

Solution

The equilibrium data is given on weight fraction basis. So the problem should be solved using the weight fraction basis.

Feed, F	=	1 000 kg
Solute content of feed (xF)	=	0.05
Solute, acetaldehyde (A)	=	50 kg
Solvent, toluene (B)	=	950 kg

Extraction solvent, water (S) for each stage $= 250$ kg

So the slope of the operating line $= -\dfrac{A}{S} = -\dfrac{950}{250} = -3.8$

The equilibrium curve is drawn using the relation, $y = 2.2\,x$

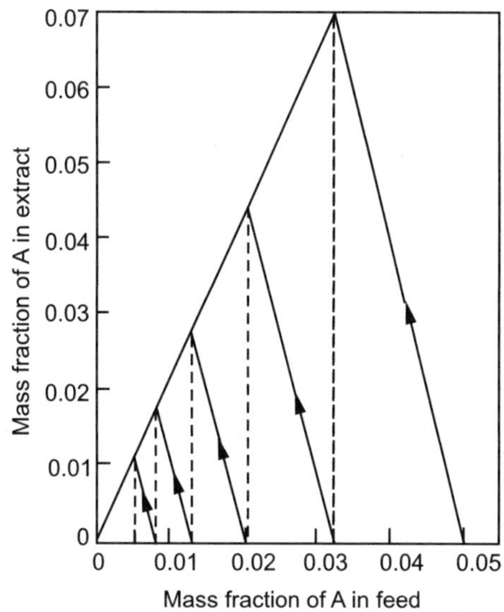

Fig. 5.21 Graphical solution for 5J

As 250 kg of water is added in each of the five stages, the operating lines will be parallel. The raffinate from the first stage is the feed to the second stage, the raffinate from the second stage is the feed to the third stage and so on. The extraction solvent, toluene is solute free. Weight fraction of solute in toluene (y_S) is zero. On the x axis, locate the feed point, which is (x_F, y_S). The operating line for the first stage passes through this point and has a slope of –3.8. Draw this line. It intersects the equilibrium line at (x_1, y_1). Locate (x_1, y_S) on the x axis. The operating line for the second stage passes through this point and has a slope of –3.8. Draw this line. It intersects the equilibrium line at (x_2, y_2). Repeat the above three more times to find x_5 which is the weight fraction of CH_3CHO in toluene after 5 stages as 0.005 5.

Number of kg of acetaldehyde per kg of toluene in the final raffinate

$$= \frac{0.005\ 5}{(1 - 0.005\ 5)} = 0.005\ 53$$

Weight of acetaldehyde in the final raffinate $= 950 \times 0.005\ 53 = 5.253\ 5$ kg

Amount of CH_3CHO extracted $=$ amount in feed – amount in final raffinate

$$= 50 - 5.253\,5 = 44.746\,5 \text{ kg}$$

Percentage of acetaldehyde extracted $= \dfrac{44.746\,5}{50} \times 100 = 89.49$

The graphical solution is given in Fig. 5.21.

5K From a water–dioxane solution, dioxane is to be separated using phenol as a solvent by extraction. Water and phenol are substantially insoluble. 1 000 kg of a 25% dioxane–75% water solution is extracted with phenol. Calculate the recovery if 1 000 kg of pure solvent is used in a single stage process and calculate the % recovery if 500 kg of solvent is used in the first stage and another 500 kg of solvent in the second stage in a cross current extraction battery. The solvent is free from dioxane. The equilibrium data is given below:

Wt% dioxane in water	5.1	18.9	25.2
Wt% dioxane in phenol	5.2	22.5	32.0

Solution

Equilibrium data is given on a weight percentage basis, which can be converted to weight fraction. So, the problem should be solved on a weight fraction basis.

Feed, F = 1 000 kg

Solute content of feed (x_F) = 0.25

Solute, dioxane (A) = 250 kg

Solvent, water (B) = 750 kg

1. Extraction solvent benzene (S) in the single stage operation = 1 000 kg

   So the slope of the operating line $= -\dfrac{A}{S} = -\dfrac{750}{1\,000} = -0.75$

   The equilibrium curve is drawn using the given data. As 1 000 kg of benzene is added in a single lot, there is only one operating line. The extraction solvent, benzene, is solute free. The weight fraction of the solute in benzene (y_S) is zero. Locate the feed point on the x axis, which is (x_F, y_S). The operating line passes through this point and has a slope of –0.75. Draw this line. It intersects the equilibrium line at (x_1, y_1). The weight fraction of the solute in benzene, x_1, after the single stage is 0.1.

   Number of kg of dioxane per kg of benzene in the raffinate $= \dfrac{0.1}{(1 - 0.1)} = 0.111$

   Weight of dioxane in the final raffinate $= 750 \times 0.111 = 83.25$ kg

   Amount of dioxane extracted = amount in feed – amount in final raffinate

   $= 250 - 83.25 = 166.75$ kg

$$\text{Percentage of dioxane extracted} = \frac{166.75}{250} \times 100 = 66.7$$

2. Extraction solvent, benzene (S), for each stage = 500 kg

So the slope of the operating line $= -\dfrac{A}{S} = -\dfrac{750}{500} = -1.5$

The equilibrium curve is drawn using the given data. As 500 kg of benzene is added in each of the two stages, the operating lines will be parallel. The raffinate from the first stage is the feed to the second stage. The extraction solvent, benzene is solute free. The weight fraction of solute in benzene (y_S) is zero. locate the feed point on the x axis, which is (x_F, y_S). The operating line for the first stage passes through this point and has a slope of -1.5. Draw this line. It intersects the equilibrium line at (x_1, y_1). Locate (x_1, y_S) on the x axis. The operating line for the second stage passes through this point and has a slope of -1.5. Draw this line. It intersects the equilibrium line at (x_2, y_2). The weight fraction of the solute in benzene, x_2, after 2 stages is 0.082 5.

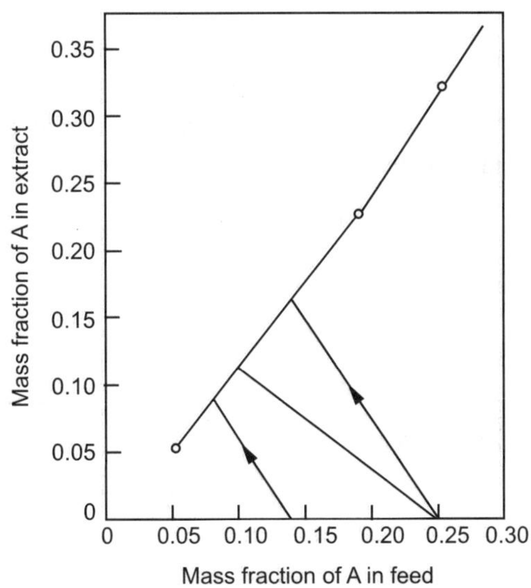

Fig. 5.22 Graphical solution for 5K

Number of kg of dioxane per kg of benzene in the final raffinate

$$= \frac{0.082\ 5}{(1 - 0.082\ 5)} = 0.089\ 9$$

Weight of dioxane in the final raffinate $= 750 \times 0.089\ 9 = 67.425$ kg

Amount of dioxane extracted = amount in feed – amount in final raffinate

$= 250 - 67.425 = 182.575$ kg

Percentage of dioxane extracted $= \dfrac{182.575}{250} \times 100 = 73.03$

The graphical solution is given in Fig. 5.22.

5L 1 000 kg h^{-1} of water–dioxane solution containing 18% dioxane is to be continuously and counter currently extracted with benzene at 298 K to recover 90% dioxane. Water and phenol are essentially insoluble and the equilibrium distribution of dioxane between them is as follows:

Wt % dioxane in water	5.1	18.9	25.2
Wt % dioxane in phenol	5.2	22.5	32.0

Determine the number of stages required, if the solvent rate is 1.5 times the minimum and pure benzene is used in the process.

Solution

Equilibrium data is given on a weight percentage basis, which can be converted to weight fraction. So, the problem should be solved on a weight fraction basis.

Feed, F = 1 000 kg

Solute content of feed (x_a) = 0.18

Solute, dioxane (A) = 180 kg

Solvent, water (B) = 820 kg

90% of solute is proposed to be recovered.

Dioxane recovered $= 180 \times 0.9 = 162$ kg

Dioxane in the extract = 162 kg

Dioxane in the raffinate = dioxane in the feed – dioxane in the extract

$= 180 - 162 = 18$ kg

As water and phenol are essentially insoluble, all the water remains in the raffinate and all the benzene remains in the extract.

Weight fraction of dioxane in the final raffinate $(x_b) = \dfrac{18}{18 + 820} = 0.021\ 5$

The extraction solvent, benzene, is solute free. The weight fraction of solute in benzene (y_b) is zero. The equilibrium curve is drawn using the given data. When the extraction solvent, benzene (S), is minimum the weight fraction of soulte in the final extract, $y_a = y_a^*$. y_a^*, found from the equilibrium curve corresponding to x_a is 0.212 5.

$$0.2125 = \frac{162}{162 + S_{\min}} \text{ and hence } S_{\min} \text{ is } 600.35 \text{ kg.}$$

Benzene rate is 1.5 times the minimum. $S = 1.5 \times S_{\text{min}} = 1.5 \times 600.35 = 900.53$ kg

Actual weight fraction of soulte in the final extract, $y_a = \dfrac{162}{162 + 900.53} = 0.152\,5$

Now the extreme ends of the operating line (x_a, y_a) and (x_b, y_b) are known. The operating line is drawn on the same graph sheet in which the equilibrium curve is drawn. The number of theoretical stages can be found by the usual staircase construction based on the McCabe–Thiele method. The number of theoretical stages required for this operation is 9.2 (Fig. 5.23).

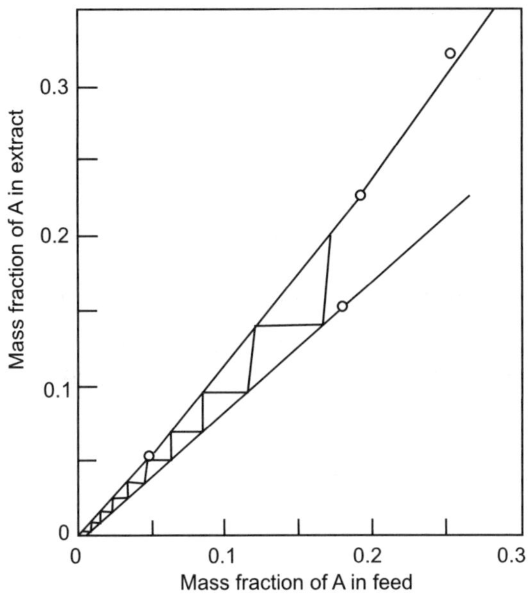

Fig. 5.23 Graphical solution for 5L

5M Nicotine in a water solution containing 1% nicotine is to be extracted with kerosene at 293 K. Water and kerosene are essentially in soluble. Determine the % extraction of nicotine if 100 kg of feed solution is extracted once with 135 kg solvent. Repeat for three theoretical extractions using 45 kg each.

Equilibrium data:

$\dfrac{\text{kg of nicotine}}{\text{kg of water}}$	0	0.0010	0.0025	0.005	0.0075	0.00998	0.0204
$\dfrac{\text{kg of nicotine}}{\text{kg of kerosene}}$	0	0.0008	0.0020	0.0046	0.0069	0.0091	0.0187

Solution

Equilibrium data is given on a solute free basis. So, the problem should be solved on a solute free basis.

Feed, F	=	100 kg
Solute content of feed (x_F)	=	0.01
Solute, nicotine (A)	=	1 kg
Solvent, water (B)	=	99 kg
Solute content of feed on solute free basis (x_F^1)	=	$\frac{1}{99} = 0.010\,1$

1. If the entire 135 kg is used in one lot, $S = 135$ kg

   Slope of operating line for this case is $-\frac{99}{135} = -\frac{11}{15}$

   Locate the feed point on the x axis, which is (x_F^1, y_S^1). The operating line for the first stage passes through this point and has a slope of $-\frac{11}{15}$. Draw this line. It intersects the equilibrium line at (x_1^1, y_1^1). Find x_1^1, which is the concentration of nicotine in kerosene after the addition of 135 kg of kerosene in one lot = 0.004 6.

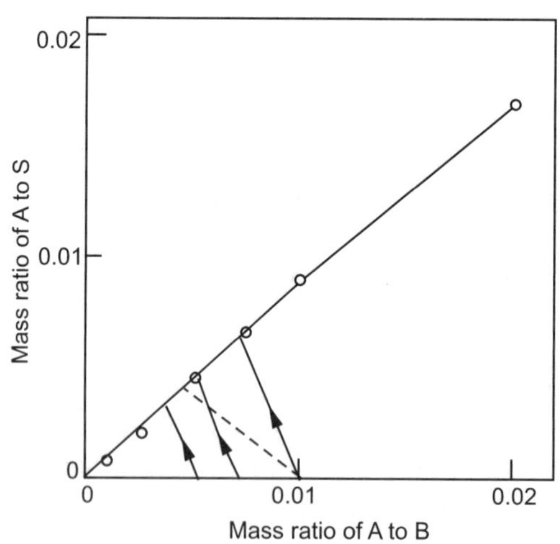

Fig. 5.24 Graphical solution for 5M

   Nicotine extracted now = 99(0.010 1 – 0.004 6) = 0.544 5 kg

   So 54.45% nicotine is extracted.

2. Extraction solvent, kerosene (S) for each stage = 45 kg

   So the slope of the operating line $= -\frac{A}{S} = -\frac{99}{45} = -\frac{11}{5}$

The equilibrium curve is drawn using the given data. As 45 kg of kerosene is added in each of the three stages, the operating lines will be parallel. The raffinate from the first stage is the feed to the second stage; the raffinate from the second stage is the feed to the third stage. The extraction solvent, kerosene, is solute free. The weight fraction of solute in kerosene (y_S^1) is zero. Locate the feed point on the x axis, which is (x_F^1, y_S^1). The operating line for the first stage passes through this point and has a slope of $-\frac{11}{5}$. Draw this line. It intersects the equilibrium line at (x_1^1, y_1^1). Locate (x_1^1, y_S^1) on the x axis. The operating line for the second stage passes through this point and has a slope of $-\frac{11}{5}$. Draw this line. It intersects the equilibrium line at (x_2^1, y_2^1). Repeat the above one more time to find x_3^1, which is the concentration of nicotine in kerosene after 3 stages as 0.003 8.

Amount of nicotine extracted $= B(x_F^1 - x_3^1) = 99(0.010\,1 - 0.003\,8) = 0.623\,7$ kg

So 62.37% nicotine is extracted. The graphical solution is given in Fig. 5.24.

5N In a counter current multistage extraction operation, 1 500 kg h^{-1} of a nicotine–water solution containing 1% nicotine is contacted with kerosene as solvent to reduce the nicotine concentration to 0.1%. Find (i) the minimum kerosene rate, and (ii) determine the number of theoretical stages required if twice the minimum rate is used. The equilibrium relation can be taken as $y = 0.92x$ where y = kg of nicotine per kg of kerosene and x = kg of nicotine per kg of water.

Solution

The equilibrium data is given on a solute free basis. So, the problem should be solved on a solute free basis.

Feed, F	=	1 500 kg
Solute content of feed	=	1.0%
Solute, nicotine (A)	=	15 kg
Solvent, water (B)	=	1 485 kg
Weight ratio of nicotine to water in the feed (x_a^1)	=	$\frac{15}{1\,485} = 0.010\,1$

The solute content is proposed to be reduced to 0.1%.

Solute in the final raffinate	=	$\frac{1\,485}{99.9} \times 0.1 = 1.486$
Nicotine extracted	=	nicotine in feed – nicotine in the final raffinate
	=	$15 - 1.486 = 13.514$

As water and kerosene are essentially insoluble, all the water remains in the raffinate and all the kerosene remains in the extract.

Weight ratio of nicotine to water in the final raffinate $(x_b^1) = \dfrac{1.486}{1485} = 0.001$

The extraction solvent, kerosene, is solute free. The weight ratio of nicotine to kerosene in the extraction solvent (y_b^1) is zero.

When the extraction solvent, kerosene (S), is minimum, the weight ratio of nicotine to kerosene in the final extract, $y_a^1 = y_a^{1*}$

y_a^{1*} is found from the equilibrium relation corresponding to x_a^1.

$y_a^{1*} = 0.92x_a^1 = 0.92 \times 0.101 = 0.009\ 292$

$0.009\ 292 = \dfrac{13.514}{S_{\min}}$ and hence $S_{\min}$ is 1 454.37 kg.

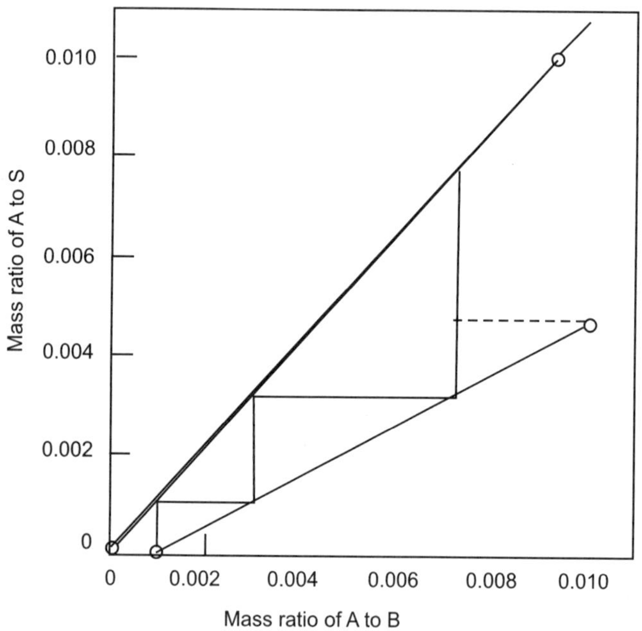

Fig. 5.25 Graphical solution for 5N

Kerosene rate is two times the minimum.

$$S = 2 \times S_{min} = 2 \times 1\ 454.37 = 2\ 908.74 \text{ kg}$$

Weight fraction of nicotine to kerosene to in the final extract, $y_a^1 = \dfrac{13.515}{2908.74} = 0.004\ 646$

Now the extreme ends of the operating line (x_a^1, y_a^1) and (x_b^1, y_b^1) are known. The operating line is drawn on the same graph sheet in which the equilibrium curve is drawn. The number of theoretical stages can be found by the usual staircase construction based on McCabe–Thiele method. The number of theoretical stages required for this operation is 2.33 (Fig. 5.25).

50 An aqueous solution containing 20 wt% acetone is to be extracted counter currently using monochlorobenzene containing 0.05 wt% acetone. Water and monochlorobenzene may be considered immiscible within the operating range. Compute the following for obtaining a raffinate containing 1 wt% acetone: (i) minimum solvent to water ratio and (ii) number of theoretical stages needed, if this ratio is 1.5 times the minimum.

Equilibrium data:

$\dfrac{\text{kg of acetone}}{\text{kg of water}}$	0.0258	0.0739	0.1605	0.267
$\dfrac{\text{kg of acetone}}{\text{kg of monochlorobenzene}}$	0.0288	0.0704	0.1560	0.237

Solution

Equilibrium data is given on a solute free or weight ratio basis. So the problem should be solved on the same basis. The problem may be solved for a feed of 100 kg.

Feed, F = 100 kg

Solute content of feed = 20 wt%

Solute, acetone (A) = 20 kg

Solvent, water (B) = 80 kg

Weight ratio of acetone to water in the feed (x_a^1) = $\dfrac{20}{80} = 0.25$

Solute content is proposed to be reduced to 1%.

Solute in the final raffinate = $\dfrac{80}{99} \times 1 = 0.808$

Acetone extracted = acetone in feed – acetone in the final raffinate

= $20 - 0.808 = 19.192$ kg

Weight ratio of acetone to water in the final raffinate (x_b^1) = $\dfrac{0.808}{80} = 0.010\,1$

As water and monochlorobenzene are essentially insoluble, all the water remains in the raffinate and all the monochlorobenzene remains in the extract. The extraction solvent, monochlorobenzene, contains 0.05 wt% acetone.

Weight ratio of acetone to monochlorobenzene in the extraction solvent (y_b^1)

$$= \frac{0.05}{99.95} = 0.000\,5$$

When the extraction solvent, monochlorobenzene (S), is minimum, the weight ratio of acetone to monochlorobenzene in the final extract, $y_a^1 = y_a^{1*}$.

y_a^{1*} is found from the equilibrium curve corresponding to $x_a^1 = 0.232\ 5$

1 kg monochlorobenzene contains 0.000 5 kg acetone at the inlet.

1 kg monochlorobenzene entering the extractor can pick up 0.232 5 – 0.000 5

= 0.232 kg acetone

Acetone to be picked up = 19.192 kg

$$0.232 = \frac{19.192}{S_{\min}} \text{ and hence } S_{min} \text{ is } 82.72 \text{ kg}$$

Minimum solvent to water ratio = 82.72 ÷ 80 = 1.034

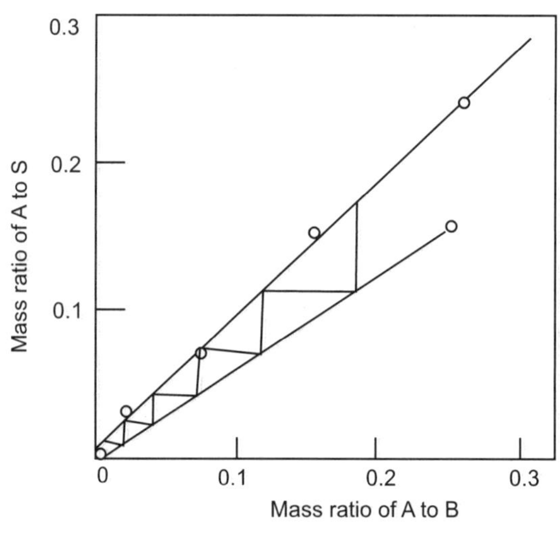

Fig. 5.26 Graphical solution for 5O

Monochlorobenzene rate is 1.5 times the minimum.

$S = 1.5 \times S_{\min} = 1.5 \times 82.72 = 124.08$ kg

Total acetone in the final extract = acetone extracted + acetone in monocholorobenzene

$= 19.192 + 124.08 \times 0.000\ 5 = 19.254$ kg

Weight fraction of nicotine to monochlorobenzene to in the final extract,

$$y_a^1 = \frac{19.192}{124.08} = 0.154\ 7$$

Now the extreme ends of the operating line (x_a^1, y_a^1) and (x_b^1, y_b^1) are known.

The number of theoretical stages can be found by the usual staircase construction based on McCabe–Thiele method. The number of theoretical stages required for this operation is 5.6 $\approx$ 6 (Fig. 5.26).

NOTATIONS

Leaching

L Mass flow rate of overflow solution, kg s^{-1}.
L_a Mass flow rate of overflow solution leaving the unit, kg s^{-1}.
L_{n+1} Mass flow rate of fresh solvent entering the unit, kg s^{-1}.
S Mass flow rate of the solution retained by the solute-free solid, kg s^{-1}.
S_a Mass flow rate of the solution contained by the feed solid entering the unit, kg s^{-1}.
S_n Mass flow rate of the solution retained by the solute-free solid leaving the unit, kg s^{-1}.
x Mass fraction of solute in the solution retained by the solute-free solid.
x_A Mass fraction of solute, A.
x_B Mass fraction of solvent, B.
x_a Mass fraction of solute in the solution contained by the feed solid entering the unit.
x_b Mass fraction of solute in the solution retained by the solute-free solid leaving the unit.
x_n Mass fraction of solute in the solution retained by the solute-free solid leaving the nth plate.
y Mass fraction of solute in the overflow solution.
y_a Mass fraction of solute in the overflow solution leaving the unit.
y_b Mass fraction of solute in the fresh solvent entering the unit.
y_{n+1} Mass fraction of solute in the overflow solution leaving the $(n+1)^{th}$ plate.

Extraction

A Solute.
B Original solvent.
C_E Solute concentration in extract.
C_R Solute concentration in raffinate.
E Extract, mass of extract, kg.
F Feed, mass of feed, kg.
m Slope of the equilibrium curve.
R Raffinate, mass of raffinate, kg
S Extraction solvent, mass of extraction solvent.
S_n Mass of extraction solvent entering the nth stage.
x Mass fraction of solute in raffinate.
x^1 Mass ratio of solute to solvent in raffinate.

x_F	Mass fraction of solute in feed.
x_F^1	Mass ratio of solute to solvent in feed.
x_1^1	Mass ratio of solute to solvent in raffinate leaving the first stage.
x_2^1	Mass ratio of solute to solvent in raffinate leaving the second stage.
y	Mass fraction of solute in extract.
y_S	Mass fraction of solute in the extraction solvent.
y^1	Mass ratio of solute to solvent in extract.
y_1^1	Mass ratio of solute to solvent in extract leaving the first stage.
y_S^1	Mass ratio of solute to solvent in extraction solvent.
y_n^1	Mass ratio of solute to solvent in extract leaving the nth stage.
y_{n+1}^1	Mass ratio of solute to solvent in extraction solvent entering the nth stage.

REFERENCES

1. Brunicke OH, *Solid–Liquid Extraction*, Copenhagen, Arnold Busch, 1962.
2. McCabe WL and Thiele EW, *Ind. Eng. Chem.*, **17**:605 (1925).
3. Treybal RE, *Liquid Extraction*, Second Ed., Newyork, McGraw–Hill Book Company, 1963.

Problems for Practice

5.1 1 000 kg h^{-1} of the water–dioxane solution containing 20% dioxane is to be continuously and counter currently extracted with benzene at 298 K to recover 80% dioxane. Water and benzene are insoluble and the equilibrium distribution of dioxane between them is as follows:

Wt% of dioxane in water	5.1	18.9	25.2
Wt% of dioxane in benzene	5.2	22.5	32.0

Determine the number of stages required if a benzene rate of 1.5 times the minimum is used. Benzene is free from dioxane.

5.2 Acetic acid is to be extracted from an aqueous solution containing 20 wt% using isopropyl ether. 8 kg of ether is to be used per kg of water for extraction. Ether is immiscible in water. The distribution equilibrium may be expressed as $x = 2.8y$ where x is number of kg of acid per kg of water and y is number of kg of acid per kg of ether. (i) Calculate the minimum percentage of the original acid remaining in aqueous solution after treatment with two successive batch equilibrium steps using fresh solvent each time. (ii) Using stepwise counter current system, how many equilibrium stages are required for the 95% recovery of acid?

5.3 A solution containing 28 wt% of acetone in water is to be extracted using mono-chlorobenzene (MCB) containing 0.5 wt% acetone by counter current extraction process. MCB and water may be considered to be immiscible within operating range. The equilibrium data are as follows:

kg of acetone per kg of water	0.0258	0.0739	0.1605	0.267
kg of acetone per kg of MCB	0.0288	0.0704	0.1560	0.237

The raffinate is to contain 1% acetone. Compute (i) the minimum solvent rate and (ii) the number of stages required if the solvent rate is 1.25 times the minimum.

5.4 A counter current extraction battery is used to extract the sludge for the reaction: $Na_2CO_3 + CaO + H_2O \rightarrow CaCO_3 + 2\ NaOH$

The quantity of solution retained by the calcium carbonate sludge varies with concentrations as follows:

kg of solution retained per kg of $CaCO_3$	0.082	0.87	0.930	1.200	1.640
Mass% of NaOH	0	5	10	15	20

The products from the reaction enter the first unit with no excess reactant but contain 0.65 kg of water per kg of calcium carbonate. It is desired to produce a 10% solution of NaOH and 98% of NaOH is to be recovered. Estimate (i) the number of stages required, and (ii) wash water to be used per kg of calcium carbonate.

5.5 In a counter current multistage liquid–liquid extraction plant, 1 500 kg h^{-1} of nicotine–water solution containing 1.5% nicotine is to be extracted with kerosene to reduce the nicotine concentration to 0.1%. Determine: (i) the minimum kerosene rate, and (ii) the number of theoretical stages, if the kerosene rate used is 1.2 times the minimum rate. The equilibrium relationship is $y = 0.89x$ where y is number of kg of nicotine per kg of kerosene and x is number of kg of nicotine per kg of water.

5.6 1 500 kg h^{-1} of a water–dioxane solution containing 20% dioxane is to be continuously and counter currently extracted with benzene at 298 K to recover 95% of dioxane. Water and benzene are insoluble. (i) Calculate the minimum solvent required. (ii) If 1 000 kg h^{-1} of solvent is used, calculate the number of theoretical stages required. Use the equilibrium data given in problem 5.1.

5.7 A solution containing 23 wt% of acetone in water is to be extracted with pure monochlorobenzene (MCB) by the counter current extraction process. MCB and water may be considered to be immiscible within the operating range. (i) Determine the minimum quantity of solvent needed per kg of feed, and (ii) the theoretical number stages if the solvent used is 1.2 times the minimum. It is desired to obtain 2.25% of acetone in the raffinate. Use the equilibrium data given in problem 5.3.

5.8 500 kg h^{-1} of a solution of acetaldehyde in toluene containing 15 wt% acetaldehyde is to be extracted by the counter current extraction process using pure water to reduce the acetaldehyde content to 10% of its initial value. Water and toluene are immiscible with each other. The equilibrium relationship is given by $y = 2.5x$ where x refers to number of kg of acetaldehyde per kg of toluene and y refers to number kg of acetaldehyde per kg of water. Calculate (i) minimum solvent rate and (ii) number of theoretical states and the weights of raffinate and extract if 1.5 times the minimum solvent rate is used.

5.9 500 kg h^{-1} of an aqueous solution containing 8% acetone is to be counter currently extracted using MCB (monochlorobenzene) to reduce the acetone content to 4% of its initial value. Water and the solvent are immiscible. (i) Determine the minimum solvent rate and (ii) number of theoretical states required if 1.3 times the minimum solvent rate is used. Use the equilibrium data given in problem 5.3.

5.10 A slurry of flaked soybeans weighing a total of 100 kg contains 75 kg of inert solids and 25 kg of solution with 10 wt% of oil and 90 wt% of solvent hexane. This slurry is contacted with 100 kg of pure hexane in a single stage. The underflow contains 1.5 kg insoluble solid per kg of solution retained. (i) Calculate the amount and composition of the overflow and underflow leaving the stage. (ii) Use the same conditions given above, but assume a constant underflow of 1.85 kg of solid per kg of solution. Calculate the exit flow rates and compositions.

5.11 1 000 kg of a 25% dioxane–75% water solution is extracted with benzene to remove 95% of the dioxane. Benzene is dioxane free. At these concentrations, water and benzene are substantially insoluble. Calculate the requirement of benzene for a single stage equilibrium operation. Use the equilibrium data given in problem 5.1.

5.12 A solution containing 20 mass% of acetone in water is to be extracted using monochlorobenzene (MCB) containing 0.5 mass% acetone by the counter current extraction process. MCB and water may be considered to be immiscible within the operating range. Compute the minimum solvent rate to obtain a raffinate containing 1% acetone. What are the suitable extractors for this operation? Use the equilibrium data given in problem 5.3.

5.13 100 kg h^{-1} of nicotine–water solution containing 1.9% nicotine by weight is to be extracted with 200 kg h^{-1} of pure kerosene solvent. The concentration in the exit stream is to be 0.3%. Determine the number of stages needed for the above operation.

kg of nicotine per kg of water	0.00101	0.00246	0.00502	0.01	0.0204
kg of nicotine per kg of kerosene	0.00078	0.00196	0.00456	0.00913	0.0187

5.14 A nicotine in water solution containing 1% nicotine is to be extracted with kerosene at 293 K. Water and kerosene are essentially insoluble. (i) Determine the % extraction of nicotine if 100 kg of feed solution is extracted once with 150 kg solvent. (ii) Repeat for three theoretical extractions using 50 kg solvent each. Use the equilibrium data given in problem 5.13.

5.15 100 kg h^{-1} of solution of B in A containing 0.014 weight fraction of component B is stripped with a solvent stream C of 250 kg h^{-1} containing 0.0004 weight fraction of B in a counter current stage tower. The solvents A and C are essentially immiscible. The equilibrium data:

kg of B per kg of A	0.00106	0.0024	0.0069	0.0096	0.02
kg of B per kg of C	0.00081	0.00178	0.0053	0.0089	0.0185

It is desired to reduce the concentration of B to 0.0010 weight fraction of the mixture. Determine the number of theoretical stages needed.

5.16 An inlet water solution of 100 kg h^{-1} containing 0.010 weight fraction of nicotine in water is stripped with a kerosene stream of 200 kg h^{-1} containing 0.000 5 weight fraction of nicotine in a counter current multistage tower. Kerosene and water are essentially immiscible with each other. It is desired to reduce the concentration of nicotine in exit water to 0.001 weight fraction. Determine the number of theoretical stages needed. Use the equilibrium data given in problem 5.13.

6 Crystallisation

Crystallisation is an important industrial operation, as it results in a highly pure form of the product convenient for direct packing. The concepts essential for designing crystallisation equipments are discussed in this chapter.

Crystallisation is the formation of solid particles within a homogeneous phase. It may be carried out from vapour (snow), from a melt (large single crystals) or from a solution. Most industrial uses of crystallisation involve solutions. The process of crystallisation from solution is important because a number of materials are marketed in the form of crystals. It is used widely as a purification step because of the high degree of purification achieved in a single step. The crystallisation process ranges from the production of pure single crystals to the production of crystalline sugar which is the most pure bulk produced chemical in the world. The world production of salt is 100 million tonnes per annum which gives an idea of the scale and importance of this operation.

CRYSTALS

A crystal is the most highly organised type of nonliving matter. It is characterised by the fact that its constituent parts (atoms or ions) are arranged in ordinary three dimensional arrays called space lattices. When crystals are allowed to form without hindrance from other crystals or outside bodies, they appear as polyhedrons having sharp corners and flat faces. Although the relative sizes of the faces and edges of various crystals of the same material may vary widely, the angle made by the corresponding faces of all crystals of the same material are equal and are characteristic of that material.

Under ideal conditions, a growing crystal maintains geometric similarity during growth. Such a crystal is called an *invariant crystal*. The rate of growth of any face is measured by the velocity of translation of the face away from the centre of the crystal in a direction perpendicular to the face. In the case of an invariant crystal, the rates of growth of the various faces are equal. Crystals are classified based on the interfacial angle. The seven different crystal forms are monoclinic, triclinic, trigonal, tetragonal, hexagonal, orthorhombic and cubic. The two phase mixture of mother liquor and crystals of all sizes which occupy the crystalliser and are withdrawn as product is called *magma*.

PRINCIPLES OF CRYSTALLISATION

Critical analysis of the crystallisation process requires a thorough knowledge of equilibrium, yield, purity of the product, energy requirements, rate of nucleation and crystal growth.

Equilibrium

Equilibrium relationships in crystallisation are expressed in the form of solubility data which are usually plotted in the form of phase diagrams. Solubility data are generally given as parts by weight of anhydrous material per 100 parts by weight of total solvent. If there is water of crystallisation, the composition of the crystal has to be specified.

Some inorganic substances which crystallise with water of crystallisation form several different hydrates depending on concentration and temperature. The phase equilibria of such systems are quite complicated. Magnesium sulphate is an example.

Figure 6.1 shows the dependence of solubility of magnesium sulphate on temperature and concentration. At high concentration and temperature, the hydrate is $MgSO_4.H_2O$. At low concentration and temperature, the hydrate is $MgSO_4.12H_2O$. At intermediate concentrations the hydrate encountered is $MgSO_4.6H_2O$ and/or $MgSO_4.7H_2O$ depending on concentration and temperature.

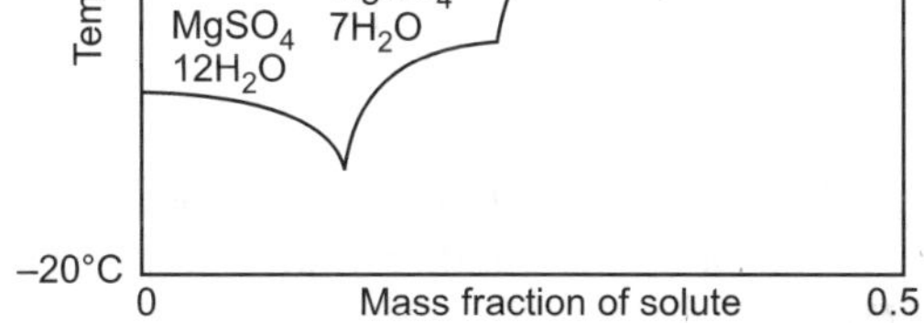

Fig. 6.1 Temperature–concentration dependence of solubility

Solubility data are temperature dependent. They may be taken from standard tables or hand books [1]. For most materials, the solubility increases more or less rapidly with temperature (for example, KNO_3). For a few substances, such as NaCl, the solubility changes very little with temperature. For a few others, solubility decreases with increase in temperature (as in $MnSO_4.H_2O$). Figure 6.2 shows the temperature dependence of solubility.

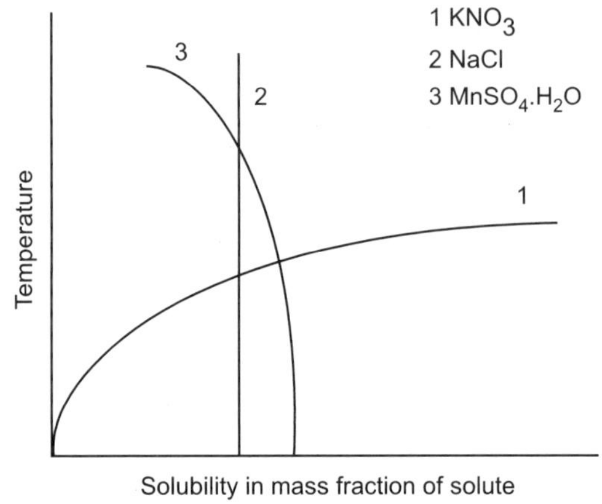

Fig. 6.2 Temperature dependence of solubility

Yield

In the crystallisation process, the final mother liquor is in contact with a sufficiently large crystal surface so that the concentration of the liquor is that of a saturated solution at the final temperature of the process. The yield of the process is calculated from the composition of the initial solution or feed and the solubility of the material at the final temperature. If appreciable evaporation has taken place during the process this must be known or estimated. The actual crop, after removal from the crystalliser, will in general retain some adhering mother liquor; this will add to the weight. In case the solid product is in the anhydrous form, calculation of yield is simple as the solid phase contains no water.

When the crop is hydrated, the water of crystallisation in the crystals must be accounted for since this water is withdrawn from the mother liquor and is not available for retaining the solute in the solution.

Problems on crystallisation can be easily solved based on material balance equations, overall balance and solute balance.

1. The input is the feed solution (F). If crystallisation is accompanied by evaporation and cooling, the outputs are, the mother liquor left (M) crystals formed (C) and evaporation loss (E).

   Overall balance:

   $$F = M + C + E \tag{6.1}$$

   If there is no evaporation

   $$F = M + C \tag{6.2}$$

2. If x_F is the weight fraction of the solute in the feed, x_M is the weight fraction of the solute in the mother liquor, x_C is the weight fraction of solute in the crystals.

   Solute balance:

   $$Fx_F = Mx_M + Cx_C \tag{6.3}$$

   It may be noted that x_C is the ratio of the molecular weight of the anhydrous solute to that of the hydrated solute.

Therefore, for hydrated solutes (solutes with water of crystallisation), $x_C < 1$ and for anhydrous solutes (solutes with no water of crystallisation), $x_C = 1$.

ILLUSTRATIONS

6A Common salt solution contains 20% sodium chloride and 80% water by weight. To recover 90% of dissolved salt, it is proposed to evaporate a part of water and then carry out the crystallisation at 303 K. At 303 K, the solubility of sodium chloride in water is 40 kg per100 kg of water. Calculate (i) weight of water to be evaporated per 1 000 kg of original solution and (ii) weight of mother liquor left after crystallisation.

Solution

Basis: 1000 kg of solution.

Weight of sodium chloride in the solution $= 1\,000 \times \dfrac{20}{100} = 200$ kg

Weight of water in the solution $=$ 800 kg

90% of sodium chloride is to be recovered as crystals.

Weight of sodium chloride to be crystallised $= 200 \times \dfrac{90}{100} = 180$ kg

Sodium chloride in mother liquor = sodium chloride in feed – sodium chloride crystallised out

$= 200 - 180 = 20$ kg

The mother liquor is saturated at the crystallisation temperature (at which the solubility of sodium chloride in water is 40 kg per 100 kg of water).

To retain 20 kg of sodium chloride in solution, the amount of water required is

$$= 20 \times \frac{100}{40} = 50 \text{ kg}$$

Weight of mother liquor = weight of water + weight of sodium chloride

$$= 50 + 20 = 70 \text{ kg}$$

Water to be evaporated = water in feed – water in mother liquor

$$= 800 - 50 = 750 \text{ kg}$$

6B After a crystallisation process, a solution of calcium chloride in water contains 50 parts of calcium chloride per 100 parts of water. Calculate the weight of this solution necessary to dissolve 200 kg of $CaCl_2.6H_2O$ crystal at a temperature of 298 K. The solubility of calcium chloride in water at 298 K is 7.38 kmol of calcium chloride per 1 000 kg of water.

Solution

Basis: 200 kg of $CaCl_2.6H_2O$ solute.

Let the solution required to dissolve the above solute be x kg. The solution contains 50 parts of calcium chloride per 100 parts of water.

Calcium chloride already present in the solution $= \dfrac{50x}{(100+50)} = 0.333\ 3x$

Solvent (water) in the solution $= 0.666\ 7x$

Solute to be dissolved $= 200$ kg

Anhydrous calcium chloride in the solute $= 200 \times \dfrac{111}{219} = 101.37$ kg

(219 is the molecular weight of the hydrated salt and 111 is the weight of calcium chloride present in it.)

Water of crystallisation in the solute $= 200 - 101.37 = 98.63$ kg

Total water = water of crystallisation in the solute + water in the solution

$= 98.63$ kg $+0.666\ 7x$

Total calcium chloride = calcium chloride in the solute + calcium chloride in the solution

$= 0.333\ 3x + 101.37$ kg

Solubility at 298 K = 7.38 kmol calcium chloride per 1 000 kg water

In the final solution, the ratio of calcium chloride to water should be $= 7.38 \times \dfrac{111}{1\ 000}$

$$\frac{\text{Solute}}{\text{Water}} = \frac{819.2}{1000} = \frac{0.3333x + 101.37}{0.6667x + 98.63}$$

Thus, weight of solution required (x) = 96.65 kg

6C A solution of potassium dichromate in water contains 15% potassium dichromate by weight. 1 000 kg of this solution is evaporated to remove some amount of water. The remaining solution is cooled to 298 K. If the yield of potassium dichromate crystals is 75%, calculate the amount of water evaporated. The solubility of potassium dichromate in water is 0.39 kmol per 1 000 kg of water at 298 K.

Solution

Basis: 1 000 kg of 15% potassium dichromate solution.

Weight of potassium dichromate in the solution = 150 kg

Weight of water in the solution = $1\,000 - 150 = 850$ kg

75% of the solute has to be crystallised out.

Potassium dichromate to be crystallised = $150 \times \dfrac{75}{100} = 112.5$ kg

The balance will remain in solution. The solution remaining after crystallisation is the mother liquor.

Potassium dichromate in mother liquor = 37.5 kg

The mother liquor is saturated at the crystallisation temperature; the solubility of potassium dichromate in water is 0.39 kmol per 1 000 kg of water.

Solubility of potassium dichromate = 0.39×294 kg per 1 000 kg water

= 114.66 kg per 1 000 kg water

Water required to retain 37.5 kg solute in mother liquor = $1\,000 \times \dfrac{37.5}{114.66} = 327.05$ kg

The remaining water has to be removed by evaporation.

Weight of water to be evaporated = water in the feed – water in mother liquor

$= 850.00 - 327.05 = 522.95$ kg

6D 2 000 kg of 30% solution of sodium carbonate is cooled slowly to 293 K. During cooling, 5% of the solution is evaporated. The carbonate precipitating out forms $Na_2CO_3.10H_2O$ crystals. The solubility of anhydrous sodium carbonate at 293 K is 21.5 kg per 100 kg of water. What is the weight of the decahydrate crystals, water loss on evaporation and mother liquor left?

Solution

Basis: 2 000 kg of feed (F)

Weight fraction of sodium carbonate solute in the feed (x_F) $= \dfrac{30}{100} = 0.3$

Weight of sodium carbonate solute in the feed $= 2\ 000 \times 0.3 = 600$ kg

Weight of water in the feed $= 2\ 000 - 600 = 1\ 400$ kg

During cooling, 5% of solution is evaporated.

Weight of water evaporated (E) $= 2\ 000 \times \dfrac{5}{100} = 100$ kg

The mother liquor is saturated at the crystallisation temperature, 293 K. The solubility of anhydrous sodium carbonate at 293 K is 21.5 kg per 100 kg of water.

Weight fraction of sodium carbonate in mother liquor (x_M) $= \dfrac{21.5}{(21.5 + 100)} = 0.177$

The composition of crystal (C) is $Na_2CO_3.10H_2O$. The molecular weight of anhydrous Na_2CO_3 is 106 and that of the hydrated crystals is 286.

Weight fraction of Na_2CO_3 in the hydrated crystals (x_C) $= \dfrac{106}{286} = 0.371$

The problem can be solved using the overall balance and solute balance.

Overall balance:

$$F = M + C + E$$

$$2\ 000 = M + C + 100 \tag{1}$$

Solute balance:

$$Fx_F = Mx_M + Cx_C$$

$$600 = 0.177M + 0.371C \tag{2}$$

From (1) and (2),

Mother liquor = 540.72 kg; Crystals = 1 359.28 kg

6E After crystallisation, crystals of $Na_2SO_4.10H_2O$ are obtained. In a particular process, 2 000 kg of $Na_2SO_4.10\ H_2O$ are obtained and the mother liquor was found to contain 20% Na_2SO_4 (anhydrous) by weight. If the feed solution contained 30% Na_2SO_4 (anhydrous) by weight and 20% of original water is lost by evaporation, calculate the weight of feed solution, weight of mother liquor left and weight of water evaporated.

Solution

Basis: As the amount of feed is not known, we have to assume the feed to be 100 kg and find the crystals obtainable. From that, we have to calculate backwards to find the other unknowns.

Weight fraction of solute in feed (x_F)	=	0.3
Weight of Na_2SO_4 in 100 kg feed	=	30 kg
Weight of water in 100 kg feed	=	70 kg

20% of original water is lost by evaporation.

Water evaporated (E) $= 70 \times \dfrac{20}{100} = 14$ kg

Weight fraction of solute in mother liquor (x_M) $= 0.2$

Molecular weight of Na_2SO_4 is 142 and that of $Na_2SO_4.10H_2O$ is 322.

Weight fraction of anhydrous solute in crystals (x_C) $= \dfrac{142}{322} = 0.441$

The problem can be solved using the overall balance and solute balance.

Overall balance:

$$F = M + C + E$$

$$100 = M + C + 14$$

$$86 = M + C \qquad (1)$$

Solute balance:

$$Fx_F = Mx_M + Cx_C$$

$$30 = 0.2M + 0.441C \qquad (2)$$

From (1) and (2)

$$C = 53.11 \text{ kg}$$

If the weight of crystals is 53.11 kg, the weight of feed is 100 kg.

If the crystals weigh 2 000 kg, the feed is $= \dfrac{100}{53.11} \times 2000 = 3\ 765.77$ kg

If the weight of feed is 100, evaporation loss = 14 kg

If the weight of feed is 3 756.77 kg, evaporation loss $= \dfrac{14}{100} \times 3\ 765.77 = 527.2$ kg

Weight of mother liquor left = Feed – crystals – evaporation loss

$= 3\ 756.77 - 2\ 000 - 527.2 = 1\ 238.57$ kg

6F Solubility of $FeSO_4.7H_2O$ is 47.5 kg and 33.8 kg in 100 kg of water at 318 K and 305 K respectively.

(i) Estimate the theoretical weight of saturated solution at 318 K to be charged to get 1000 kg of crystals by cooling to 305 K.

(ii) If 5% of the total water entering the system is lost by evaporation, what is the yield of crystals in this case?

(iii) At the conditions of (ii), how much of feed solution is required for a harvest of 1 000 kg of crystals?

Solution

Basis: 147.5 kg of saturated solution at 318 K.

(i) Solubility at 318 K = 47.5 kg

Solubility at 305 K = 33.8 kg

If a saturated solution at 318 K is cooled to 305 K, the yield of crystals will be equal to the difference in solubility.

Yield of crystals = 13.7 kg

For 13.7 kg crystals, the weight of feed required = 147.5

For 1 000 kg crystals, the weight of feed required $= 147.5 \times \dfrac{100}{13.7} = 10\ 766.4$ kg

(ii) 147.5 kg feed contains 100 kg water.

Weight of water in 10 766.4 kg feed $= 10\ 766.4 \times \dfrac{100}{147.5} = 7\ 299.3$ kg

During cooling 5% of water is lost by evaporation.

Evaporation loss $= 7\ 299.3 \times \dfrac{5}{100} = 364.96$ kg

The solute dissolved in this water will be available as additional crystals. The solubility at 305 K is 33.8 kg in 100 kg of water.

Additional yield $= 364.96 \times \dfrac{33.8}{100} = 123.4$ kg

Total yield = original yield + additional yield = 1 123.4 kg

(iii) Under conditions of (ii), yield for 10 766.4 kg feed = 1 123.4 kg

Feed, if the yield required is only 1 000 kg $= 10766.4 \times \dfrac{1\ 000}{11\ 23.4} = 9\ 584.6$ kg

6G A hot solution of barium nitrate from an evaporator contains 30.6 kg barium nitrate per 100 kg of water and goes to a crystalliser where the solution is cooled and barium nitrate crystallises. On cooling, 10% of the original water evaporates. For a feed of 100 kg, calculate (i) yield of crystals if the solution is cooled to 290 K, where the solubility is 8.5 kg barium nitrate per 100 kg water, and (ii) yield of crystals if the solution is cooled to 280 K, where the solubility is 6.9 kg barium nitrate per 100 kg of water.

Solution

Basis: 100 kg of feed

(i) Weight fraction of solute in feed (x_F) $= \dfrac{30.6}{(30.6+100)} = 0.234$

Weight fraction of solute in mother liquor $(x_M) = \dfrac{8.5}{(8.5+100)} = 0.078$

The crystals are not hydrated.

So, the weight fraction of anhydrous solute in the crystals obtained $(x_C) = 1.0$

Weight of water in the feed $= 100 \times 0.766 = 76.6$ kg

10% of water is lost during cooling.

Water evaporated (E) $= 76.6 \times \dfrac{10}{100} = 7.66$ kg

The problem can be solved using the overall balance and solute balance.

Overall balance,

$$F = M + C + E$$

$$100 = M + C + 7.66 \tag{1}$$

Solute balance

$$Fx_F = Mx_M + Cx_C$$

$$23.4 = 0.078M + C \tag{2}$$

From (1) and (2)

Yield = 17.48 kg

(ii) If the solution is cooled to 280 K,

Weight fraction of solute in mother liquor $(x_M) = \dfrac{6.9}{(6.9+100)} = 0.065$

New solute balance $23.4 = 0.065M + C$ (3)

From (1) and (3)

New yield = 18.53 kg

6H A tank holds 5 000 kg of a saturated solution of sodium bicarbonate at 333K. If 200 kg of sodium bicarbonate has to be crystallised from this solution, to what temperature must the solution be cooled? Temperature–solubility data is given in Table 6.2.

Table 6.1 Temperature–solubility data

Temperature (K)	Solubility (kg $NaHCO_3$ per 100 kg water)
323	14.45
313	12.70
303	11.10
293	9.60

Solution

Basis: 5 000 kg of saturated solution of sodium bicarbonate at 333 K.

Solubility at 333 K $=$ 16.4 kg $NaHCO_3$ per 100 kg H_2O

Weight fraction of solute $= \dfrac{16.4}{(100 + 16.4)} = 0.141$

Sodium bicarbonate in the feed solution $= 5\ 000 \times 0.141 = 705$ kg

Water in the feed solution $= 5\ 000 - 705 = 4\ 295$ kg

Sodium bicarbonate to be crystallised $=$ 200 kg

We know that the solution from which crystallisation takes place is saturated at the crystallisation temperature.

Sodium bicarbonate in the remaining solution $= 705 - 200 = 505$ kg

Solubility of the solute at that stage $= 505 \times \dfrac{100}{4295}$

$=$ 11.76 kg $NaHCO_3$ per 100 kg H_2O

From the data given in the problem, this value is between the solubility values for the temperatures 303 K and 313 K.

Solubility at 313 K = 12.7 kg $NaHCO_3$ per 100 kg H_2O

Solubility at 303 K = 11.1 kg $NaHCO_3$ per 100 kg H_2O

The temperature to which the solution should be cooled is between 303 and 313 K.

$$\text{The actual temperature is} = 303 + \left\{ 10 \times \frac{(11.76 - 11.10)}{(12.70 - 11.10)} \right\}$$

$$= 303 + 4.125 = 307.125 \text{ K}$$

6I The solubility of anhydrous manganese sulphate at 293 K is 62.9 g per 100 g of water. How much $MnSO_4.5H_2O$ must be dissolved in 100 kg of water to give a saturated solution?

Solution

Basis: 100 kg of water.

Let x kg of $MnSO_4.5H_2O$ be required for making a saturated solution at 293 K.

Molecular weight of anhydrous manganese sulphate $=$ 151

Molecular weight of $MnSO_4.5H_2O$ $=$ 241

Weight of anhydrous manganese sulphate in x kg $MnSO_4.5H_2O$ $= \dfrac{151x}{241} = 0.627x$

Weight of water of crystallisation in x kg $MnSO_4.5H_2O$ $= 0.373x$

Total water $= 100 + 0.373x$

Solute to solvent ratio should match with the solubility at 293 K.

$$\frac{\text{Solute}}{\text{Solvent}} = \frac{0.627x}{100 + 0.373x} = \frac{62.9}{100}$$

$$x = 160.46 \text{ kg}$$

Solute required is 160.46 kg.

6J The solubility of barium nitrate is 34 kg per 100 kg of water and 5 kg per 100 kg of water at 373 K and 273 K respectively. If you start with 100 kg of barium nitrate and make a saturated solution in water at 373 K, how much of water is required? If this solution is cooled to 273 K, how much of barium nitrate will be precipitated out of the solution?

Solution

Basis: 100 kg of barium nitrate solute.

Saturated solution at 373 K is prepared taking 100 kg of barium nitrate. The solubility of barium nitrate is 34 kg per 100 kg of water at 373 K. That is, 34 kg of solute requires 100 kg of water.

Water required for the dissolution of 100 kg solute $= 100 \times \dfrac{100}{34} = 294.12$ kg

As no evaporation takes place, the amount of water will remain the same and it is the water in the mother liquor.

Water in mother liquor $= 294.12$ kg

The mother liquor is saturated at the crystallisation temperature, 273 K. At 273 K, the solubility is 5 kg barium nitrate per 100 kg water. So, 100 kg water requires 5 kg solute.

Solute required by the water in mother liquor $= 5 \times \dfrac{294.12}{100} = 14.71$ kg

The rest of the solute will crystallise out.

Crystals obtained $= 100 - 14.71 = 85.29$ kg

6K A solution of 53.8 grams of magnesium sulphate per 100 grams of water is cooled from 353 K to 323 K. During this process, 6% of water is evaporated. For 100 kg of original feed solution, calculate the amount of $MgSO_4.7H_2O$ crystals obtained and the quantity of mother liquor left. At 323 K, the solution should contain 0.3 mass fraction of magnesium sulphate.

Solution

Basis: 100 kg of feed solution (F)

Mass fraction of solute in feed (x_F) $= \dfrac{53.8}{(100+53.8)} = 0.35$

$MgSO_4$ in 100 kg feed $= 100 \times 0.35 = 35$ kg

Water in 100 kg feed $= 100 - 35 = 65$ kg

During cooling, 6% water is evaporated.

Water evaporated (E) $= 65 \times \dfrac{6}{100} = 3.9$ kg

Molecular weight of $MgSO_4.7H_2O$ is 246.3 and that of the anhydrous solute is 120.3.

Mass fraction of anhydrous solute in crystals (x_C) $= \dfrac{120.3}{246.3} = 0.488$

Mass fraction of solute in mother liquor (x_M) $= 0.3$

The problem can be solved using the overall balance and solute balance.

Overall balance:

$$F = M + C + E$$

$$100 = M + C + 3.9$$

$$96.1 = M + C \qquad (1)$$

Solute balance:

$$Fx_F = Mx_M + Cx_C$$

$$35 = 0.3M + 0.488C \qquad (2)$$

From (1) and (2), yield of crystals $= 35.82$ kg

6L A batch of 1 500 kg of saturated potassium chloride solution is cooled from 360 K to 290 K in a unagitated tank. The solubility of potassium chloride is 53 kg per 100 kg of water at 360 K and 34 kg per 100 kg of water at 290 K. Water losses due to evaporation may be neglected. What is the yield of crystals?

Solution

Basis: 1 500 kg of saturated potassium chloride solution at 360 K.

Solubility of potassium chloride is 53 kg per 100 kg of water at 360 K.

153 kg of saturated potassium chloride solution contains 100 kg of water.

Water in 1 500 kg saturated potassium chloride solution $= \dfrac{1\ 500 \times 100}{153} = 980.39$

Potassium chloride in 1500 kg saturated potassium chloride solution $= 1\ 500 - 980.39 = 519.61$ kg

It is given that during crystallisation by cooling, there is no evaporation. So, water in the mother liquor is the same as water in the feed.

Water in the mother liquor = 980.39 kg

Mother liquor is saturated at the crystallisation temperature, 290 K. Solubility of potassium chloride is 34 kg per 100 kg of water at 290 K.

$$\text{Potassium chloride in mother liquor} = \frac{34 \times 980.39}{100} = 333.33$$

Potassium chloride crystallised out = KCl in the feed – KCl in the mother liquor

$= 519.61 - 333.33 = 186.28$ kg

6M A saturated solution containing 1 500 kg of potassium chloride at 360 K is cooled in an open tank to 290 K. The specific gravity of the solution is 1.2. If the solubility of potassium chloride per 100 parts of water is 53.55 at 360 K and 34.5 at 290 K, calculate (i) the capacity of the tank required and (ii) the mass of crystals obtained neglecting the loss of water by evaporation.

Solution

Basis: 1 500 kg of potassium chloride solute.

A saturated solution is prepared at 360 K using this potassium chloride. The solubility of potassium chloride is 53.55 kg per 100 kg of water at 360 K.

53.55 kg of potassium chloride requires 100 kg of water to get a saturated solution.

$$\text{Water required for 1 500 kg potassium chloride} = \frac{1500 \times 100}{53.55} = 2\ 801.12 \text{ kg}$$

Weight of saturated solution prepared = weight of KCl + weight of water

$= 1\ 500 + 2\ 801.12 = 4\ 301.12$ kg

Specific gravity of the saturated solution at 360 K is 1.2. So, the density of the solution is 1 200 kg m^{-3}. Volume of the crystalliser is found by dividing the weight of the solution by its density.

$$\text{Volume of the crystalliser} = \frac{4\ 301.12}{1\ 200} = 3.584 \text{ m}^3 \approx 4.0 \text{ m}^3$$

It is given that during crystallisation by cooling, there is no evaporation. So, water in the mother liquor is the same as water in the feed.

Water in the mother liquor = 2 801.12 kg

The mother liquor is saturated at the crystallisation temperature, 290 K. The solubility of potassium chloride is 34.5 kg per 100 kg of water at 290 K.

$$\text{Potassium chloride in mother liquor} = \frac{34.5 \times 2801.12}{100} = 966.39 \text{ kg}$$

$$\begin{aligned}\text{Potassium chloride crystallised out} &= \text{KCl in the feed} - \text{KCl in the mother liquor} \\ &= 1\,500 - 966.39 = 533.61 \text{ kg}\end{aligned}$$

Purification of the Product

Although a crystal is pure, it retains some mother liquor when removed from the final magma; the adhering liquor will carry impurities if there are any present in the mother liquor. If the adhering mother liquor dries on the crystal, there will be contamination. In practice, the crystals are usually centrifuged or filtered. The residual mother liquor after this operation amounts to 2% to 5% by weight of the crystals. Large uniform crystals from the low viscosity mother liquor will retain a minimum proportion of the mother liquor. Nonuniform small crystals from viscous solutions will retain a large amount of mother liquor. It is a common practice to wash the crystals on centrifuge or filter with fresh solvent. The use of counter current washing in multiple stages reduces loss of crystals by dissolution in the wash solvent. The purity can also be improved by recrystallisation. But, this method is not as satisfactory as washing the crystals with pure solvent.

ILLUSTRATION

6N 500 kg of 20 weight% solution of sodium nitrate is concentrated to saturation by evaporation. The solution is then cooled to 293 K. The crystals of sodium nitrate are removed by filtration. The wet crystals carry 5% by weight of mother liquor. This is dried. The solubility of sodium nitrate is 1.76 kg per kg of water at 373 K and 0.88 kg per kg of water at 293 K. Calculate (i) amount of water evaporated to achieve saturation at 373 K, and (ii) total weight of sodium nitrate obtained.

Solution

Basis: 500 kg of feed solution.

$$\text{Weight of sodium nitrate in the feed solution} = \frac{20}{100} \times 500 = 100 \text{ kg}$$

$$\text{Weight of water in the feed solution} = 500 - 100 = 400 \text{ kg}$$

The feed solution is saturated by evaporation at 373 K. The solubility of sodium nitrate is

1.76 kg per kg of water at 373 K. At 373 K, 1 kg of water is required for 1.76 kg of sodium nitrate to make a saturated solution.

$$\text{Weight of water required for saturated solution at 373 K} = 100 \times \frac{1}{1.76} = 56.82 \text{ kg}$$

The remaining water has to be evaporated.

$$\begin{aligned}\text{Weight of water to be evaporated} &= \text{water in feed} - \text{water in saturated solution}\\ &= 400 - 56.82 = 343.18 \text{ kg}\end{aligned}$$

The saturated solution at 373 K is cooled to 293 K. The resultant solution is saturated at 293 K. As the temperature has come down, the solubility also will come down. The excess solute will crystallise out. The solution remaining after the crystallisation is complete is known as the mother liquor. The mother liquor is saturated at the crystallisation temperature. In the present case there is no evaporation. So, water in the original solution and the mother liquor is the same.

Water in the mother liquor = 56.82 kg

The mother liquor is saturated at the crystallisation temperature at which the solubility of sodium nitrate is 0.88 kg per kg of water.

$$\text{Sodium nitrate in the mother liquor} = 56.82 \times 0.88 = 50 \text{ kg}$$

$$\begin{aligned}\text{Sodium nitrate crystallised out} &= \text{sodium nitrate in the original solution} - \text{sodium nitrate in mother liquor}\\ &= 100 - 50 = 50 \text{ kg}\end{aligned}$$

$$\begin{aligned}\text{Weight of mother liquor} &= \text{weight of solvent} + \text{solute}\\ &= 56.82 + 50.00 = 106.82 \text{ kg}\end{aligned}$$

Wet crystals carry 5% of the mother liquor.

$$\text{Mother liquor wetting the crystals} = 106.82 \times \frac{5}{100} = 5.34 \text{ kg}$$

106.82 kg of the mother liquor contains 50 kg sodium nitrate.

$$\begin{aligned}NaNO_3 \text{ in 5.34 kg mother liquor wetting the crystals} &= 5.34 \times \frac{50}{106.82} = 2.5 \text{ kg}\\ \text{Total sodium nitrate crystals} &= \text{sodium nitrate crystalised out} + \text{sodium nitrate from mother liquor wetting the crystals}\\ &= 50 + 2.5 = 52.5 \text{ kg}\end{aligned}$$

HEAT EFFECTS IN THE CRYSTALLISATION PROCESS

The heat effect in the crystallisation process is calculated by means of a heat balance. Such a balancc can bc computed by two methods.

1. The individual heat effects such as sensible heats, latent heats and heat of crystallisation can be combined into a heat balance equation.
2. An enthalpy balance can be taken, in which the total enthalpy of all leaving streams – total enthalpy of all entering streams is equal to the heat absorbed from external source by the process.

In the first method, heat removed from the crystallising solution by external means is equal to the sum of sensible heat lost by the cooling solution and the heat evolved in the formation of the crystalline crop (heat of crystallisation) – the radiation losses – heat of vaporisation of solvent evaporated during the process.

Heat of Crystallisation

Heat of crystallisation is the latent heat accompanying the precipitation of crystals from a saturated solution. For most substances this is exothermic, it varies with concentration and temperature. The heat of crystallisation is the negative value of heat of solution. The heat of solution is the heat evolved when a unit mass of solid is dissolved in a very large amount of water. This value can be obtained from standard tables or hand books. During crystallisation, there is a change in the concentration of the solution. Hence, accurate determination of heat of crystallisation must involve heat of dilution as well. For concentrated solutions, the heat of dilution is negligible when compared to the heat of solution. Usually, the heat of dilution is not taken into account. An enthalpy–concentration diagram may be used for calculating heat balance over crystallisation processes.

ILLUSTRATIONS

60 A Swenson–Walker crystalliser is to produce 500 kg h^{-1} of $FeSO_4.7H_2O$ crystals. The saturated solution enters the crystalliser at 322 K and the slurry leaves at 300 K. Cooling water enters the crystalliser jacket at 288 K and leaves at 294 K. The overall heat transfer coefficient has been estimated to be 200 W m^{-2} K^{-1}. There are 1.2 m^2 cooling surfaces per metre of crystalliser length. Calculate the cooling water requirement in kg h^{-1} and the number of crystalliser sections, each section being 3 m long.

Data:

1. Solubility at 322 K and 300 K are 140 parts and 70 parts of $FeSO_4.7H_2O$ per 100 parts of water.
2. Average specific heat of solution is 2.9 kJ kg^{-1} K^{-1}.
3. Heat of crystallisation is 66 kJ kg^{-1}.

Solution

Basis: 1 hour operation.

Material balance: The solubilities of $FeSO_4.7H_2O$ at 322 K and 300 K are 140 parts and 70 parts of $FeSO_4.7H_2O$ per 100 parts of H_2O. There is no information regarding evaporation during cooling. So, if we take 240 kg of saturated solution of $FeSO_4.7H_2O$ in water at 322 K and cool to 300 K, the amount of $FeSO_4.7H_2O$ crystals obtained will be given by the difference in solubility at the two temperatures.

Yield of $FeSO_4.7H_2O$ crystals for a feed of 240 kg $= 140 - 70 = 70$ kg

For a yield of 500 kg, feed required $= \dfrac{240}{70} \times 500 = 1\,714.29$ kg

Energy balance:

Heat to be removed in cooling the feed solution to 300 K from 322 K

$$= 1\,714.29 \times 2.9 \times (322 - 300) = 109\,372 \text{ kJ}$$

Heat of crystallisation $= 66 \times 500 = 33\,000$ kJ

Total heat to be removed (q) $= 142\,372$ kJ

This much heat has to be removed by cooling water. The feed enters at 322 K and the slurry leaves at 300 K. Cooling water enters the crystalliser jacket at 288 K and leaves at 294 K.

Assuming counter current flow for maximum efficiency,

$$\text{Log mean temperature difference } (\Delta T_{lm}) = \frac{28 - 12}{\ln \dfrac{28}{12}} = \frac{16}{0.842} = 18.884 \text{ K}$$

Overall heat transfer coefficient (U) has been given as 200 W m^{-2} K^{-1}

$$= 0.2 \text{ kW m}^{-2} \text{ K}^{-1}$$

$$q = UA\Delta T_{lm}$$

$$142\,372 = 0.2 \times 3\,600 \times A \times 18.884$$

Heat transfer surface (A) required $= 10.47$ m^2

There is a 1.2 m^2 cooling surface per metre of crystalliser length.

Length of crystalliser $= \dfrac{10.47}{1.2} = 8.73$ m

Each crystalliser section is 3 m long.

Number of crystalliser sections $= \dfrac{8.73}{3} = 2.91 \approx 3$

Cooling water absorbs 142 372 kJ heat and gets heated up to 294 K from 288 K.

$$\text{Cooling water required} = \frac{142\,372}{4.187 \times 6} = 5\,667.22 \text{ kg h}^{-1}$$

6P Glauber's salt, $Na_2SO_4.10H_2O$, is to be produced in a Swenson–Walker crystalliser by cooling a solution of Na_2SO_4 anhydrate which is saturated at 300 K, to 290 K. If cooling water enters and leaves the unit at 280 K and 290 K respectively and evaporation is negligible, how many sections of crystalliser, each 3 m long, will be required to process 0.25 kg s^{-1} of the product? The solubility of Na_2SO_4 anhydrate in water is 40 and 14 kg per 100 kg of water at 300 K and 290 K respectively. The mean heat capacity of the liquor is 3.8 kJ kg^{-1} K^{-1} and the heat of crystallisation is −230 kJ kg^{-1}. For the crystalliser, the available heat transfer area is 3 m^2 per metre length. The overall heat transfer coefficient is 0.15 kW m^{-2} K^{-1}. The molecular weight of $Na_2SO_4.10H_2O$ is 322 and that of Na_2SO_4 is 142.

Solution

Basis: 1 hour operation.

Yield of crystals $= 0.25 \times 3600 = 900$ kg

Material balance: As the amount of feed is not known, we have to assume the feed to be 100 kg, and find the crystals obtainable. From that, we have to calculate backwards to obtain the feed. Saturated solution of Na_2SO_4 at 300 K is cooled to 290 K. The solubility of Na_2SO_4 anhydrate in water is 40 and 14 kg per 100 kg of water at 300 K and 290 K respectively.

$$\text{Weight fraction of solute in feed } (x_F) = \frac{40}{100+40} = 0.286$$

$$\text{Weight fraction of solute in mother liquor } (x_M) = \frac{14}{100+14} = 0.123$$

Molecular weight of Na_2SO_4 is 142 and that of $Na_2SO_4.10H_2O$ is 322.

$$\text{Weight fraction of anhydrous solute in crystals } (x_C) = \frac{142}{322} = 0.441$$

Evaporation (E) is negligible. That is, $E = 0$

The problem can be solved using the overall balance and solute balance.

Overall balance:

$$F = M + C + E$$

$$100 = M + C \tag{1}$$

Solute balance:

$$Fx_F = Mx_M + Cx_C$$

$$0.286F = 0.123M + 0.441C \tag{2}$$

From (1) and (2)

$$C = 51.2 \text{ kg}$$

If the weight of crystals is 51.2 kg, the weight of feed is 100 kg.

If crystals are 900 kg, feed is $= \dfrac{100}{51.2} \times 900 = 1\ 757.812$ kg

Encrgy balance:

Heat to be removed in cooling the feed solution to 290 K from 300 K

$$= 1\ 757.812 \times 3.8 \times (300 - 290) = 66797 \text{ kJ}$$

Heat of crystallisation $= 900 \times 230 = 207\ 000$ kJ

Total heat to be removed (q)$= 273\ 797$ kJ

This much heat has to be removed by cooling water. The feed enters at 300 K and the slurry leaves at 290 K. Cooling water enters the crystalliser jacket at 280 K and leaves at 290 K.

Assuming counter current flow for maximum efficiency,

Average temperature drop $= 10$ K

Overall heat transfer coefficient (U) has been given as 0.15×3600 kW m^{-2} K^{-1}.

$$q = UA\Delta T_{lm}$$

$$273797 = 0.15 \times 3600 \times A \times 10$$

Heat transfer surface (A) required $= 50.7$ m^2

There is a 3 m^2 cooling surface per metre of crystalliser length.

Length of crystalliser $= \dfrac{50.7}{3} = 16.9$ m

Each crystalliser section is 3 m long.

Number of crystalliser sections $= \dfrac{16.9}{3} = 5.63 \approx 6$

6Q A solution of 500 kg of Na_2SO_4 in 2 500 kg of water is cooled from 333 K to 283 K in an agitated steel vessel of mass 750 kg. At 283 K, the solubility of the anhydrous salt is 8.9 kg per 100 kg of water and the stable crystalline phase is $Na_2SO_4.10H_2O$. At 283 K, the heat of solution is -78.5 MJ kmol^{-1} and the heat capacities of the solution and mild steel are 3.6 and 0.5 kJ kg^{-1} K^{-1} respectively. If during cooling, 2% of the water initially present is lost by evaporation, estimate the heat which must be removed.

Solution

Basis: Solution of 500 kg of Na_2SO_4 in 2 500 kg of water.

Material balance:

Weight fraction of solute in feed $(x_F) \quad = \dfrac{500}{500 + 2500} = 0.167$

The feed solution is cooled to 283 K, $Na_2SO_4.10H_2O$ crystallises out. At 283 K, the solubility of the anhydrous salt is 8.9 kg per 100 kg of water.

Weight fraction of solute in mother liquor $(x_M) = \dfrac{8.9}{100 + 8.9} = 0.082$

Molecular weight of Na_2SO_4 is 142 and that of $Na_2SO_4.10H_2O$ is 322.

Weight fraction of anhydrous solute in crystals $(x_C) = \dfrac{142}{322} = 0.441$

During cooling 2% of original water is evaporated.

Water evaporated = 2 500 × 0.02 = 50 kg

The problem can be solved using the overall balance and solute balance.

Overall balance:

$$F = M + C + E$$

$$3000 = M + C + 50 \quad (1)$$

Solute balance:

$$Fx_F = Mx_M + Cx_C$$

$$500 = 0.082M + 0.441C \quad (2)$$

From (1) and (2)

$$C = 720.69 \text{ kg}$$

Energy balance:

Heat to be removed in cooling the feed solution to 333 K from 283 K

$$= 3\,000 \times 3.6 \times (333 - 283) = 540\,000 \text{ kJ}$$

Heat removed from vessel = 750 × 0.5 × (333 – 283) = 18 750 kJ

Heat of crystallisation = –(heat of solution)

$= 78.5$ MJ kmol^{-1}

$= 78\,500$ kJ kmol^{-1}

$= 78\,500$ kJ per 322 kg

$= 243.79$ kJ kg^{-1}

Heat to be removed from crystals = 243.79 × 720.69 = 175 697 kJ

Total heat to be removed = 734 447 kJ

Mean value of latent heat of vaporisation of water is 2 487.5 kJ kg^{-1} and 2 357.9 kJ kg^{-1} at 333 K and 283 K respectively. The mean value is 2 418.2 kJ kg^{-1}.

Heat required in the evaporation of water = 50 × 2 418.2 = 120 910 kJ

Nett heat to be removed = 734 447 – 120 910 = 613 537 kJ $\approx$ 613.5 MJ

6R What is the evaporation rate and the yield of $CH_3COONa.3H_2O$ from a continuous evaporative crystalliser operating at 1 kN m^{-2} when it is fed with 1 kg s^{-1} of a 50 mass% aqueous solution of sodium acetate at 350 K? The boiling point elevation of the solution is 10 K and the heat of crystallisation is 150 kJ kg^{-1}. The average specific heat of the solution is 3.5 kJ kg^{-1} K^{-1} and at 1 kN m^{-2}, water boils at 280 K at which the latent heat of vaporisation is 2 482 kJ kg^{-1}. Over the range 270–305 K, the solubility of sodium acetate in water (S) at T K is given approximately by S $= 0.61T - 132.4$ kg per 100 kg of water. The molecular weight of $CH_3COONa.3H_2O$ is 136 and that of anhydrous CH_3COONa is 82.

Solution

Basis: 1 hour operation.

Material balance:

Weight of feed solution (F)	=	3 600 kg
Weight fraction of solute in feed	=	0.50
Weight of solute in the feed	=	1 800 kg
Weight of water in the feed	=	1 800 kg

The feed solution is evaporated 1 kN m^{-2}. At 1 kN m^{-2}, water boils at 280 K. The boiling point elevation of the solution is 10 K. So, the solution evaporates at 290 K. Crystallisation occurs due to evaporation (E) and $CH_3COONa.3H_2O$ crystallises out (C). The solubility at 290 K can be found by the equation given in the problem. The solubility of sodium acetate in water (S) at T K is given by $S = 0.61T - 132.4$ kg per 100 kg of water.

$$= (0.61 \times 290) - 132.4$$

$$= 44.5 \text{ kg per 100 kg of water}$$

Weight fraction of solute in mother liquor $= \dfrac{44.5}{100 + 44.5} = 0.308$

Weight fraction of water in the mother liquor $= 1 - 0.308 = 0.692$

The molecular weight of $CH_3COONa.3H_2O$ is 136 and molecular weight of anhydrous CH_3COONa is 82.

Weight fraction of anhydrous solute in crystals $= \dfrac{82}{136} = 0.603$

Weight fraction of water in the crystals obtained $= 1 - 0.603 = 0.397$

Water balance:

$$1800 = 0.692M + 0.397C + E \qquad (1)$$

Solute balance:

$$1800 = 0.308M + 0.603C \tag{2}$$

Energy balance:

Heat removed in cooling the feed solution to 350 K from 290 K

$$= 3600 \times 3.5 \times (350 - 290) = 756\ 000 \text{ kJ}$$

Heat of crystallisation	=	150 kJ kg^{-1}
Heat to be removed from crystals	=	$150C$ kJ
Total heat to be removed	=	$756000 + 150C$ kJ

This much heat is removed by the evaporation of water, as the equipment used here is an evaporative crystalliser.

Water evaporated is E kg and latent heat of vaporisation is 2482 kJ kg^{-1}.

Hence $2\ 482E = 756\ 000 + 150C$ kJ (3)

From (1), (2) and (3)

Rate of evaporation (E) = 476.23 kg h^{-1} or 0.132 3 kg s^{-1}

Rate of yield (C) = 2 840.97 kg h^{-1} or 0.789 kg s^{-1}

FRACTIONAL CRYSTALLISATION

When two or more solutes are present in the solution, crystallisation of one of the solutes, leaving the others in solution is known as fractional crystallisation. This is based on differences in solubility of the solutes.

The solubility of a material in a solution of another solute is quite different from its solubility in the pure solvent. For example, the solubility of NaCl at 293 K is 36 parts per 100 parts of H_2O and that of $NaNO_3$ is 88 parts per 100 parts of H_2O. But, a solution saturated with respect to both these salts will contain only 25 parts of NaCl and 50 parts of $NaNO_3$ per 100 parts of water.

The mutual solubilities of the above two salts is shown in Fig. 6.3. The solubilities are plotted for two different temperatures. The line DEF is for 373 K at which temperature the solubility of NaCl is 40 parts per 100 parts of H_2O (D) and that of $NaNO_3$ is 176 parts per 100 parts of H_2O (F). A solution saturated with respect to both salts contains 17 parts of NaCl and 160 parts of $NaNO_3$ per 100 parts of H_2O (E). The line ACB is the corresponding solubility curve for 293 K. CE shows the variation of the composition of a solution saturated with both components with temperature. If a solution at 373 K has a composition represented by a point on the line DE, the solution is saturated with respect to NaCl but not with respect to $NaNO_3$. If the composition of the solution is represented by a point on the line EF, the solution is saturated with respect to $NaNO_3$ and not with respect to NaCl.

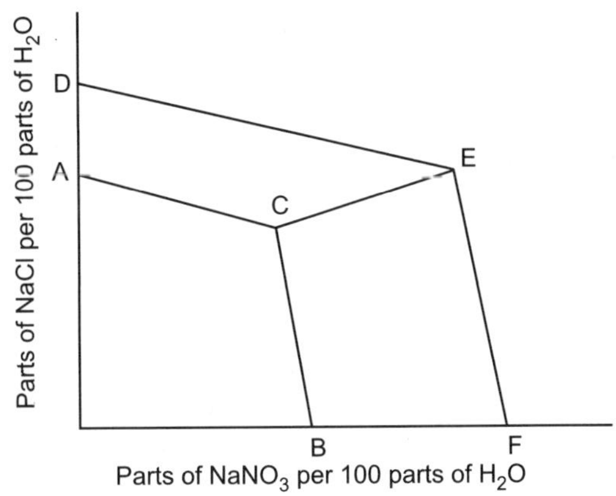

Fig. 6.3 Temperature dependence of solubilities of NaCl and $NaNO_3$ in water

CRYSTAL FORMATION

Crystallisation involves two steps—the crystals must first form and then grow to the desired size. For both steps, the degree of super saturation is the driving force.

Super saturation may be achieved by one or more of the following three methods. If the solubility of the solute increases strongly with increase in temperature, a saturated solution becomes super saturated by simple cooling and temperature reduction. If the solubility is relatively independent of temperature, super saturation may be achieved by evaporating a portion of the solvent. If neither cooling nor evaporation is desirable, super saturation may be achieved by the addition of a third component. The third component may act as a solvent in which case it will form a mixed solvent with the original solvent and the solubility of the solute in the mixed solvent will be sharply reduced. This process is called *salting*. The third component may act as a solute in which case it will compete with the original solute in dissolving in the solvent, thereby reducing the solubility of the original solute. This process is known as *precipitation*. In general, the addition of a third component rapidly creates very large super saturation.

NUCLEATION [2]

Formation of new crystals is termed *nucleation*. Uniformity of the crop of crystals depends on the relationship between nucleation and growth. If new crystals form continuously and rapidly during the process, the crop will consist of many small crystals. If only a few nuclei form or are introduced at the beginning and if subsequent crystallisation takes place on these nuclei, a crop of large uniform crystals will result without further formation of nuclei.

In any crystallisation process, the formation of nuclei should be under control. In a batch process, if uniform crystals are desired, it is advisable to form as large a proportion of crystals as possible, at the same time. Otherwise, a non-uniform crop will be obtained. In a continuous process, the number of nuclei formed per unit time will be constant and uniform, and must equal the number of crystals that are withdrawn per unit time from the crystalliser. In a continuous crystalliser, either most of the nuclei should form within a narrow zone in the unit so that the nuclei can receive the same time of growth (as in a Swenson–Walker crystalliser) or there must be a classifying section in the crystalliser which will retain the small crystals under treatment until they have grown to the proper size before they are removed from the unit (as in a continuous vacuum crystalliser).

Nucleation can be accomplished by adding the desired number of nuclei, usually in the form of crushed crystals to the crystalliser, when the solution is either saturated or super saturated; nuclei may also be formed in situ. New nuclei may originate in situ in one or more of the following ways.

1. By spontaneous nucleation from unseeded solution.
2. By attrition of existing crystals. If crystals are agitated vigorously, small corners and fragments may be broken from existing crystals. Such fragments and mutilated crystals quickly repair themselves and fragments become new nuclei.
3. New crystals may be formed because of the inoculating effect of crystals already formed or present.
4. Local variations in the concentration of the solution may cause nucleation in restricted zones. For example, withdrawal of heat through the containing wall will cause temperature gradients near the wall which can increase the super saturation enough to accelerate nucleation. Evaporation from the surface may result in abnormally high concentrations in the solution at the surface and lead to nucleation.

Spontaneous Nucleation

Crystallisers in which the solution has access to the atmosphere of the plant will in all probability be seeded by the plant dust which invariably carry tiny crystals and dust particles which will inoculate the solution.

Nucleation by Foreign Substances

Crystallisation of one substance can be initiated by crystals of a different substance, if crystal forms are similar in size and form of lattice.

CRYSTAL GROWTH [3,4]

After initial seeding has been done, further nucleation should be avoided while the crystals are growing; this results in crystals of uniform size.

The rate of deposition of crystalline material depends on the surface area of the growing crystals and on the super saturation. These must be matched to the rate of cooling or rate of solvent removal to keep super saturation below the point where nucleation takes place.

The rate of crystallisation is determined by the two processes which takes place in series. Material is transferred from the solution to the surface of the crystal by diffusion. At the surface, the material is incorporated into the crystal structure. The net rate depends on the rate of each of these processes. If the concentration of the saturated solution is C_o, that of the bulk of the solution is C and that of the solution in contact with crystal surface C', the rate of deposition has been estimated to be

$$\frac{dw}{d\theta} = k'S(C' - C_o) = kS(C - C') \tag{6.4}$$

where w is the weight of material deposited, S is the surface area, θ is the time, k is the mass transfer coefficient for diffusion and k' is the reaction rate constant for interfacial reaction. The relative importance of the two steps depends on a number of factors.

1. When the super saturation is high, the ordering reaction at the surface is relatively rapid and the diffusion step controls the rate.
2. Conversely, when the super saturation is small, the process at the surface is the rate determining step.
3. When sonic and supersonic vibrations increase the rate of diffusion, the rate depends on the diffusion rate.
4. Small amounts of impurities modify the rate of growth at the surface. Dyes, acids and various ions have been found to inhibit the growth of crystals as they are absorbed on the crystal faces and interfere with the crystallisation process. Different faces are affected to different extents and the crystal habit is modified by foreign substances.

MIER'S SUPER SATURATION THEORY [5]

Curve AB in Fig. 6.4 is the ordinary solubility curve. It represents the maximum concentration of solution that can be obtained by bringing the solute into equilibrium with the solvent. It also represents the ultimate limit to crystallisation from super saturated solutions. If a sample of solution having composition and temperature corresponding to the point C is cooled, it first crosses the solubility curve. We expect crystallisation to start immediately. If we start with a pure solution free from all solid particles (not only solute particles but also foreign solid matter), the solution will not begin to crystallise until it has super cooled considerably past the solubility curve. Crystallisation begins somewhere in the neighbourhood of point D and the concentration of the substance then roughly follows the curve DE.

In the absence of solid particles, the curve FG (called super solubility curve) represents the limit at which formation of nuclei begins spontaneously and consequently the point where crystallisation can start. Nuclei cannot form and crystallisation cannot occur short of this point. The above postulates are known as Mier's super saturation theory.

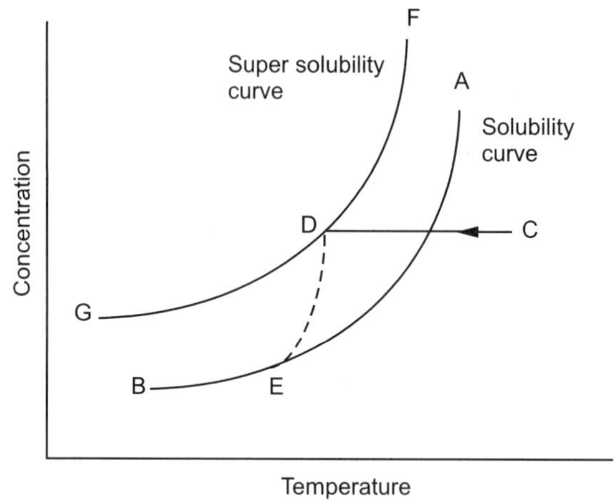

Fig. 6.4 Mier's super saturation curve

ΔL LAW [6]

All geometrically similar crystals of the same material, suspended in the same solution, grow at the same rate if growth is measured as the increase in length of geometrically corresponding distances on all crystals. The growth rate is independent of the initial size of the original crystals, provided all crystals in the suspension are treated exactly alike, that is, grown at the same temperature and uniform super saturation field.

CAKING OF CRYSTALS

A problem that is often encountered in handling crystalline products is their tendency to cake or bind together. This is troublesome in bulk storage or in barrelled products. The extent of caking may range from loose aggregates that fall apart between fingers to solid lumps that have to be crushed using considerable force.

The tendency for crystalline materials to cake is attributable to a small amount of dissolution taking place at the surface of the crystals and subsequent re-evaporation of the solvent. The crystals can then become very tightly bound together.

Because the vapour pressure of the saturated solution of a crystalline solid is less than that of pure water at the same temperature, condensation can occur on the surface of the crystals even though the relative humidity of the atmosphere is $<100\%$. The solution so formed then penetrates into the pack of crystals by virtue of the capillary action of the small spaces between the crystals and caking can occur if the absorbed moisture subsequently evaporates when the atmospheric humidity falls. Caking can also occur at constant relative humidity because the vapour pressure of a solution in a small capillary is less than that in a large capillary as a result of the Kelvin effect. As condensation takes place, small particles are the first to dissolve, the average size of the capillary is increased and the vapour pressure of the solution may increase sufficiently for evaporation to occur.

A crystalline material will cake readily if the particle size is non-uniform because of lesser porosity. Thus, the tendency for caking can be reduced by forming crystals of relatively large and uniform size. Alternately, small amounts of insoluble materials such as calcium phosphate, talc or a water repelling agent such as stearic acid or a stearate may be added.

NOTATIONS

F	Mass of feed, kg.
M	Mass of mother liquor, kg.
C	Mass of crystals, kg.
E	Mass of solvent evaporated, kg.
x_F	Mass fraction of solute in feed.
x_M	Mass fraction of solute in mother liquor.
x_C	Mass fraction of solute in the crystals obtained.

REFERENCES

1. Seidell A, *Solubilities*, Third ed., Princeton, NJ, Van Nostrand, 1940.
2. McCabe WL, *Ind. Eng. Chem.*, **21**: 30, 112 (1929).
3. Buckley HE, *Crystal growth*, New York, Wiley, 1951.
4. Van Hook A, *Crystallisation, Theory and Practice*, New York, Wiley, 1951.
5. Ting HH and McCabe WL, *Ind. Eng. Chem.*, **26**: 1201 (1934).
6. La Mer VK, *Ind. Eng. Chem.*, **44**: 1270 (1952).

Problems for Practice

6.1 An aqueous solution containing 23% sodium phosphate is cooled from 313 to 298 K in a crystalliser to form $Na_3PO_4.12H_2O$ crystals. The solubility of anhydrous sodium phosphate at 298 K is 15.5 kg per 100 kg of water and the required flow of crystals is 0.063 kg s^{-1}. The mean heat capacity of the solution is 3.2 kJ kg^{-1} K^{-1} and the heat of crystallisation is 146.5 kJ kg^{-1}. Cooling water enters and leaves at 288 K and 293 K respectively. For the crystalliser, the available heat transfer area is 1.5 m^2 per m length, the crystalliser sections are 3 m long and the overall heat transfer coefficient is 0.14 kW m^{-2} K^{-1}. How many sections of the crystalliser are required for this?

6.2 A crystalliser is charged with 7 500 kg of an aqueous solution containing 30% anhydrous sodium sulphate. The solution is cooled and the solute crystallises out as the decahydrate. The mother liquor contains 20% anhydrous solute. Compute the amount of mother liquor obtained and the yield of crystals. If 10% of initial water is lost during cooling, find the additional yield of crystals.

6.3 An aqueous solution of magnesium sulphate is cooled from 353 K to 303 K in a crystalliser to produce 1 000 kg per hour of Mg $SO_4.7\ H_2O$ crystals. The solubility of anhydrous salt in kg per 100 kg of water at 353 K and 303 K is 64.2 and 40.8 respectively. The mean heat capacity of the solution is 3.3 kJ $kg^{-1}\ K^{-1}$ and the heat of solution is -73 kJ kg^{-1}. Cooling water enters at 288 K and leaves at 295 K. For the crystalliser, the available heat transfer area is 1.5 m^2 per m length, crystalliser sections are 3 m long and the overall heat transfer coefficient is 210 W $m^{-2}\ K^{-1}$. How many sections of the crystalliser are required for this? Also compute the cooling water required. Assume that 5% of initial water is evaporated during the operation. Take the latent heat of vaporisation of water as 2 450 k J kg^{-1}.

6.4 A feed solution of 10 000 kg at 328 K containing 47 kg $FeSO_4$ per100 kg water is cooled to 298 K, where $FeSO_4.7H_2O$ crystals are removed. The solubility of the salt at 298 K is 30.5 kg per 100 kg of water. The average heat capacity of the feed solution is 3.0 kJ $kg^{-1}\ K^{-1}$, the heat of solution at 298 K is -18 kJ mol^{-1} $FeSO_4.7H_2O$. Calculate the yield of crystals and make a heat balance. Assume that no water is evaporated.

6.5 A batch of 1 000 kg KCl is dissolved in sufficient water to make a saturated solution at 363 K, where the solubility is 35 wt% KCl in water. The solution is cooled to 293 K, at which temperature the solubility is 25.4 wt%. (i) What is the weight of water required for dissolution and the weight of KCl crystals obtained? (ii) What is the weight of crystals obtained if 5% of the original evaporates on cooling?

6.6 A hot solution containing 2 000 kg of $MgSO_4$ and water at 300 K with a concentration of 30 wt% $MgSO_4$ is cooled to 293 K and $MgSO_4.7H_2O$ crystals are removed. The solubility at 293 K is 35 kg $MgSO_4$ per 100 kg water. The average heat capacity of the feed solution is 2.93 kJ $kg^{-1}\ K^{-1}$. Heat of solution at 293 K is -13.31×10^3 kJ $kmol^{-1}$ $MgSO_4.7H_2O$. Calculate the yield of crystals and make a heat balance, assuming no water is lost by evaporation.

6.7 7 500 kg of an aqueous solution containing 29.6% Na_2SO_4 is cooled. During cooling, 5% water in the solution is lost by evaporation. As a result, crystals of $Na_2SO_4.10H_2O$ crystallise out. If the mother liquor is found to contain 18.3% Na_2SO_4, calculate the weight and percent yield of crystals and the quantity of mother liquor obtained. All percentages are by weight.

6.8 300 kg of a saturated solution of silver nitrate at 373 K are cooled to 293 K and crystals are filtered out. The wet filter cake contains 80% solid crystals and 20% mother liquor. The wet cake is dried to remove water by evaporation. Calculate the fraction of silver nitrate in the feed stream eventually removed as dry crystals and the amount of water evaporated during the drying operation. The solubility of silver nitrate in water is 952 kg silver nitrate per 100 kg of water at 373 K and 222 kg silver nitrate per100 kg of water at 293 K.

6.9 35 wt% solution of Na_2CO_3 weighing 6 000 kg is cooled slowly to 293 K to yield crystals of $Na_2CO_3.10H_2O$. The solubility of Na_2CO_3 at 293 K is 21.5 parts of anhydrous salt per 100 parts of water. During cooling, 4% of the weight of the original solution is lost due to vaporisation. Determine the weight of the crystals formed.

6.10 10 000 kg of an aqueous solution containing 30.4% Na_2SO_4 is cooled. During cooling, 7.5% water in the solution is lost by evaporation. As a result, crystals of $Na_2SO_4.10\ H_2O$ crystallise out. If the mother liquor is found to contain 19.4% Na_2SO_4, calculate the weight and percent yield of crystals and the quantity of mother liquor obtained. All percentages are by weight.

6.11 A batch of 750 kg KCl is dissolved in sufficient water to make a saturated solution at 363 K, where the solubility is 38 wt% KCl in water. The solution is cooled to 293 K, at which temperature the solubility is 27.2 wt%. What is the weight of water required for the dissolution and the weight of KCl crystals obtained?

6.12 A batch of saturated Na_2CO_3 solution of 100 kg is to be prepared at 323 K. The solubility is 4.48 mole per 1 000g of water at 323 K. If monohydrates were available, how many kg of water would be required to form the solution? If the decahydrate is available how many kg of salt will be required?

6.13 A saturated solution of magnesium sulphate at 353 K is cooled to 303 K. During cooling, 4% of the original water is lost. Calculate the quantity of the original solution needed to crystallise 1000 kg of $MgSO_4.7H_2O$. The solubility in terms of grams of magnesium sulphate per 100 g of H_2O is 40.8 and 64.2 at 303 K and 353 K respectively.

6.14 In a crystallisation process, 2 500 kg of $Na_2SO_4.10\ H_2O$ crystals were obtained. The mother liquor leaving the process contained 20% Na_2SO_4 and the feed contained 36% Na_2SO_4. During the process, 25% of original water is lost by evaporation. Find the weights of feed required, mother liquor leaving and water evaporated.

6.15 A crystalliser is charged with 9 774 kg h^{-1} of an aqueous solution having 30% Na_2SO_4. The solution is cooled and 5% of the feed weight is lost as water of evaporation. $Na_2SO_4.10H_2O$ crystals are obtained and the mother liquor was found to contain 18% Na_2SO_4. Find the weight of crystals obtained, mother liquor and water loss.

6.16 5 000 kg of potassium chloride is present in a saturated solution at 353 K. The solution is cooled to 293 K in an open tank. The solubilities are 55 and 25 parts per 100 parts of water at 353 K and 293 K respectively. Assuming that 3% of the solution evaporates as water find the weight of mother liquor, water evaporated and crystals formed.

6.17 9 581 kg of 30% solution of sodium carbonate is slowly cooled to 293 K. During cooling, 10% of the original water is lost by evaporation. The crystals have ten molecules of water of hydration. The mother liquor carries 21.6 kg of salt per 100 kg of water. Find the weight of the streams leaving the crystalliser.

6.18 A solution of potassium chloride in water is saturated at a temperature of 288 K. Calculate the weight of potassium chloride that can be dissolved by 100 kg of this solution, if it is heated to a temperature of 338 K. The solubility of potassium chloride at 288 K = 1.62 kmol per 100 kg water, the solubility of potassium chloride at 338 K = 6.37 kmol per 100 kg water.

7 Humidification

Humidification refers to the simultaneous transfer of mass and heat across the interphase when a gas and a pure liquid are brought into intimate contact. When the liquid evaporates into the gas phase, the operation is humidification; when the vapour in the gaseous phase condenses, the operation is dehumidification. In both cases, the material constituting the liquid phase is being transferred across the interphase. Air conditioners and cooling towers are industrially important examples of humidification equipments. Principles governing the design of equipment of this type are discussed in this chapter.

Humidification involves the transfer of material between a pure liquid and a gas which is insoluble in the liquid. In humidification, the vapour content is increased by passing the gas over the liquid which evaporates into the gas stream. This transfer takes place by diffusion; at the interface, simultaneous transfer of heat and mass takes place. In the reverse operation, dehumidification, partial condensation is effected and the condensed vapour is removed. Calculations are based on unit mass of vapour-free gas (vfg). In these operations, vapour refers to the component which is also present as liquid and gas refers to the component which is present only in gaseous form.

In the gas phase, vapour will be referred to as component A and vfg as component B. The properties of the gas–vapour mixture vary with the total pressure. So the total pressure must be specified. Unless otherwise specified, a total pressure of 1 atm is assumed. It is also assumed that the gas–vapour mixture follows ideal gas laws. In general, humidification refers to the air–water system, but the same principles can be applied to other liquids and gases.

Drying of wet solids is different from the humidification operation. In drying, reduction in the moisture content of the solid is the main aim and humidification of the air stream is secondary. However, drying of wet solids is an example of a humidification operation.

ABSOLUTE HUMIDITY (Y)

Absolute humidity is defined as the mass of vapour associated with unit mass of vapour-free gas. It is also the mass ratio of vapour to vapour-free gas in the vapour–gas mixture. It is denoted in kg of vapour per kg of vapour-free gas.

$$Y = \frac{\text{mass of vapour}}{\text{mass of vapour free gas}} = \frac{m_A}{m_B} \tag{7.1}$$

Here m_A is the mass of vapour and m_B is the mass of vapour-free gas.

MOLAL HUMIDITY (Y_m)

Molal humidity is the molar ratio of vapour to vapour-free gas in the vapour–gas mixture. For gases, the molar ratio is also equal to the partial pressure ratio.

$$Y_m = \frac{\text{moles of vapour}}{\text{moles of vapour free gas}} = \frac{n_A}{n_B} \tag{7.2}$$

Here, n_A is the number of moles of vapour and n_B is the number of moles of vapour-free gas.

If the partial pressure of the vapour is P_A and the total pressure is P, then partial pressure of the vapour-free gas will be $P - P_A$.

$$Y_m = \frac{n_A}{n_B} = \frac{P_A}{P - P_A} \tag{7.3}$$

The relationship between absolute humidity and molal humidity can be derived as given below.

$$Y = \frac{\text{mass of vapour}}{\text{mass of vapour free gas}} = \frac{m_A}{m_B} \tag{7.4}$$

Here, m_A is the mass of vapour and m_B is the mass of vapour-free gas. The mass of any material can be found by multiplying the number of moles by the molecular weight.

$$Y = \frac{m_A}{m_B} = \frac{n_A \times M_A}{n_B \times M_B} \tag{7.5}$$

Here, M_A is the molecular weight of the vapour and M_B is the molecular weight of the vapour-free gas.

$$Y = \frac{n_A \times M_A}{n_B \times M_B} = Y_m \times \frac{M_A}{M_B} = \frac{P_A}{P - P_A} \times \frac{M_A}{M_B} \tag{7.6}$$

In the case of air–water vapour system, $Y = 0.620\ 7\ Y_m$. (7.7)

The composition of the vapour–gas mixture can be reported in terms of the mole fraction of the vapour (y). The mole fraction of the vapour is given by

$$y = \frac{\dfrac{Y}{M_A}}{\dfrac{1}{M_B} + \dfrac{Y}{M_A}} \tag{7.8}$$

SATURATION HUMIDITY (Y_s)

Saturation humidity is the vapour content of the gas–vapour mixture at saturation. The mixture is said to be saturated when the partial pressure of the vapour (P_A) is equal to the vapour pressure of the liquid (P_A^*) at that temperature.

At saturation, $P_A = P_A^*$ (7.9)

$$Y_s = \frac{P_A^*}{P - P_A^*} \times \frac{M_A}{M_B} \tag{7.10}$$

PERCENTAGE HUMIDITY (Y_p)

Percentage humidity is the percentage ratio of actual humidity to the saturation humidity.

$$Y_p = \frac{Y}{Y_s} \times 100 \tag{7.11}$$

RELATIVE HUMIDITY (Y_r)

Relative humidity is the percentage ratio of partial pressure of vapour to the vapour pressure of liquid at gas temperature.

$$Y_r = \frac{P_A}{P_A^*} \times 100 \tag{7.12}$$

RELATIONSHIP BETWEEN Y_p AND Y_r

Percentage humidity is the percentage ratio of the actual humidity to the saturation humidity.

$$Y_p = \frac{Y}{Y_s} \times 100$$

Substituting, the values of Y and Y_s in terms of partial pressures,

$$= \left[\left\{\frac{P_A}{P-P_A} \times \frac{M_A}{M_B}\right\} \div \left\{\frac{P_A^*}{P-P_A^*} \times \frac{M_A}{M_B}\right\}\right] \times 100 \tag{7.13}$$

On simplification,

$$Y_p = \left\{\frac{P_A}{P_A^*} \times 100\right\} \times \frac{(P-P_A^*)}{(P-P_A)}$$

$$= Y_r \times \frac{(P-P_A^*)}{(P-P_A)} \tag{7.14}$$

The partial pressure (P_A) will always be less than the vapour pressure (P_A^*). Hence $Y_p < Y_r$.

HUMID HEAT (C_Y)

Humid heat is the heat energy required to raise the unit mass of dry gas and its associated vapour through unit temperature difference at constant pressure.

$$C_Y = C_{P,B} + Y \times C_{P,A} \tag{7.15}$$

$C_{P,B}$ and $C_{P,A}$ are the specific heats of the gas and vapour respectively.

For the air–water vapour system,

$$C_Y = 1 + 1.9Y \text{ kJ (kg of dry air)}^{-1} \text{ K}^{-1} \tag{7.16}$$

HUMID VOLUME (V_Y)

Humid volume is the volume occupied by unit mass of dry gas and associated vapour at 1 atm pressure and gas temperature.

$$V_Y = \frac{22.4 \times T}{273}\left(\frac{1}{M_B} + \frac{Y}{M_A}\right) \tag{7.17}$$

V_Y is in m^3 (kg of dry gas)$^{-1}$ and T is in kelvin.

DEW POINT (T_{DP})

Dew point is the temperature at which a vapour–gas mixture becomes saturated when cooled at constant total pressure, out of contact with liquid. It is also the temperature at which the partial pressure of the vapour becomes equal to the vapour pressure of the liquid. At T_{DP}, $P_A^* = P_A$. For the air–water vapour system at saturation, $T_{DP} = T_{WB} = T_{DB}$.

ILLUSTRATIONS

7A At a temperature of 295 K, acetone exerts a vapour pressure of 26.66 kPa. Calculate the composition of a saturated mixture of nitrogen and acetone vapour at 295 K and a pressure of 99.3 kPa expressed in the following terms: (i) percentage composition by volume, (ii) percentage composition by weight, (iii) kg of vapour per m^3 of mixture, (iv) kg of vapour per kg of vapour-free gas and (v) moles of vapour per mole of vapour-free gas.

Solution

Basis: 1 kmol of vapour–gas mixture.

(i) Mole fraction is the ratio of partial pressure to total pressure.

Mole fraction of acetone in saturated acetone–nitrogen mixture $= \dfrac{26.66}{99.3} = 0.268$

Mole fraction of nitrogen in saturated acetone–nitrogen mixture $= 1 - 0.268 = 0.732$

For gaseous mixtures, composition in mol% $\equiv$ vol%

Mol% = mole fraction $\times$ 100

Composition of the mixture in vol%

Acetone = 26.8%

Nitrogen = 73.2%

(ii)

Constituent	Mole fraction	Molecular weight	Weight (kg)	Wt%
Acetone	0.268	58	15.54	43.12
Nitrogen	0.732	28	20.50	56.88
		Total weight:	36.04	

Composition of the mixture in wt%

Acetone = 43.12%

Nitrogen = 56.88%

(iii) Volume of 1 kmol at 99.3 kPa mm 293 K $= \dfrac{nRT}{P} = \dfrac{1 \times 0.082\,05 \times 293 \times 101.3}{99.3}$

$= 24.53 \text{ m}^3$

One kmol mixture contains 15.54 kg acetone vapour.

24.53 m^3 mixture contains 15.54 kg acetone vapour.

kg of acetone per m^3 of mixture $= \dfrac{15.54}{24.53} = 0.634$

(iv) One kmol mixture contains 20.50 kg nitrogen and 15.54 kg acetone vapour.

kg of vapour per kg of vapour-free gas $= \dfrac{15.54}{20.50} = 0.758$

(v) One kmol mixture contains 0.732 kmol nitrogen and 0.268 kmol acetone vapour.

Moles of vapour per mole of vapour-free gas $= \dfrac{0.268}{0.732} = 0.366$

7B A mixture of ether vapour and nitrogen contains 50% ether by volume. Calculate the relative saturation and percentage saturation of the mixture at 296 K and a pressure of 100 kPa. Vapour pressure of ether at 296 K is 60 kPa.

Solution

For gases, volume percentage, pressure percentage and mole percentage are the same. Mole percentage divided by 100 gives mole fraction.

Partial pressure of ether (P_A) = Total pressure × mole fraction

= $100 \times 0.5 = 50$ kPa

Vapour pressure of ether at 296 K (P_A^*) = 60 kPa

Relative saturation, $Y_r = \dfrac{P_A}{P_A^*} \times 100 = \dfrac{50 \times 100}{60} = 83.33\%$

Mole of ether per mole of ether-free nitrogen at the existing conditions (n_v) $= \dfrac{0.5}{0.5} = 1.0$

Mole of ether per mole of ether-free nitrogen at saturation (n_s) $= \dfrac{P_A^*}{P - P_A^*}$

$= \dfrac{60}{100 - 60} = 1.5$

$$\text{Percentage saturation } (Y_p) = (n_v/n_s) \times 100 = \frac{1 \times 100}{1.5} = 66.67\%$$

$$Y_p = Y_r \times \frac{(P - P_A^*)}{(P - P_A)}$$

$$= 83.33 \times \frac{(100 - 60)}{(100 - 50)} = 66.67\%$$

This proves that always $Y_p < Y_r$.

7C Hexane which is used as a solvent in an extraction process, is proposed to be recovered by evaporation into a stream of nitrogen. Nitrogen enters the evaporator at a temperature of 303 K containing hexane such that its dew point is 278 K. It leaves at a temperature of 298 K with a dew point of 293 K. The barometric pressure is constant at 100 kPa. (i) Calculate the vapour concentrations of the gases entering and leaving the evaporator expressed in moles of vapour per mole of vapour-free gas. (ii) Calculate the number of moles of acetone evaporated per mole of vapour-free gas passing through the evaporator. (iii) Calculate the weight of hexane evaporated per 1 000 m^3 of gases entering the evaporator. (iv) Calculate the volume of gases leaving the evaporator per 1 000 m^3 of entering gases. The vapour pressure of hexane is 8 kPa at 278 K and 18 kPa at 293 K.

Solution

(i) Composition of entering gas:

Entering gas has a dew point of 278 K. Hence partial pressure of hexane vapour in the entering gases is equal to the vapour pressure of hexane at 278 K.

For gases, the partial pressure ratio is also equal to the mole ratio.

Partial pressure of hexane = 8 kPa

Partial pressure of nitrogen = total pressure – partial pressure of hexane

$$= 100 - 8 = 92 \text{ kPa}$$

$$\text{Moles of hexane per mole of nitrogen} = \frac{8}{92} = 0.087$$

(ii) Composition of leaving gas:

Leaving gas has a dew point of 293 K. Hence, partial pressure of hexane vapour in the leaving gases is equal to the vapour pressure of hexane at 293 K.

Partial pressure of hexane = 18 kPa

Partial pressure of nitrogen = total pressure – partial pressure of hexane

$$= 100 - 18 = 82 \text{ kPa}$$

$$\text{Mole of hexane per mole of nitrogen} = \frac{18}{82} = 0.220$$

Moles of hexane evaporated per mole of nitrogen = hexane in the leaving gases – hexane in the entering gases

$$= 0.220 - -0.087 = 0.133$$

(iii) kmol of gases in 1 000 m^3 of gas at the entering conditions

$$= \frac{PV}{RT} = \frac{100 \times 1\,000}{101.3 \times 0.082\,05 \times 303} = 39.70 \text{ kmol}$$

At the inlet, one mole of nitrogen is accompanied by 0.087 mol hexane. For 1 mol of nitrogen or 1.087 mol of entering gases, 0.133 mol of hexane is evaporated.

kmol of hexane evaporated per 1 000 m^3 of entering gases $= 0.133 \times \dfrac{39.70}{1.087} = 4.86$ kmol

Molecular weight of hexane is 86.

kg of hexane evaporated $= 4.86 \times 86 = 417.96$ kg

(iv) kmol of gas leaving = kmol of entering gases + hexane evaporated

$= 39.70 + 4.86 = 44.56$ kmol

Volume of leaving gases at 298 K and 100 kpa pressure =

$$\frac{nRT}{P} = \frac{44.56 \times 0.082\,05 \times 298 \times 101.3}{100} = 1\ 103.69 \text{ m}^3$$

7D A solvent recovery system delivers a gas saturated with benzene vapour which analyses on a benzene-free basis as follows: carbon dioxide: 15%, oxygen: 4% and the rest is nitrogen. This gas is at 298 K and 100 kPa. It is compressed to 5 atm and cooled to 298 K after compression. How many kilograms of benzene are condensed by this process per 1 000 m^3 of the original mixture? The vapour pressure of benzene at 298 K = 10 kPa.

Solution

Basis: 1000 m^3 of original mixture.

Number of kmol of gas in original mixture $= \frac{PV}{RT} = \frac{1 \times 1\,000}{0.082\,05 \times 298} = 40.90$

The gases are saturated with benzene at 298 K. So, the partial pressure of benzene is equal to vapour pressure at 298 K.

Mole fraction of benzene $= \frac{\text{partial pressure of benzene}}{\text{total pressure}} = \frac{10}{100} = 0.1$

kmol of benzene in the original mixture $= 40.90 \times 0.1 = 4.09$

kmol of benzene free gas $= 40.90 \times 0.9 = 36.81$ kmol

The gases are compressed to 5 atm (506.5 kPa) and after compression, cooled to the original temperature 298 K. So the partial pressure of benzene in the final mixture is also 10 kPa.

Mole fraction of benzene in the final mixture $= \frac{10}{506.5} = 0.019\,7$

Mole fraction of benzene free gases in the final mixture $= 0.980\,3$

kmol of benzene free gas $= 36.81$ kmol

Benzene in the final mixture $= 36.81 \times \frac{0.019\,7}{0.980\,3} = 0.734$ kmol

Benzene condensed = benzene in the original mixture – benzene in the final mixture

$= 4.09 - 0.734 = 3.356$ kmol $= 261.77$ kg

7E What is the minimum number of m^3 of dry air at 293 K and 98.63 kPa necessary to evaporate 13.8 kg of ethanol if the total pressure remains constant. Assume that the air blown over the alcohol to evaporate it leaves at 98.63 kPa. The vapour pressure of alcohol at 293 K is 6 kPa.

Solution

Basis: 13.8 kg of ethanol

$$\text{kmol of ethanol} = \frac{13.8}{46} = 0.3$$

A minimum amount of air is required only at saturation, where partial pressure of ethanol in the mixture is equal to its vapour pressure.

Partial pressure of ethanol = 6 kPa

Partial pressure of air = total pressure – partial pressure of ethanol

= 98.63 – 6 = 92.63 kPa

For gases, partial pressure ratio is also equal to mole ratio.

$$\frac{6}{92.63} = \frac{\text{kmol of vapour}}{\text{kmol of air}} = \frac{0.3}{\text{kmol of air}}$$

kmol of air = 4.633

Volume of air at 293 K and 98.63 kPa

$$= \frac{nRT}{P} = \frac{4.633 \times 0.08205 \times 293 \times 101.3}{98.63} = 114.39 \text{ m}^3$$

7F Ambient air on a particular day at Chennai has the following conditions:

Pressure = 100 kPa, dry bulb temperature = 306 K, dew point = 295 K. Find the absolute humidity by calculation. The vapour pressure of water at 295 K is 2.64 kPa.

Solution

Dew point is a measure of humidity. Partial pressure at dry bulb temperature is equal to vapour pressure at dew point.

Partial pressure of vapour (P_A) = 2.64 kPa

Partial pressure of vapour-free gas (P_B) = total pressure – partial pressure of vapour

= 100 – –2.64 = 97.36

$$Y_m = P_A \div P_B = \frac{2.64}{97.36} = 0.027 \text{ mol } H_2O \text{ per mol DA}$$

$$Y = 0.620\,7\; Y_m$$
$$= 0.6207 \times 0.027 = 0.016\,8 \text{ kg } H_2O \text{ per kg DA}$$

7G An air–water vapour mixture of 98.66 kPa and 298 K has a dew point of 291 K. It is required to remove 70% water by cooling to 281 K and compressing. Calculate the necessary pressure required. The vapour pressure of water is 2.06 kPa at 291 K and 1.07 kPa at 281 K.

Solution

Dew point is a measure of humidity. The vapour pressure at dew point is equal to the partial pressure at dry bulb temperature.

$$\text{Initial water content of the mixture} = \frac{2.06}{(98.66 - 2.06)} = 0.021\,3 \text{ mol per mol of DA.}$$

70% of moisture is removed by cooling to 281 K and compressing. Let the final pressure be P.

If 70% H_2O is removed, the final H_2O content will be 30% of the original value.

$$= 0.0213 \times \frac{30}{100} = 0.006\,39 \text{ mol per mol of DA}$$

The final air is saturated at 281 K. So, the partial pressure of moisture in the final air will be equal to the vapour pressure at 281 K.

Molar ratio is equal to partial pressure ratio.

$$\frac{0.006\,39}{1} = \frac{1.07}{(P - 1.07)}$$

Required pressure (P) = 168.61 kPa

7H Air at a temperature of 303 K and 100 kPa pressure has a relative humidity of 80%. Calculate (i) the absolute humidity of the air, (ii) absolute humidity of this air if the temperature is reduced to 288 K and pressure is increased to 200 kPa, and (c) weight of water condensed during cooling and compression. The vapour pressure of water is 4.24 kPa and 1.70 kPa at 303 K and 288 K respectively.

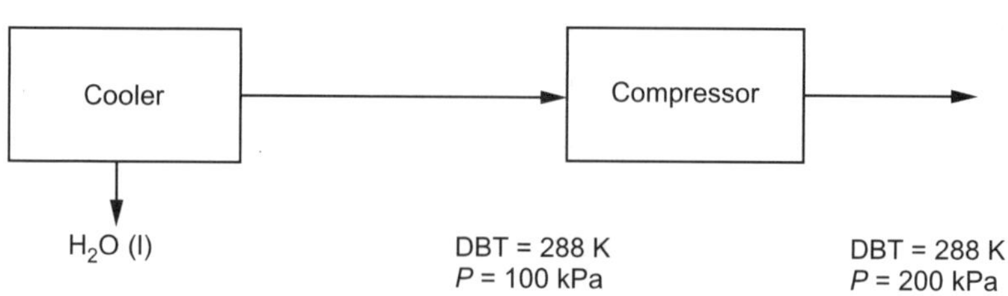

Fig. 7.1 Air conditioning operation

Solution

Figure 7.1 represents the data provided in the form of a block diagram. (i) At the inlet, the dry bulb temperature is 303 K, pressure (P) is 100 kPa and relative humidity is 80%. At 303 K, the vapour pressure of water is 1.70 kPa. The relative humidity is the percentage ratio of partial pressure of water vapour (P_A) to vapour pressure (P_A^*) at that temperature.

$$Y_r = (P_A \div P_A^*) \times 100 = 80$$

So $\quad P_A = 4.24 \times 0.8 = 3.39$ kPa

Then $Y_m = P_A \div (P - P_A) = \dfrac{3.39}{(100 - 3.39)} = 0.035\ 1$ mol per mol DA

$$Y = Y_m \times 0.6207 = 0.02176 \text{ kg per kg DA}$$

(ii) If the temperature is reduced to 288 K and pressure is increased to 200 kPa, condensing out some water, the air becomes saturated at 288 K. The partial pressure of water vapour becomes equal to the vapour pressure of water at 288 K.

Y_m at the outlet $= P_A \div (P - P_A) = \dfrac{1.70}{(200 - 1.70)} = 0.008\ 6$ mol per mol DA

$$Y = Y_m \times 0.620\ 7 = 0.005\ 3 \text{ kg per kg DA}$$

(iii) Weight of water removed in the process = moisture content of air at outlet – moisture content of air at inlet

$$= 0.021\ 76 - 0.005\ 3 = 0.016\ 46 \text{ kg per kg DA}$$

7I Air at a temperature of 311 K and atmospheric pressure has a dew point of 300 K. Estimate the molal humidity, molal humidity at saturation and percentage humidity. (ii)The air of part (i) is passed into an evaporator from where it emerges at a temperature of 322 K with a dew point of 318 K. Estimate the Y_p of air leaving the evaporator. (iii) Calculate the weight of water evaporated per 1 000 m^3 of entering air. Temperature–vapour pressure data is given in Table 7.1.

Table 7.1 Temperature–vapour pressure data

Temperature (K)	Vapour pressure of water (kPa)
300	3.70
311	6.62
318	9.58
322	11.73

Solution

Dew point is a measure of moisture content. The vapour pressure of water at the dew point is equal to partial pressure of water vapour in the mixture.

(i) Entering air:

$$Y_m = \frac{3.70}{(101.32 - 3.70)} = 0.037\,9 \text{ mol per mol DA}$$

$$Y_m \text{ at saturation} = \frac{6.62}{(101.32 - 6.62)} = 0.07 \text{ mol per mol DA}$$

$$\text{Percentage saturation} = \frac{Y_m}{Y_m \text{ at saturation}} \times 100 = 54.14$$

(ii) Leaving air:

$$Y_m = \frac{9.58}{(101.32 - 9.58)} = 0.104\,4 \text{ mol per mol DA}$$

$$Y_m \text{ at saturation} = \frac{11.73}{(101.32 - 11.73)} = 0.131\,0 \text{ mol per mol DA}$$

$$\text{Percentage saturation} = \frac{Y_m}{Y_m \text{ at saturation}} \times 100 = 79.77$$

$$\text{(iii) kmol of entering air} = \frac{PV}{RT} = \frac{1 \times 100\,0}{0.082\,05 \times 311} = 39.188$$

The water vapour picked up per kmol DA + 0.037 9 kmol water vapour or 1.037 9 kmol entering air

$$= \text{moisture in leaving air} - \text{moisture in entering air}$$

$$= 0.104\,4 - 0.037\,9 = 0.066\,5 \text{ kmol}$$

$$\text{Total water evaporated} = \frac{0.0665}{1.0379} \times 39.188 = 2.51 \text{ kmol} = 45.20 \text{ kg}$$

7J A stream of gas at 304 K and 1 bar, 50% saturated with water vapour is passed through a drying tower, where 90% of water vapour is removed. Calculate the water vapour content of the entering gas and leaving gas, weight of water removed per 1 000 m^3 of entering gas and volume of leaving gas per 1 000 m^3 of entering gas, if the gas leaves at 300 K and 0.98 bar. The vapour pressure of water at 304 K is 0.36 bar.

Solution

Basis: 1 000 m^3 of entering gas.

At saturation, the partial pressure is equal to vapour pressure at that temperature. The molar ratio is also the partial pressure ratio.

$$\text{Saturation humidity at inlet conditions} = \frac{0.36}{1-0.36} = 0.562\ 5 \text{ mol per mol DA}$$

Entering gas is 50% saturated, molar humidity of incoming air

$$= 0.5625 \times \frac{50}{100} = 0.281\ 3 \text{ mol per mol DA}$$

90% of water vapour is removed and the outgoing gas contains only 10% of initial water vapour content.

$$\text{Molal humidity of outgoing air} = 0.281\,3 \times \frac{10}{100} = 0.028\ 1 \text{ mol per mol DA}$$

$$\text{kmol of incoming air} = \frac{PV}{RT} = \frac{1 \times 1\,000}{1.013 \times 0.082\,05 \times 304} = 39.57$$

One mole of entering dry air contains 0.281 3 mol moisture.

$$\text{Dry air} = \frac{39.57}{(1+0.281\,3)} = 30.88 \text{ kmol}$$

One mole of leaving dry air contains 0.028 1 mol moisture.

$$\text{kmol of outgoing gas} = 30.88 \times 1.028\ 13 = 31.75$$

$$\text{Water removed} = \text{entering air} - \text{leaving air}$$

$$= 38.57 - 31.75 = 6.82 \text{ kmol} = 122.76 \text{ kg}$$

$$\text{Volume of outgoing gas} = \frac{nRT}{P} = \frac{31.75 \times 0.082\,05 \times 300 \times 1.013}{0.98} = 807.84 \text{ m}^3$$

7K Hot air is being used to dry a wet material. The hot air enters the drier at a total pressure of 102.65 kPa and at 433 K. The partial pressure of water vapour in the incoming air is 3.33 kPa. At the exit of the drier, the temperature is 383 K and the pressure is 101.32 kPa. In the outgoing air, the partial pressure of water vapour is 13.33 kPa. Calculate the absolute humidity of incoming air and outgoing air. Also calculate the kg of moisture picked up per 1 000 m^3 of entering air.

Solution

Basis: 1 000 m^3 entering gases.

$$\text{Molar humidity of incoming air} = \frac{\text{partial pressure of moisture}}{\text{partial pressure of dry air}}$$

$$= \frac{3.33}{(102.65 - 3.33)} = 0.033\ 6 \text{ mol per mol DA}$$

Absolute humidity = molal humidity × 0.620 7

Absolute humidity = 0.033 6 × 0.620 7 = 0.020 8 kg per kg DA

$$\text{Molar humidity of outgoing air} = \frac{\text{partial pressure of moisture}}{\text{partial pressure of dry air}}$$

$$= \frac{13.33}{(102.65 - 13.33)} = 0.149\,2 \text{ mol per mol DA}$$

Absolute humidity = molal humidity × 0.620 7

Absolute humidity = 0.149 2 × 0.620 7 = 0.093 kg per kg DA

Moisture picked up per kmol of DA = moisture at outlet – moisture at inlet

= 0.149 2 – 0.033 6 = 0.115 6 kmol

$$\text{kmol of entering air} = \frac{PV}{RT} = \frac{1\,000 \times 102.65}{0.082\,05 \times 433 \times 101.32} = 28.52$$

At the inlet, one mole of dry air is accompanied by 0.0336 mole moisture. One mole dry air or 1.0336 mole entering moist air picks up 0.115 6 mole moisture.

$$\text{Total moisture picked up} = \frac{0.1156}{1.033\,6} \times 28.52 = 3.19 \text{ kmol} = 57.42 \text{ kg}$$

7L In a mixture of benzene vapour (A) and nitrogen gas (B) at a total pressure of 106.65 kPa and at a temperature of 333 K, the partial pressure of benzene is 13.33 kPa. Express the composition of benzene in other terms.

Solution

Mole fraction or volume fraction of benzene

$$= \frac{\text{Partial pressure of benzene}}{\text{Total pressure}} = \frac{13.33}{106.65} = 0.125$$

$$\text{Absolute humidity } (Y) = \frac{P_A}{P - P_A} \times \frac{M_A}{M_B}$$

$$= \frac{13.33 \times 78}{(106.65 - 13.33) \times 28} = 0.398 \text{ kg benzene per kg of } N_2$$

$$\text{Molal humidity } (Y_m) = \frac{\text{moles of vapour}}{\text{moles of vapour free gas}} = \frac{n_A}{n_B} = \frac{P_A}{P - P_A}$$

$$= \frac{13.33}{(106.65 - 13.33)} = 0.143 \text{ moles of benzene per mole of } N_2$$

7M A benzene (A)–gas (B) mixture is saturated at 1 atm and 323 K. Calculate the absolute humidity (i) if B is N_2 (ii) if B is CO_2. The vapour pressure of benzene at 323 K is 36.58 kN m^{-2}.

Solution

The mixture is saturated at 323 K.

Partial pressure of benzene = vapour pressure at 323 K = 36.58 kN m^{-2}

$$\text{Molal humidity of the mixture } (Y_m) = \frac{P_A}{P - P_A} = \frac{36.58}{101.3 - 36.58}$$

= 0.565 mole benzene per mole of B

$$\text{Absolute humidity } (Y) \text{ when B is } N_2 = \frac{0.565 \times 78}{28} = \frac{1.574 \text{ kg benzene}}{\text{kg of } N_2}$$

$$\text{Absolute humidity } (Y) \text{ when B is } CO_2 = \frac{0.565 \times 78}{44} = 1.002 \text{ kg benzene per kg of } CO_2$$

7N A mixture of nitrogen and acetone vapour at 133.32 kPa total pressure and 298 K has a percentage saturation of 80. Calculate absolute humidity, molal humidity, relative humidity, volume% of acetone, humid volume and humid heat.

Data: SVP of acetone at 298 K = 38.66 kPa, specific heat of N_2 = 1.005 kJ kg^{-1} K^{-1}, specific heat of acetone (v) = 1.465 kJ kg^{-1} K^{-1}.

Solution

$$\text{Saturation humidity} = \frac{38.66}{94.66} = 0.408\,4 \text{ mole of acetone per mole of nitrogen}$$

Percentage saturation of the mixture is 80.

Molal humidity (Y_m) = Saturation humidity × percentage saturation

$$= 0.408\,4 \times \frac{80}{100} = 0.326\,7 \text{ moles of acetone per mole of } N_2$$

$$\text{Absolute humidity } (Y) = 0.326\,7 \times \frac{58}{28} = 0.676\,7 \text{ kg of acetone per kg of } N_2$$

$$\text{Molal humidity } (Y_m) = 0.326\,7 = \frac{P_A}{P - P_A} = \frac{P_A}{133.32 - P_A} \text{ and } P_A = 32.84 \text{ kPa}$$

$$\text{Relative humidity } (Y_r) = \frac{P_A}{P_A^*} \times 100 = \frac{32.84}{38.66} \times 100 = 84.93$$

$$\text{Mol\% acetone} = \frac{P_A}{P} \times 100 = \frac{32.84 \times 100}{133.32} = 24.63$$

Vol% acetone $=$ same as mol% $= 24.63$

$$\text{Humid volume } (V_Y) = \frac{22.4 \times T}{273}\left[\frac{1}{M_B} + \frac{Y}{M_A}\right] \times \frac{101.32}{133.32}$$

$$= \frac{22.4 \times 298}{273}\left[\frac{1}{28} + \frac{0.676\,7}{58}\right] \times \frac{101.32}{133.32} = 0.88 \text{ m}^3 \text{ per kg of N}_2$$

$$\text{Humid heat } (C_y) = C_{PA} + YC_{PB}$$

$$= 1.005 + 0.676\,7 \times 1.465$$

$$= 1.996 \text{ kJ kg}^{-1} \text{ K}^{-1}$$

DRY BULB TEMPERATURE (T_{DB})

Dry bulb temperature is the actual temperature of the gas–vapour mixture.

Wet Bulb Temperature (T_{WB})

When a stream of unsaturated gas is passed over the surface of a liquid, the humidity of the gas is increased due to evaporation of the liquid. The temperature of the liquid falls below that of the gas and heat is transferred from the gas to the liquid. At equilibrium, the rate of heat transfer from the gas just balances that required to vaporise the liquid and the liquid is said to be at the wet bulb temperature (T_{WB}). It is the steady state temperature reached by a small amount of liquid evaporating into a large amount of unsaturated vapour–gas mixture. The rate at which this temperature is reached depends on the initial temperature and the rate of flow of gas past the liquid surface. T_{WB} will always be lower than T_{DB} of the gas into which the liquid evaporates.

The rate of transfer of heat from the gas to the liquid is given by,

$$q = N_A^1 a M_A \{\lambda_{WB} + C_{PA}(T_{DB} - T_{WB})\} \tag{7.18}$$

where q is the rate of sensible heat transfer to liquid, N_A^1 is the molar rate of vaporisation in kmol m^{-2} s^{-1}. N_A^1 may be replaced by the mass transfer coefficient and concentration gradient.

$$N_A^1 = k_y \times \frac{y_i - y}{(1 - y)_{lm}} \tag{7.19}$$

Here $(1 - y)_{lm}$ is the log mean mole fraction difference for the non-diffusing component. The mole fraction of the vapour y may be replaced by

$$y_i = \frac{\dfrac{Y_{WB}}{M_A}}{\dfrac{1}{M_B} + \dfrac{Y_{WB}}{M_A}} \text{ and } y = \frac{\dfrac{Y}{M_A}}{\dfrac{1}{M_B} + \dfrac{Y}{M_A}} \tag{7.20}$$

a is the area available for heat and mass transfer.

$$q = \frac{k_y}{(1-y)_{lm}} M_A a \left\{ \frac{\dfrac{Y_{WB}}{M_A}}{\dfrac{1}{M_B} + \dfrac{Y_{WB}}{M_A}} - \frac{\dfrac{Y}{M_A}}{\dfrac{1}{M_B} + \dfrac{Y}{M_A}} \right\} \{ \lambda_{WB} + Cp_A(T - T_{WB} \} \tag{7.21}$$

The rate of heat transfer may be expressed in the usual mode as follows,

$$q = h_y(T - T_i)A \tag{7.22}$$

where, h_y = heat transfer coefficient for the gas side, T = temperature of the bulk T_{DB} and T_i = interface temperature T_{WB}.

When equilibrium is attained, the temperature of the liquid is constant. There is no temperature gradient in the liquid. The liquid is pure and hence there is no concentration gradient within the liquid. The resistance to mass and heat transfer within the liquid is thus practically nil. In the usual temperature and humidity ranges encountered, $(1 - y)_{lm}$ is nearly unity and can be neglected. The sensible heat $C_{PA}(T - T_{WB})$ will be negligible when compared to latent heat. $\dfrac{Y}{M_A}$ and $\dfrac{Y_{WB}}{M_A}$ may be neglected in the denominator when compared to $\dfrac{1}{M_B}$. When equations (7.21) and (7.22) are combined and the above conditions are applied, the equation reduces to

$$h_y(T - T_{WB}) = M_B k_y \lambda_{WB}(Y_{WB} - Y) \tag{7.23}$$

$$\frac{Y - Y_{WB}}{T - T_{WB}} = \frac{-h_y}{M_B k_y \lambda_{WB}} \tag{7.24}$$

For a given T_{WB}, Y_{WB} and λ_{WB} are constant. The relationship between Y and T depends on the ratio of h_y to k_y. The above equation predicts a linear relationship between Y and T for all mixtures of gas–vapour having the same T_{WB}. The curves of Y vs T for gases with the given T_{WB} are known as psychrometric lines. The slope of these lines is $\dfrac{-h_y}{M_B k_y \lambda_{WB}}$ and they intersect the saturation humidity line at T_{WB}.

Stanton's number for heat transfer.

$$\frac{h_y}{C_P G} = b\, Re^n Pr^{-m} = St_H \tag{7.25}$$

Stanton's number for mass transfer

$$\frac{\overline{M}k_y}{G} = b\,Re^n Pr^{-m} = St_M \tag{7.26}$$

$$\frac{(St_H)}{(St_M)} = \frac{h_y}{k_y\overline{M}} = C_P\left(\frac{Sc}{Pr}\right)^m \tag{7.27}$$

where $\overline{M}$ is the average molecular weight of the gas–vapour mixture, b, m and n are constants and $C_P \approx C_Y$. At low humidity values, $\overline{M} \approx M_B$.

Substituting this [1] in equation (7.24) and taking the value of m to be $\frac{2}{3}$,

$$\frac{Y - Y_{WB}}{T - T_{WB}} = \frac{-C_Y}{\lambda_{WB}}\left(\frac{Sc}{Pr}\right)^{\frac{2}{3}} \tag{7.28}$$

The wet bulb temperature can be measured using a thermometer or a temperature measuring device covered with a wick which is saturated with pure liquid and immersed in a stream of gas having a definite temperature T and humidity Y. During the measurement of T_{WB}, the following precautions are to be followed.

1. The wick must be completely wet and no dry spot must be present.
2. The gas velocity should be large enough to ensure that the heat transfer from the surroundings to the bulb by radiation is negligible when compared to heat transfer by conduction and convection.
3. If makeup liquid is required it must be supplied at T_{WB}.

When these precautions are taken, T_{WB} will be independent of gas velocity.

ILLUSTRATION

70 Moist air at 310 K has a wet bulb temperature of 300 K. If the latent heat of vaporisation of H_2O at 300 K is 2440 kJ kg^{-1}, estimate the absolute and relative humidity of air. The total pressure is 105 kN m^{-2} and the vapour pressure of water is 3.6 kN m^{-2} at 300 K and 6.33 kN m^{-2} at 310 K.

Solution

We know that, for the air–$H_2O(v)$ system

$$\frac{Y - Y_{WB}}{T - T_{WB}} = \frac{-h_y}{M_B k_y \lambda_{WB}} = \frac{1}{\lambda_{WB}}$$

Absolute humidity at the wet bulb temperature is the partial pressure ratio multiplied by the molecular weight ratio.

$$Y_{WB} = \frac{P_A}{P - P_A} \times \frac{M_A}{M_B} = \frac{3.6}{100 - 3.6} \times \frac{18}{29} = 0.023\ 18$$

Then, substituting the other values in the above equation,

$$\frac{Y - 0.023\ 18}{(310 - 300)} = \frac{1}{2\,440}$$

Solving, $Y = 0.027\ 27$

Absolute humidity is the partial pressure ratio multiplied by the molecular weight ratio.

$$\frac{P_A}{P - P_A} \times \frac{M_A}{M_B} = Y$$

Solving $P_A = 4.208$ kN m^{-2}

Relative humidity is the percentage ratio of partial pressure to the vapour pressure at that temperature.

$$Y_r = \frac{P_A}{P_A^*} \times 100 = \frac{4.208}{6.33} \times 100 = 66.48$$

ADIABATIC SATURATION TEMPERATURE (T_{AS})

If a gas is passed over the liquid at such a rate that the time of contact is sufficient for equilibrium to be established, the gas will become saturated and both phases will be brought to the same temperature. In a thermally insulated system, the total sensible heat falls by an amount equal to the latent heat of the liquid evaporated. As a result of the continued passage of the gas, the temperature of the liquid gradually approaches an equilibrium value which is known as adiabatic saturation temperature (T_{AS}).

These conditions are achieved in an infinitely tall thermally insulated humidification column. Gas of a given initial temperature and humidity flows through this in a counter current manner to the liquid under conditions where the gas is completely saturated at the top of the column. If the liquid is continuously circulated round the column and if fresh liquid is added at the same temperature as the circulating liquid, the temperature of the liquid at the top and bottom of the column and of the gas at the top approach adiabatic saturation temperature. The temperature and humidity differences are maximum at the bottom and zero at the top. Hence, the rate of heat and mass transfer decrease progressively from the bottom to the top of the tower. Figure 7.2 shows an adiabatic saturation tower.

A heat balance over the column shows that the heat of vaporisation of the liquid must come from the sensible heat in the gas. The temperature of the gas falls from dry bulb temperature to T_{AS} and the humidity increases from Y to Y_s at T_{AS}.

For unit mass of dry gas

$$C_Y(T - T_{AS}) = \lambda_{AS}(Y_s - Y) \tag{7.29}$$

$$(Y - Y_{S,AS}) = \frac{C}{\lambda_{AS}}(T - T_{AS}) \tag{7.30}$$

$$\frac{Y - Y_{S,AS}}{T - T_{AS}} = \frac{-C_Y}{\lambda_{AS}} \tag{7.31}$$

where C_Y is the humid heat of the gas, λ_{AS} is the latent heat of vaporisation of the liquid at T_{AS} and $Y_{S,AS}$ is the saturation humidity at T_{AS}. For small changes in humidity, C_Y is almost constant. The above equation predicts a linear relationship between Y and T for all mixtures of gas–vapour having the same T_{AS}. A curve of Y vs T for gases with a given T_{AS} is known as an adiabatic cooling line. For a range of T_{AS}, a family of curves approximating to straight lines with a slope $\frac{-C_Y}{\lambda}$ is obtainable. These lines are not exactly parallel because of variations in C_Y and λ with temperature.

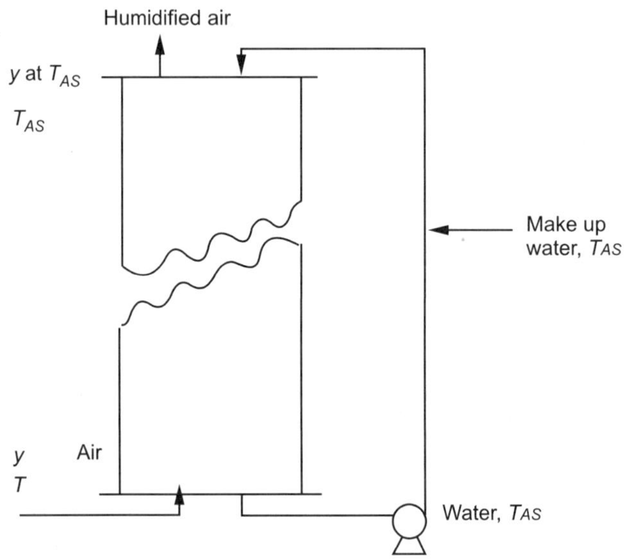

Fig. 7.2 Adiabatic saturation tower

LEWIS RELATION [2]

Psychrometric lines based on equation (7.24) and adiabatic saturation lines based on equation (7.31) intersect the saturation humidity line at the same point. For that point, $\frac{h_y}{M_B k_y} = C_Y$. This relation is known as the *Lewis relation*. In systems for which this relation holds good, psychrometric lines and adiabatic saturation lines will be the same and $T_{WB} = T_{AS}$. An example of this is the air–water vapour system. For other systems, psychrometric lines and adiabatic saturation lines are different; psychrometric lines are steeper than adiabatic saturation lines.

HUMIDITY CHART [3]

The humidity chart is a convenient diagram showing the properties of mixtures of air–water vapour. Dry bulb temperature (T_{DB}) is plotted as abscissa and absolute humidity (Y) as ordinate. Any point on the chart represents a definite mixture of air and water. The curved line gives the humidity of saturated air as a function of air temperature (Y_s vs T). These are known as saturation humidity lines. The coordinates of the points on this curve are obtained from the vapour pressure–temperature data for water using the equation

$$\frac{\text{Partial pressure of water vapour}}{\text{Partial pressure of dry air}} \times \frac{18}{29} \tag{7.32}$$

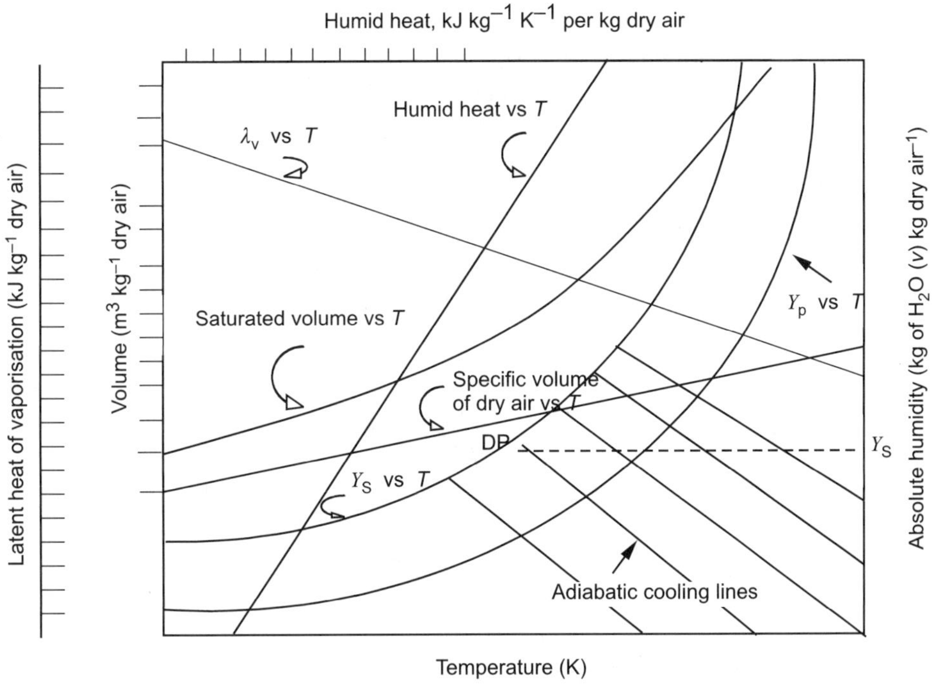

Fig. 7.3 Humidity chart

The humidity chart is shown in Fig. 7.3. Any point above and to the left of the saturated line represents a mixture of saturated air and liquid. Any point below the saturated line represents under-saturated air. Any point on the temperature axis represents dry air. Curved lines between the saturation humidity line and the temperature axis marked in % represent mixtures of air and water vapour of definite percentage humidity. They have been drawn based on

$$Y_p = \frac{Y}{Y \text{ at saturation}} \times 100 \tag{7.33}$$

Linear interpolation between the saturated line and the temperature axis can be used to locate lines of any given constant Y_p. Slanting lines running down and to the right of the saturated line are wet bulb temperature (T_{WB}) lines. The ends of these lines are identified by the corresponding T_{WB}.

Plots of specific volume of dry air and saturated volume are also available. Both are plots of volume against temperature. The volume can be read on the scale at the left. The coordinates of points on these lines are calculated using the equation.

$$V_Y = \frac{22.4 \times T}{273} \times \left(\frac{1}{29} + \frac{Y}{18}\right) \tag{7.34}$$

For dry air $Y = 0$ and for saturated air $Y = Y_s$. Linear interpolation between the two lines based on Y_p gives the humid volume of unsaturated air. A plot of C_Y vs Y is also available. This line is a plot of equation $C_Y = C_{P,\text{Air}} + YC_{P\text{Water}(v)}$. Some charts include the $\lambda_v - T$ plot as well, based on $\lambda_v - T$ data. The scale for λ_v is at the extreme left.

Use of the Humidity Chart

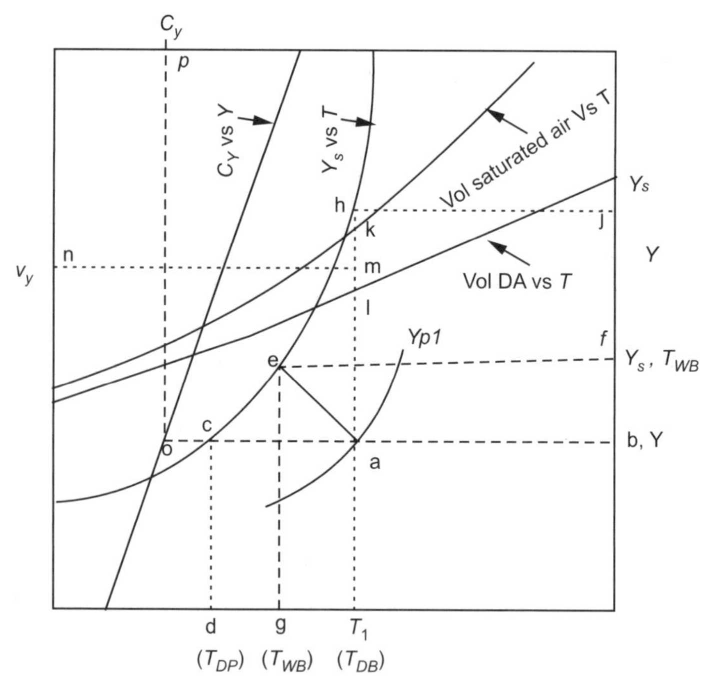

Fig. 7.4 Use of the humidity chart

The humidity chart can be used for a number of data for the air–water vapour mixture. To locate a point on the chart, two parameters are required. The rest of the data can be generated from the chart. Consider an unsaturated air–water vapour mixture at a dry bulb temperature T_1 and given Y_{p1}. The point a represents this air in the chart. It is the point of intersection of the constant dry bulb temperature line for T_1 and constant percentage humidity line for Y_{p1}. The absolute humidity Y is read at point b on the y-axis. The dew point can be found by following the constant absolute humidity line through a to meet the Y_s vs T line at c. The dew point is d on the dry bulb temperature axis. T_{WB} is the temperature of the wet bulb temperature line passing through a. Y_S at T_{WB} can be found by following the wet bulb temperature line through a to e at the Y_S vs T line and reading the value of f on the y-axis. T_{WB} can be read at g on the T-axis. If the original air is saturated at constant temperature, Y_s is found by following the constant T line to its intersection with Y_s vs T line at h and the corresponding Y_s can be read at j on the y-axis. To find V_Y, travel along the constant temperature line through T_1 to intersect the specific volume of dry air vs T line at l and saturated volume vs T line at k. Locate m between k and l such that m is at a distance of $(Y_{p1} \times kl) \div 100$ from 1. V_y is given by point n on the volume axis. To find the humid heat, extend the constant Y line through a to meet the C_Y vs Y line at o and C_Y can be read at p on the C_Y scale. Figure 7.4 explains the use of the humidity chart.

ILLUSTRATIONS

7P An air–water vapour sample has a T_{DB} of 328 K and $Y = 0.03$ kg H_2O (v) per kg of air at atmospheric pressure. Compute the other parameters using the humidity chart.

Solution

1. *Percentage humidity*: On the humidity chart, locate the constant dry bulb temperature line for 328 K and travel vertically along the line till the constant humidity line for 0.03 kg $H_2O(v)$ per kg of air is intersected. The Y_p corresponding to that point is $\approx 25\%$.

2. *Molal humidity*: This can be found using the formula $Y = Y_m \times \dfrac{M_A}{M_B}$

$$\text{Hence } Y_m = Y \times \frac{M_B}{M_A} = 0.03 \times \frac{29}{18} = 0.048\,3 \ \frac{\text{kmol}\,H_2O(v)}{\text{kmol}\,\text{DA}}$$

3. *Partial pressure of water vapour*: Molal humidity, $Y_m = \dfrac{P_A}{P - P_A}$, where P_A is the partial pressure of water and P is the total pressure. As the humidity chart is referred to, the total pressure is 1 atm.

$$Y_m = \frac{P_A}{P - P_A}$$

$$0.048\ 3 = \frac{P_A}{101.325 - P_A}$$

$$P_A = 4.67 \text{ kN m}^{-2}$$

4. *Vapour pressure of water at 328 K*: On the humidity chart, locate the constant dry bulb temperature line for 328 K and travel vertically along the line, till the Y_S vs T line is intersected. The Y_S corresponding to that point is 0.115 kg of water vapour per kg of dry air.

$$Y_S = \frac{P_A^*}{P - P_A^*} \times \frac{M_A}{M_B}$$

where P_A^* is the vapour pressure of water and P is the total pressure. As the humidity chart is referred to, the total pressure is 1 atm.

$$Y_S = \frac{P_A^*}{P - P_A^*} \times \frac{M_A}{M_B}$$

$$0.115 = \frac{P_A^*}{P - P_A^*} \times \frac{M_A}{M_B} = \frac{P_A^*}{101.325 - P_A^*} \times \frac{18}{29}$$

$$P_A^* = 15.82 \text{ kN m}^{-2}$$

5. *Relative humidity*: Relative humidity is the percentage ratio of partial pressure to vapour pressure.

$$Y_r = \frac{P_A}{P_A^*} \times 100 = 29.52\%$$

6. *Dew point*: On the humidity chart, locate the constant humidity line for 0.03 kg $H_2O(v)$ per kg of air and travel horizontally along the line, till the Y_S vs T line is intersected. The temperature corresponding to that point is the dew point, which is 304.5 K.

7. *Humid volume*: On the humidity chart, locate the constant dry bulb temperature line for 328 K and travel vertically along the line, till the specific volume of dry air vs T line is intersected. The specific volume of dry air corresponding to that point is 0.93 m^3 per kg of dry air. Continue the vertical travel till the specific volume of saturated air vs T line is intersected. The specific volume of saturated air corresponding to that point is 1.10 m^3 per kg of dry air. Then, the humid volume is obtained using the formula,

   Humid volume = specific volume of dry air + Y_p (specific volume of saturated air – specific volume of dry air)

$$= 0.93 + 0.25(1.10 - 0.93) = 0.972\ 5 \text{ m}^3 \text{ per kg of dry air}$$

8. *Humid heat:* On the humidity chart, locate the constant humidity line for 0.03 kg $H_2O(v)$ per kg of air and travel horizontally along the line, till the C_Y vs Y line is intersected. The value of humid heat corresponding to that point is the humid heat of the mixture, which is 1.05 kJ kg^{-1} K^{-1}.

7Q Air at 298 K and 70% relative humidity is cooled to 288 K and reheated to 293 K. Find (i) the weight of water removed per unit weight of dry air, (ii) the wet bulb temperature of original and final air and (iii) the percentage humidity, relative humidity and partial pressure of water vapour in the final air.

Solution

The problem has to be solved using the humidity chart.

(i) The point of intersection of the constant dry bulb temperature line for 298 K and constant relative humidity line for $Y_r = 70\%$ gives the absolute humidity, Y as 0.0140 kg per kg of dry air. This gas is cooled to 288 K. Y_s at 288 K is be found by following the constant dry bulb temperature line till it meet the Y_s vs T line. Y_s at 288 K is 0.010 6 kg per kg of dry air. The humidity of the final air is less that of the initial air.

So, water removed during cooling = 0.014 0 – 0.010 6 = 0.003 4 kg per kg of dry air.

(ii) The dew point or wet bulb temperature is the point of intersection of the constant absolute humidity line and the Y_s vs T line. The dew point is to be read on the dry bulb temperature axis.

Wet bulb temperature of original air = 294 K

Wet bulb temperature of final air = 290 K

(iii) Y of final air = 0.010 6

The final air is reheated to the original temperature 293 K.

Y_s of final air = 0.0146, as read from humidity chart for temperature 293 K.

We know that, $Y_p = \dfrac{Y}{Y \text{ at saturation}} \times 100 = 72.6\%$

Y_m of final air = $0.010\,6 \div 0.620\,7 = 0.017\,1$

Y_m of saturated air at 293 K = $0.014\,6 \div 0.620\,7 = 0.023\,5$

Y_m is molar ratio of water vapour to dry air, which is also equal to the partial pressure ratio of water vapour to dry air.

$0.0171 = P_A \div (101.3 - P_A)$ and $0.023\,5 = P \div (101.3 - P_A^*)$

So, P_A, the partial pressure of water vapour = 1.76 kPa

P_A^*, the vapour pressure of water = 2.34 kPa

Relative humidity Y_r = $P_A \div P_A^* = 75.37\%$

The partial pressure of water vapour in the final air is 1.76 kPa.

7R An air conditioning system takes the outside air at 303 K and 90% humidity, cools it to 288 K and reheats the cooled air to 298 K. Calculate (i) the kg of water vapour removed per kg of dry air in the cooling plant, (ii) the wet bulb temperature of the origin and conditioned air and (iii) the percentage humidity, relative humidity and partial pressure of water vapour in the conditioned air.

Solution

Figure 7.5 represents the data provided in the form of a block diagram. The problem has to be solved using the humidity chart.

(i) The point of intersection of the constant dry bulb temperature line for 303 K and constant percentage humidity line for $Y_p = 90\%$ gives the absolute humidity Y as 0.024 7 kg per kg of dry air. This gas is cooled to 298 K. Y_s at 298 K can be found by following the constant dry bulb temperature line till it meet the Y_s vs T line. Y_s at 288 K is 0.010 4 kg per kg of dry air. The humidity of the final air is less that of the initial air.

So, water removed during cooling = 0.0247 – 0.010 4 = 0.014 3 kg per kg of dry air

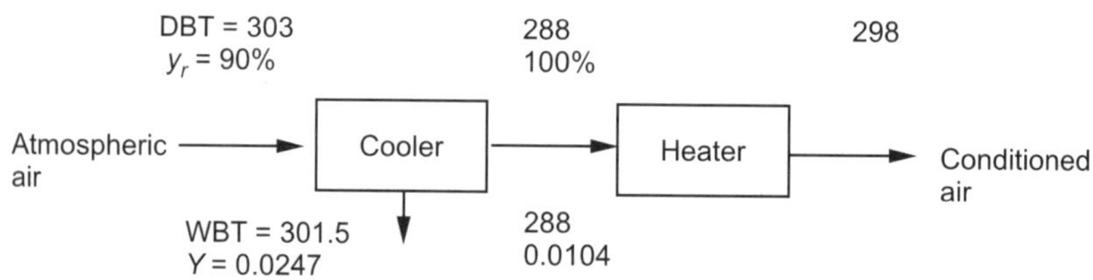

Fig. 7.5 Air conditioning operation

(ii) The dew point or wet bulb temperature is the point of intersection of the constant absolute humidity line and the Y_s vs T line. The dew point is to be read on the dry bulb temperature axis.

Wet bulb temperature of original air = 301.5 K

Wet bulb temperature of final air = 291.5 K

(iii) Y of final air = 0.010 4

The final air is reheated to 298 K.

Y_s of the final air is 0.02 as read from the humidity chart for a temperature of 298 K.

We know that, $Y_p = \dfrac{Y}{Y \text{ at saturation}} \times 100 = 52\%$

Y_m of final air $= 0.010\,4 \div 0.620\,7 = 0.016\,7$

Y_m of saturated air at 298 K $= 0.02 \div 0.620\,7 = 0.032\,2$

Y_m is the molar ratio of water vapour to dry air, which is also equal to the partial pressure ratio of water vapour to dry air.

$0.016\ 7 = P_A \div (101.3 - P_A)$ and $0.0322 = P_A^* \div (101.3 - P_A^*)$

So P_A, the partial pressure of water vapour $= 1.67$ kPa

P_A^*, the vapour pressure of water $= 3.36$ kPa

Relative humidity Y_r $= (P_A \div P_A^*) \times 100 = 52.77\%$

7S Air at 358 K with a humidity of 0.03 kg water vapour per kg of dry air at 1 bar is contacted with water at adiabatic saturation temperature and thereby humidified and cooled to 70% saturation. Find the final temperature and humidity of air.

Solution

On the humidity chart, locate the constant dry bulb temperature line for 358 K and travel vertically along the line till the constant humidity line for 0.03 kg $H_2O(v)$ per kg of air is intersected. The adiabatic saturation temperature (wet bulb temperature) corresponding to that point is 315 K. Travel along this adiabatic saturation temperature line till it intersects the 70% humidity line. The temperature corresponding to that point is the final temperature of humidified air, 319 K, and the humidity corresponding to that point is the final humidity of humidified air, 0.049 kg $H_2O(v)$ per kg of air. The procedure is shown in Fig. 7.6.

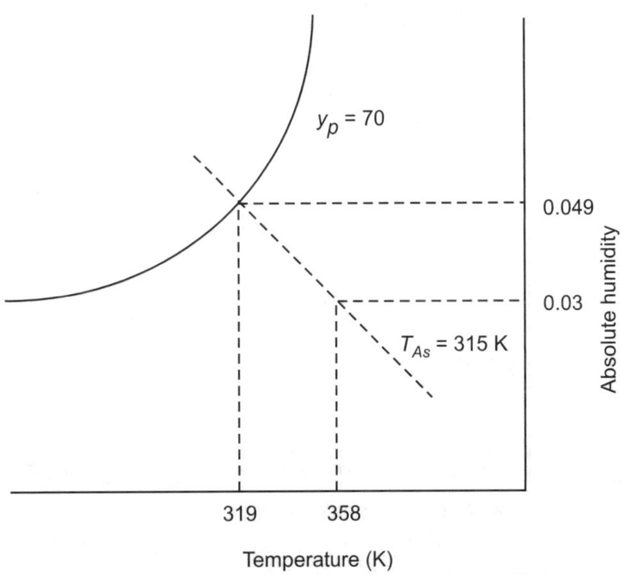

Fig. 7.6 Humidity chart solution for 7S

ENTHALPY OF HUMID GAS

In the calculations of enthalpies, it is necessary to define a reference state at which the enthalpy is taken as zero. It is most convenient to take the freezing point of the material constituting the vapour phase as the reference temperature and the liquid state of the material as its standard state. The enthalpy of the vapour gas mixture is the sum of the enthalpies of the gas and the vapour content. If the mixture is unsaturated, the vapour is in a super heated state. Let H_Y be the enthalpy of the humid gas per unit mass of dry gas, H_A the enthalpy of vapour per unit mass, H_B the enthalpy of dry gas per unit mass, C_{Av} the specific heat of the vapour at constant pressure, $C_{A,l}$ the specific heat of the liquid, C_B the specific heat of dry gas, T_o the freezing point of the liquid, T_{DP} the dew point, T_{DB} the dry bulb temperature, Y the humidity of the gas and λ_{DP} the latent heat of vaporisation of the liquid at dew point.

$$H_Y = H_B + Y_{HA} \tag{7.35}$$

Here $H_A = C_{A,l}(T_{DP} - T_o) + \lambda D_P + C_{A,v}(T_{DB} - T_{DP})$ and $H_B = C_B(T_{DB} - T_o)$. Based on this, the $H_y - Y$ diagram may be constructed.

ILLUSTRATIONS

7T An air–water vapour mixture has a $T = 328$ K and $Y = 0.03$ kg $H_2O(v)$ per kg dry air. Compute its enthalpy. C_p of air $= 1\ 005$ J kg^{-1}K^{-1}, C_P of $H_2O(v) = 1\ 884$ J kg^{-1}K^{-1}, λ_v of water $= 2\ 502.3$ kJ kg^{-1}.

Solution

From the humidity chart, the dew point of the gaseous mixture can be found to be 304.5 K. We know that $H_Y = H_B + Y_{HA}$ and $H_A = C_{A,l}(T_{DP} - T_o) + \lambda_{DP} + C_{A,v}(T_{DB} - T_{DP})$ and $H_B = C_B(T - T_o)$. Substituting the relevant values in the above equation,

$$H_Y = (1 \times 55) + 0.03\{(4.186 \times 31.5) + 2\ 502.3 + (1\ 884 \times 23.50\}$$

$$= 134.81 \text{ kJ per kg of DA}$$

7U Conditioned air at 298 K and 50% saturation is to be supplied for a laboratory of size 4 m × 20 m × 6 m with no facilities for recirculation. The air conditioner takes the outside air at 308 K and 90% saturation, refrigerates and separates out the condensed water and reheats the air using steam at 1 atm. Find the volume of air needed at the entry conditions. Also compute the weight of water condensed in the conditioner.

Solution

The humidity of the feed air and conditioned air are found using a humidity chart. The air conditioner takes outside air at 308 K and 90% saturation.

Absolute humidity of air under these conditions (Y)

$$= 0.034 \text{ kg of moisture per kg of dry air}$$

Molal humidity of this air (Y_m) $= Y \div 0.620\,7$

$$= 0.055 \text{ mol of moisture per mol of dry air}$$

Conditioned air is at 298 K and 50% saturation.

Absolute humidity of air under these conditions (Y)

$$= 0.001 \text{ kg of moisture per kg of dry air}$$

Molal humidity of this air (Y_m) $= Y \div 0.620\,7$

$$= 0.0016 \text{ mol of moisture per mol of dry air}$$

At the inlet to the laboratory, each mole of dry air contains 0.0016 mole of moisture.

Volume of conditioned air to be fed to the laboratory = 4 m × 20 m × 6 m = 480 m^3

$$\text{Dry air to be fed to the laboratory} = \frac{480}{1.0016} = 479.23 \text{ m}^3$$

$$= \frac{479.23 \times 1}{0.082\,05 \times 298} = 19.60 \text{ kmol}$$

At the inlet to the conditioner, each mole of dry air contains 0.055 mole of moisture.

Moist air to be fed to the conditioner $= 19.60 \times 1.055$ kmol

Volume of moist air to be fed to the conditioner

$$= \frac{19.60 \times 1.055 \times 0.082\,05 \times 308}{1} = 522.56 \text{ m}^3$$

Air enters the conditioner with 0.055 mole of moisture per mole of dry air and leaves with 0.0016 mole of moisture per mole of dry air. In the conditioner, 0.0534 mole of water is condensed per mole of dry air.

Water condensed in the conditioner $= 19.60 \times 0.053\,4$ kmol $= 1.046\,6$ kmol $= 18.84$ kg

7V Air is to be cooled and dehumidified by counter current contact with water in a packed tower. The tower is to be designed for the following conditions.

Conditions of air: dry bulb temperature = 300 K; wet bulb temperature = 298 K; flow rate: 700 kg h^{-1} as dry air.

Conditions of water: inlet temperature = 283 K; outlet temperature = 291 K.

For the entering air, find the absolute humidity, relative humidity, dew point and enthalpy. What is the maximum water rate which can be used to meet design requirements assuming a very tall tower?

Solution

Basis: 1 hour operation.

Using the humidity chart, absolute humidity, relative humidity and dew point can be found for air with a dry bulb temperature of 28°C and a wet bulb temperature of 25°C.

Absolute humidity = 0.022

Relative humidity = 86%

Dew point = 25°C

Enthalpy of the humid air can be found using the formula, $H_Y = H_B + Y_{HA}$

Here, $H_A = C_{A,l}(T_{DP} - T_o) + \lambda D_P + C_{A,v}(T_{DB} - T_{DP})$ and $H_B = C_B(T_{DB} - T_o)$.

$$H_Y = 1 \times (28 - 0) + 0.022 \times [4.187 \times (25 - 0) + 2500 + \{1.88 \times (28 - 25)\}]$$

Enthalpy of humid air = 85.42 kJ kg^{-1} of dry air

Total water to be removed = $700 \times 0.022 = 15.4$ kg

Latent heat to be supplied for this = $15.4 \times 2500 = 38\,500$ kJ

Air is cooled from 28°C to 18°C.

Sensible heat to be removed from air = $700 \times 1 \times (28 - 18) = 7\,000$ kJ

Total heat to be removed = 45 500 kJ

Heat is removed by water, which enters at 10° C and leaves at 18° C.

$$\text{Maximum water rate} = \frac{45\,500}{4.187 \times (18 - 10)} = 1\,358.4 \text{ kg h}^{-1}$$

DETERMINATION OF HUMIDITY

Dew Point Method

A cooled polished disk is inserted into a gas with unknown humidity and the temperature of the disk is gradually lowered. The disk reaches a temperature at which a thin mist just appears on the polished surface. That temperature is the temperature of equilibrium between the vapour in the gas and the liquid phase and is therefore the dew point. This is noted down. Then the disk temperature is slowly raised and the temperature at which the mist just disappears is noted. The average of the two temperatures may be taken as dew point and the humidity can be read from the humidity chart.

Psychrometric Method

It is a method of determining the humidity based on simultaneous wet bulb and dry bulb temperature measurements and the use of a humidity chart. The psychrometric line for the wet bulb temperature noted is located. The humidity corresponding to the point of intersection of this psychrometric line and the dry bulb temperature line is the humidity of the gas–vapour mixture.

Use of Hygrometers

Mechanical Hygrometers

Materials such as human hair, wool fibre and plastics have been used to measure humidity. These methods are based on the change in the dimensions of the material with humidity.

Electrical Hygrometers

Humidity is determined based on the measurement of electrical resistance of a film of moisture absorbing material on exposure to the gas.

Gravimetric Methods

It is the most accurate humidity measuring technique. Here, a known quantity of the gas is passed over a moisture absorbing chemical such as P_2O_5 and the increase in weight is determined.

HUMIDIFICATION

The following methods may be used to increase the humidity of the gas.

1. Live steam may be added in the required amount. This produces a slight increase in temperature. Impurities present in the steam are added to the gas stream.
2. Water may be sprayed into the gas at such a rate, that on complete evaporation it gives the required humidity. Here, the temperature of the gas will fall as the latent heat of vaporisation must be supplied by the sensible heat of the gas and liquid.
3. The gas may be mixed with a gas of higher humidity. The humidity can be controlled easily by varying the proportions of the two gas streams being mixed. This is mostly practiced in the industry.
4. The gas may be brought into contact with water in such a way that only part of the liquid is evaporated. To obtain a high rate of humidification, the area of contact between the air and the water is made as large as possible by supplying water in the form of a fine spray. Alternatively, the interfacial area is increased using a packed column. Evaporation occurs if the humidity at the surface is greater than that in the bulk of air.
5. Two methods of changing the humidity and temperature of gas from A (T_1, Y_1) to B (T_2, Y_2) can be traced on the humidity chart. The first method consists of

saturating the air by water maintained at the dew point of air of humidity Y_2 and then heating at constant humidity to T_2. In the second method, the air is heated to the adiabatic saturation temperature corresponding to the humidity Y_2. It is then saturated by water at the adiabatic saturation temperature and heated at constant humidity to T_2. In the second method, an additional operation – preliminary heating of air – is required while the temperature of water is automatically adjusted to the required value. Fig. 7.7 explains the two methods.

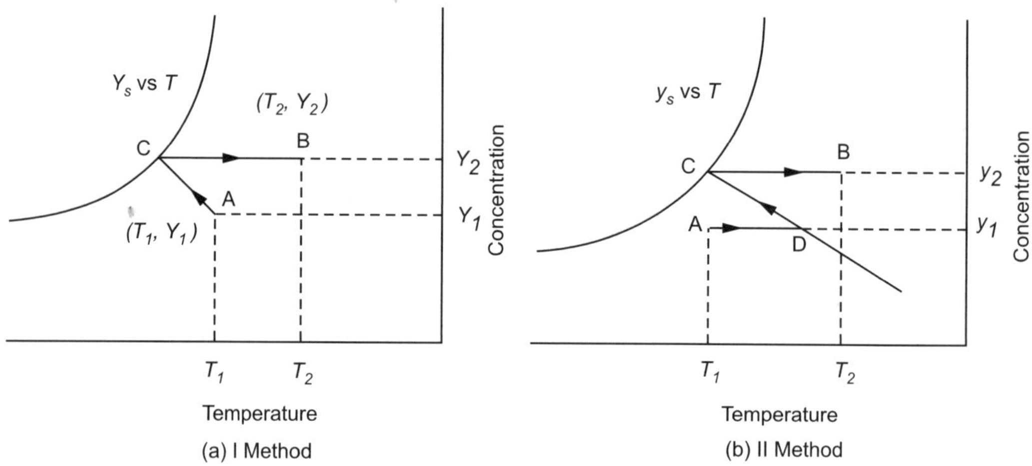

Fig. 7.7 Humidification

DEHUMIDIFICATION

Dehumidification of air can be effected by bringing it into contact with a cold surface, either liquid or solid. If the temperature of the surface is lower than the dew point of the gas, theoretically, the temperature of the gas should fall at constant humidity until the dew point is reached and subsequent cooling would be accompanied by condensation. But in practice, both humidity and temperature are reduced simultaneously throughout the process. Air in contact with the surface is cooled below its dew point and condensation of vapour occurs before the more distant air has time to cool. When the gas stream is cooled by cold water, counter current flow should be employed because the temperatures of air and water are changing in opposite directions.

Humidity can also be reduced by compressing air and allowing it to cool again to the original temperature. During compression, the partial pressure of vapour (P_A) is increased, as the partial pressure is mole fraction times total pressure. When the compressed air is cooled to the original temperature, the maximum partial pressure is the vapour pressure of the liquid at the original temperature, the gas then becomes saturated and condensation occurs and humidity drops significantly.

ILLUSTRATIONS

7W A sample of air is to be humidified and warmed. The air is initially at 30°C and 40% humidity. The final air is to be at 45°C and 60% humidity. With the help of a humidity chart, indicate two processes that can be followed to achieve this.

Solution

Initial air T_{DB} : 30°C Y_P : 40%

From the humidity chart, the absolute humidity (Y) is 0.011 kg of water vapour per kg of dry air.

Final air T_{DB} : 45°C Y_P : 60%

From the humidity chart, the absolute humidity (Y) is 0.049 kg of water vapour per kg of dry air.

$$T_{WB} = 40°\text{C}$$

1. The initial air is saturated with water maintained at 40°C and it is then heated to 45°C.
2. The initial air is preheated to 130°C and adiabatically cooled by contact with H_2O at 40°C. When 40ºC is reached, it is heated to the final temperature of 45°C.

7X Air at 300 K and 20% humidity is to be heated in two stages with intermediate saturation with water to 90% humidity, so that the final stream is at 320 K and 20% humidity. What is the humidity of the exit stream and conditions at the end of each stage?

Solution

Initial air T_{DB} : 300 K Y_P : 20%

From the humidity chart, the absolute humidity (Y) is 0.004 5 kg of water vapour per kg of dry air.

Final air T_{DB} : 320 K Y_P : 20%

From the humidity chart, the absolute humidity (Y) is 0.014 kg of water vapour per kg of dry air.

In the first stage, the initial air is heated to 318 K, (where the constant humidity line intersects the adiabatic saturation line for 293 K) and is saturated with water at 293 K, till 90% humidity is attained. At the end of this stage (intermediate stage), the humidity is 0.014 kg of water vapour per kg of dry air and the temperature is 294.5 K. In the final stage, saturated air is heated from 294.5 K to 320 K.

7Y In a process in which benzene is used as a solvent, it is evaporated into dry nitrogen. At 297 K and 1 bar, the resulting mixture has a relative humidity of 60%. It is necessary to recover 80% of the benzene present by cooling to 283 K and compressing to a suitable pressure. What should that pressure be? The vapour pressure of benzene is 12.2 kN m^{-2} at 297 K and 6 kN m^{-2} at 283 K.

Solution

Relative humidity is the percentage ratio of the partial pressure of vapour to the vapour pressure of liquid at gas temperature.

$$Y_r = \frac{P_A}{P_A^*} \times 100$$

Vapour pressure of benzene at 297 K is given as 12.2 kN m^{-2}.

Partial pressure of benzene in the benzene–nitrogen mixture can be found to be

$$60 = \frac{P_A}{12.2} \times 100 \quad \text{or} \quad P_A = 0.6 \times 12.2 = 7.32 \text{ kN m}^{-2}$$

Molal humidity of the initial benzene–nitrogen mixture is

$$Y_m = \frac{P_A}{P - P_A} = \frac{7.32}{100 - 7.32} = 0.079 \text{ mole of benzene per mole of nitrogen}$$

If 80% benzene has to be removed, the molal humidity of the final mixture should be, $0.079 \times 0.2 = 0.015\,8$ mole of benzene per mole of nitrogen. As the mixture is cooled to 283 K, the partial pressure of benzene vapour in the mixture should be equal to the vapour pressure of liquid benzene at 283 K, which is 6 kN m^{-2}.

$$Y_m = \frac{P_A}{P - P_A}$$

So, $0.0158 = \dfrac{6}{P - 6}$ and the compression pressure, $P = 385.75$ kN m^{-2}.

7Z The air supply to a drier has a dry bulb temperature of 40ºC and a wet bulb temperature of 35°C. It is heated to 120°C by coils and blown into the drier. In the drier, it cools along an adiabatic saturation line and leaves the drier at 90% saturation. Compute the dew point of the initial air, the absolute humidity and the amount of water evaporated per 10 m^3 of entering air and the temperature of air as it leaves the dryer.

Solution

For air–water vapour mixtures, the wet bulb temperature and dew point are the same. So, the dew point of the initial air is 35°C.

The operation mentioned in the problem can be followed on the humidity chart. The absolute humidity of initial air is found to be 0.035 kg of moisture per kg of dry air. Travel along this constant humidity line till a temperature of 120ºC is reached. The adiabatic saturation line for the temperature 47°C passes through this point. Travel along this line till the 90% humidity line is intersected. The absolute humidity corresponding to that point is 0.070 kg of moisture per kg of dry air and temperature is 48°C.

$$\text{Molal humidity of entering air} = \frac{0.035}{0.620\,7} = 0.056\ 4 \text{ mol moisture per mol of dry air}$$

$$\text{Molal humidity of leaving air} = \frac{0.070}{0.620\,7} = 0.113 \text{ mol moisture per mol of dry air}$$

So, 1.0565 mol of entering air picks up $0.113 - 0.056\ 4 = 0.056\ 6$ mol of moisture

$$10 \text{ m}^3 \text{ of entering air contains} = \frac{PV}{RT} = \frac{1 \times 10}{0.0820\,6 \times 313} = 0.389\,4\,\text{kmol}$$

$$\text{Moisture picked up in the drier} = \frac{0.056\,6}{1.056\,4} \times 0.389\,5 = 0.020\ 9 \text{ kmol} = 0.376 \text{ kg}$$

DESIGN OF HUMIDIFICATION EQUIPMENT [4, 5]

Consider a counter current gas-liquid contactor, as shown in Fig. 7.8. Gas at a humidity Y_b and temperature T_{yb} enters the bottom of the contactor and leaves at the top with a humidity of Y_a and temperature T_{ya}. Liquid enters the top at a temperature T_{xa} and leaves at the bottom at a temperature T_{xb}. Mass velocity of the gas is G_y^1 in terms of mass of vapour-free gas per unit area of cross section per hour. The mass velocity of the liquid at the inlet and outlet are G_{xa} and G_{xb} respectively. Let dz be the height of the small section of tower at a distance Z from the bottom of the contact zone. Let the mass velocity and temperature of the liquid at the height Z be G_x and T_x respectively and the temperature and humidity of the gas be T_y and Y. At the interface between the gas and liquid, let the temperature be T_i and humidity be Y_i. The cross sectional area of the tower is S and height of the contact zone is Z_T. Assume that the liquid is warmer than the gas. Let H_y and H_x be the enthalpies of the gas and liquid respectively.

For the small volume Sdz of the contact zone, the following design equations can be written.

Enthalpy balance:

$$G_y^1 dH_y = d(G_x H_x) \tag{7.36}$$

If the change in G_x with height is neglected,

$$G_y^1 dH_y = G_x dH_x \tag{7.37}$$

$H_x = C_x(T_x - T_o)$ where T_o is the reference temperature and freezing point of the liquid forming the vapour.

$$G_y^1 dH_y = G_x C_x dT_x \tag{7.38}$$

$$\frac{dH_y}{dT_x} = \frac{G_x.C_x}{G_y^1} \tag{7.39}$$

Rate of heat transfer from the liquid to the interface

$$G_x C_x dT_x = h_x(T_x - T_i)a_H dz \tag{7.40}$$

Here, h_x is heat transfer coefficient and a_H is the heat transfer area per unit contact volume.

$$\frac{dT_x}{T_x - T_i} = \frac{h_x a_H dz}{G_x C_x} \tag{7.41}$$

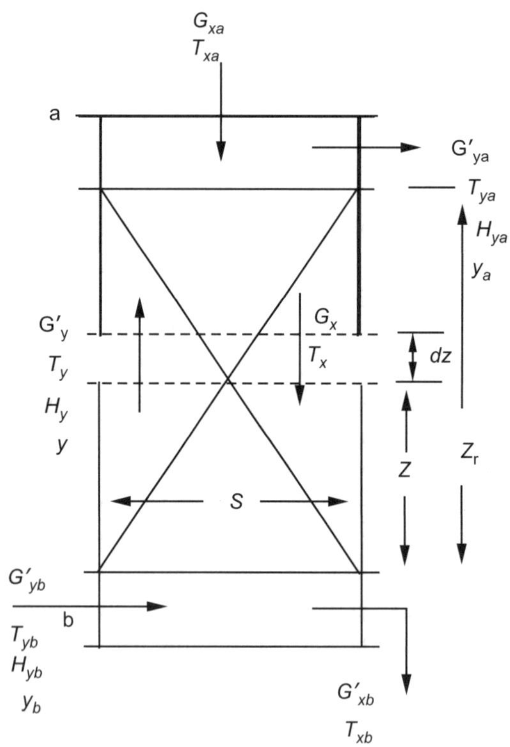

Fig. 7.8 Humidification tower

Rate of heat transfer from interface to gas is

$$G_y^1 C_y dT_y = h_y(T_i - T_y)a_H dz \tag{7.42}$$

$$\frac{dT_y}{T_i - T_y} = \frac{h_y a_H dz}{G_y^1 C_y} \tag{7.43}$$

Rate of mass transfer of vapour from the interface to the gas is

$$G_y^1 dy = k_y M_B (Y_i - Y) a_M dz \tag{7.44}$$

Here a_M is mass transfer area per unit contact volume.

$$\frac{dY}{Y_i - Y} = \frac{k_y M_B a_M dz}{G_y^1} \tag{7.45}$$

A more useful design equation can be derived by rearrangement of equations (7.42) and (7.44).

$$G_y^1 (C_y dT_y + \lambda_o dY) = \{h_y (T_i - T_y) a_H + \lambda_o k_y M_B (Y_i - Y) a_M\} dz \tag{7.46}$$

Here, λ_o is λ at T_o datum temperature which is the freezing point of the liquid. For water, λ_o is 600 kJ kg^{-1} or 2500 kcal kg^{-1}. If the packing is completely wet with liquid $a_H = a_M = a$. If the change in C_y versus Y is negligible then $dH_y = C_y dT_y + \lambda_o dY$.

Hence $G_y^1 dH_y = \{h_y (T_i - T_y) + \lambda_o k_y M_B (Y_i - Y)\} a dz$ (7.47)

For the air–water vapour system, the above expression can be further simplified by using the Lewis relation,

$$\frac{h_y}{k_y M_B} = C_Y \text{ or } h_y = k_y M_B C_Y$$

$$\begin{aligned} G_y^1 dH_y &= \{k_y M_B C_Y (T_i - T_y) + \lambda_o ky M_B (Y_i - Y)\} a dz \\ &= k_y M_B a dz \{C_Y (T_i - T_y) + \lambda_o (Y_i - Y)\} \\ &= k_y M_B a dz \{C_Y (T_i - T_o) + \lambda_o Y_i - C_Y (T_y - T_o) - \lambda_o Y\} \\ &= k_y M_B a dz (H_i - H_y) \end{aligned} \tag{7.48}$$

$$\frac{dH_y}{H_i - H_y} = \frac{k_y M_B}{G_y^1} a\, dz \tag{7.49}$$

To find the packed height, the design equations (7.41), (7.43), (7.45) or (7.49) can be integrated based on the available data. Consider equation (7.49), which is most frequently used, based on mass transfer.

$$\int_{H_{yb}}^{H_{ya}} \frac{dH_y}{H_i - H_y} = \frac{k_y a M_B}{G_y^1} \int_0^{Z_T} dz \tag{7.50}$$

$$\ln \frac{H_i - H_{yb}}{H_i - H_{ya}} = \frac{k_y a M_B}{G_y^1} Z_T \tag{7.51}$$

In the above equation, $\ln \dfrac{H_i - H_{yb}}{H_i - H_{ya}}$ is the number of transfer units (NTU) and $\dfrac{G_y^1}{k_y a M_B}$ is the height of the transfer unit (HTU).

Total packet height, Z_T = NTU × HTU

The function $\dfrac{dH_y}{H_i - H_y}$ can be integrated graphically by plotting $\dfrac{1}{H_i - H_y}$ as ordinate against H_y as abscissa as in Fig. 7.9 and determining the area under the curve between the limits H_{ya} and H_{yb}, which is the number of transfer units. H_i values required for this have to be taken from the equilibrium data.

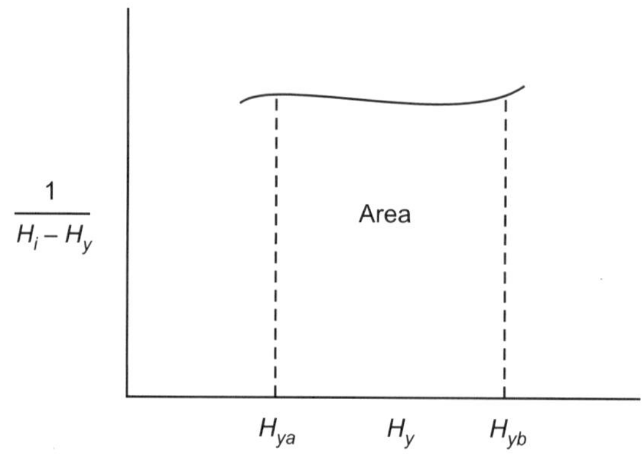

Fig. 7.9 Graphical integration for finding NTU

The H_{ya} and H_{yb} values have to be computed from the conditions at the air inlet and outlet. Other intervening values of H_y can be found by linear interpolation or from a plot of H_y versus T (Fig. 7.10).

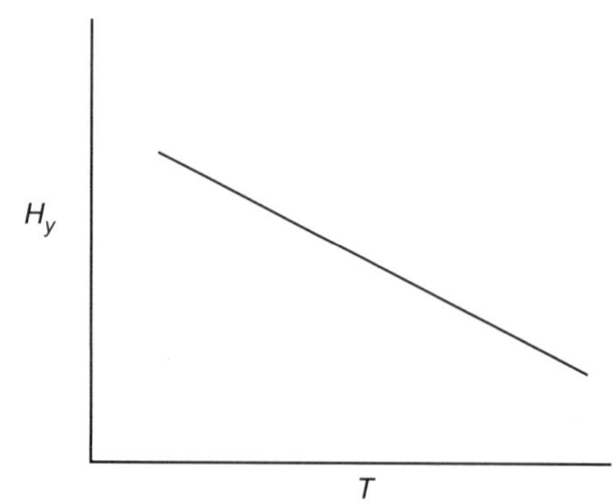

Fig. 7.10 Graphical procedure for generating H_y–T data

The total contact volume can easily be found by modifying the equation for total packed height, as given below.

$$\ln \frac{H_i - H_{yb}}{H_i - H_{ya}} = \frac{k_y a M_B S}{G_y^1 S} Z_T = k_Y \frac{a M_B}{\overset{\circ}{m}} V_T \tag{7.52}$$

V_T is the total contact volume and $V_T = Z_T S$ where S is the cross sectional area of the tower, $\overset{\circ}{m}$ is the mass flow rate of the vapour-free gas and $\overset{\circ}{m} = G_y^1 S$.
A similar useful design equation based on heat transfer is

$$\int_{T_{yb}}^{T_{ya}} \frac{dT_y}{T_i - T_y} = \frac{h_y a}{G_y^1 C_Y} \int_0^{Z_T} dz \tag{7.53}$$

The humid heat C_Y may be assumed to be temperature independent or an average value over the temperature range $\overline{C_Y}$ may be taken into consideration.

$$\ln \frac{T_{yb} - T_i}{T_{ya} - T_i} = \frac{h_y a}{G_y^1 \overline{C_Y}} Z_T \tag{7.54}$$

In the above equation, $\ln \dfrac{T_{yb} - T_i}{T_{ya} - T_i}$ is the number of transfer unit (NTU) and $\dfrac{G_y^1 \overline{C_Y}}{h_y a}$ is the height of the transfer unit (HTU). Total packet height, $Z_T = NTU \times HTU$.

ADIABATIC HUMIDIFICATION

In this case, the inlet and outlet temperatures of water are equal. The make up water is fed at T_{AS}. The volumetric area factors a_H and a_M are identical. The water temperature is constant throughout.

$$T_{xa} = T_{xb} = T_i = T_{AS} = \text{constant}$$

Equation (7.43) becomes

$$\frac{dT_y}{T_{AS} - T_y} = \frac{h_y a}{C_y G_y^1} dz \tag{7.55}$$

A similar useful design equation based on heat transfer is

$$\int_{T_{yb}}^{T_{ya}} \frac{dT_y}{T_{AS} - T_y} = \frac{h_y a}{G_y^1 C_Y} \int_0^{Z_T} dz \tag{7.56}$$

The humid heat C_Y may be assumed to be temperature independent, or an average value over the temperature range $\overline{C_Y}$ may be taken into consideration.

$$\ln \frac{T_{yb} - T_{AS}}{T_{ya} - T_{AS}} = \frac{h_y a}{G_y^1 \overline{C_Y}} Z_T \tag{7.57}$$

In the above equation, $\ln \frac{T_{yb} - T_{AS}}{T_{ya} - T_{AS}}$ is the number of transfer units (NTU) and $\frac{G_y^1 \overline{C_Y}}{h_y a}$ is the height of the transfer unit (HTU).

Total packet height Z_T = NTU × HTU

ILLUSTRATIONS

7AA Water is to be cooled from 43.3°C to 26.7°C in a forced draft cooling tower under conditions such that the height of a transfer unit is 0.53 m. The air enters the bottom of the tower at 23.9°C at a wet bulb temperature of 21.1°C. Find the height of the tower if 1.33 times the minimum air is used. The heat transfer resistance of the liquid phase may be neglected.

Enthalpy data:

Temperature of air (°C)	21.1	23.9	26.7	29.4	32.2	35	37.8	40.6	43.3
Enthalpy of moist air [kcal (kg of DA)$^{-1}$]	18.9	21.5	24.3	27.5	31.1	35.2	39.9	45.2	51.3

Solution

The absolute humidity (Y) of air at a dry bulb temperature of 23.9°C and wet bulb temperature of 21.1°C is 0.0145 kg of moisture per kg of dry air, as read from the humidity chart. The enthalpy of moist air at the inlet conditions is determined using the formula,

$$H_Y = C_B(T_{DB} - T_o) + Y\{\lambda_{DP} + C_{A,v}(T_{DB} - T_{DP})\}$$

$$H_{yb} = 0.24(23.9 - 0) + 0.0145\{597 + 0.45(23.9 - 0)\} = 14.55 \text{ kcal kg}^{-1}$$

Heat lost by the water is equal to the heat gained by air.

$$G_x C_x dT_x = G_y^1 dH_y$$

$$\frac{G_x C_x}{G_y^1} = \frac{H_{ya} - H_{yb}}{T_{xa} - T_{xb}}$$

When $\int G_y^1$ is minimum, equilibrium conditions exist in the tower and $H_{ya} = H_{ya}^*$ (enthalpy of moist air in equilibrium with entering water) $= 51.3$ kcal kg^{-1}.

$$\frac{G_x C_x}{G_y^1 \text{ min}} = \frac{51.3 - 14.55}{43.3 - 26.7} = 2.21$$

When $G_y^1 = 1.33 G_y^1$ min, H_{ya} will be different from H_{ya}^*.

$$\frac{G_x C_x}{1.33\, G_y^1 \min} = \frac{2.21}{1.33} = 1.66 = \frac{H_{ya} - 14.55}{43.3 - 26.7} \text{ and } Hy_a = 42.1 \text{ kcal (kg DA)}^{-1}.$$

The function $\frac{dH_y}{H_i - H_y}$ can be integrated graphically by plotting $\frac{1}{H_i - H_y}$ as ordinate against H_y as abscissa and determining the area under the curve between the limits, H_{ya} and H_{yb}, which is the number of transfer units. The H_i values required for this has to be taken from the equilibrium data. The H_{ya} and H_{yb} values have been computed. Other intervening values of H_y can be found by linear interpolation. Table 7.2 gives the data required for graphical integration.

NTU = $41.4 \times 0.1 = 4.14$

Figure 7.11 shows the graphical solution.

HTU is given in the problem as 0.53 m.

Total packed height, $Z_T = NTU \times HTU = 4.14 \times 0.53 = 2.19$ m

Table 7.2 Data for graphical integration

T_x	H_i	H_y	$\frac{1}{H_i - H_y}$
26.7	24.3	14.55	0.103
29.4	27.5	19.03	0.118
32.2	31.1	23.68	0.135
35.0	35.2	28.33	0.146
37.8	39.9	32.98	0.144
40.6	45.2	37.63	0.132
43.3	51.3	42.1	0.109

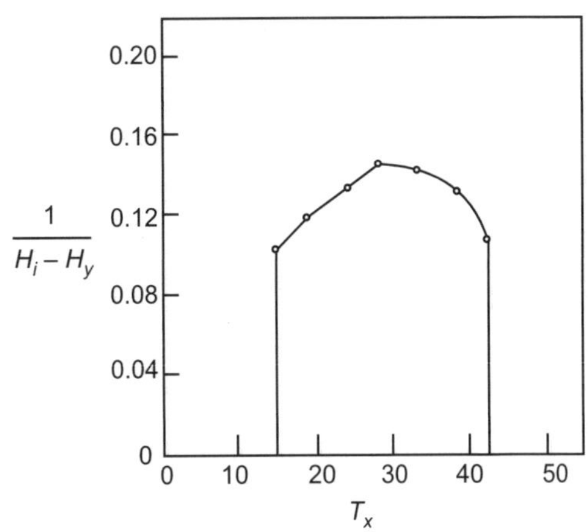

Fig. 7.11 Graphical integration for 7AA

7AB

Hot water at 45°C is to be cooled in an induced draft cooling tower by contact with air to a temperature of 29°C. Calculate the minimum dry air required in kg s^{-1} and the height of the packed tower, if the actual dry air rate is 11 kg s^{-1}.

Data:

Air: Temperature = 30°C, absolute humidity = 0.016 kg of moisture per kg of dry air.

Water: Temperature = 45°C, feed rate = 15 kg s^{-1}, heat capacity = 4.19 kJ $kg^{-1}\,°C^{-1}$.

Gas phase mass transfer coefficient (k_{ya}) = 0.9 kg m^{-3} $s^{-1}(\Delta y)^{-1}$

Equilibrium data:

Temperature of air (°C)	29	32.5	35	37.5	40	42.5	45
Enthalpy of moist air [kJ (kg of DA)$^{-1}$]	100	114	129.8	147	166.8	191	216

Solution

Enthalpy of the moist air at the inlet conditions is determined using the formula,

$$H_Y = C_B(T_{DB} - T_o) + Y\{\lambda_{DP} + C_{A,v}(T_{DB} - T_{DP})\}$$

$$H_{yb} = 1(30 - 0) + 0.016\{2\,500 + 1.88(30 - 0)\} = 70.9 \text{ kJ kg}^{-1}$$

Heat lost by water is equal to the heat gained by air.

$$G_x C_x dT_x = G_y^1 dH_y$$

When G_y^1 is minimum, equilibrium conditions exist in the tower and $H_{ya} = H_{ya}^*$ (enthalpy of moist air in equilibrium with entering water) = 216 kJ kg^{-1}.

$$15 \times 4.19 \times (45 - 29) = G_y^1 \min(216 - 70.9) \text{ and } G_y^1 \min = 6.845 \text{ kg s}^{-1}.$$

When the air rate is 11 kg s^{-1}, the enthalpy of moist air at the top of the tower is H_{ya}.

$$15 \times 4.19 \times (45 - 29) = 11 \times (H_{ya} - 70.9) \text{ and } H_{ya} = 162.25 \text{ kJ kg}^{-1}.$$

The function $\dfrac{dH_y}{H_i - H_y}$ can be integrated graphically by plotting $\dfrac{1}{H_i - H_y}$ as ordinate against H_y as abscissa and determining the area under the curve between the limits H_{ya} and H_{yb}, which is the number of transfer units. The H_i values required for this have to be taken from the equilibrium data. The H_{ya} and H_{yb} values have been computed. Other intervening values of H_y can be found by linear interpolation. Table 7.3 gives the data required for graphical integration.

$$\text{NTU} = 29.3 \times 0.01 \times 10 = 2.93$$

Figure 7.12 shows the graphical solution.

$$\text{HTU} = \frac{G_y^1}{k_y a} = \frac{11}{0.9} = 12.22 \text{ m}$$

Total packed height, Z_T = NTU × HTU = 2.93 × 12.22 = 35.8 m

Table 7.3 Data for graphical integration

T_x	H_i	H_y	$\frac{1}{H_i - H_y}$
29	100	70.9	0.034
32.5	114	90.88	0.041
35	129.8	105.15	0.041
37.5	147	119.42	0.036
40	166.8	133.69	0.030
42.5	191	147.96	0.023
45	216	162.25	0.019

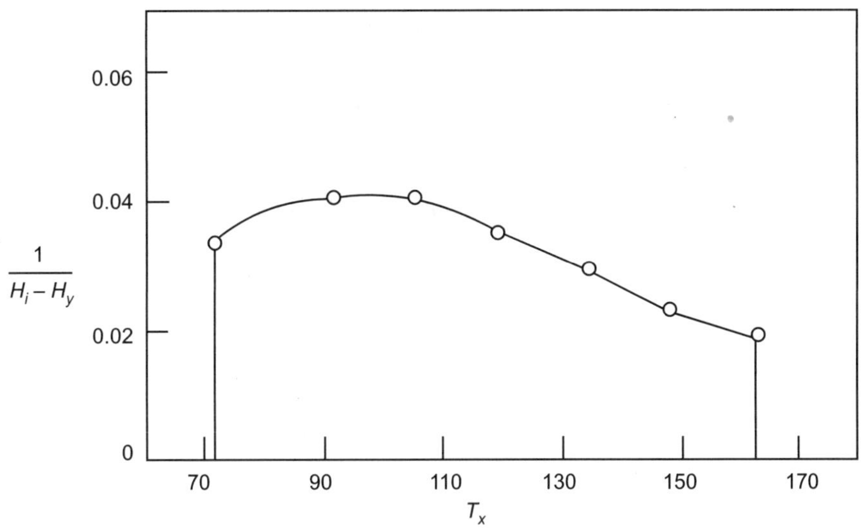

Fig. 7.12 Graphical integration for 7AB

7AC A counter current cooling unit is to be designed to cool 2 000 kg h^{-1} of water from 50°C to 30°C. Air is available at a dry bulb temperature of 30°C and a wet bulb temperature of 24°C. 20% excess air will be used and the gas phase mass transfer coefficient (k_{ya}) is 2 400 kg h^{-1} m^{-3}. Assuming the cross sectional area of the tower to be 1 m^2, estimate the height of the tower.

Temperature of air (°C)	25	30	35	40	45	50	55
Enthalpy of moist air [kcal (kg of DA)$^{-1}$]	19.1	23.9	31.8	40.4	51.3	63.1	82.1

Enthalpy of incoming air = 17.28 kcal per kg of dry air.

Solution

Enthalpy of the moist air at the inlet conditions (H_{yb}) = 17.28 kcal kg^{-1}

Heat lost by water is equal to heat gained by air.

$$G_x C_x dT_x = G_y^1 dH_y$$

Table 7.4 Data for graphical integration

H_x	H_i	H_y	$\frac{1}{H_i - H_y}$
30	23.9	17.28	0.151
35	31.8	26.83	0.201
40	40.4	36.37	0.248
45	51.3	45.92	0.189
50	63.1	55.46	0.131

When G_y^1 is minimum, equilibrium conditions exist in the tower and $H_{ya} = H_{ya}^*$ (enthalpy of moist air in equilibrium with entering water) = 63.1 kcal kg^{-1}.

2 000 × 1.0 × (50 – 30) = G_y^1min (63.1 – 17.28) and G_y^1min = 873 kg h^{-1}.

20% excess air is used.

$G_y^1 = 1.2 G_y^1$ min

$G_y^1 = 1.2 \times 873 = 1047.6$ kg h^{-1} and enthalpy of moist air at the top of the tower is H_{ya}.

$2\,000 \times 1.0 \times (50 - 30) = 1047.6 \times (H_{ya} - 17.28)$ and $H_{ya} = 55.46$ kcal kg^{-1}.

The function $\dfrac{dH_y}{H_i - H_y}$ can be integrated graphically by plotting $\dfrac{1}{H_i - H_y}$ as ordinate against H_y as abscissa and determining the area under the curve between the limits H_{ya} and H_{yb}, which is the number of transfer units. The H_i values required for this have to be taken from the equilibrium data. The H_{ya} and H_{yb} values have been computed. Other intervening values of H_y can be found by linear interpolation. Table 7.4 gives the data required for graphical integration.

NTU = $57 \times 0.025 \times 5 = 7.125$

Figure 7.13 shows the graphical solution.

$$\text{HTU} = \frac{G_y^1}{k_y a} = \frac{1\,047.6}{2\,400} = 0.4365 \text{ m}$$

Total packed height, $Z_T = NTU \times HTU = 7.125 \times 0.436\,5 = 3.11$ m

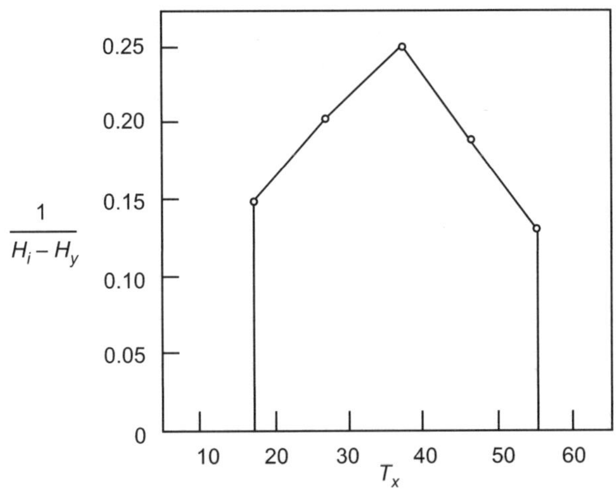

Fig. 7.13 Graphical integration for 7AC

7AD A process requires 6 000 kg h^{-1} of dry air at 20% humidity and 55°C. This air is to be obtained by conditioning air at 20% humidity and 25°C by first heating and then adiabatically humidifying to the desired humidity and finally reheating to the desired temperature. The humidifying step is carried out in a spray chamber. Assuming that the air leaving the spray chamber is to be 2°C warmer than the adiabatic saturation temperature, to what temperature must air be preheated, and at what temperature should it leave the spray chamber? How much of heat is required for preheating and reheating? If the gas phase heat transfer coefficient ($H_y a$) is 1500 Wm^{-3} $°C^{-1}$, what should be the volume of the spray chamber?

Solution

The problem has to be solved using the humidity chart.

Absolute humidity of inlet air (Y_{in}) = 0.005 kg of moisture per kg of dry air

Absolute humidity of conditioned air (Y_{out}) = 0.022 kg of moisture per kg of dry air

The final air is to be obtained by conditioning air at 20% humidity and 25°C by first heating, then humidifying adiabatically to the desired humidity (0.022 kg of moisture per kg of dry air) and finally reheating to the desired temperature, 55°C. The humidifying step is carried out in a spray chamber. The air is assumed to leave the spray chamber 2°C warmer than the adiabatic saturation temperature.

Adiabatic saturation temperature (T_{AS}), for which absolute humidity is 0.022 kg of moisture per kg of dry air at T_{AS} + 2°C, is 26°C. The air is to be preheated to 72°C before being fed to the spray chamber. Air leaves the spray chamber at 28°C.

Humid heat of air at inlet conditions = $1 + (0.005 \times 1.88) = 1.009\ 4$ kJ kg^{-1} $°C^{-1}$

Humid heat of air at the outlet of spray chamber

$$= 1 + (0.022 \times 1.88) = 1.041\ 4\ \text{kJ kg}^{-1}\ {}^\circ\text{C}^{-1}$$

Preheating duty $= 6\ 000 \times 1.0094 \times (72 - 25) = 284\ 651\ \text{kJ h}^{-1}$

Reheating duty $= 6\ 000 \times 1.041\ 4 \times (55 - 28) = 168\ 707\ \text{kJ h}^{-1}$

Total heat duty $= 453\ 358\ \text{kJ h}^{-1}$

Average humid heat $(\overline{C_Y}) = 1.025\ 4\ \text{kJ kg}^{-1}{}^\circ\text{C}^{-1}$

The volume of an adiabatic humidification chamber (V_T) can be determined using the formula derived earlier,

$$\ln \frac{T_{yb} - T_{AS}}{T_{Ya} - T_{AS}} = \frac{h_y a}{G_y^1 \overline{C_Y}} V_T$$

$$\ln \frac{72 - 26}{28 - 26} = \frac{1.5 \times 3\,600 \times V_T}{6\,000 \times 1.025\,4}$$

$$V_T = 3.572\ \text{m}^3$$

NOTATIONS

A	Component A, vapour phase of the liquid.
a	Interfacial surface area, m^2.
a_M	Area available for mass transfer, m^2.
a_H	Area available for heat transfer, m^2.
B	Component B, vapour-free gas in contact with the liquid.
C_y	Specific heat capacity of gas, kJ kg^{-1} K^{-1}.
C_x	Specific heat capacity of liquid, kJ kg^{-1} K^{-1}.
$C_{A,l}$	Specific heat of the liquid at constant pressure, kJ kg^{-1} K^{-1}.
$C_{A,v}$	Specific heat of the vapour at constant pressure, kJ kg^{-1} K^{-1}.
C_{PA}	Specific heat of vapour, kJ kg^{-1} K^{-1}.
C_Y	Humid heat, kJ (kg of dry air)$^{-1}$.
G_{xa}	Mass velocity of the liquid at the top of the contactor, kg m^{-2} s^{-1}.
G_{xb}	Mass velocity of the liquid at the bottom of the contactor, kg m^{-2} h^{-1}.
G_y^1	Mass velocity of the gas in terms of mass of vapour-free gas, kg m^{-2} h^{-1}.
G_{ya}	Mass velocity of the gas at the top of the contactor, kg m^{-2} h^{-1}.
G_{yb}	Mass velocity of the gas at the bottom of the contactor, kg m^{-2} h^{-1}.
H_A	Enthalpy of vapour per unit mass, kJ kg^{-1}.
H_B	Enthalpy of dry gas per unit mass, kJ kg^{-1}.
H_Y	Enthalpy of the humid gas per unit mass of dry gas, kJ kg^{-1}.

H_{xa} Specific enthalpy of the liquid at the top of the contactor, kJ kg^{-1}.
H_{xb} Specific enthalpy of the liquid at the bottom of the contactor, kJ kg^{-1}.
H_{ya} Specific enthalpy of the gas at the top of the contactor, kJ kg^{-1}.
H_{yb} Specific enthalpy of the gas at the bottom of the contactor, kJ kg^{-1}.
h_y Heat transfer coefficient based on the gas phase, W m^{-2} K^{-1}.
k_y Mass transfer coefficient based on the gas phase, kmol m^{-2} s^{-1} Δy^{-1}.
M_A Molecular weight of component A, liquid.
M_B Molecular weight of component B, gas.
m_A Mass of component A, kg.
m_B Mass of component B, kg.
N_A^1 Molar rate of vaporisation, kmol m^{-2} s^{-1}.
P Total pressure, N m^{-2}
Pr Prandtl number $\frac{C_P\mu}{k}$.
P_A Partial pressure of component A in the vapour–gas mixture, N m^{-2}.
P_A^* Vapour pressure of pure A in the liquid state, N m^{-2}.
q Rate of transfer of sensible heat, W.
Re Reynolds number $\frac{du\rho}{\mu}$.
S Cross sectional area of the tower, m^2.
Sc Schmidt number $\frac{\mu}{\rho D}$.
St_H Stanton number for heat transfer, $\frac{h_y}{C_P G}$.
St_M Stanton number for mass transfer, $\frac{M k_y}{G}$.
T Temperature in the bulk T_{DB}, K.
T_i Interphase temperature T_{WB}, K.
T_o Freezing point of the liquid which constitutes the vapour in the gaseous phase, K.
T_{AS} Adiabatic saturation temperature, K.
T_{DB} Dry bulb temperature, K.
T_{DP} Dew point, K.
T_{WB} Wet bulb temperature, K.
T_{xa} Temperature of the liquid at the top of the contactor, K.
T_{xb} Temperature of the liquid at the bottom of the contactor, K.
T_{ya} Temperature of the gas at the top of the contactor, K.
T_{yb} Temperature of the gas at the bottom of the contactor, K.
Y Absolute humidity, kg of vapour per kg of vapour-free gas.
Y_i Humidity at the interface, kg of vapour per kg of vapour-free gas.
Y_m Molal humidity, moles of vapour per mole of vapour-free gas.
Y_p Percentage humidity.
Y_r Relative humidity.
Y_s Saturation humidity, kg of vapour per kg of vapour-free gas.
Y_{S,A_S} Saturation humidity at T_{AS}, kg of vapour per kg of vapour-free gas.
Y_{WB} Absolute humidity at T_{WB}, kg of vapour per kg of vapour-free gas.
y Mole fraction of the vapour.
y_i Mole fraction of the vapour at the interphase.

$(1-y)_{lm}$	Log mean mole fraction difference for vfg.
V_T	Total contact volume, m^3.
V_y	Humid volume, m^3 (kg of dry gas)$^{-1}$.
vfg	Vapour free gas.
Z_T	Height of the contact zone, m.
dz	Height of a small section of tower at a distance Z from the bottom of the contact zone, m.
λ_{WB}	Latent heat of vaporisation at T_{WB}, kJ kg^{-1}.
λ_{AS}	Latent heat of vaporisation at T_{AS}, kJ kg^{-1}.
λ_{DP}	Latent heat of vaporisation of the liquid at T_{DP}, kJ kg^{-1}.
Δ	Difference.

REFERENCES

1. Parker RO and Treybal RE, *Chem. Eng. Prog. Symp. Ser.*, **57**: 132 (1960).
2. Lewis WK, *Trans A I M E.*, **44**: 325 (1922).
3. Grosvenor WM, *Trans A I Ch E.*, **1**: 184 (1908).
4. Hensley JC (ed), *Cooling Tower Fundamentals*, Second ed., Overland park, KS, Marley Cooling Tower Co., 1998.
5. McKelvey KK and Brooke M, *The Industrial Cooling Tower*, Princeton, NJ, Van Nostrand, 1940.

Problems for Practice

7.1 Air at a temperature of 293 K and pressure 0.987×105 N m^{-2} has a relative humidity of 80%. Calculate (i) the molal humidity, (ii) the molal humidity if the temperature is reduced to 283 K and pressure increased to 2.38×10^5 N m^{-2} condensing some of the water, (iii) the weight of the condensed water from 29.3 m^3 of original wet air in cooling and compressing to the conditions as mentioned in part (ii) and (iv) the final weight of wet air of part (III). The vapour pressures are 0.023×105 and $0.001\,2 \times 105$ N m^{-2} at 293 K and 283 K respectively.

7.2 In a solvent recovery unit, 50 kg of acetone is to be recovered by a stream of nitrogen. Nitrogen is admitted at 308 K and 100 kPa pressure. The partial pressure of acetone in the incoming nitrogen is 1.33 kPa. The gases leave at 303 K and 98 kPa pressure with 90% saturated vapour. Find the volume of nitrogen required and the volume of the gases leaving the unit. The vapour pressure of acetone at 303 K is 36 kPa.

7.3 Air entering a drier has a dew point of 280 K, while that of leaving air is 290 K. If 2500 kg of wet air is forced through the drier, how many kg of water is removed?

Assume that the total pressure remains the same at 100 kN m^{-2}. The vapour pressures of water at 280 K and 290 K are 1 kN m^{-2} and 2 kN m^{-2} respectively.

7.4 What is the minimum number of m^3 of dry air at 298 K and 100 kPa that is necessary to evaporate 11.7 kg of benzene if the total pressure remains constant? Assume that the air blown over the benzene for it to evaporate leaves at 100 kPa. The vapour pressure of benzene at 298 K is 10 kPa.

7.5 Air at 333 K and 101.3 kPa having a percentage humidity of 10% is fed to drier at the rate of 1 000 m^3 h^{-1}. In the drier, water is removed from a wet solid material at the rate of 20 kg h^{-1}. Air leaves the drier at 313 K and 98.6 kPa. Compute the flow rate of air leaving the drier. The vapour pressure of water at 333 K is 20 kPa.

7.6 A mixture of dry flue gases and acetone at a pressure of 100 kPa has a dew point of 298 K. It is proposed that 90% of the acetone should be condensed by cooling to 278 K and compressing to a suitable pressure. Calculate the final pressure of the mixture. The vapour pressure of acetone is 30.66 kPa and 12 kPa at 298 K and 278 K respectively.

7.7 The dry bulb temperature and dew point of ambient air were found to be 302 K and 291 K respectively. The barometer reads 100 kPa. Compute (i) the absolute molal humidity, (ii) the absolute humidity, (iii) the percentage relative humidity, (iv) the percentage saturation, (v) the humid heat and (vi) the humid volume. The vapour pressure of water is 2.062 kPa and 4.004 kPa at 291 K and 302 K respectively.

7.8 At 320 K, benzene exerts a vapour pressure of 26.66 kPa. If a mixture of 20 mol% benzene in nitrogen at 320 K and 106.63 kPa pressure is isothermally compressed until the final gaseous volume becomes 20% of the original volume, what weight of benzene is condensed per 1 000 m^3 of the original mixture?

7.9 Dry nitrogen is bubbled through benzene at 106.63 kPa and 323 K at a rate of 100 m^3 per minute. Nitrogen saturated with benzene vapour leaves at 98.63 kPa and 313 K at a rate of 138.5 m^3 per minute. Calculate the vapour pressure of benzene at 313 K and the composition of the final mixture in kg of benzene vapour per kg of nitrogen.

7.10 A mixture of carbon dioxide and benzene vapour at 160 kPa and 323 K has a percentage saturation of 60. Compute molal humidity, absolute humidity, relative humidity, mole fraction of benzene vapour, humid volume and humid heat. Data: vapour pressure of benzene at 323 K is 36.65 kPa, heat capacity values of carbon dioxide and benzene vapour are 36 J mol^{-1} K^{-1} and 74 J mol^{-1} K^{-1} respectively.

7.11 For atmospheric air of 60% humidity at 310 K temperature, what are the values of dry bulb, wet bulb, dew point and adiabatic saturation temperatures? This air is preheated to 350 K and passed through a humidifier where it is adiabatically saturated. The air leaves with 80% humidity. What is the temperature and humidity of exit air?

7.12 The air supply to a drier has a dry bulb temperature of 313 K and a wet bulb temperature of 308 K. It is heated to 393 K and blown into a drier. It cools in the drier along an adiabatic saturation line and leaves at 90% saturation. Compute the dew point of the initial air, absolute humidity, percentage humidity and the amount of water evaporated per 100 m^3 of entering air and the temperature on leaving the drier.

7.13 Air is available at a dry bulb temperature of 303 K and a wet bulb temperature of 298 K. Determine its humidity, percentage saturation, humid volume, enthalpy and dew point.

7.14 Air at 355 K having a humidity of 0.065 5 kg of water per kg of dry air is contacted in an adiabatic saturator with water. It leaves at 80% saturation. What are the final values of humidity and temperature? For 100% saturation, what will the values of humidity and temperature be?

7.15 An air–water vapour mixture has a dry bulb temperature of 328 K and a molal humidity of 0.048 at 1 atm pressure. Find the percentage humidity, relative humidity, humid heat, humid volume, enthalpy. Data: vapour pressure of water at 328 K is 118 mm Hg, heat capacity of water vapour and that of dry air are 1 884 J kg^{-1} K^{-1} and 1 005 J kg^{-1} K^{-1} respectively, latent heat of vaporisation of water is 2 502 kJ kg^{-1}.

7.16 Air enters an adiabatic saturator at a temperature of 350 K and a dew point of 314 K. It leaves the saturator at 90% saturation. What are the final values of humidity and temperature?

7.17 The air in a room has a humidity of 0.021 kg of water per kg of dry air at 305 K and 101.3 kPa. Calculate the percentage humidity and relative humidity.

7.18 A mixture of nitrogen and acetone vapour at 133 kPa and 298 K has a percentage saturation of 80. Compute the molal humidity, absolute humidity, relative humidity, vol% of acetone vapour, humid volume and humid heat. Data: vapour pressure of acetone at 298 K is 38.65 kPa. Specific heat of nitrogen and acetone vapour are 1 kJ kg^{-1} K^{-1} and 1.46 kJ kg^{-1} K^{-1} respectively.

7.19 A packed counter current cooling tower is used to cool water from 328 K to 298 K by air. The liquid flow rate is 1000 kg h^{-1} m^{-2}. The entering air is at 298 K and 20% relative humidity. The entire resistance to mass transfer lies in the gas phase. The value of $k_y a = 0.2$ kg m^{-3} s^{-1} $(\Delta y)^{-1}$. Estimate the minimum air flow rate when the vapour pressure of water at 298 K is measured as 2.53 kPa. Using a gas flow rate of 1.5 times the minimum, estimate the height of tower.

Equilibrium data is as follows:

Temperature (K)	293	303	313	323	328
Enthalpy (kJ per kg of dry air)	60.7	101.8	166.5	278.7	354.9

7.20 Air with a dry bulb temperature of 311 K and a wet bulb temperature of 300 K is to be dried by first cooling to 289 K to condense water vapour and then heated to 297 K. Calculate the initial humidity and percentage humidity. Also calculate the final humidity and percentage humidity.

7.21 Air entering a dryer has a dry bulb temperature of 339 K and a wet bulb temperature of 309 K at 1 atm. Determine its humidity, percentage humidity, relative humidity, dew point, enthalpy and vol% of water vapour.

7.22 A mixture of CS_2 vapour and air contains 23.32% CS_2 by vol. Calculate the relative saturation and percentage saturation of the mixture at 293 K and 98.63 kPa pressure. The vapour pressure of CS_2 at 293 K is 39.98 kPa.

7.23 Conditioned air at 101.3 kPa pressure, 323 K and a humidity of 0.01 kg of water per kg of bone dry air enters a dryer. It leaves the dryer at 101.3 kPa pressure and 323 K with 83% relative humidity. The vapour pressure of water at 323 K is 12.33 kPa. If 50 kg of water enters into the air stream per hour, calculate the weight of bone dry air flowing through the dryer.

7.24 Fresh air at 298 K in which the partial pressure of water vapour is 2 kPa is blown initially through a preheater at the rate of 215 $m^3 \ h^{-1}$ and then adiabatically saturated in a spray chamber to 100% saturation and again reheated. This reheated air has a humidity of 0.24 kg of water vapour per kg of dry air. It is assumed that the fresh air and the air leaving the reheaters have the same percentage humidity. Determine the temperature of air after preheater, spray chamber and reheater, and the heat requirements for preheating and reheating.

7.25 For atmospheric air of 60% humidity at 303 K, what are the values of dry bulb, wet bulb, dew point and adiabatic saturation temperatures? This atmospheric air is preheated to 348 K and passed through a drier where it is adiabatically saturated. The air leaves with 75% humidity. What is the temperature and humidity of the exit air?

7.26 An air–water sample has a wet bulb temperature 296 K and a dry bulb temperature of 329 K at 1 atm pressure. Calculate (i) percentage humidity (ii) absolute humidity (iii) volume of dry air (iv) humid heat (v) dew point (vi) humid volume (vii) enthalpy of air. Data: Specific heat of dry air = 1 005 J $kg^{-1} \ K^{-1}$, specific heat of water vapour = 1 883 J $kg^{-1} \ K^{-1}$, latent heat of vaporisation = 2 500 kJ kg^{-1}.

7.27 Calculate (i) molal humidity (ii) absolute humidity (iii) relative humidity and (iv) percentage humidity of air which is at 302 K and at 100 kPa. The dew point of air is 291 K, the vapour pressure of water at 291 K = 2.06 Kpa and the vapour pressure of water at 302 K = 4.00 kPa.

7.28 Fresh air available at a dry bulb temperature of 301 K and wet bulb temperature of 293 K is preheated at 363 K and introduced into a drier. In the drier, it cools along the adiabatic cooling line and leaves the drier 90% saturated. Estimate the (i) dew point and humidity of the inlet air, (ii) exit temperature of air leaving the drier, (iii) water removed in the drier per 100 m^3 of fresh air and (iv) heat needed to heat 100 m^3 of fresh air in the preheater.

7.29 A plant requires 2 000 kg min^{-1} of cooling water to flow through its distillation equipment condensers. The water will leave the condensers at 323 K. It is planned to design a counter current cooling tower in order to cool this water to 303 K from 323 K, by contact with air. Air is available at a dry bulb temperature of 303 K and and a wet bulb temperature of 297 K. 30% excess air will be used and make up water will enter at 288 K. For the packing to be used, the mass transfer coefficient is expected to be 2 500 kg h^{-1} $m^{-3}(\Delta Y)^{-1}$, provided the minimum liquid rate and gas rate are 12 000 and 10 000 kg h^{-1} m^{-2} respectively. Estimate the height of the cooling tower.

8

Drying

In drying of solids, a liquid (usually water) is removed by a hot and dry gas. Drying is a relative term; it merely means reduction in liquid content from an initial value to a desired final value. Background information required for designing drying equipment is provided in this chapter.

Drying generally refers to the removal of a liquid from a solid by vaporisation. It is the final operation in a manufacturing process. It often follows evaporation, filtration or crystallisation. The product from the dryer is ready for final packing or dispatch. If the material to be dried has a large amount of liquid, the major portion of the liquid is first removed by mechanical means using presses or centrifuges and the solid with residual liquid is subjected to drying to reduce the liquid content to the desirable level by vaporisation. The efficiency of the drying operation depends on the effective utilisation of heat.
The purpose of drying is

1. to reduce the transport cost,
2. to make the material more suitable for handling; for example, soap powder, fertiliser,
3. to provide definite properties such as the free flowing nature of salt, and
4. to remove moisture that may otherwise lead to corrosion; for example, drying of coal gas.

PRINCIPLES OF DRYING

When a solid dries, two simultaneous processes occur. (i) Heat is transferred to vaporise the liquid. Heat transfer may be by conduction, convection, radiation or a combination of these. Irrespective of the mode of heat transfer, heat must flow to the outer surface and then into the interior of the solid. (ii) Mass is transferred as a liquid or vapour within the solid and as vapour from the surface. Movement of moisture within the solid is the result of a concentration gradient which depends on the characteristics of the solid. The factors governing the rates of these processes determine the drying rate.

HEAT TRANSFER IN DRYERS

Drying of wet solids is a thermal process. Materials can be dried by heating them well above the boiling point of the liquid. In most drying operations, the drying rates are limited by heat transfer and not by mass transfer. Hence, most dryers are designed based on heat transfer considerations alone.

Calculation of Heat Duty

Heat must be applied to a dryer to accomplish the following:

1. to heat the feed solid and liquid to the vaporisation temperature (T_v),
2. to vaporise the liquid,
3. to heat the solids to the final temperature, and
4. to heat the vapours to the final temperature.

If $\mathring{m}_s$ is the mass of bone dry (moisture free) solids to be dried per unit time, X_a and X_b are the initial and final liquid contents in mass of liquid per unit mass of bone dry solid, the quantity of heat transferred per unit mass of solid is $\frac{q_T}{\mathring{m}_s}$.

$$\frac{q_T}{\mathring{m}_s} = C_s(T_{sb} - T_{sa}) + X_a C_l(T_v - T_{sa}) + (X_a - X_b)\lambda_{Tv} + X_b C_l(T_{sb} - T_v) + (X_a - X_b)C_v(T_{vb} - T_v) \tag{8.1}$$

where T_{sa} = feed temperature, T_v = vaporisation temperature, T_{sb} = final solids temperature, T_{vb} = final vapour temperature, λ_{Tv} = latent heat of vaporisation at T_v and C_s, C_l, C_v are the specific heats of the solid, liquid and vapour respectively. In equation (8.1), specific heat and latent heat of vaporisation are assumed to be temperature independent and the entire vaporisation takes place at T_v. Though these conditions are rarely met, the above equation gives a quantitative estimate of the heat transfer rate if the temperatures are known.

In an adiabatic drier, T_v is the wet bulb temperature (T_{WB}) and T_{vb} is the exit gas temperature (T_{gb}). The heat transferred to the solid, liquid and vapour comes from the cooling of the gas. The heat balance in this case gives

$$q_T = \mathring{m}_g(1 + Y_a)C_{Ya}(T_{ga} - T_{gb}) \tag{8.2}$$

Here, $\mathring{m}_g$ is mass rate of the dry gas, Y_a is the humidity of the gas at the inlet and C_{Ya} is the humid heat of the gas at the inlet.

Heat Transfer Coefficients

The basic heat transfer equation used in dryer calculations is

$$q_T = UA\overline{\Delta T} \tag{8.3}$$

$\overline{\Delta T}$ is the average temperature difference and not the log mean temperature difference. If U, A and $\overline{\Delta T}$ are known, the capacity of the drier can be estimated. Usually, the total surface area of the solid particles (A) exposed to a heated surface or hot gas is difficult to estimate precisely. So, driers are designed based on the volumetric heat transfer coefficient.

$$q_T = U_a V\overline{\Delta T} \tag{8.4}$$

where U_a is the volumetric heat transfer coefficient in W m^{-3} K^{-1}, V is the volume of the dryer in m^3 and $\overline{\Delta T}$ is the average temperature difference in K. Because of the wide variations in the type of dryer and the particles being dried, no universal heat transfer correlation is available for designing driers. U has to be found by experimentation at the actual conditions.

MASS TRANSFER IN DRYERS

In dryers, in which a gas is passed over or through the solids, the mass must be transferred from the surface of the solid to the gas and sometimes through the interior channels of the solid. In all such cases, the resistance to mass transfer controls the drying rate. With respect to the gas, drying is more like adiabatic humidification. With respect to the solid, it is like evaporation when the solid is very wet, and like solvent desorption from an adsorbent when the solid is nearly dry.

The average mass transfer rate, $\mathring{m}_v$ is given by

$$\mathring{m}_v = \mathring{m}_s(X_a - X_b) \tag{8.5}$$

where $\mathring{m}_v$ = mass flow rate of vapour, $\mathring{m}_s$ = mass flow rate of solid, X_a = initial moisture content and X_b = final moisture content.

If the gas enters at humidity Y_a and leaves with humidity Y_b then

$$Y_b = Y_a + \frac{\mathring{m}_s(X_a - X_b)}{\mathring{m}_g}$$

$$= Y_a + \frac{\mathring{m}_v}{\mathring{m}_g} \tag{8.6}$$

where $\mathring{m}_g$ is the mass flow rate of gas.

PHASE EQUILIBRIUM

In drying operations, the relationship between the moisture content of the solid being dried and the relative humidity (Y_r) of the gas is the equilibrium relation as shown in Fig. 8.1. When a wet solid is brought into contact with air of lower humidity than that corresponding to the moisture content of the solid, the solid tends to lose moisture and dry to attain equilibrium with the air. When air is more humid than the solid in equilibrium with it, the solid absorbs moisture from the air, until equilibrium is attained. In fluid phases, the diffusion is governed by concentration differences expressed in mole fraction. In a wet solid, the moisture content is expressed in mass of water per unit mass of bone dry solid.

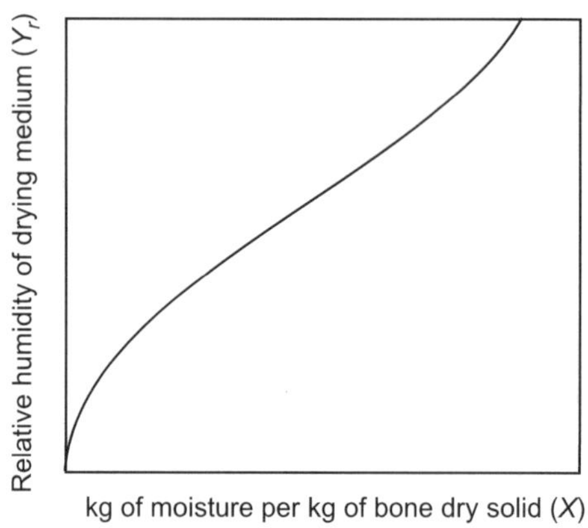

Fig. 8.1 Equilibrium curve for drying operation

Equilibrium Moisture and Free Moisture

Air entering a dryer is not always dry, but contains some moisture and has a definite Y_r. For air of definite humidity, the moisture content of the solid leaving the dryer cannot be less than the equilibrium moisture content corresponding to the humidity of the entering air. The portion of water in the wet solid which cannot be removed by the inlet air is called the equilibrium moisture (X^*). Free moisture is the difference between the moisture content of the feed solid and the equilibrium moisture content.

$$X = X_a - X^* \tag{8.7}$$

where X = free moisture and X_a = moisture content of feed solid.

Bound Water and Unbound Water

Bound water refers to the moisture contained by a substance which exerts a vapour pressure less than that of pure liquid at that temperature. Unbound water refers to the moisture contained by a substance which exerts a vapour pressure equal to that of the pure liquid at the same temperature. Substances containing bound water are hygroscopic in general. Bound water may exist under several conditions. Liquid water in fine capillaries exerts abnormally low vapour pressure because of the highly concave curvature of the surface, moisture in cell and fibre walls may suffer a lowering in vapour pressure because of the presence of dissolved solids, water in natural organic substances is in physical and chemical combination the nature and strength of which vary with the nature and moisture content of the solid. Because of all these criteria, bound moisture exerts a lower vapour pressure. On the other hand, unbound water is largely held in the voids of the solid and hence exerts its full vapour pressure.

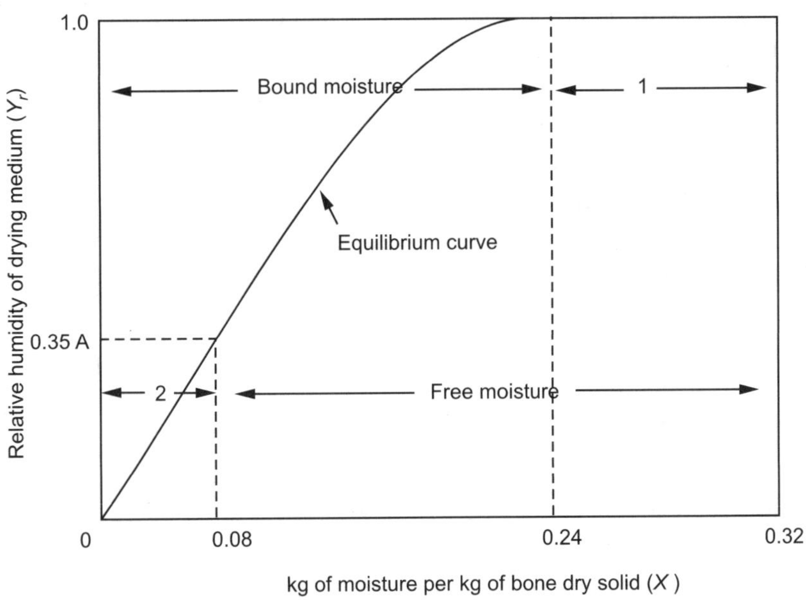

Fig. 8.2 Bound and unbound moisture (1: unbound moisture, 2: equilibrium moisture)

A typical equilibrium moisture curve for a substance is given in Fig. 8.2. If the equilibrium moisture curve for a substance intersects the 100% relative humidity line at 24% moisture, any sample of the substance that contains less than 24% water contains only bound water. Any moisture that a sample may contain above 24% is unbound water. If the sample contains 32% water, then the bound water is 24% and the unbound water is 8%. If the sample is dried with air of 35% relative humidity, the moisture content of the solid in equilibrium with the drying medium, as seen from the equilibrium moisture curve, is 8%. The equilibrium moisture content under this set of conditions is 8% which is the lowest moisture content that can be reached. If a sample containing 32% moisture content is dried with air at 35% Y_r,

$$X = X_a - X^* = 32 - 8 = 24\%$$

As evident from the above, the distinction between bound and unbound water depends on the material being dried, while the distinction between free and equilibrium moisture depends on the drying conditions.

In drying operations, moisture content may be expressed on a wet or dry basis. If nothing is specified, wet basis has to be presumed.

ILLUSTRATION

8A A wet solid is to be dried from 60% to 5% moisture on a wet basis. Compute the moisture to be evaporated per 1 000 kg of the dried product.

Solution

Basis: 1 000 kg of dried product.

$$\text{Initial moisture content} = \frac{60}{40} = 1.5\,\text{kg of water per kg of dry solid.}$$

$$\text{Final moisture content} = \frac{5}{95} = 0.052\ 7\ \text{kg of water per kg of dry solid.}$$

Dried product contains 5% moisture and the balance 95% is dry solid.

Dry solid in the product $= 1\ 000 \times 0.95 = 950$ kg

Moisture to be evaporated $= 950 \times (1.5 - 0.052\ 7) = 1\ 374.94$ kg

RATE OF DRYING [1–3]

In order to setup drying schedules and to determine the size of the equipment, the time required to dry a substance with a particular moisture content to another, under specified conditions, has to be known. The rate of drying can be determined for a sample of a substance by suspending it from a balance inside a cabinet or duct in a stream of air. The weight of the sample being dried is to be measured as a function of time. If the data are to be of maximum utility, the conditions should resemble those expected to prevail in the contemplated large scale operation as closely as possible.

1. The sample should be supported in the same manner in a tray or frame.
2. It should have the same ratio of drying to non-drying surface.
3. It should be subjected to similar conditions of radiant heat transfer.
4. The air should have the same temperature, humidity, velocity and direction of flow with respect to the sample.

Exposing the drying specimen to air of constant temperature, humidity, velocity and direction of flow constitutes drying at constant drying conditions. When the data obtained during such a test is used for plotting a curve of moisture content as a function of time, it results in a curve similar to the one shown in Fig. 8.3. A lot of information can be obtained if the data are converted into drying flux (N) expressed as mass per area in unit time and plotted against moisture content (Fig. 8.4).

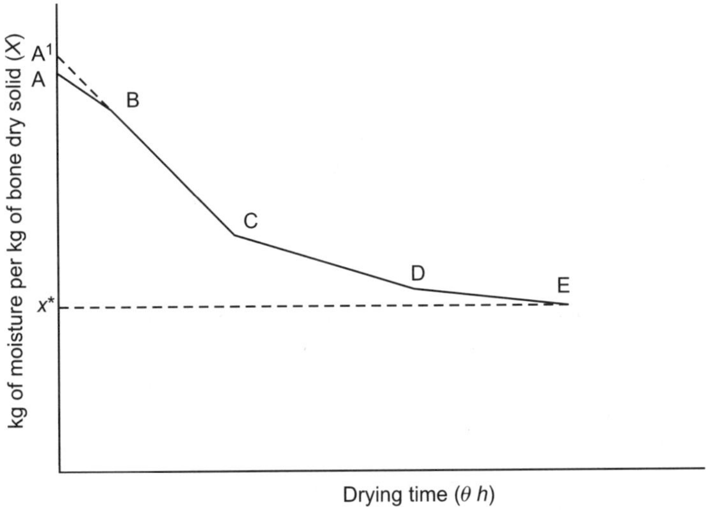

Fig. 8.3 Drying curve

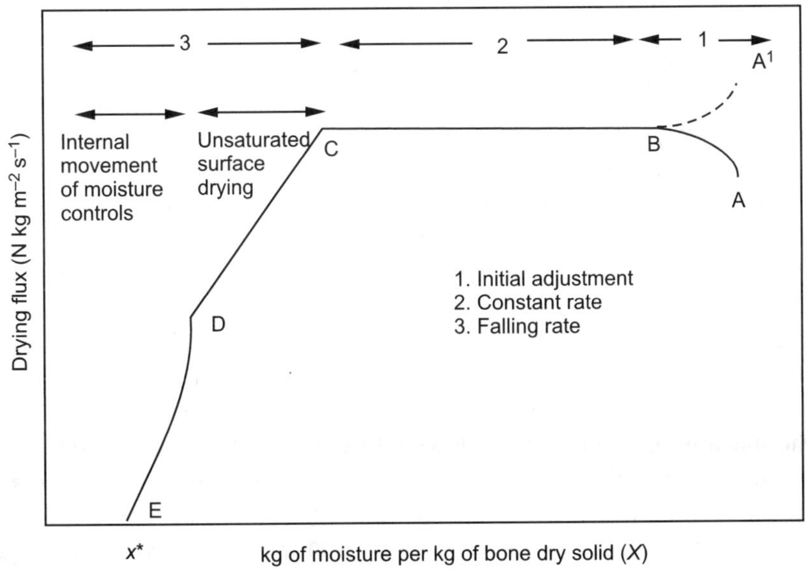

Fig. 8.4 Drying rate curve

$$N = \frac{\mathring{m}_s}{A\,\Delta\theta} \times \Delta X \tag{8.8}$$

Here, $\mathring{m}_s$ is the mass flow rate of dry solid, A is the wet surface over which the gas blows and through which evaporation takes place in the case of cross air circulation drying; A is the cross section of the bed measured at right angles to the direction of air flow in the case of thorough circulation drying, ΔX is the reduction in moisture content and $\Delta\theta$ is the drying time.

The rate curve usually has two major parts, a period of constant rate and one of falling rate. If the solid is initially very wet, the surface will be covered with a thin film of liquid which is entirely unbound moisture. When it is exposed to relatively dry air, evaporation will take place from the surface. The rate at which moisture evaporates can be described in terms of gas phase mass transfer k_y, as follows.

$$N = k_y(Y_s - Y) \text{ for cross circulation drying} \tag{8.9}$$

Here, Y is the absolute humidity of air and Y_s is the saturation humidity of air at the liquid surface temperature T_s. As evaporation of moisture absorbs latent heat, the liquid surface will attain an equilibrium temperature quickly and remain at that throughout the process. At equilibrium, rate of heat flow from the surroundings is equal to the rate of heat absorption. Hence, Y_s will remain constant. The capillaries and interstices of the solid that are filled with liquid deliver the liquid to the surface as rapidly as it evaporates. Under constant drying conditions, N should remain constant (Fig. 8.4) between B and C and it is denoted by N_c. During drying at the initial stage, both the solid and liquid surfaces will be colder than the equilibrium surface temperature T_s and the evaporation rate will increase while the surface temperature reaches the equilibrium value during the period AB. This initial period is usually so short that is ignored in subsequent analysis.

When the average moisture content of the solid has reached a value X_c, the critical moisture content, moisture has been so reduced by evaporation that further drying causes spots to appear upon the surface. These spots occupy increasingly larger proportions of the exposed surface as drying proceeds. However, the rate N is computed based on constant gross area A; the value of N must fall even though the rate per unit wet surface area remains constant. This gives rise to first part of the falling rate period, the period of unsaturated surface drying from points C to D. Ultimately, the original surface film of liquid would have entirely evaporated at an average moisture content corresponding to point D. This part of the curve may be missing entirely or it may constitute the whole of the falling rate period.

On further drying, the rate at which moisture can move through the solid as a result of concentration gradients existing between deeper parts and the surface is the controlling step. As the moisture concentration is lowered by drying, the rate of internal movement of moisture decreases. In some cases, evaporation may take place beneath the surface of the solid in a plane or zone which retreats deeper into the solid as the drying proceeds. The rate of drying falls even more rapidly than before from D to E. At point E, the moisture content of the solid has fallen to the equilibrium value X^* for the prevailing air humidity and drying stops.

TIME OF DRYING

Rate of drying by definition is

$$N - \frac{-\mathring{m}_s}{A}\frac{dX}{d\theta} \tag{8.10}$$

The time required to reduce the moisture content from X_a to X_b is

$$\int_0^\theta d\theta = \frac{+\mathring{m}_s}{A}\int_{X_b}^{X_a}\frac{dX}{N} \tag{8.11}$$

$$\theta = \frac{\mathring{m}_s}{N\,A}(X_a - X_b) \tag{8.12}$$

if N is constant. This is the general equation. But, the actual case is not this simple.

Case I

The entire drying takes place within the constant rate period. That is, X_a and $X_b < X_c$ and $N = N_c$. It follows from equation (8.12) that,

$$\theta = \frac{\mathring{m}_s}{N_c A}(X_a - X_b)$$

Case II

The entire drying takes place within the falling rate period. That is, X_a, $X_b < X_c$ and drying occurs under conditions of changing N.

General Case

The plot of $\frac{1}{N}$ versus X is a curve. Equation (8.1) can be integrated graphically by determining the area under the curve of $\frac{1}{N}$ as ordinate and X as abscissa. Figure 8.5 gives a typical graphical solution.

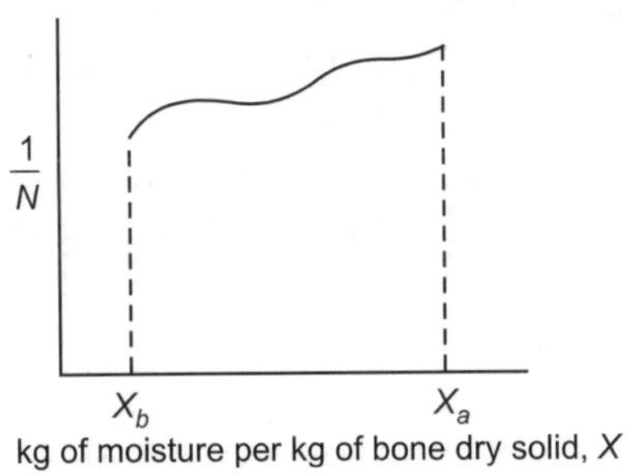

Fig. 8.5 Graphical integration for finding drying time

Special Case

N is linear in X. That is, a plot of $\frac{1}{N}$ versus X is a straight line.

$N = m_X + b$, where m is the slope of the linear portion of the curve and b is a constant.

Equation (8.1) then becomes

$$\int_0^\theta d\theta = \frac{+\mathring{m}_s}{A} \int_{X_b}^{X_a} \frac{dX}{mX + b} \tag{8.13}$$

$$\theta = \frac{\mathring{m}_s}{mA} \ln \frac{mX_a + b}{mX_b + b}$$

$$= \frac{\mathring{m}_s}{mA} \ln \frac{N_a}{N_b} \tag{8.14}$$

because $mX_b + b = N_b$ and $mX_a + b = N_a$

$$N_a - N_b = mX_a + b - mX_b - b = m(X_a - X_b) \tag{8.15}$$

$$m = \frac{N_a - N_b}{X_a - X_b} \tag{8.16}$$

$$\theta = \frac{\mathring{m}_s}{A} \frac{(X_a - X_b)}{(N_a - N_b)} \ln \frac{N_a}{N_b}$$

$$= \frac{\mathring{m}_s}{A N_{lm}} (X_a - X_b) \tag{8.17}$$

where N_{lm} is the log mean of the drying rates N_b and N_a.

Case III

The drying has both a constant rate period and a falling rate period. During the constant rate period, the initial moisture content X_a is reduced to the critical moisture content X_c and further moisture reduction to the final moisture content X_b takes place during the falling rate period. During the constant rate period, the duration of drying is denoted by θ_c and the drying flux is denoted by N_c. The duration of drying during the falling rate period is denoted by θ_f.

$$\theta_c = \frac{\mathring{m}_s}{AN_c} (X_a - X_c) \tag{8.18}$$

$$\theta_f = \frac{\mathring{m}_s}{AN_c}\frac{(X_c - X_b)}{(N_c - N_b)}\ln\frac{N_c}{N_b} \tag{8.19}$$

If the entire falling rate curve is a straight line between points C and E, then

$$N = m(X - X^*) \tag{8.20}$$

$$N_c = m(X_c - X^*) \tag{8.21}$$

$$N_b = m(X_b - X^*) \tag{8.22}$$

$$\frac{N_c}{N_b} = \frac{X_c - X^*}{X_b - X^*} \tag{8.23}$$

$$N_b = N_c\frac{X_b - X^*}{X_c - X^*} \tag{8.24}$$

$$\frac{X_c - X_b}{N_c - N_b} = \frac{(X_c - X^*) - (X_b - X^*)}{N_c - N_c\dfrac{(X_b - X^*)}{(X_c - X^*)}}$$

$$= \frac{(X_c - X^*) - (X_b - X^*)}{\dfrac{N_c[(X_c - X^*) - (X_b - X^*)]}{(X_c - X^*)}} = \frac{(X_c - X^*)}{N_c} \tag{8.25}$$

Using equations (8.23) and (8.25) in the equation for θ_f

$$\theta_f = \frac{\mathring{m}_s}{AN_c}(X_c - X^*)\ln\frac{X_c - X^*}{X_b - X^*} \tag{8.26}$$

$$\theta = \theta_c + \theta_f \tag{8.27}$$

$$= \frac{\mathring{m}_s}{AN_c}\left\{(X_a - X_c) + (X_c - X^*)\ln\frac{X_c - X^*}{X_b - X^*}\right\} \tag{8.28}$$

EMPIRICAL RELATION FOR RATE OF DRYING DURING A CONSTANT RATE PERIOD

N_c can be estimated with fair precision from correlations developed for evaporation from a free liquid surface. The calculations may be based on mass transfer or heat transfer as explained below.

$$\mathring{m}_v = \frac{M_v k_y (y_i - y)A}{(1 - y)_{lm}}$$

$$= \frac{h_y(T - T_i)A}{\lambda_i} \tag{8.29}$$

In the above expressions, $\mathring{m}_v$ is the rate of evaporation, A is the drying area, h_y is the heat transfer coefficient, k_y is the mass transfer coefficient, M_v is the molecular weight of vapour, T is temperature of the gas, T_i is the temperature of interface, y is the mole fraction of the vapour in the gas, y_i is the mole fraction of vapour at the interface and λ_i is the latent heat of vaporisation at T_i.

When the air is flowing parallel to the surface of the solid, the heat transfer coefficient can be estimated by the dimensional equation [4].

$$h_y = 14.3G^{0.8} \tag{8.30}$$

When the flow is perpendicular to the surface, the equation [5] is $h_y = 24.2G^{0.37}$, where h_y is in W m^{-2} K^{-1}and G is in kg m^{-2} s^{-1}.

The constant drying rate $N_c = \dfrac{\mathring{m}_v}{A} = h_y\dfrac{(T - T_i)}{\lambda_i}$ (8.31)

T_i may be assumed to be equal to T_{WB} of air. Heat transfer is assumed to be by convection only. When heat transfer by convection and radiation are not negligible, T_i is more than T_{WB} and N_c will increase.

ILLUSTRATIONS

8B A laboratory drying test was made on a 0.5 m × 0.5 m sample of a fibrous board-like material. The sample was suspended from a balance and the drying took place from the two large faces. Time versus weight data is given below:

Time (h)	0	0.1	0.2	0.4	1.0	3.0	5.0	6.0	8.0
Weight (kg)	10.625	10.597	10.548	10.470	10.225	9.412	8.852	8.67	8.507

Time (h)	10.0	12.0	14.0	16.0
Weight (kg)	8.448	8.423	8.420	8.420

The dry weight of the sample was 8.301 kg. Plot the rate of drying curve and tabulate the characteristics.

Solution The results are tabulated as given in Table 8.1.

The moisture content is calculated on dry basis using the following expression.

Moisture content on dry basis

$$= \frac{(\text{weight of wet sample} - \text{weight of dry sample})}{\text{weight of dry sample}} \times 100$$

The drying flux is calculated using the following expression.

$$\text{Drying flux} = \frac{\text{loss in weight of the sample}}{\text{time taken} \times \text{drying area}}$$

Table 8.1 Drying data

Time (h)	Weight (kg)	Moisture (% on dry basis)	Drying flux (kg m^{-2} h^{-1})
0	10.625	28 .00	0
0.1	10.597	27.66	0.56
0.2	10.548	27.07	0.77
0.4	10.470	26.13	0.78
1.0	10.225	23.18	0.8
3.0	9.412	13.38	0.8
5.0	8.852	6.63	0.71
6.0	8.670	4.45	0.65
8.0	8.507	2.48	0.53
10.0	8.448	1.75	0.44
12.0	8.423	1.47	0.37
14.0	8.420	1.43	0.32
16.0	8.420	1.43	0.28

Figure 8.6 shows the drying flux versus moisture content curve.

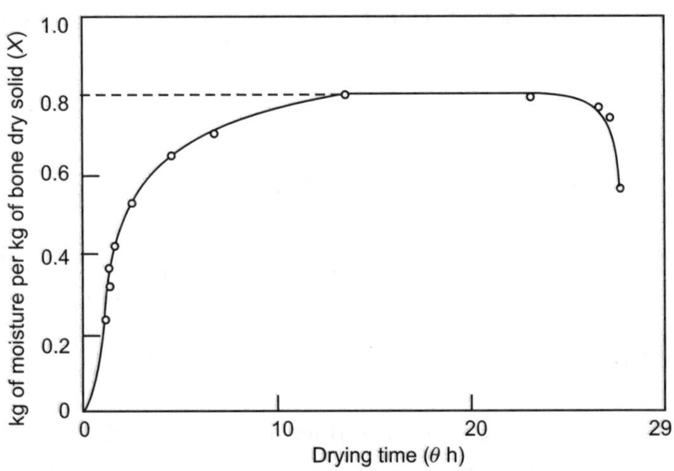

Fig. 8.6 Graphical solution for 8B

Initial moisture content = 28.00%

Final moisture content = 1.43%

Moisture content at which drying flux begins to fall is the critical moisture content. Critical moisture content = 13.38%

Rate of drying during constant rate period = 0.8 kg m^{-2} h^{-1}

8C A wet solid is dried from 40% moisture content to 10% moisture content under constant drying conditions in 5 hours. If the equilibrium moisture content is 5%, the critical moisture content is 15%. How long will it take to dry it to 7% moisture content under the same conditions? All moisture contents are on wet basis.

Solution

The moisture content is given on a wet basis. So, we have to convert it to the dry basis.

Initial moisture content (X_a) $= \frac{40}{60} = 0.666\,7$ kg of moisture per kg of dry solid

Final moisture content (X_b) $= \frac{10}{90} = 0.111$ kg of moisture per kg of dry solid

Critical moisture content (X_c) $= \frac{15}{85} = 0.176\,5$ kg of moisture per kg of dry solid

Equilibrium moisture content (X^*) $= \frac{5}{95} = 0.052\,6$ kg of moisture per kg of dry solid

The final moisture content is below the critical moisture content. Thus, we have a constant rate period and a falling rate period. Under these conditions, the total drying period has been given as 5 hours.

$$\theta = \frac{\mathring{m}_s}{AN_c}\left\{(X_a - X_c) + (X_c - X^*)\ln\frac{X_c - X^*}{X_b - X^*}\right\}$$

Substituting the values of the parameters in the above equation, we have

$$5 = \frac{\mathring{m}_s}{A\,N_c}\left\{(0.6667 - 0.1765) + (0.1765 - 0.0526)\ln\frac{0.176\,5 - 0.052\,6}{0.111\,1 - 0.052\,6}\right\}$$

$$\frac{\mathring{m}_s}{A\,N_c} = 8.5734$$

If the moisture content has to be reduced further down to 7% on a wet basis, the new final moisture content $(X_b^1) = \frac{7}{93} = 0.075\,3$ kg of moisture per kg of dry solid. Drying time under the new set of conditions (θ^1) is given by,

$$\theta^1 = \frac{\overset{\circ}{m}_s}{AN_c}\left\{(X_a - X_c) + (X_c - X^*)\ln\frac{X_c - X^*}{X_b^1 - X^*}\right\}$$

Substituting the values of the parameters in the above equation, we have

$$\theta^1 = 8.573\,4\left\{0.490\,2 + 0.123\,9\ln\frac{0.123\,9}{0.075\,3 - 0.052\,6}\right\} = 6.006 \text{ h}$$

8D A wet solid is dried from 35% moisture content to 8% moisture content under constant drying conditions in 5 hours. If the equilibrium moisture content is 5%, the critical moisture content is 15%. How long will it take to dry it to 6% moisture content under the same conditions? All moisture contents are on a wet basis.

Solution

Moisture content is given on a wet basis. So, we have to convert it to the dry basis.

Initial moisture content (X_a) $= \frac{35}{65} = 0.538\,5$ kg of moisture per kg of dry solid

Final moisture content (X_b) $= \frac{8}{92} = 0.087$ kg of moisture per kg of dry solid

Critical moisture content (X_c) $= \frac{15}{85} = 0.176\,5$ kg of moisture per kg of dry solid

Equilibrium moisture content (X^*) $= \frac{5}{95} = 0.052\,6$ kg of moisture per kg of dry solid

The final moisture content is below the critical moisture content. So we have a constant rate period and a falling rate period. Under these conditions, the total drying period has been given as 5 hours.

$$\theta = \frac{\overset{\circ}{m}_s}{AN_c}\left\{(X_a - X_c) + (X_c - X^*)\ln\frac{X_c - X^*}{X_b - X^*}\right\}$$

Substituting the values of the parameters in the above equation, we have

$$5 = \frac{\overset{\circ}{m}_s}{A\,N_c}\left\{(0.538\,5 - 0.176\,5) + (0.176\,5 - 0.052\,6)\ln\frac{0.176\,5 - 0.052\,6}{0.087 - 0.052\,6}\right\}$$

$$\frac{\overset{\circ}{m}_s}{A\,N_c} = 9.601$$

If the moisture content has to be reduced further down to 6% on a wet basis,

New final moisture content (X_b^1) $= \frac{6}{94} = 0.0638$ kg of moisture per kg of dry solid.

The drying time under the new set of conditions (θ^1) is given by,

$$\theta^1 = \frac{\overset{\circ}{m}_s}{AN_c}\left\{(X_a - X_c) + (X_c - X^*)\ln\frac{X_c - X^*}{X_b^1 - X^*}\right\}$$

Substituting the values of the parameters in the above equation, we have

$$\theta^1 = 9.601\{(0.538\,5 - 0.176\,5) + (0.176\,5 - 0.052\,6)\ln\frac{0.123\,9}{0.063\,8 - 0.052\,6}\} = 6.335 \text{ h}$$

Additional time required = 6.335 – 5.0 = 1.335 h

8E A woolen cloth is dried in a hot air drier from an initial moisture content of 100% to a final moisture content of 10%. If the critical moisture content is 55% and the equilibrium moisture content is 6%, calculate the saving in drying time if the material is dried to 16% instead of 10%. All drying conditions remain the same. All moisture contents are on a dry basis.

Solution

The moisture content is given on a dry basis. So, we have to use it as such.

Initial moisture content (X_a) = 1.00 kg of moisture per kg of dry solid

Final moisture content (X_b) = 0.10 kg of moisture per kg of dry solid

Critical moisture content (X_c) = 0.55 kg of moisture per kg of dry solid

Equilibrium moisture content (X^*) = 0.06 kg of moisture per kg of dry solid

The final moisture content is below the critical moisture content. So, we have a constant rate period and a falling rate period. Under these conditions, the total drying period is given by

$$\theta = \frac{\overset{\circ}{m}_s}{AN_c}\{(X_a - X_c) + (X_c - X^*)\ln\frac{X_c - X^*}{X_b - X^*}\}$$

Substituting the values of the parameters in the above equation, we have

$$\theta = \frac{\overset{\circ}{m}_s}{AN_c}\{(1.00 - 0.55) + (0.55 - 0.06)\ln\frac{0.55 - 0.06}{0.10 - 0.06}\}$$

$$\theta = 1.677\,7\frac{\overset{\circ}{m}_s}{AN_c} \text{ time unit}$$

If the moisture content has to be reduced to 16% instead of 10%,

New final moisture content (X_b^1) = 0.16 kg of moisture per kg of dry solid.

The drying time under the new set of conditions (θ^1) is given by,

$$\theta^1 = \frac{\overset{\circ}{m}_s}{AN_c}\{(X_a - X_c) + (X_c - X^*)\ln\frac{X_c - X^*}{X_b^1 - X^*}\}$$

Substituting the values of the parameters in the above equation, we have

$$\theta^1 = \frac{\mathring{m}_s}{A\,N_c}\{(1.00 - 0.55) + (0.55 - 0.06)\ln\frac{0.55 - 0.06}{0.16 - 0.06}\}$$

$$= 1.228\,7\frac{\mathring{m}_s}{A\,N_c} \text{ time unit}$$

$$\text{Saving time} = 1.677\,7\frac{\mathring{m}_s}{A\,N_c} - 1.228\,7\frac{\mathring{m}_s}{A\,N_c}\text{time unit}$$

$$\text{Percentage saving in time } \frac{1.677\,7 - 1.228\,7}{1.677\,7} \times 100 = 26.76$$

8F A certain material was dried under constant drying conditions and it was found that 2 hours are required to reduce the free moisture concentration from 20% to 10%. How much longer will it take to reduce the free moisture concentration to 4%? Assume that no constant rate period is encountered and the falling rate period is linear. The equilibrium moisture content is zero.

Solution

The moisture content is given on a wet basis. So, we have to convert it to the dry basis.

Initial moisture content (X_a) $= \frac{20}{80} = 0.25$ kg of moisture per kg of dry solid

Final moisture content (X_b) $= \frac{10}{90} = 0.111$ kg of moisture per kg of dry solid

Critical moisture content (X_c) is not given.

Equilibrium moisture content (X^*) = 0 kg of moisture per kg of dry solid

It is given that there is no constant rate period and that the falling rate period is linear. Under these conditions, the total drying period has been given as 2 hours.

$$\theta = \frac{\mathring{m}_s}{AN_c}\left\{(X_c - X^*)\ln\frac{X_a - X^*}{X_b - X^*}\right\}$$

Substituting the values of the parameters in the above equation, we have

$$2 = \frac{\mathring{m}_s}{A\,N_c}\left\{(X_c - 0)\ln\frac{0.25 - 0}{0.111\,1 - 0}\right\}$$

$$\frac{\mathring{m}_s X_c}{AN_c} = 2.46$$

If the moisture content has to be reduced further down to 4% on a wet basis,

New final moisture content (X_b^1) $= \frac{4}{96} = 0.042$ kg of moisture per kg of dry solid.

Drying time under the new set of conditions (θ^1) is given by,

$$\theta^1 = \frac{\overset{\circ}{m}_s}{A\,N_c}\left\{(X_c - 0)\ln\frac{0.25-0}{0.111\,1-0}\right\}$$

$$= \frac{\overset{\circ}{m}_s}{AN_c}\left\{(X_c - 0)\ln\frac{0.25-0}{0.042-0}\right\}$$

$$= \frac{\overset{\circ}{m}_s X_c}{AN_c}\ln\frac{0.25}{0.042} = 2.46 \times \ln\frac{0.25}{0.042} = 4.39 \text{ h}$$

Additional time required = 4.39 – 2 = 2.39 h

8G It is necessary to dry a fibre board of size 0.131 m × 0.162 m × 0.071 m from a moisture content of 58% to 5% on a wet basis. The rate of drying during the constant rate period was found to be 8.9 kg m^{-2} h^{-1}. The critical moisture content was 24.9% and the equilibrium moisture content was 1%. The fibre board is dried from only one side. The bone dry density was 210 kg m^{-3}. Determine the time required for drying. Assume that the rate of drying during the falling rate period is proportional to the free moisture content.

Solution

The moisture content is given on a wet basis. So, we have to convert it to the dry basis.

Initial moisture content (X_a) $= \dfrac{58}{42} = 1.380\,9$ kg of moisture per kg of dry solid

Final moisture content (X_b) $= \dfrac{5}{95} = 0.052\,6$ kg of moisture per kg of dry solid

Critical moisture content (X_c) $= \dfrac{24.9}{75.1} = 0.331\,6$ kg of moisture per kg of dry solid

Equilibrium moisture content (X^*) $= \dfrac{1}{99} = 0.010\,1$ kg of moisture per kg of dry solid

Weight of dry board ($\overset{\circ}{m}_s$) = volume of the board × dry density

= 0.131 × 0.162 × 0.071 × 210 = 0.316 kg

The board is dried from one side.

Drying area (A) = 0.131 × 0.162 = 0.021 m^2

Rate of drying during constant rate period (N_c) = 8.9 kg m^{-2} h^{-1}

The final moisture content is below the critical moisture content. So, we have the constant rate period and the falling rate period. Under these conditions, the total drying period has been given by,

$$\theta = \frac{\mathring{m}_s}{AN_c}\left\{(X_a - X_c) + (X_c - X^*)\ln\frac{X_c - X^*}{X_b - X^*}\right\}$$

Substituting the values of the parameters in the above equation, we have

$$\theta = \frac{0.316}{0.021 \times 8.9}\left\{(1.380\,9 - 0.331\,6) + (0.331\,6 - 0.010\,1)\ln\frac{0.331\,6 - 0.010\,1}{0.052\,6 - 0.010\,1}\right\}$$

$$= 2.874 \text{ h}$$

8H A slab of wet material is to be dried by flowing air at 333 K, with 10% relative humidity and at a velocity of 10 m s^{-1}. The critical moisture content is 0.35 kg free water per kg of dry solid. The rate of drying in the falling rate period can be considered linear. The slab must be dried from a moisture content of 55% to 12% (wet basis). The equilibrium moisture content at the conditions of the drier is 5% (wet basis). The slab is 6 cm thick and kept on insulated trays. The dry density of the solid is 1.38 g cm^{-3}. Calculate the time of drying. The rate of drying during the constant rate period may be taken as $N_c = 0.004V^{0.8}(P_i - P_g)$, where V is the velocity of air in m s^{-1} and P_g and P_i are the vapour pressure of water in air in mm Hg at dry bulb and wet bulb temperatures respectively.

Solution

The rate of drying during the constant rate period (N_c) has to be computed using the empirical relation given. The vapour pressure of water at the dry bulb and wet bulb temperatures can be calculated from the humidity chart. The absolute humidity (Y) at 333 K dry bulb temperature and 10% relative humidity is 0.014 kg of moisture per kg of dry air. This has to be converted to molal humidity which is also the ratio of partial pressure of moisture to dry air.

$$\text{Molal humidity } (Y_m) = \frac{Y}{0.6207} = \frac{0.014}{0.6207} = 0.023 = \frac{P_g}{760 - P_g} = P_g = 17.09 \text{ mm Hg}$$

The absolute humidity (Y) at wet bulb temperature corresponding to a dry bulb temperature of 333 K and 10% relative humidity is 0.028 kg of moisture per kg of dry air.

$$\text{Molal humidity } (Y_m) = \frac{Y}{0.620\,7} = \frac{0.028}{0.620\,7} = 0.046 = \frac{P_i}{760 - P_i} \text{ and } P_i = 33.42 \text{ mm Hg}$$

$$N_c = 0.004V^{0.8}(P_i - P_g) = 0.004 \times 10^{0.8}(33.43 - 17.09) = 0.412 \text{ g cm}^{-2}\text{ h}^{-1}$$

$$\text{Initial moisture content } (X_a) = \frac{55}{45} = 1.222 \text{ kg of moisture per kg of dry solid}$$

$$\text{Final moisture content } (X_b) = \frac{12}{88} = 0.136 \text{ kg of moisture per kg of dry solid}$$

Critical moisture content (X_c) $=$ 0.35 kg of moisture per kg of dry solid

Equilibrium moisture content (X^*) $= \dfrac{5}{95} = 0.053$ kg of moisture per kg of dry solid

Let us consider a sheet of area (A) 1×1 cm^2, the thickness of sheet is given as 6 cm.

Weight of dry board ($\mathring{m}_s$) = volume of the board $\times$ dry density

$$= 1 \times 1 \times 6 \times 1.38 = 8.28 \text{ g}$$

The final moisture content is below the critical moisture content. So, we have the constant rate period and the falling rate period. Under these conditions, the total drying period has been given by,

$$\theta = \frac{\mathring{m}_s}{AN_c}\{(X_a - X_c) + (X_c - X^*)\ln\frac{X_c - X^*}{X_b - X^*}\}$$

Substituting the values of the parameters in the above equation, we have

$$\theta = \frac{8.28}{1.0 \times 0.412}\{(1.222 - 0.35) + (0.35 - 0.053)\ln\frac{0.35 - 0.053}{0.136 - 0.053}\} = 25.14 \text{ h}$$

8I A solid is dried in a batch drier from 25% to 6% moisture (wet basis). The initial weight of the dry solid is 160 kg with a drying surface 1 m^2 per 40 kg dry solid weight. The critical moisture content is 0.2 kg of moisture per kg dry solid, the constant drying rate is 0.3×10^{-3} kg m^{-2} s^{-1} and the equilibrium moisture content is 0.05 kg of moisture per kg of dry solid. Assuming the falling rate curve to be a straight line, compute the total drying time.

Solution

The initial and final moisture contents are given on a wet basis.

Initial moisture content (X_a) $= \dfrac{25}{75} = 0.333$ kg of moisture per kg of dry solid

Final moisture content (X_b) $= \dfrac{6}{94} = 0.064$ kg of moisture per kg of dry solid

The critical and equilibrium moisture contents are given on dry basis.

Critical moisture content (X_c) $=$ 0.2 kg of moisture per kg of dry solid

Equilibrium moisture content (X^*) $=$ 0.05 kg of moisture per kg of dry solid

The rate of drying during the constant rate period is given.

$$N_c = 0.3 \times 10^{-3} \text{ kg m}^{-2} \text{ s}^{-1} = 0.3 \times 10^{-3} \times 3600 = 1.08 \text{ kg m}^{-2} \text{ h}^{-1}$$

It is given that the solid being dried has a drying surface of 1 m^2 per 40 kg dry solid weight.

That is, $\dfrac{\mathring{m}_s}{A} = 40$

The final moisture content is below the critical moisture content. So, we have a constant rate period and a falling rate period. It is also given that the falling rate curve is a straight line. Under these conditions, the total drying period has been given by,

$$\theta = \frac{\mathring{m}_s}{AN_c}\{(X_a - X_c) + (X_c - X^*) \ln \frac{X_c - X^*}{X_b - X^*}\}$$

Substituting the values of the parameters in the above equation, we have

$$\theta = \frac{40}{1.08}\{(0.333 - 0.2) + (0.20 - 0.05) \ln \frac{0.20 - 0.05}{0.064 - 0.05}\} = 18.12 \text{ h}$$

8J A batch of solids is to be dried from 25% to 8% moisture (on a wet basis) under conditions identical to those for which data is available. The initial weight of the wet solid is 200 kg and the drying surface is 1 m^2 per 8 kg of dry weight. Determine the time of drying.

X	0.35	0.25	0.20	0.18	0.16	0.14	0.12	0.10	0.09	0.08	0.064
N	0.3	0.30	0.30	0.266	0.239	0.208	0.18	0.15	0.097	0.07	0.025

where X refers to kg of water per kg of dry solid and N refers to kg of moisture evaporated per m^2 of drying surface per hour.

Solution

Perusal of the equilibrium data reveals that up to a moisture content of 20%, the drying flux is constant and it begins to fall afterwards. So the drying flux during the constant rate period (N_c) is 0.3 kg m^{-2} h^{-1} and critical moisture content (X_c) is 0.2 kg of water per kg of dry solid. It is also given that the drying surface is 1 m^2 per 8 kg of dry weight.

That is, $\dfrac{\mathring{m}_s}{A} = 8$

Initial moisture content (X_a) $= \dfrac{25}{75} = 0.333$ kg of moisture per kg of dry solid

Final moisture content (X_b) $= \dfrac{8}{92} = 0.087$ kg of moisture per kg of dry solid

Critical moisture content (X_c) $=$ 0.20 kg of moisture per kg of dry solid

The duration of drying during the constant rate period (θ_c) is given by, $\theta_c = \dfrac{\mathring{m}_s}{AN_c}(X_a - X_c)$

Substituting the values of the parameters, $\theta_c = \dfrac{8}{0.3}(0.333 - 0.20) = 3.55$ h

The duration of drying during falling rate period (θ_f) is given by

$$\theta_f = \frac{\mathring{m}_s}{A}\int_{X_c}^{X_b}\frac{dX}{N}$$

The function $\int_{X_c}^{X_b}\frac{dX}{N}$ has to be determined graphically by plotting $\frac{1}{N}$ as ordinate against X as abscissa and determining the area under the curve between the limits X_b and X_c. Then θ_f is found by multiplying the area and $\frac{\mathring{m}_s}{A}$. Table 8.2 gives the data required for the graphical integration.

From Fig. 8.7, the area under the curve is found to be 0.58 square units.

$$\theta_f = \frac{8}{1}\times 0.58 = 4.64\,h$$

Total drying time (θ) = $\theta_c + \theta_f = 3.55 + 4.64 = 8.19$ h

Table 8.2 Data for graphical integration

X	N	$\frac{1}{N}$
0.25	0.3	3.33
0.20	0.3	3.33
0.18	0.266	3.76
0.16	0.239	4.18
0.14	0.208	4.81
0.12	0.18	5.56
0.10	0.15	6.67
0.08	0.07	14.29

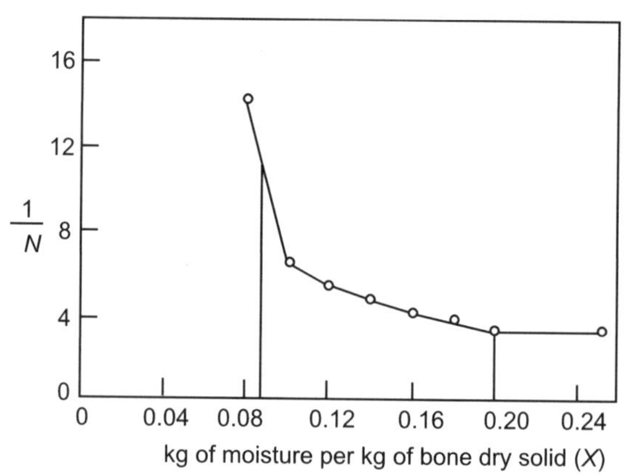

Fig. 8.7 Graphical solution for 8J

8K The weight of the dry material in the solid is 48 kg m^{-2}. Calculate the time required to dry the material from 25% to 8% moisture (dry basis).

Data:

X	0.30	0.20	0.18	0.15	0.14	0.11	0.07	0.05
N	1.22	1.22	1.14	0.90	0.80	0.56	0.22	0.05

where X is the moisture content in kg per kg dry solid and N is the drying rate in kg h^{-1} m^2.

Solution

Perusal of the equilibrium data reveals that the drying flux is constant up to a moisture content of 20% and it begins to fall afterwards. So, the drying flux during the constant rate period (N_c) is 1.22 kg m^{-2} h^{-1} and the critical moisture content (X_c) is 0.2 kg of water per kg of dry solid.

It is also given that drying surface is 1 m^2 per 48 kg of dry weight.

That is, $\frac{\mathring{m}_s}{A} = 48$

Initial moisture content (X_a) = 0.25 kg of moisture per kg of dry solid

Final moisture content (X_b) = 0.08 kg of moisture per kg of dry solid

Critical moisture content (X_c) = 0.20 kg of moisture per kg of dry solid

The duration of drying during the constant rate period (θ_c) is given by, $\theta_c = \frac{\mathring{m}_s}{AN_c}(X_a - X_c)$

Substituting the values of parameters, $\theta_c = \frac{48}{1.22}(0.25 - 0.20) = 1.97$ h

The duration of drying during the falling rate period (θ_f) is given by

$$\theta_f = \frac{\mathring{m}_s}{A}\int_{X_c}^{X_b}\frac{dX}{N}$$

The function $\int_{X_c}^{X_b}\frac{dX}{N}$ has to be determined graphically by plotting $\frac{1}{N}$ as ordinate against X as abscissa and determining the area under the curve between the limits X_b and X_c. Then, θ_f is found by multiplying the area and $\frac{\mathring{m}_s}{A}$. Table 8.3 gives the data required for the graphical integration.

Table 8.3 Data for graphical integration

X	N	$\frac{1}{N}$
0.20	1.22	0.82
0.18	1.14	0.88
0.15	0.9	1.11
0.14	0.8	1.25
0.11	0.56	1.79
0.07	0.22	4.55

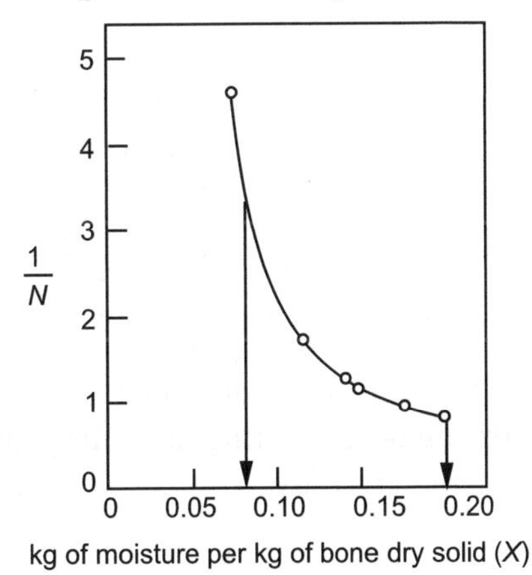

Fig. 8.8 Graphical solution for 8K

From Fig. 8.8, the area under the curve is found to be 0.15 square units.

$$\theta_f = \frac{48}{1} \times 0.15 = 7.2\,\text{h}$$

Total drying time (θ) = $\theta_c + \theta_f = 1.97 + 7.2 = 9.17$ h

8L During the batch drying test of a wet slab of material 0.35 m^2 and 7 mm thick, the drying rate N in kg m^{-2} s^{-1} was expressed as 0.95 (X – 0.01), where X is the moisture content in kg moisture per kg dry solid. The slab was dried only from one side with the edges sealed. The density of the dry material is 1 200 kg m^{-3}. It is required to reduce the moisture content from 35% to 5% on a wet basis. What is the time needed for drying?

Solution

The moisture content is given on a wet basis. So, we have to convert it to the dry basis.

$$\text{Initial moisture content } (X_a) = \frac{35}{65} = 0.538 \text{ kg of moisture per kg of dry solid}$$

$$\text{Final moisture content } (X_b) = \frac{5}{95} = 0.052 \text{ kg of moisture per kg of dry solid}$$

Weight of dry material in the slab being dried ($\mathring{m}_s$)= volume $\times$ dry density

$$= 0.35 \times 0.007 \times 1\,200 = 2.94 \text{ kg}$$

The slab was dried only from one side with the edges sealed. So, the drying area (A) is 0.35 m^2.

$$\frac{\mathring{m}_s}{A} = \frac{2.94}{0.35} = 8.4 \text{ kg m}^{-2}$$

It is given that the drying rate N in kg m^{-2} s^{-1} is expressed as 0.95 (X – 0.01), where X is the moisture content in kg moisture per kg dry solid. Using this, X versus N data is generated, which is given below.

X	0.54	0.50	0.40	0.30	0.20	0.10	0.05	0.03
N = 0.95 (X – 0.01)	0.504	0.465	0.370	0.278	0.18	0.86	0.038	0.019

Perusal of the equilibrium data reveals that there is no constant rate period and the entire drying occurs during the falling rate period. The duration of drying during falling rate period (θ_f) is given by

$$\theta_f = \frac{\mathring{m}_s}{A} \int_{X_c}^{X_b} \frac{dX}{N}$$

The function $\int_{X_c}^{X_b} \frac{dX}{N}$ has to be determined graphically by plotting $\frac{1}{N}$ as ordinate against X as abscissa and determining the area under the curve between the limits X_b and X_c. Then, θ_f is found by multiplying the area and $\frac{\mathring{m}_s}{A}$. Table 8.4 gives the data required for the graphical integration. From Fig. 8.9, the area under the curve is found to be 2.75 square units.

$$\theta_f = 8.4 \times 2.75 = 23.1 \text{ h}$$

Table 8.4 Data for graphical integration

X	N	$\frac{1}{N}$
0.54	0.504	1.986
0.50	0.465	2.15
0.40	0.37	2.703
0.30	0.278	3.597
0.20	0.18	5.556
0.10	0.86	11.696
0.05	0.038	26.316
0.03	0.019	52.632

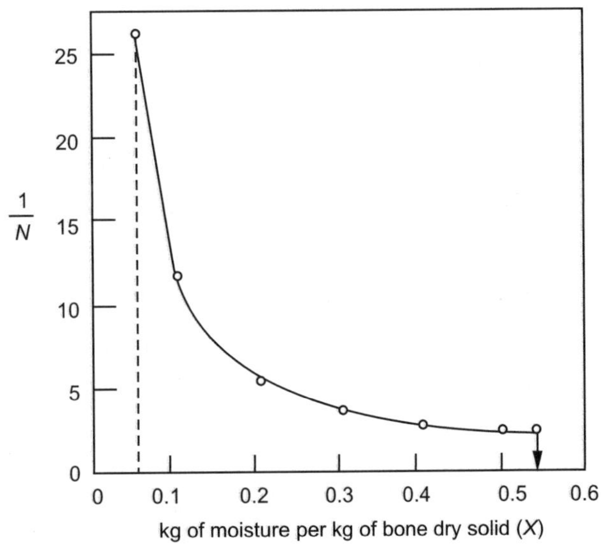

Fig. 8.9 Graphical solution for 8L

8M In order to test the feasibility of drying certain food stuff, drying data were obtained in a tray drier with air flow over the top exposed surface having an area of 0.186 m^2. The weight of the bone dry sample was 3.765 kg. At equilibrium after a long period, the weight of the wet sample was 3.955 kg. The following data were obtained during the test.

Time (h)	0	0.4	0.8	1.4	2.2	3.0	4.2	5.0	7.0	9.0	12.0
Weight (kg)	4.944	4.885	4.808	4.699	4.554	4.401	4.241	4.153	4.025	3.978	3.955

(i) Calculate the free moisture content and the drying rate. (ii) Using the above data, predict the total drying time to dry the sample from 20% to 6%.

Solution

(i) The results are tabulated as given in Table 8.5. The moisture content is calculated on a dry basis using the following expression.

$$\text{Moisture content on dry basis} = \frac{\text{weight of wet sample} - \text{weight of dry sample}}{\text{weight of dry sample}} \times 100$$

Drying flux is calculated using the following expression.

$$\text{Drying flux} = \frac{\text{loss in weight of the sample}}{\text{time taken} \times \text{drying area}}$$

Table 8.5 gives the drying data.

Initial moisture content $(X_a) = 31.31\%$

Equilibrium moisture content $(X^*) = 5.05\%$

Free moisture content is the difference between the above two values, which is 26.26%.

The moisture content at which drying flux begins to fall is the critical moisture content. Critical moisture content (X_c)= 16.89%

Average rate of drying during constant rate period $(N_c) = 1.0035$ kg m^{-2} h^{-1}

(ii) There is no mention about the basis for the moisture content. So, the wet basis has to been assumed.

$$\text{Initial moisture content } (X_a) = \frac{20}{80} = 0.25 \text{ kg of moisture per kg of dry solid}$$

$$\text{Final moisture content } (X_b) = \frac{6}{94} = 0.064 \text{ kg of moisture per kg of dry solid}$$

Table 8.5 Drying data

Time (h)	Weight (kg)	Moisture (% on dry basis)	Drying flux (kg m^{-2} h^{-1})
0	4.944	31.31	0
0.4	4.885	29.75	0.793
0.8	4.808	27.70	1.035
1.4	4.699	24.81	0.977
2.2	4.554	20.96	0.974
3.0	4.401	16.89	1.028
4.2	4,241	12.64	0.716
5.0	4.153	10.31	0.591
7.0	4.025	6.91	0.344
9.0	3.978	5.66	0.126
12.0	3.955	5.05	0.041

Critical moisture content (X_c) = 0.20 kg of moisture per kg of dry solid

Perusal of the equilibrium data reveals that for a moisture content of up to 16.89%, the drying flux is constant and it begins to fall afterwards. The drying flux during the constant rate period (N_c) is 1.003 5 kg m^{-2} h^{-1} and the critical moisture content (X_c) is 0.168 9 kg of water per kg of dry solid.

It is also given that dry weight of sample ($\mathring{m}_s$) is 3.765 kg and the drying surface (A) is 0.186 m^2.

Duration of drying during constant rate period (θ_c) is given by $\theta_c = \dfrac{\mathring{m}_s}{AN_c}(X_a - X_c)$

Substituting the values of parameters, $\theta_c = \dfrac{3.765}{0.186}(0.25 - 0.168\,) = 1.64$ h

Duration of drying during the falling rate period (θ_f) is given by

$$\theta_f = \frac{\mathring{m}_s}{A}\int_{X_c}^{X_b}\frac{dX}{N}$$

The function $\int_{X_c}^{X_b}\dfrac{dX}{N}$ has to be determined graphically by plotting $\dfrac{1}{N}$ as ordinate against X as abscissa and determining the area under the curve between the limits X_b and X_c. Then, θ_f is found by multiplying the area and $\dfrac{\mathring{m}_s}{A}$. Table 8.6 gives the data required for the graphical integration.

Table 8.6 Data for graphical integration

X	N	$\dfrac{1}{N}$
0.168 9	1.028	0.973
0.126 4	0.716	1.397
0.103 1	0.591	1.692
0.069 1	0.344	2.907
0.056 6	0.126	7.937
0.050 5	0.041	24.39

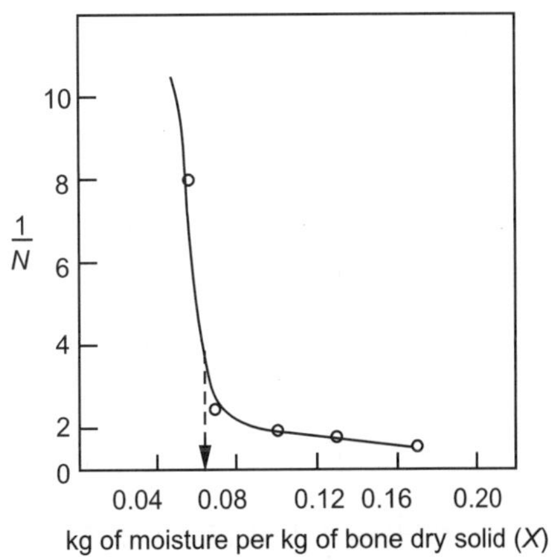

Fig. 8.10 Graphical solution for 8M

From Fig. 8.10, the area under the curve is found to be 0.166 square units.

$$\theta_f = \frac{3.765}{0.186} \times 0.166 = 3.36 \text{ h}$$

Total drying time (θ) = $\theta_c + \theta_f = 1.64 + 3.36 = 5.0$ h

8N 1 000 kg dry weight of a non-porous solid is dried under constant drying conditions with an air velocity of 1.0 m s^{-1}, so that the area of the drying surface is 50 m^2. The critical moisture content of the material may be taken as 0.125 kg water per kg dry solid. If the initial drying rate is 0.3 g m^{-2} s^{-1}, how long will it take to dry the material from 0.15 to 0.025 kg water per kg dry solid? If the air velocity were increased to 3.0 m s^{-1}, what would be the anticipated saving in time if the drying operation is controlled by surface evaporation?

Solution

Initial moisture content (X_a) = 0.15 kg of moisture per kg of dry solid
Final moisture content (X_b) = 0.025 kg of moisture per kg of dry solid
Critical moisture content (X_c) = 0.125 kg of moisture per kg of dry solid

The equilibrium moisture content (X^*) is assumed to be 0 kg of moisture per kg of dry solid. The initial rate of drying is given which may be assumed to be that during the constant rate period.

$$N_c = 0.3 \times 10^{-3} \text{ kg m}^{-2} \text{ s}^{-1} = 0.3 \times 10^{-3} \times 3600 = 1.08 \text{ kg m}^{-2} \text{ h}^{-1}$$

It is given that 1 000 kg is the dry weight of the solid and the area of the drying surface is 50 m^2.

That is $\frac{\mathring{m}_s}{A} = 20$

The final moisture content is below the critical moisture content. So, we have a constant rate period and a falling rate period. It is also given that the falling rate curve is a straight line. Under these conditions, the total drying period has been given by

$$\theta = \frac{\mathring{m}_s}{AN_c}\left\{(X_a - X_c) + (X_c - X^*)\ln\frac{X_c - X^*}{X_b - X^*}\right\}$$

Substituting the values of the parameters in the above equation, we have

$$\theta = \frac{20}{1.08}\left\{(0.15 - 0.125) + (0.125 - 0)\ln\frac{0.125 - 0}{0.025 - 0}\right\} = 4.189 \text{ h}$$

For drying controlled by surface evaporation, $N_c \propto G^{0.8}$; parallel flow of air is assumed for better mass transfer. G depends on gas velocity u and hence $N_c \propto u^{0.8}$

$$\frac{N_c}{N_c'} = \frac{u}{u'}$$

where u is the initial air velocity (1 m s^{-1}) and u' is the new, enhanced air velocity (3 m s^{-1}). The new N_c' value for the enhanced air velocity will be 2.60 kg m^{-2} h^{-1}. The new drying time based on the enhanced air velocity will be

$$\theta' = \frac{20}{2.60}\left\{(0.15 - 0.125) + (0.125 - 0)\ln\frac{0.125 - 0}{0.025 - 0}\right\} = 1.739 \text{ h}$$

Note: Increased air velocity leads to a saving in drying time.

MECHANISMS OF DRYING [6]

The mechanism depends on the nature of the solid and the method of contacting the solid and gas. Solids are of three types—crystalline, porous and non-porous.

Crystalline solids contain no interior liquid and drying occurs only at the surface of the solid.

Porous solids contain the liquid in interior channels. The drying rate of such solids depends on the way the liquid moves and on the distance it must travel to reach the surface. The moisture flows through porous solids by capillary action. A porous material contains a complicated network of interconnecting pores and channels, the cross sections of which vary greatly. Mouths of pores of various sizes are found at the surface. As water is removed by vaporisation, a meniscus across each pore is formed which sets up capillary forces by the interfacial tension between the water and the solid. The capillary forces possess components in a direction perpendicular to the surface of the solid. It is these forces that provide the driving force for the movement of water through the pores towards the surface. The strength of the capillary forces at a given point in a pore depends on the curvature of the meniscus which is a function of the pore cross section. Small pores develop greater capillary forces than the large ones and small pores therefore can pull water out of the large pores.

In non-porous solids, moisture flows through the solid by diffusion and hence the rate of drying is low. The resistance to mass transfer of water vapour from the solid surface to the air is negligible and the diffusion in the solid controls the overall drying rate. When bound moisture is removed from a colloidal non-porous solid, the material shrinks since the outer layers necessarily lose moisture before the interior portions. The concentration of moisture in these layers is less than that of the interior and the surface layers shrink against an unyielding constant volume core. This surface shrinkage causes checking, cracking and warping. In extreme cases, the shrinkage and drop in diffusivity may combine to give a skin practically impervious to moisture, which encloses the bulk of the material so that the interior moisture cannot be removed. This is known as case hardening, warping, checking and cracking.

Case hardening can be minimised by reducing the rate of drying, thereby flattening the concentration gradients in the solid. Then, the shrinkage of the surface is reduced and the diffusivity throughout the solid is nearly constant. The moisture gradient at the surface is flattened and the entire piece is protected against shrinkage.

CLASSIFICATION OF DRYERS [7, 8]

Dryers can be classified in a number of ways. Some dryers are continuous, some agitate the solids, some are essentially unagitated, some driers operate under vacuum to reduce drying time, some can handle almost any kind of material while others can handle only specified feed. A major division may be made between

1. Dryers in which the solid is directly exposed to a hot gas. They are called adiabatic or direct driers.
2. Dryers in which heat is transferred out of the solid via an external medium such as condensing steam, usually through a metal surface with which the solid is in contact. They are known as non-adiabatic or indirect dryers. Dryers heated by dielectric, radiant or microwave energy are also non-adiabatic.

Some units combine adiabatic and non-adiabatic drying. They are known as direct–indirect dryers.

In adiabatic dryers, the solids are exposed to the gas in the following ways.

1. Gas is blown across the bed or slab of solids or across one or both faces of a continuous sheet or film (Fig. 8.11a). This process is called cross circulation drying.
2. Gas is blown through a bed of coarse granular solids which are supported on a screen (Fig. 8.11b). This is known as through circulation drying. In this case and in cross circulation drying, air velocity is kept low to avoid any entrainment of solid particles.
3. Solids are showered downward through a slowly moving gas stream often with some undesired entrainment of fine particles in the gas (Fig. 8.11c).
4. Gas passes through the solid at a velocity sufficient to fluidise the bed (Fig. 8.11d). There is inevitably some entrainment of tiny particles.
5. The solids are all entrained in a high velocity gas stream and are pneumatically conveyed from the mixing device to a mechanical separator (Fig. 8.11e).

In a non-adiabatic dryer, the only gas to be removed is the water vapour or solvent, although sometimes a small amount of sweep gas (often air or nitrogen) is passed through the unit. Non-adiabatic dryers differ chiefly in the ways in which solids are exposed to the hot surface or other source of heat.

Solids are spread over a stationary or slowly moving horizontal surface which may be heated electrically or by a heat transfer fluid such as steam or hot water. Alternatively, heat may be supplied by a radiant heater above the solid.

Solids are moved over a heated surface (usually a cylindrical surface) by an agitator or a screw or paddle conveyor.

Solids slide by gravity over an inclined heated surface or are carried upward with the surface for a time and then slide to a new location as in the case of the rotary drier.

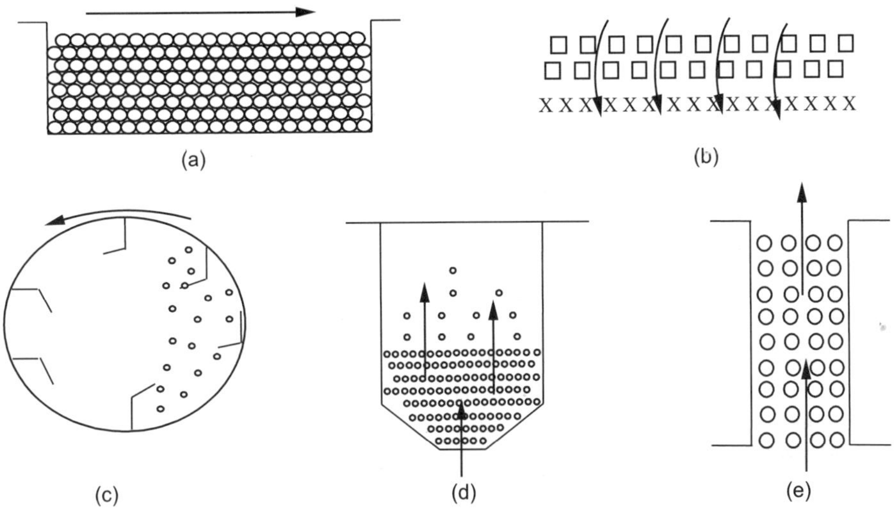

Fig. 8.11 Types of solid-drying medium interaction: (a) Cross circulation (b) Through circulation (c) Showering action (d) Fluidised bed (e) Pneumatic conveying

SELECTION OF DRYERS

Dryers for Solids and Pastes

A tray drier or screen conveyor dryer is to be used when agitation is not permitted. A tower dryer, rotary dryer, screw conveyor dryer, fluidised bed dryer or flash dryer is used when agitation is permitted.

Dryers for Solutions and Slurries

A spray dryer, thin film dryer or drum dryer is to be used.

NOTATIONS

A	Area of drying surface, m^2.
b	Constant.
C_l	Specific heat capacity of liquid, kJ kg^{-1} K^{-1}.
C_s	Specific heat of the solid, kJ kg^{-1} K^{-1}.
C_v	Specific heat of the vapour at constant pressure, kJ kg^{-1} K^{-1}.
C_{Ya}	Humid heat of gas at inlet, kJ kg^{-1} K^{-1}.
G	Mass velocity of the gas, kg m^{-2} s^{-1}.
h_y	Heat transfer coefficient based on gas phase, W m^{-2} K^{-1}.
k_y	Mass transfer coefficient based on gas phase, kmol m^{-2} $s^{-1}\Delta$ y^{-1}.

M_v	Molecular weight of vapour.
m	Slope of the linear portion of the plot of $\frac{1}{N}$ versus X.
$\mathring{m}_s$	Mass flow rate of bone dry (moisture free) solids, kg s^{-1}.
$\mathring{m}_g$	Mass flow rate of dry gas, kg s^{-1}.
$\mathring{m}_v$	Mass flow rate of vapour, kg s^{-1}.
N	Drying flux, kg m^{-2} s^{-1}.
N_a	Drying flux at the inlet conditions, kg m^{-2} s^{-1}.
N_b	Drying flux at the outlet conditions, kg m^{-2} s^{-1}.
N_c	Drying flux during constant rate period, kg m^{-2} s^{-1}.
N_{lm}	log mean of drying fluxes N_b and N_a.
q_T	Total quantity of heat transferred ,W.
T	Temperature of gas, K.
T_i	Temperature of interface, K.
T_s	Liquid surface temperature.
T_v	Vaporisation temperature, K.
T_{sa}	Solids feed temperature, K.
T_{sb}	Solids final temperature.
T_{vb}	Final vapour temperature.
T_{WB}	Wet bulb temperature, K.
T_{gb}	Exit gas temperature, K.
$\overline{\Delta T}$	Average temperature difference, K.
U	Overall heat transfer coefficient, W m^{-2} K^{-1}.
U_a	Volumetric heat transfer coefficient, W m^{-3} K^{-1}.
V	Dryer volume, m^3.
X	Free moisture content, kg of liquid per kg of bone dry solid.
X_a	Initial liquid content, kg of liquid per kg of bone dry solid.
X_b	Final liquid content, kg of liquid per kg of bone dry solid.
X_c	Critical liquid content, kg of liquid per kg of bone dry solid.
X^*	Equilibrium moisture content, kg of liquid per kg of bone dry solid.
ΔX	Reduction in moisture content, kg of liquid per kg of bone dry solid.
Y	Absolute humidity of air, kg of moisture per kg of dry gas.
Y_a	Absolute humidity of gas at the dryer inlet, kg of moisture per kg of dry gas.
Y_b	Absolute humidity of gas at the dryer outlet, kg of moisture per kg of dry gas.
Y_s	Saturation humidity of air at the liquid surface temperature,T_s.
y	Mole fraction of vapour in gas.
y_i	Mole fraction of vapour at the interface.
λ_i	Latent heat of vaporisation at T_i, kJ kg^{-1}.
λ_{Tv}	Latent heat of vaporisation at T_v, kJ kg^{-1}.
θ	Total drying time, s.
θ_c	Drying time during constant drying period, s.
θ_f	Drying time during falling rate period, s.
$\Delta\theta$	Drying time, s.

REFERENCES

1. Gilliland ER and Sherwood TK, *Ind. Eng. Chem.*, **25**: 1134 (1933).
2. Sherwood TK, *Ind. Eng. Chem.*, **21**: 976 (1929); **22**: 132 (1930); **24**: 307 (1932).
3. Sherwood TK and Comings EW, *Ind. Eng. Chem.*, **25**: 311 (1933).
4. Shepherd CB, Haddock C and Brewer RC, *Ind. Eng. Chem.*, **30**: 389 (1938).
5. Molsted MC, Farevaag P and Farrell JA, *Ind. Eng. Chem.*, **30**: 1131 (1938).
6. Hougen OA and McCauley HJ, *Trans. AIChE*, **36**: 183 (1940).
7. Dittman FW, *Chem. Eng.*, *84*: 106 (1977).
8. Keey RB, *Chem. Eng. Sci.*, *23:* 1299 (1968).

Problems for Practice

8.1 A wet solid is dried from 35% to 10% moisture in 6 hours. The critical moisture content is 14% and the equilibrium moisture content is 4%. How long will it take to dry the material from 30% moisture content to 6% moisture content under similar drying conditions? All moisture contents are on a wet basis.

8.2 A porous solid is dried in a batch drier under constant drying conditions. Seven hours are required to reduce the moisture content from 35% to 10%. The critical moisture content and the equilibrium moisture content are 20% and 4% respectively. All moisture contents are on a dry basis. Assuming that the rate of drying during the falling rate period is proportional to the free moisture content, how long will it take to dry a sample of the same solid from 35% to 5% under the same drying conditions?

8.3 Data on the drying rate curve of a particular solid are given below. The weight of the dry material in the solid is 48 kg m^{-2}. Calculate the time required to dry the material from 25% to 8% on a dry basis.

Data:

X	0.30	0.20	0.18	0.15	0.14	0.11	0.07	0.05
N	1.22	1.22	1.14	0.90	0.80	0.56	0.22	0.05

where X is the moisture content in kg per kg dry solid and N is the drying rate in kg h^{-1} m^{-2}.

8.4 The following data is available for drying a substance:

X	0.35	0.25	0.20	0.18	0.16	0.14	0.10	0.08	0.064
N	0.30	0.30	0.30	0.266	0.24	0.21	0.15	0.07	0.05

where X is the moisture content in kg of moisture per kg of dry solid and N is the drying rate in kg m^{-2} h^{-1}. Estimate the time needed for drying a similar material from an initial moisture content of 25% to a final moisture content of 12% (both on a wet basis). The drying surface is 1 m^2 per 10 kg dry weight. The weight of the wet solid is 200 kg.

8.5 A wet filter cake in a pan 0.3 m × 0.3 m square and 25 mm thick is dried on the top surface with air at a wet bulb temperature of 300 K and a dry bulb temperature of 322 K flowing parallel to the surface at a velocity of 0.75 m s^{-1}. The dry density of the cake is 2000 kg m^{-3} and the critical moisture content is 0.09 kg water per kg of dry solid. How long will it take to dry the material from a moisture of 0.2 kg water per kg dry solid to the critical moisture content?

8.6 A batch of solids is to be dried from 22% to 8% moisture (on a wet basis) under the conditions identical to those for which data are available. The initial weight of the wet solid is 300 kg and the drying surface is 1 m^2 per 12 kg dry weight. Determine the time of drying. Use the equilibrium data given in problem 8.4.

8.7 A wet solid is dried from 40% to 10% moisture in 5 hours. The critical and equilibrium moisture contents are 14% and 4% respectively. How long will it take to dry the material to 6% moisture under the same drying conditions?

8.8 A commercial drier needed 6 hours to dry a wet material from a moisture content of 30% to 8%. The critical and equilibrium moisture contents are 15% and 4% respectively. Calculate the time needed to dry this material from a moisture content of 35% to 6%, if the drying conditions remain unchanged. Assume that the falling rate curve is a straight line. All moisture contents are on a dry basis.

8.9 A porous solid is dried in a batch drier under constant drying conditions. Six hours are required to reduce the moisture content from 30% to 10%. The critical moisture content and equilibrium moisture content are 15% and 2% respectively. All moisture contents are on a dry basis. Assuming that the rate of drying during the falling rate period is proportional to the free moisture content, how long will it take to dry a sample of the same solid from 25% to 5% under the same drying conditions.

8.10 A drying time of 6 hours was taken to reduce the moisture content of a wet solid from 36% to 12% on a wet basis. The critical and equilibrium moisture contents were found to be 15% and 5% (wet basis) respectively. How much more time is taken if the solid is dried to 10% moisture content on a wet basis.

8.11 A material was dried in a tray type batch dryer using constant drying conditions. When the initial free moisture content was 0.28 kg free moisture per kg dry solid, 6 hours were required to dry it to a free moisture content of 0.08 kg free moisture per kg dry solid. The critical free moisture content is 0.14 kg free moisture per kg dry solid. Assuming that the drying rate in the falling rate region is linear to the moisture content from the critical point to the origin, predict the time taken to dry a sample from a free moisture content of 0.33 to 0.04 kg free moisture per kg dry solid.

8.12 It is required to dry a fibre board of dimensions 1.2 m $\times$ 1.2 m $\times$ 12 mm in a plant. To determine the drying characteristics, a 0.3 m $\times$ 0.3 m sample of the board with the edges sealed – so that the drying took place from only the large faces – was used. It was suspended from a balance in a laboratory dryer and exposed to a current of hot air. Initial moisture content: 70%, critical moisture content: 60%, equilibrium moisture content: 10%, constant rate of drying: 1×10^{-4} kg s^{-1}, dry mass of the sample: 0.9 kg. All moisture contents are on a wet basis. Determine the time for drying large sheets from 75% to 25% moisture under the same drying conditions.

8.13 A porous solid is to be batch dried under constant drying conditions. A trial shows that it requires 6 hours to reduce the moisture content from 30% to 10%. The critical moisture content was found to be 16% and the equilibrium moisture 2.5%. All moisture contents are on a wet basis. Assuming that the rate of drying during the falling rate period is proportional to the free moisture content, how long should it take to dry a sample of the same solid from 35% to 6% under the same drying conditions?

8.14 To determine the drying characteristics of a 0.3 m $\times$ 0. 3 m sample of fibre board – with the edges sealed so that drying took place only from the two large faces – was suspended from a balance in a laboratory cabinet dryer and exposed to a current of hot, dry air. The initial moisture content was 75%. The sheet lost weight at a constant rate of 400 g h^{-1} until the moisture content fell to 60% whereupon the drying rate fell. The equilibrium moisture was estimated as 10%. The weight of the sample was 1.0 kg. All the moisture contents are on a wet basis. Determine the time for drying to 20% moisture content.

8.15 A wet solid is dried from 32% to 8% moisture in 5 hours under constant drying conditions. The critical moisture content of the solid is 12%, the equilibrium moisture content is 5% and all moisture contents are reported on a wet basis. The density of the dry solid is 1.2 kg m^{-3}. How long will it take under the same drying conditions to dry it to a final water content of 6%? Assume any suitable data required.

8.16 A batch of solids for which the following data is applicable is to be dried from 22% to 8% (wet basis) under conditions identical to those for which the following data is given. The initial weight of the wet solid is 300 kg and the drying surface is 1 m^2 per 8 kg dry weight. Determine the time of drying. Use the equilibrium data given in problem 8.4.

8.17 A wet solid is dried from 40% to 8% moisture under constant drying rate conditions in 5 hours. If the equilibrium moisture content is 5% and the critical moisture content is 15%, how long will it take to dry to 6% moisture under the same operating conditions? All the moisture content data are on a wet basis.

8.18 A porous solid is dried in a batch dryer under constant drying conditions. It takes 6 h to reduce the moisture content from 30% to 10%. The critical moisture content was found to be 16% and the equilibrium moisture 2%. All moisture contents are on a dry basis. Assuming that the rate of drying during the falling-rate period is proportional to the free-moisture content, how long should it take to dry a sample of the same solid from 35% to 6% under the same drying conditions?

8.19 A slab with a wet weight of 5 kg originally contains 50% moisture (wet basis). The size of the slab is 600 × 900 × 75 mm. The equilibrium moisture content is 5% of the total weight when in contact with air of 293 K and 20% humidity. The drying rate is given below for contact with air of the above quality at a definite velocity. Drying is from one face. How long will it take to dry the slab to 15% moisture content (wet basis)?

Wet slab (kg)	9.1	7.2	5.3	4.2	3.3	2.9	2.7
Drying rate (kg m^{-2} h^{-1})	4.9	4.9	4.4	3.9	3.4	2.0	1.0

8.20 A batch of solids is to be dried from 28% to 6% moisture, on a wet basis. The initial weight of the solid is 380 kg and the drying surface is 0.3 m^2 per 8 kg dry weight. The critical moisture content is 18% on dry basis and the constant drying rate is 0.32 kg m^{-2} h^{-1}. For the falling rate period the following data is available.

% moisture content (dry basis)	18	16	13.6	11	8.2	7.5	6.4
Rate of drying (kg m^{-2} h^{-1})	0.32	0.24	0.18	0.15	0.07	0.044	0.025

8.21 Raw cotton of 0.7 g cm^{-3} density when dry is to be dried in a batch tray dryer from a moisture content of 1 g H_2O per g dry solids to 0.1 g H_2O per g of dry solids. The trays are 60 cm^2 and 1 cm thick and are arranged so that drying occurs only from the top surface with the bottom surface insulated. Air at 348 K with a 323 K wet bulb temperature circulates through the pan surface at a mass flow rate of 2 500 kg h^{-1} m^{-2}. Previous experience under similar drying conditions indicates that the critical moisture content will be 0.4 g H_2O per g of dry solids and that the drying rate during the falling rate period will be proportional to the free moisture content. Determine the drying time required.

8.22 A wet solid material having an initial moisture content of 40% is dried to a final moisture content of 10% in 4.5 hours. How long will it take for the moisture content to reach a value of 5%, all other conditions remaining the same? The equilibrium and critical moisture content for the material are 3.5% and 16% respectively.

8.23 A granular solid is to be dried to 0.1 kg moisture per kg of dry solid from an initial moisture content of 0.35 kg per kg dry solid. The critical moisture content is given as 0.15 kg moisture per kg of dry solid and the equilibrium moisture content is 0.06 kg moisture per kg of dry solid. The rate of drying during the constant rate period is 0.001 kg m^{-2} s^{-1}. 20 kg of the material on a dry basis is kept in a tray of 1 m^2 area. Calculate the time required for drying.

8.24 A laboratory drying test was made on 0.1 m^2 of a fibrous board. The sample was suspended from a balance with sealed edges. The dry bulb temperature of air is 333 K and the wet bulb temperature was 303 K with an average air velocity of 2.2 m s^{-1} past the board. The weights recorded at various times are:

Time (h)	0	0.5	1.0	1.5	2.0	2.5	3.0
Mass (kg)	5.0	4.62	4.42	4.31	4.28	4.12	3.9

(i) Plot the drying curve and estimate the critical moisture content.

(ii) Estimate the time required for drying the same sheets from 20% moisture (wet basis) using the air of same temperature and humidity but with 50% greater air velocity.

8.25 It is required to dry sheets of a material from 73% to 4% moisture (wet basis). The sheets are 2 m × 3 m × 5 mm. The rate of drying at a constant rate period is 0.10 kg m^{-2} h^{-1}. The base dry density of the material is 30 kg m^{-3}. The material is dried from both sides. The critical moisture content is 30% and the equilibrium moisture content is negligible. The falling rate period is linear. Estimate the time of drying.

9

Adsorption

In adsorption operations, the mixture to be separated is brought into contact with another insoluble phase, the adsorbent solid. Unequal distribution of one of the original constituents between the adsorbed phase on the solid surface and bulk of the fluid permits the separation. The fundamentals of adsorption phenomena and the procedures for designing adsorption columns are discussed in this chapter.

Adsorption involves the contact of solids with either liquids or gases and mass transfer is in the direction of fluid to solid. Here, the ability of certain solids to preferentially increase the concentration of specific substances from solution onto their surfaces is exploited. By adsorption, the components of either gaseous or liquid solutions can be separated.

APPLICATIONS OF ADSORPTION

(a) Solid–gas operations: gas separation.

1. Dehumidify air and other gases.
2. Removal of objectionable odours and impurities from industrial gases such as carbon dioxide.
3. Recovery of expensive solvent vapours from dilute mixtures with air or other gases.
4. Fractionation of hydrocarbon mixtures containing methane, ethylene, ethane, propylene and propane.

(b) Liquid–solid operations: liquid separation.

1. Removal of moisture from gasoline.
2. Decolourisation of petroleum products.
3. Decolourisation of aqueous sugar solutions.

4. Removal of objectionable taste and odour from water.
5. Fractionation of mixtures of aromatic and aliphatic hydrocarbons.

In all these operations, small particles of the adsorbent are held in a fixed bed and the fluid is passed continuously through the bed until the solid is nearly saturated and the desired separation can no longer be achieved. The flow is then transferred to the next bed until the saturated adsorbent is replaced or regenerated.

TYPES OF ADSORPTION

Adsorption is of two types—physical adsorption and chemical adsorption.

Physical Adsorption

It is a reversible phenomenon. It is the result of intermolecular forces of attraction between molecules of the solid and the adsorbed substance. When the intermolecular attractive forces between the solid and gas are greater than those existing between the gas molecules, then the gas will condense upon the surface of the solid even though its partial pressure is lower than the vapour pressure at that temperature. Such a condensation is accompanied by an evolution of heat. The amount of heat is larger than the latent heat of vaporisation and almost equal to the heat of sublimation of the gas. The adsorbed substance does not penetrate into the crystal lattice of the solid. It remains entirely upon the surface [1]. However, if the solid is highly porous and contains many fine capillaries, the adsorbed substance will penetrate into these interstices if it can wet the solid. At equilibrium, the partial pressure of the adsorbed substance equals that of the contacting gas phase. If the pressure of the gas phase is lowered or the temperature of the adsorbed gas is raised, the adsorbed gas is readily removed (desorbed) in an unchanged form. This reversible adsorption is observed in liquids also.

Chemical Adsorption or Chemisorption or Activated Adsorption

This process is the result of chemical interaction between the solid and the adsorbed substance [2]. The strength of the chemical bond may vary considerably. Identifiable chemical compounds may not actually form, but the adhesive forces are generally much greater than that found in physical adsorption. The heat liberated during chemisorption is usually large; it is of the order of the heat of chemical reactions. The process is irreversible. On desorption, the original substance will be found to have undergone a chemical change. The same substance which undergoes physical adsorption at a low temperature, may exhibit chemisorption at higher temperatures and sometimes both the phenomena may occur at the same time. Chemisorption is particularly important in catalysis.

ADSORBENTS

1. They are solids in granular form; vary in size from 50 μm to 10 mm.
2. The solids must possess certain engineering properties depending upon the application for which they are used. If they are used in a fixed bed through which a liquid or gas has to flow, they must not offer too great a pressure drop for flow, they must not be carried away by the flowing stream, they must have adequate strength and hardness so that they won't be reduced in size during handling or get crushed in supporting their own weight in beds of required thickness.
3. They must have sufficient specificity and sufficient adsorptive capacity.
4. As adsorption is a surface phenomenon, a large surface area per unit weight is the most essential requirement. Their very large surface is due to their highly porous nature. Though the pores are very small – usually of the order of few molecular diameters in width – they are extremely large in number to provide a large surface area. The surface area of treated charcoals is of the order 1000 $m^2\ g^{-1}$ [3].

Adsorbents and Their Applications

1. Fuller's earth (natural clay—$MgAlSiO_3$): in petroleum processing, decolourisation, neutralisation and drying.
2. Activated clay: decolourisation of petroleum products.
3. Bauxite: decolourisation and drying of gases.
4. Alumina (Al_2O_3): decolourisation and drying of gases.
5. Bone charcoal: refining of sugar.
6. Decolourising carbon (activated or treated by air or steam): decolourisation of solutions of sugar, industrial chemicals, drugs, dry cleaning liquids, water purification, refining of vegetable and animal oils.
7. Activated carbon: adsorption of specific gases present in extremely low amounts and fractionation of hydrocarbons.
8. Silica gel: dehydration of air gases.
9. Molecular sieves (porous synthetic zeolite crystals, metal alumino silicates): depending on their molecular size, polarity and unsaturation, they are used for a variety of applications such as dehydration of gases and liquids, separation of gas mixtures and separation of hydrocarbon mixtures.

ADSORPTION ISOTHERMS [4, 5]

It is the equilibrium relationship between the concentration of the adsorbate in the fluid phase and the concentration on the adsorbent at a given temperature. For gases, the concentration is expressed in mol% or partial pressure. For liquids, the concentration is expressed in grams per litre or parts per million. The concentration of the adsorbate on the adsorbent is expressed as mass adsorbed per unit mass of adsorbent. Figure 9.1 shows the possible equilibrium curves.

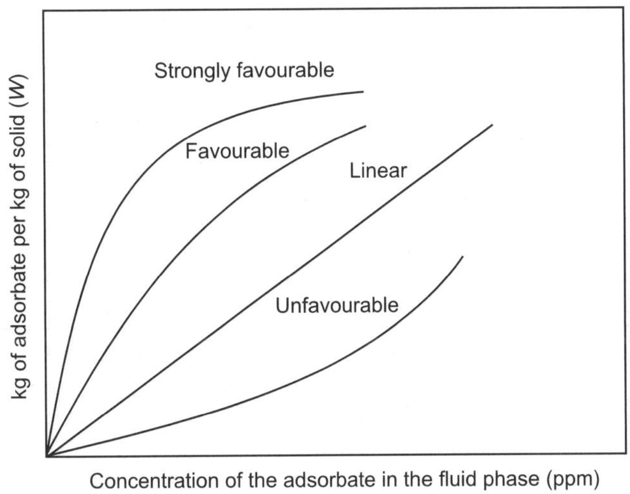

Fig. 9.1 Adsorption isotherm

The linear isotherm goes through the origin. The amount adsorbed is directly proportional to the concentration in the fluid. Isotherms which are convex upwards are favourable because a relatively high solid loading can be obtained at low concentration in the fluid. Isotherms which are concave upward are unfavourable because relatively low solid loadings are obtained and it leads to mass transfer zones that are quite long. The Langmuir isotherm is given by the relation.

$$W = W_{\max}\frac{kc}{1 + kc} \tag{9.1}$$

where W is the adsorbate loading, $W_{\max}$ is the maximum adsorbate loading, C is the concentration in the fluid and k is the adsorption coefficient. This isotherm is derived by assuming the surface to be uniform (it is not so in reality). This works fairly well for gases that are weakly adsorbed.

For strongly adsorbed gases and for adsorption in liquids, the Freundlich isotherm, $W = bc^m$ has to be used. Here, b and m are constants and m is less than 1 for liquids.

Adsorption Hysteresis

Figure 9.2a represents a completely reversible adsorption phenomenon. The conditions corresponding to point A can be obtained either by adsorption or desorption. If different equilibria result at least over a part of the isotherm depending on whether adsorption or desorption is taking place (Fig. 9.2b), hysteresis is said to occur. This is the result of the shape of the openings to the capillaries and pores of the solid or of complex phenomena of wetting of the solid by the adsorbate. If hysteresis occurs, the desorption pressure is always lower than the adsorption pressure.

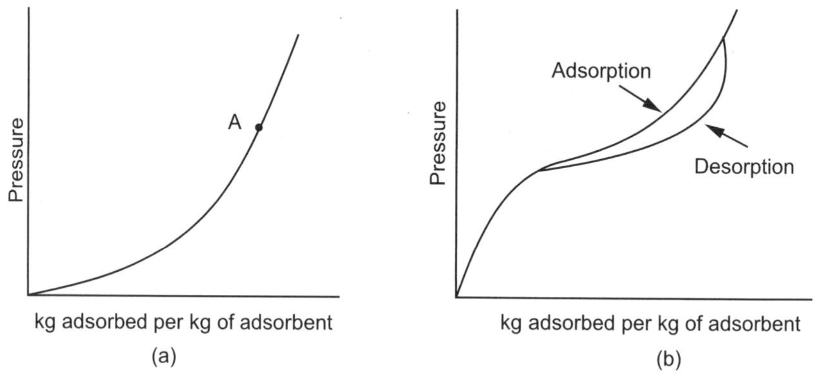

Fig. 9.2 Adsorption hysteresis

FIXED BED ADSORPTION

In fixed bed adsorption, the concentration of the adsorbate in the fluid phase and the solid phase change with time as well as with their position in the bed. At first, most of the mass transfer takes place near the inlet of the bed where the fluid first contacts the adsorbent. If the solid adsorbent contains no adsorbate at the beginning, the concentration in the fluid drops exponentially with distance, almost to zero, before the end of the bed is reached. This concentration profile is shown by curve θ_1 in Fig. 9.3a, where C/C_0 is the concentration in the fluid relative to that in the feed. After a few minutes, the solid near the inlet is nearly saturated and most of the mass transfer takes place farther from the inlet. The concentration gradient becomes S-shaped, as shown by the curve θ_2. The region where most of the change in concentration occurs is known as the mass transfer zone. With time the mass transfer zone moves down the bed, as shown by curves θ_3 and θ_4. Similar profiles could be drawn for the average concentration of adsorbate on the solid showing nearly saturated solid at the inlet, a large change in the region of the mass transfer zone and zero concentration at the end of the bed.

The concentration versus time curves for fluid leaving the bed (as in Fig. 9.3b), are called breakthrough curves. At time θ_1 and θ_2, the exit concentration is almost zero. When the concentration reaches some limiting permissible value or break point, the flow is stopped or diverted to a fresh adsorbent bed. The break point is often taken as a relative concentration of 0.05 to 0.10, and since only the last portion of fluid processed has this high concentration, the average fraction of solute removed from the start to the break point is often 0.99 or higher.

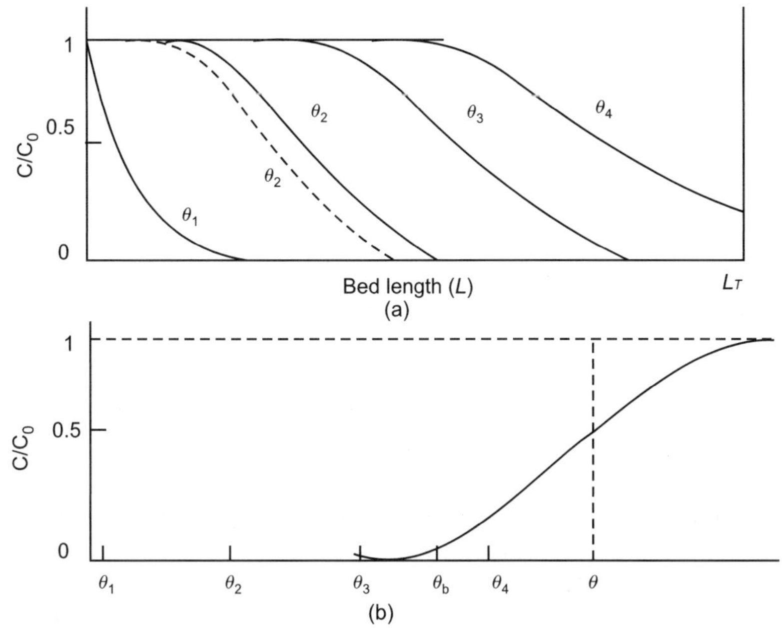

Fig. 9.3 (a) Concentration profiles (b) Breakthrough curve for adsorption in a fixed bed

If adsorption is continued beyond the break point, the concentration would rise rapidly to about 0.5 and then more slowly approach 1.0 (Fig. 9.3b). The S-shaped curve is parallel to those for the internal concentration profiles and is often symmetric. By material balance it can be shown that the area between the curve and a line at $C/C_0 = 1$ is proportional to the total solute adsorbed if the entire bed comes to equilibrium with the feed. The amount adsorbed is also proportional to the rectangular area to the left of the dashed line at θ^*, the ideal adsorption time for a vertical breakthrough curve. For a symmetric curve, θ^* is also the time when C/C_0 reaches 0.5. The movement of the adsorption front through the bed and the effect of process variables on θ^* can be obtained by a simple material balance.

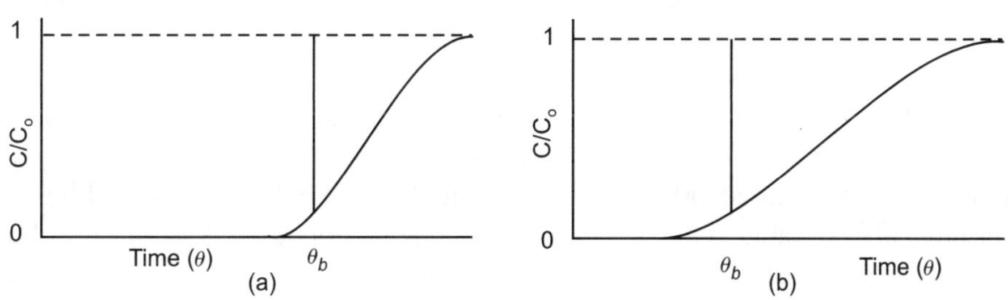

Fig. 9.4 Breakthough curves for (a) a narrow and (b) a wide mass transfer zone

For unit area of cross section of the bed, the adsorbate feed rate is the product of superficial velocity and concentration.

$$\mathring{m}_A = u_0 C_0 \tag{9.2}$$

For an ideal breakthrough curve, all the solute fed in time θ^* is adsorbed and the concentration on the solid has increased from the initial value W_0 to the equilibrium or saturation value W_{sat}. Thus,

$$u_0 C_0 \theta^* = L\rho_b (W_{\text{sat}} - W_0) \tag{9.3}$$

$$\theta^* = \frac{L\rho_b (W_{\text{sat}} - W_0)}{u_0\, C_0} \tag{9.4}$$

Here, L is the length of the bed and ρ_b is the bulk density of the bed.

For fresh adsorbent or completely regenerated adsorbent, $W_0 = 0$; but complete regeneration is prohibitively costly.

The breakpoint time θ_b is always less than θ^* and the actual amount of solute adsorbed at the break point can be determined by integrating the breakthrough curve up to the time θ_b (Fig. 9.4). If the mass transfer zone is narrow relative to the bed length, the breakthrough curve is rather steep (Fig. 9.4a) and most of the capacity of the solid will be utilised at the break point. When the mass transfer zone is almost as long as the bed, the breakthrough curve is greatly extended (Fig. 9.4b) and less than half of the bed capacity is utilised. A narrow mass transfer zone is desirable to make efficient use of the adsorbent and to reduce the energy costs in regeneration. In the ideal case of no mass transfer resistance, the mass transfer zone would be of infinitesimal width and the breakthrough curve would be a straight line when the entire solid is saturated.

Design of Fixed Bed Adsorbers [6]

Usually adsorbers are scaled up from laboratory tests in a bed of small diameter and the large unit is designed for the same particle size and superficial velocity. The bed length need not be the same; different bed lengths give breakthrough curves of the same shape. With longer beds, the mass transfer zone is a smaller fraction of the bed length and a greater fraction of the bed is utilised.

At the break point, the solid between the inlet of the bed and the beginning of the mass transfer zone is completely saturated. The solid in the mass transfer zone goes from nearly saturated to almost no adsorbate, and for a rough average the solid could be assumed to be about one half saturated. This is equivalent to having about one half of the solid in the mass transfer zone fully saturated and one half unused.

To calculate the length of unused bed from the breakthrough curve, the total solute adsorbed up to the break point is determined by integration. The capacity of the solid is obtained by integration of a complete breakthrough curve. The ratio of these two quantities is the fraction of bed capacity utilised at the break point and 1.0 minus this ratio is the unused fraction. The unused fraction is converted to an equivalent length of unused bed (LUB), which is assumed to be constant. The break point time is then calculated from the ideal time and the fraction of bed utilised.

$$\theta_b = \theta^* \left(1 - \frac{\text{LUB}}{L}\right) \tag{9.5}$$

As an example, if a 20 cm deep bed gives 60% utilisation at the break point, then the LUB is 8 cm. Increasing the bed length to 40 cm makes the unused portion $\frac{8}{40} = 20\%$. Therefore, the break point time is increased by a fraction $\frac{40}{20} \times \frac{0.8}{0.6} = 2.67$, because of the longer bed and greater fraction used.

ILLUSTRATION

9A Using molecular sieves, moisture was removed from N_2 gas in a packed bed at 301 K. The column height was 0.268 m, with the bulk density of the solid being equal to 712.8 kg m^{-3}. The initial water concentration of the solid was 0.01 kg kg^{-1} of dry solid and the mass velocity of nitrogen gas was 405 2 kg m^{-2} h^{-1}. The initial moisture concentration of the gas was $C_0 = 926 \times 10^{-6}$ kg per kg of dry gas. The breakthrough data are as follows:

Time (h)	0	9	9.2	9.6	10	10.4	10.8	11.25	11.5	12	12.5	12.8
Concentration (C) $\frac{\text{kg of } H_2O(v)}{\text{kg of } N_2} \times 10^{-6}$	<0.6	0.6	2.6	21	91	235	418	630	717	855	906	926

A value of $\frac{C}{C_0} = 0.02$ is desired at the break point. Find the break point, the fraction of total capacity used up to the break point, the length of unused bed (LUB) and the saturation loading capacity of the solid. For a proposed column length of 0.4 m, calculate the break point time and the fraction of the total capacity used.

Solution

Using the C versus θ data and C_o value given, θ versus C/C_o is generated and is tabulated as given below:

θ	9	9.2	9.6	10	10.4	10.8	11.25	11.5	12	12.5	12.8
C/C_o	0.00065	0.0028	0.023	0.098	0.254	0.451	0.680	0.774	0.923	0.978	1.0

θ^* is the ideal adsorption time for the vertical breakthrough curve, which is also the time when $C/C_o = 0.5$ can be calculated by linear interpolation.

$$\theta^* = 10.8 + \frac{(11.25 - 10.8)}{(0.68 - 0.451)} \times (0.5 - 0.451) = 10.9 \text{ h}$$

Break point time θ_b, that is, the time when $C/C_o = 0.02$, is again calculated by linear interpolation.

$$\theta_b = 9.2 + \frac{(9.6 - 9.2)}{(0.023 - 0.002\,8)} \times (0.02 - 0.002\,8) = 9.54 \text{ h}$$

$$\text{Fraction of total capacity used up to break point} = \frac{\theta_b}{\theta^*} = \frac{9.54}{10.9} = 0.875$$

Assuming a column cross section of 1 m^2, using the column height and bulk density of the solid, weight of adsorbent is calculated to be $1 \times 0.268 \times 712.8 = 191.03$ kg

Mass velocity of the gas, its moisture content and ideal adsorption time are known.

So maximum adsorbate loading can be calculated as

$$= 405\ 2 \times 10.9 \times 926 \times 10^{-6} = 40.898 \text{kg}$$

$$\text{Saturation loading capacity of the solid adsorbent} = \frac{40.898}{191.03}$$

$$= 0.214\ 1 \text{ kg of } H_2O(v) \text{ per kg of adsorbent}$$

$$\text{LUB} = \frac{L \times (\theta^* - \theta_b)}{\theta^*} = \frac{0.268 \times (10.9 - 9.54)}{10.9} = 0.033\ 4 \text{ m}$$

If the new bed is 0.4 m long, fraction of total capacity used

$$= \frac{L - \text{LUB}}{L} = \frac{0.4 - 0.033\,4}{L} = 0.916\ 5$$

Weight of adsorbent in the new bed $= 1 \times 0.4 \times 712.8 = 285.12$ kg

Maximum adsorbent loading of the new bed $= 285.12 \times 0.214\ 1 \times 0.912\ 5 = 55.703$ kg

Adsorbent flow through the bed $= 405\ 2 \times 926 \times 10^{-6} = 3.752 \text{ kg h}^{-1}$

New break point time $= \dfrac{55.703}{3.752} = 14.91$ h

HEAT OF ADSORPTION [7]

The *differential heat of adsorption* ($\overline{H}$) is defined as the heat liberated at constant temperature, when unit quantity of vapour is adsorbed upon a large quantity of solid already containing the adsorbate. The quantity of the solid used is so large that the adsorbate concentration is unchanged.

The *integral heat of adsorption* at any concentration X of the adsorbate upon the solid is defined as the enthalpy of adsorbate–adsorbent combination minus the sum of the enthalpies of unit weight of pure adsorbent and sufficiently pure adsorbate to provide the required concentration X, all at the same temperature.

SINGLE STAGE ADSORPTION

The operation is analogous to a single stage gas absorption. Figure 9.5 shows a schematic of the single stage adsorption process. The amount of adsorbent is usually very small with respect to the solution to be treated. The solute to be removed is more strongly adsorbed than the other constituents, so that their adsorption may be ignored. The adsorbent is insoluble in the solution. The solution to be treated contains L kg of unadsorbed substance or solvent and the concentration of the adsorbate or solute in it is reduced from y_0^1 to y_1^1 kg of solute per kg of solvent.

The amount of adsorbent on solute free basis is S kg and the solute content increases from x_0^1 to x_1^1 kg of solute per kg of solute free adsorbent. If fresh adsorbent is used, then x_0^1 is zero. So, solute removed from the solution equals that picked up by the solid.

$$L(y_0^1 - y_1^1) = S(x_1^1 - x_0^1) \tag{9.6}$$

$$(y_0^1 - y_1^1) = -\frac{S}{L}(x_0^1 - x_1^1) \tag{9.7}$$

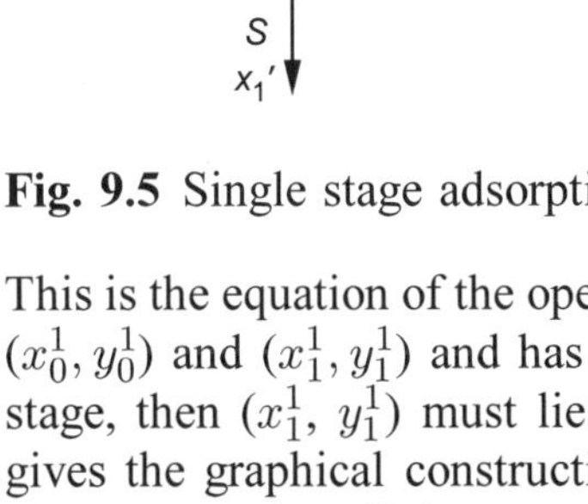

Fig. 9.5 Single stage adsorption

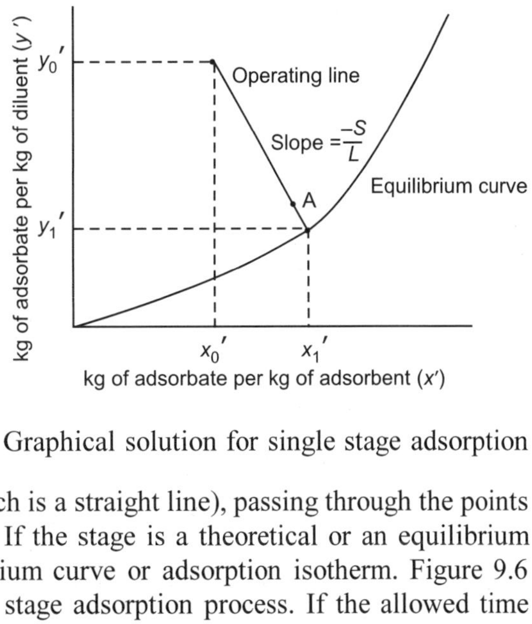

Fig. 9.6 Graphical solution for single stage adsorption

This is the equation of the operating line (which is a straight line), passing through the points (x_0^1, y_0^1) and (x_1^1, y_1^1) and has a slope of $\frac{-S}{L}$. If the stage is a theoretical or an equilibrium stage, then (x_1^1, y_1^1) must lie on the equilibrium curve or adsorption isotherm. Figure 9.6 gives the graphical construction for a single stage adsorption process. If the allowed time of contact is insufficient, equilibrium won't be reached and the solid concentration will be that of A.

MULTI-STAGE CROSS CURRENT OPERATION

The removal of a given amount of solute can be done with greater economy of adsorbent if the solution is treated with separate small batches of adsorbent rather than in a single batch with filtration between each stage. This method of operation is called *split feed treatment*. The savings are greater with increase in the number of batches. But with an increase in the batches, filtration and other handling costs are also greater. Therefore, more than two batches is not usually economical. The operation is shown schematically in Fig. 9.7. Here, the same quantity of solution is treated in each stage by amounts of adsorbents, S_1 and S_2, in two stages to reduce the solute concentration from y_0^1 to y_2^1.

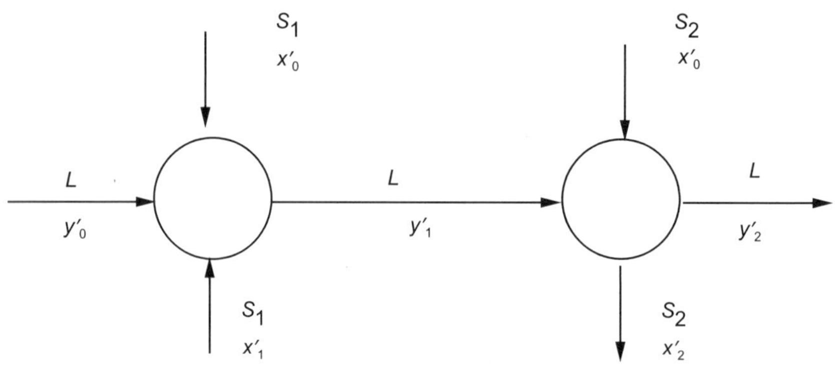

Fig. 9.7 Multi-stage cross current adsorption

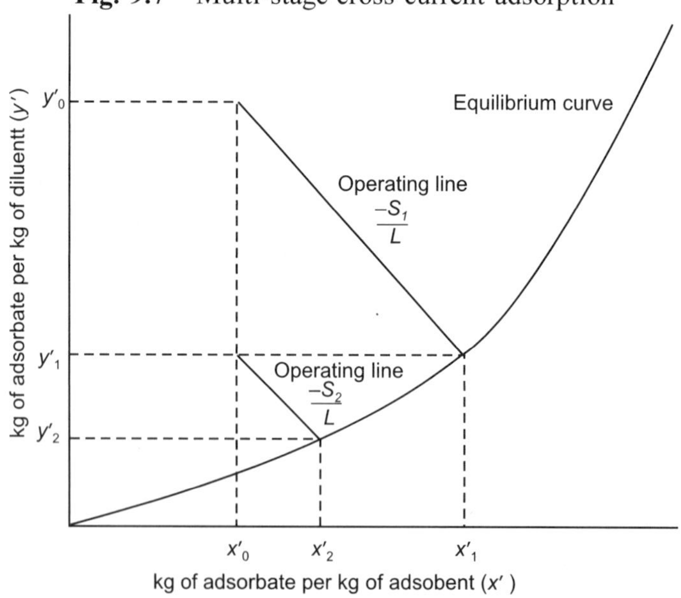

Fig. 9.8 Graphical solution for multi-stage cross current adsorption

Material balance for I stage is $L(y_0^1 - y_1^1) = S_1(x_1^1 - x_0^1)$ (9.8)

Material balance for II stage is $L(y_1^1 - y_2^1) = S_2(x_2^1 - x_0^1)$ (9.9)

These equations provide two operating lines, each with slopes appropriate to the adsorbent quantity used in the corresponding stage. If the amounts of adsorbent used in each stage are equal, the operating lines will be parallel. The least total amount of adsorbent will require unequal dosages in each stage. This can be calculated by trial and error. Figure 9.8 gives the graphical construction for a two stage cross current adsorption process.

MULTI-STAGE COUNTER CURRENT OPERATION

Counter current operation leads to still greater economy than the cross current operation. The schematic representation of the operation is shown in Fig. 9.9. A solute balance for the first n stages is

$$L(y_0^1 - y_n^1) = S(x_1^1 - x_{n+1}^1) \qquad (9.10)$$

This equation is the equation of the operating line.

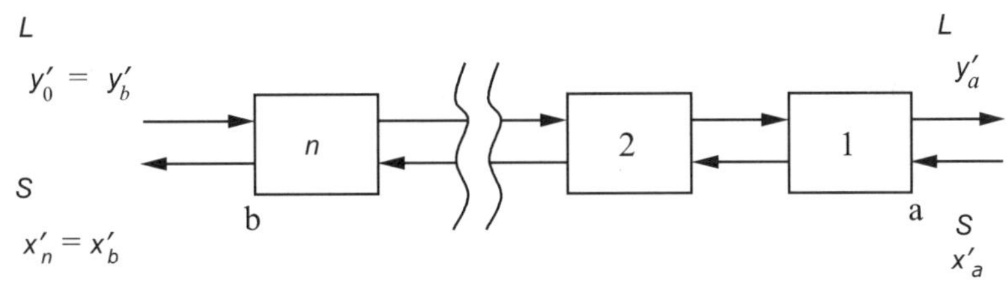

Fig. 9.9 Multi-stage counter current adsorption

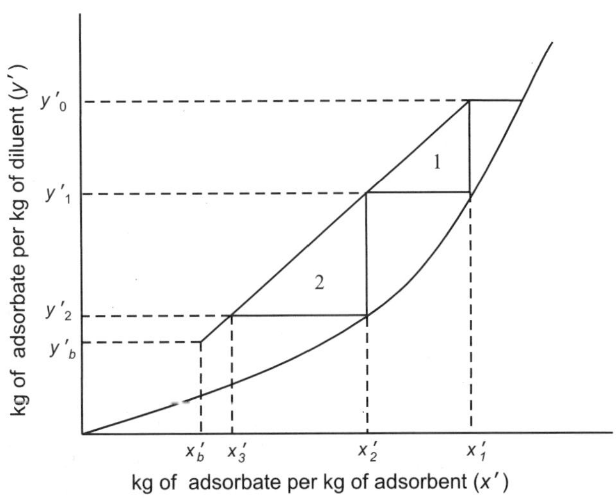

Fig. 9.10 Graphical solution for multi-stage counter current adsorption

This passes through (x_{n+1}^1, y_n^1) and (x_1^1, y_0^1) and has a slope of $\frac{S}{L}$. The equilibrium curve and the operating line are drawn on the same graph sheet. The number of theoretical stages can be found by the usual staircase construction between the equilibrium curve and the operating line. Figure 9.10 gives the graphical construction for a multi-stage counter current adsorption process.

ILLUSTRATIONS

9B Equilibrium adsorption of acetone vapour on activated carbon at 303 K is given by the following data:

g of acetone adsorbed per g of carbon	0	0.1	0.2	0.3	0.35
Partial pressure of acetone (mm Hg)	0	2	12	42	92

The vapour pressure of acetone at 303 K is 283 mm Hg. A 1 litre flask contains air and acetone vapour at 1 atm pressure and 303 K with a relative saturation of 35%. After 2 g of fresh activated carbon has been introduced into the flask, the flask is sealed. Compute the final concentration at 303 K and the final pressure. Neglect the adsorption of air.

Solution

The equilibrium data has to be converted to a weight ratio basis. The partial pressure ratio of acetone to air is multiplied by the molecular weight ratio of acetone to air to get the weight ratio of acetone to air. The data generated is given in Table 9.1.

Table 9.1 Equilibrium data

x^1 g of acetone per g of carbon	Partial pressure of acetone (mm Hg)	y^1 g of acetone per g of air
0	0	0
0.1	2	$\frac{2}{758} \times \frac{58}{29} = 0.005\,3$
0.2	12	$\frac{12}{748} \times \frac{58}{29} = 0.032$
0.3	42	$\frac{42}{718} \times \frac{58}{29} = 0.117$
0.35	92	$\frac{92}{668} \times \frac{58}{29} = 0.275$

The vapour pressure of acetone at 303 K is 283 mm Hg and the air–acetone vapour mixture has a relative saturation of 35%.

Partial pressure of acetone vapour $= 283 \times 0.35 = 99.05$ mm

Partial pressure of air $= 760 - 99.05 = 660.95$ mm

The partial pressure ratio of acetone to air is multiplied by the molecular weight ratio of acetone to air to get the weight ratio of acetone to air.

Initial weight ratio of acetone to air (y_0^1) $= \dfrac{99.05}{660.95} \times \dfrac{58}{29} = 0.3$

Initial weight ratio of acetone to carbon (x_0^1) = 0

Carbon added to the flask (S) = 2 g

Slope of operating line $= \dfrac{-S}{L} = -\dfrac{2}{1.014} = -1.972$

The equilibrium curve is drawn using the equilibrium data. The operating line for this single stage operation passes through (x_0^1, y_0^1) and has a slope of $\frac{-S}{L}$. It intersects the equilibrium curve. The y coordinate of the point of intersection, y_1^1 is 0.015. The weight ratio of acetone to air in the flask at the end of the operation = 0.015.

$$\frac{P_{\text{Acetone}}}{660.95} \times \frac{58}{29} = 0.015$$

Partial pressure of acetone $P_{\text{Acetone}} = 4.96$ mm Hg

Final pressure $= 660.95 + 4.96 = 665.91$ mm Hg

Figure 9.11 shows the graphical solution for this illustration.

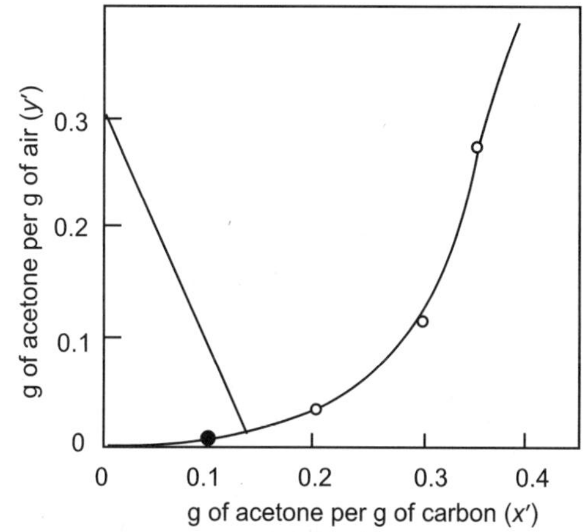

Fig. 9.11 Graphical solution for 9B

9C By correlation of experimental data, the equilibrium relation for a system was found to be $y = 0.000\,4x^2$ where x is g of coloured impurity per 1 000 g of active carbon, $y = g$ of coloured impurity per 1 000 g of solution. Calculate the amount of carbon required for 1 000 kg of solution to reduce the coloured impurity concentration from 0.9 to 0.1 g per 1 000 g of solution in (a) a single stage operation and (b) in a two stage operation with an intermediate composition of 0.32 g of impurity per 1 000 g of solution.

Solution

Single Stage Operation

1 000 kg of solution (L) is added to active carbon. Impurity content of the solution is given in g per 1 000 g, which is also g per 1 kg. Let S kg of carbon be required to reduce the coloured impurity concentration from 0.9 to 0.1 g per 1 000 g of solution.

Impurity content of the feed solution (y_0^1) = 0.9 g per kg of solution

Impurity content of the treated solution (y_1^1) = 0.1 g per kg of solution

Impurity content of the fresh active carbon (x_0^1) = 0 g per kg of carbon

Impurity content of the active carbon at the end of the single stage operation = x_1^1

The value of x_1^1 can be found from the equilibrium relation, $y_1^1 = 0.000\,4(x_1^1)^2$

$$\frac{0.1}{0.000\,4} = (x_1^1)^2 \text{ and } x_1^1 = 15.81$$

Impurity lost by the solution is picked up by active carbon.

$$S(x_1^1 - x_0^1) = L(y_0^1 - y_1^1)$$

$$S(15.81 - 0) = 1\,000(0.9 - 0.1) \text{ and hence } S = 50.6 \text{ kg}$$

Carbon required for single stage operation = 50.6 kg

Two Stage Cross Current Operation

The solution is treated in two stages. In the first stage, the impurity concentration is reduced from 0.9 to 0.32 g per 1 000 g of solution. The output from the first stage is fed to the second stage to reduce the impurity concentration further to 0.1 g per 1 000 g of solution.

Impurity content of the solution output from I stage (y_1^1) = 0.32 g per kg of solution

Impurity content of the solution output from II stage (y_2^1) = 0.1 g per kg of solution

Let the active carbon added to I stage be S_1, to II stage be S_2, the impurity content of the active carbon at the end of I stage be x_1^1 and at the end of II stage be x_2^1.

The value of x_1^1 can be found from the equilibrium relation $y_1^1 = 0.000\,4(x_1^1)^2$

$$\frac{0.32}{0.000\,4} = (x_1^1)^2 \text{ and } x_1^1 = 28.28$$

Similarly, the value of x_2^1 can be found from the equilibrium relation,

$$y_2^1 = 0.0004(x_2^1)^2$$

$$\frac{0.10}{0.0004} = (x_2^1)^2 \text{ and } x_2^1 = 15.81$$

The impurity lost by the solution is picked up by active carbon.

Material balance for I stage:

$$S_1(x_1^1 - x_0^1) = L(y_0^1 - y_1^1)$$

$$S_1(28.28 - 0) = 1000(0.9 - 0.32) \text{ and hence } S_1 = 20.51 \text{ kg}$$

Material balance for II stage:

$$S_2(x_2^1 - x_0^1) = L(y_1^1 - y_2^1)$$

$$S_2(15.81 - 0) = 1000(0.32 - 0.1) \text{ and hence } S_2 = 13.92 \text{ kg}$$

Total carbon required for the two stage cross current operation

$$= S_1 + S_2 = 20.51 + 13.92 = 34.43 \text{ kg}$$

9D The equilibrium relationship for the adsorption of colour from a carrier is given by $y = 0.6x^{0.5}$ where y is the number of grams of coloured substance removed per g of adsorbent and x is the number of grams of colour per 100 g of carrier. If a feed solution containing one part of colour per three parts of carrier is contacted with 25 kg of adsorbent, calculate the % of colour removed by (a) a single contact (b) two cross current contacts dividing the adsorbent equally per contact.

Solution

In the equilibrium relationship, the ordinate and abscissa are not on the same basis. y is the number of grams of colour per g of adsorbent and x is the number of grams of colour per 100 g of carrier. It has to be corrected so that the ordinate is the g of colour per g of adsorbent and the abscissa is the g of colour per g of carrier.

Further, the relationship is not in the usual notation, that is, y referring to the weight ratio of solute (A) to diluent (B) in the light or liquid phase and x referring to the weight ratio of solute (A) to adsorbent (S) in the heavy or solid phase.

It is given that $y = \frac{\text{g of A}}{\text{g of S}}$ and $x = \frac{\text{g of A}}{\text{g of 100 g B}}$, whereas the usual notation is

$$X = \frac{\text{g of A}}{\text{g of S}} \text{ and } Y = \frac{\text{g of A}}{\text{g of B}}$$

Hence $y = X$ and $x = 100Y$

Substituting this in the given relation

$$y = 0.6x^{0.5}$$

$$X = 0.6(100Y)^{0.5} = 0.6 \times 10(Y)^{0.5} = 6(Y)^{0.5}$$

Squaring both sides, we get,

$$(X)^2 = 36Y \text{ or } Y = 0.027\,8X^2$$

The solution to be treated is 100 kg containing one part of colour (A) per three parts of carrier (B). A = 25 kg and B = 75 kg.

Weight ratio of colour to carrier in the feed solution $(Y_0) = 0.333$

(a) Solid adsorbent (S) added in the single stage operation = 25 kg

The adsorbent is colour free. The weight ratio of colour to adsorbent, X_0 is zero. Let the weight ratio of colour to carrier in the treated solution be Y_1 and the weight ratio of colour to adsorbent at the end of the operation be X_1. In the operation, the solution loses colour which is gained by the adsorbent.

Colour lost by the feed solution = $B(Y_0 - Y_1)$

Colour gained by the adsorbent = $S(X_1 - X_0)$

$$B(Y_0 - Y_1) = S(X_1 - X_0)$$

Substituting the values, $75(0.333\,3 - Y_1) = 25(X_1 - 0)$

$$25 - 75Y_1 = 25X_1$$

But we know that $Y_1 = 0.027\,8X_1^2$

Replacing Y in terms of X we have,

$$2.085X_1^2 + 25X_1 - 25 = 0$$

Solving the quadratic equation and taking the positive root, we have $X_1 = 0.928$

Colour removed by the adsorbent = $S(X_1 - X_0) = 25(0.928 - 0) = 23.2$ kg

Percentage of colour removed $= \dfrac{23.2}{25} \times 100 = 92.8$

(b) Solid adsorbent added (S_1) to the I stage = 12.5 kg

The adsorbent is colour free. The weight ratio of colour to adsorbent X_0 is zero. Let the weight ratio of colour to carrier in the treated solution leaving the I stage be Y_1 and the weight ratio of colour to adsorbent at the end of the I stage be X_1. In the operation, the solution loses colour, which is gained by the adsorbent.

Colour lost by the feed solution = $B(Y_0 - Y_1)$

Colour gained by the adsorbent = $S_1(X_1 - X_0)$

$$B(Y_0 - Y_1) = S_1(X_1 - X_0)$$

Substituting the values, $75(0.333\,3 - Y_1) = 12.5(X_1 - 0)$

$$25 - 75Y_1 = 12.5X_1$$

But we know that $Y_1 = 0.027\,8X_1^2$

Replacing Y in terms of X, we have $2.085X_1^2 + 12.5X_1 - 25 = 0$

Solving the quadratic equation and taking the positive root, we have $X_1 = 1.583$

Colour removed by the adsorbent in the first stage $= S_1(X_1 - X_0)$

$$= 12.5(1.583 - 0) = 19.787\,5 \text{ kg}$$

Colour remaining in the feed solution at the output of the I stage

= original colour – colour removed in the I stage

$= 25 - 19.787\,5 = 5.212\,5$ kg

Weight ratio of colour to carrier in the output of I stage $(Y_1) = \dfrac{5.212\,5}{75} = 0.069\,5$

Solution output from the I stage is the feed to the second stage.

Solid adsorbent added (S_2) to the II stage = 12.5 kg

The adsorbent is colour free. The weight ratio of colour to adsorbent X_0 is zero. Let the weight ratio of colour to carrier in the treated solution leaving the II stage be Y_2 and the weight ratio of colour to adsorbent at the end of the II stage be X_2.

In the operation, the solution loses colour which is gained by the adsorbent.

Colour lost by the feed solution $= B(Y_1 - Y_2)$

Colour gained by the adsorbent $= S_2(X_2 - X_0)$

$$B(Y_1 - Y_2) = S_2(X_2 - X_0)$$

Substituting the values, $75(0.069\,5 - Y_2) = 12.5(X_2 - 0)$

$$5.212\,5 - 75Y_2 = 12.5X_2$$

But we know that $Y_2 = 0.027\,8X_2^2$

Replacing Y in terms of X, we have $2.085X_2^2 + 12.5X_1 - 5.212\,5 = 0$

Solving the quadratic equation and taking the positive root, we have $X_2 = 0.390\,8$

Colour removed by the adsorbent in the second stage $= S_2(X_2 - X_0)$

$$= 12.5(0.390\,8 - 0) = 4.885 \text{ kg}$$

Total colour removed = colour removed in I stage + colour removed in II stage

$$= 19.787\,5 + 4.885 = 24.672\,5 \text{ kg}$$

$$\text{Percentage of colour removed} = \frac{24.672\ 5}{25} \times 100 = 98.69$$

9E Active carbon is used to remove colour impurities from an aqueous solution. The original value of colour on an arbitrary scale is 48. It is required to reduce this to 10% of its original value. Using the following data, find the quantity of fresh adsorbent used for 1 000 kg of solution for (a) a single stage and (b) two stage cross current operation assuming that at the end of the first stage the colour of the solution is 21.5 at the arbitrary scale.

Equilibrium data:

g of active carbon per kg of solution	0	1.0	4.0	8.0	20	40
Equilibrium colour	48	43	31.5	21.5	8.5	3.5

Solution

The experimental data has to be converted to a suitable form for plotting the equilibrium curve. The basis for this conversion is, what the solution loses is gained by the solid. Let x be the equilibrium colour units and y be the colour units adsorbed per kg of carbon. The equilibrium data is given in Table 9.2. The equilibrium curve is plotted based on the data.

Table 9.2 Equilibrium data

kg of carbon per kg of solution	Equilibrium colour units	Colour units per kg of carbon
0	48	0
0.001	43	$\frac{48-43}{0.001\ 0} = 5\ 000$
0.004	31.5	$\frac{48-31.5}{0.004} = 4\ 125$
0.008	21.5	$\frac{48-21.5}{0.008} = 3\ 312.5$
0.02	8.5	$\frac{48-8.5}{0.02} = 1\ 975$
0.04	3.5	$\frac{48-3.5}{0.04} = 1\ 115$

Single Stage Operation

1 000 kg of solution (L) with colour concentration 48 on an arbitrary scale is treated with active carbon to reduce the colour concentration to 10% of the original value, 4.8.

Let S kg of carbon be required for this.

Colour of the feed solution on the arbitrary scale (y_0) $= 48$

Colour of the treated solution on the arbitrary scale (y_1) $= 4.8$

Colour content of the fresh active carbon (x_0) $= 0$

Let the colour content of the active carbon at the end of the single stage operation be x_1. The value of x_1 is found from the equilibrium curve corresponding to y_1 as 1 400. The colour lost by the solution is picked up by the active carbon.

$$S(x - x_0) = L(y_0 - y_1)$$

$$S(1\ 400 - 0) = 1\ 000(48 - 4.8) \text{ and hence } S = 30.86 \text{ kg}$$

Carbon required for a single stage operation = 30.86 kg

Two Stage Cross Current Operation

The solution is treated in two stages. In the first stage, the colour concentration is reduced from 48 to 21.5 on the arbitrary scale. The output from the first stage is fed to the second stage to reduce the colour concentration further down to 4.8 on the arbitrary scale.

Colour content of the solution output from I stage (y_1) = 21.5 on the arbitrary scale

Colour content of the solution output from II stage (y_2) = 4.8 on the arbitrary scale

Let the active carbon added to I stage be S_1, to the II stage be S_2, the colour content of the active carbon at the end of I stage be x_1 and at the end of II stage be x_2.

The value of x_1 is found from the equilibrium data corresponding to y_1 as 3 315. The value of x_2 is found from the equilibrium curve corresponding to y_2 as 1 400. Impurity lost by the solution is picked up by active carbon.

Material balance for I stage:

$$S_1(x_1 - x_0) = L(y_0 - y_1)$$

$$S_1(3\ 315 - 0) = 1\ 000(48 - 21.5) \text{ and hence } S_1 = 7.99 \text{ kg}$$

Material balance for II stage:

$$S_2(x_2 - x_0) = L(y_1 - y_2)$$

$$S_2(1\ 400 - 0) = 1\ 000(21.5 - 4.8) \text{ and hence } S_2 = 11.93 \text{ kg}$$

Total carbon required for the two stage cross current operation

$$= S_1 + S_2 = 7.99 + 11.93 = 19.92 \text{ kg}$$

Figure 9.12 shows the graphical solution for this illustration.

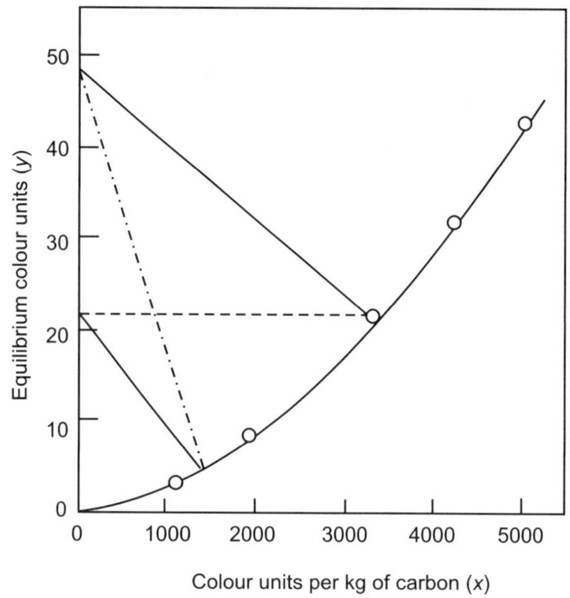

Fig. 9.12 Graphical solution for 9E

9F A solution of washed raw sugar containing 48% sucrose by weight is coloured. It is to be decolourised by treatment with adsorptive carbon. Equilibrium data based on test runs is as follows.

kg of C per kg of dry sugar	0	0.005	0.01	0.015	0.02	0.03
% colour removed	0	47	70	83	90	95

The original solution has a colour concentration of 20 measured on an arbitrary scale. It is desired to reduce the colour to 2.5% of its original value. Compute the dosage of adsorptive carbon.

Solution

The experimental data has to be converted to a suitable form for plotting the equilibrium curve. The basis for this conversion is, what the solution loses is gained by the solid and the sugar solution contains 48% by weight of sugar. Let x be the equilibrium colour units and y be the colour units adsorbed per kg of carbon. Table 9.3 gives the equilibrium data. The equilibrium curve is plotted based on the data.

Table 9.3 Equilibrium data

$\frac{\text{kg of C}}{\text{kg of dry sugar}}$	$\frac{\text{kg of C}}{\text{kg of sugar solution}}$	% colour removal	Y $\frac{\text{colour units}}{\text{kg of sugar solution}}$	X $\frac{\text{colour units}}{\text{kg of C}}$
0	0	–	20	0
0.005	$0.005 \times 0.48 = 0.002\,4$	47	$20 \times 0.53 = 10.6$	$\frac{(20 - 10.6)}{0.002\,4} = 3\,917$
0.010	$0.010 \times 0.48 = 0.004\,8$	70	$20 \times 0.3 = 6.0$	$\frac{(20 - 6)}{0.004\,8} = 2\,917$
0.015	$0.015 \times 0.48 = 0.007\,2$	83	$20 \times 0.17 = 3.4$	$\frac{(20 - 3.4)}{0.007\,2} = 2\,306$
0.020	$0.020 \times 0.48 = 0.009\,6$	90	$20 \times 0.1 = 2.0$	$\frac{(20 - 2)}{0.009\,6} = 1\,875$
0.030	$0.030 \times 0.48 = 0.014\,4$	95	$20 \times 0.05 = 1.0$	$\frac{(20 - 1)}{0.014\,4} = 1\,319$

Single Stage Operation

Let 100 kg of solution (L) with colour concentration 20 on an arbitrary scale be treated with active carbon to reduce the colour concentration to 2.5% of the original value, 0.5. Let S kg of carbon be required for this.

Colour of the feed solution on the arbitrary scale (y_0) $= 20$

Colour of the treated solution on the arbitrary scale (y_1) $= 0.5$

Colour content of the fresh active carbon (x_0) $= 0$

Let the colour content of the active carbon at the end of the single stage operation be x_1. The value of x_1 is found from the equilibrium curve in Fig. 9.13 corresponding to y_1 as 650. The colour lost by the solution is picked up by active carbon.

$$S(x - x_0) = L(y_0 - y_1)$$

$$S(650 - 0) = 100(20 - 0.5) \text{ and hence } S = 3 \text{ kg}$$

Carbon required for single stage operation = 3 kg for 100 kg feed solution.

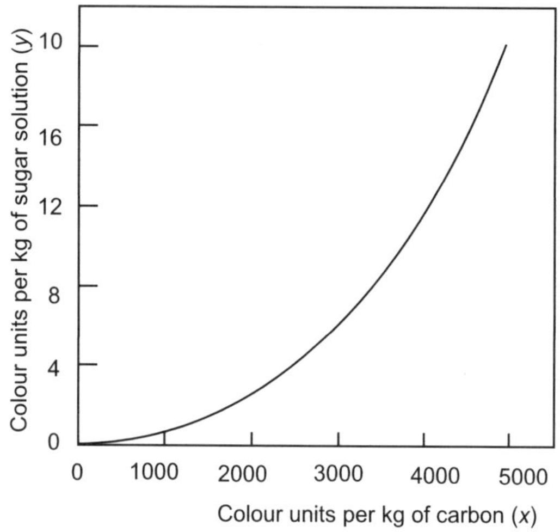

Fig. 9.13 Graphical solution for 9F

9G A counter current adsorber uses silica gel for adsorbing NO_2 from a dilute mixture with air. Gas enters the adsorber at the rate of 500 kg h^{-1} containing 1.5% NO_2 by volume and 90% of NO_2 is to be removed. The entering gel is free from NO_2.

Equilibrium data:

Partial pressure of NO_2 (mm Hg)	0	2	4	6	8	10	12
g of NO_2 per 100 g of gel	0	0.4	0.9	1.65	2.00	3.65	4.85

Calculate the minimum gel rate. Estimate the number of transfer units for twice the minimum gel rate.

Solution

Basis: 1 hour operation. Gas rate is on mass basis.

The equilibrium data has to be converted to a weight ratio basis. The partial pressure ratio of NO_2 to air is multiplied by the molecular weight ratio of NO_2 to air to get the weight ratio of NO_2 to air. Table 9.4 gives the equilibrium data.

Average molecular weight of the feed gas $= 29 \times 0.985 + 46 \times 0.015 = 29.255$

29.255 kg feed gas contains 0.69 kg NO_2

500 kg feed gas contains $= 500 \times \dfrac{0.69}{29.255} = 11.793$ kg NO_2

Air in the feed gas mixture = weight of mixture – weight of NO_2

$= 500 - 11.793 = 488.207$ kg

Weight ratio of NO_2 to air in the gas input of the adsorber (y_b) $= \dfrac{11.793}{488.207} = 0.024\ 2$

90% NO_2 is removed.

NO_2 removed $= 11.793 \times 0.9 = 10.613\ 7$ kg

Silica gel removes only NO_2. NO_2 in the gas output of adsorber (y_a) $= 1.179\ 3$ kg

Weight ratio of NO2 to air in the adsorber output (y_a) $= \dfrac{1.179\ 3}{488.207} = 0.002\ 4$

When the silica gel rate (S) is minimum, weight fraction of NO_2 in the outgoing gel $x_b = x_b^*$.

x_b^* found from the equilibrium curve corresponding to y_b is 0.0448.

$0.044\,8 = \dfrac{10.613\,7}{S_{\text{min}}}$ and hence S_{min} is 236.94 kg.

Table 9.4 Equilibrium data

Partial pressure of NO_2	kg of NO_2 per kg of air	g NO_2 per100 g of gel	kg of NO_2 per kg of gel
0	0	0	0
2.0	$\frac{2}{758} \times \frac{46}{29} = 0.004\ 1$	0.4	$\frac{0.4 \times 1\,000}{1\,000 \times 100} = 0.004$
4.0	$\frac{4}{756} \times \frac{46}{29} = 0.008\ 4$	0.9	$\frac{0.9 \times 1\,000}{1\,000 \times 100} = 0.009$
6.0	$\frac{6}{754} \times \frac{46}{29} = 0.012\ 6$	1.65	$\frac{1.65 \times 1\,000}{1\,000 \times 100} = 0.016\ 5$
8.0	$\frac{8}{752} \times \frac{46}{29} = 0.016\ 8$	2.60	$\frac{2.60 \times 1\,000}{1\,000 \times 100} = 0.026$
10.0	$\frac{10}{750} \times \frac{46}{29} = 0.021\ 2$	3.65	$\frac{3.65 \times 1\,000}{1\,000 \times 100} = 0.036\ 5$
12.0	$\frac{12}{748} \times \frac{46}{29} = 0.025\ 5$	4.85	$\frac{4.85 \times 1\,000}{1\,000 \times 100} = 0.048\ 5$

The actual gel rate is twice the minimum.

$$S = 2 \times S_{\text{min}} = 2 \times 236.94 = 473.88 \text{ kg}$$

Weight ratio of NO_2 to gel in the gel input of the adsorber (x_a) $= 0$

Weight ratio of NO_2 to gel in the gel output of the adsorber (x_b) $= \dfrac{10.613\,7}{473.88} = 0.022\ 4$

Now the extreme ends of the operating line (x_a, y_a) and (x_b, y_b) are known. The operating line is drawn on the same graph sheet in which the equilibrium curve is drawn. The number of theoretical stages can be found by the usual staircase construction based on the Mc Cabe–Thiele method. The number of theoretical stages required for this operation is 5.68~6 (Fig. 9.14).

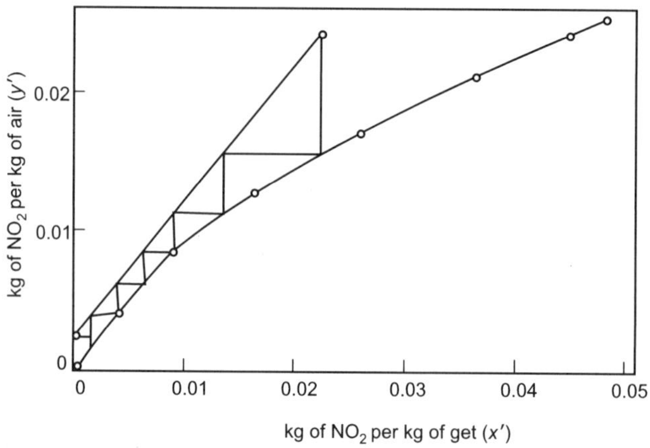

Fig. 9.14 Graphical solution for 9G

9H 600 kg min^{-1} of dry air at 293 K carrying 5 kg min^{-1} of water vapour is to be dehumidified with SiO_2 gel to 0.001 kg of water vapour per kg of dry air. The operation has to be conducted isothermally and counter currently using 25 kg min^{-1} of dry SiO_2 gel. How many theoretical stages are required and what will the water content be in the SiO_2 gel leaving the last stage?

Equilibrium data:

$\frac{\text{kg of } H_2O(v)}{\text{kg of gel}}$	0	0.05	0.10	0.15	0.20
$\frac{\text{kg of } H_2O(v)}{\text{kg of air}}$	0	0.001 8	0.036	0.005	0.006 2

Solution

Basis: 1 minute operation.

Dry air feed rate = 600.0 kg

Moisture content in feed air = 5.0 kg

Weight ratio of moisture to dry air at the gas inlet of the adsorber $(y_b) = \dfrac{5}{600} = 0.008\ 33$

25 kg of silica gel is used in the adsorber to remove moisture in the incoming air.

Weight ratio of moisture to gel in the gel input of the adsorber $(x_a) = 0$

Weight ratio of moisture to dry air in the gas output of adsorber $(y_a) = 0.001$

Moisture in the outgoing gas = $600 \times 0.001 = 0.6$ kg

Moisture adsorbed by gel = moisture in gas input – moisture in gas out put

$= 5 - 0.6 = 4.4$ kg

Weight ratio of moisture to gel in the gel output of the adsorber $(x_b) = \dfrac{4.4}{25} = 0.176$

Now the extreme ends of the operating line (x_a, y_a) and (x_b, y_b) are known. The operating line is drawn. The equilibrium line is drawn on the same graph sheet making use of the equilibrium data. The number of theoretical stages can be found by the usual staircase construction based on the Mc Cabe–Thiele method. The number of theoretical stages required for this operation is 4.43 ~ 5 (Fig. 9.15).

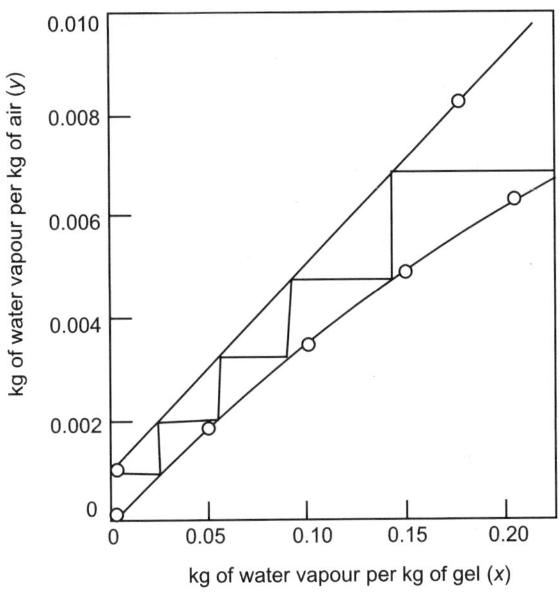

Fig. 9.15 Graphical solution for 9H

NOTATIONS

b Constant.
C Concentration in the fluid, g cm^{-3} or ppm (mg L^{-1}).
C_0 Initial concentration in the fluid, g cm^{-3} or ppm (mg L^{-1}) or kg m^{-3}.
$\overline{H}$ Differential heat of adsorption, kJ kg^{-1} of adsorbate.
k Adsorption coefficient.
L Length of the bed, m.
LUB Length of unused bed, m.

m	Constant, mass of unadsorbed substance in the feed, kg.
$\mathring{m}_A$	Mass flow rate of adsorbate, g s^{-1}.
S	Mass of the adsorbent solid, kg.
S_1	Mass of the adsorbent solid fed to the I unit, kg.
S_2	Mass of the adsorbent solid fed to the II unit, kg.
u_0	Superficial velocity , m s^{-1}.
W	Adsorbate loading, g of adsorbate per g of adsorbent.
W_0	Initial adsorbate loading on the solid adsorbent, g of adsorbate per g of adsorbent.
$W_{\max}$	Maximum adsorbate loading, g of adsorbate per g of adsorbent.
W_{sat}	Equilibrium adsorbate loading on the solid adsorbent, g of adsorbate per g of adsorbent.
x_0^1	kg of adsorbate per kg of adsorbate-free adsorbent entering the I unit.
x_1^1	kg of adsorbate per kg of adsorbate-free adsorbent leaving the I unit.
x_2^1	kg of adsorbate per kg of adsorbate-free adsorbent leaving the II unit.
x_{n+1}^1	kg of adsorbate per kg of adsorbate-free adsorbent leaving the counter current unit.
y_0^1	kg of solute or adsorbate per kg of unadsorbed substance or solvent entering the I unit.
y_0^1	kg of adsorbate per kg of unadsorbed substance entering the counter current unit.
y_1^1	kg of solute or adsorbate per kg of unadsorbed substance or solvent leaving the I unit.
y_2^1	kg of solute or adsorbate per kg of unadsorbed substance or solvent leaving the II unit.
y_n^1	kg of adsorbate per kg of unadsorbed substance leaving the counter current unit.
ρ_b	Bulk density of the bed, kg m^{-3}.
θ	Time, s.
θ^*	Ideal adsorption time, s.
θ_1	Definite period of time, s.
θ_2	Definite period of time later than θ_1, s.
θ_b	Break point or breakthrough time, s.

REFERENCES

1. Smith D and Adams NG, *Adsorption on solids*, London, Butterworth, 1974.
2. Clark A, *The Theory of Adsorption and Catalysis*, Newyork, Academic, 1970.
3. Gregg SJ and Sing KSW, *Adsorption, Surface Area and Porosity*, Newyork, Academic, 1967.
4. Hudson JB and Ross S, *Ind. Eng. Chem.*, **56(11)**: 31 (1964).
5. Dietz VR, *Ind. Eng. Chem.*, **57(5)**: 49 (1965).
6. Michaels AS, *Ind. Eng. Chem.*, **44**: 1922 (1952).
7. Othmer DF and Sawyer FG, *Ind. Eng. Chem.*, **35**: 1269 (1943).

Problems for Practice

9.1 A solution of washed, raw cane sugar, containing 48% sucrose by weight is coloured by the presence of small quantities of impurities. It is decolourised by treatment with adsorptive carbon. The equilibrium data based on test runs is given below:

kg of carbon per kg of dry sugar	0	0.005	0.01	0.015	0.02	0.03
Percentage of colour removed	0	47	70	83	90	95

The original solution has a colour concentration of 20 measured on an arbitrary scale. 1 000 kg of this solution has to be treated for 90% colour removal. Estimate the amount of carbon needed (i) for a single stage process (ii) for a two-stage process with an intermediate colour concentration of 10 units on the same arbitrary scale.

9.2 The experimental decolourisation data is observed to follow the equilibrium relation $y = 0.000\ 4x^2$, where y is the number of grams of coloured impurity per 1 000 g of solution and x is the number of grams of coloured impurity per 1 000 g of active carbon. Calculate the amount of carbon required per 1000 kg of solution to reduce its coloured impurity from 0.9 to 0.2 g per 1 000 g of solution by (i) a single stage operation and (ii) a two-stage operation with an intermediate composition of 0.5 g of impurity per 1 000 g of solution.

9.3 Experiments on decolourisation of oil yielded the following equilibrium relationship. $Y = 0.5X^{0.5}$, where Y is the number of grams of colour removed per g of adsorbent and X is the number of grams of colour per 1000g of colour-free oil. 100 kg oil containing 1 part of colour per 3 parts of oil is agitated with 25 kg of adsorbent. Calculate the % colour removal if (i) 25 kg adsorbent is used in one step (ii) 12.5 kg adsorbent is used initially followed by another 12.5 kg of adsorbent.

9.4 90% NO_2 is to be removed from a dilute mixture with air by adsorption on silica gel in a counter current adsorber. The gas enters the adsorber at a rate of 0.126 kg s^{-1} and it contains 2.0% NO_2 by volume. The operation is to be isothermal at 298 K and at 1 atm pressure.

Equilibrium data:

Partial pressure of NO_2 (mm Hg)	0	2	4	6	8	10	12
kg NO_2 per100 kg gel	0	0.4	0.9	1.65	2.6	3.65	4.85

(i) Calculate the minimum weight of gel required. (ii) For twice the minimum gel rate, calculate the number of transfer units.

9.5 500 kg min^{-1} of dry air at 293 K carrying 5 kg min^{-1} water vapour is to be dehumidified with silica gel to 0.001 kg water per kg dry air. The operation is to be conducted isothermally and by the counter current method with 25 kg min^{-1} of silica gel. How many theoretical stages are required and what will be the moisture content of silica gel leaving the last stage? The silica gel that enters is free from moisture.

Equilibrium data:

kg of water vapour per kg of gel	0	0.05	0.10	0.15	0.20
kg of water vapour per kg of dry air	0	0.001 8	0.003 6	0.005 0	0.006 2

9.6 100 kg min^{-1} of dry air at 293 K carrying 0.75 kg min^{-1} water vapour is to be dehumidified with silica gel to 0.001 kg of water per kg of dry air. The operation is to be conducted isothermally and by the counter current method with 5 kg min^{-1} of silica gel. How many theoretical stages are required and what will be the moisture content of the silica gel leaving the last stage? The silica gel that enters is free from moisture. For equilibrium data, refer problem 9.5.

9.7 The equilibrium decolourisation data for a certain system using activated carbon is given below:

x	15.81	22.36	36.2	47	63	74
y	0.1	0.2	0.5	1	1.5	2

where x is the number of grams of colouring material per kg of pure activated carbon and y is the number of grams of colouring material per kg of pure solution. Calculate the amount of activated carbon required per 1 000 kg of pure solution to reduce the colouring material concentration from 2 to 0.2 g colouring material per kg of pure solution for (i) a single stage operation (ii) a two-stage cross current operation with an intermediate concentration of 0.5 g of colouring material per kg of pure solution.

9.8 An aqueous solution is coloured by small amounts of impurity which is to be removed by adsorption on activated carbon. The colour intensity which is proportional to the concentration of the coloured substance was measured on an arbitrary scale. It is desired to reduce the colour to 10% of its original value of 9.6. Determine the quantity of fresh carbon required per 1 000 kg of solution (i) for a single stage operation (ii) for a two-stage cross current operation with an intermediate colour concentration of 4.8 on the same arbitrary scale.

Equilibrium data:

kg of carbon per kg of solution	0	0.001	0.004	0.008	0.02	0.04
Equilibrium colour	9.6	8.6	6.3	4.3	1.7	0.7

9.9 The equilibrium relationship for adsorption of colour from the carrier is given by $y = 0.57x^{0.5}$ where y is the number of grams of coloured substance removed per gram of adsorbent and x is the number of grams of colour per 100 grams of carrier. If 100 kg of carrier containing 1 part per 3 parts of carrier is contacted with 25 kg of adsorbent, calculate the percent of colour removed by (i) single contact (ii) two-stage cross contact dividing the adsorbent equally per contact.

9.10 A solid adsorbent is used to remove the colour impurities from an aqueous solution. The original value of colour on an arbitrary scale is 48. It is required to reduce this to 10% of its original value. Using the following data, find the quantity of fresh adsorbent used for 1 000 kg of solution for (i) a single stage and (ii) a two-stage cross-current operation with an intermediate value of 24 for the colour on the arbitrary scale.

Equilibrium data:

kg of carbon per kg of solution	0	0.001	0.004	0.008	0.02	0.04
Equilibrium colour	48	43	31.5	21.5	8.5	3.5

9.11 If 100 kg of a gas containing 1 part solute per 3 parts of inert is contacted with 25 kg of adsorbent (carbon), calculate the % solute removed by (i) a single stage process and (ii) a two-stage process (cross current) using 12.5 kg of carbon in each stage. The equilibrium relationship is given by $y = 0.1(x)^{0.5}$, where y is the number of kg of solute per kg of adsorbent and x is the number of kg of solute per 100 kg of inert solid.

10

Other Separation Processes

This chapter provides a brief outline of emerging separation techniques. Among these, only ion exchange and chromatography have significant use in industry right now. Where conventional techniques fail to produce the expected results, the new techniques are promising for specific requirements.

ION EXCHANGE

In ion exchange operations, the exchange of an equivalent number of similarly charged ions occurs between an immobile phase – which may be a crystal lattice or a gel – and a liquid surrounding the immobile phase. If the exchanging ions carry a positive charge the ion exchanger is termed cationic, and if they carry a negative charge, it is termed anionic. The rate at which ions diffuse between the exchanger and liquid is determined not only by the concentration differences in the two phases but also by the necessity of maintaining electrical neutrality in both phases.

The mechanism of these reactions and the techniques used to bring them about resemble those of adsorption. In short, ion exchange is a special kind of adsorption. Ion exchange capacity is measured by the total number of exchangeable ions per unit mass of material (the common unit being milliequivalents per gram).

Earlier, ion exchange solids were the naturally occurring alumino silicates also known as zeolites, $Na_2O.Al_2O_3.4SiO_2.2H_2O$. If hard water containing Ca^{2+} is passed through this solid, Ca^{2+} ions will diffuse through this material and exchange with the Na^+ ions.

$$Ca^{2+} + Na_2R \rightarrow CaR + 2Na^+ \tag{10.1}$$

The Ca^{2+} ions become immobilised in the bed. After saturation with Ca^{2+}, the zeolite can be regenerated by contact with a solution of NaCl.

$$CaR + 2NaCl \rightarrow Na_2R + CaCl_2 \tag{10.2}$$

Modern ion exchange resins are synthetic insoluble styrene–divinyl benzene polymers containing $-SO_3H$ or $-COOH$ group anions and replaceable cations. They make exchanges of the type,

$$Na^+ + HR \longrightarrow NaR + H^+ \tag{10.3}$$

The immobilised Na^+ in the resins may be exchanged with H^+ before reuse.

$$NaR + H^+ \longrightarrow RH + Na^+ \tag{10.4}$$

Similarly, synthetic insoluble polymeric resins containing large immobile $-NH_2$ group cations and anions are used for exchanging anion in solution. The following ion exchange takes place.

$$RNH_3OH + Cl^- \longrightarrow RNH_3Cl + OH^- \tag{10.5}$$

$$H^+ + OH^- \longrightarrow H_2O \tag{10.6}$$

Such resins are regenerated by NaOH.

$$RNH_3Cl + OH^- \longrightarrow RNH_3OH + Cl^- \tag{10.7}$$

Techniques and Applications

All the operational techniques used for adsorption are also used for ion exchange—batch wise, continuous and counter current operations, fixed and fluidised bed operations.

Applications

1. Treatment of ore slurries for collection of metal values.
2. Water softening.
3. Complete deionisation of water.
4. Treatment and concentration of dilute waste solutions.
5. Separations of rare earth metals.
6. Fractionation of multi-component ionic mixtures.

Ion Exclusion

Here, a resin is pre-saturated with the same ions as in the solution. It can then reject ions in such a solution but at the same time, adsorb non-ionic organic substances which may also be in the solution. The organic matter can later be washed off from the resin in the anion-free state.

Rate of Ion Exchange

It depends upon the rates of the following processes:

1. diffusion of ions from the bulk of the liquid to the external surface of the exchanger,
2. inward diffusion of ions through the solid to the site of exchange,
3. exchange of ions,
4. outward diffusion of the released ions of the solid, and
5. diffusion of the released ions from the surface of the solid to the bulk of the liquid.

Depending on the situation, the exchange reaction, the rate of diffusion or the resistance to diffusion in the liquid phase may be rate controlling.

CHROMATOGRAPHIC SEPARATIONS

Chromatographic methods of separation are distinguished by their high selectivity, that is, their ability to achieve separation between components which possess similar physical and chemical properties. Many mixtures which are difficult to separate by other methods can be separated by chromatography. The range of materials which can be processed covers a large spectrum of molecular weights from hydrogen to proteins.

Chromatographic techniques have been used for chemical analysis for over 50 years. When it is used as a commercial separation process, it is often called *large scale chromatography* or *production chromatography*. Production chromatography is an emerging unit operation available to chemical engineers. This technique has been used for the last 25 years. Its use is increasing as the demand for high purity materials is growing.

In production chromatography, the components of a mixture are separated as they pass through a column. The column contains a stationary phase which may be a packed bed of solid particles or a liquid with which the packing is impregnated. The mixture is carried through the column dissolved in a gas or a liquid stream (called the mobile phase, eluent or carrier). Separation occurs because of the differences in the distribution coefficients of the components of the mixture, between the stationary and mobile phases, resulting in differing velocities of travel.

Chromatographic methods are classified according to the nature of the mobile and stationary phases used. The terms, gas chromatography (GC) and liquid chromatography (LC) refer to the nature of the mobile phase.

Both GC and LC may be operated in several modes. The principal modes are elution, selective adsorption or desorption and counter current chromatography. Elution is the most used and best developed large scale separation technique.

Elution Chromatography

In elution chromatography, a batch of feed mixture is introduced into the column at the inlet. The mobile phase flow causes the band of feed to migrate and split progressively into its component solute bands or peaks. The emergence of the bands at the column outlet is monitored by a suitable detector and the components are collected in sequence. The velocity at which each band travels through the column is usually less than that of the mobile phase and depends on the distribution coefficient of solute between the two phases. Solute 1 will travel faster than solute 2 if it has lower affinity for the stationary phase or a higher affinity for the mobile phase than solute 2. The principle is *differential migration*.

Continuous production is achieved in elution chromatography by repetitive batch injection. The injection cycle is timed so that the emergence of one batch at the column exit is immediately followed by the emergence of the first eluted component to be collected from the next batch. At any one time, there is more than one batch moving through the column. High Performance Liquid Chromatography (HPLC) finds enormous application in the production of pharmaceuticals, biochemicals, fine chemicals and industrial chemicals. Columns of diameter 150–450 mm result in production rates of 0.06–2.00 kg h^{-1} [1].

MEMBRANE SEPARATION PROCESSES

Separation of gaseous or liquid mixtures may be accomplished by the use of a semipermeable membrane that allows one of the constituents of the mixture to pass through more readily than others. The membranes may be thin layers of rigid materials such as porous glass or sintered metal. They may also be flexible films of synthetic polymers of high permeability.

SEPARATION OF GASES

Separation of Gases Using Porous Membranes

When a gas mixture is allowed to diffuse through a porous membrane to a region of lower pressure, the gas permeating the membrane is enriched in the lower molecular weight components since they diffuse more rapidly.

Diffusivity (D_A) through pores is directly proportional to pore size and square root of temperature, and inversely proportional to the square root of the molecular weight.

$$D_A = 9700 \times r \times \sqrt{\frac{T}{M}} \tag{10.8}$$

where T is the temperature in K, r is the mean pore radius in cm, M is the molecular weight of the permeating component and D_A is the diffusivity in $cm^2\ s^{-1}$.

The flux per unit membrane area depends on the effective diffusivity (D_e) which is lower than pore diffusivity by a factor of $\frac{\varepsilon}{\tau}$, where ε is the porosity and τ is the tortuosity. For membranes with 50% porosity,

$$D_e = \frac{D_A}{\tau}, \text{ which is almost equal to } \frac{1}{4}D_e \tag{10.9}$$

The diffusion flux of each gas (N) is directly proportional to the concentration gradient or partial pressure gradient.

$$N_A = D_e \frac{\Delta C_A}{\Delta z} = D_e \frac{\Delta P_A}{RT\Delta z} \tag{10.10}$$

The composition of the permeate depends on the fluxes of all species. For a binary mixture, the mole fraction of A in the permeate is

$$y_A = \frac{N_A}{N_A + N_B} \tag{10.11}$$

Applications

Separation of uranium isotopes using the hexafluorides $^{235}UF_6$ and $^{238}UF_6$.

Separation of Gases Using Polymer Membranes

The transport of gases through dense polymer membranes occurs by a solution diffusion mechanism. The gas dissolves in the polymer at the high pressure side of the membrane, diffuses through the polymer phase and desorbs or evaporates at the low pressure side. The rate of mass transfer depends on the concentration gradient in the membrane which is proportional to the pressure gradient across the membrane, if the solubility is proportional to the pressure.

The flux for A, $N_A = -D_A \frac{\Delta C_A}{\Delta z} = -D_A \frac{C_{A1} - C_{A2}}{z}$ (10.12)

The concentrations are related to the partial pressure by the solubility coefficient which has the units mol cm^{-3} atm^{-1}.

$$C_A = P_A S_A \text{ and } C_B = P_B S_B \tag{10.13}$$

Here, S is the reciprocal of the Henry's law coefficient.

$$N_A = D_A S_A \frac{P_{A1} - P_{A2}}{z} \tag{10.14}$$

The product $D_A S_A$ is the flux per unit pressure gradient which is called the permeability coefficient (p_A).

$$N_A = p_A \frac{P_{A1} - P_{A2}}{z} \tag{10.15}$$

where p_A is the permeability and it has the units of L (STP) m^{-2} h^{-1} atm^{-1}.

The ratio of permeabilities for a binary mixture is the membrane selectivity α, which is also called the *ideal separation factor*.

$$\alpha = \frac{p_A}{p_B} = \frac{D_A S_A}{D_B S_B} \tag{10.16}$$

A high selectivity can be obtained when the diffusivity ratio is favourable or there is a large difference in solubility. For effective separation, the selectivity should be more than four [2].

Applications [3]

1. N_2 of purity 95–99 % can be obtained using permeators for air separation.
2. Separation of H_2 from CH_4, CO and N_2.
3. Removal of CO_2 from natural gas.
4. Removal of He from natural gas.

Separator Arrangement

Most commercial membranes used for gas separation operations are 0.3 m wide and 3–5 m long. For treating much larger flows, several units have to be arranged in series or parallel. The parallel arrangement is shown in Fig. 10.1a. It is important to ensure that the flow rate of feed is the same for all the units.

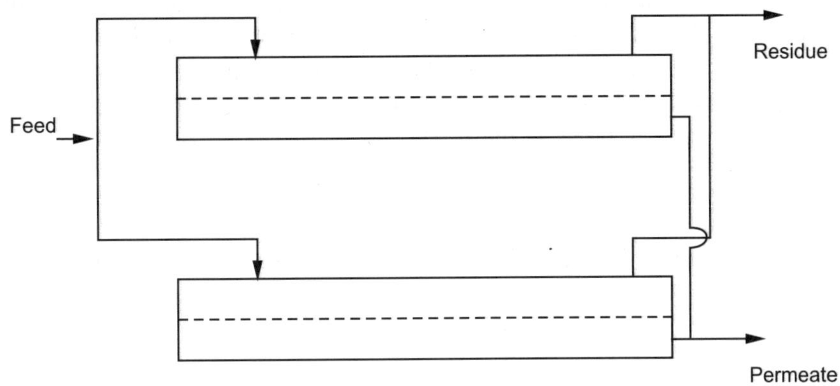

Fig. 10.1a Separator arrangement for parallel flow

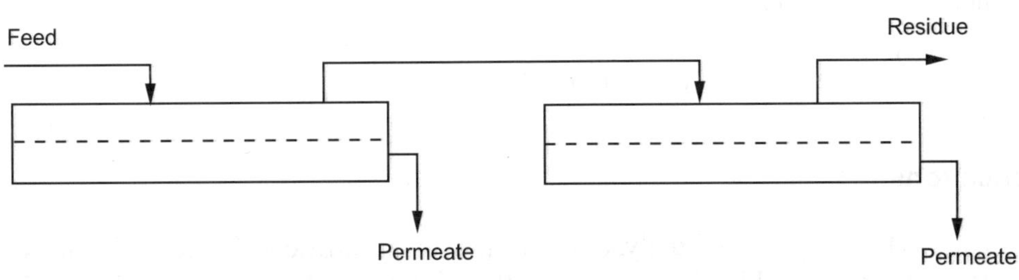

Fig. 10.1b Separator arrangement for series flow

The series arrangement is shown in Fig. 10.1b. If the pressure on the feed side is maintained high, two or three stages can be fed without any recompression between the stages. To get high purity permeate, the product from the first stage can be compressed and fed to the next stage.

SEPARATION IN LIQUIDS

For the separation of liquid mixtures, porous membranes or polymer membranes may be used and the process is known as *dialysis*. With porous membranes, the separation depends on the differences in diffusivity. When polymer membranes are used, permeation of liquids occurs by a solution–diffusion mechanism. The selectivity depends on the solubility ratio as well as the diffusivity ratio and these ratios depend to a large extent on the chemical nature of the polymer.

Dialysis

In dialysis, thin porous membranes are used to selectively separate low molecular weight solutes from a solution by allowing them to diffuse into a region of lower concentration. No pressure difference exists across the membrane. The flow of the solute is directly proportional to the concentration difference on the two sides of the membrane. Solutes of higher molecular weights are retained in the feed solution itself as their diffusivity is very low. Fig. 10.2 shows a schematic of a typical dialysis unit. Diffusion through the pores is greatly hindered when the molecules are almost as large as the pores.

$$N_A = k_A(C_{A1} - C_{A2}) \tag{10.17}$$

The solute flux experiences three resistances in series—the resistances of the feed, product and membrane.

$$\frac{1}{k_A} = \frac{1}{k_{1A}} + \frac{1}{k_m} + \frac{1}{k_{2A}} \tag{10.18}$$

Here, k_{1A} is the resistance for feed, k_m is the resistance for membrane and k_{2A} is the resistance for the product.

$$k_m = \frac{D_{e,A}}{z} \text{ and } D_{e,A} = 0.022 \text{ to } 0.164 D_A \tag{10.19}$$

Applications

1. The best application of dialysis is the use of an artificial kidney to remove waste products from the blood of persons suffering from malfunctioning kidneys. For this, hollow fibre cellulose membranes are used. Figure 10.2 shows a schematic of this application.

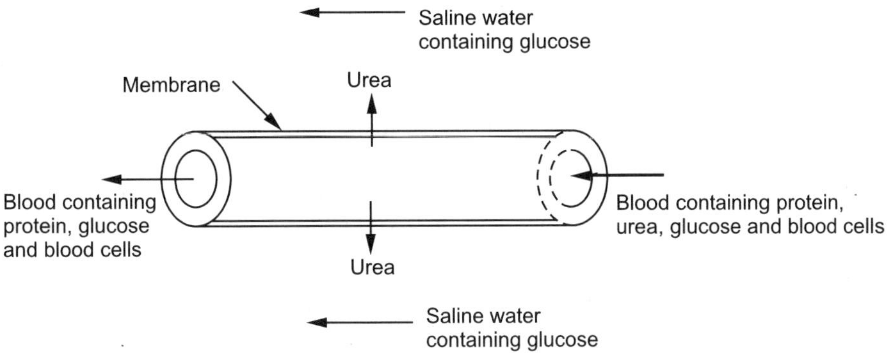

Fig. 10.2 Hemo-dialysis unit

2. An industrial application of dialysis is the recovery of the caustic from the spinning bath of the rayon industry (Fig. 10.3).

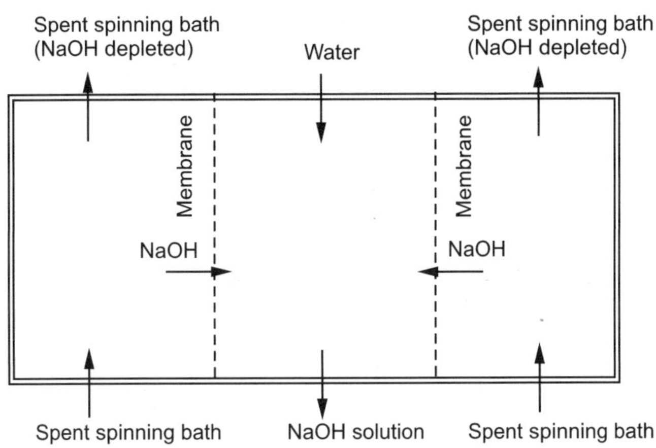

Fig. 10.3 Dialysis unit for caustic recovery

3. Recovery of salts or sugars from natural products.

Electrodialysis

This is a modified form of dialysis wherein the driving force is supplemented by the application of an electrical field and the use of ion-selective membranes. In other words, it is an electrically driven membrane separation process.

In electrodialysis, cation exchange membranes (CEM) are alternated with anion exchange membranes (AEM) in a parallel array to form solution compartments of thickness $\sim$ 1 mm. Figure 10.4 shows a schematic of an electrodialysis unit. A single stack (module) will typically contain 100–400 membranes each of area 0.5–2 m^2. The feed is pumped through the solution compartments. Cations are transported toward the anode when an electrical potential is applied to the electrodes. Cations can be transported across the CEM but not across the AEM and conversely for the anions. The net result is ion depletion and ion concentration in alternate compartments throughout the stack. The DC current requirements of the stack are 100 A at 150 V. The membranes in the ED stack are kept apart by spacers, which define the flow channels for the process feed. There are two basic types:

1. Tortuous path, causing the solution to flow in long narrow channels making several 180° turns between the entrance and the exit. The ratio of the channel length to width may typically be 100:1 and the cross flow velocity is usually 0.3–1.0 m s^{-1}.
2. Sheet flow with a straight path between the entrance and exit ports with a cross flow velocity of 0.05–0.15 m s^{-1}.

In ED stacks, the passage of DC current forces the ionic salts to pass from the dilute stream to the concentrated stream. Using a stack containing n pairs of AEM and CEM, the passage of 1 F of electricity will allow the transfer of N moles of salt [4].

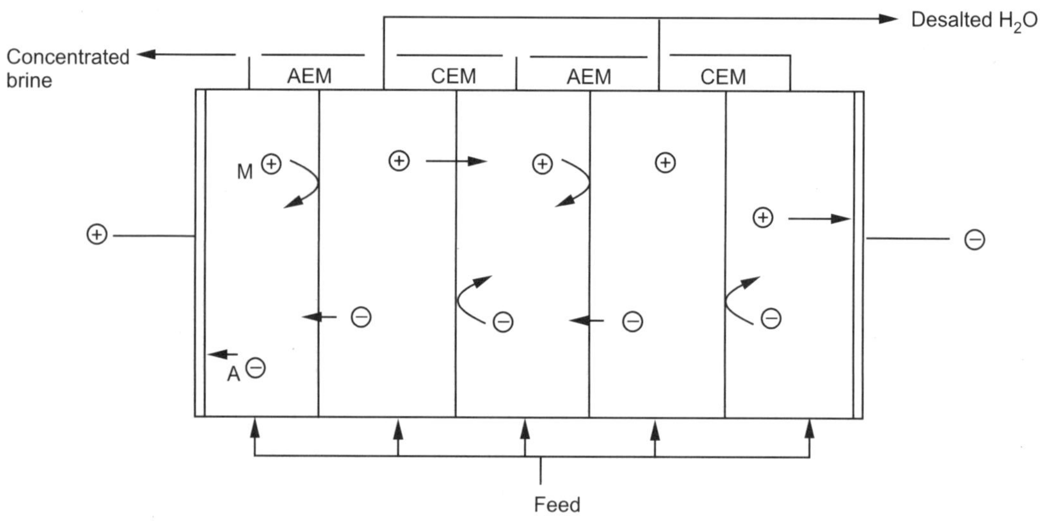

Fig. 10.4 Electrodialysis unit

Applications

1. Desalination of sea water to produce potable water.
2. Recycling of transition metal ions.
3. Salt removal from effluent water prior to reuse in industrial processes.
4. Salt splitting—removal of acidic and alkaline ions from a neutral salt solution.
5. Removal of acid from fruit juice.
6. Demineralisation of cow's milk.
7. Isolation of acids from reaction streams.
8. Manufacture of pure NaCl (10^6 TPA in Japan).

REVERSE OSMOSIS

When a solution is separated from its solvent by a membrane that is permeable to the solvent and nearly impermeable to the solute, the solvent diffuses through the membrane into the solution. The level of the solution rises gradually until it reaches a steady level. The static head developed is equal to the osmotic pressure. The pure solvent has a higher chemical potential than the solvent in the solution and so diffuses through the membrane until the difference is cancelled by the pressure head. If an additional pressure is applied to the liquid column on the solution side of the membrane, it is possible to force the solvent back through the membrane. This pressure-driven transport of solvent from a solution through a membrane is known as reverse osmosis (RO).

The phenomenon of reverse osmosis is beginning to find use for the concentration of low molecular weight solutes and especially for the desalination or demineralisation of water. For example, the osmotic pressure of brackish water containing 1.5–12 kg m^{-3} of salts is 0.1–0.7 Mpa and that of sea water containing 30–50 kg m^{-3} of salts is 2.3–3.7 Mpa. In practice, desalination plants operate at 3–8 Mpa.

Industrial RO Based Desalination Plants [5]

The largest application of RO is the desalination or demineralisation of brackish water for the production of drinking water. Typically, the water to be processed has a TDS of 1.5 kg m^{-3}, mostly salinity and hardness. This is brought down closer to a maximum TDS of 0.5 kg m^{-3}.

1. Membrane modules can be configured in various ways to produce a plant of the required separation capability. Large scale plants operate on feed and bleed basis. Figure 10.5 shows the schematic of a RO setup.

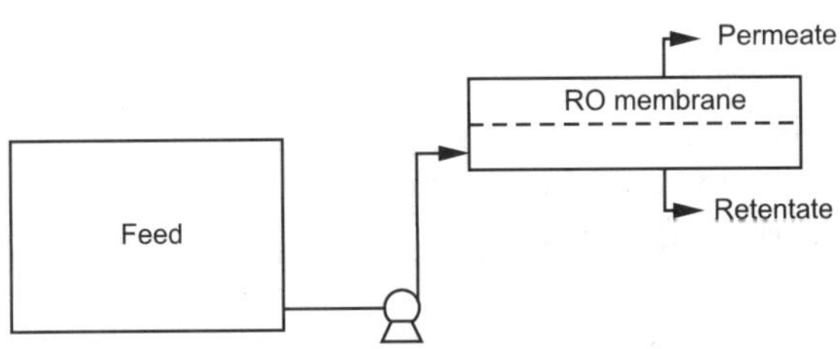

Fig. 10.5 Typical reverse osmosis setup

The overall process involves two stages—pre-treatment and demineralisation. In general, a part of the feed bypasses the pre-treatment stage as the permeate has a TDS of 0.25 kg m^{-3}, which is better than the final product specification.

Pre-treatment

1. Evaporative cooling to reduce the feed water temperature from 323–328 K to 300–308 K which is more compatible for the operation of the RO plant.
2. Precipitation softening by the addition of slaked lime [$Ca(OH)_2$] and $Na_2Al_2O_3$ or $FeCl_3$. The result is partial removal of Ca, SiO_2 and especially colloids. Clarifiers are used for the completion of the process in the tank itself.
3. Acidification to optimise the removal of residual coagulant.
4. Pre-chlorination to ensure a disinfected supply to the RO plant.
5. Rapid gravity filtration to reduce further particulate content. In the first stage, there is up flow through a 1.5 m deep gravel bed and in the second stage there is down flow through a 1 m deep sand bed with an effective particle size of 0.9 mm.
6. Acidification to reduce the pH to 5 for optimum life of RO membrane.
7. Sequestering, addition of sodium hexametaphosphate to retard the precipitation of $CaSO_4$, which will exceed its solubility limit in the reject stream.
8. Cartridge filtration with elements to retain particles of size more than 25 μm to protect high pressure pumps and RO membranes in the event of breakthrough of particulate matters.

Demineralisation by RO

Pretreated water is fed to the RO modules. The modules are of the spirally wound type. The RO plant is completely automated to control or monitor the flow rate, pH, residual Cl_2, turbidity, temperature, conductivity and other parameters. The permeate from the unit is blended with appropriate proportions of feed to maintain a final TDS ~0.5 kg m^{-3} and stored. The reject is discharged to the evaporation ponds. Figure 10.6 gives the flow sheet of the process. RO is advantageous because of

1. low capital and operating cost,
2. high water recovery rate,
3. modular in construction; can be easily expanded in capacity,
4. can cope with reasonable variations in feed salinity, and
5. well proven on a large scale.

THERMAL DIFFUSION

If a temperature gradient is applied to a homogeneous solution, a concentration gradient is established which induces diffusion. This type of diffusion is known as thermal diffusion or thermo-diffusion. The flux, $J_{TD,A}$ of component A (the component with lower molecular weight in a binary solution) is expressed in terms of the thermal diffusion coefficient, β.

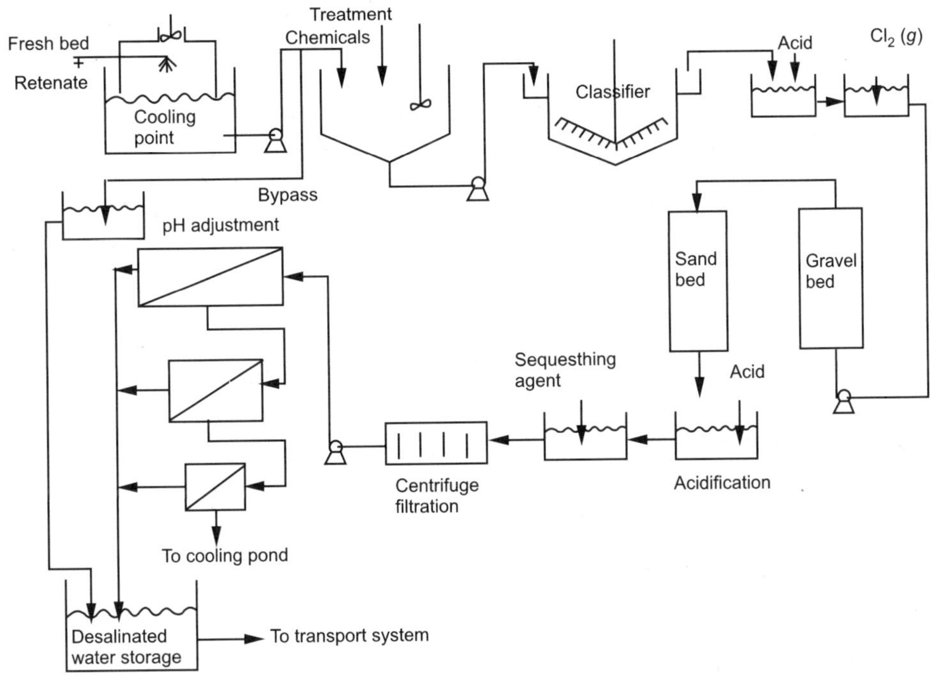

Fig. 10.6 Demineralisation by RO process

$$J_{TD,A} = \beta x_A x_B D \frac{d \ln T}{dz} \tag{10.20}$$

where x_A and x_B are the mole fractions of A and B respectively, D is the coefficient of ordinary diffusion, T is the temperature in the absolute scale and dz is the displacement in the direction of diffusion.

The phenomenon of thermal diffusion can be applied to the separation of materials. Two basic methods are available. In the static method, the thermal gradient is established in such a way that convection currents are eliminated.

In the reflux method, counter current flow of cold and hot materials is provided thereby greatly increasing the obtainable separation. Reflux is provided utilising the density gradient that results from the imposed temperature gradient. Such equipments are called thermogravitational columns. Figure 10.7 shows a schematic for the two different thermal diffusion methods.

1. The static method has been used for continuous separation of material by allowing material to flow between two horizontal flat plates while the upper plate is heated and the lower plate is cooled.
2. Reflux is usually provided by putting the hot and cold walls in vertical positions thereby providing laminar natural convention currents. An alternate form of this is made of concentric tubes with external electric heating.

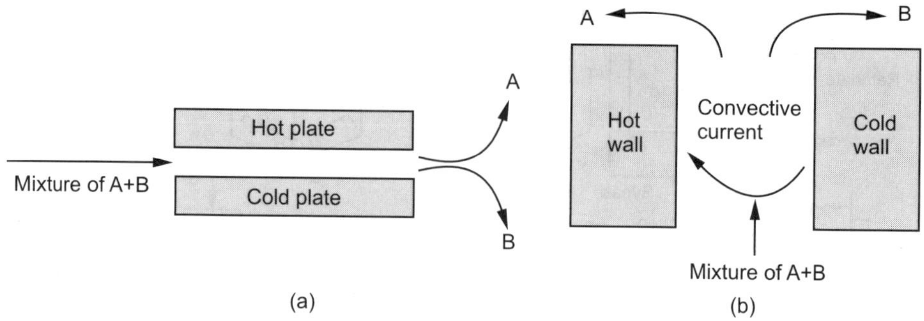

Fig. 10.7 Thermal diffusion: (a) Static method (b) Reflux method

Applications

1. Separation of isotopes of He, Ne, Ar ,Kr, Xe, U and other elements.
2. Separation of liquid organic mixtures.

SWEEP DIFFUSION

If a condensable vapour such as steam is allowed to diffuse through a gas mixture, it will preferentially carry one of the components along with it thus effecting a separation. This operation is known as *sweep diffusion.*

FOAM SEPARATION

Foam is a non-equilibrium dispersion of gas bubbles in a relatively smaller volume of liquid. Foams have important uses in separations, both physical and chemical. These processes take advantage of several different properties of foams. The buoyancy and mechanical rigidity of foam is exploited to physically separate some materials. The large volume of vapour in foam can be exploited to filter gases. The large surface area of foam can also be exploited in the separation of chemicals with different surface activities.

Froth flotation is a significant use of foam for physical separations. It is used to separate precious minerals from the waste rock extracted from mines. This method relies on the differences in wetting properties of materials. Impurities are wetted by water whereas the minerals are hydrophobic. When a mixture is immersed in water containing foam promoters and foam is formed by bubbling air and by agitation, waste rock remains in water while the minerals go to the surface with the bubbles and are entrapped in the foam. The foam rises bringing the minerals to the surface. This can be collected and the valuable mineral in high purity can be extracted.

Foam fractionation is a separation method that is chemical in nature. It relies on the preferential surface adsorption of some molecules (mainly surfactants) and hence exploits the large surface area of foams. It can be extended to other separations by coating the material to be separated with a surfactant to enhance its adsorption at the surface. In this method, foam fractionation can be applied to remove radioactive wastes. Foams can also be used to collect and separate colloidal particles, if they are coated with a surfactant to bring them to the interface.

ZONE REFINING

Zone refining is a fractional solidification technique in which separation is brought about by the crystallisation of a melt without a solvent being added. It is an improvement over progressive freezing. In progressive freezing, a melt is slowly frozen causing the impurities to be concentrated in the last melt to freeze. In this case, a single solidification does not give the required purification. Re-melting of the partially purified ingot sometimes leads to the redistribution of the impurities, thereby eliminating the purification achieved in the first solidification. The impure end is removed by cutting; but cutting introduces new impurities. These problems are solved by melting only a small part of the material and passing this molten zone down the ingot; subsequent zone passes increases purification, without requiring handling, cutting or permitting excessive back-mixing.

Zone refining is extensively used in the preparation of extremely pure Ge for semiconductor devices. In principle, zone refining can be applied to the purification of almost any type of substance that can be melted and solidified such as elements, organic and inorganic compounds. Due to low processing rate, high energy consumption and the requirement of a large temperature gradient, the cost of zone refining is prohibitively high.

NOTATIONS

A	Component A.
C_{A1}	Molar concentration of component A at plane 1, mol cm^{-3}.
C_{A2}	Molar concentration of component A at plane 2, mol cm^{-3}.
D	Diffusion coefficient, cm^2 s^{-1}.
D_A	Diffusivity of component A, cm^2 s^{-1}.
D_B	Diffusivity of component B, cm^2 s^{-1}.
D_e	Effective diffusivity of the diffusing component, cm^2 s^{-1}.
$D_{e,A}$	Effective diffusivity of component A, cm^2 s^{-1}.
$J_{TD,A}$	Thermal diffusion flux for component A, mol cm^{-2}s^{-1}.
k_m	Resistance for membrane.
k_{2A}	Resistance for product.
k_{1A}	Resistance for feed.
M	Molecular weight of the permeating component.
N_A	Rate of diffusion per unit area or diffusion flux of A, mol cm^{-2} s^{-1}.
N_B	Rate of diffusion per unit area or diffusion flux of B, mol cm^{-2} s^{-1}.

P_A	Partial pressure of component A, atm.
P_B	Partial pressure of component B, atm.
P_{A1}	Partial pressure of component A at plane 1, atm.
P_{A2}	Partial pressure of component A at plane 2, atm.
p_A	Permeability of component A, L (STP) m^{-2} h^{-1} atm^{-1}.
p_B	Permeability of component B, L (STP) m^{-2} h^{-1} atm^{-1}.
R	Universal gas constant, 8.314 J $mol^{-1}K^{-1}$.
r	Mean pore radius, cm.
S_A	Solubility coefficient of component A, mol cm^{-3} atm^{-1}.
S_B	Solubility coefficient of component B, mol cm^{-3} atm^{-1}.
T	Temperature, K.
x_A	Mole fraction of A.
x_B	Mole fraction of B.
Z	Distance between plane 1 and 2, cm.
z	Thickness of the polymeric membrane, cm.
dz	Displacement in the direction of diffusion, cm.
$\frac{\Delta C_A}{\Delta Z}$	Concentration gradient for component A, mol cm^{-2}.
$\frac{\Delta P_A}{\Delta Z}$	Partial pressure gradient for component A, mol cm^{-2}.
α	Selectivity of the membrane.
β	Thermal diffusion coefficient.
ε	Porosity.
τ	Tortuosity.

REFERENCES

1. Dal Nogare S and Juver Jr. RS, *Gas–Liquid Chromatography Theory and Practice*, Newyork, Interscience, 1962.
2. Crank J and Park GS (eds), *Diffusion in polymers*, Newyork, Academic, 1968.
3. Pan CY, *AIChE J.*, **29**: 545 (1983).
4. Walawender W and Stern SA, *Separation Sci.*, **7**: 553 (1972).
5. Reahl ER, *Desalination*, **78**: 77 (1990).

Answers to Problems

CHAPTER 1

1.1 6.51×10^{-7} kmol $m^{-2}s^{-1}$

6.19×10^{-7} kmol $m^{-2}s^{-1}$

1.2 4.18×10^{-7} kmol $m^{-2}s^{-1}$

1.3 8.06×10^{-6} m^{-2} s^{-1}

1.4 3.52×10^{-6} mol $cm^{-2}s^{-1}$

1.5 4.81×10^{-6} mol $cm^{-2}s^{-1}$

4.08×10^{-6}mol $cm^{-2}s^{-1}$

1.6 2.74×10^{-6} mol $cm^{-2}s^{-1}$

1.7 1.83×10^{-6} mol $cm^{-2}s^{-1}$

1.8 9.26×10^{-12} kmol s^{-1}

1.9 3.98×10^{-5} kmol $m^{-2}s^{-1}$

1.10 4.34×10^{-6} mol $cm^{-2}s^{-1}$

3.70×10^{-6} mol $cm^{-2}s^{-1}$

1.11 3.14×10^{-5} kmol $m^{-2}s^{-1}$

1.12 3.02×10^{-8} kmol $m^{-2}s^{-1}$

1.13 7.73×10^{-12} kmol s^{-1}

1.14 4.19×10^{-1} kg m^{-2}

1.15 1.35×10^{-7} kmol $m^{-2}s^{-1}$

1.16 2.79×10^{-6} mol $cm^{-2}s^{-1}$

1.17 3.85×10^{-6} kmol $m^{-2}s^{-1}$

1.18 1.18×10^{-5} $m^{-2}s^{-1}$

1.19 4.04×10^{-8} kmol s^{-1}

1.20 1.41×10^{-1} kmol m^{-2}

1.21 5.56×10^{-9} m^3 (STP) $m^{-2}s^{-1}$

1.22 Rs 1 926.07

1.23 7.69×10^{-6} kmol $m^{-2}s^{-1}$

12.775 kPa

CHAPTER 2

2.1 $k_g = 3.198 \times 10^{-5}$ mol $cm^{-2}s^{-1}$ atm^{-1}; $k_l = 1.688 \times 10^{-3}$ mol $cm^{-2}s^{-1}$ (mol $cm^{-3})^{-1}$
Diffusion flux = 2.158×10^{-6} mol $cm^{-2}s^{-1}$; At the interphase, the gas side contains 1.256 mol% solute and the liquid side contains 1.343×10^{-3} mol solute per cm^3 of solution.

2.2 $k_g = 1.25 \times 10^{-4}$ kmol m^{-2} s^{-1} atm^{-1}; $k_l = 4 \times 10^{-2}$ kmol m^{-2} s^{-1} (kmol $m^{-3})^{-1}$
$K_l = 8 \times 10^{-3}$ kmol m^{-2} s^{-1} (kmol $m^{-3})^{-1}$; Diffusion flux = 7.94×10^{-2} kmol m^{-2} s^{-1}
At the interphase, the gas side contains 1.645 mol% solute and the liquid side contains 2.056 kmol solute per m^3 of solution.

2.3 Rate of absorption = 2.41×10^{-5} kmol m^{-2} s^{-1}

2.4 $K_g = 3.38 \times 10^{-4}$ kmol m^{-2} s^{-1} atm^{-1}; $K_l = 2.62 \times 10^{-3}$ kmol m^{-2} s^{-1} (kmol $m^{-3})^{-1}$
$R_g = 0.165\ R_l$

2.5 $k_g = 3.4 \times 10^{-4}$ kmol m^{-2} s^{-1} atm^{-1}; $k_l = 1.27 \times 10^{-5}$ kmol m^{-2} s^{-1} (kmol $m^{-3})^{-1}$
$K_l = 2.54 \times 10^{-6}$ kmol m^{-2} s^{-1} (kmol $m^{-3})^{-1}$; Diffusion flux = 2.7×10^{-5} kmol m^{-2} s^{-1}
At the interphase, the gas side contains 2.05 mol% solute and the liquid side contains 2.19 kmol solute per m^3 of solution.

CHAPTER 3

3.1 NTU = 4, Z_T = 1.6 m

3.2 N_{Th} = 3.2, N_{Actual} = 10

3.3 NTU = 4, HTU =0.504 m, Z_T = 2.016 m

3.4 NTU = 5.26 ~ 6, Z_T = 1.8 m

3.5 1.817 wt% or 0.051 8 mol%

3.6 NTU = 6.09 ~ 7

3.7 NTU = 7, HTU = 1.584 m, Z_T = 11.088 m

3.8 NTU = 6, HTU = 0.544 m, Z_T = 3.264 m

3.9 Liquid rate = 774.09 kg h^{-1}, N_{Th} = 9

3.10 NTU = 3.647 ~ 4, Z_T = 1.2 m

3.11 $(\frac{L}{G})_{\text{actual}}$ to $(\frac{L}{G})_{\text{min}}$ = 1.325

3.12 Minimum liquid rate = 2 532.6 kg h^{-1}, N_{Th} = 8

3.13 NTU = 6.15 ~ 7

3.14 NTU = 3, HTU = 0.51 m, Z_T = 1.53 m

3.15 $(\frac{L}{G})_{\text{min}}$ =0.73 by mol, liquid rate = 365.95 kg h^{-1}, liquid concentration = 2.09 wt%

CHAPTER 4

4.1 71.73% vaporisation, $y_{D\text{ ave}}$ = 0.76

4.2 5 836 kg h^{-1}, 8 564 kg h^{-1}, 5 and 20 inclusive of reboiler

4.3 1 835.92 kg h^{-1}, 3 164.08 kg h^{-1}, 8 inclusive of reboiler, the fifth plate from the top is the feed plate.

4.4 0.4, 4 inclusive of reboiler, 7 inclusive of reboiler

4.5 12 inclusive of reboiler

4.6

x	0	0.16	0.31	0.49	0.66	1.0
y	0	0.28	0.49	0.67	0.81	1.0

Average relative volatility = 2.15

4.7 8 inclusive of reboiler

4.8 13 inclusive of reboiler

4.9 x_B = 0.31; y_D = 0.58

4.10 12 inclusive of reboiler; the sixth plate from the bottom is the feed plate.

4.11 10 inclusive of reboiler, x_2 = 0.89; y_2 = 0.94

4.12 9.1 m

4.13 11 inclusive of reboiler; the sixth plate from the bottom is the feed plate.

4.14 x_w = 0.34; $y_{D\text{ ave}}$= 0.687

4.15 341.5 K; 71 mol% benzene and 29 mol% water; benzene

4.16 13 inclusive of reboiler

4.17 x_w = 0.39; $y_{D\text{ ave}}$= 0.573

4.18 81.74 kmol h^{-1}, 78.26 kmol h^{-1}, N_{Actual} = 11 inclusive of reboiler, The fourth theoretical plate from the bottom is the feed plate.

4.19 6 inclusive of reboiler

4.20 N_{Actual} = 14 inclusive of reboiler

4.21

x	0	0.03	0.47	0.71	0.88	1.0
y	0	0.41	0.60	0.80	0.93	1.0

4.22 N_{Th} = 8 inclusive of reboiler; N_{Actual} = 16 inclusive of reboiler

4.23 Distillate = 547.05 kg; Residue = 452.95 kg, $y_{D\,ave}$ = 0.396

4.24 N_{Actual} = 10 inclusive of reboiler

4.25 5 **4.26** x_w = 0.28; $y_{D\,ave}$ = 0.83

4.27

x	0	0.157	0.312	0.488	0.655	1.0
y	0	0.280	0.492	0.674	0.810	1.0

Average relative volatility = 2.156

CHAPTER 5

5.1 3

5.2 6.72%, 3

5.3 0.826 4 kg per kg of feed, 7

5.4 1, 6.679 8 kg

5.5 1 551.37 kg h^{-1}, 33

5.6 915 kg h^{-1}, 13

5.7 0.758 kg per kg of feed, 6

5.8 155.31 kg h^{-1}, 4,431.47 kg h^{-1}, 301.49 kg h^{-1}

5.9 7

5.10 (i) Over flow = 75 kg, underflow = 50 kg,
solute content of overflow = 2.0 wt%
solute content of underflow = 2.0 wt%

(ii) Over flow = 84.5 kg, underflow = 40.5 kg,
solute content of overflow = 1.78 wt%
solute content of underflow = 2.47 wt%

5.11 554.17 kg

5.12 0.843 6 kg per kg of feed

5.13 3

5.14 56.43%, 67.32%

5.15 4

5.16 4

CHAPTER 6

6.1 3

6.2 4 387.72 kg, 3 112.28 kg, 435.66 kg

6.3 3, 8 079 kg h^{-1}

6.4 2 925.17 kg, net heat evolved = 556 410 kJ

6.5 (i) 1 857.14 kg, 357.68 kg (ii) 416.32 kg

6.6 356.52 kg, net heat evolved = 20 754 kJ

6.7 68.97%, 3 763.86 kg

6.8 0.899, 16.16 kg

6.9 5 569.48 kg

6.10 70.55%, 4 614.56 kg

6.11 1 223. 68 kg, 292.8 kg

6.12 62.335 kg, 86.865 kg

6.13 1834.19 kg

6.14 3 138.02 kg, 135.94 kg, 502.08 kg

6.15 4 830.8 kg, 4 454.5 kg, 488.7 kg

6.16 10 835.23 kg, 422.73 kg, 2 832.95 kg

6.17 Crystals obtained = 6 675.1 kg, mother liquor left = 2 235.2 kg and evaporation loss = 670.7 kg

6.18 142.62 kg

CHAPTER 7

7.1 0.019, 0.000 5, 0.388 kg, 11.52 kg **7.2** 47.064 m^3, 68.31 m^3 **7.3** 15.732 kg

7.4 33.45 m^3 **7.5** 978.76 m^3 **7.6** 283.4 kPa

7.7 0.021 06, 0.013 07, 51.51, 50.49, 1.025 kJ (kg dry air)$^{-1}$ K^{-1}, 0.884 m^3 (kg dry air)$^{-1}$

7.8 493.83 kg **7.9** 24.02 kPa, 0.897

7.10 0.178 4, 0.315, 65.94%, 0.1511, 0.45 m^3 (kg of CO_2)$^{-1}$, 49.17 J (kg CO_2)$^{-1}$ K^{-1}

7.11 310 K, 304 K, 302 K, 304 K, 313 K, 0.035 **7.12** 310 K, 0.06, 90%, 44.28 kg, 317 K

7.13 0.015, 70%, 0.878 m^3 (kg dry air)$^{-1}$, 69. kJ (kg dry air)$^{-1}$, 293 K

7.14 0.085, 327 K, 0.089, 323 K

7.15 26.12%, 29.5%, 1.061 kJ (kg dry air)$^{-1}$ K^{-1}, 0.973 m^3 (kg dry air)$^{-1}$,132.93 kJ (kg dry air)$^{-1}$

7.16 0.0625, 320 K **7.17** 63.64%, 62%

7.18 0.326 8, 0.6769, 84.93%, 24.63%, 0.88 m^3 (kg of N_2)$^{-1}$, 1.988 kJ (kg of N_2)$^{-1}$ K^{-1}

7.19 4.8 m **7.20** 0.017, 40%, 0.012, 60%

7.21 0.018, 9%, 11.5%, 300.5 K, 113.19 kJ (kg dry air)$^{-1}$, 2.82%

7.22 57.52%, 44.75% **7.23** 836.12 kg

7.24 327 K, 301 K, 310 K, 7 288 kJ, 1 175 kJ

7.25 303 K, 298 K, 294 K, 298 K, 310 K, 0.032

7.26 3%, 0.003, 0.93 m^3 (kg dry air)$^{-1}$, 1061.5 J (kg dry air)$^{-1}$$K^{-1}$, 276 K, 0.976 m^3 (kg dry air)$^{-1}$, 134.39 kJ (kg dry air)$^{-1}$

7.27 0.021, 0.013 03, 51.5%, 50.4%

7.28 290 K, 0.012, 310 K, 2.77 kg, 7 307.15 kJ

7.29 20 m

CHAPTER 8

8.1	6.38 h	**8.2**	13.53 h	**8.3**	9.17 h	**8.4**	7.04 h	**8.5**	1.41 h
8.6	10.24 h	**8.7**	6.21 h	**8.8**	8.90 h	**8.9**	8.19 h	**8.10**	0.61 h
8.11	10.04 h	**8.12**	10.12 h	**8.13**	10.16 h	**8.14**	3.14 h	**8.15**	6.15 h
8.16	6.83 h	**8.17**	5.87 h	**8.18**	10.04 h	**8.19**	14.12 h	**8.20**	50.75 h
8.21	86.93 s	**8.22**	6.28 h	**8.23**	1.41 h	**8.24**	1.52 h	**8.25**	0.66 h

CHAPTER 9

9.1	9.6 kg, 6.9 kg	**9.2**	31.31 kg, 24.74 kg	**9.3**	98.83%, 99.98%
9.4	6	**9.5**	4	**9.6**	4, 0.13
9.7	80.5 kg, 54.86 kg	**9.8**	30.86 kg, 20.4 kg	**9.9**	92.2%, 98.48%
9.10	30.86 kg, 20.38 kg	**9.11**	43.44%, 46.18%		